Nepal

THE ROUGH GUIDE

There are more than one hundred and fifty Rough Guide titles
covering destinations from Amsterdam to Zimbabwe

Forthcoming titles include
Dominican Republic • Jerusalem • Laos • Melbourne • Sydney

Rough Guide Reference Series
Classical Music • Drum 'n' Bass • European Football • House
The Internet • Jazz • Opera • Reggae • Rock Music • World Music

Rough Guide Phrasebooks
Czech • Dutch • Egyptian Arabic • French • German • Greek • Hindi & Urdu
Hungarian • Indonesian • Italian • Japanese • Mandarin Chinese
Mexican Spanish • Polish • Portuguese • Russian • Spanish
Swahili • Thai • Turkish • Vietnamese • European Languages

Rough Guides on the Internet
www.roughguides.com

ROUGH GUIDE CREDITS

Text editor: Olivia Eccleshall
Series editor: Mark Ellingham
Editorial: Martin Dunford, Jonathan Buckley, Jo
Mead, Amanda Tomlin, Kate Berens, Ann-Marie
Shaw, Paul Gray, Chris Schüler, Helena Smith,
Judith Bamber, Kieran Falconer, Orla Duane, Ruth
Blackmore, Sophie Martin, Geoff Howard, Claire
Saunders, Anna Sutton, Gavin Thomas, Alexander
Mark Rogers, Polly Thomas, Andrew Tomicic, Joe
Staines, Lisa Nellis (UK); Andrew Rosenberg, Mary
Beth Maioli (US)
Production: Susanne Hillen, Andy Hilliard, Link
Hall, Helen Ostick, Julia Bovis, Michelle Draycott,
Anna Wray, Katie Pringle
Cartography: Melissa Baker, Maxine Burke, Nichola
Goodliffe, Ed Wright
Picture research: Eleanor Hill, Louise Boulton
Online editors: Alan Spicer, Kate Hands
Finance: John Fisher, Katy Miesiaczek, Gary Singh,
Edward Downey, Catherine Robertson
Marketing & Publicity: Richard Trillo, Simon
Carloss, Niki Smith, David Wearn (UK); Jean-Marie
Kelly (US)
Administration: Tania Hummel, Charlotte Marriott,
Demelza Dallow

ACKNOWLEDGEMENTS

This book is dedicated to Krysia and Lily, who put up
with a lot when we were apart and even more
when we were together.

Special thanks for help in this edition must again go
first to my assistant and friend Dadi Ram Sapkota.
Other people who provided invaluable help includ-
ed: Rajendra Adhikari (Tour du Tarai/Bird Education
Society, Sauraha), Belinda and Sanja (Natural
Health Clinic, Pokhara), Basanta Bidari (Lumbini
Development Trust), Hikmat Bisht (Silent Safari,
Mahendra Nagar), Helen Brown, John Child
(Friends in High Places), Bhuban Kumar Chitrakar
(Thimi), Gyan Bahadur Dahal, Mike and Greta
Dalby, Hira Dhamala (Karnali Excursions), Scott
Dimetrosky (Himalayan Explorers Club), Karma
Dorji, Bill and Nora Duckworth, Sallie Fischer, Mike
Ford, Sonam Gurung (Dawn Till Dusk Bikes), Jack
Jones, Roopendra Joshi, Premi Khadga (Bardia
Jungle Cottage, Thakurdwara), Peter Knowles
(White Water Nepal), Kerry Moran, Narayan and
crew at Forest Hideaway Cottages (Thakurdwara),
Ganga Nepali and Ailsa Colston-Nepali (Hotel
Nirvana, Pokhara), Prativa Pandey (CIWEC), Om
Bahadur Pariya, Tony Parr (Nepal Village Resorts),
Krishna Kumar Pradhan (Bandipur), Madhukar and
Greta Rana, Arun Rijal (King Mahendra Trust,
Sauraha), Patricia Roberts, Ralph and Pam
Rosenberg, Gun Muni Shakya (Himalayan Music
Shop), Ellie Skeele, Woody and Penny Strong, and
Peter Stewart (Himalayan Mountain Bikes).
Readers who provided useful comments and
updates are credited separately on p.v.

Thanks, also, to all at Rough Guides who helped
produce this book, especially my editor, Olivia
Eccleshall; cartographer Mandy Muggridge,
Geographic Services Ltd; production director
Susanne Hillen; senior production controller
Michelle Draycott; typesetter Helen Ostick; proof-
reader Gillian Armstrong; and Australasian
researcher Cameron Wilson.

PUBLISHING INFORMATION

This fourth edition published July 1999 by Rough Guides
Ltd, 62–70 Shorts Gardens, London WC2H 9AB
Distributed by the Penguin Group:
Penguin Books Ltd, 27 Wrights Lane, London W8 5TZ
Penguin Books USA Inc., 375 Hudson Street, New York
10014, USA
Penguin Books Australia Ltd, 487 Maroondah Highway,
PO Box 257, Ringwood, Victoria 3134, Australia
Penguin Books Canada Ltd, 10 Alcorn Avenue, Toronto,
Ontario, Canada M4V 1E4
Penguin Books (NZ) Ltd, 182–190 Wairau Road,
Auckland 10, New Zealand
Typeset in Linotron Univers and Century Old Style to an
original design by Andrew Oliver.
Printed in England by Clays Ltd, St Ives PLC
Illustrations in Part One and Part Three by Edward Briant

Illustration on p.1 by Tommy Yamaha on p. 375 by Henry
Iles; and on p.433 by Sally Davies
© David Reed 1999
No part of this book may be reproduced in any form
without permission from the publisher except for the
quotation of brief passages in reviews.
528pp – Includes index
A catalogue record for this book is available from the
British Library.
ISBN 1-85828-438-4

Nepal

THE ROUGH GUIDE

written and researched by
David Reed

Additional contributions by
Peter Knowles and Peter Stewart

THE ROUGH GUIDES

We set out to do something different when the first Rough Guide was published in 1982. Mark Ellingham, just out of university, was travelling in Greece. He brought along the popular guides of the day, but found they were all lacking in some way. They were either strong on ruins and museums but went on for pages without mentioning a beach or taverna. Or they were so conscious of the need to save money that they lost sight of Greece's cultural and historical significance. Also, none of the books told him anything about Greece's contemporary life – its politics, its culture, its people, and how they lived.

So, with no job in prospect, Mark decided to write his own guidebook, one which aimed to provide practical information that was second to none, detailing the best beaches and the hottest clubs and restaurants, while also giving hard-hitting accounts of every sight, both famous and obscure, and providing up-to-the-minute information on contemporary culture. It was a guide that encouraged independent travellers to find the best of Greece, and was a great success, getting shortlisted for the Thomas Cook travel guide award, and encouraging Mark, along with three friends, to expand the series.

The Rough Guide list grew rapidly and the letters flooded in, indicating a much broader readership than had been anticipated, but one which uniformly appreciated the Rough Guide mix of practical detail and humour, irreverence and enthusiasm. Things haven't changed. The same four friends who began the series are still the caretakers of the Rough Guide mission today: to provide the most reliable, up-to-date and entertaining information to independent-minded travellers of all ages, on all budgets.

We now publish more than 100 titles and have offices in London and New York. The travel guides are written and researched by a dedicated team of more than 100 authors, based in Britain, Europe, the USA and Australia. We have also created a unique series of phrasebooks to accompany the travel series, along with an acclaimed series of music guides, and a best-selling pocket guide to the Internet and World Wide Web. We also publish comprehensive travel information on our Web site:

www.roughguides.com

THE AUTHOR

David Reed first entered Nepal in 1985, from Tibet, and developed an instant appreciation for its culinary advantages over China. (Six subsequent visits have deepened his love for the subtler aspects of the culture.) In 1989 he gladly left a hellish career in trade journalism to research and write the first edition of this book; he has since updated every edition of the Nepal guide. He currently lives with his wife Krysia and daughter Lily in Colorado, where he works for the Rocky Mountain Institute, an environmental think-tank.

READERS' LETTERS

Special thanks to the following readers for their letters:

Pippa Adams, Jamie Avera, J.P. Baldwin, Shannon Brandt, Karen Briggs and Clare Sansom, Marion Carter, Tom Connaly, Michael Dawson, Cheryl Douglas and Erik Jensen, Rick Dubbledam, Dave Dusgate, Anne M. Gale, Karen Gallagher, Ben Harwood, Paula Hirschoff, Ben Honey, Pam Jones, V.J. Knowles and C.M.R. Solly, Steve and Leslie Kodish, Peter Koret, Lauryl Lefebvre, Gareth Llewellyn, Tony Maguire, Timothy Nalden, P. Petit and J. Munro, Chris Phelan, Gavin Pierce, Pia Problemi, Michael Schell, Brian Scowcroft, Fiona Shenton, Eleanor Smith, Simon Smythe, Marion Taylor, Earl Thompson, Martine Thompson, Sophie Unwin, Debbie Voger, Alan Wald, Lucy Wallis, Callum Weeks, Andrew Wilkins, Pierre Willems, and Dion Williams and Carinna Castnotis.

CONTENTS

Introduction x

LIST OF MAPS

MAP SYMBOLS

▬▬	Railway	▣	Restaurant
═══	Main road	◉	Accommodation
──	Minor road	⌃⌃	Mountain range
──	Dirt track	▲	Mountain peak
─ ─	Ferry crossing	⸌⸍	Pass/bridge
■-■-■	International boundary	ⓘ	Tourist office
─ ─ ─	Chapter division boundary	⊠	Post office
⊥⊥⊥⊥	Steps	●─■	Gate/arch
═══◄	One-way street	▮	Building
------	Path	▨	Park
⋯⋯⋯	River	▨	National park
▰▰▰	Ridge line	░	Beach
✗	Airport		

INTRODUCTION

Nepal forms the very watershed of Asia. Landlocked between India and Tibet, it spans terrain from subtropical jungle to the icy Himalaya, and contains or shares eight of the world's ten highest mountains. Its cultural landscape is every bit as diverse: a dozen major **ethnic groups**, speaking as many as fifty languages and dialects, coexist in this narrow, jumbled buffer state, while two of the world's great **religions**, Hinduism and Buddhism, overlap and mingle with older tribal

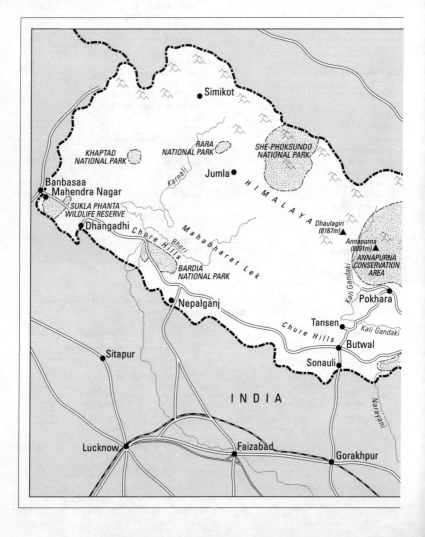

traditions – yet it's a testimony to the Nepalis' tolerance and good humour that there is no tradition of ethnic or religious strife. Unlike India, Nepal was never colonized, a fact which comes through in fierce national pride and other, more idiosyncratic ways. Founded on trans-Himalayan trade, its dense, medieval **cities** display a unique pagoda-style architecture, not to mention an astounding flair for festivals and pageantry. But above all, Nepal is a nation of unaffected **villages** and terraced hillsides – more than eighty percent of the population lives off the land – and whether you're trekking, biking or bouncing around in packed buses, sampling this simple lifestyle is perhaps the greatest pleasure of all.

But it would be misleading to portray Nepal as a fabled Shangri-la. One of the world's poorest countries (if you go by per capita income), it suffers from many of the pangs

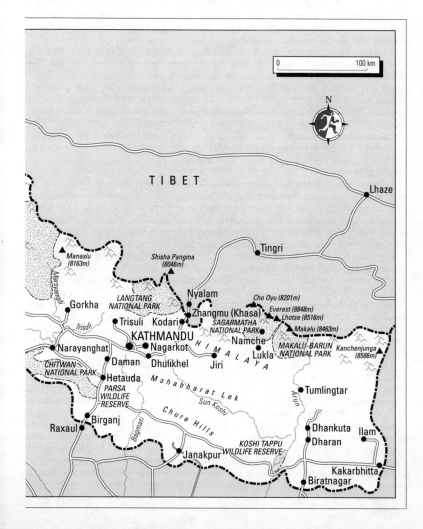

and uncertainties of the Third World, including overpopulation and deforestation; **development** is coming in fits and starts, and not all of it is being shared equitably. Heavily reliant on its big-brother neighbours, Nepal was, until 1990, run by one of the last remaining absolute monarchies, a regime that combined China's repressiveness and India's bureaucracy in equal measure. It's now a **democracy**, but corruption and frequent changes of government have led to widespread disillusion and spawned a simmering rebel insurgency; political freedom has changed little for the average struggling Nepali family.

Travelling in Nepal isn't a straightforward or predictable activity. Certain tourist areas are highly developed, even overdeveloped, but facilities elsewhere are rudimentary; **getting around** is time-consuming and sometimes uncomfortable. Nepalis are well used to shrugging off such inconveniences with the all-purpose phrase, *Ke garne?* ("What to do?"). Nepal is also a more fragile country than most – culturally as well as environmentally – so it's necessary to be especially sensitive as a traveller. Tips for minimizing your impact are given in Basics.

Topography is obviously a key consideration when travelling in Nepal. Generally speaking, the country divides into three altitude zones running from west to east. The northernmost of these is, of course, the **Himalayan chain**, broken into a series of *himal* (permanently snow-covered mountain ranges) and alpine valleys, and inhabited, at least part of the year, as high as 5000m. The largest part of the country consists of a wide belt of middle-elevation **foothills** and **valleys**, Nepal's traditional heartland; two ranges, the Mahabharat Lek and the lower, southernmost Chure (or Siwalik) Hills, stand out. Finally, the **Tarai**, a strip of flat, lowland jungle and farmland along the southern border, has more in common with India than with the rest of Nepal.

Highlights

Given the country's primitive transport network, most travellers stick to a well-worn circuit, with the result that certain sights and trekking routes have become rather commercialized. Don't be put off. The beaten track is remarkably thin and easy to escape in Nepal – and this guide is intended, first and foremost, to give you the confidence to do just that. It's the out-of-the-way places, the ones not written up in any book (even this one), that you'll remember most fondly on your return.

Everyone touches down in **Kathmandu** at some point, but for all its exotic bustle, the capital is rather rough going these days – logistically it makes a good base, but you won't want to spend lots of time there. Hindu temples, Buddhist stupas, rolling countryside and huddled brick villages provide incentives for touring the prosperous **Kathmandu Valley**, as do the historically independent city-states of **Patan** and **Bhaktapur**. The surrounding central hills are surprisingly undeveloped, apart from a couple of mountain view points, yet a few lesser routes, such as the road to the **Tibet border** and especially the **Tribhuwan Rajpath**, make for adventurous travel – especially by mountain bike or motorcycle.

The views get more dramatic, or at least more accessible, in the **western hills**. **Pokhara**, set beside a lake under a looming wall of peaks, is the closest thing you'll find to a resort in Nepal. Other hill towns – notably **Gorkha** and its impressive fortress, **Manakamana** with its wish-fulfilling temple, and laid-back **Tansen** – offer scenery with history or culture to boot.

It's in the teeming jungle and ethnic villages of the **Tarai** that Nepal's diversity really becomes apparent. Most travellers venture no further than **Chitwan National Park**, where endangered Asian one-horned rhinos are easily viewable, but **Bardia National Park** and two other rarely visited wildlife reserves are out there for the more adventurous. **Lumbini**, Buddha's birthplace in the western Tarai, is a world-class pilgrimage site, as is **Janakpur**, a Hindu holy city in the east. Rolling tea plantations, weekly markets and a rich cultural mix figure prominently in the spectacular and little-visited **east-ern hills**, most easily reached from the Tarai.

And of course Nepal is probably the most famous destination in the world for a growing range of outdoor activities, covered in a separate section of this guide. **Trekking** from village to village through the hills and up into high Himalayan valleys is an experience not to be missed. The scenery varies from cultivated terraces to lush rhododendron forests to glacier-capped peaks, but the cultural interactions are often, in retrospect, the most rewarding part of a trek. Nepal's rivers, meanwhile, are the liquid counterparts to its mountains, and **rafting** offers not only adventure but also a different perspective on the countryside and wildlife. Yet another alternative means of locomotion, **mountain-biking**, brings you in contact with the land and its people at your own pace.

Recent trends

The past decade has brought great upheaval to Nepal, and there's probably more still to come. The country's political system, economic development and mercurial relationship with India all seem to be in a worrying state of flux.

But while political instability is unlikely to have much of a direct effect on your plans, other changes inevitably will. No guidebook can reliably predict quite how things will be by the time you get to Nepal, but the following recent trends give an idea of what's in store:

• **Maoist rebels** are waging a guerrilla war against the government from their bases in remote hill areas. At the time of writing no incidents have involved tourists, and the rebels have stated publicly that they have no quarrel with foreigners, but seek the latest advice as you plan your trip.

• New **road-building** is moving trailheads further into the hinterland, making some treks shorter and the transport to them longer. This year's great trek or bike ride is next year's dirt road, and the following year's paved road (and a few years later, it may be a trail again).

• **Tourist bus** services are proliferating, making travel to certain places easier, but also turning those places into tourist traps.

• Nepal is getting more and more **packaged**: for no good reason other than heavy marketing, organized tours, treks and safaris have become common, even for budget travellers.

• The growth of **budget tourist ghettos** has been a major theme of the past decade. The commercialization is really dismaying in some areas, leading many returning travellers to complain that Nepal is "ruined". It's not, but parts of it are, so avoid them.

• Fortunately, a **Nepali cultural revival** seems to be emerging, as Nepalis discover that they need not toss out traditional ways to cater to foreigners. Thus travellers dissatisfied with pseudo-Western food and facilities now have a growing range of good, indigenous alternatives to choose from.

• **Rural electrification** is proceeding steadily, bringing not only lights but also videos, cable TV, email and a whole lot more contact with the outside world.

• **Rip-offs and theft** are on the rise, owing to an influx of Indian immigrants, high unemployment and weak law enforcement. Nepal is still one of the mellowest and safest countries in the world, but it's no longer the hassle-free paradise it once was.

• **Prices** have historically risen faster than average in the tourist areas, though oversupply is beginning to reverse this trend. Off the beaten track, prices if anything tend to decline in real terms.

PART ONE

THE

BASICS

GETTING THERE BY AIR

If Nepal is your only destination, flying direct to Kathmandu is the logical option. However, not many airlines serve this route, so you may well find yourself making several hops with two or even three different carriers. Flights in the autumn and spring high seasons (early October to mid-November, and late February to late March) fill up months ahead, so make sure you book well in advance if you plan to travel at these times.

Since it's a long way to Nepal, consider **stopping over** on the way there or back. If you're coming from North America or Australia and New Zealand, it should cost little or no extra to stop in Hong Kong, Bangkok, Singapore or a number of other Asian cities. From Europe, a stop in Karachi, Delhi or Dhaka may be free. Another option is an **"open jaw" ticket**, which entails flying into one city (in this case Kathmandu) and returning from another (say, Delhi), allowing you to travel overland in between. The price is usually calculated by halving the return fares to each destination and adding the two figures together.

If Nepal is only one stop on a longer journey, you might save money with a **round-the-world ticket**. Many discount travel agents can sell you an "off-the-shelf" RTW ticket that will have you touching down in about half a dozen cities including Kathmandu or at least Delhi (customized RTW tickets are apt to be more expensive). For greater flexibility, if not economy, buy a **one-way ticket**

to Hong Kong, Bangkok or Singapore, where onward tickets are very cheap. For typical airfares from other Asian cities to Kathmandu, see "Asian Connections" (p.14).

SHOPPING FOR TICKETS

Airline tickets are sold through many channels, and there's no magic rule of thumb for predicting which will be cheapest. For fares to Kathmandu and most of Asia, however, the best deals generally come from "consolidators" and other discount-type agents. You'll probably save time if you conduct your search in the following order.

Consolidators buy up large blocks of tickets that airlines don't think they'll be able to sell at their published fares, and sell them at a discount. Besides being cheap, consolidators normally don't impose advance purchase requirements, but they do often charge very stiff fees for date changes (airlines won't alter tickets once they've been sold through a consolidator). Also, these companies' margins are pretty tiny, so they make their money by dealing in volume – don't expect them to entertain lots of questions.

Other companies have access to different types of **discounted fares**, or sell a mix of consolidated and published fares. For example, some specialize in student and youth fares as well as ID cards, travel insurance and other deals for students and under-26s. At the time of writing, **charter flights** to Nepal were operating only out of the Netherlands and Germany, but keep an eye out in case any start up in your country.

Try the firms listed in the boxes on the following pages, or check out the ads in the Sunday newspaper travel sections. A **Web search** will turn up many other possibilities. Try as many companies as you can, since each one will have contracts with different airlines.

Check the restrictions carefully before buying any ticket, and establish exactly which airline(s) it's with – consolidators often cobble together itineraries on two or more airlines, which can mean long layovers and a greater risk of lost baggage. And remember, price isn't the only consideration: some companies are more reputable than others. Deal only with those that belong to an official travel trade association (such as ABTA

MAJOR AIRLINES IN THE UK AND IRELAND

AIRLINES SERVING NEPAL

Aeroflot, 70 Piccadilly, London W1 (☎0171/355 2233). Heathrow or Shannon to Kathmandu via Moscow and Dubai, once a week.

Austrian Airlines, 10 Wardour St, London W1V 4BJ (☎0171/434 7350). London to Kathmandu via Vienna.

Biman Bangladesh, 17 Conduit St, London W1 (☎0171/629 0252). Heathrow to Kathmandu via Paris/Frankfurt/Rome and Dhaka, four times a week.

Gulf Air, 14 Albermarle St, London W1 (☎0171/408 1717). Heathrow to Kathmandu via Bahrain, twice a week.

Pakistan International Airlines (PIA), 44 Dover St, London W1 (☎0171/290 3600).

Heathrow and Manchester to Kathmandu via Karachi, each twice a week.

Qatar Airways, 10 Conduit St, London W1 (☎0171/896 3636). London to Kathmandu via Doha, four times a week.

Royal Nepal Airlines Corporation (RNAC), 13 New Burlington St, London W1 (☎0171/494 0974). Gatwick to Kathmandu via Frankfurt and Dubai, twice a week.

Singapore Airlines, 143–147 Regent St, London W1 (☎0181/747 0007). Heathrow to Kathmandu via Singapore, twice a week.

Thai International, 41 Albemarle St, London W1 (☎0171/499 9113). Heathrow to Kathmandu via Bangkok, daily.

OTHER USEFUL AIRLINES

Air France, 177 Piccadilly, London W1 (☎0181/742 6600). London, Dublin or various other regional cities to Delhi via Paris.

Air India, Lansdowne House, 55 Berkeley Square, London W1 (☎01753/684 828). London and Manchester to Delhi nonstop, with connections to other Indian cities (and to Kathmandu on Indian Airlines).

British Airways, 156 Regent St, London W1 (☎0181/897 4000). London to Delhi nonstop, with connections to Calcutta and other Indian cities.

Egyptair, 296 Regent St, London W1 (☎0171/734 2395). London to Delhi via Cairo.

Emirates Airlines, 125 Pall Mall, London SW1 (☎0171/808 0808). London or Manchester to Delhi via Dubai.

Finnair, 14 Clifford St, London W1 (☎0171/408 1222). London to Bangkok via Helsinki.

KLM, Terminal 4, Heathrow (☎0181/750 9000).

London, Manchester or other regional cities to Delhi via Amsterdam.

Kuwait Airlines, tickets sold through Jetair, 188 Hammersmith Rd, London W6 (☎0181/970 1522). London to Delhi via Kuwait.

LOT Polish Airlines, 313 Regent St, London W1 (☎0171/580 5037). London to Bangkok via Warsaw.

Lufthansa, 7/8 Conduit St, London W1 (0345/737 747). Heathrow to Delhi and Bangkok via Frankfurt.

Qantas, 182 The Strand, London WC2 (☎0345/747 767). London to Bangkok.

Royal Jordanian Air, 177 Regent St, London W1 (☎0171/734 2557). London or Dublin to Delhi via Amman.

Swissair, Swiss Centre, Leicester Square, London W1 (☎0171/434 7300). London or Dublin to Delhi via Zurich.

in Britain or ASTA in the US) – they must uphold certain professional standards, and if they go bust you will probably be protected. Never deal with a company that demands cash up front, refuses to accept payment by credit card or won't provide written confirmation of flight details.

Once you've found the best discounted fare, it's probably still worth checking out what the **airlines** themselves are offering. Any local travel

agent will be able to access published fares, but in practice they may not have time to search out special promotions and the like, so it's worth doing your own research. Ordinarily, the cheapest way to go is with an **Apex** (Advance Purchase Excursion) ticket, although this will carry certain restrictions: you have to book – and pay – at least 21 days before departure and return within three months, and you tend to get penalized if you change your schedule. Many airlines don't offer

Apex fares to Kathmandu, but their standard excursion fares often cost no more, and they carry no advance purchase restrictions.

FROM THE UK AND IRELAND

The half-dozen airlines that fly between London and Kathmandu all make at least one stop en route, resulting in a minimum of twelve hours' total travel time. Only one (Thai) flies daily. Many other airlines fly from London and other regional cities to Delhi, where you can change planes for Kathmandu – this won't get you there any faster, and it probably won't save you any money either, but it expands your options for getting a seat on the day of your choice.

Fares to Kathmandu are **seasonal**, with airlines generally charging full whack for departures in October and early November, around Christmas and from early March to mid-April. During these months a return ticket will cost £50–200 more than during less popular times of the year, depending on the airline. (A notable exception is Biman Bangladesh, whose high season is mid-December to mid-January.) Handily, though, *indirect* tickets routed through Delhi are cheapest in the autumn and early spring. Flying on weekends will add £50 or more to a return fare; prices quoted below assume midweek travel.

FROM LONDON

From London, Qatar Airways, Gulf Air, Pakistan International Airways (PIA) and Royal Nepal Airlines Corporation (RNAC) offer the most direct routings. Of these, Qatar seems to have the most reliable and most comfortable service, with Gulf not far behind – they both charge around £470 in low season and £600 in high season. PIA is a bit cheaper at £450/550. Sad to say but RNAC, Nepal's flag-carrier, is renowned for overbooking, delays and general ineptitude, and isn't even all that cheap (£460/640).

Aeroflot's and Biman Bangladesh's services are quite cheap, but not as convenient. Aeroflot flies only once a week (around £450), and the flight entails a stopover in Moscow and usually another in some godforsaken airstrip in central Asia.

Biman offers the cheapest fare during Nepal's high season (as little as £430), but the flight routes through Dhaka, and you might have to spend the night there. Flights on Thai and Singapore aren't really worth considering from Europe because they go via Bangkok and Singapore respectively, both of which are just too far out of the way if Nepal is your sole destination.

Aeroflot is the cheapest way to get **to Delhi** (£290–400), but Gulf Air, Emirates and Royal Jordanian Air don't cost much more. Expect to pay more like £430–580 for nonstop flights on Air India or British Airways. A connecting flight to Kathmandu and back on RNAC or Indian Airlines will add about £160 to the final tab (if you're trying to save money, go overland – see below).

Several of the travel agents listed in the box on p.5 sell **round-the-world** tickets including Delhi, Kathmandu and Bangkok for £900–1000. Cheaper tickets have you travelling the Delhi–Kathmandu leg overland at your own expense. Returning to Delhi overland and then flying Delhi–Bangkok may save some money, but not much.

FROM OTHER BRITISH CITIES

PIA flies **from Manchester** to Kathmandu via Karachi, and the fare is the same as from London. Air India, KLM, Air France and Emirates all fly from Manchester to Delhi (via their capital cities), where you can pick up a Kathmandu connection on RNAC or Indian Airlines. KLM, Air France and British Airways fly indirectly from various other British cities to Delhi. However, from most places it will probably still work out cheaper to take a shuttle flight or train **to London** to take advantage of the much cheaper fares from there.

FROM IRELAND

There are no direct flights to Kathmandu **from Ireland**. Most travel agents will recommend flying to London to connect with one of the cheap flights from there (see above); figure on £80 for the Dublin–London or Shannon–London connection. Alternatively, you could fly with Royal Jordanian, Air France or Swissair from Dublin via their respective capitals to Delhi, and then on to Kathmandu on RNAC or Indian Airlines. Aeroflot flies from Shannon to Moscow, where you can connect with the once-weekly flight to Kathmandu, but it's not particularly cheap nor, as explained above, very convenient.

FROM NORTH AMERICA

Nepal is basically on the other side of the planet from North America. If you live on the East Coast it's somewhat shorter to go via Europe, and from the West Coast it's shorter via the Far East; but either way it's a long haul, involving one or more intermediate stops, and you'll arrive fresher and less jet-lagged if you can manage to fit in a few days' stopover somewhere en route.

Several airlines fly to Kathmandu from North America, although this is a fairly low-volume route and only one operates a daily service (Thai, from the West Coast). Plenty of other airlines fly to Delhi, Bangkok and other Asian cities, where you can catch a connecting flight to Kathmandu, so when seat availability is tight it's well worth asking about alternative routings.

Seasonal considerations may help determine your route. Most airlines flying east (over the Atlantic) consider high season to be summer and the period right around Christmas; low season is winter (excluding Christmas), spring and sometimes autumn. Flying west (over the Pacific), high season is generally summer and midwinter, with everything else being low season. The difference between high- and low-season fares is US$100–200. Note that flying on weekends ordinarily adds $100 or so to a round-trip fare; prices quoted below assume midweek travel in low season.

A **round-the-world** ticket originating in the US and including stops in Delhi and Bangkok will typically cost $1100 and up. From Canada, figure on Can$1750. Most off-the-shelf tickets don't include Kathmandu in the itinerary, forcing you to buy a separate Delhi–Kathmandu ticket (US$300/Can$350) or travel overland (see p.12). Some agents can put together a ticket that has you travelling overland at your own expense between Delhi and Kathmandu (always an adventure), and then flying from there to Bangkok.

FROM EAST AND CENTRAL USA

Flying **eastwards**, you'll stop over somewhere in Europe (usually London), and probably again somewhere in the Gulf. Figure on at least twenty hours' total travel time.

The cheapest deals going east tend to be with PIA out of **New York** (via Karachi). Sold through several New York consolidators (see box on p.8), these tickets can be had for as little as $1100 in

MAJOR AIRLINES IN NORTH AMERICA

AIRLINES SERVING NEPAL

Aeroflot (☎888/340-6400). Flights from several US cities and Montréal to Kathmandu via Moscow and Dubai, once a week; also to Delhi.

Pakistan International Airlines (PIA) (☎800/221-2552). New York to Kathmandu via London and Karachi, twice a week; also connections to Delhi and Mumbai.

Royal Nepal Airlines Corporation (RNAC) (☎800/266-3725 in US; ☎800/567-7622 in Toronto; ☎800/465-7622 in Vancouver). Various US and Canadian cities (through co-operative agreements) to Kathmandu via Hong Kong, Singapore, Bangkok or London.

Singapore Airlines (☎800/742-3333). Los Angeles, San Francisco and Vancouver to Kathmandu via various East Asian cities and Singapore; New York or Newark to Kathmandu via Amsterdam/Frankfurt and Singapore; twice a week.

Thai International (☎800/426-5204). Los Angeles to Kathmandu via Bangkok, daily; also connections to Delhi and Calcutta.

OTHER USEFUL AIRLINES

Air Canada (☎800/776-3000). Toronto to Delhi via London; Vancouver to Kathmandu through a co-operative agreement with Singapore.

Air India (☎800/223-2250). New York and Toronto to Delhi and Calcutta via London.

British Airways (☎800/247-9297 in US; ☎800/668-1059 in Canada). Many US and Canadian cities to Delhi via London.

Canadian Airlines (☎800/665-1177). Vancouver to Hong Kong and Bangkok.

Cathay Pacific Airways (☎800/233-2742). Los Angeles and Vancouver to Mumbai via Hong Kong.

China Air Lines (☎800/227-5118). Los Angeles and San Francisco to Bangkok and Delhi via Taipei.

Finnair (☎800/950-5000). New York and Miami to Bangkok via Helsinki.

Garuda Indonesia (☎800/342-7832 in US; ☎800/663-2254 in Canada). Los Angeles to Bangkok via Jakarta.

Gulf Air, (☎888/359-4853). Various East Coast cities (through a code-sharing agreement with American) to Kathmandu via London and Bahrain, twice a week).

KLM (☎800/374-7747 in US; ☎800/361-5073 in Canada). Major US and Canadian cities to Delhi and Calcutta via Amsterdam.

Korean Air (☎800/438-5000). Several US and Canadian cities to Bangkok via Seoul.

Kuwait Airways (☎800/458-9248). New York and Chicago to Delhi via London.

LOT Polish Airlines (☎800/223-0593 in US; ☎800/361-1017 in Canada). New York and Chicago to Bangkok via Warsaw.

Lufthansa (☎800/645-3880). Many US and Canadian cities to Delhi via Frankfurt and Karachi.

Malaysia Airlines (☎800/552-9264). Los Angeles and Vancouver to Delhi and Bangkok via Kuala Lumpur.

Northwest Airlines (☎800/447-4747). Los Angeles and Seattle to Hong Kong, Bangkok and Singapore via Tokyo.

United Airlines (☎800/538-2929). Los Angeles and San Francisco to Bangkok via Tokyo or Taipei.

---

low season, $1250 in high season. Marked-down tickets on several other carriers (notably Gulf, Air India, British Airways, Air France, KLM and Lufthansa) are frequently sold by consolidators for around $1250/1350. These tickets often have you crossing the Atlantic with one airline and then switching to another – there are any number of permutations, but it's common to change at London, Frankfurt or Delhi to connect with RNAC.

RNAC's fare from New York, which includes a connecting flight on another carrier, is $1500/1700.

The story is similar from other Eastern and Midwestern cities, but fares are $150–300 higher. In many cases the cheapest option will be to go via New York to take advantage of the rock-bottom consolidated fares from there. From the Midwest, **flying west** via Los Angeles (see below) may not cost any more, in case you've got a Far Eastern stopover in mind.

FROM WEST COAST USA

From the West Coast, it takes about the same time to fly eastwards or westwards – a minimum of 24 hours' total travel time – but **westbound airfares** are generally cheaper. Singapore and Thai fly direct from Los Angeles to Kathmandu via their respective capitals; tickets on Thai are heavily discounted through a couple of West Coast consolidators (see box above). Many other airlines (Cathay Pacific, Malaysia, Korean, China Air Lines, United and Northwest) can take you as far as Hong Kong, Bangkok or Singapore, where you'll typically switch to RNAC or Thai. The best deals through consolidators start at around $1200 in low season, $1300 in high season. RNAC charges $1400/1500.

FROM CANADA

From **Toronto** or **Montréal**, you'll almost certainly fly east. The cheapest discounted deals tend to be out of Toronto on Air India, Air Canada or Canadian (connecting with RNAC in London or Delhi), and start at around Can$1900 in low season, $2100 in high season. Consolidators can also route you through London on any number of airlines to connect with the Air India–RNAC route, or use various European carriers (British Airways, Air France, Lufthansa, KLM or Aeroflot, to name a few) to get you to Delhi or Kathmandu via their respective capitals.

From **Vancouver**, flying west is the clear choice. Singapore flies direct to Kathmandu (via Singapore), while several other airlines (Air Canada, Canadian, Cathay Pacific, Korean and Malaysia) fly to Hong Kong or Bangkok to connect with RNAC. Other options are to fly via Seattle (served by Northwest), San Francisco (for China Air Lines or United) or Los Angeles (Thai's US gateway). The cheapest fares are likely to come in at around $2100 in low season, $2300 in high season.

From **other central and eastern cities**, you can go via Toronto, Vancouver or possibly New York or Los Angeles. The latter two are worth considering because of the extremely cheap consolidator flights from there (see above). Most connecting flights to Toronto or Vancouver will add $200–300 to the above fares.

FROM AUSTRALIA AND NEW ZEALAND

Flying to Nepal **from Australia and New Zealand** invariably means stopping over in a southeast Asian city. As ever, prices depend on the season. These vary slightly from airline to airline, but generally low season runs from mid-January to late February, and from early October to the end of November; high season is mid- to late May, June, July and August, and early

December to mid-January; shoulder season comprises the rest of the year.

Return fares to Kathmandu start at about A$1450/NZ$1800, but a cheaper option might be to fly to Bangkok for about A$900/NZ$1200 (the cheapest return flight from Sydney is currently Olympic's at A$860) and pick up an onward ticket to Nepal from there. These cost around US$200 even in peak season, although obviously this option lacks the certainty of a through ticket, and you might be turned back if you don't have sufficient funds.

Fares to Delhi are about the same as to Kathmandu, so another possibility – although not the most economical one – is to fly into India and fly or travel overland into Nepal from there.

MAJOR AIRLINES IN AUSTRALIA AND NEW ZEALAND

AIRLINES SERVING NEPAL

Royal Nepal Airlines Corporation (RNAC), Level 17, 456 Kent St, Sydney (☎02/9285 6855); NZ Agent: Adventure World, 101 Great South Rd, Remuera, Auckland (☎09/524 5118). Flights to Kathmandu from Bangkok, Singapore and Hong Kong.

Singapore Airlines, 17–19 Bridge St, Sydney (local-call rate ☎13 1011); Lower Ground Floor, West Plaza Building, cnr Customs and Albert streets, Auckland (☎09/379 3209; toll-free

☎0800/808 909). Flights to Kathmandu from Singapore, and numerous connecting flights from Australian and New Zealand cities.

Thai Airways, 75–77 Pitt St, Sydney (☎02/9251 1922; local-call rate ☎1300/651 960); Kensington Swan Building, 22 Fanshawe St, Auckland (☎09/377 3886). Flights to Kathmandu from Sydney, Auckland and Perth, with a one-night stopover in Bangkok required.

OTHER USEFUL AIRLINES

Air France, 64 York St, Sydney (☎02/9244 2100); 2/143 Nelson St, Auckland (☎09/303 3521).

Air India, Level 18, 44 Market St, Sydney (☎02/9299 2022); Level 6, 214-218 Queen St, Auckland (☎09/303 1301).

Air New Zealand, 5 Elizabeth St, Sydney (☎02/9223 4666; reservations ☎13 2476); Quay St, Auckland (☎09/357 3000).

Alitalia, 9/118 Alfred St, North Sydney (☎02/9922 1555; local call-rate ☎1300/653 747); 6th Floor, Trustbank Building, 229 Queen St, Auckland (☎09/379 4457).

British Airways, Level 19, 259 George St, Sydney (☎02/8904 8800); 154 Queen St, Auckland (☎09/356 8690).

Cathay Pacific, Sydney Airport (☎02/9931 5500; reservations ☎13 1747); 11th Floor, 205–209 Queen St, Auckland (☎09/379 0861; toll-free ☎0800/800 454).

Gulf Air, 64 York St, Sydney (☎02/9244 2199); no NZ office.

Lauda Air, 11/143 Macquarie St, Sydney (☎02/9251 6155; toll-free ☎1800/642 438); Lufthansa House, 36 Kitchener St, Auckland (☎09/303 1529).

Malaysia Airlines, 16 Spring St, Sydney (local-call rate ☎13 2627); Floor 12, Swanson Centre, 12–26 Swanson St, Auckland (☎09/373 2741).

Olympic Airways, 3rd floor, 37–49 Pitt St, Sydney (☎02/9251 2044).

Qantas, 70 Hunter St, Sydney (☎02/9951 4294; local-call rate ☎13 1211); Qantas House, 154 Queen St, Auckland (☎09/357 8900; toll-free ☎0800/808 767).

Royal Brunei Airlines, Suite 5208, MLC Centre, Sydney (☎02/9223 1566); Unit 9, 25 Mary St, Brisbane (☎07/3221 7757).

DISCOUNT AGENTS IN AUSTRALIA AND NEW ZEALAND

Accent on Travel, 545 Queen St, Brisbane (☎07/3832 1777).

Anywhere Travel, 345 Anzac Parade, Kingsford, Sydney (☎02/9663 0411).

Budget Travel, 16 Fort St, Auckland; other branches around the city (☎09/366 0061; toll-free ☎0800/808 040 for nearest branch).

Destinations Unlimited, 3 Milford Rd, Milford, Auckland (☎09/373 4033).

Flight Centres Australia: 82 Elizabeth St, Sydney (☎02/9235 3522); 19 Bourke St, Melbourne (☎03/9650 2899); other branches nationwide (☎13 1600 for nearest branch). New Zealand: National Bank Towers, 205–225 Queen St, Auckland (☎09/309 6171); other branches countrywide (☎0800/FLIGHTS for nearest branch).

Harvey World Travel, 247 Pitt St, Sydney (☎02/9261 2800); branches nationwide (nearest branch ☎13 2757).

Northern Gateway, 22 Cavenagh St, Darwin (☎08/8941 1394).

Passport Travel, 401 St Kilda Rd, Melbourne (☎03/9876 3888).

STA Travel, Australia: 855 George St, Sydney (☎02/9212 1255); 256 Flinders St, Melbourne (☎03/9654 7266); other offices nationwide). New Zealand: Travellers' Centre, 10 High St, Auckland (☎09/309 0458); 90 Cashel St, Christchurch (☎03/379 9098); other branches in Wellington, Dunedin, Palmerston North, Hamilton and at major universities.

Thomas Cook, Australia: 175 Pitt St, Sydney (☎02/9229 6611); 257 Collins St, Melbourne (☎03/9282 0333); branches in other state capitals (☎13 1771 for nearest branch). New Zealand: 159 Queen St, Auckland (☎09/379 3924; nearest branch ☎0800/500 600).

Topdeck Travel, 65 Grenfell St, Adelaide (☎08/8232 7222).

Tymtro Travel, 428 George St, Sydney (☎02/9223 2211).

UTAG Travel, 122 Walker St, North Sydney (☎02/9956 8399); branches throughout Australia.

Round-the-world tickets start at around A$2100/NZ$2400. For all tickets, the best prices are usually found through the discount agents listed above.

FROM AUSTRALIA

From **Sydney**, Thai Airways serves Kathmandu with an obligatory one-night stopover in Bangkok for A$1530/1750, depending on the season. Singapore Airlines flies to Kathmandu via Singapore, for around A$1600/1850. Several airlines, among them Air New Zealand, Qantas, Alitalia and British Airways, connect with either Royal Nepal Airlines Corporation (RNAC) or Thai Airways in Bangkok, Hong Kong or Singapore, the cheapest combination being the Alitalia/RNAC package at A$1500/1700. Fares out of **Perth** may be cheaper by A$100 or so, since flying time to southeast Asia from the west coast is shorter than from the east coast.

FROM NEW ZEALAND

From **Auckland**, most flights to Nepal go via Sydney. A Thai Airways flight (via Sydney) entails an overnight stop in Bangkok, and costs NZ$1900/2200, according to season. A combined Air New Zealand/RNAC flight, also calling at Sydney and Bangkok, is NZ$1950/2150. Singapore Airlines flies direct daily from Auckland to Singapore, with an overnight stay before flying on to Kathmandu (NZ$2030/2280).

PACKAGE TOURS

Most **tours** of Nepal are based around trekking, rafting, cycling or wildlife-viewing, which are described later in "Outdoor pursuits". Sightseeing packages do exist, although most treat Nepal as an add-on to India. For a longer (not to mention cheaper) tour, wait till you get to Kathmandu and arrange a customized itinerary with one of the travel agents there. As with trekking, booking a sightseeing tour from your home country can cost as much as ten times what you'd spend by doing things independently (at least £600/US$1000 a week, excluding airfare), but this is the price of peace of mind. A few sightseeing tour operators are included in the box opposite. You could also try the travel agents listed earlier on pp.5, 8 and above. See also the "Village Tourism " section on p.62.

SIGHTSEEING TOUR OPERATORS

Although phone numbers are given below, you're better off booking through your local travel agent, who will make all the phone calls, sort out the snafus and arrange flights, insurance and the like – all at no extra cost to you.

NORTH AMERICA

Abercrombie & Kent (☎800/323-7308 or 708/954-2944).
Adventure Center (☎800/227-8747 or 510/654-1879.
Cox & Kings (☎800/999-1758 or 212/935-3935).
Himalayan Travel (☎800/225-2300 or 203/359-3669).

Inner Asia (☎800/ 777-8183 or 415/922-0448).
Journeyworld International (☎800/635-3900 or 212/247-6127).
Mercury Travels Limited (☎800/223-1474 or 212/661-0380).
Rascals in Paradise (☎800/872-7225).
Independent family tours.

UK & IRELAND

Abercrombie & Kent, Sloane Square House, Holbein Place, London SW1W (☎0171/730 9600).
Cox & Kings, St James Court, 45 Buckingham Gate, London SW1E (☎0171/873 5000).

Explore Worldwide, 1 Frederick St, Aldershot, Hants GU11 (☎01252/344 161).
Mercury Travels, 1 Thames Place, Richmond Rd, London SW15 (☎0181/780 3022).

AUSTRALIA & NEW ZEALAND

Abercrombie & Kent, 90 Bridport St, Albert Park, Melbourne (☎03/9699 9766); and 14th floor, Brookfield House, 17 Victoria St W, Auckland (☎09/358 4200).
Asia and World Travel, cnr George and Adelaide streets, Brisbane (☎07/3229 3511).
Asian Travel Centre, 126 Russell St, Melbourne (☎03/9654 8277).

Far East Travel Centre, 50 Margaret St, Sydney (☎02/9262 6414).
India/Nepal Travel Centre, Level 13, 92 Pitt St, Sydney (☎9223 6000); Level 7, 333 Adelaide St, Brisbane (☎07/3221 4788); branches in Melbourne and Perth.

OVERLAND ROUTES TO NEPAL

The classic Asia overland trip is still alive and kicking, despite periodic political reroutings. Leaving Europe behind at Istanbul, the usual approach from the west traverses Turkey, angles down through Iran, crosses Pakistan and enters India at Amritsar.

Several **overland expedition operators** (see box below) run 6- to 18-week trips in specially designed vehicles all the way through to Kathmandu. Expect to pay between £800 and £2400 for the one-way trip from London, depending on duration and level of luxury.

FROM INDIA

Transport connections between **India** and Nepal are well developed, with travel agents in Delhi, Darjeeling and other major train junctions in the north selling **bus** packages to Kathmandu. However, these are often ripoffs, and in any case it's an easy matter to ride to the border and make your own way from there – you'll almost certainly end up on the same Nepali bus anyway.

Three **border crossings** see the vast majority of travellers: **Sonauli/Belahiya**, the most popular entry point, reachable from Delhi, Varanasi and most of north India (via Gorakhpur); **Raxaul/Birganj**, accessible from Bodh Gaya and Calcutta (via Patna); and **Kakarbhitta**, serving Darjeeling and Calcutta (via Siliguri). A fourth, **Banbasaa/Mahendra Nagar**, handy for the Uttar Pradesh hill stations and Delhi, is less frequently used but is gaining in popularity. Two others (near Nepalganj and Dhangadhi) are also open to tourists, though rarely used and not easy to get to. All these official crossings are described in the relevant sections of the guide.

Other crossings near Janakpur, Biratnagar and Ilam sometimes admit foreigners, and may soon become official entry points. But since you can't be sure ahead of time that you'll be allowed

---

OVERLAND OPERATORS AND AGENTS

UK & IRELAND

Adventure Travel Centre/Top Deck Travel, 131–135 Earls Court Rd, London SW5 (☎0171/370 4555).

Colette Pearson Travel, 64 S William St, Dublin 2 (☎01/677 1029).

Encounter Overland, 267 Old Brompton Rd, London SW5 (☎0171/370 6845).

Exodus Travels, 9 Weir Rd, London SW12 (☎0181/673 0859).

NORTH AMERICA

Adventure Center (☎800/227-8747 or 510/654-1879).

Trek Holidays (☎800/661-7265 or 416/922-7584).

Safaricentre (☎800/223-6046 or 310/546-4411).

AUSTRALIA & NEW ZEALAND

Adventure World, 73 Walker St, North Sydney (☎02/9956 7766; toll-free ☎1800/221 931), plus branches in Melbourne, Brisbane, Adelaide and

Perth; 101 Great South Rd, Remuera, Auckland (☎09/524 5118).

A list of adventure travel operators and agents appears on pp.60 and 137.

through, you should probably enter the country via one of the official crossings to avoid a wasted journey; then, if you're up for adventure on the way out, check with Central Immigration in Kathmandu before setting off to find out what else is open.

BY PRIVATE VEHICLE

Nepal used to be *the* place to sell **vehicles** – particularly vans – but liberalized import policies have removed any financial incentive. Needless to say, bringing a vehicle into Nepal is a hell of a commitment, and requires nerves of steel to cope with precarious roads, drunk drivers, slow-moving vehicles, nonexistent law enforcement, horrendous city traffic, parking nightmares, sacred cows and fatalistic pedestrians (see p.36 for driving tips). The trade-off is that you don't have to deal with Nepali buses, and you get to go at your own pace, bring lots more gear and have your own personal space. You can enter Nepal via any official border crossing (see above).

If you're driving all the way from your home country, the best strategy is to obtain a **carnet de passage**, a document intended to ensure you don't illegally sell the vehicle while out of the country. A *carnet* is available from the AA or similar motoring organization. It may also be possible to get one in India if the vehicle (most likely a motorcycle) was purchased there. If you can't manage to obtain a carnet, you'll have to pay a per-diem duty rate on the vehicle when you enter Nepal; it works out to about US$1 a day for a

motorcycle, $3 a day for a car, paid in advance for however many days you think you'll be in Nepal. You'd also do well to come equipped with an **international driving licence**.

BY BICYCLE

Entering Nepal by **bicycle** involves no special paperwork. The main routes are summarized in the box below. Cycling from India is best done in December and January, when the weather is coolest. Entering via one of the far-western or far-eastern crossings, be prepared to spend one or more nights in really basic accommodation (like the floor of a teashop). Chapter Nine gives more information on biking in Nepal.

FROM TIBET

Any advice to do with travelling in **Tibet** is liable to be out of date by the time it's in print, so seek current information before going to Tibet in anticipation of being able to cross into Nepal. At the time of writing, China was allowing individuals with the proper paperwork for Tibet travel to exit at Zhangmu (Kodari on the Nepal side) on the Lhasa–Kathmandu highway, but was only allowing groups to enter there. **Landcruisers** ply a standard three- or four-day quasi-sightseeing route from Lhasa via Shigatze, Gyantse and Tingri to the border, where you'll have to walk a bit (or, if the road is washed out, a lot) and then continue for almost another full day to Kathmandu by **bus**. See p.149 for more information on seasonal considerations.

CYCLING INTO NEPAL

If you're entering Nepal by bike, here's a brief look at the main routes:

Birganj–Kathmandu. Distance 185km, elevations ranging from 90m above sea level to 2490m. A spectacular but extremely strenuous ride up and over the Tribhuwan Rajpath – the climb is so tough from the south that this is probably a better route for leaving Nepal than entering it. Unfortunately, Birganj is the least pleasant of Nepal's border crossings.

Kakarbhitta–Kathmandu. Distance 540km, elevations 80m–2490m. Adventurous route from Darjeeling through little-visited country, with an obligatory stopover in Janakpur; the final leg can be along the Rajpath or an easier way via Chitwan. (Yet a third variation, Janakpur to

Kathmandu via Dhulikhel, may be possible by the time you get to Nepal.)

Sonauli–Pokhara. Distance 185km, elevations 90–1500m. A very good introduction to Nepal: a scenic, reasonably cycle-friendly route offering side trips to Lumbini and Tansen.

Mahendranagar–Pokhara. Distance 750km, elevations 80–1500m. The most rural way from Delhi, passing two great wildlife parks and then joining the Sonauli-Pokhara route.

Kodari–Kathmandu. Distance 230m, elevations 630m–1640m. The only route from Tibet. This mostly downhill Nepal stretch will seem tame compared to the ride from Lhasa to the border.

ASIAN CONNECTIONS

One-way air fares between the following Asian cities and Kathmandu don't vary that much, although it's still always worth shopping around. Prices given are in US dollars. Note that Royal Nepal Airlines Corporation (RNAC) and Indian Airlines (IA) give a 25 percent discount to under-30s on the Calcutta, Delhi and Varanasi flights.

Bangkok ($220) – Thai, RNAC
Calcutta ($96) – IA, RNAC, Necon (the latter indirectly, via Biratnagar)
Delhi ($142) – IA, RNAC
Dhaka ($100) – Biman Bangladesh

Hong Kong ($320) – RNAC
Karachi ($189) – PIA
Mumbai ($257) – IA, RNAC
Singapore ($320–390) – RNAC, Singapore
Varanasi ($71) – IA, Necon

If you've managed to **cycle** all the way to Lhasa, you ought to be fit and acclimatized enough to make it the rest of the way to Nepal – but needless to say, this is an extremely arduous journey along an unpaved road, crossing two passes of at least 5000m, and should only be attempted in good weather.

CLIMATE AND WHEN TO GO

It's hard to generalize about the climate of a country ranging in elevation from near sea level to Mount Everest. About the only thing that can be said is that all but a few parts of Nepal are governed by the same monsoonal pattern (see box opposite), with temperatures varying according to elevation (see chart opposite).

Five **seasons** prevail in Nepal, but these are based on more than just weather: whenever you choose to go, you'll have to weigh other factors, both positive (mountain visibility, festivals, wildlife) and negative (crowds, disease).

Probably half of all tourists visit Nepal in the **autumn** (October to November), and for good reasons. The weather is clear and dry, and temperatures aren't too cold in the high country nor too hot in the Tarai. With the air washed clean by the monsoon rains, the mountains are at their most visible, making this the most popular time for trekking. Two major festivals also fall during this season. The downside, however, is that the tourist quarters are heaving and hustley, prices are higher and it may be hard to find a decent room, you'll wait ages for food and for trekking permits, and people are short on ready smiles and chat.

Winter (December and January) weather is for the most part clear and stable. It isn't especially cold at lower elevations – it never snows in Kathmandu, and afternoon temperatures are balmy – but the "mists of Indra" can make mornings dank and chilly (especially in unheated budget lodgings). Most travellers head down into India, leaving the tourist areas fairly quiet – too quiet, sometimes, as many restaurants pare down their menus for the season, and most trekking lodges close. This is an excellent time to visit the Tarai, where temperatures are relatively mild.

Spring (February to mid-April) brings warmer temperatures, longer days, weddings and more festivals. The rhododendrons are in bloom in the hills towards the end of this period, and in the Tarai the thatch has been cut, so despite the increasing heat this is the best time for viewing wildlife. All of which creates another tourist crush, albeit not quite as bad as in the autumn. The one factor that keeps people away is a disappointing haze that obscures the mountains from lower elevations, though it's usually possible to trek above it.

The **pre-monsoon** (mid-April to early June) is stifling at lower elevations, and dusty wind squalls are common. People get a little edgy with

AVERAGE TEMPERATURES AND RAINFALL

	FEB			APR			JUN			AUG			OCT			DEC		
	°C		rain	°C		rain	°C		rain	°C		rain	°C		rain	°C		rain
	Min	Max	cm	Min	Max	cm	Min	Max	cm	Min	Max	cm	Min	Max	cm	Min	Max	cm
Ilam (1200m)	10	18	0	16	25	6	18	25	32	9	25	28	16	25	8	8	18	0
Janakpur (70m)	9	24	1	16	35	4	24	36	23	25	34	24	20	29	5	10	24	0
Jumla (2420m)	-3	13	4	3	22	3	13	24	7	15	24	17	6	24	4	-5	15	0
Kathmandu (1290m)	4	20	3	11	27	6	19	29	29	20	28	36	13	26	6	2	20	0
Namche (3450m)	-6	6	2	1	12	3	6	15	14	8	16	24	2	12	8	-6	7	4
Pokhara (80m)	8	21	3	15	30	9	20	29	57	21	29	71	17	26	22	7	20	0
Sonauli (90m)	10	26	1	18	37	6	24	38	28	26	35	41	21	30	8	10	25	0

the heat; this is the time for popular unrest, but also for the Kathmandu Valley's great rainmaking festival. Trek high, where the temperatures are more tolerable.

Nepalis welcome the **monsoon** (June to September), which breaks the enervating monotony of the previous months, and makes the fields come alive with rushing water and green shoots. The rains rinse and renew the land. This can be a fascinating time to visit, when Nepal is at its most Nepali, but there are many drawbacks: mountain views are rare, leeches come out in force along the mid-elevation trekking routes, roads become impassable, flights get cancelled, and disease runs rampant as the rising water table brings the entire contents of city sewers to the surface.

More specific when-to-go advice for wildlife-viewing, trekking, rafting and mountain-biking is given in Chapters Five, Seven, Eight and Nine respectively.

THE MONSOON

Listen to these humming downpours in the night and the doors to godly pleasures will unfold themselves.
Lekhnath Poudyal (1885–1966), "Thoughts on the Rainy Monsoon"

Nepal's climate is governed by the **monsoon**, one of the world's great weather phenomena. A seasonal wind (the word derives from the Arabic for "season"; the Nepali word for monsoon is *barkhaa*), the monsoon is driven by extreme temperature fluctuations in Central Asia. As air over the Asian landmass warms in late spring and early summer, it rises, sucking air in from the ocean periphery to take its place. The air drawn from the south, passing over the Indian Ocean, is laden with moisture; as soon as it's forced aloft and cooled (whether by updrafts over hot land, or by a barrier, such as the hills and mountains of Nepal), it reaches its saturation point and drops its moisture. With the arrival of autumn, the flow reverses: cooling over the continent blows dry air outwards, bringing clear, stable conditions.

That's the theory, though in practice this huge, complex system is affected by countless variables such as land temperatures, jet-stream patterns, topography and late-season typhoons. The further inland you are, the harder it is to predict the outcome. Nepal is at the end of the line of the eastern arm of the South Asian monsoon sweeping up from the Bay of Bengal, which means it gets a month or so of **pre-monsoon** – a period of false storms and dry lightning – before the moist air arrives.

In Nepal, the **rains** generally advance from east to west in early to mid-June, and drop more precipitation overall in the east than in the west. They build slowly, reaching a peak in July and early August, then taper off again until clear weather returns by early October. Even at the monsoon's height, however, it doesn't bring continuous torrential rain – more usually it's intermittent showers and longer overnight soaks. Local terrain and other factors can affect rainfall considerably: areas lying in the "rain shadow" north of the Himalaya see very little monsoon moisture, while south-facing slopes may receive precipitation long before the plains to the south do. The latter effect is most dramatic where monsoon winds slam into high ranges with few intervening foothills, as they do around Pokhara.

RED TAPE AND VISAS

All foreign nationals except Indians need a visa to enter Nepal. Tourist visas are issued on arrival with a minimum of fuss at the Kathmandu airport and at official overland entry points. Have a passport-size photo at the ready, and if possible bring exact change for the visa fee – in US dollars if you're entering by air.

Fees may change without warning, but visas currently **cost** US$15 (or equivalent in other currencies) for fifteen days, $25 for thirty days ($40 for a double-entry visa), and $60 for a sixty-day multiple-entry visa. If you plan on border-hopping between Nepal and India (or Tibet), the double- or multiple-entry option may save some time and money, but it's not essential as you can get a re-entry stamp at any official border crossing (same prices as visas).

Getting a visa from an overseas **Nepalese embassy or consulate** will cut down on paperwork on arrival, but it's really only worth doing if you happen to be in the neighbourhood or if you're one of those people who has to have everything sorted out before you go. The fees are supposed to be the same as those given above, but are actually often higher. See the box below for embassy and consulate addresses.

NEPALESE EMBASSIES AND CONSULATES

Australia: Level 13, 92 Pitt St, Sydney 2000 (☎02/9233 6161); Level 5, 277 Flinders Lane, Melbourne 3000 (☎03/9650 6683); Suite 2, 16 Robinson St, Nedlands 6009, WA (☎08/9386 2102).

Bangladesh: Road No. 2, Baridhara Diplomatic Enclave, Baridhara, Dhaka (☎02/601790).

Belgium: 21 Ave Champel, B-1640 Rhoke St, Genese (☎32-02-3585808).

Canada: 200 Bay St, 32nd Floor, Toronto, ON M5J 2J9 (☎416/865-0200).

China: No. 1 Sanlitun Xiliujie, Beijing (☎5321795).

Denmark: 2 Teglgardsstr, DK-1452, Copenhagen (☎3312 4166).

France: 45 rue de Acacias, 75017 Paris (☎4622 4867); 7 bis Allée des Soupirs, 31000 Toulouse (☎6132 9122).

Germany: Im Hag 15, D-5300 Bonn 2 (☎0228/343097).

India: Barakhamba Rd, New Delhi 110001 (☎11/332 9969); 19 Woodlands, Sterndale Rd, Alipore, Calcutta 700027 (☎33/452024).

Italy: Piazzale Medaglie d'Oro 20, 00136 Rome (☎06/345 1642).

Japan: 14–19 Todoroki, 7-Chome Setagaya-Ku, Tokyo-158 (☎03-3705-5558).

Netherlands: Prinsengracht 687-1017-Jv, Amsterdam (☎020/241 530).

Norway: Haakon Viis Gate 5B, PO Box 1483, Vika, 0116 Oslo (☎02/283 5510).

Myanmar (Burma): 16 Natmauk Yeiktha, Yangon (☎50633).

Pakistan: 419 Qamar House, M.A. Jinnah Rd, Karachi 2 (☎021/201 113).

Sweden: Eriksbergsgatan 1A, S-114 30, Stockholm (☎08/679 8039).

Switzerland: Asylstrasse 81, 8030 Zurich (☎01/475993).

Thailand: 189 Soi 71, Sukhumvit Rd, Bangkok 10110 (☎2/391 7240).

UK: 12a Kensington Palace Gdns, London W8 4QU (☎0171/229 1594).

USA: 2131 Leroy Pl NW, Washington DC 20008 (☎202/667-4550); 820 Second Ave, Suite 17B, New York, NY 10017 (☎212/370-4188).

Tourist visas can be **extended**, up to thirty days at a time, for a maximum of 120 days in a calendar year (150 days given extenuating circumstances). Extensions are granted only at the Kathmandu or Pokhara **Central Immigration** offices – a somewhat tedious procedure, especially in high season, when queues can run to two hours or more, which is why it's best to get the longest visa you think you'll need right from the start. The cost is US$1 per day, payable in Nepalese currency only. Submit your passport and one passport-size photo with your application; instant photos are available from studios near Central Immigration offices.

The fine for overstaying is double the amount that you would have paid had you properly extended your visa. However, don't overstay more than a couple of days, and for heaven's sake *don't* tamper with your visa. Tourists have been jailed for these seemingly minor infractions.

> A trekking permit isn't required for any of the places described in this book *except* the areas covered in Chapter Seven. You'll find a more detailed discussion of trekking permits there.

TREKKING PERMITS

A tourist visa is technically valid only in the fraction of Nepal served by roads. To visit anywhere more than about a day's walk off a main road you need to get a **trekking permit** from Central Immigration – even if you don't intend to trek. For most trekking areas, the fee is the rupee equivalent of US$5 per week. Submit your passport, and two identical passport photos. Central Immigration offices will process simultaneous applications for visa extensions and trekking permits, but you still have to pay both fees.

COSTS, MONEY AND BANKS

Your money goes a long way in Nepal. Off the tourist routes, it can actually be hard to spend US$5/£3 a day, however willing you might be to pay more. On the other hand, Kathmandu and some of the other tourist traps can burn a hole in your pocket rather faster than you might have expected in the Third World. The cost of seeing Nepal, then, depends in large part on the proportion of time you spend on and off the beaten track.

While even in the capital it's still possible for a budget traveller to keep to US$8/£5 a day, the figure can effortlessly balloon to $20/£13 or more simply by trading up to slightly nicer hotels and restaurants. If you like to travel in greater luxury, you should expect to spend $40 or more per day, depending mainly on standard of accommodation.

TYPICAL COSTS

The price of **accommodation** varies considerably, depending on where you stay and when. Really basic rooms (ie, the kind Nepalis stay in) can almost always be found for $1.50/£1 or less. Prices aren't automatically higher in tourist areas, but most travellers take up the option of paying more for a few creature comforts: figure on $4–15/£2.50–10 for a budget double room in the high season. Off-season rates can plummet by 50 percent or more, but it's up to you to bargain. Prices for single rooms are usually lower, and dorm beds are often available, but you'll generally save money by doubling up. Better hotels usually cost $30 or more – a lot more, if you want international-standard features.

Food, cheap as it is, tends to be the biggest daily expense for budget travellers. Normally, a tourist dinner will run to $2–4/£1.50–2.50 per person, rising to $8/£5 or more in a really posh place. (But put that in perspective – that's about what you'd leave for a *tip* in a comparable restaurant back home.) *Daal bhaat*, the all-you-can-eat national meal of rice, lentils and curried vegetables, costs less than $1/70p just about anywhere, and you can fill up on road snacks for just pennies.

If you stick to buses, the cost of **transport** is trifling. An all-day journey on a tourist bus will cost $4–10/£2.50–6, half that on a local bus. In any case, there are only a handful of tourist bus routes to spend your money on, and the local buses are so uncomfortable that you probably won't be using many of them either. On a per-person basis, a hired private vehicle isn't much more expensive than a tourist bus if you have enough people to fill it. However, the stakes go up dramatically if you fly (one-way fares are generally in the region of $50–100/£30–60).

A **value-added tax** (**VAT**) of 10 percent is built into the prices of most goods, but many hotels and restaurants (particularly the more expensive ones) quote their prices exclusive of it. An additional two-percent tourism service fee is applicable to room and meal charges in tourist hotels, but the cheaper places roll it into their prices.

No matter how tight your budget, it would be foolish not to splurge now and then on some of the things that make Nepal unique: **trekking** on your own is quite cheap, but you might prefer to hire a porter or guide for $5–10/£3–6 a day, or even pay upwards of $20/£13 a day for a fully catered trek. **Rafting**, **biking** and **wildlife trips** also work out to be relatively expensive, but well worth it. And few visitors will be able to resist buying at least something from Nepal's rich range of **handicrafts**.

You'll inevitably pay over the odds for things at first, but don't think of it as being ripped off. So what if you pay Rs100 too much for your first night's lodging? It's all part of the process of learning the going rate of things, which you can't be expected to know right away.

A final point: some travellers make a wild show of pinching pennies, which Nepalis find pathetic – they know how much an air ticket to Kathmandu costs. Others throw money around too freely, which proves they deserve to be parted from it. Bargain where appropriate, but don't begrudge a few rupees to someone who's worked hard for them, and try to spend your money where it will do most good.

NEPALESE MONEY

Nepal's unit of currency is the **rupee**, which is divided into 100 paisa. At the time of writing, the **exchange rate** was Rs68 to the US$ (£1=Rs110). The Nepalese rupee floats freely against most other currencies but is generally pegged to a fixed rate against the Indian rupee, which at the time of writing was 160 Nepalese rupees to 100 Indian rupees. (Where confusion might arise, it's common practice to refer to the two currencies as NC and IC respectively.)

Almost all Nepali money is paper: **notes** come in denominations of Rs1, 2, 5 10, 20, 25, 50, 100, 250, 500 and 1000. **Coins** are 25 and 50 paisa and 1, 2, 5 and 10 rupees. The smaller, aluminium coins are used mainly for almsgiving.

One minor annoyance of travelling in Nepal is **getting change**. Even in tourist areas, business people will hem and haw about breaking a large note – "You have smaller money?" they'll ask, peering into your wallet. Trying to pass even a Rs100 note to a village merchant or a riksha driver is sure to invite delays, since few Nepalis can afford to keep much spare change lying around. It gets to be a game of bluff between buyer and seller, both hoarding a wad of small notes for occasions when exact change is vital.

TRAVELLERS' CHEQUES AND CREDIT CARDS

Travellers' cheques are of course more secure than cash, and in Nepal they bring a slightly higher official exchange rate, just about offsetting the one-percent commission you pay when buying them. Any major brand will do. **US dollar** cheques are most widely accepted, though cheques denominated in other currencies are easy enough to change in tourist areas. Make sure to keep the purchase agreement and a record of cheque serial numbers safe and separate from the cheques themselves. In the event that cheques are lost or stolen, the issuing company will expect you to report the loss immediately to their office in Kathmandu (see "Police and trouble", p.71). Most companies claim to replace lost or stolen cheques within 24 hours.

Some hard-currency **cash** may also come in handy – again, US dollars are best. Bring a selection of small and medium denominations, and make sure the bills are relatively new.

Travel agents, luxury hotels and some of the midrange guest houses accept major **credit cards**, but budget outfits don't. An increasing number of retailers take plastic, but they typically add a three- to five-percent processing fee onto the amount – a practice that's illegal in developed countries, but Nepal is not a developed country. You should be able to use the fee as a bargaining chip. Manual transactions (ie, those not submitted by an electronic swipe device) may take months to appear on your bill. Be wary if a proprietor insists on taking your card out of sight for processing: a con artist can add an extra zero to the amount, or make duplicate impressions to bill fictitious transactions against your account.

A credit card is also worth having in case you need a cash advance (see below).

BANKS AND MONEYCHANGERS

Using **banks** in Nepal is, by South Asian standards, surprisingly hassle-free. Numerous private banks and two quasi-government ones (Nepal Bank and Rastriya Banijya Bank) all vie for tourists' business, as do a horde of government-registered **moneychangers**. The government banks give slightly better rates and/or charge less commission than the private ones. The private banks and moneychangers offer very similar rates once you've factored in commissions, which vary considerably, but some work out better for large transactions, others for small ones.

Moneychangers can be found wherever there are significant numbers of tourists. Private bank branches are located mainly in larger cities, with government banks typically providing the only service in smaller, untouristed places. **Hours** for foreign exchange vary: at least one Kathmandu airport branch operates around the clock, Nepal Bank's central Kathmandu (New Road) branch stays open seven days a week and some private banks keep extended hours, but lesser branches generally change money only Sunday to Thursday 10am–2pm, Friday 10am–noon. Specific timings are given in the guide where they're notable. Moneychangers, confined to tourist areas, keep generous hours – usually 8am–8pm, seven days a week.

Hold onto all exchange receipts, as you'll need them for **changing money back** when you leave. Some private banks in Kathmandu will buy rupees back, as will banks at the Kathmandu airport and at official border crossings. However, they may have trouble giving the exact change equivalent in foreign currency, and they may be able to give it only in US dollars. If you're entering India, changing NC into IC is no problem.

Nepal's currency **black market** has been all but killed off by the government's move to make the rupee fully convertible and its lifting of a ban on Nepalese citizens taking hard currency out of the country. All that's left of the black market now is a few touts offering no better than the official rate, and usually a bit worse. The only reason to change unofficially would be if all official outlets were closed. If you do it, haggle hard (make sure you know the official rate) and be on your guard for sleight-of-hand tricks.

GETTING MORE MONEY

If you run low on funds in Nepal, by far the best way to replenish them is with a **credit card cash advance**. Some private banks (notably Nepal Grindlays) issue cash advances against Visa/Mastercard, and they typically charge no commission if you take the money in rupees. You'll still end up paying interest on the advance to your credit card company, of course. American Express cardholders can similarly draw money at the Amex office in Kathmandu.

Having money wired from home is never cheap or convenient, and should be considered a last resort. Funds can be sent via Western Union (☎1800/649 565 in Australia; ☎0800/833 833 in the UK; ☎800/543-4080 in the US or Canada; ☎09/302 0143 in New Zealand), and can be collected at Annapurna Travels & Tours on Durbar Marg in Kathmandu. It's also possible to have money wired directly from a bank in your home country to a bank in Nepal, although this is somewhat less reliable because it involves two separate institutions. If you go this route, the person wiring the funds to you will need to know the fax or telex number of the bank the funds are being wired to (see p.141 for a list of major banks in Kathmandu).

HEALTH AND INSURANCE

Hygiene is not one of Nepal's strong points. Sanitation is poor, and a lot of bugs make the rounds, especially during the monsoon and immediately after it. But don't panic – by coming prepared and looking after yourself while you're in the country, you're unlikely to come down with anything worse than the local version of Delhi belly.

This section deals with health matters mainly in the context of Western-style medicine. Traditional ayurvedic and Tibetan practices are discussed later in the "Spiritual pursuits and alternative therapies" section. For more detailed health advice, refer to the books recommended on p.486, or visit the Web sites listed in the box below.

BEFORE YOU GO

No **inoculations** are required for Nepal, but hepatitis A, typhoid and meningitis jabs are recommended, and it's worth ensuring that you're up to date with tetanus, polio, mumps and measles boosters. Malaria tablets and injections for Japanese B encephalitis and rabies may also be in order, depending on where and when you go. All of these can be obtained in Kathmandu, often more cheaply than at home, but obviously it's better to get nasty things like injections out of the way before starting your trip.

If you have any medical conditions or concerns about your health, don't set off to a place like Nepal without first seeing a **doctor**. Medicines are sold over the counter everywhere, but obviously bring any prescribed medications. Also, consider having a dental checkup before you go. If you wear eyeglasses, bring an extra pair; if you wear contacts, bring a backup pair of glasses because of the dust and pollution.

RECOMMENDED INOCULATIONS

There are some diseases that are ghastly or fatal, but rare. There are others that are just moderately awful, but more common. Deciding which to protect yourself against is a matter of risk management. Only you can decide which sorts of risks you're prepared to take.

Hepatitis A is one of those not-so-bad-but-common diseases in Nepal. It won't kill you, but it'll put a swift end to your travels, and it may lay you up for several months after your return. It's transmitted through contaminated food and water, so sensible hygiene will reduce your risk of catching it, but you can't count on fastidiousness alone. A newly developed vaccine affords the best protection, which lasts for a year, or ten years if followed up by a booster within six to twelve months. This vaccine has superseded immunoglobulin (gammaglobulin), a serum of hepatitis antibodies whose protection wears off quickly, though some local clinics that aren't experienced in travel medicine may not yet know this. Note that children under the age of about ten don't need to be vaccinated against hepatitis A because the disease is very mild in childhood and getting it confers lifelong immunity.

Typhoid and paratyphoid are endemic in Nepal, and like hepatitis A, they're spread through contaminated food and water, and are almost as common. These nearly identical diseases produce a persistent high fever, headaches, abdominal pains and diarrhoea, but are treatable and rarely fatal. Vaccination can be by a couple of different kinds of injection or by a series of tablets taken orally. The tablets are not as effective against typhoid and don't protect against paratyphoid at all, but may be worth considering if you've had an allergic reaction to the injections in the past or if you want to minimize the number of holes in your arm.

Flu is no more prevalent in Nepal than elsewhere, but you might consider getting a flu shot before you leave just to reduce the risk of spending several days sick during your time in Nepal. A new flu vaccine is formulated each

MEDICAL RESOURCES FOR TRAVELLERS

WEB SITES

CIWEC Clinic (*www.bena.com/nepaltrek/ ciwec/ciwec.html*). This Kathmandu-based clinic is the most authoritive source of information on Nepal-related travel medicine, and its Web site contains excellent articles on rabies, inoculation, diarrhoea and other health matters.

Centers for Disease Control (*www.cdc.gov/travel.travel.html*). Outbreak alerts, suggested inoculations, precautions and other background information for travellers.

ADDRESSES

UK

British Airways Travel Clinic, 156 Regent St, London W1 (☎0171/439 9584), with other branches throughout the country. Gives inoculations and sells travel-related health accessories.

Medical Advisory Service for Travellers Abroad (MASTA), London School of Hygiene and Tropical Medicine, Keppel Street, London WC1. Operates a 24-hour travellers' health line (☎0891/224100), giving written information tailored to your needs by return of post.

Tropical Diseases Hospital, 4 St Pancras Way, London NW1 (☎0171/530 3500). Travel clinic offering inoculations and travel health advice.

NORTH AMERICA

Canadian Society for International Health, 170 Laurier Ave W, Suite 902, Ottawa, ON K1P 5V5 (☎613/230-2654). Distributes a free pamphlet, "Health Information for Canadian Travellers", containing an extensive list of travel health centres in Canada.

International Association for Medical Assistance to Travellers (IAMAT), 417 Center St, Lewiston, NY 14092 (☎716/754-4883; *www.sentex.net/~iamat*) and 40 Regal Rd, Guelph, ON N1K 1B5 (☎519/836-0102). A nonprofit organization supported by donations, it can provide a list of English-speaking doctors in Nepal, climate charts and leaflets on various diseases and inoculations.

Travelers Medical Center, 31 Washington Square, New York, NY 10011 (☎212/982-1600). Consultation service on immunizations and treatment of diseases for people travelling to developing countries.

AUSTRALIA & NEW ZEALAND

Auckland Hospital, Park Road, Grafton (☎09/797 440).

Travellers' Medical and Vaccination Centre Australia: Level 7, 428 George St, Sydney (☎02/9221 7133); Level 2, 393 Little Bourke St, Melbourne (☎03/9602 5788); Level 6, 29 Gilbert Place, Adelaide (☎08/8212 7522); Level 6, 247 Adelaide St, Brisbane (☎07/3221 9066); 5 Mill St, Perth (☎08/9321 1977). New Zealand: 1/170 Queen St (☎09/373 3531); 6 Washington Way, Christchurch (☎03/379 4000). General info/health line (Australia: ☎1902/261 560), inoculations/medications, area-specific advice, lists of English-speaking doctors in Nepal, first-aid/medical kits and post-travel examinations.

Travellers Immunization Service, 303 Pacific Hwy, Lindfield, Sydney (☎02/9416 1348). Offers inoculations and general advice.

Travel-Bug Medical and Vaccination Centre, 161 Ward St, North Adelaide (☎08/8267 3544). Consultations, inoculations, first-aid/medical kits, post-travel examinations.

year and is usually available starting in mid- or late October.

You should have a **tetanus** booster every ten years, whether you travel or not. Assuming you were vaccinated for **polio** in childhood, only one booster is necessary during your adult life. Immunizations against **mumps** and **measles** are recommended for anyone who wasn't vaccinated as a child and hasn't already had these diseases.

OPTIONAL INOCULATIONS

The following diseases all fall into the potentially-fatal-but-rare category. They're discussed in descending order of how much you should be concerned about them.

Meningicoccal meningitis, spread by airborne bacteria (through coughs and sneezes, for example), is indeed a very unpleasant disease that attacks the lining of the brain, and can be fatal. However, while localized epidemics are occasionally reported in Nepal, normally the chances of catching meningitis are fairly remote. The injection causes few side effects, and lasts for three to five years.

Although **rabies** is a problem in Nepal, the best advice is just to give dogs and monkeys a wide berth. True, rabies is a scary disease, but unlike other diseases, it can be cured by an after-the-fact ("post-exposure") series of five injections that are essentially 100-percent effective if administered in reasonable time. The post-exposure series is available in Kathmandu, although it's very expensive. The *pre*-exposure vaccine involves a series of three injections over a four-week period, which produces a protective antibody level for three years; if you get bitten, you'll still have to get two more boosters. It's probably not worth it except for children, who may not report every contact with animals to their parents.

Japanese B encephalitis, though potentially fatal, is confined to the more jungly portions of the Tarai during the monsoon, when few foreigners are likely to go there. In fact, there are no known cases of tourists catching the disease in Nepal, although some aid workers have caught it. The inoculation is in the form of three injections given over a three- to four-week period.

Don't bother with the **cholera inoculation** – few authorities now believe it's worthwhile, and the risk of catching cholera in Nepal is minimal.

MALARIA PROPHYLAXIS

Malaria hasn't been eradicated in Nepal – as is sometimes claimed – and the effectiveness of mosquito-control measures appears to be waning. Fortunately, malaria doesn't occur above 1000m, and Kathmandu and most hill areas are higher than this. However, you need to guard against it if you're planning to travel in the Tarai, especially during and immediately after the monsoon. It has a variable incubation period of a few days to several weeks, so you can become ill long after being bitten. The best prevention is mosquito netting or repellent (see below). There is no vaccination against malaria, but taking regular "prophylactic" doses of tablets will provide a fair degree of immunity.

Advice on malaria **prophylaxis** changes from year to year, so seek the latest information from one of the medical organizations listed in the box on p.21. The basic drug used is chloroquine (trade names include Nivaquin, Avloclor and Resochin),

For advice on altitude sickness and other **trekking hazards**, plus a first-aid checklist, see p.386.

a weekly tablet that you must start taking one week *before* entering the malarial area and continue until four weeks *after* leaving it. However, Nepal has chloroquine-resistant strains, so doctors there also recommend taking daily doses of proguanil (Paludrine) or weekly doses of mefloquine (Lariam).

It's important to keep taking the tablets after you leave the malarial area, as the parasite isn't susceptible to the medicine for its first four weeks of incubation: the most common way of catching malaria is when travellers forget to do this.

However, these drugs may produce **side effects**, and you really have to weigh the risks and consequences of these against those of getting malaria. Chloroquine and proguanil can cause itching, rashes, hair loss and vision problems. Mefloquine is worse – many people have experienced severe psychological depression, psychosis or palpitations, some for long after they've stopped taking the drug. Chloroquine is safe during pregnancy, but the others should be avoided. As an alternative, some doctors recommend a regimen of doxycycline (Vibramycin) or chloroquine/halofantrine. Finally, it's not advisable to use any malaria prophylaxis for more than two or three months at a stretch.

Incidentally, all these medicines are much cheaper and more readily available in Kathmandu than in Europe or North America.

PRECAUTIONS

The lack of sanitation in Nepal is sometimes overhyped – it's not worth getting too uptight about it or you'll never enjoy anything, and run the risk of rebuffing Nepalese hospitality.

A few common-sense precautions are in order, though, starting with the **water**: stick to tea or bottled drinks, or purify water with iodine (for more on this, see the trekking chapter). Many guest houses provide water in drip-filter units, but you can't always be sure the water was boiled first, or that the filters are clean. Clean or dirty, water is regarded as a purifying agent, and plates, glasses and cutlery are customarily rinsed just before use: if you're handed wet utensils it might not be a bad idea to give them a discreet wipe.

When it comes to **food**, usually it's flashy tourist restaurants and "Western" dishes that bring the most grief: more people get sick in Kathmandu than anywhere else. Be particularly wary of fruit juices and lassis (which often contain water or ice), prepared dishes that have to be reheated, and any food that's been sitting out where flies can land on it. Nepali food is usually fine and you can probably trust anything that's been boiled or fried in your presence, although meat can sometimes be dodgy. Raw, unpeeled fruit and vegetables should always be viewed with suspicion, and you should verify that salads in tourist restaurants have been soaked in an iodine or potassium permanganate solution.

Kathmandu's **polluted air** gives many people respiratory infections within a few days of arrival. Asthmatics and others with breathing problems are particularly affected. Minimize your exposure by staying off the main boulevards, or wear a face mask if necessary, and avoid breathing around people who are hacking and wheezing tubercularly. You can help your immune system by keeping warm, dry and well rested (especially if jet-lagged). Most importantly, get out of the valley to where the air is fresh as quickly as possible.

You need to be particularly vigilant about **personal hygiene** while travelling in Nepal. That means, above all, washing your hands often. Keep any cuts clean, and treat them with iodine to prevent infection. If you're staying in cheap guest houses, bring a sleeping sheet to keep fleas and lice at bay. Wear shoes at all times, since scabies and hookworm can be picked up through bare feet.

When travelling in the Tarai, minimize your exposure to malaria by depriving **mosquitoes** of the opportunity to bite you. They're hungriest from dusk to dawn: during these times, wear repellent and/or long-sleeved clothes (watch out especially for ankles), and sleep under netting or use mosquito "mats" (small tablets that release a mosquito-repelling scent when heated in an electric device) or old-fashioned coils. Remember, though, that very few mosquitoes carry malaria, so you don't need to worry over every bite. If you do get bites or itches, try not to scratch them as infection may result. Tiger balm and even dry soap may relieve the itching.

Take the usual precautions to avoid **sunburn** and **dehydration**. Obviously susceptibility to sunburn varies by individual, but during the sunny times of year you'll probably want at least medi-

um protection, and high protection will be necessary while trekking. Sunscreen is available in tourist areas.

AIDS

Nepal's isolation gave it a decade's grace period from the **AIDS** epidemic, but the disease is now becoming a significant health problem. It's being transmitted mainly by heterosexual contact, especially in the context of prostitution. Indian brothels, where many Nepali women work (see p.468), are full of HIV-positive sex workers, and the disease is quickly spread from there to Nepal by businessmen and long-distance drivers. However, prostitution in Nepal is not generally aimed at tourists, and your main sexual threat is apt to be other foreigners – use the same precautions that you would at home. Carry condoms with you (preferably brought from home, though the Nepali ones are getting more reliable) and insist on using them. Condoms also protect you from other sexually transmitted diseases such as hepatitis B.

If you get a shave from a barber, make sure he uses a clean blade, and don't submit to processes such as ear-piercing, acupuncture or tattooing unless you can be sure the equipment is sterile. Should you need an injection, make sure that new, sterile equipment is used. Try not to bleed too much in Nepal because the blood supply isn't adequately screened; if you do need a transfusion, any blood you receive should be from voluntary rather than commercial donor banks.

SELF-DIAGNOSIS

Chances are, at some point during your travels in Nepal you'll feel ill. In the vast majority of cases, it won't be something you need to see a doctor about, and sod's law says it will happen somewhere remote and inconvenient anyway. The following information should help with **self-diagnosis**, although it is *not* presented as a substitute for professional medical advice.

Antibiotics definitely shouldn't be taken lightly: they pre-empt the body's ability to develop its own immunity to the disease, and can increase susceptibility to other problems by killing off "good" as well as "bad" organisms in the digestive system (yoghurt can replenish them to some extent). Some may cause allergic reactions or other unpleasant side effects. Also, the more a particular antibiotic is used, the sooner organisms build up a resistance to it. It's not a bad idea to travel with a course of one or more of the drugs mentioned here, but make sure you have the dosage explained to you. In the case of serious or persistent intestinal problems, you're strongly urged to have a **stool test** done at a clinic (see below), where the doctor can make an authoritative diagnosis and prescription.

INTESTINAL TROUBLES

Diarrhoea is the most common bane of travellers. If it's mild and not accompanied by other major symptoms, it probably won't require any treatment and should pass of its own accord within a few days. In the meantime, however, it's essential to replace the fluids and salts you're losing – Jeevan Jal, sold in packets everywhere, is a cheap and effective oral rehydration formula. (Bananas and Coke are also supposed to be good for replacing electrolytes.) Some people recommend starving the bug, which will at least slow the flow, but the best advice is simply to follow your appetite. Diarrhoea tablets such as Lomotil and Immodium will plug you up if you have to travel, but they undermine the body's efforts to rid itself of the infection.

If the diarrhoea comes on suddenly and is accompanied by bad **cramps** and **vomiting**, there's a good chance it's food poisoning, which is brought on by toxins secreted by foreign bacteria. There's nothing you can do for food poisoning other than keep replacing fluids, but it should run its course within 24 to 48 hours. If it doesn't, a course of antibiotic such as ciprofloxacin, norfloxacin or cotrimoxazole may be necessary (note that overuse of the latter has reduced its effectiveness in Nepal).

If the diarrhoea is more severe, or if you see **blood** or **mucus** in your stools, the cause may be amoebic dysentery or giardiasis (giardia). These also frequently produce a **temperature** alternating with chills. Occasionally, dysentery can even produce **constipation**, while giardiasis is often recognizable by rotten-egg belches and farts. Giardia is more commonly contracted while trekking, and involves one to two weeks' incubation time, which may help you rule it out if you haven't been in the

country that long. Both giardia and dysentery are treatable with tinidazole or metronidazole. If the diarrhoea is associated with fatigue and appetite loss over many days, it may be the result of a cyclospora infection, which is treated with cotrimoxazole. Again, be sure to keep rehydrating.

Finally, bear in mind that oral drugs, such as malaria pills or the contraceptive pill, are rendered less effective or completely ineffective if taken while suffering from diarrhoea.

FLU AND FEVER

Flu-like symptoms – fever, headache, runny nose, fatigue, aching muscles – may mean nothing more serious than the latest virus floating around on Kathmandu's bad air. Rest and aspirin or other pain reliever should do the trick. However, strep throat or a bronchial infection will require an antibiotic course such as erythromycin or amoxycillin. Flu symptoms and **jaundice** (yellowing of the eyes) point to hepatitis, which is best treated with rest and a plane ticket home.

A **serious fever** or delirium is cause for real concern. Diagnosis is tricky, but safe to say the sufferer needs to be got to a doctor as quickly as possible. To begin with, try bringing the fever down with aspirin or paracetamol. If the fever rises and falls dramatically every few hours, it may be malaria, which, in the absence of medical help, can be zapped with three tablets of pyralfin (Fansidar). If the fever is consistently high for four or more days, it may be typhoid – again, only if no doctor is available, treat with ciprofloxacin/norfloxacin or chloramphenicol.

MINOR SYMPTOMS

Minor **muscle cramps**, experienced after heavy exercise or sweating, may indicate you're low on salt – a teaspoon of salt will bring rapid relief. Likewise, a simple **headache** may just mean you're dehydrated. (However, a severe headache, accompanied by eye pain, neck stiffness and a temperature, could mean meningitis – in which case get to a doctor pronto.)

Itchy skin is often traced to insect bites – not only obvious ones like mosquitoes, but also fleas, lice or scabies picked up from dirty bedclothes. The latter, a burrowing mite, goes for the webbed spaces between fingers and toes. Shampoos and lotions are available locally. Air out your bedding and wash your clothes thoroughly.

Worms may enter your body through the skin (especially the soles of the feet) or food. An itchy

---

Some of the illnesses and parasites you can pick up in Nepal may not show themselves immediately. If you become ill within a year of returning home, tell the physician who treats you where you've been.

TRAVEL INSURANCE COMPANIES

Most travel agents will arrange travel insurance with no commission to you, and their policies are usually the best value for basic coverage. The following insurance companies tend to offer more deluxe coverage.

UK

Activecard (☎01327/262 805).
Columbus Travel Insurance (☎0171/375 0011).
Direct Travel Insurance (☎01903/893 333).

Endsleigh Travel Insurance (☎0171/436 4451).
Worldwide Travel Insurance Services (☎01892/833 338).

NORTH AMERICA

Access America (☎800/284-8300).
Carefree Travel Insurance (☎800/323-3149).
International SOS Assistance (☎800/523-8930).

Travel Assistance International (☎800/821-2828).
Travel Guard (☎800/826 1300).
Travel Insurance Services (☎800/937 1387).

AUSTRALIA & NEW ZEALAND

Cover-More (Australia: ☎02/9202 8000; toll-free ☎1800/251 881).
Ready Plan (Australia: ☎1300/555 017; New Zealand, through STA Travel: ☎09/379 3208).

UTAG (Australia: ☎02/9956 8399; toll-free ☎1800/809 462).

---

anus is a common symptom, and you may even see them in your stools. They are easy to treat with worming tablets, available from any pharmacy.

ANIMAL BITES

For **animal bites** or scratches, *immediately* wash the wound with soap and water for as long as half an hour, depending on severity, then treat it with iodine, 40–70 percent alcohol or 0.1 percent quaternary ammonium compound (brand name Cetrimide). If there's any suspicion that the animal is rabid, hightail it to one of the Kathmandu clinics for a series of five very expensive rabies injections over the course of a month. The disease's incubation period is between ten and ninety days. Ideally, you're supposed to capture the animal alive for observation.

GETTING MEDICAL HELP

In a non-emergency situation, make for one of the traveller-oriented **clinics** in Kathmandu. Run to Western standards, these can diagnose most common ailments, write prescriptions, and also give inoculations. A veritable cornucopia of Indian-manufactured medicines is available without prescription from **pharmas** (pharmacies) in all major towns, but always check the sell-by date.

In the event of a serious injury or illness, contact your embassy (see p.142) for a list of recommended **doctors** in Kathmandu, which is where virtually all qualified GPs and specialists are based. Most speak English.

Hospitals are listed in the Kathmandu and Pokhara sections of the guide; other hospitals are located in Dhulikhel, Tansen and the bigger Tarai cities. Most are poorly equipped and the standard of care is variable. Should you be unlucky enough to have to spend time in a Nepali hospital, note that nursing staff do not perform many of what we would consider to be routine functions: relatives are expected to feed patients, change bedpans, monitor IVs and so on.

INSURANCE

In the light of all this, **travel insurance** is too important to ignore. Your travel agent can usually recommend a company, otherwise see the box above.

Policies vary: some are comprehensive while others cover only certain risks (accidents, illnesses, delayed or lost luggage, cancelled flights, etc). The most important part of any policy is its medical evacuation provision: believe it or not, the cost of evacuating a really sick person from Nepal

EARTHQUAKE DANGER IN NEPAL

Nepal lies along one of the earth's great geological fault zones, where the Indian subcontinent plate joins the greater Asian plate. The collision of these two plates, which formed the Himalaya, continues to this day at a rate of 2cm per year. Most of this compression is absorbed in the process of mountain-building, but some of it is stored as temporary tension in the earth's crust and then released in the form of **earthquakes**.

Nepal's historical record shows a pattern of infrequent but catastrophic quakes. The most recent major one, in 1988, registered a whopping 8.3 on the Richter scale and killed 800 people in the eastern part of the country; its effects would have been much worse had it struck further west. The last big one to hit Kathmandu, in 1934, was probably nearly as great in magnitude.

The next time a major earthquake hits Nepal – particularly if it hits Kathmandu – there will be major loss of life. In the past few decades ever taller, more slipshod buildings (many of them tourist guest houses) have been erected in the capital. A national building code that's supposed to set mandatory standards still has yet to be implemented, so essentially no attention is paid to earthquake resistance in construction. Moreover, the Kathmandu Valley's soils are apparently of the sort that turn to soup in an earthquake, magnifying the damage.

Maybe the next big one won't be until 2030, maybe it will be tomorrow. It's not something that should stop you from going to Nepal, but it might provide yet another reason to spend most of your time outside of Kathmandu.

---

to his or her home country can be as high as £30,000/$50,000, which would be a catastrophic expense if not covered by insurance. Coverage of medical expenses is less important because treatment in Nepal is cheap. It's nice if the policy has a provision for lost or stolen baggage, but standard per-article limits are usually quite low and supplementary coverage is prohibitively expensive. Note that it's almost impossible to buy or extend a travel insurance policy once you're overseas.

The best **premiums** are usually to be had through student/youth travel agencies such as STA, USIT/Council Travel or Travel CUTS – see the earlier "Getting there" sections for contact information. These policies cost about £35–55/US$85–105 for a month (depending on coverage), £65–100/$150–200 for two months, on up to £230–400/$500–700 for a year. If you plan to go **trekking or rafting**, check whether the policy specifically excludes such **"dangerous activities"**. You might have to pay extra for this coverage, but without it you could be left footing the bill for an expensive helicopter rescue – worse, the chopper might not even be sent if it looks like you won't have the funds to pay for it. If you plan to climb a trekking or expedition peak, you'll probably have to get a policy through your national mountaineering organization, such as the British Mountaineering Council or American Alpine Club.

Before you spend money on a travel insurance policy, though, find out what coverage you already have or might qualify for. For example, if you're eligible for certain student/teacher/youth **ID cards**, by all means sign up, as the health insurance benefit more than pays for the cost of the card (inquire at student travel agencies). Students also may find that their **student health coverage** extends for one term beyond the date of last enrolment. **Bank and credit cards** (particularly American Express) often provide certain levels of medical or other insurance, and travel insurance may also be included if you use a major credit card to pay for your trip (but usually only while you're actually travelling to and from your destination). **Homeowners' or renters' insurance** may cover theft or loss of documents, money and valuables while overseas. **Canadian provincial health plans** include some overseas medical coverage, although this is unlikely to pick up the full tab in the event of a mishap.

Keep **receipts** for any treatment or medicines paid for while overseas. Similarly, should you have anything stolen, report the theft to the police (see "Police and trouble", p.71) as soon as possible, and keep a copy of your statement to substantiate any later claim.

INFORMATION, MAPS AND GUIDES

Nepal's Tourism Department runs on a shoe-string budget, letting the free market fill the gap with a confusing welter of advertising. There are no tourist offices outside the country, and those few in Nepal are chronically starved of printed materials and generally bereft of maps. They can, however, sometimes come up with information on festival dates, local bus schedules and the like.

You'll always get the most useful information from other travellers. Check the informal **notice boards** in restaurants around the tourist quarters for news of upcoming events or to find travelling or trekking companions. In Kathmandu, the neighbouring offices of the **Kathmandu Environmental Education Project** and the **Himalayan Rescue Association** can help out

with information on trekking routes and conditions. Despite its shameless advertiser bias, *Travellers' Nepal*, a free monthly magazine distributed to the big hotels and travel agencies, is the best of several sources of what's-on information.

MAPS

While **maps** published in Nepal have their quirks and errors, they're generally more accurate and up-to-date, not to mention cheaper, than those published overseas.

The best **country map** you'll find in the tourist bookshops is the colour one produced by Mandala on a scale of 1:800,000, which is reasonably reliable for roads and towns but not at all helpful for trails. A larger-scale (1:500,000) three-sheet road map of Nepal is available in a few shops.

Free **city maps** of Kathmandu, available at the airport and through tourist offices, are adequate for most purposes. Bookshops and street vendors sell somewhat better maps of Kathmandu and Pokhara and their valleys. Maps of other cities simply don't exist.

Maps of **trekking areas and wildlife parks** are recommended in the relevant sections of the guide. One series worth mentioning in particular here is the one produced by the government of Nepal with assistance from FINNIDA, the Finnish aid agency. These 1:25,000 and 1:50,000 maps, which are comparable in quality to those published by the British Ordnance Survey and the USGS, are being released region by region starting in the east, and the whole series should be available by 2000.

A NOTE ON PLACE NAMES

Even though Devanaagari (the script of Nepali and Hindi) spellings are phonetic, transliterating them into the Roman alphabet is an inexact science. Some places will never shake off the erroneous spellings bestowed on them by early British colonialists – for instance Durbar Square, which according to widely accepted phonetic rules (see p.488) should be spelled "Darbaar". Where place names are Sanskrit- or Hindi-based, the Nepali pronunciation sometimes differs from the accept-

ed spelling – the names Vishnu (a Hindu god) and Vajra (a tantric symbol) sound like "Bishnu" and "Bajra" in Nepali. This book follows local pronunciations as consistently as possible, except in cases where this would be out of step with every map in print. Having said that, it's often hard to get a consensus on pronunciation – some people say Hetauda, others Itaura; some say Trisuli, others Tirsuli – so keep an open mind while map-reading.

MAP AND TRAVEL BOOK SUPPLIERS

BRITAIN

Daunt Books, 83 Marylebone High St, London W1 (☎0171/224 2295).

John Smith and Sons, 57–61 St Vincent St, Glasgow G2 (☎0141/221 7472).

National Map Centre, 22–24 Caxton St, London SW1 (☎0171/222 2466; www.mapsworld.com).

Stanfords, 12–14 Long Acre, London WC2 (☎0171/836 1321; sales@stanfords.co.uk); 29 Corn Street, Bristol BS1 (☎0117/929 9966). Maps available by phone, mail or email order.

The Travel Bookshop, 13–15 Blenheim Crescent, London W11 (☎0171/229 5260; www.thetravelbookshop.co.uk).

IRELAND

Easons Bookshop, 40 O'Connell St, Dublin 1 (☎01/873 3811).

Fred Hanna's Bookshop, 27–29 Nassau St, Dublin 2 (☎01/677 1255).

Hodges Figgis Bookshop, 56–58 Dawson St, Dublin 2 (☎01/677 4754).

Waterstone's, Queens Bldg, 8 Royal Ave, Belfast BT1 1DA (☎01232/247355).

UNITED STATES

Book Passage, 51 Tamal Vista Drive, Corte Madera, CA 94925 (☎415/927-0960).

Chessler Books, PO Box 399-122, Kittridge, CO 80457 (☎303/670-0093). Mail-order mountaineering books and trekking maps.

The Complete Traveler Bookstore, 199 Madison Ave, New York, NY 10016 (☎212/685-9007).

Map Link, 30 S La Petera Lane, Unit 5, Santa Barbara, CA 93117 (☎805/692-6777).

Phileas Fogg's Books & Maps, #87 Stanford Shopping Center, Palo Alto, CA 94304 (☎800/533-FOGG).

Rand McNally, 444 N Michigan Ave, Chicago, IL 60611 (☎312/321-1751); 150 E 52nd St, New York, NY 10022 (☎212/758-7488); 595 Market St, San Francisco, CA 94105 (☎415/777-3131); call 800/333-0136 (ext 2111) for other locations, or maps by mail order..

Sierra Club Bookstore,6014 College Ave, Oakland, CA 94618 (☎510/658-7470).

Travel Books & Language Center, 4931 Cordell Ave, Bethesda, MD 20814 (☎1-800/220-2665).

Traveler's Bookstore, 22 W 52nd St, New York, NY 10019 (☎212/664-0995).

Maps by mail or phone order are available from **Rand McNally** (☎1-800/333-0136, ext 2111).

CANADA

Open Air Books and Maps, 25 Toronto St, Toronto, ON M5R 2C1 (☎416/363-0719).

Ulysses Travel Bookshop, 4176 St-Denis, Montréal (☎514/843-9447).

World Wide Books and Maps, 714 Granville St, Vancouver, BC V6Z 1E4 (☎604/687-3320).

AUSTRALIA & NEW ZEALAND

Mapland, 372 Little Bourke St, Melbourne, VIC 3000 (☎03/9670 4383).

The Map Shop, 16a Peel St, Adelaide, SA 5000 (☎08/8231 2033).

Perth Map Centre, 884 Hay St, Perth, WA 6000 (☎08/9322 5733).

Specialty Maps, 58 Albert St, Auckland (☎09/307 2217).

Travel Bookshop, Shop 3, 175 Liverpool St, Sydney, NSW 2000 (☎02/9261 8200).

Worldwide Maps and Guides, 187 George St, Brisbane, QLD 4000 (☎07/3221 4330).

GUIDES

Hiring a **guide** is a great way to get under the skin of Nepal. You'll have instant introductions everywhere you go, and will probably be invited home to meet the family, which will give a perspective on Nepalis' lives that you couldn't possibly gain on your own. You'll also learn all sorts of things you won't get from a book (Nepali swear words, for instance).

Most people only think of hiring a guide for a **trek** (more on this in Chapter Seven), but a guide is even more essential when tracking **wildlife** in the Tarai parks. A growing number of travellers are discovering that they can escape the crowds of Chitwan by hiring a guide there and then moving on to remoter parks, which are otherwise accessible only on an expensive package. A guide can also save you money when **shopping**.

Would-be guides often position themselves strategically at temples and palaces, but these "pay me what you will" characters often end up blackmailing you for more than they're worth. Better to find one through an innkeeper, travel agent or someone you've already done business with.

An inexperienced guide hired informally may accept as little as Rs300 a day; someone with better English will demand upwards of Rs700 a day, and an agency will charge even more for a licensed guide. Generally, you get what you pay for.

For a list of recommended **books** on Nepal, see p.482.

NEPAL ONLINE

A growing amount of information about Nepal can be found on the **Web**. Most of it's pretty self-serving, but a couple of the sites listed below are very good clearinghouse-type resources, and others have some excellent content on specific Nepal-related topics. A few more sites are recommended in other sections, where relevant. For interactive advice from fellow travellers, try the Usenet discussion groups.

Needless to say, this list won't remain current for long, but you only have to find one Nepal site to find the rest, since they're well linked.

AAMA Network Consultant (*www.catmando.com/nepal.htm*). A potpourri of reference information and links to hotels, trekking companies, etc.

Himalayan Explorers Club (*www.hec.org*). A resource for trekkers and other travellers, featuring a logbook, newsletter and other useful stuff.

Mercantile Communications (*www.south-asia.com*). Commercial site representing the *Kathmandu Post, Rising Nepal, Independent Weekly, Himal Magazine* and other Nepal-based publications, as well as some Radio Nepal programming through Real Audio.

Nepal Home Page (*www.info-nepal.com/homepage*). The premier Nepal site, with an extensive FAQ on travel in Nepal, the Nepal white pages, directories of trekking agencies and embassies, news services, a festival calendar, and more.

Nepal Information Center (NICE) (*www.uni-mainz.de/~baadj000/nepal.htm*). Very comprehensive (if unfiltered) selection of Nepal-related links.

Nepal Trekking Home Page (*www.bena.com/nepaltrek/*). A mix of useful info and links to trekking companies.

rec.travel.asia. Unmoderated news group with a small portion of postings devoted to Nepal matters. Can be excellent for getting answers to specific questions, though bear in mind that first-hand information isn't necessarily accurate or up-to-date information.

Shangri La Home Page (*aleph0.clarku.edu/rajs/Shangri_La.html*). Extensive information on Himalayan natural history and the environment.

soc.culture.nepal. Another unmoderated news group, used more by academics and expat Nepalis.

Travel-Nepal.com (*www.travel-nepal.com*). Online reservations, general information on Nepal, and links.

US State Department travel advisory (*travel.state.gov/travel_warnings.html*). Warns of epidemics or unrest when appropriate.

GETTING AROUND

Getting around is one of the biggest challenges of travelling in Nepal. Distances aren't great, but the roads are poor and extremely slow, and public transport is uncomfortable. If you can afford it, occasionally flying or hiring a private vehicle makes life easier.

Nepal has one of the least developed **road** networks in the world. Of the few highways that are paved, only one is wide enough for two buses to pass without having to slow down or go over onto the shoulders. Highways are irregularly maintained, and each monsoon takes a toll on road surfaces, so in the space of one year a stretch of road can go from wonderful to hellish (or vice versa). Whenever and wherever you travel, the route will probably be new in parts, disintegrated in parts, and under construction in parts.

The state of Nepal's roads has had an unfortunate effect on tourism. Most travellers just aren't willing to endure the long, bumpy, cramped journeys it takes to get far afield in Nepal, so they stick to a circuit of a few easily accessible destinations in the middle of the country. In response, private operators have created tourist bus services between these destinations, making them even easier to get to, and making everywhere else seem even more out of reach. The result is a well-worn path between a few rather un-Nepali tourist ghettoes. Ironically, while most "independent" travellers are packing themselves together in these budget barrios, nowadays it's the group tourists who are doing a better job of getting off the beaten path by air and private vehicle.

If you're on a budget, don't allow yourself to be limited by the tourist buses. There are other, increasingly affordable options. For example, in the main cities you can hire a motorcycle, or club together with two or three others to charter a taxi on a daily rate. For longer journeys, consider going by hired jeep or van, or if you've got the time, by mountain bike. And don't rule out **flying**, even if only one way, which can make possible itineraries that would otherwise seem out of the question.

BUSES

Public **buses** ply every paved road in Nepal, as well as quite a few of the unpaved ones. The bus network is completely and chaotically privatized – there seem to be as many bus companies as there are buses – but all fares are fixed for public services (not for tourist ones). Fares depend less on distance than on the state of the road and the time it takes to make the journey; for express buses it works out to about Rs15 per hour, somewhat more for night services (see box on p.32).

Open-air **bus stations** (*bas park* or *bas istand* in Nepali, and referred to as "bus parks" throughout the guide) are typically located in the smelliest, dustiest and muddiest parts of town. Some cities have more than one bus park to handle services along different routes. Tickets are often sold through syndicates – for example, all night bus tickets from one window or booth, all day buses from another. Destinations may not be written in English, in which case you just have to ask around. In Kathmandu and Pokhara you may find it easier to make arrangements through a ticket agent (but heed the warnings given in the box opposite), while in other cities with inconveniently located bus stations you can ask your hotel to send someone to buy a ticket for you.

Few travellers are ever quite prepared for the sheer **slowness** of bus travel in Nepal. Allowing for bad roads, overloaded buses, tea stops, meal stops, police checks, constant picking up and letting off of passengers, and the occasional flat tyre or worse, the average speed in the hills is barely 25km per hour, and on remote, unpaved roads it can be as little as 10kph. In the Tarai, it's more like 40kph on a good road.

TOURIST BUSES

Regularly scheduled **tourist buses** connect Kathmandu with Pokhara, Chitwan National Park,

TICKET AGENTS

With their funfair signs advertising "Bus and Train to India" and "Exciting Jungle Safari", **ticket agents** are the used-car salesmen of Nepal, preying on travellers' faith in the apparently limitless possibilities of the Orient. Though they make themselves out to be budget travel agencies, they're not registered with the government and they offer very limited services. Many are inept, and some are downright dishonest. Even the honest ones often make promises they're in no position to fulfil. Naturally, they all mark up the price of the tickets they sell.

For a seat on a public bus, a ticket agent can save you the trouble of making an extra trip to the bus station, and his commission will be money well spent. For tourist bus services, whose offices are often located just down the street, an agent doesn't provide much value for his fee, although in Nepal it's so hard to tell agents from actual service providers that you'll probably end up booking through an agent anyway. Ticket agents are also useful for hiring vehicles, but shop around.

Be wary when ticket agents try to sell you anything more complicated than the above. *Don't* book a trek or river trip through an agent – deal directly with the tour operator, who can give you straight information and will be accountable if anything goes wrong. Wildlife packages (see p.298) and tickets to India (see p.147) booked through an agent have additional drawbacks. Finally, go to a registered travel agent to arrange air tickets or anything involving computerized bookings.

Nagarkot and Dhulikhel, and Pokhara with Chitwan and Sonauli. Additional services may start up in time.

The vehicles are usually in good condition, and the drivers know what they're doing, making for a much **safer** ride than in a public bus. Tourist buses aren't supposed to take any more passengers than there are seats (though they may pick up a few anyway), so the journey should also be more comfortable and somewhat faster. There should be just two **seats** on either side of the aisle ("2x2"), making for a roomier ride than on public 2x3 buses, and the seats should be reasonably well padded. Some buses are better, and more expensive, than others. The most luxurious ones are operated by Greenline Tours; of the rest, those billed as minibuses are somewhat faster than the full-sized ones. **Luggage** is kept safely stowed under a tarpaulin on the roof or in a cargo compartment, but put a lock on your bag just to be sure, and keep valuables with you inside.

Tickets are widely touted in Kathmandu and Pokhara. Buses depart from the tourist quarters of those cities, which saves you the trouble of hoofing it down to the bus station (or the expense of taking a taxi). Book seats at least one or two days in advance. Since tourist fares aren't regulated, and ticket agents often add an undisclosed commission onto the price, it's worth shopping around.

PUBLIC EXPRESS BUSES

Public long-distance services generally operate on an **express** basis. Not that they don't make any stops: besides calling at all major towns en route, an "express" bus will stop as often as necessary on the way out of town until it's full, and will also let passengers off all over the place as it approaches its final destination. Still, this is a lot better than a local bus (see below), and an express bus will also be less crowded. Vehicles are less comfortable and less safe than tourist buses, but not too awful.

In addition to the private bus companies, the quasi-government **Sajha** ("cooperative") service is also worth mentioning. Its distinctive blue buses, donated by Japan, aren't well maintained, nor are they very comfortable, and they have only limited luggage capacity, but in some cases they provide particularly useful connections.

Express buses fall into two functional categories. **Day buses** usually cover the medium-distance routes (approximately 6–12 hours) and set off in the morning to arrive at their destination before nightfall or not long after. That means if a given journey takes, say, eight hours, you can be pretty sure that the last bus will depart no later than midday. Day buses may be 2x2s or 2x3s and can vary a lot in comfort level – some are fiendishly short on legroom.

Night buses, which operate on the longest routes (10–20+ hours), depart in the afternoon or early evening to arrive the following morning. On these you're assured of 2x2 reclining seats with padding and adequate legroom, although a few hours in the seat will reveal the extent of the padding, and the legroom may be taken up by other people's luggage. Between all the lurching,

SAMPLE BUS FARES

These express bus fares were compiled when the exchange rate was Rs68=$1. Use them for relative purposes only.

Kathmandu to:	Tourist Bus Public Bus (Day)	Public Bus (Night)
Birganj	Rs114	Rs150
Chitwan (Tadi)	Rs150–200	Rs76
Gorkha	Rs63	–
Janakpur	Rs158	Rs204
Jiri	Rs170	–
Kakarbhitta	Rs337	–
Nagarkot	Rs100	Rs20
Nepalganj	Rs224	Rs280
Pokhara	Rs200–275	Rs98 Rs113
Sonauli	Rs125	Rs165
Tansen	Rs131	–
Trisuli	Rs45	–

honking, tea stops and blaring music you won't get much sleep (bring earplugs and something to cover your eyes). Note that night journeys are also more dangerous, since it's not uncommon for drivers to fall asleep at the wheel. The main advantage of travelling by night is that it frees up time during the day and saves on the cost of accommodation (a prime consideration for Nepali passengers).

Like tourist buses, and unlike local buses, express buses allow you to **reserve seats** in advance. Do this, or you could end up in one of the whoopee seats along the back bench. Fortunately Nepalis don't plan very far ahead, so you can usually get away with buying a ticket just a few hours beforehand; the exception is during the big autumn festivals, when buses are packed with people heading back to their villages and seats get booked up several days in advance. Check the seating chart to see what's available – there will always be one for night buses, though not necessarily for day buses. The ticket should indicate the vehicle number, which is useful for verifying that you're on the right bus. Normally seats can be reserved only at the bus's point of origin; getting on at a major junction along the route may be possible, but you'll probably have to stand.

Most express buses give you the choice of stowing your **baggage** on the roof or in a locked hold in the back. The exception is Sajha buses, which have neither facility, and passengers must keep their luggage with them inside. Having all your things with you is of course the best insur-

ance policy against theft, but inconvenient. Putting bags in the hold is usually the next-safest option, especially on night buses. You'll have to make the arrangements and pay a fee (up to 50 percent of the seat price) at the bus's point of origin; make sure you get a receipt, and have any valuables noted on it. Baggage stowed on the roof is probably okay during the day, but you can never be completely sure – if possible, lock your bag to the roof rack, and keep an eye out during stops.

LOCAL BUSES

Serving mainly shorter routes or slow, remote roads, **local buses** are ancient, battered contraptions with seats designed for midgets. Lack of safety is a real concern in these buses, which are often overworked, overloaded and poorly maintained. When you read a newspaper story about a bus plunging into a river, drowning some infeasibly large number of people, chances are it was a local.

With local buses, the idea is to cram as many passengers in as possible – indeed, a bus isn't making money until it's nearly full to bursting, and it can get awfully suffocating inside. This can lead to infuriating false starts, as the driver inches forward and the conductor runs around trying to round up customers, since no local bus will leave the station with empty seats. Once on the road, the bus will stop any time it's flagged down.

Almost all local buses are day services, so as with express day buses, departures tend to be in the early part of the day to arrive at the final destination before dark. They often depart from their own bus park or widening in the road. Tickets are bought on board, and since seats can't be reserved, the only way to be sure of getting one is to board the bus early and wait.

Unless your **bag** is small, it will have to go on the roof; during daylight hours it should be safe there as long as it's locked, but again, keep all valuables on your person. **Riding on the roof** can actually be quite pleasant in good weather, but it's illegal and you'll only be allowed to do it in remote areas between checkposts (except during big holidays, when the rules are relaxed). Note that if the bus gets in an accident, passengers on the roof turn into human projectiles.

TRUCKS

If no buses are going your way, you may be able to get there by **truck**. Most trucks in Nepal are ungainly Indian-built Tatas, ferrying fuel to Kathmandu or building materials to hill boomtowns, or "Public Carriers", gaily decorated hauliers-for-hire on both sides of the Indian border. Many do a sideline in hauling passengers, and charge set fares comparable to what you'd pay on a bus. Fully laden, they go even slower than buses. The ride is comfortable enough if you get a seat in the cab, and certainly scenic if you have to sit or stand in the back — either way, the trip is bound to be eventful.

However, trucks aren't licensed as passenger vehicles, and so take little interest in passenger **safety** and are unaccountable for losses: watch your luggage. Women journeying by truck will probably prefer to join up with a companion.

If you're really stuck, you could try **hitching**. There aren't many private vehicles in Nepal, though, and anyone you manage to flag down will expect money.

PLANES AND HELICOPTERS

Internal flights aren't such a bargain for foreigners in Nepal, who are charged inflated dollar prices. Even so, there may be times when $75 seems a small price to pay to avoid spending 24 hours on a bus, or a week retracing your steps along a trail. The so-called "**mountain flight**" — an hour-long scenic loop out of Kathmandu — is also very popular among tourists who want to get an armchair view of Everest.

Given Nepal's mountainous terrain, aircraft play a vital role in the country's transport network, especially in the west, where planes are often used to carry in food during the winter. Of the 29 cities and towns with **airstrips** served by scheduled flights (see map), almost half are two or more days' walk from a road. Most flights begin or end in Kathmandu, but two other **airports** in the Tarai — Nepalganj in the west, Biratnagar in the east — serve as secondary hubs. Popular destinations, such as Lukla in the Everest region, get up to ten flights a day, while obscure airstrips may receive only one flight a week. For frequencies and flight times, see the relevant sections in the guide.

Three makes of propeller **planes** designed for mountain flying are principally used in Nepal: 44-seat Avros, 18-seat Dornier 228s and 17-seat Twin Otters. Flying in one of these small craft is a splendid way to get clear views of the Himalaya and the incredible maze of Nepal's middle hills. Thermals can make the ride bumpy, and landings on mountain airstrips are always memorable. Many runways double as pastures, and a klaxon is sounded a few minutes before the arrival of aircraft to warn locals to get their livestock out of the way.

AIRLINES AND TICKETING

Government deregulation of the domestic air sector has made life easier for air travellers in Nepal. An ever-changing line-up* of **airlines** provide services within the country, and competition between them has helped reduce the delays and uncertainty that marked the former monopoly of Royal Nepal Airlines Corporation (RNAC), the somewhat dysfunctional national carrier. Of the private airlines, Necon Air is by far the biggest, but Buddha Air also has a good reputation; a complete list is given on p.146. The choice of airlines is greatest on tourist routes, since they're the most lucrative ones, while RNAC remains the only option for more obscure destinations.

Book **tickets** through a travel agent, who will have a handle on who's flying where, and when. At off-peak times or away from the trekking routes — in the Tarai, for instance — you shouldn't have any trouble getting a seat. However, during the trekking season, flights out of airstrips along the popular trails may be booked up months in advance by trekking agencies. If you're finding

---

*Most exist mainly to take advantage of special tax advantages, which become less lucrative after a few years.

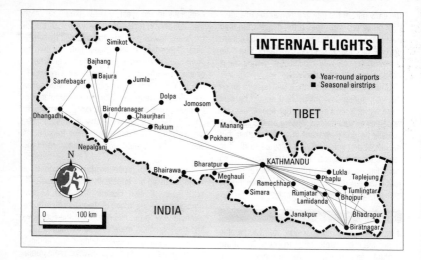

you can't get a seat, all is not lost. Agencies often overbook, releasing their unused tickets on the day of departure, so you may be able to buy a returned ticket from the airline that morning. Otherwise, adjust your schedule and go a week or two later, by which time the agency peak should have tapered off.

Check in early for popular flights, which are often overbooked by the airlines. Getting there early will also improve your chances of getting a seat on the side of the plane with the best mountain views.

SAFETY AND DELAYS

Government oversight of the airline industry is minimal, and while it's true that most of the aircraft are leased from overseas companies that set maintenance and pilot performance requirements, the fact is that there have been several fatal crashes in recent years. Baggage overloading seems to be one problem. It's a close call whether flying is more or less dangerous than travelling by tourist bus (it's certainly safer than going by *local* bus), but all of this is perhaps a moot point because your whole attitude toward risk will change about five minutes into your first taxi ride in Nepal.

Another problem with flying in Nepal is **delays and cancellations**, usually due to weather. Most airstrips have no instrument-landing facili-

ties, and are surrounded by potentially dangerous terrain, so there must be good visibility to land – if there's fog or the cloud ceiling is too low, the plane won't fly. (An old Nepali pilots' adage: "We don't fly when it's cloudy because the clouds have rocks in them.") When planes are grounded, delays multiply throughout the system. Since clouds usually increase as the day wears on, delays often turn into cancellations. If your flight is cancelled, rather than getting on the next available flight, you may be placed at the bottom of a waiting list; in busy times or during extended periods of bad weather, the wait can be several days. Pad your schedule accordingly.

HELICOPTERS

A half-dozen companies offer charter **helicopter** services in Nepal. What they'd like to sell you is a three- or four-hour sightseeing junket up to a mountain meadow and back. At $100–200 per hour per person, that's a pretty expensive picnic – the mountain flight is a better deal (see above). More commonly, though, these services are used by trekking parties with more money than time, who charter a chopper to pick them up at a pre-arranged spot to save them several days' back-tracking. Most companies operate French-made Ecureuils, which seat four or five passengers and are designed for mountain flying. Asian Airways also has a bigger Russian Mi-17, which carries up

---

SAMPLE INTERNAL AIR FARES

The following are one-way fares on RNAC at the time of writing – other carriers' prices may vary slightly, and they're all bound to go up.

Kathmandu to:	Meghauli $72	**Nepalganj to:**
Bharatpur $50	Nepalganj $99	Jumla $57
Bhairawa $72	Pokhara $61	Simikot $88
Biratnagar $77	Tumlingtar $57	**Biratnagar to:**
Dhangadhi $149		Taplejung $60
Janakpur $55	**Pokhara to:**	
Lukla $83	Jomosom $50	

---

to 27 passengers and in high season flies scheduled services between Kathmandu and Lukla.

PRIVATE VEHICLES

It's really liberating to have your own wheels in Nepal. Besides being faster and more comfortable than a bus, a **private vehicle** will enable you to get to places you'd never go by bus, stop wherever and whenever you like, and carry more cargo. A motorcycle requires more nerve, but is even more versatile.

CARS, JEEPS AND LAND ROVERS

Rented vehicles always come with a driver in Nepal. This is just as well: you'll probably be happier not having to grapple with the country's chaotic roads (see box on p.36).

In Kathmandu and Pokhara, chartering a **taxi** by the day is the cheapest option for short or medium-distance journeys – worth considering to get to certain trekking trailheads with your wits intact. The going rate for trips within the Kathmandu or Pokhara valleys is about US$20 a day, including petrol. On longer trips, petrol becomes a more significant expense, so the driver will probably prefer to quote a price for a particular destination or itinerary, plus an extra $8 or so for every night he's away from home. However, most taxis aren't roadworthy for long distances, and usually aren't permitted to travel beyond certain checkpoints anyway. **Jeeps, Land Rovers and vans** are better for longer journeys and larger parties, and also for toting kayaks, bikes or other bulky gear. They can be rented through some travel agents in Kathmandu, Pokhara and the bigger Tarai cities, and cost proportionately more than cars. Prices for all vehicle rentals are by negotiation, so it's a good idea to have your lodge-owner help.

Avis and Hertz have representatives in Kathmandu, but renting a vehicle through them is much more expensive (about $50 a day).

MOTORCYCLES

You won't exactly be helping Nepal's smog problem by renting a **motorcycle**, but there's no denying it's a fun and flexible way of getting around Nepal.

Indian-made street bikes can be rented in Kathmandu and Pokhara for about $5 a day; petrol is extra. These small (100cc or 135cc) two-stroke models aren't suitable for covering hundreds of kilometres a day but are quite sufficient for doing day trips or even touring the country at a leisurely pace. Top speed is about 70km per hour, which is about as fast as you really want to be going on Nepali highways anyway. Two people can share a bike – heck, you'll often see three or even four Nepalis riding together – but doubling up can be rather nerve-racking over long distances and on rough roads. Riding solo, you can handle just about anything a four-wheel-drive vehicle can. Some places also rent dirt bikes, though these are quite a bit more expensive, and the only reason to take one would be to really tear up the trails, which isn't appropriate in Nepal.

Quite a few travellers bring 350cc or 500cc Enfields into Nepal from India, where they can easily be purchased and later resold to other travellers. These bikes have a lot more heft for long-distance cruising, and can easily carry two riders and gear, but are heavy and hard to handle off-road.

To rent a motorcycle you're supposed to produce a driving licence from your home country or an international driving licence, and you'll be

DRIVING IN NEPAL: A CRASH COURSE

Driving a vehicle or motorcycle in Nepal is sometimes fun, sometimes terrifying, and always challenging. Most advice can be summed up in two words: drive defensively. Nepalis, normally so unhurried, become impatient maniacs behind the wheel, and in their brinkmanship often pull dangerous stunts. Many are new to driving, and few have had any real driving instruction.

The hairiest driving is in Kathmandu, where the roads are incredibly congested not only with vehicles but also pedestrians, cyclists, cows, pushcarts, street vendors and what have you. Observance of traffic regulations is fairly lax, with drivers constantly jockeying for position irrespective of lane markings or traffic signals. On **roundabouts**, confusion arises (for visitors) because priority officially goes to vehicles *entering* the intersection, not those already going around it. Drivers use their turning indicators only haphazardly: tempos and minibuses will often pull over without warning, so you have to learn to anticipate their moves.

Use your **horn** liberally – when overtaking other vehicles, when rounding sharp corners, or just to alert other vehicles and pedestrians that you're there. Drivers of commercial vehicles will expect you to beep when you come up from behind and want to overtake. Most will want you to wait for their signal – a hand wave or (confusingly) a right-turning indicator.

Watch your **speed** on the highways, which are rarely free of unmarked hazards: potholes, landslides, washed-out bridges, speed bumps, road construction and the like. For this and other reasons, don't drive after dark if you can help it. Drunk drivers may be encountered at all hours of the day, and even the sober ones often try to overtake on blind curves. Cyclists can be particularly erratic. Take special care around pedestrians, who, even in cosmopolitan Kathmandu, sometimes behave as if they've just walked out of the forest. If you're on a bike, children will try to throw things under your wheels. Dogs and chickens frequently behave suicidally. And watch out for those **cows**: the penalty for killing a cow is up to twelve years in prison, the same as for killing a person.

expected to leave an air ticket, passport or large sum of money as a deposit. Check brakes, oil and fuel level, horn, lights and indicators before setting off, and make sure to get a helmet.

Filling stations can be found on main roads at the outskirts of all major towns. Some sell only diesel, but they'll show you where you can get petrol – in smaller towns it's dispensed unofficially by small shops. At the time of writing, the cost of petrol was Rs40–45 per litre.

Motorcycling carries some **risk**. See the box on driving safety tips, which apply doubly for motorcyclists. Also note that rented bikes carry no insurance – if you break anything, you pay for it. Stick to back roads (they're more pleasant anyway), and take care on wet dirt roads, which can be extremely slick.

BICYCLES

A rented **bicycle** (*saikal*) is the logical choice for most day-to-day getting around. One-speeders (usually Indian-made Hero models) are good enough for most around-town cycling: they're incredibly heavy and their brakes are poor, but they're sturdy and have built-in locks.

For more money, a **mountain bike** will get you there in greater comfort, and is essential for longer distances or anything steep. Even a one-speed mountain bike, with its fatter tyres, better geometry and grabbier brakes, makes an improvement over the old sit-up-and-beg design. A few shops in Kathmandu and one in Pokhara rent decent mountain bikes, but most of the models available are cheap Indian and Taiwanese imitations of their Western namesakes that don't stand up well to rough roads or off-road use. (More tips on mountain-biking are given in Chapter Nine.)

Bike rental **shops** are rare outside of Kathmandu, Pokhara and Chitwan, but you may be able to strike a deal with a lodge owner or cycle repairman. Check brakes, spokes, tyres and chain carefully before setting off – the last thing you want is for something to break on a remote mountain road. A bell is pretty well essential. Repair shops are everywhere, but they won't have mountain bike parts. Theft is a concern, especially with a flashier bike – be sure to take it inside your guest house compound at night.

CITY TRANSPORT

Taxis, identified by black number plates, are confined mainly to Kathmandu and Pokhara, and you'll find details on their idiosyncrasies in the relevant sections. A metered ride will cost about

Rs15 per kilometre, but on popular tourist routes, fixed fares work out to be around twice that. You can hire a taxi by the day (see above).

Tempos – three-wheeled, passenger-carrying scooters also known as autorikshas or tuk-tuks – are nasty little beasts, putting out noxious fumes and jamming city streets, nevertheless they're sometimes the best way to get from A to B. They come in three forms. Metered tempos have room for two or three passengers (only one if you've got a lot of luggage) and are more common than taxis, though only slightly cheaper and quite a bit less comfortable. Vikram tempos (so named for their manufacturer), which operate on fixed routes, fit eight or ten (or more), set off when they're full, and usually charge only a few rupees

per head. Battery-powered Safaa ("clean") tempos make a more pleasant alternative in Kathmandu.

Pedal-powered cycle **rikshas**, common in Kathmandu and the Tarai, are slow and bumpy, but may come in handy for short distances along narrow, crowded streets. Be sure to establish the fare before setting off (Rs5–20 per kilometre, depending on how touristy the place is).

Few cities in Nepal are so large that you're dependent on public transport. Where available, **city buses** and minibuses are usually too crowded, slow or infrequent to be worthwhile, but you may find yourself using them to visit certain sights in the Kathmandu Valley. Fares are just a few rupees.

ACCOMMODATION

Finding a place to sleep is hardly ever a problem in Nepal, although only the established tourist centres offer much of a choice.

GUEST HOUSES

Most places to stay in Nepal call themselves **guest houses** (this is for the benefit of foreigners; the Nepali word is "lodge"). This category covers everything from primitive flophouses to fairly well-appointed small hotels. By and large, those that cater to foreigners do so very efficiently: most innkeepers speak excellent English, and can arrange anything for you from laundry to bus

tickets to trekking-porter hire. Those that serve a mainly Nepali clientele are usually (though not always) more basic, and are less attuned to the peculiar needs of Westerners.

Most guest houses offer a choice of **common or attached bath**. This is an important distinction in Nepal. It can cost twice as much or more to get a room with an attached (or "inside") bath, but the advantages are obvious: you don't have to wait when the "common" bath is in use (a disaster if you've got the runs), leave your valuables while you shower, or walk up and down halls in partial undress. Note, however, that in cheaper places an attached bath isn't necessarily an asset, as it can make the room damp and smelly if not properly maintained.

Even in upmarket guest houses, despite assurances to the contrary, you can't necessarily count on constant hot water (many rely on solar panels) nor uninterrupted electricity (power cuts are common). If constant hot water is important to you, ask what kind of water-heating system the guest house has – the correct answer is "geyser" (pronounced "geezer"), which means an electric immersion heater or backup.

All but the really cheap guest houses will have a safe for valuables, and better places have lockboxes in each room. It's a good idea to leave your passport, air ticket and most of your money there;

TO BOOK OR NOT TO BOOK?

Hotels and the more popular guest houses in the Kathmandu Valley, Pokhara and Chitwan take **bookings**, and if you want to be sure of getting a room in one of these then yes, you should book ahead. It's more of a consideration in the busy seasons and during local festivals, and if you expect to arrive late in the day.

At most time of year, however, the advantages of having a confirmed room are not that great, and are usually outweighed by the hassle of making the booking. Many innkeepers in Nepal are only just learning to use the telephone, and have absolutely no concept of room reservations. The person on the other end of the line may not speak English, or may speak just enough to get both of you in a complete muddle. Even Nepali-speakers find it difficult to make arrangements over the phone. On top of that, phone numbers change often in Nepal, circuits are often busy and trunk calls are expensive, all of which means that you might be better off just showing up.

Listings in the guide give phone numbers and either email addresses or fax numbers for all lodgings that have them. The advantage of booking by fax or email is that you'll receive a written confirmation; by phone, even with the best hotels, there's a greater chance of miscommunication.

a photocopy of the relevant pages of your passport will suffice for moneychanging (but not for getting visas or trekking permits).

The cheeriest and most efficiently run guest houses are highlighted throughout the guide, but remember that recommendations are often self-defeating and can result in instant price hikes. Also, watch out for name changes, which suggest a change in ownership or an attempt to escape a bad reputation.

TOURIST GUEST HOUSES

Kathmandu and Pokhara have their own tourist quarters where fierce competition among budget **guest houses** ensures great value for money — typically Rs200–300 for a double room with common bath. In these enclaves, all but the very cheapest places provide hot running water (though perhaps only sporadically), flush toilets, foam mattresses and (usually) clean sheets and quilts — a sleeping bag should not be necessary. In the Tarai, a room fan is normally provided. Most also offer some sort of roof terrace or garden, a supply of (supposedly) boiled and filtered water and a phone. They're never heated, however, which makes them rather cold in winter.

Upmarket guest houses (for lack of a better term) are becoming increasingly popular. These tend to be more spacious buildings where there's a lobby of sorts (often with a TV), the rooms have carpeting, nicer furniture, a fan and maybe a phone, toilet paper is provided in the bathrooms, and daily maid service is available. The better ones will provide a portable electric heater in winter. Most quote their prices in dollars (about

$5–15 for a double with attached bath), though you can pay in rupees, and add 10 percent VAT on top. Many of them even accept payment by credit card.

Nepal has only one **youth hostel**, in Patan. **Trekking inns** are another matter altogether, and are described in Chapter Seven.

NEPALI-STANDARD LODGES

Off the beaten track, lodgings are geared for **Nepali** travellers. Some are luxurious – in bigger Tarai cities there will usually be at least one upscale place with creature comforts (even air conditioning) – but for the most part Nepalis are more concerned about the quality of the rice than the cleanliness of the bathrooms, so you may have to settle for something less salubrious. Stark concrete floors, cold-water showers and smelly squat toilets are the rule. Often not much English is spoken. Sheets and cotton quilts are usually provided, but it's a good idea to bring your own sleeping sheet to protect against bedbugs and lice. Noise is always a problem: bring earplugs. In the Tarai, mosquito netting (or mosquito coils) and a ceiling fan that works are crucial.

This is not to say that Nepali lodges are to be avoided. Sometimes the most primitive places – the ones with no electricity, where you sit on the mud floor by a smoky fire and eat with your hosts – can be the most rewarding of all.

HOTELS, RESORTS AND JUNGLE LODGES

It's hard to generalize about the more expensive **hotels and resorts**. You have to pay a lot of money – at least $100 a night – to get truly inter-

ROOM PRICE SCALES

All guest houses and hotels in this book have been price-graded according to the scale outlined below. The rates quoted represent the cheapest available double room in high season – at other times, you should be able to secure a room at a rate of one or even two grades below that given. You should also be able to negotiate a better rate for longer stays. In the lowest categories, the cheapest rooms will generally be those with a "common" (shared) bathroom. Where all rooms come with their own attached bath, this is denoted by a B prefix to the code. Where both common and attached baths are available, two codes are given – for example, ①/B②. Codes prefixed by AC refer to air-conditioned rooms.

Single travellers can usually expect a discount of 20 to 40 percent off the price of a double.

① Less than Rs140 ($2 if quoted in US dollars)

② Rs140–200 ($2–3)	③ Rs200–350 ($3–5)
④ $5–8	⑤ $8–12
⑥ $12–20	⑦ $20–40
⑧ $40–75	⑨ Over $75

national-quality facilities in Nepal, and it's questionable whether it's worth it, since such places tend to insulate guests from the Nepal they came to see. However, there are a few admirable exceptions in Kathmandu and Pokhara, which, in their own way, offer unique experiences of the country. This guide also recommends several smaller hotels in the $25–75 price range that are in many ways even better. After a trek or a long spell of roughing it, a night or two in one of these hotels can be just what the doctor ordered.

Jungle lodges and **tented camps** inside the Tarai wildlife parks are the most expensive hotels of all. A stay in one is indeed the experience of a lifetime, but if $100–200 a night is beyond your reach there are plenty of more affordable outfits just outside Chitwan and Bardia national parks.

A government rating system awards hotels and resorts from one to five stars, but this is a less reliable guide to quality than the price. **Rated hotels** add 10 percent VAT and 2 percent tourism tax to all bills.

CAMPING

Perhaps surprisingly, **camping** doesn't come high on the agenda in Nepal. Much of the country is well settled, every flat patch of ground is farmed, and rooms are so cheap that camping offers little saving. The only developed commercially operated campground is in Pokhara.

It's a different story, of course, if you're **rafting or trekking**, and camping is also possible in certain jungle areas near the Tarai wildlife parks. Long-distance cyclists might find it useful to bring a tent along to avoid spending nights in roadside flea-pits en route to more interesting places. Between October and May many terraces in the hills are left fallow, and you can pitch a tent if you ask permission and keep out of the owner's way. Set up well away from villages, unless you want to be the locals' entertainment for the evening. Don't burn wood – the locals need it more than you do. An unattended tent will probably be safe if zipped shut, but anything left outside is liable to disappear.

EATING AND DRINKING

Nepal – specifically Kathmandu – is renowned as the budget eating capital of Asia. Sadly, its reputation is based not on Nepali but pseudo-Western food: pizza, chips (fries), "sizzling" steaks and apple pie are the staples of tourist restaurants. Outside the popular areas, travellers' chief complaint is the blandness of the diet.

Yet Nepal lies at the intersection of two great culinary traditions, Indian and Chinese, and if you know what to look for you'll find good, native renditions of everything from tandoori to stir-fried dishes. The simple cooking of the hills – Nepal's heartland – is essentially a regional variation of north Indian, comprising rice, lentils, curried vegetables and meats, and chutneys. In the Kathmandu Valley, the indigenous Newars have their own unique cuisine of spicy meat and vegetable dishes. In the Tarai, *roti* (bread) and the vast range of Indian curries, snacks and sweets comes into play, while in the mountains the diet is essentially Tibetan, consisting of soups, pastas, potatoes and breads.

WHERE TO EAT

Enterprising budget **tourist restaurants** in Kathmandu and Pokhara show an uncanny knack for sensing exactly what travellers want and simulating it with the most basic ingredients. Some specialize in Italian, German, Chinese, Tibetan, Indian, Mexican, Thai, Korean or even Japanese food, but the majority attempt to do a little of everything. Display cases full of extravagant cakes and pies are a standard come-on. There's no denying that the food is tasty – especially after

a trek – but the scene has grown progressively more gross and surreal over the years, and quite a few travellers end up getting sick from the food in such places (see the health section, p.20). And while they won't necessarily admit it, virtually all tourist restaurants rely heavily on monosodium glutamate as a flavour enhancer, which tends to make all tourist food taste the same, and of course can cause allergic reactions (if MSG gives you trouble, try asking for food without "tasting powder").

Tourist restaurants are notoriously hard to recommend, as chefs are forever jumping ship and taking their menus with them. And don't assume that a crowded place must have good food: tourists tend to judge restaurants by their ambience, and in any case the more diners there are, the slower the service will be. (That said, a popular restaurant's high turnover should ensure fresher ingredients.)

Local **Nepali diners** (*bhojanalaya*) are traditionally humble affairs, offering a limited choice of dishes (or no choice at all). Menus don't exist, but the food will normally be on display or cooking in full view, so all you have to do is point. Utensils should be available on request, but if not, try doing as Nepalis do and eat with your hand – the right one only. (See "Cultural hints" for more on social taboos relating to eating.) In towns and cities, eateries tend to be dark, almost conspiratorial places, unmarked and hidden behind curtains. On the highways they're bustling public and spill outdoors in an effort to win business. Tarai cities always have a fancy (by Nepali standards) restaurant or two, patronized by businessmen and Indian tourists, and lots of *dhaba* (the Indian equivalent of *bhojanalaya*). Confusingly, restaurants are also often called "hotels".

It might take some time before you start appreciating the fine differences between *bhojanalaya* and other traditional establishments. **Teahouses** (*chiya pasal*) really only sell tea and basic snacks, while the simple **taverns** (*bhatti*) of the Kathmandu Valley and the western hills put the emphasis on alcoholic drinks, but also serve basic Nepali meals. Trailside, both *chiya pasal* and *bhatti* are typically modest operations run out of family kitchens. **Sweet shops** (*mithai pasal*), found in bigger towns and identified by their shiny display cases, are intended to fill the gap between the traditional midmorning and early evening meals; besides sweets and tea, they also do savoury South Indian and Nepali snacks.

Street vendors sell fruit, nuts, roasted corn, fried bread and various fried specialities. When you're travelling, as often as not the food will come to you – at every bus stop, vendors will clamber aboard or hawk their wares through the window.

Vegetarians will feel at home in Nepal, since meat is considered a luxury. Imaginative preparations are rare, though: rice, lentils, vegetable curry and noodles are the standard offerings everywhere. As a rule, vegetarian dishes get more interesting and varied the closer you get to India, with some orthodox Hindu restaurants in border towns billing themselves as vegetarian-only. Tourist menus invariably include meatless items, which are often excellent.

Nepalis generally start the day with nothing more than a cup of tea, eat a full meal around mid-morning, then carry on until the second big meal of the day at dinnertime. The Western concept of breakfast doesn't tie in very well. Again, tourist restaurants have this covered – many do excellent set breakfast deals, with eggs, porridge, muesli and the like – but out in the sticks you'll have to adjust your eating schedule, or make do with a greasy omelette or packet noodles.

NEPALI FOOD

Daal bhaat tarkaari (lentil soup, white rice and curried vegetables) isn't just the most popular meal in Nepal – for many Nepalis it's the *only* meal they ever eat, twice a day, every day of their lives. Indeed, in much of hill Nepal, *bhaat* is a synonym for food. The *daal bhaat* served in restaurants ranges from pretty good to derisory – it's a meal that's really meant to be eaten at home – so if you spend much time trekking or travelling off the beaten track you'll probably quickly tire of it. That said, a good **achhaar** (chutney) – made with tomato, radish or whatever's in season – can liven up a *daal bhaat* tremendously. The food will be served on a gleaming steel platter divided into compartments; one price covers unlimited refills, except in a few establishments that adhere to the "plate system". Add the *daal* and other condiments to the rice in the main compartment, a little at a time, knead the resulting mixture into mouth-sized balls with the right hand, then push it off the fingers into your mouth with the thumb.

You'll usually be able to supplement a plate of *daal bhaat* with small side dishes of *maasu* (meat) – chicken, goat or (in riverside bazaars) fish – marinated in yoghurt and spices and fried in oil or **ghiu** (clarified butter). In Indian-influenced Tarai towns you can often get *taareko daal*, fried with *ghiu* and spices to produce a tastier variation, and *roti* instead of rice. **Sokuti** (dried, spiced meat fried in oil) is popular in eastern hill areas. **Soups** (*surwa*) are sometimes available: *tama surwa*, made with bamboo shoots, and *gundruk*, a sour/tangy concoction of fermented vegetables, are favourites. You could make a meal out of rice and **sekuwa** (kebabs of spicy marinated meat chunks) or **taareko maachhaa** (fried fish), both common in the Tarai. If you're invited into a peasant home in the hills you might be served **dhedo** (a dough made from water mixed with toasted corn, millet or wheat flour) instead of rice.

Nepali **desserts** include *khir* (rice pudding), *sikarni* (thick, whipped yoghurt with cinnamon, raisins and nuts) and versions of Indian sweets (see below). Other traditional Nepali dishes are more localized, or reserved for special occasions, but well worth the effort of tracking them down.

NEWARI FOOD

Like many aspects of Newari culture, **Newari food** is all too often regarded as exotic but too weird for outsiders. It is indeed like no other cuisine on earth: complex, subtle, delicious and devilishly hard to make (most dishes require absolutely fresh ingredients and/or very long preparation times).

Most Newari specialities are quite spicy, and based around four mainstays: buffalo, rice, pulses and vegetables (especially radish). The Newars use every part of the buffalo: **momocha** (meat-filled steamed dumplings), **choyila** (buff cubes fried with spices and greens), **palula** (spicy buff with ginger sauce) and **kachila** (a paté of minced raw buff, mixed with ginger and mustard oil) are some of the more accessible dishes; others are made from tongue, stomach, lung, blood, bone marrow and so on. Rice, besides being boiled, is also made into **chiura** (beaten rice, a common dry substitute for cooked rice) and **chataamari** (a sort of pancake made with rice flour). Pulses and beans play a role in several other preparations, notably **woh** (fried lentil-flour patties, also known as *baara* in Nepali), **kwati** (a soup made with several varieties of sprouted beans), **musya palu** (a dry mix of roasted soya beans and ginger) and

A GLOSSARY OF FOOD TERMS

BASICS

Bread	*Roti*	Oil	*Tel*
The bill	*Bil*	Pepper (ground)	*Marich*
Butter	*Makhan*	Plate	*Plet*
Chutney, pickle	*Achhaar*	Rice (cooked)	*Bhaat*
Egg	*Phul*	Rice (uncooked)	*Chaamal*
Food	*Khaanaa*	Rice (beaten)	*Chiura*
Fork	*Kaata*	Salt	*Nun*
Glass	*Gilaas*	Spoon	*Chamchaa*
Innkeeper (male)	*Sahuji*	Sugar	*Chini*
(female)	*Sahuni*	Sweets, candy	*Mithaai*
Knife	*Chakku*	Water	*Paani*
Milk	*Dudh*	Yoghurt, curd	*Dahi*

COMMON NEPALI DISHES

Daal bhaat tarkaari	Lentil soup, white rice and curried vegetables	*Samosa*	Pyramids of pastry filled with curried vegetables
Dahi chiura	Curd with beaten rice	*Sekuwa*	Spicy, marinated meat kebab
Pakauda	Vegetables dipped in chickpea-flour batter, deep fried	*Taareko maachhaa*	Fried fish

COMMON NEWARI DISHES

Chataamari	Rice-flour pancake, usually served with curry	*Momocha*	Meat-filled steam dumplings
Choyila	Buff cubes fried with spices and greens	*Pancha kol*	Curry made with five vegetables
Kachila	Paté of minced raw buff meat mixed with ginger and oil	*Woh*	Fried lentil-flour patties served plain (*mai woh*) or topped with minced buff (*la woh*) or egg (*khen woh*)
Kwati	Soup made with sprouted beans		

COMMON TIBETAN DISHES

Momo	Pasta shells filled with meat, vegetables and ginger, steamed	*Thukpa*	Soup containing pasta, meat and vegetables
Kothe	The same, fried	*Tsampa*	Toasted barley flour

bhuti (boiled soya beans with spices and herbs). Various vegetable mixtures are available seasonally, including **pancha kol** (a curry made with five vegetables) and **alu achhaar** (boiled potato in a spicy sauce). Radish turns up in myriad forms of *achhaar*. Order two or three of these dishes per person, together with *bhaat* or *chiura*, and share them around.

INDIAN FOOD

A full description of Indian dishes isn't possible here. The ones you're most likely to encounter in Nepal are from **northern India**, such as **Mughlai** curries (thick and mildly spiced, often topped with boiled egg) and **tandoori** meats (baked in a clay oven, called a *tandoor*, with spe-

VEGETABLES (*Tarkaari* or *Saabji*)

Aubergine	*Bhanta*	Lentils	*Daal*
Beans	*Simi*	Mushroom	*Chyaau*
Cabbage	*Banda Kobi*	Onion	*Pyaaj*
Carrot	*Gaajar*	Peas	*Kerau, Matar*
Cauliflower	*Kaauli*	Potato	*Alu*
Chickpeas	*Chaana*	Pumpkin	*Pharsi*
Chili pepper	*Khursaani*	Radish	*Mulaa*
Coriander (Cilantro)	*Dhaniyaa*	Spinach, Greens	*Palungo, Saag*
Corn	*Makai*	Tomato	*Golbheda*
Garlic	*Lasun*		

MEAT (*Maasu*)

Beef	*Gaiko maasu* (usually euphemized as "buff")	Chicken	*Kukhuraako maasu*
		Goat	*Khasiko maasu*
Buffalo ("Buff")	*Raangaako maasu*	Pork	*Bungurko maasu*

FRUIT (*Phalphul*) AND NUTS

Apple	*Syaau*	Orange, Mandarin	*Suntalaa*
Banana	*Keraa*	Papaya	*Mewaa*
Cashew	*Kaaju*	Peanut	*Badaam*
Coconut	*Nariwal*		(*Mampale* near India)
Date	*Chhokada*	Pineapple	*Bhuikatahar*
Guava	*Ambaa*	Pistachio	*Pista*
Lemon	*Kagati*	Raisin	*Kismis*
Lime	*Nibuwaa*	Sugar cane	*Ukhu*
Mango	*Aaph*		

SPICES (*Masaala*)

Aniseed	*Sop*	Clove	*Lwang*
Cardamom	*Sukumel, Elaaichi*	Ginger	*Aduwaa*
Chili	*Khursaani*	Saffron	*Kkesari*
Cinnamon	*Daalchini*	Turmeric	*Besaar*

SOME COMMON TERMS

A little	*Alikati*	Hot	*Taato*
A lot	*Dherai*	I'm full	*Pugyo*
Another	*Aarko*	More	*Aru*
Boiled (water)	*Umaaleko (paani)*	Spicy	*Piro*
Cooked	*Paakeko*	Stir-fried	*Bhuteko*
Cold	*Chiso*	Sweet	*Guliyo*
Deep-fried	*Taareko*	Vegetarian	*Sahakaari*
Delicious	*Mitho*	I don't eat meat	*Ma maasu khaanna*

cial spices). **Roti** (bread) is the accompaniment to north Indian cuisine: chapati (round, flat pieces of unleavened bread) are always available in Indian restaurants, *naan* (bigger, chewier versions of the same), *paratha* (fried bread) and *puri* (puffy fried chapatis) usually so. In the Tarai the best bets are **masaala** (meaning spicy, although it isn't really) curries, and you generally can't go wrong with **kofta**, spiced vegetable dumplings in curry.

In Kathmandu you'll also run across **South Indian** canteens, which serve a completely different and predominantly vegetarian cuisine. The staple dish here is the **dosa**, a rice-flour pancake rolled around curried potatoes and vegetables, served with **sambar** (a savoury tamarind sauce) and coconut chutney. You can also get *idli* (mashed rice, usually accompanied with *sambar*), *dahi vada* (lentil-flour dumplings in curd) and various vegetable curries.

And as for the incredible array of Indian **sweets**, well, that could fill a book in itself. A selection: *laddu*, yellow-and-orange speckled semolina balls; *jelebi*, deep-fried pretzels of battered treacle; *barphi*, fudgy diamonds made from reduced milk, often decorated with edible silver leaf; *koloni*, a softer version of the same; *kudpak*, a thick molasses pudding; *lal mohan*, brown spongy balls in sweet syrup; and *ras malai*, curd cheese blobs in sweet spiced cream. Really good sweets are found only in the bigger towns.

TIBETAN FOOD

Strictly speaking, "Tibetan" refers to nationals of Tibet, but the people of the Nepal Himalaya, collectively known as Bhotiyas, together with the people of several other highland ethnic groups, all eat what could be called **Tibetan food**.

Momo, arguably the most famous and popular of Tibetan dishes, are available throughout hill Nepal. Distant cousins to ravioli, the half-moon-shaped pasta shells are filled with meat, vegetables and ginger, steamed, and served with hot tomato *achhaar* and a bowl of broth. Fried *momo* are called *kothe*. Put the same stuffing ingredients inside a flour pastry shell and fry it and you get *shyaphagle*, a sort of Tibetan meat pie. Tibetan cuisine is also justly celebrated for its excellent hearty soups, usually called **thukpa** or **thenthuk**, consisting of noodles or homemade pasta strips, meat and vegetables in broth.

For a special blow-out, try **gyakok**, a huge meal for two that includes chicken, pork, prawns, fish, tofu, eggs and vegetables, and which gets its name from the brass container it's served in; *gyakok* is only found in tourist restaurants and has to be ordered several hours ahead. In trekking lodges you'll encounter frisbee-shaped items called **Tibetan bread**, which, though unappealing on their own, are made more interesting by the addition of honey or peanut butter.

The average Bhotiya peasant seldom eats any of the above: the most common standbys in the high country are **potatoes**, boiled or made into pancakes (*riki kur*), and **tsampa** – toasted barley flour, mixed with milk or tea to make a sort of paste, or eaten plain.

ROAD FOOD AND SNACKS

There's certainly no need to go hungry when you're travelling – **fast food and snacks** are available at every stop. Since these dishes are prepared ahead of time, what you see is what you get. Common sit-down fare includes **pakauda**, fried, bready nuggets of battered vegetables, served with hot sauce, and **tarkaari ra roti**, vegetable (usually bean) curry served with *puris*. Another refreshing possibility is **dahi chiura**, a mixture of yoghurt and beaten rice that isn't so different from the "muesli curd" served in tourist restaurants. If you're in more of a hurry, you can grab a handful of **samosa**, fried pyramids of pastry filled with curried vegetables, or carry away *papar* (*pappadums* – crispy fried discs made from chickpea flour), *baara* (fried lentil patties), *chap* (potato and garlic, battered and fried), *chana* (curried chickpeas), *taareko phul* (boiled egg, battered and fried) or other titbits on a leaf plate.

If nothing else, there will always be packet **noodles** (usually referred to by brand name: Rara, Maggi, Waiwai, Yum Yum, etc), which can either be boiled as a soup or stir-fried as **chow mein**. Roadside vendors peddle **chat** (a mixture of peas or soya beans, radish, chilli, salt and lemon, all whisked together and served in a paper cone or on a leaf), roasted peanuts, coconut slivers, corn on the cob, *sel roti* (doughnuts) and lots more.

FRUIT

Which fruits are available depends on the season, but there's usually a good choice. Lovely mandarin **oranges**, which ripen throughout the late autumn and winter, grow from the Tarai up to around 1200m and are actually sweetest near the upper end of their range. Winter also brings **papaya** in the Tarai and lower hills, **apples**, grown in higher valleys but widely sold lower down, and **sugar cane**, a low-elevation crop that requires strong jaw muscles to appreciate. **Mangoes** from the Tarai start ripening in May and are available throughout most of the summer, as are **litchis**, **watermelons** and **guavas**. **Bananas** are harvested year-round at the lower elevations and range in size from little stubbies to jumbo plantains.

OTHER PROVISIONS

Imported **chocolates** are sold in tourist areas, and waxy Indian substitutes can be found in most towns. **Biscuits** and cheap boiled sweets are sold at roadside stalls everywhere. Kwality **ice cream**, available throughout the Kathmandu Valley and Pokhara, is safe. **Cheese**, produced from cow, buffalo and occasionally yak milk, comes in several styles and is sold in tourist areas and "factories" along trekking routes. (In the hills you might also come across *churpi*, a native version of cheese made from dried buttermilk or yoghurt – it's inedibly hard, and is normally softened by being added to soup.)

DRINKS

Water (*paani*) is automatically served with food in Nepali restaurants – sometimes it's been boiled, but verification is difficult, so it's best to pass unless you really know what you're doing. Various brands of bottled water are widely available, although bottlers aren't very strictly regulated, and some tests have found unhealthy levels of germs in supposedly sterilized water. Check that the seal is intact, as refilling of bottles is not uncommon. Furthermore, the plastic bottles that water comes in are not recyclable in Nepal. You'd do well to minimize your reliance on bottled water by treating tap water with iodine drops (sold in tourist stores).

Inexpensive **soft drinks** are safe and sold in "cold stores" just about everywhere, but prices rise steadily as you move into roadless areas; Coke, 7-Up and most other international brands are available. Fresh lemon soda, made with soda water and a shot of lemon (or lime) juice, makes a good alternative if you want to cut out sugar.

Tea (*chiya*), something of a national beverage in Nepal, is traditionally brewed by boiling tea dust with equal parts milk (*dudh*) and water, along with heaps of sugar (*chini*) and a bit of ginger, cardamom or cinnamon. In tourist restaurants you'll be offered the choice of "black" or "milk" tea, both usually brewed from a bag – you have to specify "Nepali" or "*masaala*" tea if you want it made the traditional way. (You can also ask for lemon tea – "hot lemon".) Tibetans and Bhotiyas take their tea with salt and yak butter, which is definitely an acquired taste.

Locally produced **coffee** is increasingly available in Nepal, and the beans aren't bad. Most restaurants make it with instant, though, and very milky, almost like a latte. Indian-made espresso machines are getting to be in vogue, but they're usually only used to boil the milk.

Roadside stalls and tourist restaurants serve freshly squeezed **fruit juices**, according to the season, but the practice of adding water and sugar is widespread even among reputable restaurants – if the water comes from the tap, as is usually the case with roadside vendors, your chances of catching something are high. Tinned juice and fruit drinks in cartons are sold in many shops. A **lassi**, a blend of yoghurt, water or ice (beware), sugar and fruit (or salt), always goes down nicely, and helps take the heat out of a curry.

ALCOHOL

Beer (*biyar*) makes another fine accompaniment to Nepali and Indian food. Foreign brands brewed by local joint ventures – San Miguel, Carlsberg, Tuborg, Kingfisher, Guinness and so on – have captured much of the market previously held by domestic lagers. Of the local beers, Real Gold is a fairly smooth premium ale, Iceberg is full-bodied but heavy, while Star, the cheapest, is on the rough side. All of these come in 650ml bottles and less often in (non-recyclable) aluminium cans.

An amazing and amusing selection of **spirits** is bottled in Nepal, ranging from Ruslan vodka to Ye Grand Earl whisky ("Glasgow – London – Kathmandu"). They're cheap and rough, but tolerable when mixed with soft drinks. Shops sell them in convenient quarter-litre bottles, restaurants by the "peg" (30ml). Look out for regional specialities like the apricot and apple brandies of Marpha, north of Pokhara, and the aniseed-based *dudhiya* (so called because it goes milky when added to water) of the eastern Tarai. Unless you're desperate, though, give so-called "country liquors" such as Urvashi a miss. Imported spirits and wine are available in supermarkets and convenience stores at practically duty-free prices; many tourist restaurants and bars serve wine by the glass, and do cocktails with local or imported spirits.

Nepalis are avid home brewers and distillers. **Chhang** is the generic term for any beer made from rice or other grains, typically fermented in cast-off mountaineering expedition barrels; cloudy (sometimes almost porridgy) unfiltered *chhang* is called *jaar*. **Raksi**, the most popular alcoholic drink in Nepal, is a distilled version of the same and bears a heady resemblance to tequila. Harder to find, but perhaps the most pleasant drink of all, is a brew-it-yourself highland concoction called **tongba**. The ingredients are a jug of fermented millet, a straw and a flask of hot water: you pour the water in, let it steep,

TOBACCO AND PAAN

Ñepalis love their **cigarettes** (*churot*). Even if you don't smoke, consider carrying a pack – cigarettes are much appreciated as tips. Factories in Janakpur and Birganj manufacture dozens of cheap brands, most of them from a mixture of Nepali and Indian tobacco. The most popular domestic filter cigarettes are Surya, Shikhar, Yak and Khukuri, although these are starting to give way to imported brands like Marlboro. Cheap non-filters such as Bijuli and Deurali are still big with porters. Cheapest of all are **bidi**, rolled single leaves of the poorest tobacco, tied together in bundles of twenty (ask for *ek muthaa*). After the evening meal, old men may be seen smoking tobacco in a **hookah** (hubble-bubble), or occasionally passing around a **chilam** (clay pipe).

Many Nepali men make quite a production of preparing tobacco **snuff** (*surti*), slapping and rubbing it in the palm of the hand and mixing it with lime before placing a pinch behind the lower lip.

Surti comes in little foil packets hung outside *kiraana pasal*, village stalls that sell cigarettes, matches, biscuits and the like.

At least as popular, particularly near India, is **paan**, the digestive and mild stimulant that Westerners often wrongly call "betel". *Paan* sellers sit like priests in their little booths, and ordering *paan* is a hallowed ritual. The *paan* wallah starts with a betel leaf, upon which he spreads four basic ingredients: *katha* (a paste that produces *paan's* characteristic red colour), *supaari* (chopped or shredded areca nut), *mitha masaala* (a mixture of sweet spices) and *chuna* (slaked white lime, to leach the other ingredients). After that, the possibilities are endless, although in general most *paan* will be either of the *jharda* (tobacco) or *mitha* (sweet) variety. For those who haven't got time for the whole performance, *paan* wallahs also sell foil packets of *paan parag*, a simple, ready-made mix.

and suck the mildly alcoholic brew through the straw until you reach the bottom; repeat four or five times. Two *tongba* can easily lubricate an entire evening.

POST, PHONES AND THE MEDIA

Nepal isn't nearly as isolated as it once was. Email access and international direct dialling are available in all the tourist spots, and you can keep up with news via satellite TV and international newspapers. The post is still as slow and patchy as ever, though.

TELECOMMUNICATIONS

There can be no better illustration of the emerging electronic village than the private **telecommunications** centres that have sprouted in Kathmandu and other tourist areas. Like glittering electronic oases, they offer Internet and email access, international direct dialling and fax services. Most accept payment by credit card, too. Simpler telephone-only outfits, which advertise themselves with the acronyms **ISD/STD/IDD** (international subscriber dialling/standard trunk dialling/international direct dialling), can be found in nearly every town of consequence. Most district headquarters have government-operated telephone offices, which are slightly cheaper but considerably less user-friendly.

Just remember that all these options for keeping in touch are just that – optional. Nepal is still a great place to fall *out* of touch.

EMAIL AND THE INTERNET

Even if you don't use **email** at home, it's a good way to communicate with friends and family who do when you're travelling overseas. Email is huge in Nepal because it's much cheaper than phoning and faxing, and much quicker and more reliable than the post. In tourist areas, there are abundant places to go online, ranging from little mom-and-pop shops with a single PC to swish cybercafés. You can even email photos as attachments – this is easiest if you're travelling with a digital camera, but if not you can have conventional prints scanned at some shops. Email charges are cheapest in Kathmandu (see p.142), but they can be expected to come down in other places as competition increases.

There are a few different strategies for using email while travelling, so it's a good idea to decide on one before you go. **Free Web-based email** services such as Hotmail, Excite and Rocketmail are handy because they travel wherever you do. However, while the service itself is free, accessing the Internet **costs** about Rs6–10 per minute in Nepal. You can minimize access time by going online only to check and print out your incoming messages, then logging off and composing messages offline.

It's also possible to continue using your own email account back home. Using this technique, you avoid the bother of having to inform lots of people of your new address, and can continue receiving all the regular mailings you get at home. A major drawback, however, is that unlike when you access your account on your home computer, and unlike with a Web-based email service, you won't be able to retain and file sent and received messages. It's also a bit fiddly, since you have to enter your personal POP settings manually each time you log on from a computer away from home – if you plan to go this route you'll have to make a note of all the settings before leaving home.

A third approach is what might be termed "**email poste restante**", where you collect incoming messages at one or more local email addresses during your travels. The messages will be held for your arrival, just as in a physical poste restante facility. This strategy is most practical if you plan to use email in only one city during your travels, or if you have a precise itinerary and trust

The international code for Nepal is 977. When dialling a number in Nepal, drop the "0" at the beginning of the area code, which will leave a seven-digit number.

your friends and family to send messages to you care of different addresses at different times. Alternatively you can inform people of your new address each time you arrive in a new place. Email addresses of businesses that accept incoming messages for travellers are given in the Kathmandu and Pokhara sections, but be sure to send them a test message before you go because email addresses change frequently.

INTERNATIONAL PHONE AND FAX SERVICES

Phoning home from Nepal is expensive: about Rs 165–180 per minute from Kathmandu and Pokhara, even more from other places. However, nearly all phone services will allow you to receive a call back on the same line. With the **"call-back"** system, you pay the full whack for the initial call to tell your party the number where you can be reached (you should be able to do that in a minute), but then only Rs5–10 per minute for the incoming call. You can also call **collect** to many countries, but the per-minute charge to you is the same as with a callback, and much higher for the person at the other end.

Sending a **fax**, you'll be charged by the minute of transmission time, not by the page. Rates for international faxes are around Rs10 per minute more than the applicable telephone rate. A standard page takes less than a minute to go through. It costs Rs25–50 per page to collect an incoming fax (**fax back**).

TRUNK AND LOCAL CALLS

Private phone centres charge Rs15–50 per minute for **trunk** (domestic long-distance) calls, depending on the distance. Your hotel or guest house should let you make **local calls** for a few rupees. (Public phones in Nepal are for now confined to the airport, but this could change.)

While this guide gives local **phone numbers** where they exist, numbers in Nepal change so frequently as to be almost useless. (Nepalis, accustomed to phone numbers being changed on them without notice, often start conversations with the phrase *Kaahaa pariyo?* – "Where have I reached?"). If the number has changed, **directory enquiries** (☎197 throughout Nepal) might be able to help, but have a Nepali translate.

POST

Post takes at least ten days to get to or from Nepal – if it arrives at all. Postcards and aerogrammes go through fine, but envelopes or parcels that look like they might contain anything of value may go astray; even sending things registered offers no guarantees. During holiday times, when backlogs develop, postal service employees are rumoured to throw out what they don't have time to process.

If you know in advance the address(es) of where you'll be staying in Nepal, you can receive post there. Otherwise, have people send letters to you care of **poste restante** in Kathmandu or (less reliably) Pokhara. Mail should be addresed: Name, Poste Restante, GPO, Kathmandu (or Pokhara), Nepal. To reduce the risk of misfiling, your name should be printed clearly with the surname underlined or capitalized. Mail is held for about two months, and can be redirected on request. American Express handles mail in Kathmandu for cardholders and those carrying Amex cheques. US citizens can receive mail c/o the Consular Section of the American Embassy in Kathmandu.

When sending mail in Nepal, there's rarely a need to deal directly with the postal system. Hotels and most guest houses will take mail to the post office for you. Book and postcard shops in tourist areas sell stamps for a nominal extra fee, and many also have their own mail drop-off boxes (just make sure they're reliable). Where no such services exist, take your letters or cards to the post office yourself and have the stamps franked before your eyes, or wait to send them from Kathmandu, where they've got a higher probability of reaching their destination. Never use a public letterbox: the stamps will be removed and resold, and your correspondence will be used to wrap peanuts.

SENDING PARCELS

Parcels can be sent by air or sea. Obviously sea mail is cheaper but takes a lot longer (three months or more) and, as it first has to go by land to Calcutta, there are more opportunities for it to go missing.

Again, the private sector is much easier to deal with than the offical postal service. **Shipping agents** and **air freight services** in Kathmandu will shield you from much of the frustration and red tape, and they provide packing materials to boot, but for this they charge almost twice as much as the post office. Be sure you're dealing with a reputable company, though (a few are recommended on p.143). Don't entrust shipping to a handicrafts shop.

THE MEDIA

Despite only 40-percent literacy, Nepal boasts more than 1000 **newspapers** – an outgrowth of two noble Brahmanic traditions, punditry and gossip. A few are published in English. Of these, however, only two dailies – the *Kathmandu Post* and the *Rising Nepal* – are widely circulated, and outside the Kathmandu Valley even they are hard to find. The *Post* is marginally the better of the two; the *Rising Nepal* carries mainly government and palace press releases. Several English-language weeklies are stronger on analysis than news, and are aimed principally at political insiders. The *Independent* (published Wednesdays) is the most readable.

A number of **magazines** are published in English, the most interesting and easy to find being *Himal*, a bimonthly journal of environmental and development issues that's published in Kathmandu but covers all of South Asia. *Spotlight*, a weekly, tries to be a sort of Nepali *Time* or *Newsweek*, and actually carries some good features on Nepalese current affairs.

In Kathmandu and Pokhara you can get a wide range of **international publications** such as the *International Herald Tribune, USA Today, Asian Wall Street Journal, Time* and *Newsweek.*

The rapid spread of **cable and satellite TV** is sending tremors through Nepalese society – Indian pop videos, Hollywood movies and all the advertising broadcast with them are having a strong influence on youth culture, and will undoubtedly challenge traditional values and attitudes about morality and parental authority. At any rate, more and more hotel and guest house rooms have TVs, and you can catch CNN, BBC World Service, ESPN, Nepal TV and movies and sitcoms in both English and Hindi.

Despite the rise of TV, the government-run **Radio Nepal** is probably still the most influential of the nation's media, catering to the illiterate majority of Nepalis and reaching villages well beyond the circulation of any newspaper. With a daily format of traditional and pop music, news bulletins, English language lessons, dramas and development messages, it has been a powerful force for cultural and linguistic unity, though in recent years various ethnic groups have pressured the government to provide programming in their native tongues. The station carries English-language news bulletins daily at 8.15am and 8.15pm.

There are also local FM stations, including a couple of English-language ones in the Kathmandu Valley. If you're travelling with a short-wave radio, you can pick up the BBC World Service at 15.31 MHz (19.6m) between about 8.45am and 10.45pm. Alternative frequencies include 11.75 and 9.74 MHz.

OPENING HOURS AND HOLIDAYS

Shops in Nepal keep long hours, and in tourist areas usually stay open seven days a week. But when dealing with officialdom remember that Saturday, not Sunday, is the day of rest – and bureaucrats like to knock off early on Friday, too.

In theory, **government offices** and **post offices** are open Sun–Thurs 10am–5pm, Fri 10am–3pm; in winter (mid-Nov to mid-Feb), the Sun–Thurs closing time is 4pm. These schedules often get truncated at either end, though. Most **museums** keep roughly the same hours, except some close on Tuesdays instead of Saturdays.

Moneychangers and **some banks** in tourist areas are generous with their hours, but elsewhere you'll have to do your transactions between 10am and 2pm Sun–Thurs, 10am–noon

on Fri. **Travel agents** tend to work a five-day week, 9 or 10am to 6pm, Mon–Fri; airline offices are the same but they take a lunch break at 1–2pm. **Embassy** and consulate hours are all over the place.

Complicating matters is Nepal's hectic calendar of **festivals and holidays**, which can shut down offices for up to a week at a time. Dates vary from year to year – Nepal has its own calendar, beginning in mid-April and consisting of twelve months that are completely out of step with the Western ones. (The Vikram Sambat calendar began in 57 BC. Thus the Nepali year beginning in April 2000 is 2057 VS.) Religious festivals, meanwhile, are calculated according to the *lunar* calendar (see the next section). Tibetan festivals follow yet a different calendar.

NATIONAL HOLIDAYS

Prithvi Narayan Shah's Birthday – January 10 or 11.
Basanta Panchami – late January or early February.
Shiva Raatri – late February or early March.
Democracy Day – February 18 or 19.
Nawa Barsa (Nepali New Year) – April 13 or 14.
Guru Purnima – late June or early July.

Janai Purnima – late July or early August.
Dasain – late September or early October (3–6 days).
Tihaar – late October or early November (3 days).
Queen's Birthday – November 7 or 8.
Constitution Day – December 15 or 16.
King's Birthday – December 28 or 29.

FESTIVALS AND ENTERTAINMENT

Stumbling onto a local festival may prove to be the highlight of your travels in Nepal (and given the sheer number of them, you'd be unlucky not to). Though most are religious in nature, merrymaking, not solemnity, is the order of the day, and onlookers are always welcome. However, some celebrations, while public, are also personal: don't photograph worshippers without asking permission.

Music and dance are also integral parts of the culture – so much so that they can only be briefly introduced here. For more detailed coverage, see p.452.

FESTIVALS AND OTHER RITES

Festivals are a sophisticated brand of performance art in Nepal, as exotic as the religions that underlie them, which may be Hindu, Buddhist, animist or a hybrid of all three (see Contexts). **Hindu events** can take the form of huge pilgrimages and fairs (*mela*), or more introspective gatherings such as ritual bathings at sacred confluences (*tribeni*) or special acts of worship (*puja*) at temples. Many involve animal sacrifices and jolly family feasts afterwards, with priests and musicians usually on hand. Parades and processions (*jaatra*) are common, especially in the Kathmandu Valley, where idols are periodically ferried around on great, swaying chariots. **Buddhist festivals** are no less colourful, typically bringing together maroon-robed clergy and lay pilgrims to walk and prostrate themselves around stupas (domeshaped monuments, usually repainted specially for the occasion).

Knowing **when and where** festivals are to be held will not only enliven your time in Nepal, it will also help you avoid certain annoyances such as closed offices and booked-up buses. Unfortunately, festival dates vary from year to year, as most are governed by the **lunar calendar**, and determining them more than a year in advance is a highly complicated business best left to astrologers. Each lunar cycle is divided into "bright" (waning) and "dark" (waxing) halves, which are in turn divided into fourteen lunar "days". Each of these days has a name – *purnima* is the full moon, *astami* the eighth day, *aunsi* the new moon, and so on. Thus lunar festivals are always observed on a given day of either the bright or dark half of a given Nepali month. Confused? The easiest strategy is just to consult a **tourist office** when you arrive. There are also Nepali festival calendars on the **Web**, though they're not very comprehensive – try Friends in High Places (*www.fihp.com/festivals.html*) or the Nepal Home Page (*www.info-nepal.com/homepage*).

Similarly jubilant (and public), Nepali **weddings** are always scheduled on astrologically auspicious days, which fall in the greatest numbers during the months of Faagun, Magh, Chaitra, Baisaakh and Mangsir (see the festival box opposite). The approach of a wedding party is often heralded by the sound of a hired brass band – one of colonialism's stranger legacies, sounding like a Dixieland sextet playing in a pentatonic scale – and open-air feasts go on until the early hours. The bride usually wears red – an auspicious colour – and for the rest of her married life she will colour the parting of her hair with red *sindur*.

Funeral processions are understandably sombre and should be left in peace. The body is normally carried to the cremation site within hours of death by white-shrouded relatives; white is the colour of mourning for Hindus, and the eldest son is expected to shave his head and wear white for a year following the death of a parent. Many of the hill tribes conduct special shamanic rites to guide the deceased's soul to the land of the dead.

NEPAL'S MAJOR FESTIVALS

Nepal doesn't have any truly national festivals, but the following are the most widely observed events, plus a few notable local ones worth trying to coincide with. Many other local festivals are listed in the relevant chapter.

MAGH (Jan–Feb)

Magh (or Makar) Sankranti Looking forward to warmer weather and lengthening days, the first day of Magh (Jan 14 or 15) is an occasion for ritual bathing at all sacred river confluences, especially at Devghat.

Basanta Panchami A one-day spring festival celebrated on the fifth day after the new moon in most Hindu hill areas. The day is also known as Saraswati Puja, after the goddess of learning, so school playgrounds are decorated with streamers and children have their books and pens blessed.

FAAGUN (Feb–March)

Losar Tibetan New Year falls on the new moon of February and is celebrated with three days of drinking, dancing and feasting. This is the highlight of the calendar in Buddhist highland areas, as well as in Boudha and other Tibetan settlements near Kathmandu and Pokhara.

Shiva Raatri Falling on the new moon of Faagun, "Shiva's Night" is marked by bonfires and evening vigils in all Hindu areas, but most spectacularly at Pashupatinath, where tens of thousands of pilgrims and sadhus (holy men) gather for Nepal's best-known *mela* (religious fair). Children collect firewood money by holding pieces of string across the road to block passers-by – foreigners are considered easy prey. Nepalis say the festival is usually followed by a final few days of winter weather, which is Shiva's way of encouraging the Indian sadhus to go home.

Faagun Purnima (or Holi) Nepal's version of the spring water festival, common to many Asian countries, is an impish affair lasting about a week. During this period, anyone – bus passengers included – is a fair target for water balloons and coloured powder (usually red, the colour of rejoicing), and it culminates in a general free-for-all on the full-moon day of Faagun.

CHAITRA (March–April)

Seto Machhendranth Jaatra A four-day chariot procession through Kathmandu, starting on the eighth day after the new moon; similar to Patan's Machhendranath Raath festival.

BAISAAKH (April–May)

Nawa Barsa Nepali New Year, which always falls on the first day of Baisakh (April 13 or 14), is observed with local parades and the like. Bhaktapur's celebration, known as Bisket Jaatra, is the most colourful, combining religious processions with a rowdy tug-of-war.

Machhendranath Raath Jaatra Arguably Nepal's most spectacular festival: thousands gather to watch as the image of Machhendranath, the Kathmandu Valley's rain-bringing deity, is pulled around the streets of Patan in a swaying, sixty-foot-high chariot. It moves only on astrologically auspicious days, taking four weeks or more to complete its journey.

Buddha Jayanti Anniversary of the Buddha's birth, enlightenment and death, celebrated at Swayambhu and Boudha on the full-moon day of Baisakh.

SAAUN (July–Aug)

Janai Purnima The annual changing of the sacred thread (*janai*) worn by high-caste Hindu men takes place at various sacred bathing sites throughout the country on the full-moon day of Saaun. Mass observances are held at Gosainkund, a holy lake high in the mountains north of Kathmandu, and Patan, where it's an occasion for serious splashing.

Gaai Jaatra A Kathmandu festival in honour of cows (*gaai*), who are said to guide dead souls to the underworld with their tails. On the day after Janai Purnima, revellers wear whimsical costumes and young boys are dressed up in fanciful cow costumes and followed by family and friends through the streets of the old city.

Nag Panchami A day to propitiate the *nag* (snake spirits), who are traditionally held to control the monsoon rains and earthquakes in the Kathmandu Valley. Devotees paste pictures of *nag* over their doorways with cow dung and offer milk (the *nag*'s favourite food) to the pictures.

Continues over

NEPAL'S MAJOR FESTIVALS (cont')

BHADAU (Aug–Sept)

Tij On the third day after the new moon of Bhadau, Hindu women fast and ritually bathe to wash away their sins and make offerings to their husbands. The most popular bathing site is Pashupatinath, near Kathmandu.

Indra Jaatra A wild week of chariot processions and masked-dance performances in Kathmandu, held around the full moon of Bhadau. On the last day, the king receives a special *tika* (an auspicious mark on the forehead) from the "living goddess" and beer flows from the mouth of an idol in Durbar Square.

Yartung A swashbuckling fair held at Muktinath, in the Annapurna trekking area, featuring horse-racing, dancing, drinking and gambling.

ASHOJ (Sept–Oct)

Dasain (known as Dashera near India) Although Hindu in origin, Nepal's greatest festival is enthusiastically embraced by members of almost all religious and ethnic groups. It stretches over ten days leading up to the full moon of Ashoj, but the liveliest action, as far as outside observers are concerned, takes place on Durga Puja, the ninth day, when animals are sacrificed to the goddess Durga in honour of her victory over demons. On Bijaya Dasami (the "Victorious Tenth Day"), elders bestow *tika*, which on this day consist of a red powder mixed with curd and rice. Dasain is a time for families to gather (buses can get very crowded with homeward-bound passengers), and you'll see makeshift swings and miniature ferris wheels set up to entertain the kids.

KHATTIK (Oct–Nov)

Tihaar (Diwali near India) The "Festival of Lights" lasts for five days, starting two days before the new moon of Kartik. On the first, crows are honoured as the messengers of death, while on the next three days dogs, cows and bulls are garlanded. More significantly, houses throughout the hills and Tarai are trimmed with hundreds of candles and oil lamps on the third night, called Lakshmi Puja, in the hope of attracting Lakshmi, the goddess of wealth. Trusting in her, many Nepalis gamble on street corners and student groups make the rounds singing "*Diusire*", a form of musical fundraising, during this festival. On the fifth day, Bhaai Tika, sisters give their younger brothers *tika* and sweets. Firecrackers have become a big part of the fun for kids (and a source of stress for everyone else) for weeks around Tihaar time.

Chhath Coinciding with the third day of Tihaar, this festival in honour of Surya, the sun god, is one of the most important festivals for the Maithili-speaking people of the eastern Tarai. It's celebrated most ardently in Janakpur, where women gather by ponds and rivers to greet the sun's first rays with prayers, offerings and ritual baths.

MANGSIR (Nov–Dec)

Biwaha Panchami As many as 100,000 pilgrims converge on Janakpur for this five-day gathering, five days after the new moon of Mangsir. The highlight is the re-enactment of the wedding of Ram and Sita, the divine, star-crossed lovers of the *Ramayan*, one of the great Hindu epics.

Mani Rimdu Held at Tengboche in the Everest trekking region around the full moon of the ninth Tibetan month (usually Nov), this colourful Sherpa masked dance dramatizes Buddhism's victory over the ancient Bon religion in eighth-century Tibet. A similar event is held in May or June at Thami

---

MUSIC AND DANCE

Music is as common as conversation in Nepal. In the hills, travelling minstrels (*gaaine*) make their living singing ballads and accompanying themselves on the *sarangi*, a hand-carved, four-stringed fiddle. Teenagers traditionally attract the attention of the opposite sex by exchanging teasing verses. After-dinner singalongs are popular, even in Kathmandu, and of course music is indispensable in all festivals.

Traditional Nepali music often gets drowned out by the rising tide of **Indian film music**, with its surging strings and hysterically shrill vocals, and **ghazal**, a more languorous, crooning style of music often performed live in Indian and Nepali restaurants. Yet Nepali folk music still gets a good airing; in contrast, it sounds mercifully calm and villagey. A few tourist restaurants in the budget quarters of Kathmandu and Pokhara host regular free performances by local folk groups.

Nepali music is almost inseparable from **dance**, especially at festivals. Nepali dance is an unaffected folk art – neither wildly athletic nor subtle, it depicts everyday activities like work and courtship. Each region and ethnic group has its own distinct traditions, and during your travels you should get a chance to join a local hoedown or two, if not a full-blown festival extravaganza. Look out, too, for the muscular stick dance of the lowland Tharus, performed regularly at lodges outside Chitwan National Park.

Staged **culture shows** in Kathmandu and Pokhara are a long way from the real thing, but they do provide a sampling of folk and religious dances, and hint at the incredible cultural diversity contained in such a small country. Most troupes perform such standards as the dance of the *jhankri* (shaman-exorcists still consulted by many, if not most, hill Nepalis); the sleeve-twirling dance of the Sherpas; the flirting dance of the hill-dwelling Tamangs; the Tharus' fanciful peacock dance; perhaps a formal priestly dance, to the accompaniment of a classical *raga* (musical piece); and at least one of the dances of the Kathmandu Valley's holiday-loving Newars.

CINEMA

Nepal's love-hate relationship with India is perhaps best illustrated by its **cinema**: Nepalis might grouse about India's cultural imperialism, but that doesn't stop them rushing to see the latest schmaltz and pyrotechnics from Bollywood. Nepali and Hindi are similar enough that movies aren't usually dubbed. Nepali films are still the exception, and are less slick than Indian productions, but much more popular when they're on. **Video** rental shops are commonplace in the main cities, though less so since the advent of satellite TV. Some tourist restaurants screen Hollywood flicks on video, many of them amazingly current – bootleg tapes often hit the streets in Kathmandu long before their official release on video.

SHOPPING

Nepal's handicrafts are as rich and varied as its culture, having been influenced by hundreds of years of trade and religious exchange with Tibet and India. In addition, the influx of Tibetan artisans since 1959 has enriched the marketplace immeasurably, while tourist demand, ironically, has helped fuel something of an artistic renaissance. You can pick up distinctive gifts, souvenirs and clothes for a song, or if your budget runs to it, spend a fortune on carpets and *objets d'art*.

WHERE TO SHOP

Ninety-nine percent of crafts outlets are concentrated in the Kathmandu Valley and Pokhara: that's where the buyers are, and just about all of the mass-produced stuff is actually made there. Competition is intense. You can't stroll the tourist strips without being importuned by **curio sellers** cradling "priceless" goods in white cloths, or beckoned from the sidelines by operators of makeshift stalls; their overheads are low and so, at least in theory, should be their prices. More reputable **shops**, galleries, "emporiums" and boutiques have better selections and aren't so hard-driving (many have fixed prices). In Patan – Nepal's handicrafts capital – you'll also find **"factory" showrooms**, where you can watch the wares being made.

One of the most encouraging developments in recent years has been the rise of **non-profit (or "fair trade") shops** in Kathmandu and Patan. By providing outlets for women, disadvantaged people and workers' cooperatives in some of Nepal's remotest hill areas, they increase employment and channel money where it's most needed. They also appear to avoid the pitfalls of other development projects in the hills, where lavish foreign aid has often led Nepalis to expect something for nothing.

Quite a few items sold in tourist areas are made elsewhere, and needless to say it's more fun (and cheaper) to pick them up at their source. Best buys are noted in the relevant sections of the Guide, along with a few local specialities that can't be found anywhere else.

No matter what the seller says, very few items are older than last week. Genuine **antiques** – anything over 100 years old, or anything customs officials might think is that old – have to be cleared for export by the Department of

Archaeology in Kathmandu. Get the dealer to take care of the paperwork.

BARGAINING

Except where prices are clearly marked as fixed (and sometimes even then), you'll be expected to **bargain**. Bargaining is very much a matter of personal style, but in Nepal it's always lighthearted, never acrimonious. Sellers always speak English in tourist areas, but prices are always cheaper for those who speak a few words of Nepali.

There's no firm guide as to what to expect to have knocked off, although prices are usually softer on the street than in shops. The initial asking price may be anywhere from 10 to 1000 percent over the going rate, depending, to a certain extent, on how much like a tourist you look. All the old chestnuts still hold true: never show the least sign of interest, let alone enthusiasm; and walking away will usually cut the price dramatically. But most important is to know what you want, its approximate value, and how much you're prepared to pay. Never start to haggle for something you definitely don't intend to buy – it'll end in bad feeling on both sides. Similarly, don't let a figure pass your lips that you're not prepared to pay. Having mentioned a price, you are obliged to pay it.

If you're contemplating making a big purchase, hiring a knowledgeable **guide** may save you money many times over what you spend on the guide's fee – but make absolutely sure you're getting independent counsel, and not just being taken on a tour of brother-in-laws' shops.

STATUES AND OTHER METALWARE

Artisans of the Kathmandu Valley have been casting bronze, brass and copper **statues** of Buddhist and Hindu deities for at least 1300 years – an unbroken artistic tradition with few parallels worldwide. The images are produced by the lost-wax process, in which a model is carved out of wax, surrounded by clay and then fired, melting the wax and leaving a terracotta mould. Small pieces can be cast from a single mould, but larger ones have to be assembled from up to a dozen pieces, the joins concealed by ornate embellishments.

Statues are cast mainly in the **style** of Tibet (Nepal's main customer for centuries), depicting a tremendous variety of Buddhas, *bodhisattva* and defenders of the *dharma*, as well as Hindu and indigenous deities. Each is characterized by a certain posture, weapon or other identifying feature. If you're shopping for a metal statue, the Handicraft Association of Nepal's inexpensive booklet, *A Short Description of Gods, Goddesses and Ritual Objects of Buddhism and Hinduism in Nepal*, sold in some bookshops, can help in figuring out the iconography.

Patan is the traditional casting centre. **Prices** depend on size, metal and workmanship, but are never cheap – at least Rs5000 for a 20cm-tall image. The best-quality images will have carefully detailed fingers and eyes, and the metal will be without pits or spots.

Many brass **pots and vessels** are wonderful pieces of design. *Ghada*, the brass water jugs that Nepali women cradle against one hip, may be too big to tote home, but small incense holders, *raksi* pourers, *puja* trays, oil lamps and *jal* urns are all attractive and relatively cheap.

So-called **"singing" bowls** are popular both as domestic and ritual objects. Made from an amalgam of various (traditionally seven) metals, these vessels produce a continuous harmonic ringing when rubbed around the rim with a wooden pestle. When held near the navel, the singing bowl is said to resonate with the body and aid in meditation.

JEWELLERY

Every hill bazaar has its metalsmiths who sell **gold and silver** at the going rate and, for a modest charge, will tap it into an earring, nose ring, necklace clasp, bracelet or any other form in which a woman wants to display the family wealth. Common to almost all hill women are *malla*, necklaces consisting of strands of glass beads drawn together with a cylindrical gold ornament. Shops in Kathmandu sell **jewellery** made of silver, white metal and semiprecious stones, which, though designed entirely for the tourist market, are nonetheless attractive.

Gem sellers in Kathmandu deal in a wide range of cut and uncut stones at reasonable prices. Garnet, tourmaline, ruby, aquamarine, citrine ("golden topaz") and cat's eye come from mines in Nepal's Ganesh Himal and eastern hills; turquoise, amethyst and sapphire come from Tibet; coral from India; and lapis lazuli from Afghanistan. Most stones are cut and polished in India. Take care when buying, as gem quality and cut can make a vast difference to value. Turquoise is often fake (bite it to see if the colour comes off).

WOOD AND PAPIER-MÂCHÉ

Nepali **woodcarving** reaches its apex in Bhaktapur, where you'll find everything from modest Buddha busts and Ganesh figures to exquisite, full-size window frames. Miniature replicas of Bhaktapur's famed Peacock Window are ubiquitous, and artisans are increasingly turning out non-traditional items such as animals, CD boxes and chess sets. Pieces are carved with mallet and chisel out of one of several types of wood, most of them from the Tarai. The most common are *sal*, a hard, heavy, chocolate-coloured wood like teak; *sisu*, similar but with more grain to it; *chaab*, a cheaper, softer, honey-coloured wood; and *korma*, also light in colour but harder than *chaab*. Prices depend not only on size but also the type of wood and the quality of carving: Rs1000 should get you a finely detailed 20cm figure. Sandalwood figures, carved in extremely intricate designs after the Indian style, are considerably more expensive.

Wooden masks are used by Tibetans and highland Nepalis in religious dances and shamanic rituals. The genuine articles are rarely sold, but replicas are widely available in tourist areas; in the never-ending battle for tourists' attention, craftsmen are now souping up their masks with overlain metal designs.

Thimi is famous for its **papier-mâché masks**, copies of those used in the masked dances of the Kathmandu Valley in which dancers take on the persona of the deity represented. The Nawa Durga (Nine Durgas) and their attendant deities Ganesh, Shiva and Bhairab are the ones most commonly recreated for tourist consumption, ranging from full size down to bite size. The Nawa Durga also take the form of **puppets** with papier-mâché or clay heads and multiple wooden arms.

Separately, Kashmiri shops sell little laquered papier-mâché boxes, incense holders, napkin rings and ornaments – they're not Nepali, but they make great cheap gifts.

PAPER ITEMS

Items made from *lokta*, an indigenous form of handmade **paper**, make excellent, lightweight purchases. Traditionally *lokta* was made by hill people in winter, when there was nothing going on, and was valued for official documents because of its strong, cross-fibrous texture. In the past decade or so, many aid organizations have seized on *lokta* as a year-round opportunity to generate income, and it has blossomed into a thriving industry carried out by an internationally famous UNICEF operation in Bhaktapur and increasingly in other places.

Lokta is often confused with rice paper. Actually it's made from the bark of a shrub (genus *Daphne*) that grows wild in Nepal's eastern and central hills between the elevations of 2000 and 3000 metres (it's not cultivated, so the increasing popularity of *lokta* products may eventually lead to its depletion). The fibrous bark is boiled, beaten to a pulp, mixed with water, poured into floating frames, and finally sun-dried on fallow terraces. The result is a rough but richly textured parchment which is then block-printed to produce beautiful greeting cards, lampshades, calendars, gift wrapping, boxes and a growing range of other products.

CARPETS

Tibetan-style hand-woven **carpets** have come a long way from their folk roots. What started out, thirty years ago, as a modest income generator for Tibetan refugees has become Nepal's biggest export item – and a multi-ethnic creative collaboration. The traditional Tibetan form has been reinvented, with a unique look and lustrous, hard-wearing texture brought about by the use of synthetic dyes, blended Tibetan and New Zealand wool, standardized manufacture and modern chemical washing processes. In recent years the field has been enlivened by an explosion of contemporary colour schemes and designs.

Many foreigners prefer carpets in earthy, pastel **colours**, assuming them to be traditional and presumably coloured with vegetable dyes. Actually, traditional Tibetan carpets come in bright, almost gaudy hues – the earth tones are in vogue because of foreign demand. Synthetic dyes can produce any colour or shade, whether muted or bright, whereas vegetable dyes have a more limited range. Carpets made of all-Tibetan lamb's wool and/or vegetable dyes are less common, and more expensive.

Traditional Tibetan **designs** are bold and simple – angular dragons, flowers, clouds or various auspicious symbols, usually against a plain field and contained within a geometric border. Many carpets being produced these days are further simplified, using large, open fields, and combining traditional motifs with abstract patterns.

Carpets are woven throughout the Kathmandu and Pokhara valleys. Compared to Middle Eastern makes, Tibetan-style carpets have deeper, more luxuriant pile, but lower knot densities and coarser patterns. One of the best **shopping** areas is in Patan, and you'll find more information about their manufacture in that section (see p.185). The choice is vast, so take your time. Start by getting an idea of what different knot counts (usually 60, 80, 100 or 144 per square inch) and wool mixes (50-, 80- or 100-percent Tibetan wool) and sizes look like. Sizes aren't standardized, but many carpets are 3x6 feet; 18-inch squares, which make fine seat covers, are also common. Make sure the ratio of vertical to horizontal knots isn't less than 2:3.

Prices are of course subject to bargaining, but the carpet seller won't go below a certain price per square metre or foot. For carpets made in Nepal, the going **rates per square metre** seem to be $120 for 100-percent Tibetan wool at 100 knots per square inch; $80 for 100-percent Tibetan wool at 80 knots per inch; $55 for a 50–50 wool mix at 100 knots per inch; and $35 for 50–50 wool and 80 knots per inch.

Nepali carpets are often made with child labour. At least one organization based in Kathmandu (Rugmark) certifies that its carpets aren't, and some others say theirs aren't, though you have no way of verifying their claims.

Nepali carpet factories are also increasingly imitating **Kashmiri and Afghan styles**, though these tend not to be as fine as the originals. Imported Kashmiri carpets are sold in many boutiques run by traders fleeing the tourist meltdown in Kashmir. These rugs are among the world's finest, but Kashmiri rug salesmen are among the world's wiliest, so proceed with great caution. A *pukka* carpet is a major investment, costing $600–2000 for a decent 3x5, depending mainly on knot count. It should have a label on the back stating that it was made in Kashmir, what it's made of (wool, silk, or "silk touch" – wool combined with a little cotton and silk to give it a sheen), its size, number of knots per inch, and the name of the design. To tell if it really is silk, scrape the carpet lightly with a knife and burn the fluff: real silk shrivels to nothing and leaves a distinctive smell.

TEXTILES AND CLOTHING

Nepali designers are applying their creative talents to **textiles** and, as with carpets, adapting indigenous designs in stylish new ways. Most of these items are produced by tiny cottage-industry outfits and have yet to find their way overseas, but the fleeting success of certain fashions shows there's a receptive market.

Dhaka, a brightly patterned **cotton weave** made on hand looms in the eastern and western hills, has long been used to make *topi* (men's caps), *cholo* (women's half-length blouses) and shawls. Palpali *dhaka*, the preferred make for *topi*, comes from Tansen (Palpa), and you'll find more about it in that section. Women's cooperatives are now producing *dhaka* in colour schemes and patterns aimed squarely at Western tastes, and turning it into scarves, ties, placemats, jackets, handbags – you name it.

Other cotton weaves, including *khadi* (traditional homespun) and many forms of sari material, are produced locally all over Nepal. These, too, turn up in innovative incarnations – block-printed, quilted and hand-stitched – from pot holders and tea cosies to cushion covers and bedspreads.

Hemp products are appearing in many outlets. For clothing, hemp fibres are usually mixed with cotton, wool or silk to produce linen-look garments (pure hemp is rather rough on the skin). Hemp is also being used in handbags, totes, caps and hats, and even shoes and slippers. At least one group also markets *allo*, a wool-like material woven from the pounded bark of nettle stems.

Pashmina, a cashmere-like **wool** gleaned from the softest hair of goats, is made into shawls which are worn by many Kathmandu Valley residents in winter. These are good purchases, but be sure you're not buying acrylic. Rub off some fibres and burn them: *pashmina* will smell like burning hair, acrylic won't smell of anything. Kashmiri shops sell more elaborate embroidered shawls and various items decorated with chain-stitch patterns, including cushion covers, tea cosies and garments far too magnificent to wear in public. You can also pick up nice **leather** jackets and other clothing items at reasonable prices.

Silk is a relatively new industry in Nepal, with a few manufacturers in the Kathmandu Valley producing thread and raw material. Others weave Indian thread into *dupian*, which looks like raw silk but is softer, shinier and more expensive, or fine *crepe de Chine*.

Nepal's burgeoning **garment industry** has been quick to experiment with all these materials and more, producing everything from cheap readymade Punjabis and the like to designer fashions purchased by foreigners and a growing clientele of wealthy Nepalis. Boutiques in Kathmandu and Patan display some stunning original pieces melding Western and local influences; in global fashion terms, these are quite cheap, and all the more exciting for their obscurity.

Tibetan wrap-around dresses, called *chuba*, can be bought off the peg or custom-made by shops in Kathmandu and Boudha. Intricate Tibetan and Bhutanese brocade also turns up in specialist shops in Kathmandu and Boudha.

Sweaters, socks and other woollens, knitted in the home by women, are amazingly cheap and sold all over tourist areas. The cheaper ones suffer from quality-control problems – many will quickly fall apart at the seams. Ask which grade of wool the garment is made from. For more durability and better styling, it's worth paying more at one of the pricier boutiques in Kathmandu or Patan.

Other cheap clothes sold in tourist areas are usually of very poor quality, but they'll do for holiday wear – cotton dresses are good choices for trekking. Lots of travellers seem to think they're going native by wearing baggy pajamas and the like, which amuses Nepalis. Machine-embroidered T-shirts are inescapable. Tibetan-style black felt with rainbow trim is another budget-wear staple, finding its way into caps, jackets, bags and the like.

PAINTINGS

Like so many things in Nepal, **thangka** – Tibetan ritual paintings – are now cranked out for the tourist market, yet the best ones remain undiminished by commercialization, and even the cheapest can't hide the dense Buddhist symbolism inherent in the form. The production process and subject matter of these vibrant, intricate paintings is discussed on p.135.

Thangka are produced not only by Tibetans but also by Tamangs and, increasingly, by artisans of other Nepali ethnic groups. In addition, **paubha** – paintings in the style of the Kathmandu Valley's Newars – are undergoing a modest revival after near-extinction earlier this century. *Paubha* are created in much the same way as *thangka*, but they tend to contain less background detail, focusing instead on a central deity, who may just as easily be Hindu as Buddhist. Some *thangka* dealers also carry other Tibetan-style paintings depicting herbs, animals, medical charts and so on.

Before **buying** a *thangka* or *paubha*, first watch a painter at work in Patan or Bhaktapur – the main production centres – to get an appreciation for how painstaking the art is, and try to get someone to explain the imagery and the meanings behind it. When you see one you like, examine the detail of the eyes, facial expression and fingers of the main figure; background figures should also stand up to scrutiny. Many paintings aimed at tourists make a great show of their "gold" paint: real gold won't come away when a moist finger is pressed against it. Most "old" *thangka* have been aged with wood smoke. A halfway decent small (15cm x 30cm) *thangka* will cost at least Rs1500, though poor ones will go for much less than that. A large (90cm x 120cm) one, using microscopic brushstrokes and genuine gold paint, will cost hundreds or even thousands of dollars.

So-called "**Maithili**" art has caught on in the past few years. These brightly coloured folk paintings, which keep alive age-old religious and fertility symbols, are created by women in the villages surrounding Janakpur in the eastern Tarai (you can read more about them in that section). However, they're most easily bought in the non-profit shops of Kathmandu or Patan, where Maithili motifs are reproduced not only on paper but also pottery and papier mâché.

Other non-traditional artforms are gaining in popularity. Notable are the *thangka*-influenced naive maps of Nepal and the Kathmandu Valley that are found primarily in Patan, and the water-colour (and occasionally acrylic or oil) street scenes and ethnic portraits sold in all the tourist areas. **Batiks**, depicting typical Nepali scenes, are an inexpensive artform introduced in the past two decades as an income-generator for disabled people in the Kathmandu and Pokhara valleys.

MISCELLANEOUS CRAFTS AND POTTERY

Khukuri, the deadly knives of Nepal's feared Gurkha soldiers, are Nepal's most ubiquitous souvenirs. Bhojpur, in the eastern hills, is the traditional forging centre, but knives are heavily peddled in Kathmandu. An authentic one will have a moon-shaped notch at the base of the blade to channel the blood away, and its sheath will contain two small tools for sharpening and honing. Prices start at Rs400, but a city-slicker model with a buffalo-horn handle will cost several times that.

The Kathmandu Valley and Pokhara are awash with **Tibetan curios**, though the vast majority of these are manufactured in Nepal or India. The range of items is formidable: prayer wheels, amulets, charm boxes, bracelets (usually inscribed with the mantra, *Om mani padme hum*), prayer-flag printing blocks, *chhang* pots, *phurpa* (ritual daggers), masks, turquoise and coral jewellery, musical instruments and many other religious artefacts. Much of it has been artificially aged, and the turquoise is often fake. Tibetan chests and other furniture, if genuine, are quite expensive. The sale of human skulls and bowls (which are quite real), ornamented with metalwork and baubles and traditionally used for tantric purposes, is illegal and such items are now sold only in secret; decorated goat skulls are easy enough to come by.

Some shops in Kathmandu sell nothing but **musical instruments**, including *sarangi* (Nepal's version of a fiddle), *murali* (flutes) and *jhankri* (shaman) drums. Tibetan instruments can be purchased in Boudha.

Simple, unglazed **pottery** is produced by *kumal* (potters) throughout the hills. Very little of it rises above the level of mundane implements, but the potters of Bhaktapur and Thimi turn out ornamental items – candlesticks, elephant-shaped plant pots and so on. Some of the non-profit shops sell non-traditional, glazed pieces. Ceramics don't travel well, though, so you'll have to wrap them carefully.

OTHER ITEMS

Attractive embroidered pouches and wooden "caddies" of Nepali **tea** make great presents or souvenirs. They're sold mainly in the Kathmandu Valley, but the tea itself is cultivated in the eastern hills around Ilam (just over the border from Darjeeling), and you'll find an account of processing and grading in that section (p.373). Two principal varieties are grown for export: Ilam, which has a full flavour much like Darjeeling, and Kanyam, smokier but considered superior by many. If you're not bothered about presentation, loose tea is much cheaper than the packaged stuff and can be sealed in plastic for travelling.

Incense can also bring back fond memories of Nepal after your return. Literally dozens of varieties manufactured in Nepal, and still others imported from India, are available in every bazaar. Tibetan mixtures, made in Nepal and sold mainly in Tibetan neighbourhoods such as Boudha and Swayambhu, are redolent of juniper. Essential oils, used for aromatherapy, massage and other purposes, come in a wide variety in tourist-quarter shops – like incense, they're extracted from a variety of plants in India and Nepal.

There's no need to lug a library along when travelling in Nepal: Kathmandu and Pokhara each have dozens of **bookshops** devoted to travel, fiction and classics. Kathmandu, especially, seems to have more booksellers per capita than anywhere in the English-speaking world. You can get new and used books in English and other European languages, usually as Western imports but sometimes in cheaper Indian imprints. Most shops will buy books or trade as well.

A burgeoning number of music stores stock **CDs and cassettes**. Those catering to foreigners offer a range of traditional and contemporary Nepali, Tibetan and Indian music, plus some Western stuff. The tapes are usually of poor quality, and the CDs can't always be trusted either, but they're fairly inexpensive so it's worth taking the chance on a few. Cheaper tapes produced for the home market are available in local shops and stalls. See "Music and dance" in Contexts for a recommended discography.

Things **not to take home** include ritual objects made from human bones (or even animal bones that a customs officer might mistake for human ones), and anything made from a rare or protected species (including ivory, certain furs and peacock feathers). These are illegal to export from Nepal. So are *shaligram* (fossil-bearing stones), though nobody seems to care much about their export. As for drugs, see "Police and trouble".

OUTDOOR PURSUITS

Long a magnet for outdoor enthusiasts, Nepal (and especially Pokhara) is now developing into a kind of big Outward Bound centre. Operators are set up to offer just about every kind of outdoor pursuit – not only trekking and climbing but also rafting, kayaking, mountain-biking, bird-watching and more.

Many travellers come to Nepal specifically to try these activities for the first time. And why not: if you're going to learn to climb or kayak or mountain bike, why not do it in the most spectacular place in the world for it, the Himalaya? Many packages are built around instruction for first-timers, with all equipment provided. On top of that, prices are quite cheap by international standards.

Most of these activities are described in greater detail in later chapters – this section just gives an overview of the possibilities.

TREKKING AND HIKING

Even if you're not the outdoor type, **trekking** is a rare pleasure that shouldn't be passed up: it's the only way to get *into* the Himalaya, as opposed to looking at them from a distance, and it's an excellent way to experience Nepal's constantly changing landscape and people-scape. Though trekking can be physically demanding and sometimes uncomfortable, few people experience any real difficulties. A trek normally lasts at least four or five days, but you'll get more out of it if you can set aside two or more weeks. Most people don't trek with a group, and wait until they get to Kathmandu before making any arrangements, but those with lots of money and little time may want to book through a trekking agency in their home country (see box on p.60). Equipment can be rented cheaply in Nepal, and it's no problem to store unneeded stuff while you're on the trail. Note that travel insurance is all the more essential if you plan to trek. For a full rundown on trekking **preparations** and **routes**, see Chapter Seven.

If you're up for a bigger challenge and can afford to go with a group, consider bagging a **trekking peak**. Or learn to **climb** – at least one company offers a climbing course in the Everest region.

Day hikes – which offer many of the rewards of trekking without the red tape – are described throughout the guide. While the scenery on a day hike will seem rather tame compared with a trek, the cultural interactions on these uncommercialized trails are often more genuine.

RAFTING AND KAYAKING

Of all the outdoor activities on offer in Nepal, **rafting** probably tops the list for excitement. Nepal's rivers are truly world-class, yet outside of the monsoon the whitewater is fine for first-timers. Rafting is one of the best ways to experience Nepal's lower hills and valleys, providing fresh angles on villages and religious gatherings at sacred confluences.

Most rafting companies offer standard three- or four-day trips, and provide all gear; some organize longer trips and raft/wildlife or raft/trek packages. On most trips, the guide steers the raft while the crew – that's you – provides the paddle-power. Nights are spent camping on riverside beaches, usually far from roads or commercial centres.

Kayaking is now a popular alternative river activity in Nepal. If you already know how, you can rent gear in Pokhara or Kathmandu and take off on your own. If you've never done it before, you can join one of the four-day kayak schools on the Seti River, near Pokhara. Kayaking is also an option on some rafting trips, since several companies use safety kayaks for support. At least one

ADVENTURE TRAVEL OPERATORS AND AGENTS

The following are some of the most established overseas companies running trekking, rafting, mountain-biking and wildlife-viewing trips in Nepal, along with a few big sales agents. Booking directly with operators in Kathmandu (see p.137) will save money but may increase complexities.

NORTH AMERICA

Above the Clouds Trekking (☎800/233-4499 or 508/799-4499). Trekking, family treks.
Adventure Center (☎800/227-8747 or 510/654-1879). Trekking, trekking peaks, rafting, wildlife.
Friends in High Places (☎800/OK-NEPAL or 781/396-0272). Trekking, custom treks.
Geographic Expeditions (☎800/777-8183 or 415/922-0448). Trekking, trekking peaks, wildlife, customized trips.
Himalayan Travel (☎800/225-2380 or 203/359-3669). Trekking, trekking peaks, rafting, wildlife.
Journeys (☎800/255-8735 or 734/665-4407). Trekking (including women's, health-profession

and tree-planting treks), rafting, wildlife; some trips suitable for children.
Mountain Travel-Sobek (☎800/227-2384 or 510/527-8100). Trekking, wildlife.
Safaricentre (☎800/223-6046 or 310/546-4411). Trekking, wildlife, rafting.
Trek Holidays (☎800/661-7265 or 416/922-7584). Trekking, trekking peaks, rafting, wildlife.
Wilderness Travel (☎800/368-2794 or 510/558-2488). Trekking, trekking peaks.
Worldwide Adventures (☎800/387-1483 or 416/221-3000). Trekking, trekking peaks, rafting, wildlife.

UK & IRELAND

Adrift Whitewater Rafting, Collingbourne House, Spencer Court, 140–142 High Street, London SW18 (☎0181/874 4969; *www.adrift.co.nz*). Rafting.
Adventure Travel Centre, 131–135 Earls Court Rd, London SW5 (☎0171/370 4555). Trekking, mountain-biking, wildlife.
Classic Nepal, 33 Metro Ave, Newton, Derbyshire (☎01773/873497). Trekking, trekking peaks, rafting, wildlife.
Colette Pearson Travel, 64 S William St, Dublin 2 (☎01/677 1029). Trekking, trekking peaks, rafting, mountain-biking, wildlife.
Encounter Overland, 267 Old Brompton Rd, London SW5 (☎0171/370 6845). Trekking, rafting, wildlife.
Exodus Travels, 9 Weir Rd, London SW12 (☎0181/675 5550). Trekking, trekking peaks, rafting, mountain-biking, wildlife.

Explore Worldwide, 1 Frederick St, Aldershot, Hants (☎01252/344 161). Trekking, trekking peaks, rafting, wildlife.
High Places, Globe Works, Pennestone Rd, Sheffield (☎0114/275 7500). Trekking, rafting, wildlife.
Himalayan Kingdoms, 20 The Mall, Clifton, Bristol (☎0117/923 7163). Trekking, trekking peaks, expedition peaks, rafting, wildlife.
Naturetrek, Arlesford, Hampshire (☎01962/733051). Birdwatching.
Sherpa Expeditions, 131a Heston Rd, Hounslow, Middx (☎0181/577 2717). Trekking, trekking peaks, rafting, wildlife.
Terra Firma, 63 Holmesdale Rd, Teddington TW11 (☎0181/943 3065). Trekking, trekking peaks, rafting, mountain-biking.

AUSTRALIA & NEW ZEALAND

Adrift, Christchurch, NZ (☎03/442 1615). Rafting.
Adventure World,73 Walker St, North Sydney NSW 2060 (☎02/9956 7766; toll-free ☎1800/221 931), other offices in Adelaide, Brisbane, Melbourne and Perth; 101 Great South Rd, Remuera, Auckland NZ (☎09/524 5118). Trekking, trekking peaks, rafting, wildlife.
Destinations Adventure, 2nd Floor, Premier Bldg, Auckland NZ (☎09/309 0464). Trekking, mountain-biking, wildlife.
Journeys Worldwide, Level 7, 333 Adelaide St, Brisbane (☎07/3221 4788). Trekking, trekking peaks, rafting, wildlife.

Outdoor Travel, 55 Hardware St, Melbourne 3000 (☎03/9670 7252). Trekking, rafting, wildlife.
Peregrine Adventures, 258 Lonsdale St, Melbourne 3000 (☎03/9663 8611); offices in Brisbane, Sydney, Adelaide and Perth. Trekking, trekking peaks, rafting, wildlife.
Sun Travel, 407 Great South Rd, Penrose, Auckland (☎09/525 3074). Trekking, trekking peaks, rafting, wildlife.
Sundowners Adventure Travel, Suite 15, 600 Lonsdale St, Melbourne (☎03/9600 1934; toll-free ☎1800/337 089). Trekking, trekking peaks, rafting, wildlife.

shop in Pokhara also rents **hydrospeeds** (sort of whitewater boogie boards).

For a more detailed discussion of **costs**, **equipment** and **safety**, as well as descriptions of the main rafting **rivers**, see Chapter Eight.

MOUNTAIN-BIKING

Nepal was made for **mountain bikes**: there are plenty of uncrowded and spectacular back roads, the cycling is challenging, and the alternative mode of getting from A to B – buses – is unpleasant. On a bike you can stop where you like, enjoy the scenery, make detours and amaze the locals. A degree of fitness is required, but if you can handle a one-speed Hero you should have no trouble with a mountain bike.

Like trekking (and unlike rafting) mountain-biking can be done **independently**. As explained on p.36, good bikes are hard to find in Nepal, though a few shops in Kathmandu rent them out by the day; if you're serious about mountain-biking then consider bringing your own bike. Some hardy cyclists with plenty of time make a whole circuit of Nepal, usually combined with India or (less commonly, and more expensively) Tibet. However, most people will probably opt to join a **tour**. These range from easy one-day cultural jaunts and downhill road rides to strenuous off-road cycle treks and multi-day, long-distance trips taking in hill stations and/or Tarai wildlife parks.

Advice on **bikes and equipment** (including bringing your own) and a list of likely **itineraries** is given in Chapter Nine.

WILDLIFE-VIEWING

Viewing **wildlife** in Nepal's Tarai is safariing with a distinctly Asian flavour: the animals most commonly seen include rhinos, monkeys, several kinds of deer and the occasional bear – tigers are spotted only rarely – and the most fun way to see them is atop an elephant. **Bring** lightweight clothes (neutral colours are best), a sun hat, swimsuit, sunscreen, insect repellent, shoes you don't mind getting wet, and binoculars if you have them. From November to February you'll also need warm clothes and a jacket for chilly evenings and early-morning walks. More **seasonal advice** is given at the beginning of Chapter Five.

Chitwan National Park (p.296) is the easiest of Nepal's **game reserves** to get to, and the one most geared for budget travellers, although it's heavily used. Bardia National Park (p.331) and Sukla Phanta Wildlife Reserve (p.341) provide less touristed alternatives. Mammals aren't as easy to see in the hills and mountains, most of the interesting ones being nocturnal or extremely reclusive, but while trekking you might see monkeys, various small rodents or (if you're lucky) goat-like tahr or blue sheep. Nepal is also famous for its **birds**, which are best viewed along the Narayani River in Chitwan National Park and in Koshi Tappu Wildlife Reserve (p.360); see also the Phulchoki and Ilam (Mai Valley) sections.

For an overview of Nepal's wildlife, see "Natural history" in Contexts.

OTHER OUTDOOR ACTIVITIES

Canyoning – rock climbing and abseiling (rapelling) in and around waterfalls – is a European sport that's just starting to catch on in Nepal. Nepal has lots of likely canyons, very few of which have been reconnoitred. The *Borderland* resort, located along the Arniko Highway near the Tibet border, offers canyoning as one of its activities; it has trained guides and a developed course with fixed anchors, and wetsuits are provided.

A company in Pokhara arranges **paragliding** for experienced pilots, and may soon start offering accompanied flights for beginners. Another Pokhara operator does short piloted trips around the valley in **ultralight** aircraft. Yet another company in Kathmandu offers early-morning **balloon flights**.

Nepal occasionally hosts **triathlons** and marathons. These events are usually staged by international organizers, so the best way to find out about them is to check with clubs in your home country, or do a Web search.

ORGANIZED SPORTS

It's often said that Nepalis are a martial race. Certainly military parade grounds are more common than playing fields, and the **martial arts** are big among urban youth. Nepali athletes have placed well in international karate and taekwando competitions, and many young men are taking up boxing and weight training as well.

Cricket is enjoying a huge rise in popularity in Nepal, thanks to the recent arrival of satellite TV. Nepal has no historical connection with the sport, since it was never part of the British empire, but cricket is broadcast incessantly on South Asian sport channels, and Nepalis are quick to follow the lead of their southern neighbours.

Other team sports aren't common, though district-level **football** (**soccer**) teams often square off at the National Stadium in Kathmandu – check the English-language daily papers for news of upcoming matches. Basketball is beginning to catch on in schools. Volleyball, badminton and table tennis are all fairly popular, since they don't require large playing areas, and equipment can be improvised. **Elephant polo** is a joke sport invented by and for expats, but the "world championships" each December at Chitwan certainly make for a fun spectator event.

The big tourist hotels in Kathmandu have **swimming** pools and **tennis** courts, and some of them allow outsiders to use their facilities for a fee (usually steep). There's also a health club in Kathmandu, as well as **golf** courses in the Kathmandu Valley, Pokhara and Dharan.

VILLAGE TOURISM

Nepal is a predominantly rural society, and its rich culture and ethnic diversity are best experienced in its villages. A growing number of programmes enable visitors to stay overnight in private homes in traditional villages far from the tourist trails.

Village stays (or **village tourism**, as this relatively new activity is called in the business) offer a unique opportunity for comfortable cultural immersion. The idea is that a tour operator contracts with a whole village to accommodate and entertain guests; rooms in local houses are fitted with bathrooms and a few tourist-style comforts, host families are trained to prepare meals hygienically, and a guide accompanies the guests to interpret. Participating villages tend to be located a couple of hours' walk from the nearest road – close enough to be easily accessible for less-than-fit visitors, yet far enough to be culturally intact and shielded from outside influences. (You'd never find these places on your own.)

Village tourism differs from trekking in a couple of important ways. First, although some walking is involved, and a trekking permit may even be required, exercise is secondary to the cultural experience: the whole point is to stay in one village and get to know its people, not to cover distances between villages. Second, accommodation is in an actual home, not a trekking inn filled with other backpackers, so the cross-cultural exchange is more authentic. And while participating villages obviously do get tourists, they get far fewer than even the most minor halt along a standard teahouse trek, and are completely uncommercialized.

Tourism and its economic benefits are far too concentrated in a few areas of Nepal, so village tourism is seen as a promising way to disperse visitors and spread the wealth. Under the best programmes, local people get to keep 50 percent of the proceeds – that's big money, given the high rates charged by operators – and since all food and services are locally produced, virtually all of the money stays in the community. However, if village tourism catches on, get-rich-quick operators can be expected to dive in with cut-price packages that give locals a much smaller portion of the cut, so if you're considering a village stay, question prospective operators closely about where the money's going.

Village tourism was pioneered in **Sirubari**, a Gurung settlement southwest of Pokhara. Nepal Village Resorts, Sirubari's operator, is in the process of developing several other villages northeast of Pokhara and in the Everest region. Another operator, Lama Adventure Treks and Expeditions, has created a similar programme in the Tamang village of **Thulo Purselgaun**, southeast of Kathmandu. Both these operators are based in Kathmandu – for contact information and prices, see p.138. Note that they prefer groups of at least three or four people, so if you're an individual or couple you should contact the companies well in advance and adjust your schedule to coordinate with already-scheduled departures.

A few language institutes and other organizations in Kathmandu also organize informal **homestays** with individual families in and around the valley. Most of these are intended specifically to provide Nepali language immersion, but at least one programme is set up for tourists just wanting to spend a weekend with a Nepali family. Again, see p.138.

SPIRITUAL PURSUITS AND ALTERNATIVE THERAPIES

Nepal is a great place to go to challenge your Western assumptions, study other systems of thought and open yourself to other ways of experiencing life. The tolerant atmosphere encourages experimentation and provides several traditional disciplines to delve into.

Moreover, Nepal is turning into quite a spiritual supermarket. The past few years have seen an explosion of outfits teaching yoga and meditation in the Kathmandu Valley, and centres are starting to pop up in the other tourist watering holes. The allied health fields of ayurvedic and Tibetan medicine are also attracting a growing interest among travellers in Nepal. Many programmes are designed for those who are just starting out and don't require a lengthy commitment, although some do. Note that it's advisable to book any residential courses well in advance – fax numbers or email addresses are given in the guide where possible.

This section provides a quick introduction to a few major practices. For general background on Hinduism and Buddhism, which provide their philosophical bases, be sure to see the section on religion in Contexts.

YOGA

Contrary to what's often put about in Western manuals, **yoga** does not just comprise exercises – it's a system of spiritual, mental and physical self-discipline, designed to bring about mastery of the self and true awareness of the self's oneness with the universe. There are several classical schools of yoga, but the ones that fit most easily into Western lifestyles come under the category of **raja yoga** and share eight "limbs" or steps (*astanga*), which represent an ascending path to self-control. The first two are the moral limbs, divided into dos and don'ts; after that come the three external limbs, *asana* (correct posture), *pranayama* (correct breathing) and *pratyahana* (control of the senses); followed finally by the three internal limbs, *dharana* (concentration), *dhyana* (meditation) and *samadhi* (super-consciousness).

Yoga's reputation for headstands and the like comes from **hatha yoga**, which places special emphasis on the three external methods to purify the body as an aid to developing the self. The term comes from the syllables *ha* and *tha*, representing inhalation and exhalation, since breath-control techniques, along with various postures, form an important part of this practice. Another popular variant, **kundalini yoga**, stresses meditation. The individual visualizes the process of enlightenment as a serpent, coiled near the base of the spine, rising through six psychic centres (*chakra*) in an ascending progression of consciousness, finally reaching the seventh, highest level.

Several **yoga centres** are located in and around Kathmandu, and are rounded up on p.139.

BUDDHIST MEDITATION AND STUDY

Meditation is closely related to yoga, and the two often overlap: much of yoga (*kundalini*, for example) involves meditation, and Buddhist meditation draws on many Hindu yogic practices. However, meditation centres in Nepal generally follow the Buddhist – particularly Tibetan Buddhist – tradition.

Buddhist meditation is a science of mind. To Buddhists, mind is the cause of confusion and ego, and the aim of meditation is to transcend these. **Vipassana** ("insight") is the kernel of all forms of Buddhist meditation; related to *hatha yoga*, it emphasizes the minute observation of physical sensations and mental processes to achieve a cool, clear understanding of mind. Another basic practice common to most schools of Buddhism, **shamatha** ("calm abiding" – co-opted by New Agers as "be here now") attunes and sharpens the mind by means of coming back again and again to a meditative discipline (breathing, visualization, etc). Theravada Buddhists consider *vipassana* to be sufficient for the attaining of enlightenment. At least two centres in the Kathmandu Valley run rigorous residential courses in this practice – see p.139 for details on one that caters to foreigners.

Tibetan Buddhist centres start students out with *vipassana* and *shamatha*, which form the foundation for a large armoury of meditation practices. An adept will cultivate Buddha-like qualities through visualization techniques – meditating on the deity that manifests a particular quality, while chanting the *mantra* and performing the *mudra* (hand gesture) associated with that deity. The Tibetan Buddhist path also involves numerous rituals, such as prayer, offerings, circumambulation and other meritorious acts, and committed followers will also take vows. Kathmandu has several centres offering introductory courses.

A big part of Tibetan Buddhism is the teacher–disciple relationship. More advanced students of the *dharma* will want to **study** under one of the lamas at Boudha (see p.163), some of whom give discourses in English.

AYURVED

Ayurved (often spelled *ayurveda*) is the world's oldest form of medicine still being practised. Dating back five thousand years, the "knowledge of life" is a holistic medical system that assumes the fundamental sameness of self and nature. Unlike the allopathic medicine of the West, which is all about finding out what's ailing you and then killing it, *ayurved* looks at the whole patient: disease is regarded as a symptom of imbalance, so it's the imbalance that's treated, not the disease.

Ayurvedic theory holds that the body is controlled by **three forces** (*tridosha*), which are a reflection of the forces within the self: *pitta*, the force of the sun, which is hot and rules the digestive processes and metabolism; *kapha*, likened to the moon, the creator of tides and rhythms, which has a cooling effect and governs the body's organs, fluids and lubricants; and *vata*, wind, which relates to movement and the nervous system. The healthy body is one that has the three forces in balance. To **diagnose** an imbalance, the ayurvedic doctor goes not only by the physical complaint but also family background, daily habits and emotional traits.

Treatment of an imbalance is typically with **herbal remedies** designed to alter whichever of the three forces is out of whack. Made according to traditional formulas using indigenous plants, ayurvedic medicines are cheaper than imports, which is why the Nepali government encourages their production. In addition, the doctor may prescribe various forms of **yogic cleansing** to rid the body of waste substances. To the uninitiated, these techniques will sound rather offputting – for instance, swallowing a long strip of cloth, a short section at a time, and then pulling it back up again to remove mucus from the stomach.

You'll find **ayurvedic doctors** and clinics throughout the Hindu parts of Nepal, but those who are able to deal with foreigners are confined mainly to Kathmandu.

TIBETAN MEDICINE

Medicine is one of the traditional branches of study for Tibetan Buddhist monks, and **Tibetan medicine** is based on the same philosophical and magical principles as Tibetan Buddhism.

Like *ayurved*, from which it derives, Tibetan medicine promotes health by maintaining the correct balance of **three humours**: *beken*, inert matter or phlegm, which when out of balance is responsible for disorders of the upper body; *tiba*, heat or bile, which is associated with intestinal diseases; and *lung*, meaning wind, which may produce nervousness or depression.

Tibetan medicine is as much a spiritual discipline as a physical one. Part of a Tibetan doctor's regular practice is to meditate on the "medicine Buddha", a manifestation of the Buddha's compassion, wisdom and healing power. The physician **diagnoses** the patient's imbalance by examining the tongue, pulse and urine, and by determining the patient's psychological state through questioning. He'll then prescribe a **treatment** to counteract the imbalance, which initially may only be a change of diet or behaviour (for instance, "cold" disorders – those to do with wind – are treated with "hot" foods and activities). For quicker relief, he'll prescribe one of a range of herbal-mineral tablets, which have been empowered by special rites.

Recommended **clinics** specializing in Tibetan medicine are listed in the Kathmandu and Boudha sections.

MASSAGE AND OTHER THERAPIES

Nepal, like many Asian countries, has its own indigenous form of **massage**. So-called Nepali "hard" massage is a deep, therapeutic treatment that works mainly on the joints and insertions (the places where muscles meet bones). It's not all that relaxing, but it can be just the job for sore shoulders after a trek. Nepalis themselves rarely receive massages after the age of about three, and would find it hard to conceive of paying for one, but numerous masseurs ply their services to foreigners in Kathmandu and Pokhara. A few practitioners also offer yogic, shiatsu and Swedish or Thai massage.

Dubious-looking signs in the tourist areas frequently advertise "Yoga & Massage", which has become a sort of shorthand for a long menu of un-Nepali services: steam baths (usually a makeshift box with a hole in the top for your head to stick out), reflexology, herbal treatments and the like. Some of these serve as fronts for prostitution (see p.141). Caveat emptor.

CULTURAL HINTS

Customs and traditions run deep in Nepal. Few Nepalis get the chance to travel abroad, so their only exposure to the outside world is through travellers. This puts a great responsibility on visitors to be sensitive to Nepali ways and values, and to project a favourable image of foreigners.

Many different ethnic groups coexist in Nepal, each with their own complex customs. In the Kathmandu Valley, where they mix the most, there's a necessarily high degree of tolerance of different clothes and lifestyles – a fact that travellers sense, and often abuse. Away from the tourist areas, however, these groups are quite parochial, and foreign ways may cause offence.

The dos and don'ts listed here are more flexible than they sound. You'll make gaffes all the time and Nepalis will rarely say anything. The list is hardly exhaustive, either: when in doubt, do as you see Nepalis doing. The important thing is to show a willingness to adapt and learn.

COMMON COURTESIES

Namaste ("I salute the god within you"), the standard Nepali greeting for strangers, acquaintances and friends, is traditionally delivered with palms together as if praying. *Namaskar* is a more formal or subservient variant. The height to which the pressed-together hands are raised roughly corresponds to the degree of deference being shown. Nowadays younger Nepalis are pretty informal about their *namaste*-ing, and often just flip the right hand in front of the forehead like a vertical salute. Returning a *namaste* with the appropriate gesture is a complex social calculation, but as a foreigner you need not worry too much about it – a middle-of-the-road *namaste* with hands at chest level will suffice for most situations.

One of the many delightful aspects of Nepali culture is the familiar **forms of address** that Nepalis use when speaking to each other: *didi* ("older sister"), *bhai* ("younger brother"), *buwa* ("father") and so on. To a large extent these are used to avoid speaking another person's name, which Nepalis are somewhat superstitious about, but they are also used between strangers.

Nepalis don't automatically **thank** people for rendering services that they're paid to do, especially not servants or employees. The word *dhanyabaad* is normally reserved for a person of higher rank or someone who has gone above and beyond the call of duty – it's inappropriate to toss it around as casually as we say "thank you". Nepalis who aren't used to dealing with foreigners find it a bit disconcerting to be thanked for simply bringing a plate of food, although the practice is accepted in tourist areas.

The gestures for **"yes"** and **"no"** may also cause confusion, since Nepalis don't nod or shake their heads. To indicate agreement, rock your head slightly to one side and then back the other way. To tell a tout or a seller "no", hold one hand in front of you, elbow pointing towards the ground, and swivel your wrist subtly, as if you were adjusting a bracelet. (Shaking the head in the Western fashion looks too much like "yes".)

CASTE AND STATUS

In Nepal, where Hinduism is tempered by Buddhist and other influences, caste doesn't dominate social interactions to quite the extent that it does in India. Nevertheless, caste *is* deeply engrained in the national psyche, as even non-Hindus were historically assigned places in the hierarchy based on ethnic affiliation or occupation. Following India's lead, Nepal "abolished" the official caste system in 1963, but a millennia-old system cannot be dismantled overnight. For most Nepalis, **caste and status** continue to determine what they do for a living, whom they may (or must) marry, where they can live and with whom they can associate.

In a Hindu society, foreigners are technically **casteless**, and their presence is polluting to orthodox, high-caste Hindus. In Nepal, this is really only a big deal in the remote far western hills, but wherever you travel you should be sensitive to minor caste restrictions: for example, you will not be allowed to enter the kitchen of a high-caste Hindu home.

However, status (*ijat*) is an equally important factor in Nepalese society, and as a foreigner you have a lot of it: you are fabulously wealthy, in the eyes of most Nepalis, and your culture dominates the world. Status adds extra complexity and nuance to interactions between strangers. Meeting for the first time, Nepalis observe a ritual of asking each other's name, home town, education, profession and age, all to determine relative status and therefore the correct form of address and level of deference. When you meet Nepalis you, too, will be subjected to this twenty-questions treatment. Incidentally, business cards now streamline this process, so it might not be a bad idea to bring a handful with you to Nepal (and indeed to most Asian countries).

EATING

Probably the greatest number of Nepali taboos – to an outsider's way of thinking – have to do with **food**. One underlying principle is that once you've touched something to your lips it's polluted (*jutho*) for everyone else. If you take a sip from someone else's canteen, try not to let it touch your lips (and the same applies if it's your own canteen – you're expected to share). Don't eat off someone else's plate or offer anyone food you've taken a bite out of (with one exception: a wife may eat her husband's leftovers), and don't touch cooked food until you've bought it.

Another all-important point of etiquette is **eat with your right hand only**. In Nepal, as in most Asian countries, the left hand is reserved for washing after defecating; you can use it to hold a glass or utensil, but don't eat, wipe your mouth, pass food or point at someone with it. It's considered good manners to give and receive everything with the right hand – or, to convey respect, with both hands. Sherpas and some other highland groups regard the family hearth as sacred, so don't throw rubbish or scraps into it.

CLOTHING AND THE BODY

Nepalis are innately conservative in their attitudes to **clothing**. Not a few are still shell-shocked from the hang-loose styles of the hippy era, and wary of all budget travellers as a result. A woman is expected to dress modestly, with legs and shoulders covered, especially in temples and monasteries: a dress or skirt that hangs to mid-calf level is best; trousers are acceptable, but shorts or a short skirt are offensive to many. A man should always wear a shirt in public, and long trousers if possible (men who wear shorts are assumed to be of a low caste). It's equally important to look clean and well groomed – travellers are rich, Nepalis reckon, and ought to look the part. You can flout these traditions, but you'll only shut yourself off from the happy encounters

with locals that make travelling in Nepal so pleasant.

Nudity is a sensitive issue. Only women with babies or small children in tow bare their breasts. When Nepali men bathe in public, they do it in their underwear, and women bathe fully clothed. Foreigners are expected to do likewise. Nepal has some idyllic hot springs, but most are heavily used as bathing areas; don't scare the locals off by stripping. Paradoxically, it's deemed okay to defecate in the open, as in many villages there are no covered toilets – but out of sight of others, in the early morning or after dark. Men may urinate in public away from buildings – discreetly – but women have to find a sheltered spot.

Still other conventions pertain to **the body**. In Nepal, the forehead is regarded as the most sacred part of the body and the feet the most unclean. It's impolite to touch an adult Nepali's head, and it's an insult to kick someone. (The Nepali equivalent of tarring and feathering is to force a person to wear a garland of shoes.) Don't put your feet on chairs or tables, and when sitting, try not to point the soles of your feet at anyone. On a related note, it's bad manners to step over the legs of someone seated: in a crowded place, Nepalis will wait for you to draw in your feet so they can pass.

Nepali views about **displays of affection** are the opposite of what most of us are used to. It's considered acceptable for friends of the same sex to hold hands or put their arms around each other in public, but not for lovers of the opposite sex. Couples shouldn't cuddle or kiss in public, nor in front of a Nepali host. Don't shake hands with a Nepali woman, as this form of contact is not traditional.

TEMPLES AND HOMES

Major Hindu **temples** or their inner sanctums are usually off-limits to non-believers, who are technically outcastes. Respect this: what seems like elitism is just Hindus' way of keeping a part of their culture sacred in a country where nearly everything is open to inspection by outsiders. In most cases, you can see everything from outside anyway.

Where you are allowed in, be respectful, take your shoes off before entering, don't take photos unless you've been given permission, and leave a few rupees in the donation box. Leather is usually not allowed in temple precincts. Don't touch offerings, nor people when they're on their way to

THE ECOTOURISM TRAVELLER'S CODE

These tips come courtesy of the Nepal Tourist Watch Centre, an organization established to preserve Nepal's heritage and environment through responsible tourism.

1. Travel in a spirit of humility and with a genuine desire to meet and talk with the local people.

2. Be aware of the feelings of other people, thus preventing what might be seen as offensive behaviour. Remember this especially with photography.

3. Get acquainted with local customs; respect them; people will be happy to help you.

4. Remember that you are one of thousands of visiting tourists. Do not expect special privileges.

5. Make no promises to local people unless you are certain you can fulfill them.

6. Cultivate the habit of asking questions instead of knowing all the answers.

7. If you really want a home away from home, why travel?

shrines or are in the process of worshipping. The front of a shrine is usually marked by a pedestal supporting the deity's carrier, and/or a lotus-carved stone embedded in the ground: these define the territory of the shrine, where it's particularly important to be reverent.

Similar sensitivity is due at Buddhist temples and monasteries. If you're granted an audience with a lama, it's traditional to present him with a *kata* (a ceremonial white scarf, usually sold nearby). Walk around Buddhist stupas and monuments clockwise – that is, keep the monument on your right.

If invited for a meal in a private **home**, bring an appopriate gift such as fruit. Take your shoes off when entering, or follow the example of your host. When the food is served you'll be expected to serve yourself first, so you won't be able to follow your host's lead. Don't take more than you can eat – it *is* polite to ask for seconds. The meal is typically served at the end of a gathering; when the eating is done, everyone gets up and leaves.

PRIVACY

Nepalis do not have the same concept of **privacy** that Westerners do. Nepali families are large and close-knit, and houses are small. Nepalis grow up constantly surrounded by other people (and noise). They like to be with other people, and they will assume you do, too.

Moreover, as a foreigner you will be an object of great curiosity as soon as you step off the beaten track. People may stare, point at you and even talk about you (in Nepali) among themselves. Nepalis will constantly be befriending you, wanting to exchange addresses and extracting solemn promises that you will write to them. Sometimes they will ask you point-blank to help them travel

to your country, assuming you to be wealthy enough to pay their airfare and powerful enough to fix their visa.

There will be days when you feel that if you're asked the question "What is your country?" one more time you'll hit someone. Give yourself time off when you need it. But Nepalis are the best thing about Nepal, so don't close yourself off to meeting them.

OTHER THINGS

Try to convey an accurate impression of your home country – both its good and bad points – and play down materialistic standards of success. Don't rub Nepalis' noses in technology and fashions they can't afford. Nepali society is rich in the traditions of family and community that are so often mislaid in the West, but like traditional societies worldwide it is under attack, and we are only now beginning to see that tourism is a corrupting agent.

You may be dismayed by the amount of **rubbish** in the streets. There are few rubbish bins in Nepal (although they're starting to appear in tourist areas), and people throw their litter on the ground, where it may or may not be swept up by other people whose job it is to do so. If you're uncomfortable throwing your litter on the street, follow the *Alice's Restaurant* technique – find a big pile that's already there and add your handful to it.

Where they exist, **toilets** range from "Western" (sit-down) flush jobs to two planks projected over a stream. In lodges – tourist ones aside – the norm is a squat toilet, usually pretty stinky and flyblown. When travelling by bus, there will almost always be a bathroom available at rest stops, but sometimes the public toilet will be nothing but a designated field. When in doubt, ask *Chaarpi kahaa chha?* ("Where is the toilet?"). Don't throw paper down squat toilets: put it in the basket provided. Toilet paper is not provided in more basic guest houses and restaurants, so bring your own. Nepalis use a jug of water and the left hand (try it yourself – it's no more or less disgusting than the toilet paper method).

Finally, **be patient**. Nepal is a developing country and things don't always work or start on time. It's unrealistic to expect things to be like they are at home, even if the menu or brochure makes it sound as if they will be. If a restaurant is slow in filling your order, it may be because they've only got one stove. Getting angry or impatient will only confuse Nepalis and won't resolve the problem. The Nepali way of dealing with setbacks isn't to complain, or even to keep a stiff upper lip, but to laugh. It's a delightful, infectious response.

You can't change Nepal, and even if you could, it is not yours to change. Many things in Nepal are slow, inefficient or downright nutty, but that's just the way things are. Taking the attitude that "somebody's got to teach them a lesson" or "if nobody complains it'll never change" (real-life dialogue overheard in Kathmandu) will only make you and everyone around you miserable. Go with the flow. It's Nepal you've come to experience – let it be Nepal.

To get by with a minimum of disappointment, the best strategy is to scale back your expectations, always double- and triple-check important arrangements, take all assurances with a pinch of salt (Nepalis will sometimes tell you what they think will make you happy rather than the truth), and find something interesting to do while you're waiting.

PHOTOGRAPHY

Everyone's a National Geographic photographer in Nepal – mountains, wildlife, temples, ethnic peoples and festivals all make winning subjects. But beware of experiencing your trip through a lens. The camera can provide great memories, but don't hesitate to put it away when it's getting in the way of the real thing.

EQUIPMENT

The first rule of packing photo gear is to keep it to what you can realistically carry. For many travellers, this will mean sticking to a pocket-sized **point-and-shoot** model with a built-in flash. These cameras are unobtrusive, lightweight and easy to use, and the digital ones make it particularly easy to send pictures home by Internet. The drawback is a lack of versatility, since the lens only zooms so much, and you can't usually override the automatic functions.

Bringing an **SLR (single lens reflex) camera** involves a tradeoff between higher performance versus extra bulk and security precautions. To get the most out of your SLR you'll want a decent selection of accessories. Zoom **lenses** lighten your load, minimize lens changes and give you a whole range of focal distances to choose from. Two or three should do it: something in the 35–80mm range, an 80–200mm, and a wide angle (24mm or even 20mm). On longer lenses, the lower the f-stop available, the more flexibility you'll have but the greater the bulk (and price). It's also good to have polarizing or split-density **filters** to cut down on glare, plus UV filters to protect lenses. A **flash** is useful for filling in shadows, and a **tripod** for long exposures. And if you're carrying all that booty, you'll want to make sure it's protected in some sort of **bag** – either over the shoulder, strapped to the chest or around the waist – which you shouldn't let out of your sight.

In some situations a cheap **disposable camera** (sold in tourist areas) may be your best bet. On a raft trip, for example, you can take pictures with a disposable without worrying about ruining it in the water, whereas a regular camera will have to be kept stowed away in a storage box most of the time while on the river.

If you're thinking of **buying** a camera for your trip to Nepal, you might consider waiting until you get there, since equipment is quite reasonably priced in Kathmandu (see p.136). Shops there also

sell most camera accessories – batteries, lens filters, tripods – but it's probably best to bring these
with you just in case they don't have the exact
thing you need. Remember that batteries go flat
more quickly in cold temperatures.

Most major brands of **film** (prints and slides)
are easily obtainable in Nepal's tourist areas, and
prices are about the same as or even cheaper
than back home. Off the beaten track, though, the
selection is pretty thin. Have a selection of both
fast (ASA/ISO 200–400) and slow (100, 64 or even
25) film on hand to deal with different conditions.
If you're bringing film into the country, pack it in a
lead bag (available in camera shops) or carry it as
hand baggage and have it hand-checked – new
airport X-ray machines are coming into service
worldwide that are programmed to turn up the
power if they spot suspicious-looking items, and
this can fog film (high-speed film is more vulnerable).

Labs in the main cities and towns **process**
most types of film; they usually do an okay job
with prints, but can't be trusted with slides. Have
important photos processed outside Nepal if possible.

All the comments about bulk and security for
still cameras apply even more so to **video cameras**. Note that you have to pay a steep extra fee
to bring a video camera into certain parks and
sights. Nepal's electricity is 220V/50 cycles,
which means North Americans won't be able to
recharge battery packs without an adapter (available locally).

TECHNIQUE

People always make good photos, but be sensitive. Always ask first, and if they say no, don't
press it. Try to make photography a fun, two-way
process: let people take pictures of their friends,
or of you with their friends. It also helps if you can
show pictures of your own family or home. Take
time to establish intimacy, rather than just barg-
ing in and "taking" pictures. Unless you've got a
Polaroid, don't mislead people into thinking they'll
get an instant portrait of themselves. Never offer
money, and if someone demands *bakshish* for a
photo, just put the camera away – this is a form
of begging (see p.70) and should be discouraged.
That said, sadhus in certain tourist spots make
their living from the *bakshish* they earn posing for
photos (and if you try to steal a photo they'll visit
holy wrath upon you). Never photograph masked
festival dancers, who are believed to embody the
deities they represent. Don't use a flash in a temple while someone is worshipping.

Postcard-perfect shots of **scenery** with clear
blue skies aren't always the ones that stand out
when you get home. Clouds, fog and rain often
add more drama. Look for unusual images, things
you've never seen before. Rather than trying to
make big, sweeping statements with your photos,
try zooming in on **details** that capture something
essential about the scene or culture. Go for action
shots that will serve as a springboard for a story.

Light levels and contrast can be very high on
sunny days in Nepal – especially at high elevations. To get around this, plan on doing most of
your shooting in the early morning or late afternoon. Tones are especially mellow at these times,
producing the best results, and in any case some
of the most interesting scenes occur just after
dawn. If you can't avoid midday conditions, use a
flash to fill in shadows on faces, especially if the
subject is relatively dark against a bright background. To get the correct exposure without a
flash, walk up close or zoom in, so the subject fills
the frame, before reading the meter. For snow
shots, meter off something of a neutral shade,
like your hand or the darkest part of the sky.

BEGGARS AND TOUTS

Dealing with beggars is part of travelling in Nepal, as in most developing countries. The pathos might initially get to you, as well it should, but you will probably adjust to it fairly quickly. A thornier dilemma, which will plague you as long as you're in Nepal, is how to cope with panhandling kids and pushy touts.

A small number of bona fide **beggars** make an honest living from *bakshish* (alms). Hindus and Buddhists alike have a long and honourable tradition of giving to lepers and the disabled, as well as sadhus and monks. Destitute women make up another large contingent of the begging population: it's terrifyingly easy for a Nepali woman to find herself alone in the world, either widowed or divorced – perhaps for failing to bear a son or because of a dowry dispute. There are no unemployment benefits in Nepal, and the state pension for senior citizens is just Rs100 a year; anyone who can't work and has no family for support generally turns to begging. Few would choose to do so if they had an alternative.

Giving is, of course, a personal decision. You might resolve only to give to the most needy-looking, or the most persistent, or the most dignified. You might conclude that almsgiving only treats the symptoms of poverty, and decide to support a charity trying to address the causes instead. On the other hand, you could argue that direct giving gets 100 percent of the money to the target, with no administration, red tape or corruption. At any rate, it's important to give the matter some thought (see also "Development dilemmas" in Contexts).

In the hills, ailing locals will occasionally approach foreigners for **medicine**, knowing that they usually carry first-aid kits. It's probably best not to make any prescriptions unless you're qualified to diagnose the illness. However, before leaving the country you can donate unused medicines to the dispensary at Kathmandu's Bir Hospital, which distributes them to the destitute, or to the Himalayan Buddhist Meditation Centre in Kathmandu, which gives them to monks.

CHILDREN

Throughout Nepal – but principally along the tourist trails – **children** will hound you for money, sweets and pens. Sometimes they're cute, usually they're a pain. They're not orphans or beggars, they're just ordinary Nepali schoolkids having a go. Unless they're collecting money for a festival – which is a legitimate tradition – **don't give them anything**.

Giving to children only encourages obnoxious behaviour, takes away their dignity and starts them on a life of toadying to tourists. Worse, it turns them into breadwinners before their time, which makes them more valuable to their family on the street than in school, thus perpetuating a cycle of lack of education, lack of opportunity and poverty. Don't even try to rationalize it by thinking you'll give only to well-behaved kids: that's how monsters are created. It's natural and noble to want to share your wealth with less well-off people, but dispensing rupees and pens only leads Nepalis to expect something for nothing and saps the country's traditional self-reliance. Instead, consider sponsoring a child through an international charity.

Saying no isn't easy. Kids will sometimes tag along for hours, giving you the Chinese water-torture treatment. In groups, after school, they can be unbearable. Remember that for them it's a game – they're just out for entertainment. The best defence is a sense of humour. If you can speak a little Nepali, try teasing them back. They're either going to laugh *at* you or *with* you, and you might as well make it the latter.

Kathmandu's **street children** are another matter. They're begging for real, but you should still think twice before giving to them – see p.108.

TOUTS AND OTHER MIDDLEMEN

Indian-style hustle is on the rise in Nepal. You'll get a major dose of it at the airport or any major bus station, where packs of **touts** lie in wait to accost arriving tourists with guest-house cards. They also cruise the tourist strips of Kathmandu, offering drugs. However, Nepali touts for the most part aren't as parasitic as their Indian brethren, and if you're entering Nepal from north India, where aggressive touts have to be dealt with firmly, adjust your attitude: they'll usually leave you alone if asked nicely, whereas they'll take a rude brush-off personally. That said, many touts in Nepal these days are in fact Indian, and may require more drastic measures.

Kathmandu and Pokhara are full of other lone entrepreneurs and **middlemen** – touts by any other name. Ticket agents (see p.31), riksha wallahs, innkeepers and guides are ever anxious to broker services and information. Naturally they take a cut, but as with touts, they usually get their commission from the seller; your price is bumped up correspondingly. Is it a ripoff? Rip-off is a relative term. If you don't know where to spend the night or change money, a tout's services are certainly worth a few rupees. In general, though, cutting out the middleman gives you more control over the transaction. You should find, without being too mercenary about it, that a few rupees (and smiles) given to people whose services you may require again will grease the wheels and make your stay much more pleasant.

POLICE AND TROUBLE

Nepal is one of the safest countries in the world, which is all the more remarkable when you consider the gulf between rich and poor. However, theft is on the rise, and political instability seems to be bringing a general rise in lawlessness.

The only real concern is **petty theft**, and then chiefly from fellow travellers. Common sense suggests a few precautions. Store valuables that you're not using in your hotel's or guest-house's safe, and carry the rest in a money belt or pouch around your neck at all times. In a dormitory, keep your bag locked up and any expensive items with you. A padlock can be purchased cheaply in Nepal; it doesn't have to be big – deterrence is the main thing. Pickpocketing happens in a few crowded places frequented by tourists, and some bus routes have reputations for baggage theft – see the "Getting around" section for advice.

If you're robbed, report it as soon as possible to the **police** headquarters of the district in which the robbery occurred. They're apt to be friendly and consoling, if not much help. For insurance purposes, go to the Interpol Section of the police headquarters in Durbar Square or Naksal, Kathmandu, to fill in a report, a copy of which you'll need to keep for claiming from your insurer once you're back home. Bring a photocopy of the pages in your passport containing your photo and your Nepalese visa, together with two passport photos. Dress smartly and expect an uphill battle – they're jaded by stolen-travellers'-cheque scams.

Violent crime is extremely rare, and the danger of getting raped or assaulted in a populated area is statistically insignificant. The only real concern is a certain amount of hooliganism in the Kathmandu tourist bars; fortunately the government is ploughing back some tourist tax revenue into maintaining a police presence in those areas in the evenings. The countryside is for the most part equally safe, although several Western women have been raped by trekking guides in recent years (see p.380). There has always been a small risk of violent attack by bandits on remote trekking trails, so it's advisable not to walk alone.

There are several ways to get on the wrong side of the law, none of them worth it. **Smuggling** is the usual cause of serious trouble – drugs and gold are the big no-nos, and if you get caught with commercial quantities of either you'll be looking at a more or less automatic five to twenty years in prison (see p.109 for a description of that edifying experience). While it would be incredibly stupid to go through immigration control with **drugs**, discreet possession inside the country carries virtually no risk; flash dope around, though, and you could conceivably get shopped by an innkeeper.

In Nepal, where government servants are poorly paid, a little **bakshish** sometimes greases the wheels. Nepalese police don't bust tourists simply in order to get bribes, but if you're accused of something it might not hurt to make an offer, in an extremely careful, euphemistic and deniable way. This shouldn't be necessary if you're the *victim* of a crime, although you may feel like offering a reward.

WOMEN'S NEPAL

Nepal is a relatively easy place for a woman to travel. In most parts of the country you'll be of interest mainly as a foreigner rather than as a woman, and, as such, the atmosphere is tolerant and inquisitive rather than threatening or dangerous.

DEALING WITH MEN

Nepali society is on the whole chaste, almost prudish; **men** are almost universally respectful, and perhaps a little in awe, of foreign women. **Sexual harassment** is on the whole low-key, and need rarely upset your travels. Staring and catcalling happen sometimes, but it's nowhere near as bad as in India, or indeed most of the world, and it rarely goes any further than words. Your chief danger comes from a few predatory trekking guides (see p.380).

However, wearing revealing clothes will up the chances of receiving unwelcome advances. It's easy for Nepali men to get the idea that foreign women are wanton – relatively speaking, they are. Wearing a short dress, shorts or loose-fitting top may reinforce this stereotype for some men. That doesn't mean you have to wear Nepali clothes, it just means that you ought to wear more modest foreign clothes that don't reveal thighs or shoulders. In tourist areas you can buy cheap calf-length dresses and skirts that fill the bill.

If you trek on one of the popular routes and see how many trekkers wear skimpy clothes, you might wonder whether this is obsolete advice. It isn't. It's true that Nepalis along the main routes have seen everything by now, and in any case they're too polite to say anything. So you can get away with it, but you'll definitely widen the distance between you and the Nepalis you meet, and you can pretty much forget about any rewarding cross-cultural interactions.

A woman travelling or trekking **alone** won't be hassled so much as pitied. Going alone (*eklai*) is most un-Nepali behaviour. Locals (of both sexes) will ask if you haven't got a husband – the question is usually asked out of genuine concern, not as a come-on. Teaming up with another female stops the comments as effectively as being with a man.

If you find yourself without a reserved seat on a **public bus**, you can make your way to the front compartment, where preference is usually given to women and children. About the only form of discrimination you'll encounter is during toilet stops, when you'll have to hunt around for a sheltered place while men are free to pee by the side of the road (yet another reason to wear a long skirt).

Tarai cities and border towns are another matter, unfortunately. Some men here, as in northern India, have some real misconceptions about Western women, and may try for a surreptitious grope or even expose themselves. Travelling with a man generally shields you from this sort of behaviour. If that isn't possible, or if you resent having to do so, don't be afraid to make a public scene in the event of an untoward advance – that's what a Nepali woman would do. Though he'll pretend it wasn't him, all eyes will be upon him and he won't try it again.

Of course, you may find you want to strike up a **relationship** with a Nepali man. If so, you should have no trouble finding eligible candidates in the tourist bars. Quite a few women travellers fall for trekking or rafting guides – the men of highland ethnic groups, such as Sherpas, have very similar views to ours on sexual equality – and

Kathmandu has a small but growing community of women who have married and settled there. However, be aware that Nepali men are not without their own agendas: exotic romance, conquest, perhaps even a ticket out of Nepal. If you suspect ulterior motives, let him down gently but firmly and he'll usually retreat gracefully.

MEETING WOMEN

A frustrating aspect of travelling in Nepal is the difficulty of making contact with **Nepali women**. The tourism industry is controlled by men; women, who are expected to spend most of their time in the home and are given fewer educational opportunities, have little contact with foreigners and speak much less English. If you're lucky enough to be invited to a Nepali home for a meal, chances are the women of the house will remain in the kitchen while you eat, only emerging to clear the plates and eat the leftovers. Upper-class women are free of these restrictions and are often well educated, but of course they don't have to work so they, too, have few dealings with travellers.

The sexual politics are different among highland ethnic groups, which is as good a reason as any for going **trekking**. Along trekking routes, many women run teahouses single-handedly while their husbands are off guiding or portering. Proud, enterprising and flamboyant, these "*didis*" are some of the most wonderful women you're likely to meet anywhere. Language may be a problem off the popular trails, but that doesn't rule out all communication. On buses, women will be much more approachable in the front compartment. And anywhere you go, having a child with you will always open doors.

For more on **women's issues** in Nepal, see "Development dilemmas" (p.468). The Rough Guide Special, *Women Travel*, gives one Western woman's account of travelling in the country.

TRAVELLING WITH CHILDREN

Kids always help break the ice with strangers, and in Nepal they unleash even more than the usual hospitality (although the lack of privacy may prove to be a problem). They can also open a door into the often closed world of Nepali women.

However, parents will have to take extra **precautions** in the light of Nepal's poor sanitation, dogs, crowds, traffic, pollution, bright sun and steep slopes. It may be hard to keep hands clean and yucky stuff out of mouths. Small children will have to be kept a firm grip on most of the time. Drum into them the necessity of keeping away from dogs and only drinking clean water. If your child comes down with diarrhoea, it's extremely important to keep him or her hydrated and topped up on salts – have oral rehydration formula on hand.

Naturally you'll want to plan a more **modest itinerary** and travel in greater comfort with children than you would on your own. Nepal's winding, bumpy roads are likely to make kids travelsick, so take bus journeys in very small doses, or rent a car. Most cheap lodgings will be out of the question on account of their bathroom arrangements. In tourist areas it should be no problem finding food that kids will eat, but they're bound to turn their noses up at "spicy" food. Baby food and disposable nappies/diapers are available in Kathmandu and Pokhara, but are hard to come by elsewhere.

Trekking is logistically awkward with children, especially ones who are too old to ride in a backpack and too young to hike on their own. You'll need one or more porters for all the kiddie paraphernalia; porters can also carry young ones in modified *doko* (wicker baskets). Trekking with an agency can alleviate some of the hassles. A couple of companies that run treks and tours especially for families with children are listed on p.60.

DISABLED TRAVELLERS

Although disability is common in Nepal, it's a poor country without the means to cater for disabled travellers. If you walk with difficulty, you will find the steep slopes, stairs and uneven pavements hard going. Open sewers, potholes, crowds and a lack of proper street crossings will all make it hard for a blind traveller to get around.

With a companion, however, there's no reason why you can't enjoy many of Nepal's activities, including elephant rides, scenic mountain flights, and sightseeing by private car. Nepalis are also likely to be very helpful. **Guides** are readily available and should be prepared to provide whatever assistance you need. If you rent a taxi for the day, the driver is certain to help you in and out, and perhaps around the sites you visit.

Basic wheelchairs are available for use in the airport in the Kathmandu airport, and the Pokhara airport is mostly at ground-level. Generally, however, facilities for the disabled are nonexistent, so you should bring your own wheelchair or other necessary walking aids or equipment. Hotels aren't particularly geared up for disabled guests, though the most expensive ones have lifts and ramps.

A safari in one of the Tarai wildlife parks should be feasible, and even a trek, catered to your needs by an **agency**, might not be out of the question. Try Himalayan Holidays, PO Box 5513, Kathmandu (☎01/410482; *namaste@himhols. wlink.com.np*).

DISABLED ORGANIZATIONS

Australia ACROD, PO Box 60, Curtin, ACT 2605 (☎02/6282 4333); 24 Cabarita Rd, Cabarita (☎02/9743 2699).

Canada Jewish Rehabilitation Hospital, 3205 Place Alton Goldbloom, Chomedy Laval, PQ H7V 1R2 (☎450/688-9550). *Guidebooks and travel information.*

Ireland National Rehabilitation Board, 25 Clyde Rd, Ballsbridge, Dublin 4 (☎01/668 4181).

New Zealand Disabled Persons Assembly, 173 Victoria St, Wellington (☎04/801 9100).

UK Royal Association for Disability and Rehabilitation (RADAR), 250 City Rd, London EC1V 8AS (☎0171/250 3222).

USA Mobility International USA, PO Box 10767, Eugene, OR 97440 (☎541/343-1284); and Society for the Advancement of Travel for the Handicapped (SATH), 347 5th Ave, New York, NY 10016 (☎212/447-7284; *www.sittravel.com*).

STAYING ON

Volunteering, studying or working while in Nepal can add a satisfying focus to your trip, and deepen your understanding of another way of life.

Unfortunately, the Nepalese government doesn't make it easy to stay on legitimately, the main obstacle being that you can't stay longer than four months in any calendar year on a tourist visa without special permission (though that means you can stay up to eight months if your trip straddles two calendar years). To stay longer, you generally have to get a non-tourist visa through a recognized work or study programme *before* entering the country.

ON A TOURIST VISA

If you feel you've received a lot from Nepal, **volunteering** is a good way to give something back. The Himalayan Explorers Club (*www.hec.org*) publishes an excellent *Nepal Volunteer Handbook* that gives information on more than fifty programmes and opportunities. The club also runs its own volunteer programme for teachers in the Khumbu region. Other overseas organizations worth contacting include Educate the Children, which takes volunteers for three-month teaching stints (*ETCithaca@aol.com*), and Volunteer Nepal (*www.web1.pipemedia.net/nepal/*), another teaching programme of two to six months' duration.

You can volunteer on a less formal basis at the old people's hospices in Pashupatinath and Chabahil run by Mother Teresa's Sisters of Charity, who welcome walk-in help on a day-to-day basis. Tulsi Meher Ashram, a training centre for destitute women located out beyond the international airport, can use people with design experience or creative handicraft ideas – contact them through Mahaguthi outlets in Kathmandu or Patan. The Kathmandu Environmental Education Project, Himalayan Explorers Club and Himalayan Rescue Association offices in Kathmandu can always use volunteers.

People with **medical qualifications** are always needed. The Himalayan Rescue Association accepts four doctors each autumn and spring to staff its high-altitude aid posts; the waiting list is two or three years long, but it can't hurt to write (*HRA@aidpost.mos.com.np*; GPO Box 495, Kathmandu, Nepal). The Banepa Hospital welcomes foreign doctors on temporary placement, and no doubt other hospitals would gladly accept help.

It's against the rules to work on a tourist visa, but plenty of people do – notably as **trekking and rafting guides**. However, you'd have to have made several trips to Nepal, or already be experienced and well connected in the adventure-travel business, to find work as a guide. Guides are usually hired on a freelance basis, so the work is only seasonal, and immigration restrictions make it hard for non-Nepalis to make a career out of it. Qualified **masseurs and yoga/meditation instructors** may be able to find work in Kathmandu or Pokhara – try contacting the places listed towards the end of those sections.

If you just want an open-ended arrangement for a few weeks or so, **teaching English** is a good way to become a temporary local. Language schools in Kathmandu and Pokhara take people on with no previous experience, although the pay is negligible.

A few language schools in Kathmandu offer intensive courses in Nepali, Newari or Tibetan – see p.143. Opportunities to study yoga and Tibetan Buddhism are summarized in "Spiritual pursuits and alternative therapies", on p.63.

STAYING LONGER

Postings with the Peace Corps, VSO and other **national voluntary agencies** abound, providing you've got the relevant skills and the determination to stay two or more years. People with experience in education, health, nutrition, agriculture, forestry and other areas are preferred. Such organizations don't instigate their own projects, but place volunteers in existing projects where technical help is needed. Many other aid agencies (such as Action Aid, Save the Children, CARE and Oxfam) operate in Nepal and occasionally take on specialists. See "Development dilemmas" (p.460) for an idea of what to expect.

If you can persuade the Finance Ministry that you've got a good business idea that will help Nepal's development, and you have a Nepali business partner, you may qualify for a **business visa**. They generally expect you to invest at least $50,000 start-up capital.

Several American universities run **study programmes** in Nepal. The University of Wisconsin-Madison's School of South Asian Studies places students in Nepal for a full year. The School for International Training (☎800/336-1616) in Brattleboro, Vermont, has its own campus in Kathmandu. The Naropa Institute in Boulder, Colorado, runs a thirteen-week course on Tibetan Buddhism each autumn at Boudha. Other programmes are out there – check at *www.studyabroad.com*.

The only known way to get a non-tourist visa after you've already arrived in Nepal is to study at Tribhuwan University's Campus of International Languages in Kathmandu. One-year courses in Nepali, Tibetan, Sanskrit and Newari begin in July. Classes run for two hours a day, five days a week, and a year's tuition costs $525. Apply no later than June with a letter of recommendation from your embassy or university to: Campus Chief, Campus of International Languages, Exhibition Road, Bhrikuti Mandap, Kathmandu, Nepal (☎226713). The university will sort out your visa.

DIRECTORY

Airport departure tax is Rs1000 (Rs900 if flying within South Asia).

Addresses don't exist in Nepal: few streets even have names, and houses are never numbered. In cities, though, intersections or neighbourhoods (*tol*) usually have names and these are gradually lending themselves to the major streets nearby.

Contraceptives Condoms and birth-control pills are available in pharmacies everywhere. Consult one of the clinics in Kathmandu for other contraceptive advice.

Customs Officers are fairly lax on entry, but they might note fancy video gear in your passport so you can't sell it in Nepal. They check more thoroughly on departure, mainly to make sure you're not smuggling antiques out.

Drugs are illegal, of course. However, cannabis grows wild throughout hill Nepal, and old folks sometimes smoke it as an evening tonic. Touts in Kathmandu – shady characters, but not informants – mostly peddle local hash, and also whisper offers of opium and heroin from the Golden Triangle. See the section on "Police and trouble" on p.71 for legalities.

Electricity is 220 volts/50 cycles per second, when you can get it: virtually all power in Nepal is generated by hydroelectric projects, so power cuts ("load shedding") are common, especially in spring when water levels get low. Most places tourists go are now electrified.

Embassies and consulates are all in Kathmandu: see p.142.

Emergencies Where there's a phone, dial ☎100 for the police or ☎102 for an ambulance – but it's better to get a Nepali-speaker to do the talking. Registering with your embassy can expedite things in the event of an emergency.

Gay Nepal Nepalis will tell you gay sex doesn't happen, or it's "something that Indians do". There are no gay bars or meeting places or any support network whatsoever, even in the capital. Yet in a society where the sexes are kept well apart before marriage, and men routinely hold hands and sleep together, it obviously goes on. Gay cou-

ples will certainly feel a certain freedom in being able to be close in public – but obviously not *too* close. The only approach a gay traveller is likely to get is from touts who might offer, at the end of a long inventory of drugs, "nice Nepali girls", and if that doesn't work, boys. But it's nothing like the scene in, say, Thailand.

Laundry Tourist guest houses will generally send laundry out for you, although the turn-around time depends on the weather. Rates are reasonable. If you're doing your own, detergent is sold in inexpensive packets in Kathmandu.

Left luggage Guest houses will always store bags for you, an invaluable service if you go

---

WHAT TO BRING

As a rule, travel light. You can buy or rent most things in Kathmandu. This box goes over the essentials that are worth bringing from home or picking up specially in Nepal. (If you think you might go trekking, rafting or mountain-biking, see the relevant chapters for an additional list of recommended items.)

An internal-frame **backpack** is probably best for heaving your things around on buses and rikshas, especially if you're also travelling in other parts of Asia as well. A **travel pack**, with shoulder straps that can be zipped out of sight, will help dispel lingering "hippy" prejudices when dealing with officialdom; best of all is one in which all compartments can be secured with a single padlock. A lightweight **daypack** also comes in handy for short excursions.

The **clothes** you bring will depend very much on the time of year, and where you expect to be going. For warm weather you'll want lightweight cotton garments – loose-fitting but modest, and covering enough to ward off sun and bugs. Shorts and a swimsuit are worth bringing (especially for rafting), but heed the advice given in "Cultural hints", p.66. A lightweight waterproof jacket or poncho is advisable at any time of year. For cooler seasons, try to dress in layers: a T-shirt, long-sleeved shirt, sweater or fleece jacket and shell will set you up for almost any weather. Trainers or any sort of durable, lightweight footwear will be adequate for most conditions in Nepal, even on a trek, though higher up you'll need something sturdier. You'll also need a back-up pair of shoes in case those get wet. Flipflops, available locally, will do in warm weather; sport

sandals are better, and perfect for rafting.

For the **sun**, bring sunscreen, lip balm, sunglasses and a brimmed hat; an umbrella (available locally) acts as an effective parasol at low elevations, and is indispensable during the monsoon. If you're heading to the Tarai, especially between April and October, bring **mosquito repellent** and/or mosquito **netting** (you can buy coils locally). **Toiletries** are pretty easy to come by in Kathmandu, but bring anything out of the ordinary. Alcohol-based antibacterial gel is good for keeping hands clean.

Carry valuables in a **money belt or neck purse**; a small **padlock** (available locally) is an effective deterrent to would-be thieves. **Earplugs** are a must for shutting out the ubiquitous honking vehicles, barking dogs and general commotion at night. In cheap lodgings, a **sleeping sheet** is an insurance policy against bedbugs and the like (unnecessary if you bring a **sleeping bag** for trekking). A **musical instrument**, **juggling balls** (can be purchased in Nepal), **portable game** or **photos of home** will help break the ice and while away some dead hours. **Binoculars** are great to have in the Tarai wildlife parks.

And finally, some odd essentials (all of which can be purchased in Nepal): a **flashlight** (torch), small **towel**, **sewing kit**, a length of **cord for drying clothes**, a pocket **alarm clock** (for early-morning departures), sealable **plastic bags** for keeping things separate in your pack, **passport-size photos** for visa and trekking applications, and **photocopies of the pages in your passport** containing personal data and your Nepalese visa.

trekking or any time you just want to travel light. The usual charge is a few rupees per item per day, but some places waive this if you take a room when you return.

Time Nepal is 15 minutes ahead of India – just to be contrary, one suspects. That makes it 5 hours 45 minutes ahead of London, 10 hours 45 minutes ahead of New York, 13 hours 45 minutes ahead of Los Angeles, and 19 hours 45 minutes ahead of Sydney. Nepal doesn't observe daylight saving time, so daylight saving time elsewhere reduces the time difference by one hour.

Tipping In Nepal, tipping isn't compulsory, but rather a reward to be bestowed for good service or withheld for bad. It has become standard to tip waiters in tourist restaurants (it may be their only pay), but Rs20 or so should be sufficient in all but the fanciest places. Don't tip taxi drivers, except maybe to round up the fare to the nearest Rs5 or Rs10. Trekking porters and guides have their own expectations – see Chapter Seven. Don't tip anyone until full completion of the service.

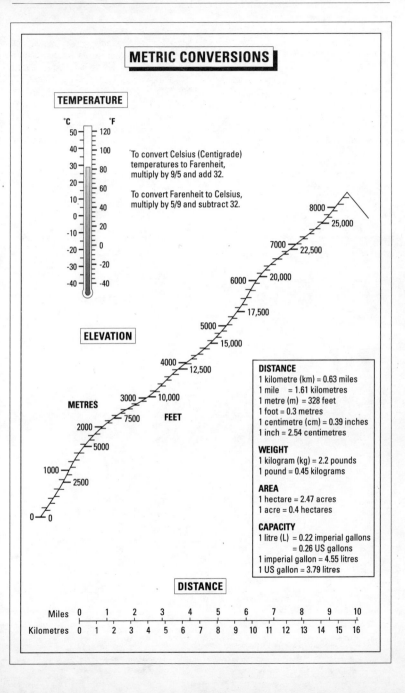

METRIC CONVERSIONS

TEMPERATURE

°C °F

To convert Celsius (Centigrade) temperatures to Farenheit, multiply by 9/5 and add 32.

To convert Farenheit to Celsius, multiply by 5/9 and subtract 32.

ELEVATION

METRES FEET

DISTANCE
1 kilometre (km) = 0.63 miles
1 mile = 1.61 kilometres
1 metre (m) = 328 feet
1 foot = 0.3 metres
1 centimetre (cm) = 0.39 inches
1 inch = 2.54 centimetres

WEIGHT
1 kilogram (kg) = 2.2 pounds
1 pound = 0.45 kilograms

AREA
1 hectare = 2.47 acres
1 acre = 0.4 hectares

CAPACITY
1 litre (L) = 0.22 imperial gallons
= 0.26 US gallons
1 imperial gallon = 4.55 litres
1 US gallon = 3.79 litres

DISTANCE

Miles	0	1	2	3	4	5	6	7	8	9	10
Kilometres	0 1	2	3 4	5	6 7	8	9 10	11	12 13	14	15 16

PART TWO

THE

GUIDE

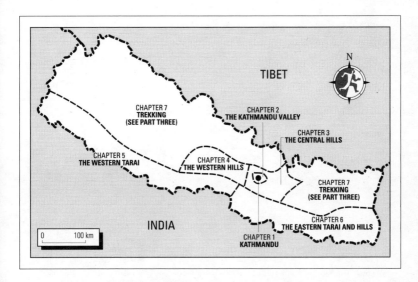

TIBET

N

CHAPTER 7
TREKKING
(SEE PART THREE)

CHAPTER 2
THE KATHMANDU VALLEY

CHAPTER 3
THE CENTRAL HILLS

CHAPTER 5
THE WESTERN TARAI

CHAPTER 4
THE WESTERN HILLS

CHAPTER 7
TREKKING
(SEE PART THREE)

INDIA

0   100 km

CHAPTER 6
THE EASTERN TARAI AND HILLS

CHAPTER 1
KATHMANDU

CHAPTER ONE

KATHMANDU

How to describe **KATHMANDU**? A medieval time capsule? An environmental disaster area? A pleasure dome? A tourist trap? A holy city, a dump, a beautiful illusion? All of the above. There are a thousand Kathmandu's, all layered and dovetailed and piled on top of one another in an extravagant morass of chaos and sophistication. With nearly half a million people, Nepal's capital is far and away its biggest and most cosmopolitan city: a melting pot of a dozen ethnic groups, and the home town of the Newars, Nepal's master craftsmen and traders extraordinaire (see p.95). Trade, indeed, created Kathmandu – for at least a thousand years it controlled the most important caravan route between Tibet and India – and trade has always funded its Newar artisans. Little wonder, perhaps, that Nepal's capital has so deftly embraced the tourist business.

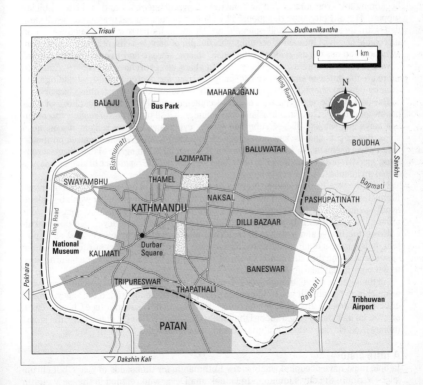

The Kathmandu most travellers experience, **Thamel**, is like a thumping, Third World theme park, all hotels and hoardings and promises, promises, with croissants and cakes beckoning from restaurant windows, and touts flogging tiger balm and hashish to holiday hippies. The **old city**, though squeezed by traffic and commercial pressures, is still studded with ageless temples and splendid architecture. Its narrow lanes seethe with an incredible crush of humanity, echoing with the din of bicycle bells, religious music, construction and car horns, reeking of incense, spices, sewage and exhaust fumes. Sacred cows still roam the streets, as do holy men, beggars, street urchins and coolies. And then there are the outcaste shantytowns down by the river, the decrepit ministry buildings, the swanky five-star shopping streets, the sequestered suburbs, the burgeoning bazaars.

But perhaps the predominant images of contemporary Kathmandu are those of what passes for progress: hellish traffic jams and pollution; a jostling skyline of rooftop water-storage tanks and satellite dishes; suburban sprawl, cybercafés, leather jackets, discos, neon signs, power cuts and backup generators, chauffeured Land Cruisers, families on motorbikes, advertisements for kitchen appliances. Kathmandu is joining the global village at ramming speed. It hasn't abandoned its traditional identity, but the rapid pace of change has produced an intense, often overwhelming, urban environment.

Nevertheless, Kathmandu is likely to be your first port of call in Nepal – all overseas flights land in the capital, and most roads lead to it – and you probably won't be able to avoid spending at least a couple of days here. It's the obvious place to sort out your affairs: it has all the **embassies** and airline offices, Nepal's best-developed **communications facilities**, and a welter of **trekking and travel agencies**. At least as important, in the minds of long-haul travellers anyway, are the capital's **restaurants** and the easy social scene that surrounds them, all of which makes Kathmandu the natural place to get your initial bearings in Nepal.

All things considered, though, you'd be well advised to get your business here over with as quickly as possible. If you're intending to do any sightseeing around the valley, consider basing yourself in the healthier surroundings of Patan or Bhaktapur (see Chapter Two), or even further out in Nagarkot or Dhulikhel (see Chapter Three). These days, the smart money is on staying *outside* Kathmandu and making day trips *in*, not vice versa.

A little history

People must have occupied what is now Kathmandu for thousands of years, but chroniclers attribute the city's founding to Gunakama Deva, who reigned in the early eighth century – by which time sophisticated urban centres had already been established by the **Lichhavi** kings at Pashupatinath and other sites in the surrounding valley. Kathmandu was originally known as Kantipur, but it later took its present name from the Kasthamandap ("Pavilion of Wood") that was constructed as a rest house along the main Tibet–India trade route in the late twelfth century, and which still stands in the city centre.

The city rose to prominence under the **Malla** kings, who took control of the valley in the thirteenth century and ushered in a golden age of art and architecture that lasted more than five hundred years. All of Kathmandu's finest buildings and monuments, including those of its spectacular Durbar Square, date from this period. At the start of the Malla era, Kathmandu ranked as a sovereign state alongside the valley's other two major cities, Bhaktapur and Patan, but soon fell under the rule of Bhaktapur. The cities were again divided in the fifteenth century, and a long period of intrigue and rivalry followed.

Malla rule ended abruptly in 1769, when Prithvi Narayan Shah of Gorkha, a previously undistinguished hill state to the west, captured the valley as the first conquest in his historic unification of Nepal. Kathmandu fared well in defeat, being made capital of the new nation and seat of the new **Shah** dynasty. The Shahs rule to this day, although from 1846 to 1951 they were politically outmanoeuvred by the powerful **Rana** family, who ruled as hereditary prime ministers and left Kathmandu with a legacy of enormous white (now mouldy grey) Neoclassical palaces. The capital remains the focus of all national political power – the 1990 democracy movement led, inevitably, to the palace gate – while its industrial and financial activities continue to fuel a round-the-clock building boom.

Orientation and arrival

Despite chaotic first appearances, Kathmandu is surprisingly easy to get to grips with; the touts, like everything else, become much more manageable once you've dumped your bags. The following, along with the map overleaf, should help with **orientation**.

Tradition has it that old Kathmandu (1290m) was laid out in the shape of a *khukuri* knife. Positioned at what would be the hilt of the knife is **Durbar Square** – a non-stop carnival set amidst temples, monuments and the former royal palace – while the city's oldest neighbourhoods stretch northeast and (to a lesser extent) southwest. **New Road**, the city's best-known shopping street, runs east from the square. The minaret-like **Bhimsen Tower** provides a useful landmark south of New Road. Kathmandu's budget hotels are concentrated in two areas: **Thamel**, north of Durbar Square in a newer part of town, and Jhochhen, better known as **Freak Street**, immediately south of the square.

Suburban Kathmandu sprawls mainly east of **Kantipath**, the main north–south thoroughfare, and is dominated by two landmarks, the **Royal Palace** and the **Tudikhel** (parade ground). Many of Kathmandu's expensive hotels, restaurants, boutiques and airline offices are located along **Durbar Marg**, the broad boulevard running south from the palace gate. West of the Bishnumati River is not, strictly speaking, part of Kathmandu, but the hilltop temple of **Swayambhu** is close enough to be reached easily on foot. The city is encircled by a none-too-scenic **Ring Road**, which pretty much defines the boundaries of this chapter.

Arriving by air
Arriving by air at **Tribhuwan International Airport**, 5km east of the city centre, you'll first have to deal with **immigration**. If you haven't already got a visa, fill out an application form and join the relevant queue. You'll need one passport-size photo and the

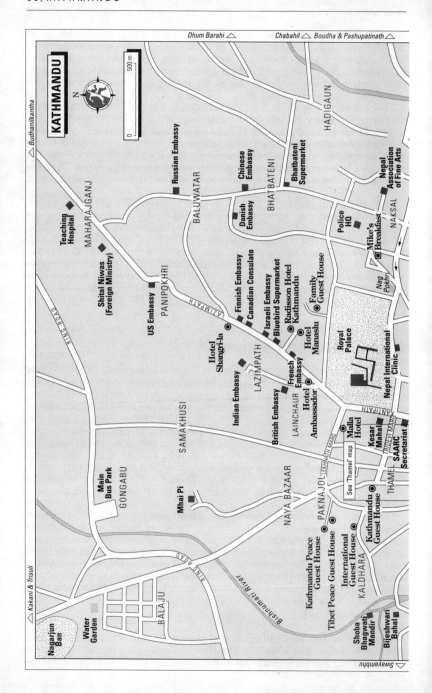

KATHMANDU

N

500 m

△ Budhanilkantha

△ Kakani & Trisuli

Dhum Barahi △   Chabahil △ Boudha & Pashupatinath △

△ Swayambhu

Teaching Hospital

Shital Niwas (Foreign Ministry)

MAHARAJGANJ

Russian Embassy

BALUWATAR

Chinese Embassy

Danish Embassy

Bhatbateni Supermarket

Nepal Association of Fine Arts

BHATBATENI

HADIGAUN

NAKSAL

Police HQ

Mike's Breakfast

US Embassy

PANIPOKHRI

RING ROAD

LAZIMPATH

Finnish Embassy

Canadian Consulate

Israeli Embassy

Bluebird Supermarket

Radisson Hotel Kathmandu

Family Guest House

Hotel Mamastu

Nag Pokhri

Royal Palace

Hotel Shangri-la

LAZIMPATH

French Embassy

SAMAKHUSI

Indian Embassy

British Embassy

LAINCHAUR

Hotel Ambassador

Nepal International Clinic

KANTIPATH

TRIDEVI MARG

Malla Hotel

Kesar Mahal

SAARC Secretariat

THAMEL

Main Bus Park

GONGABU

Mhai Pi

NAYA BAZAAR

PAKNAJOL LEKHNATH MARG

See Thamel map

Kathmandu Guest House

KALDHARA

Kathmandu Peace Guest House

International Guest House

Tibet Peace Guest House

BALAJU

RING ROAD

Bishnumati River

Nagarjun Ban

Water Garden

Shoba Bhagwati Mandir

Bijeshwari Bahal

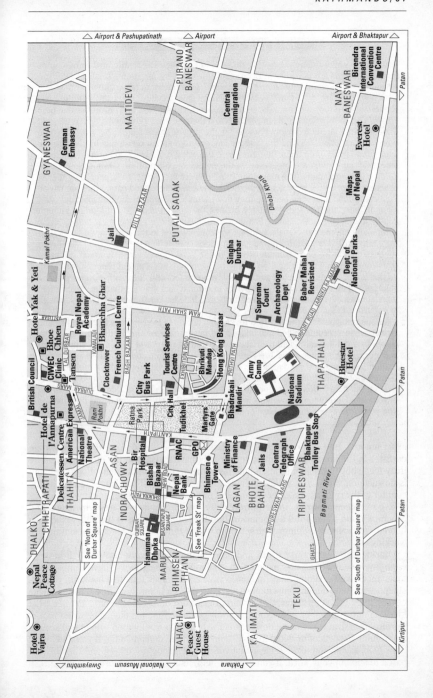

THIS AIN'T NO SHANGRI-LA

Kathmandu ranks among the world's most polluted cities. The **traffic and fumes** on its main boulevards are as bad as in Bangkok or Mexico City, albeit on a smaller scale. You wouldn't think it possible, let alone permissible, for vehicles to be so filthy.

In point of fact all motor vehicles (except motorcycles) registered in greater Kathmandu are supposed to undergo an annual **emissions test**, and only those that pass are entitled to drive on the main roads. Nevertheless, most vehicles pass, and the rest drive anyway. There are many reasons for the programme's failure, but they all come down to corruption. It's said that anyone can get a green sticker simply by slipping the appropriate *bakshish* to the tester. Tempos – the worst offenders – get around the regulations because most are registered in the names of police officers, whose job it is to enforce the regulations. The emissions standards are set low because, according to government logic, if they were set any higher too few vehicles would pass. Fines are trivial. Politicians don't intervene because they don't want to antagonize the transport industry.

For its part, the transport industry blames the government for not buiding enough **roads**, and suppliers for selling **low-grade fuel**. And there's some truth to their arguments. Sixty percent of Nepal's vehicles are concentrated in the Kathmandu Valley, and their number has tripled in a decade, so the density of vehicles sharing the limited road space is increasing unsustainably. Result: traffic jams, slower circulation and still more emissions from idling engines. As for the fuel supply, a government report has estimated that 25–30 percent of petrol and diesel is adulterated with cheaper kerosene, causing vehicles to run even dirtier. It was partly to combat this practice that the government mandated a fuel-colouring system (red for petrol, blue for kerosene), but it's easy enough to get around that.

All this contributes to **particulate levels** that are up to twelve times the World Health Organization's recommended maximum level in some areas. The particulates are themselves harmful to health, and they also carry lead (since petrol in Nepal is still leaded) and germs. The whole toxic brew not only irritates lungs and eyes, it also weakens immune systems and increases the long-term risk of various health problems (see "Development Dilemmas" on p.460 of Contexts).

If you can help it, don't stay more than a couple of days in Kathmandu at the beginning of your trip. Otherwise you're likely to come down with a chest or sinus infection that will dog you for days and may be hard to shake if you go trekking.

exact amount (see p.16) in cash US dollars – you can get dollars at the **exchange counter** in the immigration hall. If you already have a visa, join the other queue. The **duty-free** shop in the immigration hall has some pretty good bargains. Baggage claim is downstairs, where you should be able to grab a trolley. There's another exchange counter to the right as you exit customs, but rates are somewhat better in town. Nearby is a government **tourist information** desk, which hands out free city maps and brochures, and a free **hotel association booking service** (mostly the more expensive hotels). You can call lodgings yourself from one of the free courtesy phones, if they're working.

Outside, the guest-house **touts** and other hangers-on can be awful. You'll have an edge if you've made an accommodation booking because you will have removed the touts' incentive (a commission) to hassle you. If you haven't made a booking, you can still pretend that you have: just name a place where you know there'll be other fallbacks nearby if it's full. Alternatively, entertain offers from touts, choose one, and see what kind of room you end up with (you can always change the next day). The worst part of the airport arrival experience, however, is the leech-like young men who crowd around and render all sorts of unasked-for assistance and then demand a tip. If you don't want their help, say so and make it clear that you will be giving no money, and then be prepared to stick to your word. If you do want help, Rs20 should be more than enough.

Most **taxis** at the airport operate on a voucher system. Vouchers are sold from the drivers' syndicate booth just inside or just outside the arrivals exit. Prices are fixed in the high season and are posted on a board; at the time of writing they were Rs200 to most parts of Kathmandu, Rs250 to Patan and Rs400 to Bhaktapur (50 percent higher after 9pm). Touts may offer a "free" ride if you stay in their lodge, but of course the fare and the tout's commission will just get added on to the room charge – this will roughly double the price of the room, which is why you'll probably end up moving the next day.

Local **buses** offer a cheap (Rs3) but inconvenient alternative. They depart from the main intersection at the end of the airport drive – a 200m walk – and terminate at the City Bus Park, nearly 2km from most guest houses. Forget it.

Arriving by bus

Tourist **buses** from Pokhara and Chitwan let passengers off on Kantipath near Tridevi Marg (for Thamel) and near Bhimsen Tower (for Freak Street). That's if they get to Kathmandu before the afternoon rush hour starts – if your bus enters the city after about 3.30pm it may be redirected to Balaju, farther northwest of Thamel. Coming from the Indian border or Pokhara by public bus, you'll arrive at the New (Naya) Bus Park, located at Gongabu at the extreme north end of the city; taxis and tempos (see below) charge Rs75–100 to most tourist destinations. If you happen to be travelling by Sajha bus, stay on board and the bus will continue on to Bhimsen Tower. Buses from the Tibet border terminate at the City Bus Park, also known as the Old (Purano) Bus Park, east of the city centre and a Rs50 taxi ride to most lodgings.

Information and maps

The government **tourist office** at the airport (Sun–Thurs 10am–5pm, 4pm in winter; Fri 10am–3pm) gives out general brochures and can answer only the most straight-forward of questions. They're pretty clueless, but may be useful for information on upcoming festivals and public transport. The **Kathmandu Tourist Services Centre** (same hours) has a few more freebies, but it's located in Bhrikuti Mandap, the government's exhibition ground east of the Tudikhel, which is not very close to anything else.

Free **magazines** such as *Nepal Traveller* and *The Valley Bulletin* are probably the best all-around sources of information on tourist services and upcoming events. They're distributed to the bigger hotels, travel agents and supermarkets. For even more current information, as well as advertisements for trekking gear and trekking partners, check the **notice boards** in many tourist guest houses and restaurants (notably the *Kathmandu Guest House* and *Pumpernickel Bakery*).

The nonprofit **Kathmandu Environmental Education Project** (summer Sun–Fri 10am–5pm; winter Mon–Fri 9am–4pm), **Himalayan Explorers Club** (same office and hours) and **Himalayan Rescue Association** (Sun–Fri 10am–5pm, closes 4pm in winter) specialize mainly in trekking matters, but staff may be able to help with other travel questions. They also have useful trekking-related notice boards. All are on Jyatha Thamel.

The advertiser-supported city **maps** given away at the airport and tourist offices should suffice for most purposes. More detailed maps, as well as country and trekking maps, are sold in bookshops and by street vendors – specific ones are recommended where relevant elsewhere in the guide. One shop, Maps of Nepal, located 300m west of the *Everest Hotel* on the Airport Road, is notable for being the primary sales outlet for a series of extremely high-quality area maps produced by HMG (His Majesty's Government) and FINNAID, the Finnish overseas aid agency.

Getting around

You'll probably find that you do most of your moving around Kathmandu on foot, especially in the old city. Here's a rundown of other transport options.

Taxis, tempos and rikshas

Taxis are fairly cheap and are the most comfortable way to travel longer distances in Kathmandu and around the valley, though they don't work well in the crowded old city. A number of companies operate fleet taxis, which can be requested by phone (have your guest house make the call for you). Older freelance cabs tend to wait in designated areas, such as Tridevi Marg, the main Thamel intersection, at the top of Freak Street, along Dharma Path, and at the Jamal end of Durbar Marg. Both types have meters and drivers are supposed to use them, but will often try to quote a fixed price – for certain destinations, such as the airport and Central Immigration, they won't budge on this. For longer journeys, especially return journeys with some waiting time, it may be to your advantage to negotiate a fixed price. A surcharge is usually added after 8pm. Taxis start getting scarce around then, too – try the night taxi service (☎224374).

Metered tempos (also known as tuk-tuks or autorikshas) are slower, bumpier and less roomy than taxis, though their meter rates work out to be somewhat cheaper. **Fixed-route tempos** ply various routes throughout the city, generally following the main radial arteries. Get on where they start – many originate from two locations along Kantipath, near the National Theatre and just north of the GPO. On most routes there's a choice between fume-belching Vikram tempos and battery-powered Safaa ("clean") ones. The latter, which are proliferating thanks to a Danish grant, are one of the most tangible signs of development in Nepal, and they're also a more comfortable ride.

Pedal **rikshas** are really only worthwhile for short distances on narrow, crowded streets (where you'll feel every bump). The price should be about the same as for a metered tempo, but the wallahs charge whatever they can, so establish terms before setting off.

Local buses

Local **buses** and minibuses cover some of the same city routes as the fixed-route tempos, but they're really meant for longer journeys around the valley. They're cheap (no more than Rs10), but slow and extremely crowded, so they're easiest to cope with if you get on at the starting point. Refer to the box for useful routes.

LOCAL BUS ROUTES

Most buses run every 10–15 minutes during the day.

From City Bus Park to:

1. Chabahil and Airport	11. Banepa and Panauti
2. Gaushala (for Pashupatinath) and Boudha	12. Banepa and Dhulikhel
3. Sundarijal	13. Godavari
4. Sankhu	14. Patan (Lagankhel)
5. Budhanilkantha	19. Swayambhu
7. Bhaktapur	21. Kirtipur
9. Sano Thimi and Bhaktapur	22. Pharping and Dakshin Kali
	23. Balaju and Naya Bus Park
	25. Patan Gate

A separate electric **trolley bus** service also operates to Bhaktapur every fifteen minutes during the day. The starting point is on Tripureswar Marg near the National Stadium.

Bicycles

Cycling is still a good way to get to many outlying sights, but Kathmandu's traffic and pollution make it more hazardous and less fun than it used to be. Consequently rental bikes are harder to find, especially in Thamel, where most of the cycle wallahs have been pushed out by redevelopment. Some guest houses have their own bikes for rent, or can arrange them.

Old-fashioned **one-speed bikes** rent for Rs40–75 a day. **Mountain bikes**, often of disappointing quality (see p.36 and p.61), range from Rs60–80 a day for a one-speed model to Rs150–200 for an eighteen-speeder without helmet. Thamel mountain-bike operators (see p.138) may be able to set you up with something better for Rs250–500, including helmet. Shop for bikes early, or even the night before, and bargain for a long-term discount. If riding on the main roads, wear a mask (sold in pharmacies) or a dampened handkerchief.

The lane south of the National Theatre, just west of Kantipath, is the place to go to buy a new bike. An Indian-made gear bike will cost you upwards of Rs6000, depending on quality.

Motorcycles and vehicles

Riding a **motorcycle** isn't much fun inside the Ring Road, but it's a great way to explore the Kathmandu Valley and beyond. Several operators in Thamel and Freak Street rent out 100cc motorcycles for Rs300–400 a day, not including petrol. Some places also rent dirt bikes (about Rs800/day, though these rates should come down as competition increases). Again, you should be able to get a discount for multiple days. You'll need to leave a plane ticket or passport as security, and you're supposed to show a driving licence. Refer to the driving tips on p.36 of Basics.

The cheapest way to rent a **car** is to hire a taxi by the day, which will cost about $20 a day for touring around the valley (petrol included). Prices for longer journeys are based on the distance to be travelled, or are quoted exclusive of petrol; make sure the taxi has permission to travel where you want to go, since many are restricted. **Jeeps** and **vans** can also be hired for about $30 a day (petrol excluded) through certain agents – ask around. Renting a vehicle through an official agency is much more expensive: Yeti Travels (☎221234) and Gorkha Travels (☎224895), both on Durbar Marg, are the agents for Avis and Hertz respectively.

If you've driven your own car or van to Nepal, beware: central Kathmandu is a nightmare for driving. You'd have to be very brave or very foolish to enter with a camper or other large vehicle. The streets are narrow and crowded, and you'd be constantly defeated by the one-way system.

The City

The scene on Thamel avenue today: a very pretty pale-brown cow standing on the sidewalk, between a cigarette stand and an umbrella repairman, her head lifted straight up, perpendicular with the ground, while a ten-year-old boy heading home from school stood there, reaching up and scratching the animal's neck. Meanwhile all the tourists pointing to the fruit-bats hanging in the trees. The smell of bat shit and garbage and day-old murk, literally Another Shitty Day in Paradise. Shangri-la's getting wasted, but you can still stand on the street corner in Kathmandu and scratch her heavy velvet throat.

Jeff Greenwald, *Mister Raja's Neighborhood*

The Kathmandu most travellers come to see is the **old city**, a tight tangle of narrow alleys and numerous temples immediately north and south of the central Durbar Square. It's a bustling, intensely urban quarter where tall, extended-family dwellings block out the sun, while dark, open-fronted shops crowd the lanes, and vegetable sellers clot the intersections. Though the city goes to bed early, from before dawn to around 10pm there's always something happening somewhere. Early morning is the best time to watch people going about their daily religious rites (*puja*), adorning idols with red paste (*sindur*), marigold petals and other offerings. If you walk around after dinner, especially in the neighbourhoods of Indrachowk, Asan or Chhetrapati, you'll frequently run across mesmerizing devotional hymn-sings (*bhajan*).

This is only one side of Kathmandu, though, and not necessarily representative of the rest. Across the Bishnumati River, just west of town, is a more newly settled and rapidly developing area. The famous **Swayambhu stupa**, magnificently set on a conical hill here, has attracted a large community of expatriate Tibetans whose culture is a world apart from that of Kathmandu's indigenous Newars.

Most commerce these days is conducted east of the old quarter. The boulevards around the Royal Palace are wide and businesslike, lined with airline offices and five-star hotels. Tinny, congested bazaars sprawl further to the south, while the southeastern sector contains the national parliament and many other government buildings. The northeast is given over to relatively quiet, shaded suburbs.

Durbar Square

Teeming, touristy **Durbar Square** is the natural place to begin sightseeing. The old royal palace (*durbar*), running along the eastern edge of the square, takes up more space than all the other monuments here combined. Kumari Chowk, home of Kathmandu's "living goddess", overlooks the square from the south. The square itself is squeezed by the palace into two parts: at the southern end is the Kasthamandap, the ancient building that probably gave Kathmandu its name, while the northern part is taken up by a varied procession of statues and temples.

A small outfit called Tourism Promotion Nepal, which operates out of a handicrafts shop near the Taleju Bell, sells an excellent map of the square that contains a wealth of archeological and historical detail (Rs25 donation).

Hanuman Dhoka (Old Royal Palace)

The rambling **Old Royal Palace** (Mon, Wed, Thurs & Sun 10.30am–4pm, 3pm in winter; Fri 10.30am–2pm; closed Tues; Rs250) is usually called **Hanuman Dhoka**, after its main entrance.

Its oldest, eastern wings date from the mid-sixteenth century, but in all likelihood there was a palace on this spot before then. Malla kings built most of the rest by the late seventeenth century, and after capturing Kathmandu in 1768, Prithvi Narayan Shah added (in characteristically martial fashion) four lookout towers at the southeastern corner. Finally, the Ranas left their mark with the garish Neoclassical facade along the southwestern flank. Nepal's royal family last lived here in 1886, before moving to the northern end of town, retaining the complex for ceremonial and administrative purposes. Only a fraction of the five-acre palace and grounds is open to the public.

THE ENTRANCE
Entrance to the palace is through *the* Hanuman Dhoka (Hanuman Gate), a brightly decorated doorway at the east side of the northern part of Durbar Square. The gate is named after the popular monkey god **Hanuman**, whose statue stands outside, so smothered in *sindur* paste that it just looks like an orange blob. Ram's right-hand man in the Hindu *Ramayan* epic, Hanuman has always been revered by Nepalese kings, who, like Ram, are

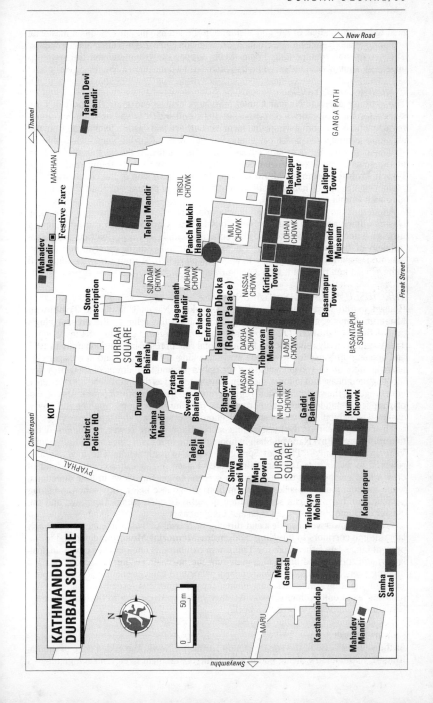

KATHMANDU
DURBAR SQUARE

0   50 m

N

New Road

Thamel

MAKHAN

Festive Fare

Tarani Devi
Mandir

Mahadev
Mandir

Stone
Inscription

DURBAR
SQUARE

Taleju Mandir

TRISUL
CHOWK

Panch Mukhi
Hanuman

SUNDARI
CHOWK

MOHAN
CHOWK

MUL
CHOWK

Jagannath
Mandir

Palace
Entrance

Hanuman Dhoka
(Royal Palace)

NASSAL
CHOWK

Kirtipur
Tower

DAKHA
CHOWK

Tribhuwan
Museum

LAMO
CHOWK

LOHAN
CHOWK

Bhaktapur
Tower

Lalitpur
Tower

GANGA PATH

Mahendra
Museum

Basantapur
Tower

Freak Street

Kala
Bhairab

Pratap
Malla

Sweta
Bhairab

Bhagwati
Mandir

MASAN
CHOWK

NHU CHHEN
L CHOWK

Gaddi
Baithak

BASANTAPUR
SQUARE

Drums

Krishna
Mandir

District
Police HQ

KOT

Chhetrapati

PYAPHAL

Taleju
Bell

Shiva
Parbati Mandir

Maju
Dewal

DURBAR
SQUARE

Kumari
Chowk

Kabindrapur

Trailokya
Mohan

Maru
Ganesh

MARU

Swayambhu

Kasthamandap

Mahadev
Mandir

Simha
Sattal

held to be incarnations of the god Vishnu. On the left as you enter stands a masterful sculpture of another Vishnu incarnation, the man-lion **Narasingh**, tearing apart a demon. The seventeenth-century king Pratap Malla supposedly commissioned the statue to appease Vishnu, whom he feared he had offended by dancing in a Narasingh constume.

INTERIOR COURTYARDS

The entrance opens to **Nassal Chowk**, the large central courtyard that provided the setting for King Birendra's coronation in 1975, and which is still used for important royal functions. The brick wings that form its southern and eastern flanks date from the sixteenth century and boast painstakingly carved wooden doorways, windows and struts – check out the door jambs beaded with tiny skulls. At the northeastern corner of the square, the five-tiered pagoda-like turret, notable for its round roofs, is the **Panch Mukhi Hanuman Mandir**. Along the northern side of the courtyard is the Malla kings' audience hall, now adorned with a series of portraits of Shah kings, beginning with Prithvi Narayan Shah.

Altogether the palace boasts ten courtyards, but visitors are allowed to enter only Nassal Chowk and one other, **Lohan Chowk**. **Mul Chowk**, which can be glimpsed through a doorway off Nassal Chowk, contains a temple to Taleju Bhawani, the ancestral deity of the Malla kings, and sacrifices are made to her in the courtyard during the autumn Dasain festival. To the north, but not at all visible, **Mohan Chowk** is supposed to have a sunken royal bath with a golden waterspout.

THE MUSEUMS AND BASANTAPUR TOWER

Housed in the west and south wings overlooking Nassal Chowk, the **Tribhuwan Museum** features a collection of memorabilia from the reign of the present king's grandfather, Tribhuwan. Often referred to as *rashtrapita* ("father of the nation"), Tribhuwan is fondly remembered for his pivotal role in restoring the monarchy in 1951 and opening up Nepal to the outside world. Looking at the photos and newspaper clippings in this exhibit, you get a sense of the upheavals and high drama of 1950–51, when the king sought asylum in India and then, having served as the figurehead for resistance efforts against the crumbling Rana regime, returned triumphantly to power. Also on display are jewel-studded coronation ornaments, royal furniture, guns, trophies and even a casket. The exhibit ends with a small selection of salvaged wooden temple carvings.

The museum leads to the massive nine-storey **Basantapur Tower**, the biggest of the four raised by Prithvi Narayan Shah in honour of the four main cities of the Kathmandu Valley. (Basantapur – "Place of Spring" – refers to Kathmandu. The tower is also referred to as Nautele Durbar, "Nine-Storey Palace".) You can ascend to a kind of crow's nest enclosed by pitched wooden screens to get fine views in four directions, while the sound of flute sellers drifts up from the square below. If weather and smog permit, from here you can see (from left to right) Ganesh Himal, Langtang, and the cluster of Dome Blanc, Dorje Lakpa and Lengpogang.

From the tower you can descend directly to Nassal Chowk, but carry on through labyrinthine corridors to the **King Mahendra Memorial Museum**, dedicated to the present king's late father. Like the Tribhuwan exhibit, this one marches chronologically through the life and times of a monarch, the most interesting attractions being a hunting scene, recreations of Mahendra's office and cabinet room, and two thrones (one for the king's immediate ascension, the other for his formal coronation). The museum exits onto Lohan Chowk. Another museum dedicated to the present king, Birendra, is supposed to be in the works.

Kumari Chowk

At the southern end of the square stands **Kumari Chowk**, the gilded cage of the Raj Kumari, Kathmandu's "living goddess" and the pre-eminent of eleven such goddesses

KATHMANDU CULTURE: THE NEWARS

Although only a minor ethnic group in national terms, the **Newars** account for three-quarters of Kathmandu's population and exert a cultural influence in Nepal far beyond their numbers. Some scholars make the Newars out to be descendants of the Kiratas, who ruled the Kathmandu Valley between the seventh century BC and the second century AD, while others say they go back even further than that. In any case, the Newar community has had to absorb successive waves of immigrants, overlords, traders and usurpers ever since, resulting in a complex cultural matrix.

Centuries of domination by foreign rulers have, if anything, only accentuated the uniqueness of Newar culture. For 1500 years the Newars have sustained an almost continuous artistic flowering: under the Lichhavis they produced acclaimed stone carvings, and under the Mallas and Shahs they've excelled in wood, metal and brick. They're believed to have invented the pagoda, and it was a Newar architect, **Arniko**, who led a Nepali delegation in the thirteenth century to introduce the technique to the Chinese. The pagoda style of stacked, strut-supported roofs finds unique expression in Nepali (read Newar) temples, and is echoed in the overhanging eaves of Newar houses.

The shape of Newar settlements goes right to the roots of Newar civilization: farming and trade. As farmers, Newars build their **villages** in compact, urban nuclei to conserve the fertile farmland of the valley. As traders, they construct their houses with removable wooden shutters, so that the ground floor can double as a shop. Scattered, in part, by the shortage of land in the valley, Newar traders have colonized lucrative crossroads throughout Nepal, recreating bustling **bazaars** wherever they go.

But above all, Newars are consummate city-builders. The fundamental building block of old Newar **cities** is the **bahal** (or *baha*) – a set of buildings joined at right angles around a central courtyard. Kathmandu is honeycombed with *bahal*, many of which were originally built as Buddhist monasteries but have reverted to residential use during two centuries of state-sponsored Hinduism. (*Bahal* architecture was applied to palaces as well, as a look at a map of Durbar Square will readily demonstrate.) Another uniquely Newar invention is the **guthi**, a benevolent community trust based on caste or kinship links that handles the upkeep of temples (*mandir*) and fountains (*hiti*), organizes festivals, arranges cremations and, indirectly, ensures the transmission of Newar culture from one generation to the next. *Guthi* have been on the decline since the 1960s, however, when land reform deprived them of much of their income from holdings around the valley, and with young Newars losing interest in traditional ways they are gradually being marginalized into social clubs.

Newars are easily recognized. Traditionally they carry heavy loads in baskets suspended at either end of a **shoulder pole** (*nol*), whereas other Nepali hill people carry things on their backs, supported by a tumpline from the forehead. As for **clothing**, you can usually tell a Newar woman by the fanned pleats at the front of her sari; men have mostly abandoned traditional dress, but some still wear distinctive waistcoats.

Newars generally speak among themselves in **Newari** (known among purists as Nepal Bhasa), a Tibeto-Burman language with many borrowings from Nepali (see p.494). Several Newari-language newspapers are published in Kathmandu. Once repressed by the government, Newari has undergone a strong revival since the 1990 restoration of democracy, with schools offering courses in it and Radio Nepal broadcasting Newari programming. However, Newari and other minority languages are still a source of controversy in Nepal: in 1998 the Supreme Court raised hackles when it ruled that the Kathmandu city government couldn't declare Newari an "official" language.

For information on Newar **religion**, see Contexts, p.448. A description of Newar **food** is given on p.41.

in the valley. In case there was any doubt, Kumari Chowk proves Kathmandu is no stuffy, dead museum: no other temple better illustrates the living, breathing and endlessly adaptable nature of religion in Nepal, with its freewheeling blend of Hindu, Buddhist and indigenous elements.

For background information on the various gods, their symbols and styles of worship, see "Religion" in Contexts (p.443). Definitions of various Nepali religious terms are also given in the glossary on p.495.

The cult of **the Kumari** – a prepubescent girl worshipped as a living incarnation of Durga, the demon-slaying Hindu mother goddess – probably goes back to the early Middle Ages. Jaya Prakash, the last Malla king of Kathmandu, institutionalized the practice when he built the Kumari Chowk in 1757. According to legend, the king either committed some sexual indiscretion against a Kumari, or disbelieved a girl who claimed to be the goddess – in any case Jaya Prakash, who is remembered as a particularly paranoid and weak king, was so consumed by guilt that he erected the building as an act of atonement. He also established the tradition – continued to this day – that each year during the festival of Indra Jaatra, the Kumari should bestow a *tika* (auspicious mark) on the forehead of the king who was to reign for the coming year. In 1768, the hapless Jaya Prakash was driven into exile on the eve of Indra Jaatra, and the conquering Prithvi Narayan Shah slipped in and took the *tika*.

Although the Kumari is supposed to be a Hindu goddess, she is chosen from the Buddhist Shakya clan of goldsmiths, according to a **selection process** reminiscent of the Tibetan Buddhist method of finding reincarnated lamas. Elders interview hundreds of Shakya girls, aged three to five, short-listing those who exhibit 32 auspicious signs: a neck like a conch shell, a body like a banyan tree, eyelashes like a cow's and so on. Finalists are placed in a dark room surrounded by freshly severed buffalo heads, while men in demon masks parade around making scary noises. The girl who shows no fear and can correctly identify belongings of previous Kumaris, and whose horoscope doesn't clash with the king's, becomes the next Kumari. She lives a cloistered life inside the Kumari Chowk and is only carried outside on her throne during Indra Jaatra and four or five other festivals each year; her feet are never allowed to touch the ground. Durga's spirit leaves her when she menstruates or otherwise bleeds, whereupon she's retired with a modest state pension. The transition to life as an ordinary mortal can be hard, and she may have difficulty finding a husband, since tradition has it that the man who marries an ex-Kumari will die young. The present Kumari was installed in 1993, when she was four and a half years old.

Non-Hindus aren't allowed past the Kumari Chowk's *bahal*-style **courtyard**, which is decorated with exquisitely carved (if weathered) windows, pillars and doorways. When someone slips enough cash to her handlers, the Kumari, decked out in exaggerated eye makeup and jewellery, shows herself at one of the first-floor windows. (Your chances of a sighting are higher in the morning or late afternoon, when she's not busy with her studies.) She's believed to answer her visitors' unspoken questions with the look on her face. Cameras are okay inside the courtyard, but photographing the Kumari is strictly forbidden.

The chariot that carries the Kumari around during the Indra Jaatra festival is garaged next door to the Kumari Chowk. The big wooden chariot yokes from past processions, which according to tradition may not be destroyed, are laid out nearby. The broad, bricked area to the east is **Basantapur Square**, once the site of royal elephant stables, where souvenir sellers now spread their wares.

Other temples and monuments

Dozens of *mandir*, *dewal* (stepped platforms) and statues litter Durbar Square. The following stand out as highlights.

THE KASTHAMANDAP

If legend is to be believed, the **Kasthamandap**, standing at the southwestern end of the square, is Kathmandu's oldest building, and one of the oldest wooden buildings in

INDRA: JAILBIRD AND RAINMAKER

In the Kathmandu Valley the story is told that **Indra**, the Vedic "King of Heaven", wanted to buy some flowers for his mother. Unable to find any flowers in heaven, he descended to the valley and stole some, but was caught and imprisoned. When Indra's mother came looking for him the people realized their mistake and were mortified, and so to appease him they commenced an annual festival in his honour.

Basically a harvest festival, **Indra Jaatra** is an occasion to give thanks to the god for bringing the monsoon rains that make the all-important summer rice crop possible. It's usually held in late August or early September, determined by the lunar calendar. Most of the action centres on Kathmandu's Durbar Square, where His Majesty presides over special festivities on the feverish third day. Masked dancers whirl through the streets, temple images go on display, *das avatar* performances are held at the base of the Trailokya Mohan to commemorate the ten incarnations of Vishnu, rice beer literally flows from the mouth of Sweta Bhairab, and the Kumari and two companions are wheeled around in chariots. There's even a temporary "jail" set up near the Kasthamandap to hold an effigy of Indra.

the world. It's said to have been constructed from the wood of a single tree in the late twelfth century (Singha Sattal, the smaller version to the south, was made from the leftovers), but what you see is mostly the result of several renovations since 1630. An open, pagoda-roofed pavilion (*mandap*), it served for several centuries as a rest house (*sattal*) along the Tibet trade route, and probably formed the nucleus of early Kathmandu. This corner of the square, called Maru Tol, still has the look of a crossroads, with sellers hawking fruit, vegetables and flowers. Many of the city's indigents sleep in the Kasthamandap at night.

The Shah kings converted the Kasthamandap into a temple to their protector deity*, **Gorakhnath**, whose statue stands in the middle of the pavilion. A Brahman priest usually sets up shop here to dispense instruction and conduct rituals. In four niches set around are shrines to Ganesh, the elephant-headed god of good fortune, which supposedly represent the celebrated Ganesh temples of the Kathmandu Valley (at Chabahil, Bhaktapur, Chobar and Bungamati), thus enabling Kathmandu residents to pay tribute to all four at once.

The building to the southeast of the Kasthamandap is **Kabindrapur**, a temple to Shiva in his role as Nataraj ("Lord of the Dance"), which is mostly patronized by musicians and dancers. Opposite Kabindrapur, occupying its own side square, is a brick *shikra* (Indian-style, corncob-shaped temple) to Mahadev (Shiva).

MARU GANESH AND TRAILOKYA MOHAN

Immediately north of the Kasthamandap stands yet another Ganesh shrine, the unassuming but ever-popular **Maru Ganesh**. A ring on Ganesh's bell is usually the first stage in any *puja*, and this shrine is the first stop for people intending to worship at the other temples of Durbar Square, royalty included. Ganesh's trusty "vehicle", a rat, is perched on a plinth of the Kasthamandap, across the way. The lane heading west from

*A word about the confusing matter of royal deities. Gorakhnath, a mythologized Indian guru, is revered as a kind of guardian angel by all the Shah kings. Taleju Bhawani, to whom many temples and bells are dedicated in the Kathmandu, Patan and Bhaktapur Durbar Squares, played a similar role for the Malla kings. The Kumari has been worshipped by the kings of both dynasties, but mainly as a public gesture to secure her *tika*, which lends credibility to their divine right to rule. Finally, the present king, Birendra, exercising the prerogative of all Hindus, has taken as his own family deity Dakshin Kali, whose shrine is at the southern edge of the Kathmandu Valley here used to be called Pie Alley – in its heyday in the 1970s it boasted many pie shops, but they've now gone the way of hash shops and hippies.

The three-roofed pagoda between the Kasthamandap and the Kumari Chowk is the seventeenth-century Trailokya Mohan, dedicated to Vishnu. A much-photographed statue of the angelic Garud, Vishnu's man-bird vehicle, kneels in his customary palms-together *namaste* position in front of the temple.

GADDI BAITHAK

The part of the Royal Palace facing the Trailokya Mohan is the **Gaddi Baithak**, a ponderous early-twentieth-century addition that pretty much sums up Rana-era architecture. If you didn't know Nepalese history you might say it had a whiff of the Raj about it, and in a way you'd be right: while India was under British rule, Nepal was labouring under its own home-grown colonialists, the Rana line of isolationist prime ministers. Purists bemoan the Neoclassical building's distorting effect on Durbar Square's proportions, but you've got to admit it adds a bit of spice to the mix. The west-facing balcony once served as the royal reviewing stand.

The antiquity of the Durbar Square area was confirmed during the construction of the Gaddi Baithak, when workers uncovered what is believed to be remnants of a Lichhavi-era temple. The find spot is enclosed by a small grate in the middle of the road near the southwest corner of the Gaddi Baithak.

MAJU DEWAL AND SHIVA PARBATI MANDIR

North of the Trailokya Mohan, the huge seventeenth-century **Maju Dewal** sits high atop a pyramid of nine stepped levels. Climb to the top for a god's-eye view of the square and all its hubbub, but don't expect to escape the would-be guides, roving bangle-sellers and students anxious to practise their English.

From this height you can look straight across at the rectangular **Shiva Parbati Mandir**, erected in the eighteenth century by one of the early Shah kings. Painted figures of Shiva and his consort Parbati lean out of the first-floor window, looking like they're about to toss the bouquet and dash off to the honeymoon suite. Despite the temple's popular name, the actual objects of worship inside are the Nawa Durga (Nine Durgas). The exterior woodwork is especially fine.

AROUND THE TALEJU BELL

North of the Shiva Parvati temple, the square narrows and then opens out to another temple-clogged area. Ranged along the left (western) side are the **Taleju Bell**, an octagonal **Krishna Mandir**, and a pair of ceremonial **drums** from the eighteenth century. The bell and drums were historically sounded as an alarm or call to congregate, but are now used only during the festival of Dasain.

Next to the palace opposite the bell, a small bas relief depicts **Jambhuwan**, the legendary teacher of Hanuman the monkey god. Just to the north of this, look up to see the **Kun Jhyal**, a gold-plated window frame flanked by two ivory ones, once used by Malla kings to watch processions in the square below.

SWETA AND KALA BHAIRABS

Just beyond, set against the palace wall but not very visible behind a wooden screen, is the snarling ten-foot-high gilded head of **Sweta Bhairab** (White Bhairab), a terrifying, blood-swilling aspect of Shiva. One day a year, during Indra Jaatra, the screen comes down and men jostle to drink rice beer flowing out of a pipe in Bhairab's mouth. The column nearby supports a gilded statue of **King Pratap Malla** and family, a self-congratulatory artform that was all the rage among the Malla kings of the late seventeenth century.

North of this, on the other side of the small Degu Taleju Mandir, the massive, roly-poly image of **Kala Bhairab** (Black Bhairab) dances on the corpse of a demon. Carved from a single twelve-foot slab of stone, it was found in a field north of Kathmandu during the reign of Pratap Malla, but probably dates to Lichhavi times. It used to be said that anyone who told a lie in front of it would vomit blood and die. One story has it that when the chief justice's office stood across the way, so many witnesses died while testifying that a temple had to be erected to shield the court from Kala Bhairab's wide-eyed stare.

THE JAGANNATH MANDIR AND EROTIC CARVINGS
East of Pratap Malla's column stands the sixteenth-century pagoda-style **Jagannath Mandir**, dedicated to the god whose runaway-chariot festival in India gave us the word "juggernaut". The struts supporting the lower roof of this temple contain Kathmandu's most tittered-about **erotic carvings**, although such carvings are actually quite common in Nepali temples: once you know where to look, you start noticing them everywhere.

Scholars can't seem to agree on the significance of these little vignettes, which often feature outrageous athletics, threesomes and bestiality. Some suggest that sex in this context is being offered as a tantric path to enlightenment, and as evidence they note that such scenes generally appear on the lower portions of struts, separated from the gods and goddesses above by lotuses (symbolic of transcendence). A more popular belief is that the goddess of lightning is a chaste virgin who wouldn't dare strike a temple so decorated. In any case, Hanuman, who guards the nearby palace entrance, is spared the sight by the globs of *sindur* over his eyes.

Nearby, along the palace outer wall, is a **stone inscription** in fifteen languages, carved in 1664 by King Pratap Malla, the prime architect of Durbar Square's temples, who also fancied himself something of a linguist. The inscription is a poem to the goddess Kali, and the story goes that if anyone can read the whole thing, milk will gush from the tap. There are two words in French and one in English.

THE TALEJU MANDIR
Set atop a twelve-tiered plinth and rising 40m above the northeast end of the square, the magnificent **Taleju Mandir** was erected in the mid-sixteenth century by King Mahendra Malla, who decreed that no building should exceed it in height – a ban that remained in force until the middle part of this century. Kathmandu's biggest temple, it looks down on you with haughty grandeur. It's open only on the ninth day of Dasain, and then only to Nepalis, who make sacrifices to Durga in the courtyard.

Taleju Bhawani, a south Indian goddess imported in the fourteenth century by the Mallas, is considered by Hindus to be a form of the mother goddess Durga, while Buddhist Newars count her as one of the Taras, tantric female deities. Behind the Taleju Mandir, reached by a doorway from Makhan Tol (see below), sits the brick godhouse of **Tarani Devi**, Taleju's "older sister".

THE REST OF THE NORTHERN SQUARE
Other, minor temples dotting the northern square belong mainly to Shiva. Inside each, the god is worshipped as a *linga*, a stone phallus that to a Shaiva (follower of Shiva) is as potent a symbol as the cross is to a Christian. The Mahadev (Shiva) temple at the very north of the square is particularly busy on Saturdays, when a *pujari* (priest) attends.

The infamous **Kot Courtyard**, which once lay northwest of the square, is now taken up by a walled police compound. It was here that the Machiavellian general Jang Bahadur Rana engineered a grisly massacre of 55 of the king's top brass in 1846, thereby clearing the way to proclaim himself prime minister and establish the hereditary line that was to rule Nepal until 1951. Blood again flows here each year on the ninth day of Dasain, when soldiers attempt to sever the heads of sacrificial buffaloes with a single sword stroke.

North of Durbar Square

Kathmandu's oldest, liveliest streets lie north and northeast of Durbar Square. You could make a more or less circular swing through the area (as this section does), but you'll almost certainly be diverted somewhere along the way. At any rate, the sights described here are only a backdrop for the old city's fascinating street life.

Indrachowk

The old trade route to Tibet passes through Durbar Square and becomes a narrow lane after it rounds the Taleju Mandir. Passing through **Makhan Tol** – the name harks back to a time when butter (*makhan*) was sold here – it runs a gauntlet of *thangka* (Buddhist scroll painting) sellers and then takes a northeasterly bearing towards Kathmandu's traditional goldsmiths' neighbourhood.

The first big intersection you reach is **Indrachowk**, named in honour of the Vedic (early Hindu) king of the gods. A sort of Asian Zeus, complete with thunderbolt, Indra fell from grace in India centuries ago, but in the Kathmandu Valley he's still revered as a rainmaker and rates his own festival (see p.97). The gaudy house-like temple on the

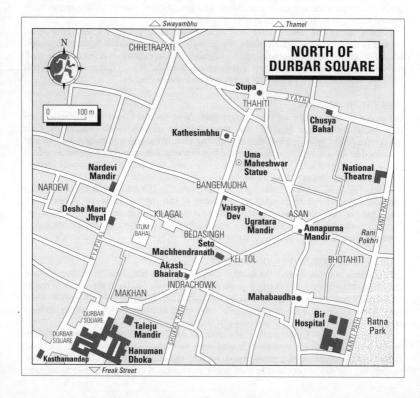

west side of the crossroads – its front decorated with European ceramic tiles, a common practice earlier this century – is that of **Akash Bhairab** (Sky, or Blue, Bhairab), whom Nepalis consider to be equivalent to Indra. The upstairs temple is out-of-bounds to non-Hindus, but you can see the scary black mask of Bhairab through the open window; it's paraded around Kathmandu during Indra Jaatra.

Shopping is good around Indrachowk. *Pashmina* (and acrylic) shawls are sold from the steps of shrines in the intersection, and colourful bead necklaces (*pote*) and tassels (*dhaago*) hang in curtains from the stalls of the **Pote Bazaar**, a small market area to the southeast. *Pote*, worn by virtually all married women in hill Nepal, typically consist of numerous strands of glass beads, all of the same colour, drawn together with a cylindrical gold ornament known as a *tilhari*. Many married women also weave *dhaago* into their hair – these are always red, a colour that indicates married status. The stalls here are owned mainly by Muslims, descendants of Kashmiri traders who migrated to the valley three centuries ago. You can watch them deftly making *pote*, using a big toe or a nail to anchor each strand while stringing it.

Kel Tol and Seto Machchendranath

The tumultuous street heading north from Indrachowk is the direct route to Thamel, but the old Tibet road continues diagonally to the small square of **Kel Tol** and the seventeenth-century temple of **Seto** (or Sweta) **Machchendranath**, one of two main shrines to the protector god of the Kathmandu Valley. Like his "red" cousin in Patan (see p.181), "White" Machchendranath is feted in a great chariot festival during the month of Chaitra (March–April).

Newars know this god as Karunamaya Lokeshwar, the *boddhisattva* of compassion, while Tibetans consider him Jowo Dzamling Karmo, White Lord of the World. Yet another name, **Jama-dyo**, traces back to a legend in which the white mask of Machchendranath was stolen by marauders from the west during ancient times. The invading king's family is said to have been afflicted with incurable diseases for six generations, until one of them took the idol back to Kathmandu and buried it in a field near what is now Durbar Marg. When a farmer rediscovered the image in the fifteenth century, it was immediately hailed as Jama-dyo – God of Jamal – and installed in this location, which is accordingly known as **Jamal** (or Jana) **Bahal**.

The entrance to the well-concealed courtyard is a gate at the west side of Kel Tol. Among the many votive *chaityas* and figures can be seen a weathered old stone figure of Amitabha (one of the *panchabuddha*, the five personifications of Buddhahood), a Victorian bronze statue converted into an incense holder, three Tara figures on pillars, and the Kanaka Chaitya, a Lichhavi-era stone hemisphere that was the original centrepiece of this *bahal* before Machchendranath stole the show. The main temple features some beautiful gilt-copper repoussé work on the outside, but an iron grille, installed to thwart temple thieves, robs it of its aesthetic appeal. This kind of precaution is still unusual in Nepal, a country whose artistic riches are all the more remarkable for being so public. Unfortunately, the risk of theft, driven by demand from Western collectors, has made it necessary here.

To Asan Tol

Beyond Kel Tol, the street is known mainly for its brass, copper and stainless steel wares: you'll see a bewildering array of incense holders, *thaal* (trays), water jugs, and vessels designed to hold water or cow's urine for *puja*. On the left, **Tilang Ghar**, a former Rana general's residence, is decorated with a stucco frieze of marching soldiers. The three-tiered octagonal **Krishna Mandir** just beyond is no longer active, and has been half obscured by the encroachments of surrounding buildings.

The last and most exuberant intersection along this route is **Asan Tol**, historically Kathmandu's principal gathering point and hiring centre for labourers (*kuli* in Nepali and Hindi – hence "coolie"). Until recently Asan was also the old city's main fruit and vegetable market, but authorities now bar such trade in an effort (often futile) to prevent gridlock. Produce is still sold in the streets leading east and north from here, while the trade in spices, homemade balls of soap, candles, oil, incense and other household wares has shifted to Kel Tol and Indrachowk.

The gilt-roofed pagoda at the south side of the square is the temple of **Annapurna**, the goddess of grain and abundance, and a manifestation of Lakshmi, the popular goddess of wealth. A lavish little affair, the pagoda bristles with icons and imagery, and in festival seasons its roof is strung with electric bulbs like a Christmas tree. Annapurna is represented by a silver *kalash*, or vessel.

Mahabaudha and Bangemudha

From Asan, the trade route angles up to Kantipath and the modern city, while an alley heading south leads to **Mahabaudha**. This plain white stupa, stuck in a rather unattractive square, takes its name from the big, harlequin-painted statue of the Buddha in an adjacent shelter, which was undergoing restoration at the time of writing. The stupa is supposed to date back to the sixth-century king Basantdeva. Just east of Mahabaudha, Kathmandu's removal men wait for work: you see them all over town, pushing loads around on rubber-wheeled flatbed carts (*thela*), almost always in bare feet and shorts. Like hill porters, they are usually of the Tamang tribe.

Walk westwards from Asan and you'll first pass the small three-tiered pagoda of **Ugratara**, a goddess believed to cure eyesight problems, before returning to the main Indrachowk–Thamel lane at **Bangemudha**. Just south of this square is the odd shrine to **Vaisya Dev**, the Newar toothache god. Commonly billed as the "Toothache Tree", it's actually the butt end of a log, embedded in the side of a building, and locals believe you can cure toothache by nailing a coin to the log. (Bangemudha – "Crooked Stick" – refers to the legendary tree from which the log was cut.) If toothache sufferers don't have any luck with Vaisya Dev, they can try one of the nearby dentists, who advertise their services with grinning signs.

At the north end of Bangemudha, a priceless fifth-century **Buddha figure** stands all but neglected in a tacky, tiled niche. Continuing north another 100m, a lattice doorway on the right opens to a small niche housing a ninth-century **Uma Maheshwar**, a standard motif depicting Shiva and Parbati as a cosy couple atop Mount Kailas. The private house across the lane boasts fine woodwork and, it's said, Kathmandu's first glass window panes.

Kathesimbhu, Thahiti and Bhagwan Bahal

Kathesimbhu, central Kathmandu's biggest stupa, stands in a square off to the left about 200m north of Bangemudha. The temple is only a modest replica of the more impressive Swayambhu stupa (its name is a contraction of "Kathmandu Swayambhu"), but for those too old or infirm to climb to Swayambhu, rites performed here earn the same merit. According to legend it was built from the earth left over after Swayambhu's construction; Lichhavi-era sculptures roundabout attest to the antiquity of the site, but the stupa itself probably dates to the seventeenth century. Like its namesake, Kathesimbhu has an associated shrine to Harati, the smallpox goddess, located in the northwestern corner of the square. The square doubles as the playground for a local school, so watch out during playtime.

Traffic circulates around another stupa at **Thahiti**, the next square north on the way to Thamel. Because they're continually replastered, stupas never look very old and are hard to date, but this one probably goes back to the fifteenth century. One of Kathmandu's finest old *bahal*, the seventeenth-century **Chusya Bahal** stands about two blocks east of Thahiti. You'll recognize it by the two stone lions out in front and a meticulously carved wooden *torana* (decorative shield) above the doorway, both standard features of a *bahal*. The building is now privately owned and undergoing renovations, but if the door's open you can peek in from the threshhold.

In the tourist zone north of Thahiti, old buildings are few and about the only sights are the goodies in the restaurant windows. The only temple of note in the Thamel vicinity is **Bhagwan Bahal**, a little-used pagoda that lends its name to an area north of Thamel Chowk (a sign in front calls it "Bikrama Sila Mahabihar"). A notable feature of this temple is the collection of kitchen pans and utensils nailed to the front wall, placed there as offerings to the deity.

Mhai Pi

Rarely visited by foreigners, the shrine of **Mhai Pi** sits atop a small, wooded hill twenty to thirty minutes' walk north of Thamel. Local people ascend the hill in early morning to do *puja* and sing hymns at the modest temple, which honours a local manifestation of Ajima, the Newar grandmother goddess. However, these low-key rituals belie this Ajima's importance in the Kathmandu Valley's religious protocol, for tradition has it that the clay used to refinish the mask of Rato Machhendranath and certain other idols must be collected from seven sacred points around Mhai Pi's hill. In addition, a colourful *jaatra* (festival) takes place here around the full moon of Bhadau (August–September).

The shrine is reached by either of two long flights of stairs, a steep one from the west and a newer one with switchbacks from the south. The western approach is reminiscent of Swayambhunath's main staircase, and monkeys in the trees add to the similarity.

Chhetrapati and Nardevi

At the southwestern fringe of Thamel lies boisterous **Chhetrapati**, a six-way intersection of almost perpetual motion. Though the neighbourhood lacks any ancient monuments, it supports a central *pati* (open shelter) resembling an Edwardian bandstand around which religious processions and impromptu musical jamborees are frequent occurrences. During Shiva Raatri in February, sadhus build fires on the platform and light up their chilams, and during Tihaar the iron railings are decorated with oil lamps.

From Chhetrapati it's a straight run south to the Kasthamandap; this street is favoured as an assembly point for protest marches, since the police can't easily secure it. On the right if you're walking south, the **Nardevi Mandir** is easily recognizable by its checkerboard-painted exterior; the lavishly decorated interior enshrines three silver images of Kali. The Nardevi area to the west of the temple has a reputation as an important centre of ayurvedic medicine, with a college, hospital and many doctors' practices and pharmacies.

Kilagal, Bhedasingh and back to Durbar Square

A short walk east of Nardevi, **Kilagal Tol** is marked by a widening in the road with a handsome central *chaitya* and a bas relief of Bhairab. A small passage nearby leads to the large flagstoned piazza of **Itum Bahal**, a remarkable sanctuary from the noise of the modern city. Though many of the buildings surrounding the square have been modernized, the neighbourhood still has a villagey atmosphere, especially at harvest time when grain is spread out to dry. At the southern end of the square, a doorway surmounted by a weathered but still splendid *torana* leads to the fourteenth-century Kichandra Bahal.

Bhedasingh, the next junction east of Kilagal, is the domain of fruit, vegetable and spice sellers, and a few potters who sell their wares from the steps of a squat Mahadev temple erected in memory of King Tribhuwan. The name Bhedasingh, which means "Sheep Horn", is a legacy of the days when livestock was traded here.

From Bedasingh you can return to Durbar Square either via Indrachowk (see above) or by backtracking to Nardevi and heading south from there. The latter route soon re-enters atmospheric eighteenth-century neighbourhoods, with several large *bahal* dating back as far as the fourteenth century tucked away down dark alleys. Keep an eye out on the east side of the street for the **Desha Maru Jhyal** – literally, the "Country Nowhere Window" – a window grille of staggering complexity which, even in a country abounding in outstanding woodwork, is considered unique. Carved from a single block of wood, it obviously predates the house in which it's now set.

South of Durbar Square

Except for the zone from Freak Street across to the GPO (General Post Office), the area south of Durbar Square is relatively untouristed and in parts desperately poor – a fair representation of reality in modern, urban Nepal. The older parts of it are less picturesque and commercial than the quarters north of Durbar Square, but New Road, which bristles and throbs with high-end consumerism, is as lively a street as any in Kathmandu.

Bhimsenthan

A small square southwest of the Kasthamandap, down a lane leading to the Bishnumati River, **Bhimsenthan** is named after one of Nepal's favourite gods. Bhimsen was one of the famous five brothers of the Hindu epic *Mahabharat*, a mortal hero who has been adopted as the patron saint of Newar merchants: you'll see pictures of him in shops everywhere. According to legend, Bhimsen came to Kathmandu as the manservant of a bride from eastern Nepal, who was married off to a farmer who lived on the west bank of the Bishnumati. Unaware of his new servant's identity, the farmer put Bhimsen to work in the fields; Bhimsen proceeded to work miracles with the rice, and the farmer, finally recognizing the god, granted him a plot of land he could reach in three strides. Bhimsen bounded across the river and settled at Bhimsenthan.

The Bhimsen temple here was built in the early eighteenth century, but is frequently renovated to look much newer. The shrine on the upper floor is open only to Hindus, while the ground floor is, fittingly, occupied by shops.

Jaisi Dewal to Tripureswar Marg

Jaisi Dewal, a seventeenth-century Shiva temple, stands in a square several blocks south of the Kasthamandap down a different road. A three-tiered pagoda without much ornamentation, its size alone is impressive. *Linga*-spotters can ogle the eight-foot-high monster at the foot of the temple, which, though only a raw, uncarved stone, has to be the biggest in the kingdom.

A *bahal* just to the southwest of the Jaisi Dewal contains a small **Ram Chandra Mandir**, surrounded by higgledy-piggledy brick buildings and stables. Hanuman, Ram's monkey helper, kneels before the temple. Further to the south, **Tukum Bahal** and its newly restored Swayambhu-style stupa are reached through a passage on the left. The road continues south to **Tripureswar Marg**, an important east–west thoroughfare and one of Kathmandu's strongest entries in the Bangkok lookalike sweepstakes.

Pachali Bhairab

The most interesting part of south Kathmandu begins with **Pachali Bhairab**, an open-air shrine marooned among the city's maintenance facilities south of Tripureswar Marg. To find it, follow the back road to Patan, Kathmandu's sister city just south of the Bagmati River, and bear left at a fork marked by a small park.

After the awfulness of what you've just walked through, you won't believe how peaceful it is here. The tiny gilded idol of Bhairab stands in a sunken sanctuary, dwarfed by

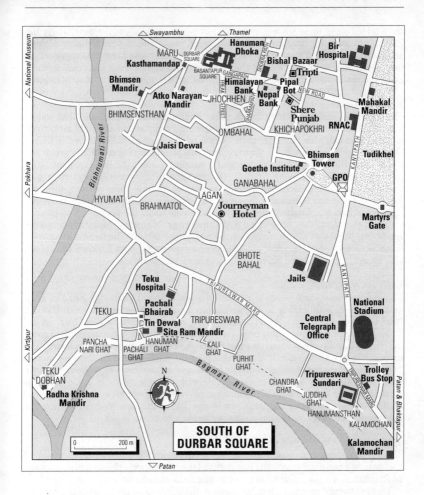

SOUTH OF
DURBAR SQUARE

0   200 m

a huge pipal tree and a life-sized human figure laid out like a pharaoh's casket. The repoussé figure is a **betal**, Bhairab's vehicle and a likeness of death which, in Nepali Hinduism, is believed to protect against death (the old principle of fighting fire with fire). *Betal* normally take the form of miniature skulls or skeletons at temple entrances, so this one is unusual for being so large and fleshed out.

Historically, all treaties were signed with Pachali Bhairab as witness, in the belief that the god would strike dead anyone who broke the agreement. An esoteric parade involving Bhairab and other gods converges here on the fifth day of Dasain before moving on to Durbar Square.

The Bagmati ghats

A path from Pachali Bhairab leads to the **ghats** of the Bagmati River, which stretch as far as the eye can see in either direction. Statues, temples and all manner of artefacts are jumbled along these stone-paved embankments – especially to the west, where the Bishnumati joins the Bagmati – and you could easily spend several hours picking around among them. The entire area is the subject of a proposed restoration project, so maybe someday (probably around the time the rivers run clean) it will enjoy a much-deserved renaissance. For the time being, though, it's in a pretty sorry state of neglect.

PACHALI GHAT

The path forks before reaching the river, but both ways lead to **Pachali Ghat** and its remarkable collection of Hindu and Buddhist statuary. If you take the right fork, you'll enter an area that's like a primer of the Newar pantheon of gods. Statues set in niches along the righthand wall depict (from right to left) Hanuman, Saraswati, the green and white Taras, Bhairab, Ganesh, a *linga/yoni*, a standing Vishnu, the Buddha, Ram, Shiva as sadhu, and a flute-playing Krishna. On the left are many more, concluding with depictions of the ten incarnations (*das avatar*) of Vishnu: fish, tortoise, the boar Baraha, the man-lion Narasingh, the dwarf Vaman, the Brahman Parasuram, the mythical heroes Ram and Krishna, the Buddha, and finally Kalki, the saviour yet to come.

Off to the right, the three-tiered **Lakshmishwar Mahadev Mandir** occupies a crumbling *bahal* that's been taken over by a language school. The temple's construction was sponsored by the late-eighteenth-century queen Rajendra Laskhmi Devi Shah, who apparently considered Shiva (Mahadev) her lord (*ishwar*).

PANCHA NARI GHAT

Continuing downstream (westwards), you pass under an old footbridge and a modern motorable one, both leading to Patan's northern suburb of Sanepa. Beyond, **Pancha Nari Ghat** used to be one of Kathmandu's most important sites for ritual bathing, but no longer, because as you can see the Bagmati has receded far from the embankment: the river is literally shrinking as its water is siphoned off for ever-growing industrial and domestic needs. Consequently the several pilgrims' shelters (*sattal*) and rest houses (*dharmsala*) along here have either fallen into disuse or been converted into residences.

A small **sleeping Vishnu** in this area recalls in miniature the great statue at Budhanilkantha (see p.169). Cremations are infrequently held at the nearby **burning ghats**. Butchers slaughter animals down by the river in the early morning – the buffalo you see here today could turn up in your *momo* tomorrow.

THE CONFLUENCE AREA

The embankment ends just short of **Teku Dobhan**, the confluence (*dobhan*) of Kathmandu's two main rivers, the Bagmati and the Bishnumati. The spot is also known as Chintamani Tirtha – a *tirtha* is a sacred place associated with *nag*, snake spirits.

This confluence area is ancient, and feels it, though none of the temples or buildings is more than a century old. The most prominent is the **Radha Krishna Mandir**, a brick *shikra* built in the 1930s; flute-playing Krishna is the middle of three figures inside. The rest house behind the temple, the **Manandhar Sattal** is named after a wealthy nineteenth-century trader who was forced to retire here after his property was confiscated by the prime minister. The next-door building is an electric crematorium built in the 1970s, but never used.

The Teku area, which extends from here northwards, is best known for being the terminus of a pioneering **ropeway** system built in the 1940s to transport heavy goods, back in the days before the valley was connected to the outside world by road. Truck transport has made the ropeway obsolete, but it's retained as an emergency supply line.

TIN DEWAL

Returning to Pachali Ghat and heading upstream (to the east), you reach the atmospheric **Tin Dewal** by an entrance from the river side. The temple's popular name refers to its three brick *shikra* sharing a common base and ground floor – an unusual combination of Indian and Nepali styles, with some fine brick detailing.

A sign identifies the site by its official name, which is transliterated into English as Bomveer Vikalashora Shibalaya. The complex was erected in 1850 by Bom Bahadur Kunwar, brother of Jang Bahadur Rana, who'd seized power in a bloody coup four years earlier. A *shivalaya* is a shrine containing a *linga*, one of which can be seen behind each of the temple's three lattice doors.

MORE GHATS

A statue of Hanuman the monkey god, wearing his customary gold-trimmed robe and coating of *sindur*, overlooks **Hanuman Ghat**, just to the east. Behind him is a newish and relatively popular **Ram Sita Mandir**.

Things get less interesting further east. **Purhit Ghat** is marked by another small Hanuman statue and a fine old *bahal* now used as a residence. Beyond that there's a 300-metre break in the embankment, as a path makes its way through a semi-permanent shantytown. Its residents – many of them low-caste rubbish-pickers, butchers and sweepers – have moved in as the river has receded, but they still take their chances each monsoon.

The embankment resumes at **Chandra Ghat**, where former pilgrims' quarters have been converted into a school. **Juddha Ghat** is flanked on the north by a long police barracks, and to the south, where the river used to flow, by a shady park. Another large Hanuman statue gives its name to **Hanumansthan**, a site dating to Lichhavi times. An Uma Maheshwar statue and a few old *linga* are also grouped here. Dying people used to be laid out on the angled, tombstone-like slab here so that their feet touched the Bagmati's holy water.

TRIPURESWAR SUNDARI AND KALAMOCHAN MANDIR

From Hanumansthan a path leads away from the river to Tripureswar Marg via the **Tripureswar Sundari**, a derelict quadrangle that has been squatted by a collective of low-caste families. The square's central temple, a massive three-tiered pagoda dedicated to Mahadev (Shiva), was erected in the early nineteenth century by Queen Lalit Tripura Sundari in memory of her husband Rana Bahadur Shah, who was assassinated in one of the period's many episodes of court intrigue.

Continuing north on this path brings you back to the buzzing, sputtering crosstown traffic of Tripureswar Marg. To the southeast lies the marvellously hideous **Kalamochan Mandir**, a study in Rana excess and faded glory. Resembling a grotesque white wedding cake, it was completed in 1852 by the first of the Rana prime ministers, the ruthless Jang Bahadur, who is said to have buried the ashes of those killed in the Kot massacre in its foundation, mafia-style. The gargoyles snarling at its four corners are fitting testaments to his ambition.

New Road, Freak Street and Bhimsen Tower

Rebuilt after a disastrous 1934 earthquake, **New Road** (Juddha Sadak) cuts a swathe of modernity through the old city. Wealthy Nepalis and Indian tourists regard it as a magical duty-free bazaar and swarm its shops for perfume, jewellery, kitchen appliances, consumer electronics and myriad other imported luxury goods. Security guards stand watch in front of department store entrances, well-heeled matrons stroll the pavements with shopping bags, and peasants visiting the capital stand transfixed at the sight of holiday snaps rolling off automatic photo-processing machines. This is what economic prosperity looks like in one of the world's poorest nations: materialistic, elite and very localized.

The statue at the west end of New Road commemorates Prime Minister Juddha Shamsher Rana, who is credited with rebuilding the road (and much of Kathmandu)

SURVIVORS: KATHMANDU'S STREET CHILDREN

The plight of street children, like so many urban problems, is a relatively recent phenomenon in Kathmandu. Ground down by rural poverty, and abetted by new roads and bus services, growing numbers of children are running away to the capital in search of a better life. Some are lured there by men promising high-paying jobs in tourism. These promises often prove false.

The charity Child Workers in Nepal (CWIN) estimates that 5000 children – some as young as five, and invariably male – live or spend most of their time on Kathmandu's streets, with nearly 1000 more joining their ranks each year. They call themselves *khate*, a word that may be translated as "survivor". Most are lone runaways or orphans, though some live with their squatter families. The young beggars who roam Thamel and Durbar Marg, barefoot and clutching dirty cloths for warmth, are perhaps the more conspicuous face of homelessness. Living relatively well off tourist handouts, however, they spurn training programmes and education, and grow up illiterate, unskilled and unemployable – your alms will do more good if given to a charity working with beggars, rather than to the beggars themselves. The majority of street children scrounge a more anonymous and meagre existence as rubbish pickers, selling what salvageable materials they can find. Some get work as casual labourers or *kanchha* (errand boys), but in such a vulnerable position they run a high risk of exploitation. Some pick pockets, or drift into drugs or prostitution. About the best a *khate* can hope for is to find steady work as a labourer, bus conductor or perhaps a riksha wallah.

In a country where 60 percent of the population is living below the poverty line, it's easy to overlook the plight of street kids. Yet the conditions Kathmandu's *khate* endure are far more debilitating than mere rural poverty. Homeless, they sleep in doorways, *pati* (open shelters) or unfinished buildings. Hungry, they often subsist on food thrown out by tourist restaurants, and many suffer from malnutrition. Weakened by toxic chemicals in the rubbish piles, pollution and contaminated water, few are without disease (CWIN reports that 20 percent have tuberculosis). They're regularly beaten by the police, who regard them as bad for tourism, and during visits by foreign delegations they may be thrown in prison or loaded into buses bound for India. And perhaps most damaging of all, they are deprived of the traditionally supportive environment of family and community, and instead must deal with daily rejection.

CWIN, one of several organizations working with Nepali street children, operates a "common room" near its office off Tripureswar Marg to provide food, education, health care and play for children. Volunteers and donations are needed. For more information, contact CWIN (☎282255; *cwin@mos.com.np*).

after the earthquake. **Pipal Bot**, a venerable old tree about midway along the road's south side, provides a natural canopy for newspaper and magazine vendors, and is a favourite gathering place for Kathmandu's intelligentsia and gossipmongers.

Freak Street (Jhochhen Tol), like Thamel, isn't prime sightseeing territory, but it has unique historical associations. For a few foggy years in the late 1960s and early 1970s, this was an important station along the hippy trail through Asia. In those days, before the invention of Thamel, Jhochhen was the place to hangout. Grass and hash were legal and sold openly, and "freaks" had the freedom of the city. It all ended suddenly in 1974, when the present king, then new to the throne, passed a series of stricter immigration and drug laws.

A lane heading east from Freak Street leads to Kathmandu's main fish market and on to **Dharahara**, the tall minaret-like tower overlooking the GPO. Commonly known as **Bhimsen Tower**, it was built in 1832 by the prime minister, Bhimsen Thapa, possibly in imitation of Calcutta's Ochterlony Monument, which had been erected only four years earlier. A story is told that Bhimsen Thapa, sitting astride his horse, leapt off the tower, creating the nearby **Sun Dhara** (Golden Water Tap) where he landed.

THE JAILS

One of the more thought-provoking things you can do while in Kathmandu is to visit Westerners held in the capital's four **jails**. Since families are expected to provide for most of the prisoners' needs, foreigners may be particularly badly off. Most are held in one of the jails south of the GPO (Central, Badragol or Women's); a fourth facility is located in Dilli Bazaar.

At any given time, as many as half a dozen **Westerners** are imprisoned or awaiting trial in Kathmandu, usually on charges of smuggling drugs. Most Westerners' cases never come to trial, since the government basically waits for someone to buy the accused out of jail. **Nepalis** receive the same rough justice, plus they are liable to be imprisoned for political reasons. Although human rights in Nepal have improved since the establishment of democracy, Amnesty International noted in its 1998 annual report that the Nepalese government continues to detain its people by the hundreds for participating in strikes and demonstrations, and occasional reports of torture and ill-treatment by police continue. Some women are imprisoned for having had abortions, which are illegal. Nepal also does not hesitate to imprison **children** when the family breadwinner is jailed and the family is without any other means of support.

Conditions in the jails are grim. For food, inmates receive a half-kilo of "black" (fermented) rice and *daal* each day, plus a few rupees with which to buy vegetables at the prison shop. They sleep on the floor, with up to fifty to a room. No clothes or bedding are provided. Still, the prisoners here can consider themselves lucky they aren't locked away in provincial jails, beyond the normal range of human rights organizations.

Daily **visiting hours** are 10am–4pm (but check: times may vary). You must ask for prisoners by name – check posters around Thamel and Freak Street to find out who's being held where. Inmates appear at the barred doorway of what looks like an animal stable, while visitors must stand behind a chain, so conversations are far from private. Don't go unless you're prepared to offer assistance, such as making telephone calls or passing along messages. And bring something tangible: food, vitamins, toiletries, books, clothes, blankets and cash are all appreciated.

Three of Kathmandu's four **jails** (see above) are located south of here, down a side street off Kantipath – bear right just after the Ministry of Finance.

West of the city: Swayambhu and around

Even if temple-touring makes your eyes glaze over, don't miss **Swayambhu** (or Swayambhunath), perched on a hill 2km west of Thamel. To begin with, it's a great place to get your bearings, geographically and culturally, in your first few days in Nepal: the hill commands a sweeping view of the Kathmandu Valley, and the temple complex, overrun with pilgrims and monkeys, is a real eye-opener.

But there's much more if you dig for it. The ancient stupa is the most profound expression of Buddhist symbolism in Nepal (many *bahal* in the valley contain a replica of it), and the source and central location of the valley's creation myth. There's evidence to believe the hill was used for animist rites even before Buddhism arrived in the valley two thousand years ago. Tantric Buddhists consider it the chief "power point" of the Kathmandu Valley, and one chronicle states that an act of worship here carries thirteen billion times more merit than anywhere else. To call it the "Monkey Temple" (its tourist nickname) is to trivialize it, as if the monkeys were its most noteworthy feature.

Since the Chinese invasion of Tibet in 1959, the area surrounding Swayambhu has become home to hundreds of Tibetans in exile. You'll see them and many other Buddhist pilgrims making a full circuit around the hill, queueing up to spin the gigantic fixed prayer wheels and frequently twirling their own hand-held ones. The place is so steeped in lore and pregnant with detail that you'll never absorb it all in a single visit.

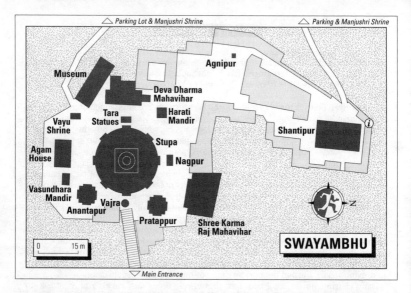

Try going early in the morning at *puja* time, or at night when the red-robed monks pad softly around the dome, murmuring mantras and spinning the prayer wheels. Make a final visit on your last day in Nepal and see how your perceptions of it differ from your initial trip.

Swayambhu's main **festivals** are Buddha Jayanti (April or May) and Losar (in February or March), when pilgrims throng around the stupa and monks splash arcs of saffron paint over it in a lotus-flower pattern. Many also flock here each morning during the month-long Gunla festivities (August or September) to mark the "rain's retreat" with music and offerings to the monks.

A visit to Swayambhu can be turned into a longer hike or bike trip by continuing on to Ichangu Narayan (see p.172).

Getting there

The main entrance is at the eastern foot of the hill and **getting there** is a simple matter on foot or cycle. From Thamel the easiest way is via Chhetrapati, where a small road heads straight towards Swayambhu, passing the *Hotel Vajra* en route. From Freak Street or Durbar Square, take the lane running northwestwards from the Maru Ganesh shrine. Either way, it should take about twenty minutes to walk it. If you're cycling, the local kids will expect you to cough up a few rupees' protection money for your bike. Buses run at irregular intervals between the City Bus Park and the eastern entrance, but they're unlikely to be of much help except for the journey back. A taxi can drive you all the way up to a small car park near the top, just west of the stupa. **Admission** is Rs50.

A paved road circles the base of the hill. Although there are several other ways up the hill, the steep main path from the **eastern entrance**, with its 365 centuries-smoothed steps, is the most dramatic. The **Buddha statues** near the bottom are from the seventeenth century, while a second group further up was donated in the early part of this century. The slates heaped up along the path are *mani* stones, inscribed, in Tibetan script, *Om mani padme hum* ("Hail to the jewel in the lotus"), the ubiquitous Buddhist mantra.

You can get **food** at a few lunch/snack places near the eastern entrance (*Pilgrim's Terrace* is good) and at the far (northwestern) side of the stupa precinct. There are also several Nepali–Tibetan eateries at the southern base of the hill, among them the *Rainbow* and *Iko* cafés, sedate descendants of the hippy hangouts that once thrived here.

The stupa
According to Buddhist scriptures, the Kathmandu Valley was once a snake-infested lake (geologists agree about the lake: see "Natural History" in Contexts). Ninety-one aeons ago, a perfect, radiant lotus flower appeared on the surface of the lake, which the gods proclaimed to be Swayambhu ("Self-created"), the abstract essence of Buddhahood. Manjushri, the *bodhisattva* of knowledge, drew his sword and cut a gorge at Chobar, south of Kathmandu, to drain the lake and allow humans to worship Swayambhu. As the water receded, the lotus settled on top of a hill and Manjushri established a shrine to it, before turning his attention to ridding the valley of snakes* and establishing its first civilization. Another legend tells how, when Manjushri cut his hair at Swayambhu, the hairs that fell on the ground grew into trees, and the lice turned into monkeys.

The apparently simple structure of **the stupa** belies an immensely complex physical representation of Buddhist cosmology, and the purpose of walking round it is to meditate on this. The solid, whitewashed dome symbolizes the womb or creation. Set in niches at the cardinal points, statues of **dhyani** (meditating) **Buddhas** correspond to the four elements (earth, air, fire and water) and a fifth, placed at an angle, to the sky or space. Like the rainbow colours produced by the refraction of pure white light, each represents a different aspect of Buddhahood: the hand positions, colours and "vehicles" (the animal statues below) of each are significant. The *dhyani* Buddhas are the same characters who appear on virtually every *chaitya* around the Kathmandu Valley. At each of the sub-cardinal points sit **female counterparts**, who in tantric Buddhism represent the wisdom aspect that must be united – figuratively speaking – with the compassionate male force to achieve enlightenment.

The gilded cube surmounting the stupa surrounds a thick wooden pillar, which may be considered the phallic complement to the female dome. The **eyes** painted on it are those of the all-seeing Adi-Buddha (primordial Buddha), staring in all four directions. Between the eyes is a curl of hair (*urna*), one of the identifying features of a Buddha, and the thing that looks like a nose is a miraculous light emanating from the *urna* (it can also be interpreted as the Nepali figure "one", conveying the unity of all things). A **spire** of gold disks stacked above the pillar represents the thirteen steps to enlightenment. The *torana*, or gold plaques above the painted eyes, also show the five *dhyani* Buddhas, known collectively as the *panchabuddha*. Finally, the umbrella at the top symbolizes the attainment of enlightenment: some say it contains a bowl filled with precious gems.

Shrines around the stupa
The stupa is surrounded by an incredible array of shrines and votive items, most of which have been donated over the past four centuries by merit-seeking kings and lamas. The bronze sceptre-like object at the top of the steps is a vastly oversized **vajra**,

---

*The Kathmandu Valley harbours a powerful *nag* (snake spirit) cult. During the summer festival of Nag Panchami, emblems are placed above each doorway to appease the *nag*, who are able to release or withhold the life-giving monsoon rains. They're also considered the rightful owners of everything under the earth, which explains why the authorities are loath to allow archeological excavations. Upset a *nag* and you could bring on an earthquake.

a tantric symbol of power and indestructibility; its pedestal is carved with the twelve animals of the Tibetan zodiac. The twin bullet-shaped *shikra* on either side of this, known as **Pratappur** and **Anantapur**, were installed by King Pratap Malla during a seventeenth-century dispute with Tibet, on the advice of an Indian guru. The story of the king's gift, and his subsequent victory over the Tibetans, is engraved on the twin bells in front of the *shikra*.

Moving around clockwise, as is the custom at all stupas, the brick hut to the south of Anantapur is **Vasundhara Mandir**, dedicated to the earth goddess Vasundhara, who's more or less synonymous with Annapurna and Lakshmi, the goddesses of grain and wealth respectively. Further on – past the priests' quarters and a number of *chaitya* – is a small marble-faced shrine to **Vayu**, the Vedic god of wind and storms.

The **museum** behind (daily except Sat 11am–4pm; donation) contains a formidable range of bas-relief statues of gods, Hindu as well as Buddhist, which are beautiful to look at but are so tersely identified that they'll leave you hopelessly confused by the Nepali pantheon. Next door and up a flight of steps, the **Deva Dharma Mahavihar** is a small, uneventful monastery that's open to the public. In front of this, close to the stupa behind protective caging, stand two acclaimed bronze statues of the **White and Green Taras**, princess wives of an eighth-century Tibetan king.

A few paces further on squats a gilt-roofed temple built to appease **Harati**, the small-pox goddess, whom Newars worship as a form of **Ajima**, or Grandmother, a more general protectress of children. A legend relates how Harati was originally an abductor of children: when the people complained to the Buddha, he stole one of Harati's own children, forcing her to realize the pain she caused humans and repent of her ways. Harati/Ajima's shrine is extremely popular, and you'll see queues of mothers with kids in tow, waiting to make offerings. The nineteenth-century idol was carved to replace an earlier one smashed by King Rana Bahadur Shah after his wife died of smallpox. Following rites observed throughout hill Nepal, petitioners toss handfuls of flower petals and rice at the image, sprinkle a bit of consecrated water (*jal*) onto the image and themselves, and finally receive a *tika* from the resident priest.

Agnipur, an insignificant-looking lump on the pavement in the extreme northwest corner of the complex, marked by two tiny lions in front, is a seldom-visited shrine to the Vedic fire god Agni, the relayer of burnt offerings to heaven. **Nagpur**, a bathtub-sized tank at the north point of the stupa, propitiates the valley's snake spirits, and when it's not filled with water you can see the idol (looking more like a draught excluder than a snake) at the bottom. Finally, the **Shree Karma Raj Mahavihar**, an active monastery at the northeast corner of the compound, contains a big Buddha and numerous butter candles, which Tibetan Buddhists light in much the same way Catholics do. You can catch the sonorous chanting of the monks at around 3 or 4pm every day.

Shantipur

A 1500-year-old mystery surrounds **Shantipur**, the otherwise plain, box-like building northwest of the stupa. Shanti Shri, a fifth-century holy man, is supposed to have sealed himself in a vault beneath the temple to meditate, vowing not to emerge until the valley needed him. Commentators write that he subsequently attained a mystic state of immortality, and according to devout believers he's still in there.

King Pratap Malla, who entered the chamber in 1658 to seek magical help in ending a drought, experienced adventures worthy of Indiana Jones. According to scholar Keith Dowman, the king recounted how he entered alone and descended to the second sub-terranean level. In the first room "bats as large as kites or hawks came to kill the light", while in the second room "ghosts, flesh-eating spirits and hungry ghosts came to beg", clutching at anyone who failed to pacify them. Of the third room he said, "if you cannot pacify the snakes by pouring out milk, they chase and bind you. Having pacified them you can walk on their bodies". Finally, Pratap Malla found the saint in an almost skeletal form, and was rewarded with a *nag* rain-making emblem.

Faded frescoes on the walls of the outer sanctum show scenes from the *Swayambhu Purana*, a recent (seventeenth-century) scripture that recounts the story of Manjushri's sword act and other creation myths. Shantipur, also known as Akashpur ("Sky-place"), completes a cycle of shrines to the five elemental spirits: earth, air, fire, water (snakes) and sky.

The Manjushri Shrine

The **Manjushri Shrine**, located on a western spur of the hilltop, comes second only to the main stupa in antiquity – the canopied *chaitya* is reckoned to be 1500 years old. Manjushri, the Buddhist god of wisdom and founder of civilization in the valley, is traditionally depicted by an empty niche in the *chaitya*, but an image of Saraswati, the Hindu goddess of learning, was placed in the niche three hundred years ago, and so the shrine is now on the pilgrimage circuit for Hindus as well. Schoolchildren make a special trip here on Basanta Panchami, in late January or early February, to have their books and pencils blessed.

The rest of the hilltop is littered with other obscure monuments. In addition, several **Tibetan monasteries**, which as a rule welcome visitors, have been built in the area since 1959, and more seem to be going up all the time. Many Westerners study Tibetan Buddhism here (see "The Dharma Scene", p.163).

Natural History Museum

The morbidly amusing **Natural History Museum** (daily except Sat 10am–4pm; Rs10) also lurks nearby, on your right as you follow the road from the car park down the south side of Swayambhu hill. Its jumbled collection of stuffed birds and shrivelled animals in old-fashioned display cases looks like it was cobbled together from the trophy rooms of hoary old Rana hunters. The weirdness is fun for its own sake though, and the specimens might give you an idea of what to look for when you get to the mountains or jungle. (See also "Natural History" in Contexts.)

Bijeshwari

Bijeshwari, along the west bank of the Bishnumati on the way to Swayambhu, used to be Kathmandu's execution ground; Henry Ambrose Oldfield, one of the few Europeans allowed to tour Nepal in the nineteenth century, attended a beheading here and pronounced the place "a regular Golgotha". While Tibetan immigrants have broken the taboo against settling near the cursed ground, a fear of ghosts still endures, as do two important but little-visited temples.

Bijeshwari Bahal, perched at the top of a flight of steps above the river, is the centre of worship of an esoteric Buddhist goddess, Bijeshwari (Lord of Victory), who is also known as Akash (Sky) Jogini and sometimes counted as the fifth of the valley's Bajra Joginis, the wrathful aspects of the tantric Tara goddesses. The inner courtyard is thick with *chaitya* and stone figures, and doors around the perimeter are painted with probing pairs of eyes – a reminder to worshippers that the Buddha is watching, and an injunction to look inward.

Just upstream stands a new cremation pavilion, and beyond that, the Hindu **Shobha Bhagwati Mandir**. Bhagwati is a common Nepali name for the mother goddess, and this idol of her is considered to be among the most powerful manifestations in the valley: early in the morning you might see political candidates, students preparing for exams, or anyone requiring quiet strength coming here to do *puja* to her. According to legend, the sculptor of the Shobha Bhagwati image here carved it with his feet, his hands having been cut off by a jealous king to prevent him from reproducing an earlier masterwork in the king's collection.

The National Museum

Museums may seem redundant in Nepal, given the wealth of heritage displayed out in the open. But theft and modernization are forcing a belated move to safeguard national treasures, many of which can be seen in the **National Museum**, based in an old Rana armoury 1km south of Swayambhu (Mon, Wed, Thurs, Sat & Sun 10.30am–4pm, 3pm in winter; Fri 10.30am–2.30pm; closed Tues; Rs50, Rs50 extra for camera). It's no curatorial coup, and shouldn't be considered a substitute for the valley's countless living exhibits, but you'll come away with a better appreciation of the intertwining of religion, art, myth and history in Nepal.

THE ART BUILDING

Count on spending most of your time in the **art building**, the white plaster one on your left as you enter. The collection of **stone sculptures** showcases an amazing artistic consistency spanning almost two thousand years, from the Lichhavi period through the tantric-influenced Malla dynasties: though motifs and styles change, the common element is a wild diversity of gods and themes inspired by the vast and imaginative canon of Hindu mythology. The images seem to celebrate not only the power of the deities, who loom up in their "universal" forms or act out Herculean labours, but also the divinity that resides within each worshipper. The most recent addition to this exhibit is a life-size statue of King Jaya Varma from 184 AD (derived from the Lichhavi date clearly inscribed on the pedestal). The oldest known statue in Nepal, it was discovered in 1992 during the excavation of a house in Malegaun.

The **metalwork** exhibit pays tribute to a later art form which blossomed under patronage from Tibet. A trio of absolutely stunning fourteenth-century bronzes of the tantric deity Samvara and his consort form the centrepieces of this exhibit. To Western eyes, the tantric *yab yum* (sexual intercourse) motif and its gory attendant imagery (skull cups, daggers, blood) may seem pretty peculiar, yet on an intuitive level it's a powerful celebration of life in all its creativity, weirdness and danger. More accurately, it's meant to be symbolic of the necessary union of wisdom (*prajna*), associated with the female aspect, and compassion (*upaya*), the male.

Other exhibits feature exceptional images, window frames and *torana* (ornate shields mounted over the doors of temples) carved from **wood**, as well as terracotta images and a few Tibetan Buddhist ritual objects. A final room on the ground floor displays a couple of dozen rare **paubha** (Nepali scroll paintings) from the sixteenth century on, and a later series of miniatures exhibiting a marked Rajasthani influence. Upstairs is a desultory collection of Tibetan Buddhist images and more ritual objects.

THE BUDDHIST ART GALLERY

The red brick building at the back of the museum compound houses the **Buddhist Art Gallery**, which gives a patchy overview of artistic traditions from three distinct parts of the counry. The **Tarai room** represents the most ancient and archeologically important area in Nepal – the environs of Lumbini, the Buddha's birthplace – but other than a few artefacts unearthed in recent digs, its contents are rather meagre and short on explanation. The **Kathmandu Valley room** is much better, though it's really only a smattering of items displayed to better effect in the art building and the Patan Museum. Among its treasures is an eighth-century bas relief of the Buddha's birth. Finally, the **Himalayan room** contains *thangka*, bronzes and ritual objects – the same sort of stuff that you see in all the souvenir shops, only authentic.

THE HISTORY BUILDING

The **history building**, a Rana-style mansion on the right as you enter the compound, is aimed mainly at school groups. The downstairs natural history section is a terrible hodgepodge of animal carcasses, bones, dolls (check out the embarrassing specimens donated by your country!) and a moon rock. Upstairs, endless displays of weaponry do little to dispel the stereotype of the Nepalis as a "martial" race (although a pair of leather cannon, captured during a skirmish with Tibet in 1792, is a genuine rarity). More interesting than what's included, perhaps, is what's left out. This is Nepalese history as written by the Shahs and Ranas, who've ruled Nepal for the past two centuries; the country's lower classes and ethnic groups, and any history prior to the Shah conquest, receive hardly a mention.

Eastern neighbourhoods

Old aerial photographs of Kathmandu show the area east of Kantipath dominated by the palaces and residences of the ruling Rana family. The palaces have now been taken over by government ministries, their lawns and gardens filled in by commercial development. You'll probably come here to do errands or window shop – as you do, notice how the old buildings and development patterns have been integrated into the new.

Kesar Mahal

On the corner of Tridevi Marg and Kantipath, **Kesar Mahal**, the residence of Field Marshal Kesar Shamsher Rana (1891–1964), now serves as the compound of the Ministry of Education and Culture. Inside, the **Kesar Library** (Sun–Thurs 10am–5pm, 4pm in winter, Fri 10am–3pm; free) looks like a featured spread in the Nepali edition of *Better Homes and Gardens*. Long shelves of European books, a suit of armour, a stuffed tiger and portraits of all the famous people the field marshal ever shook hands with shed intriguing light on a member of Nepal's pre-1951 ruling elite.

A man who appreciated the good things in life, Kesar Shamsher Rana is said to have laid out the grounds of his mansion as a "dream garden" with areas devoted to each of the six seasons. Trees were planted to ensure that different fruits ripened year-round. Although the garden has gone downhill over the years, the fruit still attracts thousands of **giant fruit bats**, which in the daytime can be seen hanging like handbags from the taller trees here and across the way at the royal palace.

Another sort of colonial landmark, Fora Durbar, the swish R&R compound for American expats, hides behind high brick walls at the southeastern corner of the Tridevi Marg–Kantipath roundabout. Across Kantipath is the oversized secretariat building of the South Asian Association for Regional Cooperation (SAARC).

The Royal Palace and Durbar Marg

An architectural travesty from the 1960s, the creepy new **Royal Palace** looks like something out of Buck Rogers, with echoes of the Mormon Tabernacle. Built in front of an earlier palace dating from the turn of the century, it was inaugurated in 1970 for King (then Crown Prince) Birendra's wedding. Its Nepali name, **Narayanhiti Durbar**, refers to a water tap (*hiti*) east of the main entrance. Guarded by soldiers, the palace is open to the public only on the tenth day of Dasain, when Nepalis queue up to receive *tika* from the king and queen.

Running south from the palace, **Durbar Marg** is the capital's premier commercial address. A single building on one *ropani* of land (about an eighth of an acre) here sold in the early 1990s for the staggering sum of Rs96 million. Land prices in Kathmandu have declined somewhat since then, but there have been no transactions on Durbar Marg recently to confirm this.

Around Rani Pokhri

Rani Pokhri (Queen's Pool), the large square tank east of Asan, is older than it looks. It was built in the seventeenth century by King Pratap Malla to console his queen after the death of their favourite son; the shrine in the middle, which is opened one day a year during the Tihaar festival, is more recent. The pavements around the pool and nearby **Ratna Park** are active centres for small-time trade (including prostitution).

West of Rani Pokhri stands the mouldering edifice of **Durbar High School** (now renamed after the Nepali poet Bhanu Bhakta Acharya), established in 1853 to educate the children of the Rana aristocracy and their hangers-on for jobs in a nascent bureaucracy. To the east rise the turn-of-the-century **Ghanta Ghar** (clocktower) – like Bhimsen Tower, a landmark only in the functional sense – and Kathmandu's two **mosques**. Muslims first settled in Kathmandu as traders five centuries ago, and now represent only a tiny fraction of Nepal's half-million "Musalmans". Nearby Tri-Chandra College, whose students have a reputation for militancy, was a flashpoint of anti-government riots in 1990, when its walls were painted with such slogans as "Do or Die for Democracy".

Around the Tudikhel

Kathmandu's **Tudikhel** is the biggest military parade ground in Nepal. Percival Landon, an early twentieth-century traveller, proclaimed it "level as Lord's", and indeed the expanse seems quixotically flat in so mountainous a country. An institution rooted in Nepal's warring past, the *tudikhel* is a feature of every town of consequence throughout the hills. The king turns out to review occasional displays of pomp and circumstance here (notably during Ghoda Jaatra in March or April), and bronze statues at each corner of the parade ground depict past Rana prime ministers on horseback striking suitably swashbuckling poses. Unfortunately, although Kathmandu's Tudikhel provides a sizable chunk of open space in the middle of the city, it's no green lung: it has few trees, and it actually adds to the city's pollution problem by forcing traffic to bottleneck around it.

On the Kantipath side of Tudikhel stands the **Mahakal Mandir**, whose modern surroundings have in no way diminished the reverence of its worshippers: passing pedestrians and motorists almost always touch a hand to the forehead. Mahakal – to Hindus a form of Bhairab, to Buddhists a defender of *dharma* – is depicted here trampling a corpse (signifying ignorance), holding a skull-cup of blood and wearing what look like glacier goggles. The **Bhadrakali Mandir**, at the southeast corner of Tudikhel, has been turned into a traffic roundabout but remains a popular wedding venue. The nearby **Martyrs' Gate** commemorates the four ringleaders of a failed 1940 attempt to overthrow the Rana regime.

Singha Durbar and Baber Mahal

Undoubtedly the most impressive structure ever raised by the Ranas, **Singha Durbar** dominates the governmental quarter in the southeastern part of the city. Once the biggest building in Asia, the prime ministers' palace of four hundred rooms was built in 1901 by Chandra Shamsher Rana, who employed workers round the clock for two years to complete the pile and fill it with such European extravagances as Carrara marble floors, crystal chandeliers and gilt mirrors, all for the then unconscionable sum of Rs2.5 million. It's said that the entire population of Kathmandu abstained from *daal*, an ingredient in traditional mortar, during the construction. While it was in use as a palace, up to 1500 servants were required to keep the prime minister and his household in the style to which they were accustomed.

The complex was mostly destroyed by fire in 1973, but has since been partially rebuilt. It's suprisingly accessible to the public. During visiting hours (Sun–Thurs 1–4.30pm, Fri 1–3.30pm; free) anyone can go through the sweeping front gate to have a look at the luxurious gardens and the gleaming white colonnaded main wing. (However, due to the threat of Maoist terrorism the government may in time enact stricter security procedures.) Numerous governmental ministries and departments are housed here and in crumbling old mansions nearby.

If you're down this way, make a point of calling in at **Baber Mahal Revisited**, located off a tree-lined street that heads east 300m south of the Singha Durbar gate. Yet another former Rana Prime Minister's palace, it has been gorgeously restored into an exclusive shopping mall. It's a heavenly retreat from the noise outside, where you can grab lunch, window-shop, hang out in the courtyards, and check out before-and-after photographs of temple restorations around the valley.

Dilli Bazaar, Baluwatar and Maharajganj

While Kathmandu's eastern and northeastern neighbourhoods don't have much of scenic interest, they provide insights into contemporary life in the capital.

Crowded **Bagh Bazaar** and **Dilli Bazaar** pretty much sum up one end of the spectrum, with their computer institutes, lawyers' cubbyholes and shops selling office furniture and "suitings and shirtings". ("Fine Art", incidentally, means sign-painting – there's always work for sign-painters in ever-changing Kathmandu.) Dilli Bazaar is also the home of Nepal's budding stock exchange. The other extreme is found further north in the shady lanes of **Bhatbateni**, **Baluwatar** and **Maharajganj**, where old money, new money and foreign money hide in walled compounds, along with embassies, aid organizations and corporate mansions.

Between the two lie the hopeful settlements of a burgeoning middle class, who build their houses one floor at a time, as funds allow, and send their children off in uniforms to "English boarding schools" with names like "Bright Future" and "Little Flower". An "English" education is almost universally viewed as the key to success in the capital.

Hadigaun and Dhum Barahi

Like most ancient cities, Kathmandu was formed by the gradual merging of what were once separate villages. Archeological excavations suggest that **Hadigaun**, now a northeastern suburb, is one of the oldest of Kathmandu's original settlements, though it has now been pretty well absorbed by the metropolis.

Evidence of Hadigaun's age comes from the overgrown shrine of **Dhum Barahi**, located in a schoolyard a further 1km northeastwards (head north out of Hadigaun, and when in doubt always take the right fork). Inside the small brick shelter, which is completely engulfed in the roots of an enormous pipal tree, a whimsical fifth-century image illustrates the tale of Barahi (Vishnu in his incarnation as a boar) rescuing the earth goddess Prithvi from the bottom of the sea. Scholars rave about this sculpture because it dates from a time when there were no established rules for depicting Vishnu as a boar, nor for how a boar should look while fishing the earth from the sea. Locals say the shrine was built at the same time as the nearby Boudha stupa to appease Vishnu, who out of jealousy had caused the stupa's spire to collapse while under construction.

Accommodation

Kathmandu is well stocked with all kinds of **accommodation**. The lists below are just to give you something to go on when you first arrive, but you'll soon discover that there are literally hundreds of other options, and they're almost all perfectly fine.

In the autumn high season the prominent Thamel lodges fill up early, but there'll always be vacancies at smaller places nearby. Book ahead if you can, but if that's not possible (phone numbers and email addresses change often) then just show up. At the budget end of the spectrum, the guest houses are all cheek by jowl, so if one's full you can just try the next.

ROOM PRICE SCALES

Lodging prices change from season to season, so it would be misleading to quote exact prices in a guidebook. Instead, all guest houses and hotels have been price-graded according to the scale below, which is based on the price of the cheapest double room in high season. Codes prefixed by B denote the cost of the cheapest room with attached bathroom, and those prefixed by AC refer to air-conditioned rooms. See p.39 for a fuller explanation.

① Less than Rs140   ⑤ $8–12
   ($2 if quoted in US$)   ⑥ $12–20
② Rs140–200 ($2–3)   ⑦ $20–40
③ Rs200–350 ($3–5)   ⑧ $40–75
④ Rs350–550 ($5–8)   ⑨ Over $75

This section starts off by running through all the budget to midrange options, by area. High-end hotels – those with rooms starting at around $25 or more – are listed at the end. Bear in mind that most places have a range of rooms and prices, some from budget right on up to high-end, but this book categorizes them based on the price of their *cheapest* double room.

One last reminder: **you don't have to stay in Kathmandu**. You can just as easily ask the taxi driver to take you to Pashupatinath (p.154), Boudha (p.160), Patan (p.172) or Bhaktapur (p.199). Before committing to Kathmandu, you owe it to yourself to glance through those sections – or at the very least, the Bhaktapur section – to see what you'd be missing.

Budget to midrange

Budget tourism in Nepal was born on **Freak Street** (Jhochhen Tol) in the late 1960s, and, being the least modern area nowadays, its prices are the lowest. In the 1980s, **Thamel** emerged as a smarter, more respectable alternative both for basic guest houses and more upmarket establishments. In the past few years, with land prices in Thamel going through the roof, guest houses have started springing up in unlikely **off-the-beaten-track** locales, and these may well be your best bet for avoiding the tourist treadmill.

Prices are influenced by supply and demand, and thus fairly fluid. Rates given here are for high season, but in slow times expect discounts of up to 50 percent or more. You should also be able to negotiate a better rate for longer stays. Take all recommendations with a pinch of salt, because maintenance in the budget category is pretty much nonexistent and so anywhere that's clean and good value one year may not be the next.

As a rule, Kathmandu innkeepers are tremendously helpful and good-humoured people. During the winter, when Kathmandu can be quite chilly, guest houses will provide cotton quilts, but only the more upmarket places have heaters. Finally, try to get a room that doesn't overlook the street: Kathmandu's barking dogs, banging pots and clattering shutters are enough to wake the dead.

The telephone code for Kathmandu and the Kathmandu Valley is ☎01.

Freak Street

Freak Street beats Thamel in many ways: it's quieter and less touristy, it's much more authentically Nepali, and it's closer to the sights of the old city (it's actually *part* of the old city). And everything's cheaper in Freak Street – not only lodging but also food, provisions, services and so on.

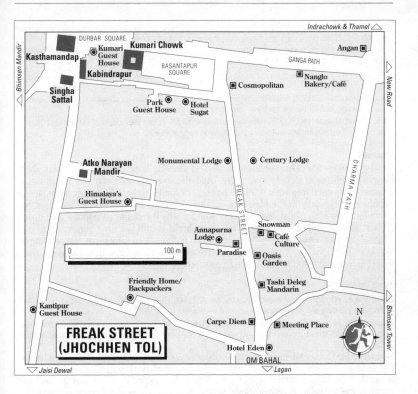

Indrachowk & Thamel △

DURBAR SQUARE

Kumari Chowk

Angan ■

Kasthamandap

Kumari
Guest
House

GANGA PATH

BASANTAPUR
SQUARE

Kabindrapur

Nanglo
Bakery/Café ■

Cosmopolitan ■

Bhimsen Mandir

**Singha
Sattal**

New Road ▷

Park ◉
Guest House

◉ Hotel
Sugat

Atko Narayan
■ **Mandir**

Monumental Lodge ◉

◉ Century Lodge

DHARMA PATH

Himalaya's
Guest House ◉

Snowman

Annapurna
Lodge ◉

■ ■Café
Culture

■

Paradise

■ Oasis
Garden

0 ——— 100 m

Friendly Home/
Backpackers
◉

■ Tashi Deleg
Mandarin

◉ Kantipur
Guest House

Carpe Diem ■

■ Meeting Place

N

Bhimsen Tower ▷

**FREAK STREET
(JHOCHHEN TOL)**

Hotel Eden ◉

OM BAHAL

▽ Jaisi Dewal

▽ Lagan

FREAK STREET

However, Freak Street has fewer of the restaurants, trekking shops, travel agencies and other facilities that make Thamel so convenient. In fact, Freak Street is shrinking – some say dying. Thamel's dominance is only part of the story. The main reason is that Freak Street is strongly Newar, and the Newar system of inheritance is to divide the property among all the sons, which produces very fragmented landholdings and makes redevelopment difficult. But then that's part of what makes Freak Street an interesting place to stay.

INEXPENSIVE

Annapurna Lodge (☎247684). The biggest of the old Freak Street pack, with a large in-house restaurant. ②/B③.

Century Lodge (☎247641). A warren of tiny cubicles with plywood walls, but the building has a nice, lived-in feel and some fine traditional features. (If it's full, try *Pagoda Lodge*, which shares the same courtyard.) ②/B③.

Friendly Home/Backpackers Guest House (☎220171). Kathmandu's longest-running guest house, and invariably packed in high season. Pretty basic, but friendly and social. ②/B②.

Himalaya's Guest House (☎246555, fax 258222). A very spiffy place in a secluded location, with helpful management, a good in-house restaurant and great views from the roof. Some rooms have TVs. ③/B④.

Kantipur Guest House (☎254953). Unpretentious place in a less touristed street, although rooms in this old building are chilly in winter. ①/B②.

Kumari Guest House (☎263498). Staying here is an intensely Nepali experience: it's a traditional, grotty old building with a dynamic *didi* and views right onto Durbar Square. ③.

Monumental Lodge (☎247864). A dive, albeit a traditional one, whose chief recommendation is its low prices. ①/B②.

Hotel Sugat (☎245824; *maryman@mos.com.np*). Great location overlooking Basantapur Square, and good value for money. ③/B③.

MIDRANGE

Hotel Eden (☎252331). Originally conceived as a posh hotel (it has an elevator), it's come down a bit in the world but so have its prices. Good rooftop restaurant. B④.

Park Guest House (☎247487). Like the next-door *Sugat*, it has fine views of Basantapur Square from the rooftop restaurant, but more comfortable rooms. ④/B④.

Thamel

Tourist ghettos like **Thamel** follow a sort of circular logic. Most people stay there because, well, most people stay there. And the more people stay there, the more Thamel turns itself into what it thinks foreigners want it to be, which only increases its popularity. Especially in the high season, there's so much hype, and so little that has anything to do with Nepal, that you may wonder why it remains as popular as it does.

That said, if you've just arrived and your brain is still six time zones out to sea, Thamel can help ease you into things until you feel ready to sally forth. It's painting by numbers here, with every imaginable convenience at your fingertips. But don't think that this is Nepal – you're still in the transit lounge.

INEXPENSIVE

Hotel the Earth, J.P. School Road (☎229039, fax 223194). The place does have a sort of earthy feel. Rooms are pretty good, if you can avoid the street-facing ones. ③/B⑤.

Hotel Earth House, Bhagwan Bahal (☎418197, fax 418436). Located on an interesting (but rapidly modernizing) street. Rooms are only so-so, but the ones in back are quiet. Nice roof terrace. ③/B④–⑤.

Hotel Florid, Thamel Northwest (☎416155; *florid@wlink.com.np*). Located on a quiet cul-de-sac. Rooms range from decent to splendid; small garden area, good service. ③/B③–⑥.

Hotel Horizon, J.P. School Road (☎220904, fax 252999). Very secluded down a quiet side lane, with decent rooms and plenty of rooftop seating. ③/B③–⑥.

Mini Om Guest House, Thamel (☎259036, fax 220143). Basic, but cheap and, considering its central location, reasonably insulated from the Thamel hubbub. ②/B③.

Mom's House Lodge, J.P. School Road (☎252492, fax 260094). The way Thamel guest houses used to be, before everything got so damned fashionable: small, funky, sociable and basic. ③/B③–④.

Mustang Guest House, Thamel Northwest (☎426053; *chitaure@mos.com.np*). Rooms are quite nice for the price, though the place is rather dark on account of being surrounded by taller buildings. ③/B③.

Pheasant Lodge, off J.P. School Road (☎417415). A very cheap and basic outfit tucked away in a quiet yet central cul-de-sac. ②.

Hotel Puska, Thamel South (☎262956, fax 250200). A bit of a monolith, but economical, central, and with a small courtyard restaurant. ③/B④.

Hotel Red Planet, Thamel Northwest (☎432879, fax 427972). Comfortable rooms with balconies, rooftop seating. Located right in the heart of Thamel's nightlife, so you can just stagger home. B④–⑤.

Shangrila Guest House, Jyatha Thamel (☎ & fax 250118). Quiet location. Basic rooms, but plenty of balcony and roof space. ④/B④.

Shiddartha Guest House, Jyatha Thamel (☎227119; *mugi@ccsl.com.np*). Not a great location (across the street from motorcycle-repair shops), but it has a peaceful courtyard shaded by pomelo trees. Rooms are only rudimentary. ③/B④.

Tara Guest House, Thamel South (☎259634). Small but pleasant garden, central location, basic rooms. ③/B④.

Thamel Guest House, Thamel (☎426747). Economical choice if you want to be where the action is. ③/B③.

MIDRANGE

Hotel Blue Diamond, Jyatha Thamel (☎226320, fax 226392). An older upmarket hotel that's now a bit tatty, but reasonably priced (especially for air conditioning). B ④–⑤/AC⑥.

Hotel Garuda, Thamel Northwest (☎416340; *garuda@mos.com.np*). A very professional establishment that has served as Kathmandu headquarters for many a mountaineering expedition. Snug rooms, central location, rooftop seating, small libary, all facilities. B⑤–⑥/AC ⑦.

Kathmandu Guest House, Thamel Northwest (☎413672; *kgh@thamel.mos.com.np*). Thamel's original and best-known guest house is set well back from the noisy street, with efficient management and a gorgeous garden. It's a huge and social place: exciting or pretentious, depending on your outlook. Rooms are always in demand, and booked up well ahead during the high season. ⑤/B⑥/AC ⑦.

Mustang Holiday Inn, Jyatha Thamel (☎249041, fax 249016). A long-standing favourite with a quiet location, well-appointed rooms, garden and roof seating, and professional management. B⑤–⑦.

Potala Guest House, Chhetrapati (☎220467, fax 223256). Central, with a gorgeous little garden. B⑤.

Hotel 7 Corner, Satghumti (☎415588, fax 260456). Nicely furnished rooms with phone and TV, and small sheltered courtyard. Located on a less commercial lane. B⑤, some with AC.

Hotel Shree Tibet, Thamel North (☎419902, fax 425938). Small, Tibetan-themed rooms and a rooftop garden. B⑤–⑦.

Thorong Peak Guest House, Thamel South (☎253458, fax 251008). Friendly, efficient and quiet, with well-appointed rooms (all with phones) and a great roof terrace. B⑤.

Tibet Guest House, Chhetrapati (☎214383). Friendly, and with a really lovely roof garden. ⑤/B⑥/AC ⑦.

Hotel Utse, Jyatha Thamel (☎257614; *utse@wlink.com.np*). Comfortable Tibetan decor, helpful staff, neat as a pin, great restaurant, roof garden. All rooms with phone, some with TV and heat. B⑦.

Thamel fringes

If you're not into the Thamel scene but you still want to be within easy walking distance of Thamel's facilities, one of these places might be what you're looking for.

INEXPENSIVE

Nepal Peace Cottage, Dhalko – see main Kathmandu map (☎248974). Average rooms, rooftop views. Arguably overpriced, but the street is interesting: pilgrims pass through on their way to Swayambhu, and riverside temples are nearby. B⑤.

Kathmandu Peace Guest House, Paknajol – see main Kathmandu map (☎415239, fax 411932). Secluded, friendly place, with a garden, parking and excellent views north and west from rooftop. ③/B④–⑥.

Souvenir Guest House, Bhagwan Bahal – see Thamel map (☎410277). Unusually low-rise building with a small courtyard garden, roof terraces and tidy rooms. ④/B⑤.

Thahity Guest House, Thahiti – see Thamel map (☎226252). Great location if you want equal access to the old city and Thamel. Excellent rooftop terrace, but the rooms are undistinguished and overpriced unless you can haggle a good discount. B⑤.

Tibet Peace Guest House, Paknajol – see main Kathmandu map (☎415026, fax 420165). An extraordinary little haven with great gardens, funky layout, cosy restaurant and good views. ②/B②–⑤.

MIDRANGE

Hotel Blue Horizon, off Tridevi Marg – see Thamel map (☎413028, fax 423855). A quiet, friendly place in a leafy neighbourhood, though rates are a bit high for the calibre of rooms. B⑤–⑥.

International Guest House, Paknajol – see main Kathmandu map (☎410533, fax 416613). Spacious hotel with plenty of outdoor seating on balconies, roof and in garden. Popular with Japanese, hence the restaurant's Japanese menu. ⑤/B⑦.

Pilgrims Hotel, Thamel Northeast – see Thamel map (☎416910; *hotel@pilgrims.mos.com.np*). Spacious rooms, many with balcony. Plenty of seating areas on the roof and in the delightful garden. Good restaurant and small library. ⑤/B⑥–⑦.

Hotel Yeti, Bhagwan Bahal – see Thamel map (☎418436). Very secluded, with plenty of shaded and sunny places to sit – but it's overpriced, so bargain. ④/B⑤.

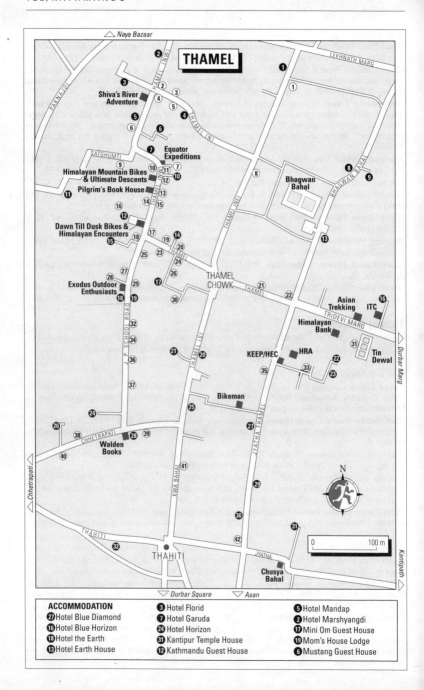

ACCOMMODATION CONTINUED

㉓ Mustang Holiday Inn
⑮ Pheasant Lodge
① Pilgrims Hotel
㉘ Potala Guest House
⑳ Hotel Puska
⑩ Hotel Red Planet
⑪ Hotel 7 Corner
㉒ Shangrila Guest House
㉚ Shiddartha Guest House
④ Hotel Shree Tibet
⑧ Souvenir Guest House
㉕ Tara Guest House
㉜ Thahity Guest House
⑭ Thamel Guest House
㉑ Thorong Peak Guest House
㉖ Tibet Guest House
㉙ Hotel Utse
⑨ Hotel Yeti

RESTAURANTS & BARS

⑧ Annapurna
② Bamboo Club
⑤ B.K.'s Place
㉙ Casablanca
㉒ Da Hua
⑰ La Dolce Vita
㊵ Everest Steak House
㉛ Fire and Ice
㊱ Green Leaves
⑭ G's Terrace
㉓ Helena's
⑱ Hot Breads
⑪ Just Juice & Shakes
㉞ Kathmandu
⑳ K.C.'s
㉝ Kilroy's
㊲ Koto
④ Krua Thai
㊴ Laxmi Narayan's Steak House
㉖ Maya Cocktail Bar
⑦ Micky Pizza Hut
⑫ Nargila
㊳ Nepalese Kitchen
⑮ New Orleans
⑥ Nirmala
③ North Beach Café
⑩ Northfields Café
㉑ Old Vienna/Gourmet
㉟ Omei
⑯ Pilgrim's Feed 'n Read
㉔ Pumpernickel Bakery
⑨ Rum Doodle
㊷ Solu
⑲ Tashi Deleg
① Thamel House
㉕ Third Eye
⑬ Tom and Jerry Pub
㉘ Tripti
㉚ Tunnel Club
㉜ Weizen Bakery
㊶ Yak
㉗ Yin Yang

Off the beaten track

There are many cheap to moderately priced guest houses all over Kathmandu, but most are situated in uninteresting parts of the city to serve the particular needs of Nepali or Indian travellers. Here are a few that are of interest to Western travellers, by virtue of either their location or facilities. But if you're trying to get off the beaten track, again, consider staying in Pashupatinath or one of the other areas described in Chapter Two.

Note that "off the beaten track" does not necessarily mean cheaper or better. In fact, most of the places listed here charge more than they would if they were in the established tourist areas because they run at lower occupancies. (*Peace Guest House* and *Hotel Vajra* are notable exceptions.)

INEXPENSIVE

Journeyman Hotel, Lagan – see South of Durbar Square map (☎253438, fax 226444). Reasonably clean and quiet facilities in a workaday area south of Freak Street. ②/B④.

Peace & Kathmandu View Guest House – off the map, about 1km west of Swayambhu (☎273230). Adventurous location near Tibetan monasteries, good views of Swayambhu, modest garden. The downside is it's overpriced, and they don't have their act together to deal with foreigners. Follow signs from the Ring Road behind Swayambhu. ③.

Peace Guest House, Tahachal – see main Kathmandu map (☎271093). This place outfreaks Freak Street: a longtime hippy haunt that's sort of gone to seed. It's grotty but the management is friendly and there's nothing cheaper. A short but fairly wretched walk to Durbar Square. ①/B①.

Hotel Shrestha, Tahachal – off the main Kathmandu map, about 1km west and south of *Peace Guest House* (☎271336, fax 270528). Quiet and out of the way, this might be a good choice if you've got kids with you. B④.

MIDRANGE

Family Guest House, Lazimpath – see main Kathmandu map (☎420853, fax 410239). A very cosy place that feels like a *pension* or bed-and-breakfast, with lovely rooms and accommodating management. Popular with Japanese for its restaurant and (modest) bath. ⑥.

Hotel Manjushree Swayambhu Peace, Swayambhu – off the map, about 200m to the north of the eastern entrance (☎ & fax 275544). Currently the only accommodation right at Swayambhu. A big, rather stark building, but the rooms are nice enough and there's a meditation hall and great views from the roof. All profits support Tibetan resettlement projects. B⑤.

Sukeyasu Guest House, Battisputali – off the map, about 300m south of the Gaushala intersection (☎472481, fax 410899). A long-established place in a quiet location within walking distance of Pashupatinath, with a well-kept garden and helpful staff. (Compare this with *Shree Shankar Guest House* – see p.160.) ⑤/B ⑥.

Hotel Vajra, Bijeshwari – see main Kathmandu map (☎272719; *vajra@mos.com.np*). Unquestionably the best in its class: beautifully appointed, with a library, theatre and art gallery, and views of Swayambhu from the roof terrace. Definitely worth a splurge. ⑥/B⑦.

Camping

Kathmandu has no developed **campsites**, which is probably just as well since it would be pretty nerve-wracking to drive a camper into the city. If you're determined to camp, try Nagarjun Ban (see p.171), which has zero facilities but a wonderful jungly setting (Rs50–100 per vehicle). Or drive up to Changu Narayan (Chapter Two), Nagarkot, Dhulikhel or Kakani (Chapter Three), all within an hour or so of Kathmandu.

High end

Kathmandu's **high-end hotels** are found mainly in **Durbar Marg**, **Kantipath** and **Lazimpath**, with a few dotted in other parts of the city. If you plan to stay in one, you'll probably already have a booking with free airport pickup. If not, you can book through the Nepal Hotel Association, which operates a reservation desk at the airport.

Most of these hotels will have central heating, air conditioning, top-notch restaurants, TVs in the rooms, and other facilities as mentioned. Tax of 12 to 15 percent (rising with the number of stars) is extra. Except where indicated, refer to the main Kathmandu map for locations.

$25–$75

Hotel Ambassador, Lazimpath (☎410432; *rajan@mos.com.np*). All mod cons at a reasonable price. B⑦/AC⑧.

Kantipur Temple House, Jyatha – see Thamel map (☎250131; *kantipur@tmplhouse.wlink.com.np*). An interesting new tower-like building done in traditional Nepali brick and woodwork. Poor grounds. B⑧–⑨.

Hotel Manaslu, Lazimpath (☎410071, fax 416516). Pleasant oasis with a nice front lawn, popular with aid workers and their visitors. B⑦–⑧.

Hotel Mandap, Thamel Northwest – see Thamel map (☎413321, fax 419734). Comfortable retreat in a popular part of Thamel, which for some people might represent the best of both worlds. AC⑦.

Hotel Marshyangdi, Thamel Northwest – see Thamel map (☎414105, fax 410008). Swanky hotel that sits strangely amidst the budget fracas of Thamel. AC⑧–⑨.

Over $75

Hotel de l'Annapurna, Durbar Marg (☎221711; *apurna@taj.mos.com.np*). Pool, sauna, casino. AC⑨.

Bluestar Hotel, Tripureswar (☎228833; *hotel@bluestar.mos.com.np*). Pool, health club, supermarket. AC⑨.

Dwarika's Kathmandu Village Hotel, Battisputali – off the main Kathmandu map, near Pashupatinath (☎470770; *dwarika@mos.com.np*). A hidden gem: this is without a doubt the most beautifully traditional of Kathmandu's deluxe hotels. B⑨.

Everest Hotel, Naya Baneswar (☎488100; *everest@vishnu.ccsl.com.np*). Big hotel with pool, tennis, gym, disco, casino. AC⑨.

Malla Hotel, Lekhnath Marg (☎418383; *malla@htlgrp.mos.com.np*). Located just north of Thamel. Pool, health club. AC⑨.

Hotel Shangri-la, Lazimpath (☎412999; *hosang@mos.com.np*). Tucked away in embassyland. Pool, health club. AC⑨.

Radisson Hotel Kathmandu, Lazimpath (☎411818; *radkat@mos.com.np*). Kathmandu's newest big-league hotel, with pool, health club, etc. AC⑨.

Soaltee Holiday Inn Crowne Plaza, Tahachal – off the main Kathmandu map, west of Kalimati (☎272555, fax 272205). Kathmandu's biggest hotel, with five restaurants, health club, pool, tennis, casino. AC⑨.

Hotel Yak & Yeti, Durbar Marg (☎248999; *yakti@vishnu.ccsl.com.np*). Kathmandu's most expensive hotel: pool, tennis, opulent restaurants, casino. AC⑨.

Eating

Scores of **restaurants** and **cafés** line the lanes of Kathmandu's tourist quarters, and more spring up after each monsoon. Quite a few carry on in a funky, student-coffee-house style – they're like relics from the early 1970s – but a growing number are going upmarket, and some are even emulating French bistros, American diners and even English pubs.

While **Tibetan**, **Chinese** and **Indian** food have long been taken for granted in Kathmandu, all-purpose **"Continental"** menus predominate nowadays. These cater to Western travellers, and they're all pretty samey, featuring "buff" steaks*, pasta and pizza, and even a few pseudo-Mexican and Greek dishes, plus, of course, ever-popular **pies and cakes**. A few restaurants specialize in **Japanese**, **Thai** and **Korean** dishes, highlighting Nepal's connections to the rest of Asia. Sometimes the food is ingeniously authentic, sometimes you have to use your imagination. Terms like "French onion soup", "enchilada" and "moussaka" get thrown around pretty casually here.

The best news of all is that fine **Nepali** and **Newari** food – not just *daal bhaat,* but also special dishes traditionally only served in private homes – are increasingly available in tourist restaurants as well as in reasonably sanitary local eateries, and are slowly taking their place among the other distinguished regional Indian cuisines.

As with lodgings, **Thamel** has all the newest, trendiest and most professional budget restaurants – though some have become so stylish that they've priced themselves out of the budget category. **Freak Street** is noticeably cheaper for eating, but it's got a smaller and less interesting selection of establishments. Kathmandu's best and most expensive restaurants are generally found in the **Durbar Marg** and **Kantipath** areas and inside the expensive hotels.

Even at the top end, **prices** are reasonable. As a guide, places decribed here as cheap will charge less than Rs150 per person for a full dinner, not including alcohol (proportionately less for breakfast or lunch). Inexpensive restaurants will run to Rs150–250, moderately priced ones Rs250–500, and expensive ones Rs500 and up. Unless you're on a really tight budget, have at least one special meal at one of the posh restaurants to get the full maharaja experience.

Restaurants move or go out of business often, so don't set off for a far-flung place without first verifying it's still there. Phone numbers are given for restaurants where it's advisable to book ahead for dinner. For locations, see the Thamel or Freak Street maps unless noted otherwise.

Not many tourist restaurants are all-**vegetarian**, but quite a few of the Indian ones are, and needless to say, every Nepali restaurant does *daal bhaat* (the Nepali national meal, which is vegetarian unless you specifically request meat). For that matter, almost

---

* A euphemism: actually it's almost always beef, imported from India. It's against the law to slaughter cattle in Nepal, but not to eat beef. It's called "buff" on menus so as not to antago-nize orthodox Hindus.

every restaurant serves at least a few meatless dishes. Even Tibetan places will usually do vegetable *momo*.

It's all too easy to overemphasize food in Kathmandu – it can also be the greatest peril of staying here. More travellers get **sick** in the capital than anywhere else, and eating in "reputable" restaurants doesn't necessarily guarantee hygiene. Indeed, Nepali restaurants are arguably safer, since chefs know what they're doing when they prepare Nepali food. Heed the words of caution given in Basics (p.40), and don't be taken in by an apparently clean dining room or shiny cutlery.

Nepali and Newari

Most of the places listed here are geared for tour groups and tend to be on the expensive side, but worth it. At the other extreme are Kathmandu's many dirt-cheap *bhojanalaya*, which advertise themselves with a curtain (usually green) hung over the entrance and are impossible to recommend by name. If you go to one of the expensive places first, you can familiarize yourself with the offerings before taking on the (menuless) *bhojanalaya*.

Most *bhojanalaya* are merely the Newar equivalents of a greasy spoon, but the best ones are fantastic. Ask your innkeeper for suggestions, or try the places north and east of Asan or along the lane from Asan to Chhetrapati. Many tourist restaurants advertise "special Nepali meals", which usually turn out to be rather ordinary *daal bhaat*. See Basics (p.41) for a rundown of Nepali and Newari dishes.

Bhanchha Ghar, Kamaladi – see main Kathmandu map (☎225172). Nepali nouvelle cuisine, featuring such delicacies as wild boar, wild mushroom curry and buckwheat chapatis – truly wonderful. Expensive.

Bhoe Chhen, off Durbar Marg in front of the *Yak & Yeti* – see the main Kathmandu map. Varied and quite good Newari food in a small, traditionally decorated dining room. Moderately priced (but the set menu is expensive).

Las Kus, in the *Kathmandu Guest House*, Thamel North. Does a set meal that provides a good introduction to Newari cuisine. Moderate.

Naachghar, in the *Hotel Yak & Yeti* off Durbar Marg – see main Kathmandu map (☎248999). Topflight Nepali, Indian and Western cooking; set dinner in a palatial setting with nightly culture shows in season. Expensive.

Nepalese Kitchen, Chhetrapati. A serviceable budget restaurant demonstrating that there's more to Nepali cuisine than *daal bhaat*. Outdoor seating, a fireplace and live music some evenings. Inexpensive.

Thamel House, Thamel Northeast (☎410388). A somewhat cheaper version of *Bhanchha Ghar* (above). Great ambience in a lovely old building. Moderate to expensive.

Tibetan and Chinese

Tibetan restaurants offer some of the cheapest tourist food in Kathmandu; cheaper still are the many *momo* kitchens throughout the old city, notably around **Mahabaudha**. Again, see Basics for descriptions of popular Tibetan dishes.

The Tibetan places usually do some Chinese dishes as well. Proper Chinese restaurants tend to be more expensive, especially the better ones in deluxe hotels like the *Malla*.

Da Hua, Bhagwan Bahal. Good all-round Chinese. Inexpensive.

Lhasa, Thamel Northwest, next door to Equator Exhibitions. Excellent Tibetan soups, *momo* and *tongba* (do-it-yourself millet beer). Cheap to inexpensive.

Mountain City, in the *Hotel Malla* on Lekhnath Marg – see main Kathmandu map. Delicious Chinese food; Szechuan a speciality. Moderate.

Nanglo, Ganga Path (northeast of Freak Street). Passable Chinese food. Inexpensive to moderate.

Omei, Jyatha Thamel. Convincing Beijing and Cantonese cuisine on white linen. Moderate.

Solu, Jyatha Thamel. A Sherpa locals' hole-in-the-wall. Cheap.

Tashi Deleg/New Mandarin, Freak Street. Cramped but cosy, and good for both Chinese and Tibetan dishes. Cheap.

Utse, Jyatha Thamel. An old standard, in the hotel of the same name, with reliable and reasonably priced Tibetan and Chinese food. Cheap to inexpensive.

Yak, Kwa Bahal. Good value for standard Tibetan offerings (including butter tea and *tongba*), plus a fair range of Indian dishes. Cheap.

Indian

Perhaps the best measure of the Indian population in Kathmandu is the number of Indian restaurants – they're everywhere. The more expensive ones serve food every bit as good as you'll find in India, and it comes with *ghazal* (see p.132) and five-star service. Even the cheapies (mostly around New Road) do some fine pure vegetarian dishes. Indian cuisine is also summarized in Basics.

Annapurna, Thamel Northeast. Excellent, unpretentious tandoori diner – the real deal. Inexpensive.

Ghar-e-Kebab, Durbar Marg in front of *Hotel de l'Annapurna* – see main Kathmandu map (☎221711). Superlative North Indian food, *ghazal*, strange nightclub interior. Expensive.

Mangalore Coffee House, corner of Jamal and Durbar Marg, near American Express – see main Kathmandu map. Great South Indian vegetarian food in an efficient upstairs canteen – authentic, right down to the toilets. Cheap.

Moti Mahal, Durbar Marg next to *Tansen* (below) – see main Kathmandu map. Tandoori food rivalling that of the expensive places, though the decor isn't as swanky. *Godavari* is a sister all-vegetarian restaurant. Moderate.

Pilgrim's Feed 'n Read, just north of the *Kathmandu Guest House*, Thamel Northwest. Pretty good South Indian and tandoori entrees (also Tibetan food and a good range of sandwiches and burgers for lunch). Inexpensive.

Shere Punjab, off New Road – see South of Durbar Square map. Basic in-and-out Punjabi canteen. Cheap to inexpensive.

Tansen, Durbar Marg – see main Kathmandu map (☎224707). Top-notch tandoori and other Indian dishes served on burnished copper in minimalist surroundings. Expensive.

Third Eye, J.P. School Road (☎260478). The food is overrated – the main reason to come here is for the retro-1970s "Rice Terrace" room in back. Moderate.

Tripti, J.P. School Road. Lively little pure vegetarian place serving north and South Indian fare. Cheap.

Other Asian: Thai and Japanese

Thai food in Kathmandu is good, but expensive. Japanese isn't always expensive, but you get what you pay for. Try miso soup if your stomach's acting up.

Fuji, Kantipath. Good food, beautiful decor. Expensive.

Koto, J.P. School Road and Durbar Marg (☎226025). A full range of Japanese dishes, excellently prepared. Probably the best value for money on the Japanese front. Moderate.

Krua Thai, Thamel Northwest. The food won't astound anyone who's just flown in from Bangkok, but it's tasty and reasonably authentic. Sprawling, multilevel, indoor/outdoor facility. Expensive.

Yin Yang, J.P. School Road (☎425510). Very popular for its combination of authentic Thai food and sophisticated atmosphere. Expensive.

European

Keep telling yourself: this is not what I came to Nepal for… Still, there are times when you feel like you've eaten a lifetime's worth of lentils and you could just murder a pizza. Many of these places serve wine.

Chez Caroline, Baber Mahal Revisited – see main Kathmandu map. A classy French café/patisserie, serving crêpes, quiche, soups and sandwiches for lunch (moderate) and fancier main courses for dinner (expensive).

Fire and Ice, Tridevi Marg. Really good pizza from an authentic pizza oven, plus homemade ice cream and other fancy desserts. Moderate.

G's Terrace, Thamel North. High-cholesterol Bavarian specialities (would you believe *Zwiebelrostbraten*?), popular with Germanics. Moderate.

La Dolce Vita, Thamel. Pretty-close-to-the-mark Italian food in a big restaurant on three floors: choose from the trattoria, bar or rooftop terrace. Moderate.

Micky Pizza Hut, Thamel Northwest. Small dining room, good atmosphere and pretty good thin-crust pizza. Inexpensive.

New Orleans, Thamel Northwest. Improvised but tasty cajun cuisine. Tremendous atmosphere after dark – sort of like an American bar transported to a Nepali courtyard. Moderate.

Old Vienna, Thamel. Schnitzel, goulash, crêpes and other rich, tasty Austrian dishes. Moderate.

Simply Shutters, Baber Mahal Revisited – see main Kathmandu map. Upscale bistro with a *menu du jour*, featuring French and other Continental specialities. Good for a romantic meal. Expensive.

All-rounders

The overwhelming majority of budget restaurants fall into this catch-all category: jacks of all trades and usually masters of none. The following places rise above the ordinary in one way or another.

Casablanca, J.P. School Road. Excellent Italian and Indian food – a handy choice if one of you wants curry and the other doesn't. Very pleasant patio area. Moderately priced.

Cosmopolitan, Freak Street. Tolerable pasta and steaks, good crêpes, hip Freak Street atmosphere. Inexpensive.

Everest Steak House, Chhetrapati. Renowned as the home of Thamel's best steaks. Inexpensive to moderate.

Green Leaves, J.P. School Road. Organic salads are the main attraction; also Indian and some Tibetan dishes. Lovely outdoor seating under a banyan tree and nightly live music. Inexpensive.

Helena's, Thamel. The cake display window here is one of Thamel's most popular tourist sights; the usual menu otherwise. The interior is gloomy, but there's seating outside. Inexpensive.

Kathmandu, J.P. School Road. Continental, Indian and Nepali food, all of it consistently good. Too bad about the atmosphere (or lack thereof). Moderate.

K.C.'s, Thamel. A perennial favourite: cosy surroundings, reliable menu, generous portions. Big on "sizzling" dishes and killer desserts. Moderate.

Kilroy's of Kathmandu, Jyatha Thamel. A gourmet restaurant serving a limited menu of entrees, desserts and drinks in a secluded courtyard. Another good option for a romantic meal. Expensive.

Laxmi Narayan's Steak House, Chhetrapati. Popular for steaks, pasta and pies. Inexpensive to moderate.

Meeting Place, Freak Street. Surprisingly good Indian food, sizzling steaks and Newar and Tibetan snacks in a cosy, neo-hippy setting. Inexpensive.

Nargila, Thamel Northwest. Middle Eastern dishes (falafel, hummus, couscous) in a relaxed atmosphere. Cheap.

Nirmala, Thamel Northwest. Vegetarian restaurant serving tasty meals from a short but varied menu. Inexpensive.

North Beach Café, Thamel North. An eclectic menu of soups, meat dishes, pasta, curries and desserts, and pleasant garden seating, set this place apart. Moderate.

Rum Doodle, Satghumti. Trusty steaks, chicken, vegetarian dishes, pizzas and pasta, salads, desserts and cocktails. Moderate.

Tashi Deleg, Thamel. A cheap and cheerful formica-table kind of place – the food isn't great, but it's reliable and good value. Cheap to inexpensive.

Breakfast, lunch and snack places

You can't beat Kathmandu's cafés for breakfast or lunch on a warm day. Most restaurants have some outdoor seating, but the places listed below stand out. Likewise, there are countless bakeries in Thamel – all "German", and all pretty interchangeable. And just about every restaurant offers set breakfasts, which usually represent great value for money (especially if you like eggs).

Bakery Café, Ganga Path (northeast of Freak Street). Nepali yuppie hangout, serving pizza, *momo*, ice cream, etc. Inexpensive.

B.K.'s Place, Thamel North. Stand-up snack bar serving chips and other takeaway food. Cheap.

Delicatessen Center, Kantipath – see main Kathmandu map. An eye-popping cornucopia of deli meats, cheeses, breads, pastries, salads and fixings. Inexpensive to moderate.

Festive Fare, Makhan Tol – see Durbar Square map. Good Nepali and Newari food with an excellent rooftop view of the Taleju end of Durbar Square. Moderate (though the set menu is expensive).

The Gourmet, Thamel (inside *Old Vienna*). Spotless German deli, serving authentic *wurst* and pâté. Inexpensive.

Hot Breads, Thamel. A bakery/café with big-time people-watching from a terrace overlooking the main Thamel intersection. *Le Bistro*, next door, has the same view and a greater range of food. Inexpensive.

Just Juice & Shakes (aka **JJ's**), Thamel Northwest. Smoothies, shakes and fresh juice, all reliable. Also coffee and pastries. Cheap.

Mike's Breakfast, Naksal – see main Kathmandu map. Absolute bliss for breakfast – garden tables, classical music and spot-on food. Americans' eyes will mist over at the *huevos rancheros*, waffles and fresh coffee. Moderate.

Northfields Café, Thamel Northwest. A somewhat less accomplished Thamel version of *Mike's*. Inexpensive to moderate.

Oasis Garden, Freak Street. Probably the most pleasant breakfast/lunch spot in this area, with indoor and outdoor seating. Cheap to inexpensive.

Pumpernickel Bakery, Thamel. A sort of Mecca for skinflints. Immensely popular for croissant sandwiches and sticky buns, with seating in a pleasant garden out back. Queuing for food is a drag, though. Cheap.

Weizen Bakery, J.P. School Road. A spin-off of *Pumpernickel* – similar offerings, less of a scrum. Cheap to inexpensive.

Desserts

K.C.'s, Helena's, Laxmi Narayan's and many other restaurants listed above produce spectacular confections, some of which actually taste as good as they look. If none of those hits the spot, try one of the following.

Angan, corner of Ganga Path and Shukra Path – see Freak Street map. Divine Indian-style sweets (buy them by the piece), also ice cream. (Other purveyors of fine Indian sweets include *Dudh Sagar* on Kantipath and *Trishna Mithai* on Lazimpath.) Inexpensive.

Delicatessen Center, Kantipath – see main Kathmandu map. Decadent cake and pie slices, pastries, crème brulée, chocolates and ice cream. Inexpensive.

Snowman, Freak Street. Operating continuously since 1968, this is the only one of Freak Street's original pie shops still going, and it's got a kind of cool that doesn't go out of fashion. Superior pies, cakes and crème caramel. Amazingly eclectic tunes. Cheap.

Nightlife and entertainment

For a capital city, Kathmandu is pretty sleepy: most restaurants start putting up their chairs around 9.30pm, and except in a few designated nightclubs, drinking is supposed to stop at 10pm. Given that, you might just decide to retire early and rise early the next morning, when the city is at its best.

However, there are things to do if you're up for them. What follows is an overview of permanent attractions – check the notice boards to find out about special events in the high season.

Bars and nightclubs

Kathmandu's nightlife scene is growing. The area around the *Kathmandu Guest House* has mutated into quite a throbbing little quarter in the evenings, with duelling sound

KATHMANDU'S FESTIVALS

Your chances of coinciding with a festival while in Kathmandu are good, since the capital spends about a month out of every year partying. Those listed here are just the main events; neighbourhood festivals happen all the time. Dates are determined according to the lunar and Nepalese calendars, and vary from year to year – enquire at a tourist office for dates, or consult a Nepalese calendar (*patro*), available in some bookshops.

MAGH (JAN–FEB)

Basanta Panchami The spring festival is marked by a VIP ceremony in Durbar Square on the fifth day after the full moon. Children celebrate Saraswati Puja on the same day at Swayambhu.

FAAGUN (FEB–MARCH)

Losar Tibetan New Year, observed at Swayambhu on the full moon of February, but more significantly at Boudha (see p.160).

Shiva Raatri "Shiva's Night" is celebrated with bonfires in Kathmandu on the new moon of Faagun, but the most interesting observances are at Pashupatinath (see p.154).

Faagun Purnima (Holi) Popular week-long water-splashing festival, reaching a climax on the full moon.

CHAITRA (MARCH–APRIL)

Seto Machhendranath Jaatra A flamboyant four-day chariot procession in which the white mask of Machhendranath is placed in a towering chariot and pulled from Jamal to an area south of Freak Street. The festival starts on the eighth day after the full moon.

Ghora Jaatra Equestrian displays at the Tudikhel.

BAISAAKH (APRIL–MAY)

Nawa Barsa Nepali New Year (April 13 or 14): Kathmandu holds parades, but Bhaktapur's festivities are more exciting (see Chapter Two).

Buddha Jayanti The anniversary of the Buddha's birth, enlightenment and death, celebrated on the day of the full moon at Swayambhu.

SAAUN (JULY–AUG)

Ghanta Karna Demon effigies are burned on street corners throughout the city on the new moon of Saaun.

Nag Panchami A day set aside for the propitiation of snake spirits with offerings and worship on the fifth day after the new moon.

Gaai Jaatra The Cow Festival, marked by processions through the old city, led by garlanded boys costumed as cows, on the day after the full moon.

BHADAU (AUG–SEPT)

Indra Jaatra A week of chariot processions and masked-dance performances held around the full moon of Bhadau (see p.97).

ASHOJ (SEPT–OCT)

Dasain A mammoth ten-day festival celebrated in most parts of Nepal, concluding on the full moon of Ashoj. In Kathmandu, mass sacrifices are held at the Kot courtyard near Durbar Square on the ninth day, Durga Puja, and the king bestows *tika* on all and sundry at the Royal Palace on the last day.

KHATTIK (OCT–NOV)

Tihaar The Festival of Lights, celebrated here (as in most places) with masses of oil lamps throughout the city and five days of special observances. Lakshmi Puja, falling on the full moon of Khattik, is the highlight. Newars celebrate the fourth day as their new year.

systems blaring across the alleyways, noisy bands of revellers looking for action, and the cops and the riksha wallahs waiting outside for closing time.

Bars in Thamel and Freak Street serve up beer, improvised cocktails and music. As with the tourist restaurants, they're more like a Nepali's imagined idea of what a bar must be like than the real thing, but on the whole they're fine for meeting, mixing and prolonging an otherwise short evening. Many have "happy hours" in the early evening, which generally means free popcorn. In the high season, bars often keep serving until the wee hours behind drawn curtains and locked doors. Don't forget to warn your innkeeper if you think you're going to stay out late, or you could get locked out. Reputations rise and fall from season to season, but the establishments listed below appear to be in for the duration.

The Thamel and Freak Street bars attract mainly budget travellers, and a few young Nepali men hoping to hook up with Western women. A handful of fancier **nightclubs** elsewhere in the city attract a more diverse clientele – Nepali men and women, expats, upmarket tourists – and are busiest at weekends. They stay open late, and typically have a cover charge.

Snooker and **pool** are becoming quite popular with young Nepalis. A number of nightspots have tables, which provide congenial common ground for foreigners and Nepalis to mix.

BARS

Bamboo Club, Thamel North. Occasional live music (usually weekends).

Carpe Diem, Freak Street. The downstairs bar section is more like a coffeehouse really, but very social in the high season.

Maya Cocktail Bar, Thamel. Two small bars on two floors, intimate atmosphere.

Rum Doodle Restaurant's "40,000 1/2-Foot Bar", Satghumti. Kathmandu's oldest nightspot (though it wasn't always in this location), cultivating a cluttered *après trek* atmosphere. The story behind the name is a long one (a novel, in fact).

Tom and Jerry Pub, Thamel Northwest. An established and surprisingly bar-like bar.

Tunnel Club, Narsingh Camp. Pool and snooker, relaxed atmosphere and a nice Nepali–Western fusion.

NIGHTCLUBS

Club Dynasty, in the *Dynasty Plaza Hotel Woodland* on Durbar Marg. DJ mixes for 25 and overs.

Moon Sun Disco, Heritage Plaza, Kamaladi (north of *Bhachha Ghar* on the map). Dancing, snooker, video games.

The Underground, Thamel. Dance tunes and throbbing lights.

Culture shows

Music and dance are essential parts of Nepali culture, and perhaps nowhere more so than in Kathmandu, where neighbourhood festivals and parades (not to mention weddings) are an almost daily occurrence. Touring other regions of the country, you'll encounter other, markedly different styles of music and dance, and while it's more fun to see these performances in their native context, it might be worth checking out a **culture show** before you leave the capital to get a sampler of Nepal's folk and performing arts.

Several Thamel restaurants (notably *Green Leaves* and *Nepalese Kitchen*) host free regular folk music performances in the high season. Most of the deluxe hotels do pricey dinner shows. Infrequent cultural evenings are held at the Royal Nepal Academy, off Kamaladi, although they're not well publicized.

The following groups do regularly scheduled shows. Admission is about Rs300; call for times.

Everest Cultural Society, at the *Hotel de l'Annapurna*, Durbar Marg (☎228787). Conventional folk performances, nightly in high season.

Hotel Vajra, Bijeshwari (☎271545). The *Vajra*'s resident Kala Mandapa ensemble does a superb classical Nepali dance and dance-drama programme every Tuesday evening.

New Himalchuli Cultural Group, at a space near the Bluebird Supermarket in Lazimpath (☎415280). Nightly folk performances in high season.

Ghazal

In recent years Kathmandu has been quick to embrace **ghazal**, an Indian popular style of music, as it has so many other cultural imports from south of the border. Troupes tend to work the better Indian restaurants, where they provide dinnertime accompaniment from a platform over to the side somewhere. A typical ensemble consists of amplified tabla, guitar, harmonium and/or synthesizer. The singer, who gets top billing, croons in a plaintive voice. Love is the theme, and the sentimental lyrics – typically in Urdu or Hindi, but increasingly in Nepali – draw from a long tradition going back to the great Persian poets.

To catch a *ghazal* act, try *Hotel Manang* in Thamel Northwest; *Amber, Ghar-e-Kebab* or *Moti Mahal* in Durbar Marg; *Raj Gharana* on Kamaladi; or *Ghoomti* in the Bishal Bazaar on New Road.

Theatre, cinema and other performances

Outside the tourist arena, scheduled performances of the arts are rare, but that's hardly surprising considering how much goes on all the time in public.

Despite stiff competition from satellite TV, Kathmandu's several **cinemas**, showing the latest Indian blockbusters in Hindi, are still popular. The easiest ones to get to are the Jai Nepal Chitra Ghar, one block east of the Royal Palace entrance, and the Bishwa Jyoti on Jamal. Showtime is generally noon, 3pm and 6pm daily and tickets cost just pennies.

Some Thamel restaurants show pirated Hollywood **videos** and laser discs to bring in customers. They're often of poor quality, but they're free. For recent English-language releases on a bigger screen (but still video disc), go to Kathmandu Mini Vision in the Kathmandu Plaza building at the east end of Lal Durbar (☎253140).

In the high seasons, the *Kathmandu Guest House* hosts **slide shows** by visiting authors and adventurers. The rafting companies do their own promotional shows. The Indigo Gallery sometimes does impromptu slide shows on fine-art subjects – email *indigo@wlink.com.np* to get on their mailing list.

Casinos

Doubtless you didn't come to Nepal to gamble, but a night at one of Kathmandu's **casinos** is a weirdly memorable experience. The casinos are off-limits to Nepalis, and frequented mainly by avid Indians and bored Westerners staying at the affiliated deluxe hotels. Admission is free, and players get complimentary food and drinks. There are casinos at the *Soaltee Holiday Inn Crowne Plaza*, *Hotel de l'Annapurna*, *Yak & Yeti*, and *Everest Hotel*.

Sports and recreation

The National Stadium, at the southern end of Kantipath, hosts frequent **football (soccer)** matches, and is also the headquarters for various martial arts clubs. The *Soaltee Holiday Inn*, *Everest Hotel* and *Yak & Yeti* all have **tennis** courts, open to non-residents for a fee. For **golf**, make for the Royal Nepal Golf Club, near the airport, Nepal's only eighteen-hole course, where hazards include monkeys from nearby Pashupatinath (☎472836; temporary memberships available).

Kathmandu's public **swimming** pool, behind the National Stadium, is open daily (except winter) for morning and afternoon sessions (women only on Sundays), and admission is Rs20. The *Hotel de l'Annapurna*, *Woodlands-Dynasty Plaza* and *Yak & Yeti* all allow non-guests to use their pools for about Rs400.

Shopping

Kathmandu is the obvious place to do some serious **shopping**, especially if it's your last stop before leaving the country. For an overview of handicrafts available in Nepal, see

Basics. Just about all of them are sold in or around Kathmandu. Usually items will be cheaper where they're actually made, but keen competition keeps prices low in the capital. The majority of wool, metal, wood and "Tibetan" items are made in the valley anyway.

Traditional souvenirs and curios

If you're in the market for a **khukuri** knife, you won't have to go far: street vendors and shops sell them wherever there are tourists, and there are several shops in Thamel devoted exclusively to them. Brass sets of **bagh chal**, Nepal's own "tigers and goats" game, are almost as common. Stalls and shops between Indrachowk and Asan sell all manner of household **brassware**. Small shops in Thamel, Chhetrapati and Khichapokhri (south of New Road) stock Nepalese **musical instruments**, while hack minstrels peddle *sarangi* (traditional fiddles) around Thamel and cheap bamboo flutes in Durbar Square.

Vendors in Basantapur Square and Thamel flog vast arrays of **Tibetan-style curios**. It's all attractive stuff, but much of what is claimed to be silver, turquoise, coral or ivory is fake, and virtually none of it is antique. (If it is, have the seller clear it with the Department of Archeology for you.) Gold- and silversmiths in the old city (mainly north and west of Indrachowk) produce fine ethnic **jewellery**; tourist shops sell cheaper but perhaps more wearable ornaments, usually made with white metal. **Gem** sellers are grouped mainly at the east end of New Road. The Pote Bazaar near Indrachowk is the place to go for traditional **glass beads**.

Boxes and embroidered bags of Nepalese **tea**, found in many shops in the tourist areas, make good gifts. **Incense** is also exotically packaged and quite cheap – you can choose from dozens of varieties at street stalls and in shops. You can also pick up many types of **essential oils** and relatively inexpensive saffron and other **spices**.

Certain handicrafts, though widely sold in Kathmandu, are better bought elsewhere in the valley: **metal statuettes** are a Patan speciality, **wood carvings** are best in Bhaktapur, and **papier-mâché masks**, **puppets** and **pottery** are all better represented in Thimi and Bhaktapur. Kathmandu **carpet**-sellers offer some good deals, but don't buy until you've had a chance to see carpets being made in one of the many factories in the Kathmandu Valley or around Pokhara (see p.55 for background on the carpet industry). The Nepal Rugmark Show Room in the Sanchaya Kosh Building on Tridevi Marg is the retail outlet of a charity that supports child-labour-free carpet manufacture.

Countless boutiques sell identical ranges of **Kashmiri**-style handicrafts, predominantly expensive silk carpets and chain-stitch tapestries, and cheaper items made out of papier-mâché, leather, soapstone and sandalwood. The proprietors of these shops are particularly adept at fleecing unwary tourists. Equally unrelated to Nepal are the **Afghan** and **Rajasthani** tribal clothing and mirrored textiles sold in some shops.

Contemporary crafts

Nepali artisans are turning out an ever-expanding range of **contemporary crafts** that adapt traditional materials or motifs to foreign tastes: unusual forms of *dhaka* and other textiles, beautiful handmade paper products, Maithili-style paintings and papier-mâché items, toys, dolls in ethnic dress, ready-made clothes, woollens, leather goods, batiks, scented candles, and ingenious articles out of bamboo and pine needles. The impetus for most of these innovations has come from a few income-generation projects supported by aid organizations, although many products are now widely imitated.

A number of shops in the tourist areas claim or imply that they're outlets for women's skill-development programmes. There's no doubt that they employ women – the question is on what terms. The following shops represent local nonprofit organizations that subscribe to fair-trade principles. For a better selection of outlets, go to Patan's "Fashion Row" (see p.186).

Mahaguthi, Durbar Marg (just north of *Hotel de l'Annapurna*) and Lazimpath. Aided by Oxfam, it supports a home for destitute women; mainly textiles, some jewellery and other gift ideas.

Nepal Woman Crafts, Naksal (near *Mike's Breakfast*). Traditional handmade paper and paper products.

Sana Hastakala, Lazimpath. Woollens, *dhaka* and other textiles, also ceramics, toys and paper.

Clothing and fashion

Thamel and Freak Street are full of shops selling **wool sweaters**, jackets, mittens and socks, which are among Nepal's best bargains – just steer clear of the cheap garments, which fall apart at the seams. Similarly inescapable around here are **kit bags**, **caps** and other fashion items with Tibetanoid rainbow fringes. Hardly fashionable, though many people lap them up, are **T-shirts** and **ready-made clothes**; watch out when you wash them because the cheap fabrics shrink and the colours run. Tailors, usually found inside the same clothing shops, are skilled at machine-**embroidering** designs on clothing.

Shawls and scarfs made of **pashmina**, the Nepali equivalent of cashmere, are cheapest at Indrachowk. **Topi**, the caps that Nepali men wear in much the same way Westerners wear ties, are sold around Asan Tol. You'll find **sari material** in New Road and around Indrachowk. Other traditional textiles are sold in the nonprofit shops (see above).

A number of boutiques in Durbar Marg and Lazimpath sell **designer fashions** with a Nepali flavour, usually in silk or other natural materials. Here are a few:

Chrysalis, Thamel South.

Kee, Chhetrapati.

Mandala, Tindhara (off Durbar Marg).

Nepalese Handloom Silk, J.P. School Road.

Oriental Creations, Makhan Tol.

Rage, Durbar Marg.

Yasmine, Durbar Marg.

Thangka

It's hard to say where to look for bargains on **thangka** and **paubha** (ritual paintings in the Tibetan and Newari styles, repectively), since there are so many standard depictions and levels of quality that any comparison of prices is an apples-and-oranges exercise. To get a grounding in styles and prices without pressure, visit the handicrafts emporium on New Road near the eastern gate. There are many dealers along Tridevi Marg and elsewhere in Thamel. The biggest grouping is in Makhan Tol, north of Durbar Square, but their prices are apt to be inflated. As with carpets, don't commit yourself to a *thangka* until you've shopped around and seen them being painted (Patan and Bhaktapur are good for this).

Other fine art

Some Kathmandu artists are starting to produce more individualistic works, usually in **watercolours**. Shops in the tourist areas sell mostly traditional street scenes and ethnic portraits – quality ranges from naff to impressive.

Kathmandu also has a growing number of fine-art **galleries**, including:

Bamboo Gallery, Panipokhari (opposite the American Embassy). Temporary exhibits generally featuring Nepali subjects.

Indigo Gallery, at *Mike's Breakfast*, Naksal. Hosts temporary shows and has a small permanent display of interesting non-standard *thangka* and *paubha* and other indigenous fine art.

Nepal Association of Fine Arts (NAFA) Gallery, Naksal (daily except Sat 10am–3pm; Rs75). Exhibits of contemporary works by Nepali painters and sculptors.

October Gallery, inside the *Hotel Vajra*, Bijeshwari. Works by Nepali artists.

Siddhartha Gallery, Baber Mahal Revisited. Temporary shows by expats and Nepalis.

THANGKA

A good **thangka** is the product of hundreds or even thousands of hours of painstaking work. A cotton canvas is first stretched across a frame, gessoed and burnished to a smooth surface that will take the finest detail. The desired design is next drawn or traced in pencil using a grid system and precise proportions; there is little room for deviation from accepted styles, for a *thangka* is an expression of religious truths, not an opportunity for artistic licence. Large areas of colour are then blocked in, often by an apprentice, and finally the master painter will take over, breathing life into the figure with lining, stippling, facial features, shading and, finally, the eyes of the main figure. Mineral- and vegetable-based paints are still used for the best paintings, but most nowadays are acrylic. Gold paint is also used, often to excess.

For discussion purposes, *thangka* can be grouped into four genres. The **Wheel of Life**, perhaps the most common, places life and all its delusions inside a circle held firmly in the clutches of red-faced Yama, god of death. The wheel's "rim" depicts the twelve causes of misery, while its "spokes" show the six sensual realms, where dwell the damned, ghosts, animals, humans, demigods and gods. All are caught in Yama's grip – even the gods – and only the Buddha exists outside the wheel. A second standard image is the **Buddha's life story**, tracing the major events of his life starting in the upper right and proceeding clockwise, dominated by an enlightened Buddha in the centre. Many *thangka* feature tantric **deities**, either benign or menacing; Avalokiteshwara, the Lord of Compassion, is a favourite. Such an image serves as a meditation tool in visualization techniques, in which the subject identifies with the deity's godly attributes or recognizes its demonic ones in him or herself. **Mandala**, too, are used in meditation. Symbolically, the subject moves through the three rings of the outer circle (representing the three parts of human nature that must be controlled), through the inner hexagram, towards the figure of the Buddha at the centre.

That's just the tip of the iceberg. A full exposition of *thangka* iconography would fill volumes – ask a dealer or artist to lead you through a few images step by step.

Books

Kathmandu has one of Asia's greatest concentration of English-language **bookshops**, and browsing them is one of the city's main forms of nightlife – many stay open till 10pm. Most are nameless holes-in-the-wall. These are the bigger ones:

Mandala Book Point, Kantipath. Good selection of reference, fiction and maps.

Pilgrim's Book House, Thamel, north of the *Kathmandu Guest House*. Extensive reference sections on all things Nepali: religion, mysticism, health, travel, language, development; also maps, postcards, paper, cassettes, incense, supplies.

Walden Books, Chhetrapati. Good for fiction, both new and used.

Music

There's no lack of **music** around Kathmandu to keep your Walkman humming. Many shops in Thamel sell East-West mood music and cheap rock/pop reissues on tape and CD, as well as some traditional Nepali folk and classical compilations on tape. Countless cassette stalls throughout the city sell Nepali folk and pop, and Indian pop and movie soundtracks. Prices at these stalls will be less than half what the tourist places charge, but finding what you're looking for will be harder if you don't speak (or read) Nepali. See Contexts for information on Nepali music.

Outdoor equipment

You can buy or rent almost any sort of **outdoor equipment** in Kathmandu. Most of the new gear is locally produced and of low quality (see box on p.136). You'll also find some legitimate name-brand stuff made in the Far East, but it's not necessarily of export qual-

---

IS IT REALLY GORE-TEX?

In Kathmandu, as in many Asian cities, authentic name-brand items and counterfeits exist side by side in a disorienting jumble. Except that here the fakes aren't watches or handbags, they're backpacks and sleeping bags.

The tailors of Kathmandu are ingenious – give them any garment and they can copy it. A few years ago they realized there was a business opportunity in making cheap knock-offs of imported trekking gear for the local tourist market. The idea took off and there's now a considerable cottage industry in producing local imitations of backpacks, day-packs, fleece clothing, waterproof outerwear, down sleeping bags and parkas, rain covers, tents…you name it. The designs are loosely based on actual name-brand products, but in a fanciful sort of way, sort of like the relationship between Thamel's pseudo-Western food and the real thing. Logos for Lowe Alpine, North Face, Patagonia and other well-known brands – often pathetically bogus – are brazenly stitched onto the items.

Does it do the job? Yes, but not as well. Things have too little padding or don't hang quite right. The zips are of poor quality, and you can't trust the stitching. The fleece quickly pills, the down loses its loft. The "Gore-Tex" isn't – it's just a generic waterproof layer with no particular breathable properties. Still, it'll probably do for a standard trek in the autumn or spring, and you can't beat the price.

---

ity. For example, many trekking shops sell Korean-made lightweight hiking boots, which are cheaper here than back home, but they're not very durable and they delaminate easily. The imitation Swiss Army knives dull quickly.

A few shops specialize in quality second-hand gear – generally expedition cast-offs (given to guides as tips and promptly resold) and stuff sold by other trekkers. You can pick up climbing hardware, gas stoves, water bottles, glacier glasses, plastic boots, authentic name-brand clothing, packs and so on. Except for the climbing hardware, it will cost at least as much as in your home country.

More expensive gear can be **rented** in Thamel or Freak Street, and for most people this is a better way to go. Figure on about Rs20–25 per day for a good sleeping bag, pack or parka.

For a full trekking equipment checklist, see p.385.

Cameras, film and film processing

With close trading links to the Far East, Kathmandu has relatively cheap prices on consumer gadgets. **Cameras** and accessories cost about half what they do in Europe, and somewhat less than in North America, so if you're planning to buy any gear for your trip you might as well wait till you get here. New Road is the place to go – there are at least a dozen little camera shops in and around the Bishal Bazaar. The selection is patchy and models may be obsolete, but if one shop doesn't have what you're looking for they'll send a guy down the street to get it from another shop that does.

Likewise, **film** is cheaper than in Europe, or about the same price as in North America, and it's available all over. As for film **processing**, plenty of labs in Thamel and on New Road offer same-day service. They usually do an adequate job on prints, but they're unreliable when it comes to slides. Have important photos processed outside Nepal if possible.

Provisions

Stores in Thamel sell just about all the **provisions** you could want – toiletries, batteries, chocolate, bread, cheese, beer and the like. Places like *The Gourmet* and *The Delicatessen Center* are ideal for picnic ingredients. For a wider selection of imported goods, go to the Bhatbhateni Supermarket, north of *Mike's Breakfast*, or the Bluebird Supermarkets in Lazimpath and Tripureswar Marg.

Trekking, rafting and other activities

Most people book organized outdoor activities like trekking, rafting, mountain-biking and wildlife-viewing in Kathmandu because that's where most of the operators and agents are. Or maybe it's the other way around. You don't have to join an organized trip, of course, but here's a rundown of recommended Kathmandu-based companies should you choose to do so. A list of companies that arrange homestays and cultural tours is also included.

Trekking companies

For a full discussion of the pros and cons of trekking with a group versus doing it independently, see Chapter Seven. As explained there, individual budget trekking companies can't be recommended because the quality of their service can vary so much from year to year (or trip to trip). The following more expensive outfits have reputations for maintaining high standards.

Ama Dablam Trekking, Kamal Pokhari (☎415372, fax 416029). Scheduled and custom treks – mostly teahouse routes, plus a few trips to more remote areas and trekking peaks.

Above the Clouds Trekking, Thamel North (☎416909; *atct@wlink.com.np*). Scheduled and custom teahouse treks, remote-area treks (eg, Jaljale Himal), expeditions.

Asian Trekking, Bhagwan Bahal (☎424249; *asianadv@mos.com.np*). A wide range of scheduled treks on standard and remote routes, expedition support treks, also rafting. Affiliated with Asian Airlines Helicopters, so flights are no problem.

Equator Expeditions, Thamel Northwest (☎415782; *equator@mos.com.np*). Runs a mountaineering school in the Khumbu (see p.406).

Guiding and Trekking Expedition Services (GATES), Gairidhara (☎410417; *gates@dendi.mos. com.np*). Specializes in short, custom treks – especially good for treks with children.

Himalaya Expeditions, Kantipath (☎226622; *himalaya@mos.com.np*). Nepal operator for Classic Nepal, Karakoram Experience and others. Scheduled and custom teahouse treks, fully supported treks, trekking peaks, expeditions.

Journeys Mountaineering & Trekking, Baluwatar (☎412898; *journeys@mos.com.np*). Nepal operator for US-based Journeys International. Does scheduled teahouse and remote-area treks such as Mustang, Dolpo and Kanchenjunga.

Sherpa Co-operative Trekking, Durbar Marg (☎224068; *sherpaco@trekk.mos.com.np*). Long-established outfitter that does numerous scheduled treks in standard and remote areas.

River operators

Because of the extra safety considerations when rafting (see Chapter Eight), it's even riskier to recommend budget **river operators**. The ones listed here are more reputable, hence more expensive. All run the most popular rivers (scheduled departures in season) and can organize trips on other rivers on demand.

RAFTING

Equator Expeditions, Thamel Northwest (☎415782; *equator@mos.com.np*). Well-respected, medium-sized rafting operator and kayaking specialist, concentrating on longer multi-day trips. Experienced Western and Nepali guides, good equipment.

Exodus Outdoor Enthusiasts, J.P. School Road (☎251753, fax 259244). An up-and-coming outfit run by very experienced Nepalis, somewhat cheaper than the competition.

Himalayan Encounters, Thamel Northwest, in the forecourt of the *Kathmandu Guest House* (☎417426; *raftnepl@himenco.wlink.com.np*). Nepal's longest-serving rafting operator, with experienced Nepali guides.

Shiva's River Adventure, Thamel Northwest (☎417685, fax 414167). A more affordable Nepali-run outfit that runs some out-of-the-way rivers.

Ultimate Descents, Thamel Northwest (☎419295; *rivers@ultimate.wlink.com.np*). Nepal's biggest river operator, concentrating on longer and more remote rivers and kayaking. Good equipment and safety record, mainly Western guides, relatively expensive.

White Magic, Jyatha (☎253225, *wmagic@wlink.com.np*). A small, well-established operator whose main business is with groups from overseas.

KAYAKING

Equator, Ultimate Descents and Shiva's River Adventure above have **kayaks** available on all their trips. These companies also run four-day **kayak schools** on the Seti River, near Pokhara (see p.421), and several other river operators are expected to follow suit.

Kayak rental is easier in Pokhara. Equator, Ultimate Descents and Drift Nepal (near *Hot Breads* in Thamel; ☎425797; *advnepal@wlink.com.np*) will rent out kayaks at slow times of year for $15–20 a day (including skirt, paddle and helmet).

Mountain-bike tours

The following established companies operate **mountain-bike tours** out of Kathmandu. There may be others by the time you get there. Advice on tours, independent biking, equipment and routes is given in Chapter Nine. For information on renting mountain bikes in Kathmandu, see "Getting around" on p.91.

Bikeman, Jyatha Thamel (☎240633; *srai@mos.com.np*). A small outfit that runs tours of the Kathmandu Valley, Nagarkot, Dhulikhel/Namobuddha, Daman and the Tarai. Older equipment.

Dawn Till Dusk, Thamel Northwest, in the forecourt of the *Kathmandu Guest House* (☎418286; *info@frontier.wlink.com.np*). Kathmandu Valley backroads, Nagarkot, Dhulikhel/Namobuddha, customized off-road itineraries. Good bikes and repair facilities. Sonam, the owner, is an old hand who embodies the spirit of mountain-biking in Nepal.

Himalayan Mountain Bikes, Thamel Northwest (☎419295; *info@hmb.wlink.com.np*). Nepal's original mountain-bike operator, with the most highly developed range of itineraries: Namobuddha, Nagarkot, Daman back route, Kathmandu Valley single tracks, Daman, western Tarai, Lhasa to Kathmandu; also Ladakh, Sikkim, Bhutan. Good equipment and repair shop.

Wildlife package tours

Although most of the **budget lodges** near Chitwan and Bardia national parks are represented by agents in Kathmandu, their packages are not recommended. See the Chitwan and Bardia sections (pp.296 & 331) for full details on doing it yourself.

For **luxury jungle lodges and tented camps**, you *do* need to book ahead. See the relevant listings for Chitwan National Park (p.307), Bardia National Park (p.335), Sukla Phanta Wildlife Reserve (p.342) and Koshi Tappu Wildlife Reserve (p.361).

Victoria Travels (☎226130, fax 224237), with offices in Kamaladi, specializes in **bird-watching** itineraries.

Village tourism

A few Kathmandu-based organizations run **village tourism** and **homestay** programmes (see p.62), in which participants stay in a private home living and eating with the family. This is a great way to connect directly with Nepali culture, and it's of particular interest to foreigners wanting to learn Nepali. Host families are trained in health standards for foreigners.

Cultural Destination Nepal, Dilli Bazaar (☎426996; fax 416417). This is a language institute, so homestays are intended to complement Nepali language study.

Himalayan Explorers Club, Jyatha Thamel (☎259275; *info@hec.org*). Keeps a file of families that accommodate club members in their homes for $3-7 per day (depending on the family), including two meals a day.

Intercultural Training & Research Centre, on a lane leading north of the Tin Dewal on Tridevi Marg (☎412793; *raj@itc.mos.com.np*). Another homestay programme intended mainly for those studying Nepali.

Lama Adventure Treks & Expeditions, Thamel (☎413959; *late@mos.com.np*). Offers a village tourism programme in Thulo Purselgaun, a Tamang settlement southeast of Dhulikhel. A four-night package costs $160–200 per person, depending on group size.

Mahendra Jyoti Homestay Program (book through Asia Travels Service in *Hotel Eurasia*, Thamel South: ☎258327; *asiacomm@wlink.com.np*). Spend the weekend with a family in a village near Dhulikhel for Rs800; you can stay on for Rs150 a day.

Nepal Village Resorts, Naksal (☎430187; *village@nep.mos.com.np*). The pioneer of village tourism in Nepal. Organizes stays in Sirubari, a Gurung village near Pokhara, and is developing other programmes in Junbesi (along the trail to Everest) and in the Annapurna area. A two-night all-in package costs $72–132 per person, depending on group size.

Ballooning
Yes, **ballooning**. Balloon Sunrise Nepal (☎424131) does early-morning flights from points in the Kathmandu Valley. The price is $195 per person ($150 if you're willing to go standby) – an expensive way to get above the smog.

Meditation, yoga and astrology

Not surprisingly, Kathmandu is an important centre for spiritual pursuits. This section sketches out the general possibilities, concentrating on established outfits that cater specifically for Westerners; a scan through the posters in the popular lodges and restaurants will no doubt turn up others. See also the organizations listed in the next section on alternative therapies, as there's a lot of overlap between all these disciplines. You'll find brief introductions to meditation and yoga in "Spiritual Pursuits" (p.63).

Meditation
The **Himalayan Buddhist Meditation Centre** (☎221875; *hbmc@casnov.attmail.com*) conducts regular meditations and introductory *dharma* teachings, hosts a revolving schedule of day-long workshops and courses on Tibetan Buddhist meditation and related Tibetan arts, and offers three- to five-day meditation courses during the autumn and spring (about Rs1000 per day, including food and lodging). The centre's restful headquarters is located in Kamaladi Ganesthan, behind the Ganesh temple in the street running east from Durbar Marg at the clocktower. HBMC is affiliated with Kopan Monastery, north of Boudha (see p.274), and another monastery in Pokhara (see p.282).

Nepal Vipassana Centre (☎250581, fax 224720) runs twelve-day courses on *vipassana* at its centre in Budhanilkantha. These aren't for the frivolous: daily meditation begins at 4.30am, and silence is kept for the duration. To register or pick up a pamphlet on the course, visit the centre's Kathmandu office (Sun–Fri 10am–5.30pm) in the courtyard of Jyoti Bhawan, behind Nabil Bank on Kantipath. All courses are funded by donations.

The **Kathmandu Buddhist Centre** (PO Box 5336, Kathmandu) holds introductory talks on Western Buddhism a few times a week during the tourist seasons – check notice boards for the location. One-day courses in Buddhism, two-day meditation workshops and longer residential courses are offered.

Opportunities also exist for **individual study** under Tibetan lamas – see "Boudha" (p.163).

If you're of the Rajneesh persuasion, you'll be pleased to learn that Kathmandu supports a thriving Osho industry which includes a travel agency, a bimonthly magazine and two meditation centres. The **Asheesh Osho Meditation Centre** (☎271385) in Tahachal conducts one-hour dynamic meditation sessions every morning; these open to all and the fee is a donation. The second venue, **Osho Tapoba... Retreat Centre** (☎353762; PO Box 278, Kathmandu), located in a b... north of Nagarjun Ban, hosts occasional retreats as well as daily medita... courses, and can provide accommodation (③/B⑤) and meals. If you can't to the centres themselves, contact Star Tours and Travels on Tridevi Marg (☎423446; *startour@vishnu.ccsl.com.np*).

Yoga

Patanjali Yoga Centre (☎278437, fax 245231; *saptayoga@hotmail.com*), east of the National Museum in Chhauni, offers classes and residential courses in pure *astanga yoga*, a balance of the eight traditional yoga systems. Contact the centre for information on short meditation/*hatha yoga* sessions, residential study, and month-long yoga programmes based in Pokhara.

Also in Chhauni, **Shakti Healing Yoga Centre** (☎282856, fax 225184) specializes in *hatha* and *raja yoga* under the direction of a female teacher. The centre offers daily morning and evening classes, four- and six-day introductory courses ($60–90) and longer training courses, plus yogic and herbal therapies.

The Yoga Studio (☎417900; *chrissieg@wlink.com.np*) teaches *hatha yoga* in the Iyengar method, a gradual path espoused by B.K.S. Iyengar, a key figure in bringing yoga to the West. The resident instructors teach a regular schedule of classes (Rs300 for one and a half hours), as well as one- and two-week intensive courses in season. The studio is located in Tangal, about a ten-minute bike ride east of Thamel, but it's hard to find – call or check posters for directions.

Ananda Yoga Centre (☎311048; *Ananda@yoga.wlink.com.np*), a nonprofit retreat facility in a lovely setting in the valley 8km west of Kathmandu, caters for both beginners and advanced students of yoga. The centre brings an eclectic approach to *hatha yoga*, *pranayama*, meditation, yogic cleansing, diet and naturopathy. The centre does four-day programmes for $75, including room and board. For more information, contact Star Tours & Travels on Tridevi Marg.

The only real yoga centre in Thamel, **Holistic Yoga Ashrama** (☎419334; PO Box 4783), just south of the *Kathmandu Guest House*, offers daily morning and afternoon yoga/meditation sessions (Rs150 per hour) and various yogic therapies. Simple accommodation is available here and at another branch near Pashupatinath.

The **Himalayan Buddhist Meditation Centre** (see "Meditation" above) also does one-day beginners' workshops on *hatha yoga* (Rs275).

Astrology

It's best not to single out **astrologers** in the Kathmandu area, partly because few of them speak English, but mostly because they all have their own flocks to look after and it wouldn't be fair to rain hordes of foreign horoscope-seekers down on them. Try offering your innkeeper or a guide a commission to take you to his astrologer and to translate for you – you'll get a fascinating glimpse into an extremely important but behind-the-scenes aspect of Newar life (see p.95).

To have a **horoscope** prepared you'll need to make an appointment first, and when you go you'll be expected to provide the exact time and place of birth (if you don't know the time, the astrologer may be able to improvise by reading your palm). It'll take the astrologer up to a week to produce an annual chart, even longer for a full span-of-life chart. You'll need to schedule a separate session for him to interpret it for you and answer any questions you may have. The fee for the entire service may run to Rs500 or more. Whatever you may think of astrology or your particular reading, at the least you'll come away with a beautiful and unique work of art.

Alternative therapies

Many of what we in the West call alternative therapies are, of course, established practice in Nepal. The full range of remedies is actually quite a bit greater than what you see in this section, which, like the previous one, focuses on what's accessible to the average visitor. Again, refer to "Spiritual Pursuits" in Basics for a bit of background on these practices.

Ayurved

For private consultations, try the **Ayurveda Health Home & Research Centre** (☎414843), a group practice located north of Tridevi Marg near *Hotel Blue Horizon*, or the **Holistic Ayurvedic Centre**, operating out of the *Hotel Gaia* (next to *Weizen Bakery*) on J.P. School Road. **Dr Ram Narayan Shah** at the Ayurvedic Hospital in Nardevi, about 200m west of the Nardevi Mandir on the left, will also treat foreigners.

To fill ayurvedic prescriptions, visit the **Gorkha Ayurved Company**, south of Chhetrapati Chowk, or if your Nepali is up to it, try any of the ayurvedic *pharmas* lining the lane running west from the Nardevi Mandir.

Tibetan medicine

Kunphen Tibetan Medical Centre (☎251920), north of Chhetrapati Chowk, is basically a front office for a Tibetan medicine company, whose products it sells, but its services come highly recommended. It's open Monday through Friday, 9am to noon and 2pm to 5 pm. **Kailash Medical & Astro Society** (☎251994), in Dhobichaur (the road leading northwest from Chhetrapati Chowk), offers a similar range of treatments and keeps similar hours.

Massage

A few legitimate **masseurs** practise in Thamel and other tourist/expat areas, though they come and go – again, check the notice boards. Some are Westerners here temporarily on a tourist visa, others are Nepalis who have received professional training at a certified yoga school. Ask to see their credentials. The price of a Nepali massage should be somewhere around Rs200 per hour; other types of massage (shiatsu, Thai, etc) may cost more.

The **Kathmandu Center of Healing** in Maharajganj (☎425946; *kch@mos.com.np*) offers Thai massage and also conducts training courses. It's located off of Lazimpath, on the road to the Russian Embassy. Some of the deluxe hotels have their own in-house masseurs.

Most of the "Yoga & Massage" signs around Thamel have been put there by charlatans attracted by the princely sums tourists will pay to have their bodies rubbed. Some offer "special" massages. **Prostitution** isn't very obvious in places like Thamel because the police keep it in check with periodic raids, but it happens and it seems to be on the increase. The same factors that fuel the sex industry in countries like Thailand (rural poverty, low status of women, tourism) are also present in Nepal. Fortunately, Nepali society doesn't condone it in the open, so Thamel is unlikely to become another Patpong.

Listings

American Express The Amex office is on Jamal (daily except Sat 10am–1pm & 2–5pm). As usual, you can receive mail at the office if you can produce an Amex card or travellers' cheques.

Banks and moneychangers In Thamel, the most convenient bank is Nepal Grindlays, with branches on J.P. School Road (at Hotel the Earth) and Kantipath (both Sun–Thurs 9.45am–3.30pm, Fri 9.45am–12.45pm). Also useful is Himalayan Bank in the Sanchaya Kosh Building on Tridevi Marg, which keeps extra-long hours (daily except Sat 8am–8pm). Many other private banks can be found along Durbar Marg and Kantipath. In the Freak Street area, your best bets are Nepal Bank on New Road (daily 10am–4pm, limited service available 7–10am & 4–7pm) and Himalayan Bank

CENTRAL IMMIGRATION

Central Immigration in Baneswar handles all trekking permit and visa extension applications in Kathmandu. Application hours are Sunday through Thursday, 10am to 2pm (1pm in winter), and Friday 10am to noon. You can retrieve your passport later the same day. The queues can be distressingly long in the busy seasons – especially on either side of the Dasain holiday in October, when the office closes for at least a couple of days. All fees are payable in rupees, and at the time of writing there was no bank anywhere nearby. Roving guys with Polaroid cameras can supply instant passport-sized photos for about Rs150. See p.16 for general information on visa extensions, and p.384 for info specific to trekking permits.

Travelling out to Baneswar and back twice in one day is a drag. By bike it takes about fifteen minutes each way from Thamel, but watch out for the one-way streets. Taking taxis adds up because it'll cost about Rs80 each way, and that's if you can get the driver to use the meter. By tempo, you have to get on at Kantipath near the GPO, and ride until Purano Baneswar. A few agencies in Thamel and along Tridevi Marg will do the whole job for you for an extra fee of anywhere between $3 and $10 (it's negotiable), plus whatever outrageous *bakshish* the immigration wallahs are demanding for back-door service (currently $11) – a lot of money in anybody's book. The whole process involves much less brain damage in Pokhara, so do it there if you can.

This Central Immigration location was chosen in haste in 1998, so there's a good chance that it will change again. The office used to be on Tridevi Marg, just east of Thamel, in a building that the government had seized from an accused drug smuggler. The alleged smuggler challenged the seizure, the case went to the High Court, and the government was ordered to give the building back.

next to the Bishal Bazaar on New Road (Mon–Fri 10am–3pm). Note that Nepal Bank requires you to show your purchase receipt for travellers' cheque transactions. Many registered moneychangers in Thamel and Freak Street keep longer hours (generally daily 8am–8pm).

Credit cards Amex, Visa and Mastercard are accepted at major hotels and many boutiques. Cash advances can be made at the major banks such as Nepal Grindlays and Himalayan Bank (see above) and through Alpine Travel Service (J.P. School Road, Durbar Marg and Bishal Bazaar/New Road). See "Costs, money and banks" in Basics for details on having funds wired to Nepal.

Email Many communication centres and cybercafés provide email and efax services. Most will allow you to receive email – major ones in Thamel include EasyLink Cybercafés (*www.visitnepal.com/easylink*), Global Communications (*glocom@mos.com.np*), ATM Telelinks (*postfax@mos.com.np*) and Cybertrek (*ctic@wilink.com.np*). The Himalayan Explorers Club (see p.138) prints out members' incoming messages for free. Charges at the time of going to press were Rs6–10 per minute for online access, Rs2 per minute to work offline, Rs15 per kilobyte to send messages, and Rs10–15 per page to print out incoming messages. See p.47 for general advice on sending and receiving email in Nepal.

Embassies and consulates It's a good idea to register with your embassy or consulate on arrival in Nepal. If you get into any legal or medical trouble, being registered will expedite assistance, and it's especially important if you go trekking or rafting to ensure prompt evacuation if necessary. HRA and KEEP (see p.384) have registration forms for many countries. For a list of Asian embassies and consulates, see p.149. Western ones include: Australia, Bansbari, on the road to Budhanilkantha (☎371678); Belgium, Durbar Marg (☎228925); Canada, Lazimpath (☎415193); Denmark, Baluwatar (☎413010); Finland, Lazimpath (☎416636); France, Lazimpath (☎412332); Germany, Gyaneswar (☎416832); Israel, Lazimpath (☎411811); Italy, Baluwatar (☎412280); Mexico, Baluwatar (☎412971); Netherlands, Kopundol Heights, Patan (☎522915); New Zealand, Dilli Bazaar (☎412436); Norway, Jawalakhel, Patan (☎538746); Poland, Ganabahal (☎250004); Spain, Battisputali (☎470770); Sweden, Khichapokhri (☎220939); Switzerland, Jawalakhel, Patan (☎538488); UK, Lainchaur (☎411590); US, Panipokhari (☎411179).

Emergencies For an ambulance, call ☎244121. See also "Police" below.

Hospitals, clinics and pharmas Two Western-standard clinics in Kathmandu do inoculations, stool tests and other diagnostics. Unquestionably the best is CIWEC Clinic, off Durbar Marg on the way to the *Yak & Yeti* (Mon–Fri 9am–4pm; ☎228531), which has very proficient Western and Nepali staff, and is a great source of information on all matters pertaining to health in Nepal. The Nepal International Clinic (NIC), a block east of the Royal Palace entrance (daily except Sat 9am–5pm; ☎434642), is also good, and a bit cheaper. Several other clinics in Thamel pretend they're of the same standard, but they're really just glorified pharmacies and often don't know what they're talking about. Medicines can be purchased at *pharma* (pharmacies) everywhere, with or without prescription. Sajha Swastha Sewa, opposite the Mahakal temple on Kantipath, is open 24 hours. CIWEC and NIC can refer you to a specialist if need be. A number of small private hospitals operate in the valley; B&B Hospital (☎531930) has a good reputation among expats, although it's located in Patan, way down at the southern edge of the Ring Road. Of the public facilities, Patan Hospital (☎522266) is reasonably modern but again fairly far from Kathmandu, while Bir Hospital (☎223807) is central but very Third World. If you're in really bad shape, you'll be sent to Bangkok anyway.

Language courses Learn some Nepali and see how the country opens up for you. The ITC School (☎412793; *raj@itc.mos.com.np*), located up a lane north of the Tin Dewal on Tridevi Marg, is professional and has enough teachers to offer scheduling flexibility. Cultural Destination Nepal (☎426996, fax 416417), a smaller outfit in Dilli Bazaar, is also recommended. Both offer short-term one-on-one sessions (about Rs200 per hour), longer intensive courses, and homestays with Nepali families. The Peace Corps (☎410019) or Experiment in International Living (☎414516) might be able to suggest other language teachers. For long-term study opportunities, see "Staying on" in Basics.

Newspapers and magazines Tourist bookshops stock a wide variety of international newspapers and magazines, including the Asian editions of the *International Herald Tribune, USA Today, Time, Newsweek* and the like, and many glossy magazines imported from Europe and North America. The local English-language dailies sell out early at the main bookstores, supermarkets and at pavement vendors on New Road.

Police If you're the victim of a crime, first contact the Tourist Police (☎247041), which is supposed to have an English-speaking officer on duty from 11am to 5pm. They also staff little booths in the centre of Thamel, in Durbar Square and in other tourist areas. Outside regular hours, have a Nepali-speaker call ☎100. You'll need to report thefts to the district police headquarters, which in Kathmandu is on the west side of Durbar Square; ask for the Interpol section. The national police HQ and Interpol office is in Naksal.

Post The Poste Restante section at Kathmandu's GPO (General Post Office) is open Sunday to Thursday, 10.15am to 4pm (winter to 3pm), Friday 10.15am to 2pm. Letters are filed alphabetically in self-serve pigeonholes; it's always a good idea to check under both your first and last initial. You can buy stamps and aerogrammes and have outgoing mail franked at the GPO (Sun–Thurs 7am–5pm, Fri 7am–3pm). However, it's probably more convenient to use one of the book- or postcard shops in the tourist areas, which also sell stamps (small surcharge) and take mail for franking. Some phone/email places will also do this. Shipping agents can take the headache out of sending parcels home. A few that can be recommended are Mountain Packers & Movers, Thamel Northwest (☎424974; *kcmount@wlink.com.np*); Ritual Freight, Thamel (☎251942); and Speedway Cargo, Thamel North (☎410595). Air-freight services include DHL International, Kamaladi and Thamel (☎222358); United Parcel Service, Thamel (☎423300); and Federal Express, Ramshah Path (☎228861). Sending parcels through the Foreign Post Section (Sun–Thurs 10.15am–1pm, Fri 10.15am–12.30pm), around the corner from the GPO on Kantipath, is cheaper but completely exasperating – set aside the whole morning.

Radio and TV Numerous FM radio stations operate in the Kathmandu Valley, including the bilingual Namaste Kathmandu/Hits 100, with a real *masaala* format of country and western, pop, Indian and Nepali tunes, and Kantipur 96.1, with endless chat. Radio Nepal, heard on several medium-wave frequencies, reads English-language news bulletins at 8am and 8pm. Cable and satellite TV serviccs carry CNN, BBC World Service, and English-language movie and sports channels, as well as Nepal TV and plenty of Indian programming. Programme guides are sold in supermarkets.

Telephones and faxes Making phone calls and sending faxes is easy at any of countless communication centres and ISD/STD/IDD places (see p.46). They're generally open daily 8am–11pm, and many accept credit cards. It costs Rs160–180 a minute to call most countries, and the charge for receiving calls ("callback") or making collect calls is Rs5–10 per minute. Shop around, because prices vary. The Central Telegraph Office is open 24 hours a day, seven days a week, but it's inconveniently located on Kantipath, opposite the National Stadium, and queues can be long.

Moving on

Life in Kathmandu is easy – too easy. Get out before you start gathering moss; later, you'll wonder why you stayed so long. What follows is a full rundown on buying tickets, arranging transport and trips, and getting visas. If you can't find what you're looking for here, try the "Listings" above.

Travel within Nepal

For better or worse, most people make Kathmandu their base for travels within Nepal. The country is so centralized, with Kathmandu its transport hub, that a grand tour easily becomes a series of trips out from the capital and back again. This, admittedly, has its advantages: you can make good use of the tourist bus services and choose from the most reputable trekking, rafting and cycle-touring companies. It's also easy to leave luggage with your guest house in Kathmandu, allowing you to travel lightly around the country.

For advice on renting a private **vehicle**, see p.35.

Buses

Various companies operate regular tourist minibuses and buses to Pokhara, Sauraha (for Chitwan National Park) and Nagarkot. The Pokhara and Chitwan services are worth considering if your destination lies anywhere along the routes to those places. Even though tickets cost roughly double the public bus fare, they're still cheap: Rs200–300 to Pokhara, Rs150–200 to Chitwan, Rs100–150 to Nagarkot. Minibuses cost more because they're a bit faster and more comfortable. One company, Greenline Tours (☎253885), operates still more expensive luxury coaches to Pokhara, Chitwan and Dhulikhel. Tickets for tourist services are available through any agent (although not every agent will be able to sell tickets for every bus). Buses depart from Kantipath near Tridevi Marg, usually in the early morning.

Most private **express and night buses** depart from the Naya (New) Bus Park in Gongabu, 3km north of Thamel on the Ring Road. Those serving destinations along the Arniko Highway (such as Dhulikhel, Barhabise, Tatopani and Jiri) leave from the Purano (Old) Bus Park on the east side of the Tudikhel. Buses operated by the quasi-government Sajha service originate at Bhimsen Tower near Freak Street, but you can also catch them at Gongabu as they're heading out of town. You'd have to be a real do-it-yourselfer to go all the way out to Gongabu to buy your own ticket – book through an agent, and consider his commission money well spent. See the box opposite for approximate frequencies and journey times.

Local buses (including buses to all destinations in the Kathmandu Valley) originate at the City Bus Park (also known as Purano – "Old" – Bus Park), east of the Tudikhel. Get on there to have any hope of getting a seat. See the box on p.90 for routes.

Flights

Flight schedules are seasonal and fairly volatile, so consult a travel agent for the latest information. The box on p.146 gives a rough idea of services to the most notable of the thirty-odd airstrips that can be reached directly from Kathmandu (others require plane changes, usually in Pokhara, Nepalganj or Biratnagar).

AIRLINES

Locations, telephone numbers and destinations for the domestic airlines are as follows, though you're better off making bookings through a travel agent.

BUS SERVICES FROM KATHMANDU

See also "Local bus routes", p.90.

TOURIST BUSES

	Frequency (per day)	Time (minimum)
Dhulikhel	1	2hr
Nagarkot	3	2hr
Pokhara	2–12*	6hr
Sauraha/Chitwan	0–3*	6hr

EXPRESS BUSES

	Frequency (day)	Frequency (night)	Time (minimum)
Barhabise	20	–	7hr
Besisahar	5	–	8hr
Bhairawa	8#	10#	8hr
Biratnagar	–	6	14hr
Birganj	2#	10#	8hr
Butwal	5	17	8hr
Dhangadhi	–	2	18hr
Dhankuta	–	1	17hr
Dharan	–	6	14hr
Dhunche	3	–	8hr
Gorkha	10#	–	6hr
Hetauda (via Daman)	1–3#	–	8hr
Hetauda (via Narayanghat)	12	–	7hr
Hile	–	1	18hr
Ilam	–	1	20hr
Jagatpur	2#	–	7hr
Janakpur	2#	7#	11hr
Jiri	4	–	10hr
Kakarbhitta	–	10	16hr
Lumbini	2	2	10hr
Mahendra Nagar	–	3	20hr
Meghauli	2#	–	7hr
Narayanghat	9#	–	5hr
Nepalganj	1#	4	12hr
Pokhara	20#	14#	7hr
Sonauli	7	8	9hr
Tadi Bazaar (Chitwan)	2#	–	6hr
Tansen (Palpa)	2#	1	12hr
Tatopani	1	–	8hr
Taulihawa	1#	1	12hr
Trisuli	9#	–	4hr

*Depending on season.
Sajha service available.

INTERNAL FLIGHTS FROM KATHMANDU

	Frequency	Time	Fare ($)
Bhadrapur	2–3/day	1hr	99
Bhairawa	2–4/day	50min	72
Bharatpur	4/day	25min	55
Biratnagar	10/day	50min*	77
Dhangadhi	1–2/week	1hr 50min	149
Janakpur	1–2/day	35min	55
Lamidanda	1/day	35min	66
Lukla	up to 10/day	40min	83
Meghauli	1/day	30min	72
Mountain flight	4–7/day	1hr	99
Nepalganj	4–5/day	1hr 10min*	99
Phaplu	1–2/day	25min	77
Pokhara	10–20/day	35min	61
Simara	4–5/day	30min	44–50
Tumlingtar	3–4/week	55min	57

* Indirect flights will take longer.

Buddha Air, Hattisar (☎418864). Bhairawa, Biratnagar, Nepalganj, Pokhara.
Cosmic Air, Kamaladi (☎246882). Bhadrapur, Bharatpur, Pokhara, Simara.
Gorkha Airlines, Hattisar (☎435121). Bharatpur, Pokhara, Tumlingtar.
Lumbini Airways, Kamaladi (☎221523). Bhairawa, Bharatpur, Lukla, Phaplu, Pokhara, Simara, Surkhet.
Necon Air, Sinamangal (☎480565). Bhairawa, Biratnagar, Janakpur, Nepalganj, Pokhara.
Royal Nepal Airlines (RNAC), New Road & Kantipath. Flies all routes on map shown on p.34. Tourist sales office (☎226574) handles flights to Bharatpur, Lukla and Pokhara. Domestic sales office (☎223453) handles all other internal flights.
Yeti Airways, Lazimpath (☎421215). Lamidanda, Lukla, Phaplu, Pokhara, Simara, Tumlingtar.

HELICOPTER SERVICES
If you find yourself in a helicopter, it will almost certainly be a charter arranged by a trekking agency, but here are the companies' contact details just in case.
Asian Airlines Helicopter, Thamel (☎423273).
Cosmic Air, Kamaladi (☎246882).
Dynasty Aviation, Lazimpath (☎414625).
Fishtail Air, Tikune (☎485186).
Gorkha Airlines, Hattisar (☎435121).
Karnali Air Service, Sinamangal (☎473141).

Leaving Nepal

Overland connections between Nepal and India are well developed, not to say comfortable. Kathmandu is the usual setting-off point, since it's the only place in Nepal to get an Indian visa. For all other countries you'll almost certainly **fly**: see the box opposite for details on recommended travel agents and international airline offices. It's worth shopping around, as even supposedly standard airfares may vary from one agent to the next.

By air

If you're flying out of Nepal, don't forget to **reconfirm** your flight at least 72 hours prior to departure or you may lose your seat. It's best to reconfirm in person, but this can be a hassle (especially with RNAC). A travel agent will do it for you for about Rs100.

The **airport departure tax** is an astronomical Rs1000 (Rs900 if you're flying within South Asia) – you'll have to hand that over on departure so make sure you set aside at least that much in rupees. On top of that, corruption is rife at Tribhuwan Airport, so you may get hit for trumped-up **overweight charges** (ie, *bakshish*) – baggage handlers know you're in a hurry, and they're counting on you not having any small change. Your best line of defence: check in early and don't cash in your rupees till after your bags are gone. If someone makes noises about your bags being overweight, ask to see them being weighed. Most airlines flying out of Kathmandu allow 20kg of checked luggage per person.

Overland to India

If you're travelling on to **India**, you can arrange your transport in one of two ways. The first is to buy a bus ticket to the border and then make your own onward arrangements from there. The second is to book a package deal from a ticket agent that takes you all the way to your first Indian destination.

RECOMMENDED TRAVEL AGENTS

Everest Travel, Kantipath (☎221216).
Jaya Travel, Durbar Marg (☎220282).
Magnificent Travel, Thamel Northeast (☎424865).

Natraj Tours & Travels, in the forecourt of the *Kathmandu Guest House* (☎222906, fax 227372).
President Travels & Tours, Durbar Marg (☎228873; *ptt@mos.com.np*).

INTERNATIONAL AIRLINES

See p.14 for sample air fares between Kathmandu and other Asian cities.

Aeroflot, Kamaladi (☎227399).
Air France, Durbar Marg (☎223339).
Air India, Hattisar (☎415637). Flights from Kathmandu are handled by Indian Airlines (see below).
Austrian Airlines, Kamaladi (☎241470).
Biman Bangladesh, Nag Pokhari (☎434982).
British Airways, Durbar Marg (☎222266).
Cathay Pacific, Kamaladi (☎248944).
China Airlines, Hattisar (☎412778).
China Southwest Airlines, Kamaladi (☎419770).
Delta Airlines, Durbar Marg (☎220759).
Dragon Air, Durbar Marg (☎223502).
Druk-Air, Durbar Marg (☎225166).
Emirates, Kantipath (☎252048).
Gulf Air, Hattisar (☎430456).
Indian Airlines, Hattisar (☎410906).

KLM, Lekhnath Marg (☎410089).
Korean Air, Kantipath (☎252048).
Kuwait Airways, Kantipath (☎249884).
Lufthansa, Durbar Marg (☎223052).
Northwest Airlines, Lekhnath Marg (☎423145).
Pakistan International Airways (PIA), Durbar Marg (☎223102).
Qantas, Durbar Marg (☎220245).
Qatar Airways, Kantipath (☎256579).
Royal Nepal Airlines (RNAC), corner of Kantipath & New Road (☎220757).
SAS, Kopundol, Patan (☎524232).
Singapore Airlines, Durbar Marg (☎220759).
Swissair, Hattisar (☎434607).
Thai, Durbar Marg (☎223565).
Transavia, Kamaladi (☎247215).
TWA, Baneswar (☎491483).

The first way is easy, and as the rest of this section will show, it's cheaper and probably more reliable than the second. Seven **border crossings** between Nepal and India are open to foreigners. The most popular are Sonauli and Birganj, which are served by day buses from Kathmandu. Other border crossings can be reached by night buses, but unless you're in a big hurry you'll probably want to stop at other places en route. See the relevant sections in Chapters Five and Six for details on the various border crossings.

The second way has been known to cause a lot of heartache, especially where reserved train tickets are involved. Given that a typical bus–train package to India involves three different tickets and as many as six companies or agents, the chances of something going wrong are high. Ticket sellers in Kathmandu know that few travellers will come back to complain.

All **bus–train packages** to India involve travelling by public bus to the border at Sonauli, and then by Indian bus to Gorakhpur, the nearest broad-gauge train station to Kathmandu. It's probably worth paying double in Kathmandu to have a confirmed sleeper out of Gorakhpur, since tickets are hard to obtain there, but Kathmandu ticket sellers require at least a week to arrange train tickets and they demand money up front. When you return to pick up your ticket, you may be told that it's being held at the border – and when you get to the border, you may be told it's in Gorakhpur. If the ticket isn't ready when it was promised, demand your money back and take your chances with the ticket scalpers in Gorakhpur. Be particularly careful when booking first-class sleepers, as there's a racket in replacing them with second-class sleepers or first-class seats. Never surrender your receipt to anyone – without it, you've got no proof of what you paid for.

There is some talk of Indian Railways opening up a booking office in Kathmandu, possibly in association with Air India's office in Hattisar (east of Durbar Marg). If it happens, it will render the above warnings unnecessary.

Bus-only deals to Darjeeling, Delhi and a few other Indian cities are less chancey. On the other hand, there's less reason to book an Indian bus so far in advance. At least one company runs a regular **direct bus** to Delhi; other outfits lay on occasional direct services to Goa and such places, but they're overpriced and must be horrendously long journeys.

Just a handful of **companies** package tickets to India from Nepal, and all other agents deal through them. The most reliable appear to be:

Avis Tours & Travels, Thamel (☎411564).
Pagoda Travels & Tours, Basantapur Square (☎252266).
Shikhar Nepal Tours & Travels, Chhetrapati (☎241669).

The Indian visa two-step

The **Indian Embassy** (☎410900) is located northeast of Thamel, off Lazimpath – take a left at *Hotel Ambassador*. Application hours are 9.30am to noon, Monday to Friday (with lots of holidays).

A 15-day **transit visa** can be obtained on the same day. Note, however, that a transit visa is not extendable, and its validity starts on the date of issue (not the date that you enter India). The cost is Rs350.

Applying for an Indian **tourist visa** in Kathmandu has to be one of the world's most convoluted processes – allow *one week* to work your way through it. The time-consuming part is obtaining "clearance" from your home country, which is needed before your visa application can even be considered. Just getting your hands on a clearance form, filling it in and paying the fee will kill the better part of a morning. After waiting a week for the clearance, you spend another morning actually applying for the visa, which you'll finally be able to collect later that day. The Kathmandu embassy issues only six-month and one-year tourist visas. The six-month visa costs Rs2100 for most nationalities (the fee may be more or less depending on what your country charges Indians for visas), plus Rs300 for the clearance telex or fax. Bring a passport-sized photo. Note that a multiple-entry visa costs no more than a single-entry one.

Travelling to Tibet

China's official policy is that foreigners wanting to enter **Tibet** from Nepal must join a **tour**. The tours are expensive – at least $650, and that's staying in budget accommodation. Flying both ways adds another $100 or so. Travel agents arrange the group Chinese visa and Tibet endorsement for an extra $10–80 per person, depending on your nationality (ie, how nice your country has been to China recently). Visa processing normally takes a week unless you pay a rush fee.

The Tibet high **season** is from May to September; monsoon landslides make the overland route less predictable in the latter part of that period, but there's always a way to get through. Tours aren't run between the middle of December and early March – the roads are usually okay, but the operators don't want to risk groups getting stranded in a snowstorm for days without proper facilities. China Southwest Airlines also suspends its twice-weekly flights to Lhasa between late November and early March.

A typical tour **itinerary** is to fly from Kathmandu to Lhasa, spend two days in Lhasa, and then travel overland for five days back to Kathmandu. (Travelling overland to Lhasa is not recommended unless you're already acclimatized to high elevations.) See p.13 for advice on crossing the border. Once in Tibet, it may be possible for your tour operator to have the group visa "split" so that you can carry on travelling independently. Let the operator know that you want to do this before leaving Kathmandu. There will of course be a hefty fee for this service. **Cycle** tours can be arranged.

The Chinese embassy in Kathmandu does not issue visas to individuals. Some travellers have reported **getting into Tibet independently** on a Chinese visa issued in another country, but others have been turned back at the border or the check-in counter, and enforcement of the tour-only policy seems to be getting stricter over time. Check locally to see if the situation has changed.

Only about ten travel agencies operate Tibet tours – book with them directly, not through an agent. Operators include:

Arniko Travel, Baluwatar (☎414594; *arnikotv@ccsl.com.np*).

Explore Nepal Richa Tours & Travels, J.P. School Road near the *Third Eye* (☎423064; *explore@enrtt.mos.com.np*).

Green Hill Tours, Thamel Northwest, just north of the *Kathmandu Guest House* (☎414803, fax 424065).

Shiva Travels, Chhetrapati (☎260356; *shivatrv@arjun.mos.com.np*).

Tibet Travels & Tours, corner of Jyatha Thamel and Tridevi Marg (☎249140; *kalden@tibet.wlink.com.np*).

Visas for other Asian countries

If you're moving on to other parts of Asia, the following embassies and consulates in Kathmandu issue **visas**. Call ahead to find out application times and procedures, as they change often.

Bangladesh, Mahrajganj (☎372266).

China, Baluwatar (☎411740). Visas issued only through travel agents (see "Travelling to Tibet", above).

India, Lainchaur (☎410900). See "The Indian visa two-step", above.

Myanmar (Burma), Chakupat, Patan (☎521788).

Pakistan, Maharajganj (☎374011).

Thailand, Bansbari, north of the Ring Road on the way to Budhanilkantha (☎371410).

CHAPTER TWO

THE KATHMANDU VALLEY

O nce you've experienced Kathmandu, it should come as no surprise that the **Kathmandu Valley** is not the natural paradise it once was. It's the country's economic engine, after all, supporting numerous industries and with a smoggy capital city right in the middle of it. Yet this broad, undulating, fertile basin – so unlike the steep-sided hills that ring it – still displays a unique combination of natural and man-made beauty. Only a few miles outside the capital, traditional brick villages maintain their rural ways, and the countryside shimmers in an undulating patchwork of paddy fields – brown, golden or brilliant green, depending on the season.

But above all, it's the valley's incredible wealth of art and architecture that over-whelms visitors, just as it did the early explorers: "The valley consists of as many tem-ples as there are houses, and as many idols as there are men," gushed William Kirkpatrick, the first Englishman to reach Kathmandu, and generations of travellers since have accurately (if patronizingly) described it as a "living museum". Its geogra-phy is largely spiritual: most of its places are named after gods, and many were liter-ally put on the map by ancient myths. The valley's one-time name, Nepal Mandala, recalls how for millennia its pilgrimage sites have together formed a kind of gigantic meditation tool. If most of this chapter is devoted to temples and holy sites – there are no forts, you'll notice– it's because religion is the best and most fascinating window on Nepali culture.

Until two hundred years ago, this protected bowl *was* Nepal (and for many hill peo-ple outside the valley, it still is). At that time, Kathmandu was only one of three major city-states constantly battling for dominance: **Patan**, just across the Bagmati River, con-trolled the southern part of the valley, while **Bhaktapur** ruled the east. These histori-cal divisions are profoundly ingrained in valley society and live on in distinct religious practices, festivals and even dress. This chapter divides the valley into three sections, as much for practical reasons as historical ones, since roads and transport developed out of the old patterns of settlement.

The sheer density of sights in the valley is phenomenal. Hindu holy places abound: the great pilgrimage complex of **Pashupatinath**, the sleeping Vishnu of **Budhanilkantha**, the sacrificial pit of **Dakshin Kali** and the hilltop temple of **Changu Narayan** are the most outstanding. If Buddhism is your main interest, head for the great stupa of **Boudha**, the centre of Tibetan Buddhist worship and study in Nepal, or the *bahal* of **Patan**, the valley's most Buddhist city. For medieval scenes, try **Kirtipur**, **Bungmati** or, best of all, **Bhaktapur**. For solitude and views, hike up **Shivapuri**, **Jamacho**, **Phulchoki** or any high point on the valley rim.

All of the places described in this chapter are within day-tripping range of Kathmandu, although in several cases you're urged to stay overnight. Some can be treated as stops along the longer, multi-day routes described in the next chapter.

BIKING AND HIKING IN THE VALLEY

Most of the valley's main historic and religious sites are connected to Kathmandu and Patan by radial arteries, which nowadays handle a lot of commercial and commuter traffic. For more enjoyable **cycle touring**, stick to the lateral roads and lesser radial ones. **Hiking** is best in the rural outer fringes of the valley floor and along the valley rim. Here's an index of routes described in later sections. For more ideas and fuller route descriptions, pick up a copy of *Kathmandu Bikes & Hikes* (see "Books" in Contexts).

DAY TRIPS

Shivapuri (p.170). Hike up to the crest of the valley's north rim for views, or ride along the traffic-free roads within the Shivapuri Watershed.

Nagarjun Ban (p.171). Hike or bike to a hilltop stupa and explore sacred caves; on foot, you can descend to Ichangu Narayan and Swayambhunath.

Ichangu Narayan (p.172). A pretty good walk or ride from Swayambhu, with further cycling possibilities beyond.

Kirtipur and beyond (p.189). Good cycling on back roads from Kirtipur to Godavari, via Chobar Gorge, Bungmati and Chapagaun.

Dakshin Kali Road (p.191). A varied ride through the southern valley, taking in several sacred sites.

Champadevi (p.192). Another hike to a high point along the valley rim.

Godavari to Tika Bhairab (p.197). Great cycling country, and you can continue south beyond Tika Bhairab.

Phulchoki (p.198). A trail and a rough, winding road pass through splendid forest to the highest point along the valley rim.

Bishanku Narayan (p.199). An interesting shrine reached by foot or bike from Godavari.

Lakuri Bhanjyang (p.199). This pass is the high point on a long, lovely ride from Lubhu to Panauti, or a shorter loop returning to Godavari and Bishanku Narayan.

Changu Narayan (p.213). Hike or bike up to this ancient temple site; hiking trails also connect to Nagarkot and Sankhu.

LONGER ITINERARIES

Several multi-day hikes and bike trips start (or end) in the Kathmandu Valley. These are described in Chapter Three – see the following sections:

Nagarkot (p.221). Loads of options down from here: hike or bike to Bhaktapur via Changu Narayan or Nala, or connect up with Dhulikhel-area routes via Nala.

Dhulikhel (p.226). A very popular route leads to the stupa of Namo Buddha and on to Paunauti; longer, less-travelled roads go from Namo eastwards and from Panauti to Lubhu.

Kakani (p.236). Follow the ridge east through the Shivapuri Watershed to the summit of Shivapuri, Budhanilkantha, or all the way to Nagarkot.

Daman (p.240). Cycle down to Naubise or over a pass and down to the Tarai; or hike from Daman to Kulekhani Reservoir and on to Pharping or Thankot in the Kathmandu Valley.

Depending on where you're going, certain ways of getting around the valley are definitely better than others – making the wrong choice can kill an otherwise fun outing. A **taxi** is probably the way to go if you're aiming for a specific destination, especially if the journey there is along a main road. Negotiate for a return trip with ample waiting time if your destination isn't one of the main tourist sites. **Buses** and fixed-route **tempos** are obviously cheaper and bring you into (very) close contact with real Nepal, but they're slow and uncomfortable. In the sections that follow, bus routes are mentioned where they exist (fares are usually just a few rupees) – see also the table of Kathmandu-

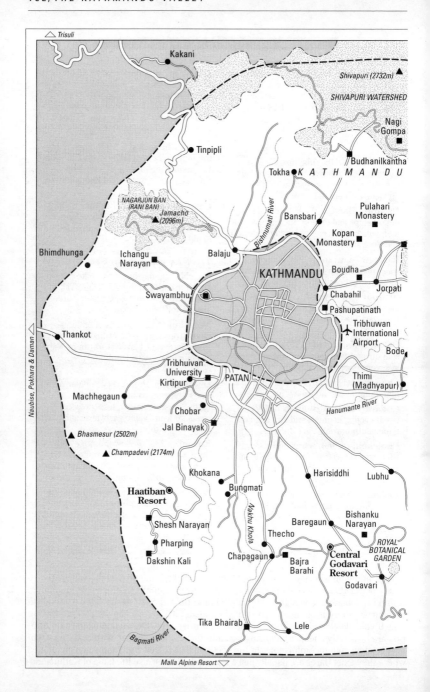

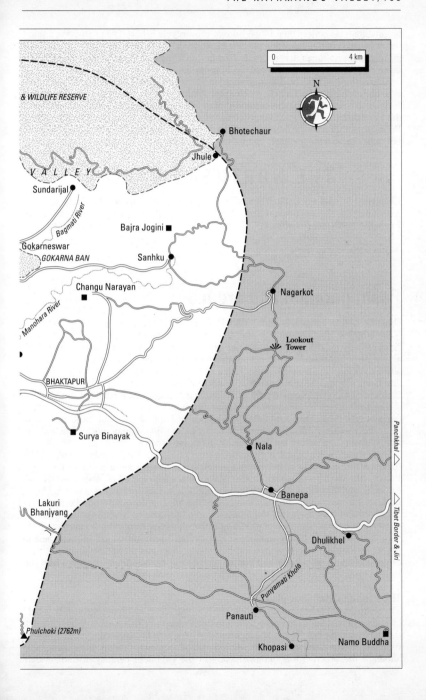

originating bus services on p.145. A **bike** or **motorcycle** is best if you're touring around the rural parts of the valley and you want maximum flexibility to stop and go. However, getting out of Kathmandu is not part of the fun, so if you're cycling, consider loading the bike in a taxi at least to get beyond the Ring Road.

The Kathmandu city/valley **maps** sold in tourist areas will probably suffice for general sightseeing. For serious walking or biking, try to get your hands on the HMG/FINNIDA 1:25,000 sheets for the valley – Maps of Nepal, on Airport Road west of the *Everest Hotel*, is the main sales agent, but some Thamel bookshops also have them. Failing that, there are the excellent but dated Schneider map of the valley or other newer but rather inaccurate versions, such as the one published by Himalayan Map House.

THE NORTHERN VALLEY

Chapter One covered Kathmandu within the Ring Road; this section deals with the remainder of the northern valley. The most important cultural sights here are **Pashupatinath** and **Boudha**, both of which have facilities for staying overnight.

> The telephone code for the Kathmandu Valley is ☎01.

Pashupatinath and around

Often likened to Varanasi in India, **PASHUPATINATH** (pronounced Posh-*potty*-not) is Nepal's holiest Hindu pilgrimage site: an amazing enclave of temples, cremation ghats, ritual bathers and half-naked sadhus. The sacred complex lies just beyond the Ring Road, 4km east of Kathmandu – incongruously close to the modern airport, but fortunately sheltered from it in a wooded ravine. Together with the associated temples of Gorakhnath and Ghujeshwari, Pashupatinath is a heady cocktail of Hindu (and to a lesser extent Buddhist) proceedings, spiked with some of the most colourful mythology on earth.

The site's layout favours an anticlockwise circuit on foot, first around Pashupatinath's temples and ghats, then up to Gorakhnath, on to Ghujeshwari and back. Instead of returning to Pashupatinath, however, you might want to continue on to Boudha (see p.160), about 2km further northeast along an unpaved road.

Pashupatinath is a relatively short **taxi** ride from central Kathmandu (about Rs100). It's not a terrible **cycle**, either: from Thamel, follow Tridevi Marg east past the Royal Palace, take the first right after Durbar Marg, then a left on the first main road (Kamal Pokhari), and follow that road over the Dhobi Khola and all the way to Gaushala, a busy, modern intersection on the Ring Road. The lane angling downhill from the northeast corner of Gaushala leads to a small built-up area (also known as Pashupatinath) at the western side of the temple complex. You'll probably have to pay a few rupees to have your bike "watched". Battery-powered Safaa ("clean") **tempos**, which originate next to RNAC on Kantipath, go to nearby Chabahil and will let you off on the Ring Road west of Pashupatinath. Boudha-bound Vikram tempos will do the same. To catch a **bus** you have to go to the City Bus Park, by which time you're already halfway there.

The Pashupatinath complex

The **temples** of Pashupatinath straddle the Bagmati River, which despite its filth is held by conservative Hindus to be the holiest in the Kathmandu Valley – this specific stretch the most sacred of all. To die and be cremated here is to be released from the cycle of rebirths. Wives used to commit *sati* on their husbands' funeral pyres here, and although the practice was outlawed early in the twentieth century, it's still widely believed that husbands and wives who bathe here together will be remarried in the next life. **Bathing** is considered especially meritorious on full-moon days, on Magh Sankranti (usually Jan 14) and Bala Chaturdashi (late Nov or early Dec), and, for women, during the festival of Tij (late Aug or early Sept). The entire complex overflows with pilgrims from all over the subcontinent during the **festival** of Shiva Raatri (held on the new moon of Feb–March). Devout locals also come for special services on full-moon days and on the eleventh lunar day (*ekadashi*) after each full and new moon.

Foreigners are free to observe most of these rituals, but it's important to respect the privacy of bathers and worshippers. Be especially sensitive about photographing people and cremation pyres: you wouldn't want tourists snapping away at your mother's funeral, would you?

Shiva is the principal deity here, in one of his more benign forms: **Pashupati, Lord of the Animals**, in whose name the king of Nepal ends all his public addresses, and to whom

praises are sung on Radio Nepal at the start of each broadcasting day. Several tales are told of how Shiva came by this title. Nepali schoolchildren are taught that Shiva, to escape his heavenly obligations, assumed the guise of a one-horned stag and fled to the forest here. The other gods pursued him and, laying hold of him, broke off his horn, which was transformed into the powerful Pashupati *linga*. The *linga* was later lost, only to be rediscovered at its present site by a cow who magically began sprinkling the spot with her milk.

THE PASHUPATI MANDIR

Approaching from the west, a lane leads past trinket stalls and sweet shops to the main gate of the **Pashupati Mandir** – the holy of holies for Nepali Shaivas, followers of Shiva. As in many temples in Nepal, admission is for Hindus only (which in practice means anyone who looks Nepali or South Asian, but not Tibetan). From the outside, though, you can glimpse the two symbols that are found in front of almost every Shiva temple, their gargantuan proportions here a measure of the temple's sanctity: a two-storey-high *trisul* (trident), and the enormous golden backside of Nandi, Shiva's faithful bull, the latter yet another reminder of the god's procreative power.

Hidden inside, the famous **Pashupati linga** displays four carved faces of Shiva, plus a fifth, invisible one on the top (Buddhists claim one of the faces is that of the Buddha). The *linga* is a fourteenth-century replacement of the original one, which was damaged by Muslim crusaders. Hindus associate this *linga* with yet another Shiva myth, in which the god transformed his phallus into an infinite pillar of light and challenged Brahma and Vishnu – the other members of the Hindu trinity – to find the ends of it. Brahma flew heavenward, while Vishnu plumbed the depths of hell. Both were forced to abandon the search, but Brahma falsely boasted of success, only to be caught out by Shiva. Shaivas say that's why Brahma is seldom worshipped, Vishnu gets his fair share, and Shiva is revered above all.

The gold-clad pagoda dates from the early seventeenth century, but inscriptions indicate that a temple has stood here since at least the fifth century, and some historians suspect it goes back to the third century BC, when the ancient village of Deopatan is said to have been founded just west of here. The temple apparently emerged as a hotbed of tantric practices in the eleventh century and remained so for four hundred years, until King Yaksha Malla reined things in by importing conventional Brahman **priests** from south India. This arrangement continues to this day, although there have been calls to end it since a scandal in which the *mul bhatta* (high priest) was forced to resign in 1998 amid charges that he had siphoned off millions of rupees in temple donations to build a resort hotel in his native Karnataka.

Wearing the ceremonial orange robes of the Pashupata sect, the priests array the *linga* in brocade silk and bathe it with curd, ghee, honey, sugar and milk. Hindu pilgrims are expected to distribute offerings to the priests and then make a circuit of the temple and the 365 *shivalinga* and other secondary shrines scattered about the precinct. Most also distribute alms to beggars lined along some of the nearby lanes. If you choose to give, arm yourself with a sufficient stockpile of small change (*saano paisa*), available from nearby vendors.

ALONG THE WEST BANK

Hindus exit the temple via a back way leading down to the west bank of the Bagmati at **Arya Ghat**, a cremation area reserved for members of the higher "twice-born" castes. Housed in a small stone reliquary beside the ghat is a famed seventh-century statue of **Virupaksha**, the "Three-Eyed Shiva". The image is also associated with Kalki, the tenth and final incarnation of Vishnu, a sort of messiah figure who will bring the present Kali Yuga (Age of Kali) to a close and usher in a new, virtuous cycle of history. Some claim that the idol is gradually sinking into the earth, and its final disappearance will mark the end of the age.

SADHUS

Sadhus, those dreadlocked holy men usually seen lurking around Hindu temples, are essentially an Indian phenomenon. However, Nepal, being the setting for many of the amorous and ascetic exploits of sadhus' favourite deity, Shiva, is a favourite stomping ground for them. Sadhus are especially common at Pashupatinath, which is rated as one of the subcontinent's four most important Shaiva pilgrimage sites. During the festival of Shiva Raatri, Pashupatinath hosts a full-scale sadhu convention, with the government laying on free firewood for the festival.

Shaiva sadhus follow Shiva in one of his best-loved and most enigmatic guises – the wild, dishevelled **yogin**, the master of yoga, who sits motionless atop a Himalayan peak for aeons at a time and whose hair is the source of the mighty Ganga (Ganges) River. Traditionally, sadhus live solitary lives, always on the move, subsisting on alms and owning nothing but what they carry. They bear Shiva's emblems: the *trisul* (trident), *damaru* (two-sided drum), a necklace of furrowed *rudraksha* seeds, and perhaps a conch shell for blowing haunting calls across the cosmic ocean. Some smear themselves with ashes, symbolizing Shiva's role as the destroyer, who reduces all things to ash so that creation can begin anew. The trident-shaped *tika* of Shiva is often painted on their foreheads, although they may employ scores of other *tika* patterns, each with its own cult affiliation and symbolism.

Sadhus have a strange role model in Shiva, who is both a mountaintop ascetic and the philandering god of the phallus. Some, such as the members of the Gorakhnath cult (which has a strong presence at Pashupatinath), follow the tantric **"left-hand" path**, a reference to the hand used for unclean tasks. Beyond the pale of orthodox Hindu practice, they employ esoteric and sometimes deliberately deviant practices to free themselves of sensual passions and transcend the illusory physical world. Occasionally sadhus may be seen tying heavy stones to their penises in an effort to destroy the erectile tissues; of one famous sadhu it was said that he had so completely marshalled his sexual energies that he bled semen. **Aghoris**, the most extreme of the left-hand practitioners, subject themselves to horrific disciplines to overcome the fear of death: cremation grounds like Pashupatinath are their temples. Some also make a practice of eating every form of disgusting thing – including, it's said, human flesh – to experience the undifferentiated oneness of true reality.

Like Shiva, sadhus also make liberal use of **intoxicants** as a path to spiritual insight. It was Shiva, in fact, who supposedly discovered the transcendental powers of *ganja* (cannabis), which grows wild throughout Nepal. Sadhus usually consume the weed in the form of *bhang* (a liquid preparation) or *charas* (hashish, smoked in a vertical clay pipe known as a chilam). With each toke, the holy man intones *"Bam Shankar"*: "I am Shiva".

Many of the buildings around the main temple, including the tall, whitewashed ones overlooking the river, are *dharmsala* (pilgrims' rest houses), set aside here for devout Hindus approaching death. In their final hour, the dying will be laid out on a sloped stone slab with their feet in the Bagmati and given a last drink of the holy river water, which probably finishes them off.

Non-Hindus must go around the temple to the south, reaching the river just downstream of Arya Ghat and a pair of footbridges. The small pagoda between the bridges is the **Bachhaleshwari Mandir**, dedicated to Shiva's consort Parbati in one of her mother-goddess roles. Next to it stands a newish ten-foot terracotta frieze of Narayan (alias Vishnu) and other sculptures of Ganesh and Gauri (Parbati).

Cremations are held almost continuously at the next embankment downstream, **Ram Ghat**, which is used by all castes. It's lined by another string of metal-roofed *dharmsala*, which you can explore in a limited way. A small eleventh-century **Buddha statue**, looking rather out of place in this Hindu Lourdes, sticks out of the embankment in front of the next-to-last building. Just beyond, a neglected bumper-sized *linga* ensconced in a round brick battlement is believed to date from the fifth century. The southernmost building shelters two temples in its courtyard, the oval **Raj Rajeshwari** and the gilded pagoda of **Nawa Durga**.

Behind the *dharmsala* broods the gothic bulk of **Pancha Dewal**, whose five Mughal-style cupolas are visible from high up on the opposite bank. This now serves as an old people's home, one wing of which is operated by **Mother Teresa's Missionaries of Charity** (the government runs the rest), and though emphatically not a tourist site, it is an excellent place to experience a different side of Nepal as a volunteer. The sisters need help each morning changing and cleaning sheets, helping residents wash, clipping nails, scrubbing pots and so on – real humble work, but that's the whole idea of it. They also run a second nursing home in nearby Chabahil. The entrance to the compound is on the north side of Pancha Dewal; look for the sisters (who speak English) in their trademark white saris with blue trim.

THE EAST BANK

You can cross the river to the east bank just downstream of the *dharmsala*. As you head upstream, the walled-off forested area on your right is a **cemetery** set aside for Nepal's few "burying" groups, which include Rais and Limbus of the eastern hills and members of one Hindu sect.

Moving northwards and uphill, you'll enter a wide, paved enclosure, which during Shiva Raatri is chock-a-block with sadhus and other spiritual exhibitionists. Of the two small temples found here, the one with a statue of Garud in front is called **Lakshmi Narayan**, in honour of Vishnu (Narayan) and his wealth-bringing wife Lakshmi. The other is the **Ram Janaki**, containing statues of Ram – Vishnu's incarnation as a mortal in the *Ramayan* epic – and his whole family, including Hanuman the monkey king, who helped rescue Ram's wife Sita from the clutches of a Sri Lankan demon. Sita is popular among Nepali Hindus, since she was born in Janakpur in the eastern Tarai (see p.353). These temples, along with the **Ram Mandir** in the next compound, are disappointingly recent and un-Nepali, however. Temples at Pashupatinath are built and rebuilt often, renovations being the standard way of winning favour with gods and mortals, and wealthy Indian patrons are among the principal contributors to the development fund.

Further upstream, the eleven great **shivalaya** (boxy *linga* shelters) were erected in honour of women who committed *sati* on the pyres opposite; photo-me sadhus stake out lucrative perches around them. Great views of the whole area are afforded from the observation deck above, which contains a one-faced *shivalinga* from the fifth century at its northern end.

Gorakhnath

The main stairway up the east bank carries on through Mrigasthali Ban, the forest where Shiva is supposed to have cavorted as a stag, to the mellow **Gorakhnath Mandir** at the top of the hill. Visiting this compound, after the sensory overload below, is like entering a soundproofed room. The temple itself, a medium-sized *shikra* structure dedicated to the patron deity of the Shah kings, isn't that interesting – what will amaze you is the sight of scores of **shivalaya** arranged in crumbling rows in the forest, mottled by shade and shafts of sunlight. The place has the romantic, ruined feel of an overgrown cemetery, with broken statuary lying undisturbed and stone inscriptions recording long-forgotten decrees. You could easily mistake the *shivalaya* for tombs, but their iconography – the *trisul*, statues of Nandi and Shiva (always with an erection), the *linga* atop the *yoni* – proclaims them to be Shiva shrines. It would be a fine spot for a picnic if it weren't for the thieving monkeys.

The onion dome rising above the trees to the southeast of Gorakhnath is the **Bishwarup Mandir** (entrance only to Hindus), dedicated to Vishnu in his many-limbed "universal form". Dominating the sanctum, however, is a six-metre-tall statue of Shiva and Parbati in the state of *yab-yum* (sexual union).

KATHMANDU VALLEY'S MAJOR FESTIVALS

Some of the festivals listed in the Kathmandu chapter are also celebrated in the valley. Again, most are reckoned by the lunar calendar, so check locally for exact dates.

MAGH (JAN–FEB)

Magh Sankranti The first day of Magh (Jan 14 or 15), marked by ritual bathing at Patan's Sankhamul Ghat and at Sankhu.

FAAGUN (FEB–MARCH)

Losar Tibetan New Year, the new moon of February, celebrated at Boudha with processions, horn-blowing and *tsampa*-throwing on the big third day.

Shiva Raatri On the full moon of Faagun, the Pashupatinath *mela* (fair) attracts tens of thousands of pilgrims and holy men, while children everywhere collect money for bonfires on "Shiva's Night".

CHAITRA (MARCH–APRIL)

Balaju Jaatra Ritual bathing at the Balaju Water Garden on the day of the full moon.

BAISAAKH (APRIL–MAY)

Bisket Bhaktapur's celebration of Nepali New Year (April 13 or 14) – see box, p.205. Thimi and Bode have their own idiosyncratic festivities.

Buddha Jayanti The anniversary of the Buddha's birth, enlightenment and death, celebrated at Boudha.

Machhendranath Raath Jaatra An amazing, uniquely Newar extravaganza in which an immense chariot is pulled through old Patan in stages over a period of several weeks (see p.180).

ASAAR (JUNE–JULY)

Dalai Lama's Birthday Observed informally at Boudha (July 6).

SAAUN (JULY–AUG)

Janai Purnima The annual changing of the sacred thread worn by high-caste Hindu men, involving bathing and splashing at Patan's Kumbeshwar Mahadev on the day of the full moon.

BHADAU (AUG–SEPT)

Krishna Jayanti Krishna's birthday, marked by an all-night vigil at Patan's Krishna Mandir on the seventh day after the full moon.

Gokarna Aunsi Nepali "Father's Day", observed at Gokarneswar with bathing and offerings on the day of the new moon.

Tij A day of ritual bathing for women on the third day after the new moon, mainly at Pashupatinath.

KHATTIK (OCT–NOV)

Haribondhini Ekadashi Bathing and *puja* on the eleventh day after the new moon. The main action takes place at the Vishnu sites of Budhanilkantha, Sesh Narayan, Bishanku Narayan and Changu Narayan.

MANGSIR (NOV–DEC)

Indrayani Jaatra Deities are paraded through Kirtipur on palanquins on the day of the new moon.

Bala Chaturdashi All-night vigil at Pashupatinath on the night of the new moon, involving candles and ritual seed-offerings to dead relatives.

Ghujeshwari and back

The **Ghujeshwari** (or Ghuyeshwari) **Mandir** sits at the bottom of the path that continues downhill from Gorakhnath. Here, too, non-Hindus can only peek from outside. The legend behind this temple is one of the all-time masterpieces of Hindu surrealism. The story goes that Shiva's first wife, Sati, offended by some insult, threw herself onto a fire (giving rise to the term *sati*, or *suttee*). Shiva retrieved her corpse and, blinded by grief, flew to and fro across the subcontinent, scattering parts of the body in 51 sacred places. Ghujeshwari is where Sati's vagina (some say her anus) fell. As a consequence, the temple here represents the female counterpart to the Pashupati *linga* and is held to be every bit as sacred, its chief focus being a *kalash* (vessel) kept in a sunken pit and containing an "odiferous liquid". Buddhists consider Ghujeshwari to be one of the valley's four mystic Bajra Joginis – powerful tantric goddesses – and the site to be the seed from which the Swayambhu lotus grew.

From Ghujeshwari a lane follows the river downstream past the **Kirateshwar Mahadev Mandir**, which hosts Nepali classical music concerts on full-moon evenings, and **Gauri Ghat**, a peaceful spot where the river enters the Pashupatinath ravine and monkeys leap from branches and cliffs into the water. The road crosses the river here and circles around to the village of Pashupatinath, while a path past the river crossing takes a more direct route up and over **Kailash Hill**. This grassy knoll, named after the Tibetan mountain where Shiva does his meditating, is used both as a playing field and public toilet. It overlooks the Pashupatinath complex to the south, and on a clear day affords good views of the mountains to the northeast.

From the eastern edge of Kailash, a steep staircase leads down to **Surya Ghat**, the site of several caves hewn out of the cliffs. These caves have been used for meditation for centuries, and are sometimes still occupied by latter-day yogins.

Pashupatinath practicalities

At last a hot-water **guest house** has opened in Pashupatinath, making it possible to experience this amazing area much more intimately. The *Shree Shankar Guest House* (☎470374; ③), just up from the main temple on a quiet lane, couldn't be better located; the rooms leave something to be desired, but the place is clean enough, it has a decent roof, and it's a start – other guest houses are sure to follow. For the time being, though, the only other lodgings within range of Pashupatinath are on the other side of the Ring Road, around the Gaushala intersection and further south in Battisputali. *Sukeyasu Guest House*, listed in the Kathmandu chapter (p.124), is the only one worth recommending, but it's really not all that convenient for Pashupatinath.

For **food**, there's a small tourist restaurant, *Kafleko*, on the east bank of the Bagmati, and various *daal bhaat* and sweet shops in Pashupatinath village and around Gaushala.

Handicrafts peddlers sell the usual range of Tibetan curios and *khukuri* knives, most of which are totally irrelevant here. If you're looking for an authentic souvenir of Pashupatinath, check out the things Nepalis buy: cheap votive icons, statuettes, *linga* replicas, conch shells, *shaligram* (fossil-bearing stones), *rudraksha* necklaces, offertory vessels and bangles.

Boudha (Boudhanath) and around

To ancient travellers along the Kathmandu–Tibet trade route, the ten-kilometre corridor from Pashupatinath to Sankhu was known as the zone of *siddhi* (supernatural powers), where guardian deities dwelt and all wishes were granted. The biggest, most auspicious landmark along this route was – and still is – the great stupa at **BOUDHA** (or **BOUD-HANATH**), about 5km northeast of downtown Kathmandu.

One of the world's largest stupas, Boudha is generally acknowledged to be the most important Tibetan Buddhist monument outside Tibet. Tibetans simply call it Chorten Chempo – "Great Stupa" – and since 1959 it has become the Mecca of **Tibetan exiles** in Nepal. Tibetans now run most of the businesses along the main road and around the stupa, while the construction of monasteries has created a regular suburban sprawl to the north. Despite the tour groups and souvenir sellers, Boudha gives you a thorough dunking in Tibetan culture, past and present. Early morning and dusk are the best times to be here, when the resonant chanting of monks and the otherworldly cacophony of their music drifts from the upper rooms of the houses that ring the stupa, and pilgrims perform *kora*, shuffling and prostrating their way around the dome.

If you want an extra helping of Tibetan culture, go during the **festival** of Losar in February or March, when Boudha hosts the biggest Tibetan New Year celebration in

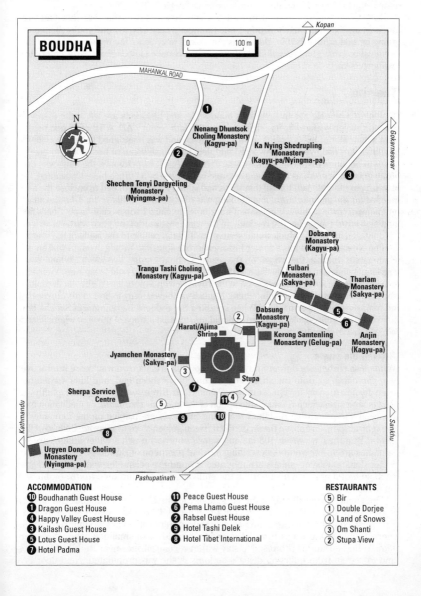

BOUDHA

0   100 m

△ Kopan

MAHANKAL ROAD

N

△ Gokarneswar

Nenang Dhuntsok Choling Monastery (Kagyu-pa)

Ka Nying Shedrupling Monastery (Kagyu-pa/Nyingma-pa)

Shechen Tenyi Dargyeling Monastery (Nyingma-pa)

Dobsang Monastery (Kagyu-pa)

Trangu Tashi Choling Monastery (Kagyu-pa)

Fulbari Monastery (Sakya-pa)

Tharlam Monastery (Sakya-pa)

Dabsung Monastery (Kagyu-pa)

Harati/Ajima Shrine

Kerong Samtenling Monastery (Gelug-pa)

Anjin Monastery (Kagyu-pa)

Jyamchen Monastery (Sakya-pa)

Stupa

Sherpa Service Centre

△ Kathmandu

△ Sankhu

Urgyen Dongar Choling Monastery (Nyingma-pa)

Pashupatinath ▽

ACCOMMODATION
⑩ Boudhanath Guest House
❶ Dragon Guest House
❹ Happy Valley Guest House
❸ Kailash Guest House
❺ Lotus Guest House
❼ Hotel Padma

⑪ Peace Guest House
❻ Pema Lhamo Guest House
❷ Rabsel Guest House
❾ Hotel Tashi Delek
❽ Hotel Tibet International

RESTAURANTS
⑤ Bir
① Double Dorjee
④ Land of Snows
③ Om Shanti
② Stupa View

Nepal. Other busy times are Buddha Jayanti (the Buddha's birthday), the full moon of April–May, when an image of the Buddha is paraded around the stupa aboard an elephant, and the full moon of March–April, when ethnic Tamangs – the original guardians of the stupa – converge here to arrange marriages, and hundreds of eligible brides are sat around the stupa for inspection. Full moon and new moon days in general attract more pilgrims, since acts of worship earn more merit on these days.

From Kathmandu, crowded **minibuses** and buses depart the City Bus Park frequently for Boudha, and **tempos** from Kantipath near RNAC, but you're better off going by **taxi** (about Rs150). Boudha is not a place to cycle to: the main road along here is one of the valley's most polluted. However you choose to go, set out early, before the traffic gets bad.

The site

Assigning a reliable age to Boudha is impossible, and historians are left at the mercy of legends, which seem to fix its origins around the fifth century AD. A **Tibetan text** relates how a daughter of Indra stole flowers from heaven and was reassigned to earth as a lowly poultryman's daughter, yet prospered and decided to use some of her wealth to build a stupa to honour a mythical Buddha of the Previous Age. She petitioned the king, who cynically granted her only as much land as could be covered by a buffalo hide. Undaunted, the woman cut the hide into thread-thin strips and joined them end to end to enclose the area needed for the gigantic stupa, and the king was obliged to keep his word. Tibetans attach great importance to this tale because it's attributed to Guru Padma Sambhava, Tibet's first and best-loved evangelist. Interestingly, in the same manuscript the guru warns of an invasion by a giant enemy, which would scatter the Tibetan people to the lands of the south.

The **Newar legend** has a firmer historical grounding, involving a drought that struck Kathmandu during the reign of the early Lichhavi king, Vrisadeva. When court astrologers advised that only the sacrifice of a virtuous man would bring rain, Vrisadeva commanded his son Manadeva to go to the royal well on a moonless night and decapitate the shrouded body he would find there. Manadeva obeyed, only to find to his horror that he had sacrificed his own father. When he asked the goddess Bajra Jogini of Sankhu how to expiate his guilt, she let fly a bird and told him to build a stupa at the spot where it landed, which was Boudha.

Around the stupa

While less embellished than Swayambhu, Boudha is in its own way more interactive: you can climb up onto the stupa's base from its northern end, and kids sometimes even fly kites from it. The dome is elevated on three twenty-cornered plinths of decreasing size, which reinforce the notion of the stupa as a *mandala*, or meditation tool. As usual, the primordial Buddha's searching blue eyes are painted on the four sides of the central spire, and above them rise the thirteen golden steps to *nirvana*. Instead of five *dhyani* Buddhas, however, 108 (an auspicious number) much smaller images are set in niches around the dome, describing a broad pantheon of Buddhas, lamas and protector deities. Prayer wheels are mounted around the perimeter wall – it's said that each spin of a prayer wheel here is the equivalent of reciting the *mantra* embossed on it 11,000 times.

The small **Ajima shrine** at the far side of the stupa shelters the image of a nasty goddess literally sucking the guts out of a corpse. Ghoulish though she may look, Buddhist Newars worship Ajima as a grandmother-protectress of children. She is more popularly known as Harati, the one-time goddess of smallpox, who after a sermon from the Buddha promised to stay within certain shrines near Buddhist temples and to refrain from inflicting disease so long as she was propitiated. Next door is a

BOUDHA'S DHARMA SCENE

Boudha's **Western community** is well established, though to become a part of it you need either an introduction or a lot of time, since serious Western students of *dharma* tend to regard tourists as spiritual interference. But as those in the know say, if you're ready you will find a teacher here. Many Westerners rate Boudha as the best place in the world to **study** Tibetan Buddhism, for although **Dharmsala** in India is better known because the Dalai Lama is based there, the presence of the Tibetan government-in-exile creates a politically charged atmosphere that can distract from serious study. Moreover, Dharmsala is heavily dominated by the Dalai Lama's Gelug-pa order, whereas at Boudha all four sects are well represented, making it easier to sample the different traditions.

Western monks wear the same maroon robes and have taken the same monastic vows as Tibetan monks but, partly because of visa restrictions, aren't expected to make the same commitment to a monastery. While Tibetan monks live at their monastery, maintaining the building and making visits to the local community, Westerners are free to come and go. Given a maximum five-month stay, most cram as much personal instruction as possible into their time, and then try to maintain a long-distance teacher–disciple relationship from home. Some follow their lama on speaking tours overseas, which are conveniently scheduled during the soggy monsoon months.

A separate wing of the *dharma* crowd consists of Westerners living in Boudha for a season of **individual study**. Some are just trying Buddhism on for size, others are earnestly shopping around for a teacher. Most teachers at Boudha give occasional open talks – with or without English translation – and normally agree to one-on-one meetings with anyone who shows a keen interest.

The Chinese occupation of Tibet killed or drove away an entire generation of lamas, and Boudha's line-up of **teachers**, though formidable, reflects this: most are either very old or rather young. Perennially popular among the *dharma* set is **Chokyi Nyima**, abbot of Ka Nying Shedrupling Monastery, who speaks excellent English and holds open teachings most Saturday mornings. He also runs meditation courses during the tourist season (for a profile of Chokyi Nyima, see "Tibetan Exiles in Nepal" in Contexts). His younger brother, **Tsokney Rinpoche**, who's abbot of a monastery near Swayambhu, is also accessible and frequently gives teachings at Ka Nying Shedrupling. The death in 1991 of **Dilgo Khyentse** of Shechen Tenyi Dargyeling Monastery has left a large gap, but this may in time be filled by his grandson, **Shechen Rabjam Rinpoche**, and **Trangu Rinpoche** of the Trangu Tashi Choling Monastery, who teaches a course each December–January. Shechen Rabjam also serves as tutor of Dilgo Khyentse's *yangsi* (reincarnated successor), who was enthroned at the monastery in 1997 at the age of four.

Kopan Monastery (2km north of Boudha), whose **Yeshe Lama** passed away in 1986, remains as busy as ever with a full schedule of Gelug activities; a Spanish boy is being groomed as Yeshe's *yangsi*. Pulahari Monastery (east of Kopan) is another hotbed of Western study, despite the death in 1994 of its abbot **Jamgon Kongtrul Rinpoche** and the subsequent installation of his young *yangsi*. Other teachers include **Chogye Trichen**, who runs Jyamchen Monastery and is also abbot of the Tibetan *gompa* at Lumbini, and **Kenpo Tsultrim Gyamtso** of the Marpa Institute on Mahakal Road (1km northwest of Boudha).

To find out about upcoming teachings, check out the restaurant notice boards around Boudha, or try asking some of the regulars at the *Bir* or the *Double Dorjee*. But if you've had no prior experience with Buddhism, you'll probably want to test the waters first by enrolling in a **meditation course**. The courses run by the Himalayan Buddhist Meditation Centre (☎221875; *hbmc@casnov.attmail.com*) are the usual place to start. Kopan Monastery (☎481268; *tsultim@hhm.wlink.com.np*) also holds a month-long course each November that attracts literally hundreds of Western participants.

room-sized prayer wheel – all are welcome to spin it – and on the other side of the shrine you'll see the tanks where whitewash is mixed during festivals.

Boudha's **pilgrims** are arguably its greatest attraction, as the stupa is famed throughout the Himalayan region for its wish-fulfilling properties. Prayer wheels, heavy silver jewellery and rainbow-striped aprons are good general indicators of a pilgrim's Tibetan origins. The men of Kham, in eastern Tibet, wear red tassels in their long hair, as do the Dolpo-pa of northwest Nepal, many of whom winter here. Nomads from the central Tibetan plateau wear sheepskin *chuba* (coats) with extra-long sleeves. Bhutanese men and women keep their hair cropped short and wear distinctive embroidered robes. Ladakhi women are distinguished by their velvet dresses, and high-crowned silk hats with small wings on either side. In addition, Nepali Bhotiyas (p.396) and Tamangs (p.232) visit Boudha in force, but the stupa has no special attraction for Buddhist Newars.

The monasteries and back lanes
The past decade has seen quite a spate of monastery-building at Boudha, and at the last count there were 31 *gompa* (monasteries) scattered around the neighbourhood. All four of the major Tibetan Buddhist sects (see "Religion" in Contexts) are represented at least twice – for a partial listing of names and sects, refer to the Boudha map. A map painted on a wall near the Ajima shrine, though not to scale, gives a complete and up-to-date tally.

The older, smaller **monasteries** around the stupa keep their doors open most of the time, and welcome spectators during their morning and dusk *puja*. Furnishings and icons are broadly similar in each. The gilded statues at the front of the assembly hall (*lhakang*) will usually represent the Buddha, various *bodhisattva*, or the founder of the monastery's sect. Spread out in front of these are likely to be oil lamps, which monks and pilgrims continually replenish; heaps of rice piled onto three-tiered silver stands, which are objects of meditation; conical dough-cakes (*torma*) symbolizing deities; and offerings of fruit, coins, flowers and incense. Frescoes on the walls depict fearsome guardians of the faith, symbolic deities and historical figures, or, like *thangka* (see p.135), express the complex cosmology of Tibetan Buddhism.

If you follow either of the two lanes heading **north of the stupa**, the romance evaporates in short order: this is Boudha the boomtown, an unplanned quagmire of garbage-strewn lanes, unlovely new buildings, schools, carpet factories and the mansions of their nouveau riche owners. The area from Boudha to Gokarneswar accounts for the largest share of the valley's carpet manufacture, a dubious distinction that contributes to serious water pollution as well as the awful congestion out on the main road in front of the stupa. Yet the carpet industry has brought undreamt-of wealth to the Tibetans of the Kathmandu Valley, who are piously donating much of it for the construction of new monasteries here. Sequestered behind high walls and iron gates, these monasteries have been deliberately named after *gompa* in Tibet that were destroyed by the Chinese, and it's hoped that, besides keeping the flame of Tibetan Buddhism alight and preserving traditional art forms, they'll help bring about the resurrection of their namesakes. It's a telling picture of the bittersweet present – and foreseeable future – of the Tibetan diaspora. With each new carpet factory or monastery, Boudha's Tibetans find themselves more comfortable in exile, and more deeply enmeshed in the difficult development-related dilemmas of their hosts.

Further afield
Boomtown aside, Boudha makes a good springboard for several walks and bike rides in this part of the valley. **Kopan Monastery**, occupying a beautifully leafy ridge about 3km due north of the stupa, is an easy target. Further along this ridge to the east lies **Pulahari Monastery** (also accessible from Gokarneswar – see below), where a stupa containing the remains of the late Jamgon Kongtrul Rinpoche (see above) has the makings of an important pilgrimage stop. From either of these points, it's a pleasant two- or

three-hour hike north along the ridge to **Nagi Gompa**, and another hour's descent to Budhanilkantha.

In the opposite direction, Pashupatinath (see above) is only about a half-hour's walk southwest of Boudha. A path sets off from the main road almost opposite the entrance to the stupa. Sankhu and Gokarneswar, described in the next section, can be reached by bike.

Straddling the Ring Road west of Boudha, the ancient settlement of Chabahil is unfortunately now blighted by traffic and characterless construction. However, Tibetans have long been drawn to its stupa (known locally as **Dhando Chaitya**), which despite its newish appearance dates to Lichhavi times. One chronicle states it was constructed by Dharmadeva, a fifth-century king, although legend attributes it to Charumati, who settled here and married a local prince after accompanying her father Ashoka on his apocryphal pilgrimage to the Kathmandu Valley in the third century BC. The prince, Devapala, is credited with founding Deopatan, one of the valley's ancient capitals and now the site of Pashupatinath. In a brick shelter at the south end of the compound stands a sixth-century statue of Padmapani Lokeshwar, carved in black stone. Chabahil's Nepalis rally round the **Chandra Binayak Mandir**, one of the valley's four principal Ganesh temples, located in the reasonably atmospheric bazaar west of the main Chabahil intersection.

Accommodation

There's a good range of budget and moderately priced **accommodation** in Boudha, so it's well worth staying overnight to enjoy the place after the day-trippers and overflying helicopters are gone. Most lodgings are within easy walking distance of the stupa; those located away from the busy main road are preferable. Except where indicated, refer to the map for locations.

Budget

Bir (☎470790). In the restaurant of the same name. Economical but uninspiring – a long-time favourite of Western *dharma* types, but it's gone downhill of late. ③/B③.

Dragon Guest House (☎479562, fax 486744). A very comfortable little establishment with a nice atmosphere, excellent views and a small garden. It's a good place to meet people. Call ahead, as it's often full. ③/B④.

Kailash Guest House (☎480741). A cheaper option with no-frills facilities. ③/B③.

Lotus Guest House (☎472432, fax 478091). Operated by the next-door monastery, this motel-like guest house is clean, quiet, spacious and minimalist. ③/B④–⑤.

Peace Guest House (no phone). A tiny, cold-water flophouse with dorm beds. ①.

Hotel Tashi Delek (☎471380). Crappy location out on the main drag, but it'll do if the others are full. ③.

ROOM PRICE SCALES

Lodging prices change from season to season, so it would be misleading to quote exact prices in a guidebook. Instead, all guest houses and hotels have been price-graded according to the scale below, which is based on the price of the cheapest double room in high season. Codes prefixed by B denote the cost of the cheapest room with attached bathroom, and those prefixed by AC refer to air-conditioned rooms. See p.39 for a fuller explanation.

① Less than Rs140 ($2 if quoted in US$)	⑤ $8–12
	⑥ $12–20
② Rs140–200 ($2–3)	⑦ $20–40
③ Rs200–350 ($3–5)	⑧ $40–75
④ Rs350–550 ($5–8)	⑨ Over $75

Midrange and expensive

Happy Valley Guest House (☎471241, fax 471876). Cavernous five-storey pile with fabulous views of the stupa (and the airport) from its rooftop terrace. B⑦–⑧.

Hyatt Regency Kathmandu, off the map – nearly 1km west of the stupa. A huge new five-star hotel – Nepal's biggest – that will exert a major upmarket influence on Boudha. AC⑨.

Maya Guest House, off the map – 400m east of the stupa on the main road (☎470266, fax 470261). Gorgeous garden, ugly and inconvenient location. Price includes breakfast and transport from Kathmandu. B⑦.

Hotel Padma (☎479052, fax 481550). A quirky little *pension* directly overlooking the stupa, with well-appointed rooms (all with TV and phone) and a small restaurant. B⑦.

Pema Lhamo Guest House (☎495662, fax 487545). A large, ornate tower with an excellent lawn and balconies. ④/B⑤.

Rabsel Guest House (☎479009, fax 470215). Quiet and good for making contact with monks at the adjacent monastery, but a bit desolate. B④–⑤.

Hotel Tibet International (☎470378; *nepcar@paljor.wlink.com.np*). Big complex used mainly by tour groups. Carpet-weaving centre and large restaurant on premises. B⑤–⑦.

Eating

Numerous **restaurants** around the stupa plaza target day-trippers, with outdoor seating and standard tourist menus. Most are lacklustre, but stick to Tibetan food and enjoy the view and you can't go wrong. Other, more authentic Tibetan places – with trademark curtained windows, dim lighting and white cotton seat covers – are tucked away in the back lanes and on the main road.

Bir Restaurant. A popular meeting place for Tibetans and long-term Westerners, though the food is unremarkable.

Double Dorjee. A cosy hole-in-the-wall that's popular with insiders. Excellent Tibetan and some Western food.

Land of Snows. Good Tibetan and Indian dishes in a clean setting, with rooftop seating available.

Om Shanti. Ditto.

Stupa View. Boudha's premier restaurant, with prices to match. All-vegetarian and fairly imaginative dishes (good pasta and tofu), plus there's a full bar and a roof terrace.

Shopping and other practicalities

Run-of-the-mill souvenirs at Boudha are notoriously overpriced, but this is the place to come if you're seeking genuinely obscure or **antique** items. Keep an eye out for tea tables, jewellery, flasks, butter-tea churns and prayer-flag printing blocks. The Tibet Musical Cultural Center, on the north side of the stupa plaza, sells traditional **musical instruments** and provides instruction. Boudha is also a good place to buy prayer flags, brocade banners, Tibetan incense, *chuba* (Tibetan wrap-around dresses) and maroon monks' garb.

For **books** on Buddhism, try the Tibet Book Centre in front of *Hotel Tibet International*. Cassette **tapes**, not only of music but also teachings by local lamas, are sold at a couple of places around the stupa and on the main road. You can buy **film** at many shops, and one or two places do processing.

There's at least one **moneychanger** in the vicinity of the stupa, just inside the entrance, and Nabil Bank has a branch about 500m east of the stupa on the main road. You can send **email** and make **phone calls** from places along the main road and northeast of the stupa plaza.

For **Tibetan medicine**, there's a branch of the Kunphen Tibetan Medical Centre on the main road just opposite the stupa entrance, inside the *Boudhanath Guest House*. Long-term residents might be able to recommend other doctors who treat foreigners.

The Sankhu and Sundarijal roads

The paved road past Boudha – one of the old trade routes to Tibet – rolls eastwards as far as **Sankhu** and its Bajra Jogini temple, from where there are unpaved tracks to points on the valley rim. A second road forks left at Jorpati, 1km east of Boudha, and makes for **Sundarijal** in the extreme northeastern corner of the valley.

Both roads are rather blighted by carpet-industry build-up for some distance past Jorpati, but the Sankhu road then becomes a fairly gentle ride on a **bicycle**, and it can be combined with visits to Nagarkot or Changu Narayan (for which you'll need a mountain bike). The Sundarijal road is mainly of interest for starting a **trek** in the Helambu region; its most interesting feature, the Gokarna Mahadev temple, is better reached by bike or foot from the Kopan and Pulahari monasteries (above). Regular **buses** from Kathmandu's City Bus Park ply both roads.

The road to Sankhu

Crossing the Bagmati River beyond noxious Jorpati, the Sankhu road first passes **Gokarna Ban**, a former royal game reserve that was open to the public but is now under long-term lease to a members-only golf club. Further on, a right fork leads to the Kathmandu Valley's controversial **landfill**. Residents of nearby Mulpani staged a much-publicized revolt in 1995, protesting that they were being made to suffer high rates of disease because the rubbish wasn't being properly buried. The landfill also violates international civil aviation standards by being too close to Tribhuwan Airport – landfills attract large numbers of birds, which can endanger air traffic.

About 5km from Jorpati, a trail to the south crosses the Manohara River on a temporary bridge (dry season only) and ascends the ridge to Changu Narayan. The road carries on to **SANKHU**, an important trade and spiritual centre in ancient times that now drifts on as a Newar backwater in a far corner of the valley. A large but unhurried town, it's not especially well preserved, but neither is it at all touristy. The oldest part is the bazaar area to the east of the main north–south road. Sankhu's main **festivals** are Magh Sankranti (Jan 14 or 15), observed with bathing just upstream of the town, and Sankhu Jaatra (the full moon of March–April), when the image of Bajra Jogini is paraded. **Food** is scarce here, but you should be able to get snacks in the bazaar and at the Bajra Jogini temple (see below).

Two roads connect Sankhu with Nagarkot (see p.217): the more travelled route leaves Sankhu from the old bazaar area, heading north, while a steeper back way branches off on a more easterly bearing. The main road from Boudha continues northwards partway to the Bajra Jogini temple.

Sankhu Bajra Jogini

Sankhu's main claim to fame is its temple to **Bajra Jogini**, whose gilded roof glints from a grove of trees on the sparsely wooded hillside north of town. To make the two-kilometre hike, follow the main road through the arch at the north end of town, then bear left after 400m on a cobbled path. If you're on wheels, continue on the road for another 1km to where it peters out at a cold-drinks stall, where you can leave your bike and walk up the remaining steps.

Sankhu Bajra Jogini is the most senior of a ferocious foursome of tantric goddesses specially venerated in the Kathmandu Valley. To Buddhist Newars – her main devotees – she is identified with Ugratara, the wrathful, corpse-trampling emanation of Tara, one of the female aspects of Buddhahood. Hindus identify her as Durga (Kali) or one of the eight mother goddesses. She's also known as Khadga Jogini, since her distinctive feature is a sword (*khadga*) held in the right hand. The main **temple** dates from the seventeenth century, but inscriptions elsewhere record that a shrine stood here a thousand years earlier. A smaller building next to it contains a replica of the Swayambhu stupa, whose natural stone dome may well be the original seventh-century object of worship at this site. The stone just to the right of the temple door is a *nag* (snake) shrine. In the back wall of the compound, a small square opening indicates a **cave** carved out of the rock where tantric yogins conduct long-term meditations. Another cave behind the *pati* west of the compound is known as Dharma Pap Gupha: those who can squeeze through the opening into the inner chamber demonstrate their virtue (*dharma*), and those who can't their vice (*pap*). The area is pleasantly shaded, but overrun by monkeys – the place literally stinks of them.

Steps lead up to a second compound, now occupied by a school, where more ritual objects relating to the temple, including a large **Buddha head** and an overturned **frying pan**, are still kept. The Buddha head is popularly said to be that of Vrisadeva, whose legendary decapitation led to the founding of Boudha (see p.162). The frying pan is associated with another wonderful legend, in which an ancient king's great success aroused the jealousy of a rival. Wanting to learn the king's secret, the rival spied on him during his daily devotions and watched as the king offered his own body, fried in a pan, as a sacrifice to Bajra Jogini; the goddess then restored him to life and endowed him with supernatural powers. When the rival copied the trick, the goddess accepted his flesh as a one-time offering, with no resurrection, and then turned over the frying pan to indicate that she would no more require blood sacrifice. Animal sacrifices are now performed only in front of the triangular stone of **Bhairab**, beside the path up to the temple, and not to the goddess herself.

The road to Sundarijal

Located 4km up the Sundarijal road, **GOKARNESWAR** overlooks the Bagmati River where it cuts through a low ridge (Gokarna Ban is just across the river). A tranquil spot, it has been an important cremation and pilgrimage site since ancient times, and is marked by the imposing **Gokarna Mahadev Mandir**, dedicated to Shiva. It's best known for its **festival** of Gokarna Aunsi, Nepali "Father's Day", held in late August or early September.

The recently restored fourteenth-century **temple** boasts excellent wood carving along the top of the ground floor, around the doors and on the roof struts. Inside stands a beefy natural-stone *linga*, though non-Hindus aren't allowed to approach close enough to the door to get much of a look at it. The temple's most unusual feature is an outdoor gallery of stone **sculptures** representing an ecumenical cross-section of the Nepalese pantheon, including unusual depictions of Brahma and the Vedic gods Surya, Chandra and Vayu, as well as more standard iconographies. The building closest to the river, an open hall called the **Vishnu Paduka**, is used for special rituals such as *shradha* (the rite performed by a son for a deceased parent); at the height of the monsoon, the river rises right up to its base. Another, smaller temple in the compound contains an eighth-century statue of Parbati, Shiva's consort.

From Gokarneswar you can **hike** up to Pulahari Monastery on the long ridge to the west, and from there northwards to Nagi Gompa or westwards to Kopan.

Although **SUNDARIJAL**, 5km beyond Gokarneswar, isn't a brilliant destination in itself, it's the most accessible trailhead for treks in the Helambu region. The steep climb up alongside the cascading Bagmati River – a small, reasonably clean stream here – would be much prettier without the hulking iron pipe that criss-crosses the trail: much of Kathmandu's water supply comes from the upper Bagmati. After a half-hour or so, the trail leaves the pipe and civilization behind and enters the forested Shivapuri Watershed (see below; admission Rs250).

Budhanilkantha and Shivapuri

A paved road leads 8km north from Kathmandu to **BUDHANILKANTHA** (pronounced *Bu*da-nil-*kan*ta), site of a monolithic sleeping Vishnu statue that is one of the valley's most impressive reminders of its semi-mythic early history. The surrounding bazaar supports a lively trade in religious paraphernalia, sweets and tea, but the Vishnu statue, set in a walled compound, is the only real attraction of the place. Try to make it here in time for the morning *puja* (9–10am), when things are most interesting.

A visit to Budhanilkantha can be combined with a **hike** or **mountain-bike** ride in the Shivapuri Watershed (see below). However, the ride from Kathmandu cannot be recommended, at least not on the main road – it's better via Tokha. **Buses** to Budhanilkantha (#5) leave from the City Bus Park every fifteen minutes or so. **Tempos** depart from Jamal, on the north side of Rani Pokhari.

The Sleeping Vishnu (Jalasayana Narayan)

The valley's largest stone sculpture, the five-metre-long **Sleeping Vishnu (Jalasayana Narayan)**, reclines in a recessed water tank like an oversized astronaut in suspended animation. Carved from a type of basalt found miles away in the southern hills, it was apparently dragged here by forced labour during the reign of the seventh-century Lichhavi king Vishnugupta. Many locals maintain that it was self-created, believing no human being could have fashioned such a masterpiece. According to legend the image was lost and buried for centuries, only to be rediscovered by a farmer tilling his fields – priests show worshippers the spot where the spade struck. Its pristine condition seems to confirm a long period of protection from the elements.

Hindus may enter the sanctum area to do *puja* before the Sleeping Vishnu; others may only view it from between concrete railings. Priests and novices continually tend, bathe and anoint the image and chant the thousand names of Vishnu.

Budhanilkantha's name has been a source of endless confusion. It has nothing to do with the Buddha (*budha* – or *burha* – means "old"), though that doesn't stop Buddhist Newars from worshipping the image as Lokeshwar, the *bodhisattva* of compassion. The real puzzler is why Budhanilkantha (literally, "Old Blue-Throat"), a title which unquestionably refers to Shiva, has been attached here to Vishnu. The myth of **Shiva's blue throat**, a favourite in Nepal, relates how the gods churned the ocean of existence and inadvertently unleashed a poison that threatened to destroy the world. They begged Shiva to save them from their blunder and he obliged by drinking the poison. His throat burning, the great god flew up to the range north of Kathmandu, struck the mountainside with his trident to create a lake, Gosainkund, and quenched his thirst – suffering no lasting ill effect except for a blue patch on his throat. Shaivas claim a reclining image of Shiva can be seen under the waters of Gosainkund during the annual Shiva festival there in August, which perhaps explains the association with the waterborne figure of Budhanilkantha. The water in this tank is popularly believed to originate in Gosainkund.

Nonetheless, the Budhanilkantha sculpture bears all the hallmarks of Vishnu or, as he's often called in Nepal, **Narayan** (pronounced Nuh-*rai*-uhn). It depicts Vishnu at his most cosmic, floating in the ocean of existence upon the snake Sesh (or Ananta, which in Sanskrit means "never-ending"); from his navel will grow Brahma and the rest of creation. Each year the god is said to "awaken" from his summer slumber during the Haribondhini Ekadashi **festival** in late October or early November, an event that draws thousands of worshippers.

One person who never puts in an appearance here, as a matter of policy, is the king of Nepal. Some say the boycott goes back to the seventeenth-century king

Pratap Malla, who was visited by Vishnu in a dream and warned that he and his successors would die if they ever visited Budhanilkantha. Others say it's because the king, who is half-heartedly held to be a reincarnation of Vishnu, must never gaze upon his own image.

Up to Shivapuri

At 2732m, **Shivapuri** (or **Sheopuri**) is the second-highest point on the valley rim. It offers excellent views of the Himalaya off to the west, from Jugal and Ganesh Himal out to Himalchuli, and eastwards from Langtang Lirung to Dorje Lakpa, not to mention intense rhododendron blossoms in March and April. The summit can be reached in about four hours by one of at least two **trails** from Budhanilkantha. You'll need to pack a lunch and sufficient water, and the vertical gain, nearly 1200m, shouldn't be taken lightly. You can camp on the flat, grassy summit to catch the best views first thing in the morning; clouds often move in by lunchtime.

Shivapuri and the Shivapuri Lek (the ridge that forms the northern rim of the Kathmandu Valley) lie within the **Shivapuri Watershed and Wildlife Reserve**, a huge walled area set aside to protect the valley's water supply and critical forest. As with several other parks and reserves in Nepal, this one was initially created without much regard for the needs of local people, who were summarily prohibited from gathering wood and other forest products. More recently, the government and foreign aid agencies have recognized the need to add social programmes to their original environmental agenda, but the residents of some villages are still irate that the reserve is preventing them from getting road access.

The road past Budhanilkantha continues steeply upwards for another 2km to the watershed gate, where you have to pay a Rs250 **admission charge**. From there, follow the dirt road to the right, contouring around and up the ridge to the east. Where the road finally rounds this ridge, take a trail up to **Nagi Gompa**, a former Tamang monastery now run by the renowned lama Urgyen Rinpoche, and continue along the ridge to Shivapuri (when in doubt, bear left). Near the top is the hermitage of Swami Chandresh, a Hindu sage who is following in the tradition of the celebrated Shivapuri Baba, who established the site in the early twentieth century and, it's said, lived to be 137.

It's also possible to hike to Shivapuri from Gokarna or by a more direct route from Budhanilkantha – see *Kathmandu Valley Bikes & Hikes* (see "Books" in Contexts).

BIKING IN THE SHIVAPURI WATERSHED

The **Shivapuri Watershed and Wildlife Reserve** contains some superb mountain-biking possibilities. The little-used road network begins at the Budhanilkantha entrance, where two main routes present themselves. The dirt road to the left snakes generally westwards for at least 15km, at which point the hill resort of Kakani (see p.235) is only about 2km further east along the ridge by trail (some carrying required). This ride is better done from Kakani to Budhanilkantha. For a shorter loop starting and ending in Budhanilkantha, ride to the Tokha Hospital and then descend along a steep, sandy road.

The road to the right (east) of the main entrance contours and climbs out of the valley, rounding the Shivapuri Lek and reaching the watershed's easternmost point at Jhule after about 20km. It may be possible to continue further around to the north side of Shivapuri – ask at the Kathmandu bike shops – but most people cycling this route leave the watershed at Jhule, spend the night at the nearby *Banar Top Resort* (☎411605; B⑤) or in Bhotechaur, and then continue on to Nagarkot and beyond (p.217). The HMG/FINNIDA "Shivapuri" and "Sundarijal" maps are the most accurate for route-finding in the watershed.

Balaju, Nagarjun Ban and Ichangu Narayan

The road to Trisuli (see p.235) passes a couple of worthy sights before it climbs out of the valley. **Buses** (departing from the City Bus Park) and **tempos** (from the Kantipath side of Rani Pokhari) follow fixed routes to **Balaju** and almost as far as the Nagarjun Ban gate, but both of these destinations are within easy **cycling** distance of Kathmandu – and a mountain bike will stand you in good stead once you get to Nagarjun Ban.

Simple **food** – snacks, *momo* and *daal bhat* – is available from diners in Balaju. If you're cycling or walking to Nagarjun Ban, you can eat in more pleasant surroundings at a few outdoor cafés along the main road beyond the forest entrance (the Rajneeshis' idiosyncratic vegetarian restaurant, *Zorba the Buddha*, is 4km beyond).

Balaju

If **BALAJU**'s "Water Garden" isn't as ravishing as its name suggests, neither is the Balaju Industrial Estate as awful as it sounds. The water garden is where Kathmandu comes to picnic and paddle on Saturdays, and for the jaded traveller it can provide some welcome relief from the commotion of the city. The park is only 2km northwest of Thamel along the road to Trisuli, behind a municipal-looking fence at the foot of a wooded hill. Admission is Rs3, plus about the same to park your bike.

In the northeast corner of the grounds lies a **Sleeping Vishnu** statue now known to be contemporaneous with the famous and much larger seventh-century image at Budhanilkantha. An earlier theory held that this was only a copy, commissioned in the seventeenth century by King Pratap Malla when he was barred from visiting the original, leading to its nickname Balanilkantha ("Young Blue-Throat"). Balaju's other claim to fame – for Nepalis, at least – is **Baaisdhara**, a bathing tank fed by twenty-two (*baais*) stone spouts (*dhara*), which really rocks with bathing worshippers during the **festival** of Lhuti Punhi, observed on the day of the full moon of March–April.

Nagarjun (Rani) Ban and Jamacho

Once in Balaju, you might as well continue on up the road another 2km to the entrance of **Nagarjun Ban** (also known as **Rani Ban**), a large and surprisingly wild royal forest preserve (daily 7am–10pm; pedestrians and cyclists Rs5, motorcyclists Rs15, cars and elephants Rs125). An unpaved road winds to the summit of 2096-metre **Jamacho**, but you can hike more directly up the ridge along a five-kilometre trail starting at the entrance. The north side of this ridge is riddled with limestone **caves**, including one where the famous second-century Buddhist saint Nagarjuna meditated and died, or so it's said. At the summit, a **stupa** decorated with fluttering prayer flags and penetrating eyes marks the spot where the Buddha sat during an apocryphal visit to the Kathmandu Valley, and a small **lookout tower** commands a panoramic (but sometimes hazy) view of the valley and of Ganesh Himal, Langtang and the peaks to the east.

Several **alternative routes** return to the valley below. If you can find it, the most interesting one is an obscure trail that starts from the road southeast of the lookout tower and descends in a southeasterly direction through thick forest and past several limestone caves, one of which contains a large image of the Buddha. The trail eventually meets the Jamacho road, which you can either follow back to the entrance (3km), or part of the way to a military post (1km), from where you can leave the forest reserve for the village of Rani Ban and muddle back down to Balaju or Swayambhu. Another trail from Jamacho makes for the slightly higher summit 1km to the west, then curves south down to Ichangu Narayan (below).

Ichangu Narayan

According to tradition, a Narayan temple occupies each of the four cardinal points of Kathmandu Valley. The western one, **Ichangu Narayan**, nestles in a small side valley at the southern base of Jamacho.

The newish temple is crudely fashioned and not particularly interesting, but it's a good excuse to get out into an area that's surprisingly rural considering how close it is to Kathmandu. Starting at the Ring Road west of Swayambhunath, the route quickly becomes quite rough before crossing a very steep little saddle at the village of Halchok, then descends past a rock quarry to reach Ichangu after about 3km. By backtracking to the base of the quarry, you can **hike** or **mountain-bike** westwards to Bhimdhunga and all the way to the Prithvi Highway near the valley rim.

PATAN AND THE SOUTHERN VALLEY

The hub of the southern valley is **Patan**, just across the Bagmati River from Kathmandu. Paved roads fan out from there to the hilltop outpost of **Kirtipur**, the holy places of **Chobar** and **Dakshin Kali**, and the wilds (well, sort of) above **Godavari**. Things get more rural the farther south you go, and off the main routes you'll find some of the valley's best remaining countryside.

Consider basing yourself in Patan: the valley's second city and a world apart from Kathmandu, it deserves more than just an afternoon's visit. There are also places to stay near Dakshin Kali, Lele and Godavari, though most of them are in the middle and upper price ranges.

Patan (Lalitpur)

Although now largely absorbed by greater Kathmandu, **PATAN** was once the capital of a powerful independent kingdom, and still maintains a defiantly distinct identity. Compared to Kathmandu it's quieter, less frenetic and more Buddhist (there may be a correlation). Sophisticated and, in a Nepali sort of way, bohemian, it's Kathmandu's Left Bank: while Kathmanduites are busy amassing power and wealth, Patan's residents appreciate the finer things of life, which perhaps explains Patan's poetic alternate name, **LALITPUR** ("City of Beauty"). Above all, it remains a proud city of **artisans**. Patan produces much of Nepal's fine metalwork (the sounds of tapping and filing ring out from workshops all over town), and its craftspeople have created some of the most extraordinarily lavish temples, *hiti* and *bahal* in the country. *Bahal* – their doorways here always guarded by cuddly stone lions with unscary overbites – are a particular feature of Patan, and a few still function as active monasteries. In the past two decades, Patan has also emerged as the de facto **foreign aid** capital of Nepal: the UN offices and diverse smaller organizations are scattered around the western suburbs, as are the residences of many expats who commute to the big USAID headquarters just across the river.

In legend and fact, Patan is the oldest city in the valley. **Manjushri**, the great lake-drainer, is supposed to have founded Manjupatan, the forerunner of Patan, right after he enshrined Swayambhu, while the so-called Ashokan stupas, earthen mounds standing at four cardinal points around Patan, seem to support the legend that the Indian emperor **Ashoka** visited the valley in the third century BC (historians are sceptical). More reliable legend ascribes Patan's founding to **King Arideva** in 299 AD. By the seventh century Patan had emerged as the cultural and artistic capital of Nepal, if not the entire Himalayan region. It maintained strong links with the Buddhist centres of learning in Bengal and Bihar – thereby playing a role in the transmission of Buddhism to Tibet – and when these fell to the Muslims in the twelfth century, many scholars and artists fled to Patan, setting the stage for a renaissance under the later **Malla kings**. Patan existed as part of a unified valley kingdom until the late fifteenth century, then enjoyed equal status with Kathmandu and Bhaktapur as a sovereign state until 1769,

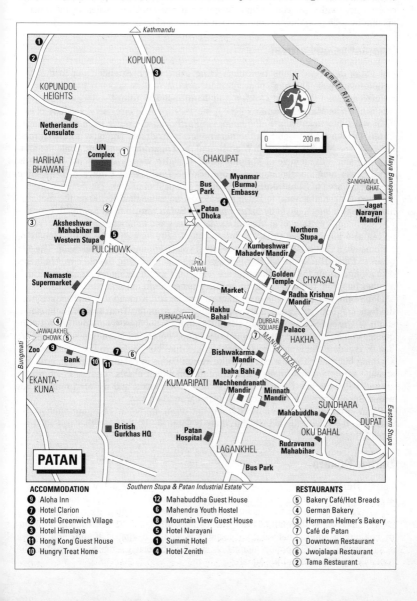

PATAN

ACCOMMODATION		RESTAURANTS
9 Aloha Inn	**12** Mahabuddha Guest House	**5** Bakery Café/Hot Breads
7 Hotel Clarion	**6** Mahendra Youth Hostel	**4** German Bakery
2 Hotel Greenwich Village	**8** Mountain View Guest House	**3** Hermann Helmer's Bakery
3 Hotel Himalaya	**5** Hotel Narayani	**7** Café de Patan
11 Hong Kong Guest House	**1** Summit Hotel	**1** Downtown Restaurant
10 Hungry Treat Home	**4** Hotel Zenith	**6** Jwojalapa Restaurant
		2 Tama Restaurant

when Prithvi Narayan Shah and his Gorkhali band conquered the valley and chose Kathmandu for their capital.

One of Patan's charms is that its historic core is frozen much as it was at the time of defeat. However, see it while you can. Although a number of temples and public monuments have been skilfully restored in the past decade, the city has lost many of its older private buildings. Here, as in Kathmandu, most owners of traditional old houses hope to replace them with more comfortable, modern concrete ones, and to finance the redevelopment by selling off their antique wooden window and door frames.

Orientation and arrival

Old Patan developed along two intersecting axes, which extended out to the four **Ashokan stupas**. The quasi-pedestrianized northern route takes in Patan's **Durbar Square** and also the famed **Golden** and **Kumbeshwar temples**. Patan's east–west axis (known as **Mangal Bazaar** where it meets Durbar Square) serves as one of two main ways into town from Kathmandu, via Pulchowk; the other main entry point is **Patan Dhoka** (Patan Gate), in the northwestern quadrant. The busy southern road runs past the **Machhendranath Mandir** and the **Lagankhel** bus park, while the eastern road skirts the temple of **Mahabuddha**. Broader, more conventional boulevards serve newer neighbourhoods from **Kopundol** to **Jawalakhel Chowk** to Lagankhel; the Tibetan area of **Ekantakuna** lies south of Jawalakhel Chowk.

A **taxi** from Kathmandu to Patan should cost no more than Rs100 on the meter. A much cheaper way to go is by battery-powered **Safaa tempo** from Kantipath near the RNAC building, getting off at Mangal Bazaar. **Buses** and minibuses are not only crowded but also inconvenient to catch, unless you already happen to be in the vicinity of Kathmandu's City Bus Park, or conceivably if you're coming from Bhaktapur. The #25 buses to Patan Dhoka are a better bet, assuming you're visiting the old city; #14 buses take a longer route to Lagankhel, and are really only worth taking if your aim is to catch another bus from there to Godavari or other places south of Patan.

Don't **bike** to Patan via the main Bagmati bridge and Kopundol – you'll expire from the fumes. A better alternative is to cross the river from the Teku area of Kathmandu, south of Durbar Square, entering Patan through its northwestern suburbs. It's even quieter coming from the international convention centre on Naya Baneswar (Airport Road), crossing the footbridge to Sankhamul Ghat, but getting to Naya Baneswar is anything but quiet. There aren't any **bike rental** shops in Patan, but you can probably arrange something informally with one of the bike fix-it places south of Pulchowk or around Patan Dhoka. Patan itself has some resident taxis and metered tempos, but within the old part of town you can easily get around on foot.

Patan officials have announced their intention to begin charging tourists an **entrance fee** to visit the old city, but there is some doubt as to whether this will ever actually happen.

Durbar Square

Patan's **Durbar Square**, while smaller and less monumental than Kathmandu's, comes across as more refined, not to mention less touristy. Maybe it's because the city of artisans has a better eye for architectural harmony; or because Patan, which hasn't been a capital since the eighteenth century, has escaped the continuous meddling of monument-building kings. That said, the formula is similar to that in Kathmandu, with a solemn royal palace looming along one side and assorted temples grouped in the remaining public areas of the square.

The Royal Palace

Patan's richly decorated **Royal Palace** was largely constructed during the second half of the seventeenth century, but substantially rebuilt after the Gorkhali invasion of 1769 and the 1934 earthquake. It consists of three main wings, each enclosing a central courtyard and reached by a separate entrance.

The courtyard of the small, southernmost wing, **Sundari Chowk**, contains what must surely be one of the grandest bathtubs in the world, although it seems to be closed indefinitely for renovations. **Tusha Hiti**, the seventeenth-century sunken royal

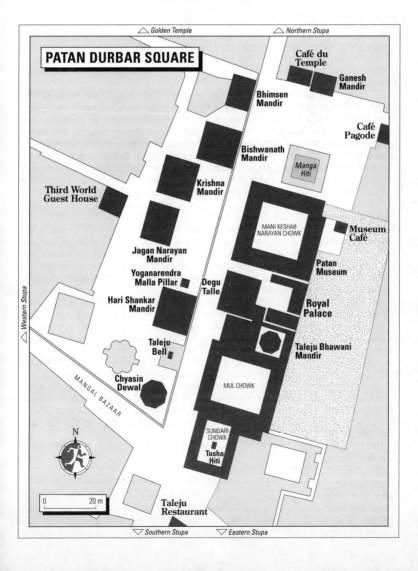

△ *Golden Temple*　　　△ *Northern Stupa*

PATAN DURBAR SQUARE

Café du Temple

Ganesh Mandir

Bhimsen Mandir

Café Pagode

Bishwanath Mandir

Manga Hiti

Krishna Mandir

Third World Guest House

MANI KESHAB NARAYAN CHOWK

Museum Café

Jagan Narayan Mandir

Patan Museum

Yoganarendra Malla Pillar

Degu Talle

Hari Shankar Mandir

Royal Palace

Western Stupa

Taleju Bell

Taleju Bhawani Mandir

Chyasin Dewal

MUL CHOWK

MANGAL BAZAAR

N

SUNDARI CHOWK

Tusha Hiti

0　　20 m

Taleju Restaurant

▽ *Southern Stupa*　　▽ *Eastern Stupa*

bath, is done up like a hall of fame of Hindu gods and goddesses. Its brass spout, the only bit of metal here, is decorated with Shiva and Parbati, while the bath itself is shaped like a *yoni*, the symbol of female sexuality, and ringed with serpents. Fittingly, Bernardo Bertolucci used it as Prince Siddhartha's bath in his 1995 film *Little Buddha*. At one end of the basin stands the obligatory statue of Hanuman the monkey god, plus a "holy stone" on which the kings of Patan performed *puja* after bathing, and at the other end a replica of the Krishna Mandir, one of the temples outside. The courtyard is covered in ornate woodwork, including many fabulous carved doorways, windows, *torana*, and images of deities individually set into niches.

Mul Chowk, the next wing to the north, served as the actual royal family residence. A sadly deteriorated gilt door in the right-hand wall of the courtyard, leading to the private Taleju Mandir, is flanked by statues of the Indian river goddesses **Ganga** and **Jamuna**, the latter riding a *makana* – a mythical cross between a crocodile and an elephant, whose curling snout decorates almost every public water spout in Nepal. Behind and to the left of Mul Chowk rises the octagonal, three-tiered **Taleju Bhawani Mandir**.

Yet another Taleju temple, the monolithic **Degu Talle** towers just north of Mul Chowk. Seven storeys high and the tallest building on the block, the temple was erected in 1640 by Siddhi Narsingh Malla, during whose reign much of the palace and square were built. It had to be completely rebuilt after being razed in the 1934 earthquake. The tower is kept locked except during the autumn Tihaar festival, when a priest is supposed to refill a pipe with ganja for the departed king. Behind it, just off a small *chowk* once used for courtly performances, you'll find a small branch of the non-profit Mahaguthi handicrafts shop. This *chowk* retains its connection with dance since it also contains the headquarters of Patan's autumn festival committee.

THE PATAN MUSEUM

The palace's northernmost wing, Mani Keshab Narayan Chowk, once served as the palace of another noted seventeenth-century king, Yoganarendra Malla. It, too, suffered in the 1934 quake and at the time was only clumsily rebuilt. With assistance from the Austrian government, it has recently been restored to house the splendid **Patan Museum** (daily except Tues, 10.30am–4pm; Rs120), a tasteful space that does honour to this city of artisans.

The museum displays a well-curated permanent collection of important bronzes, stone sculptures and wood carvings, and a gilded Malla throne, plus an assortment of archival photographs. The exhibits are arranged thematically to lead you through Hindu, Buddhist and Tantric iconography, temple construction, ritual objects and metallurgical processes, all supported by excellent explanatory text. If that's not enough for you, there's the building itself, which, with its newly stuccoed walls and artful lighting, suggests the royal palace Yoganarendra Malla might have built had he reigned at the beginning of the twenty-first century. You can ascend to the corner belfries, their eaves decorated with *kinkinimali*, leaf-shaped tin cut-outs designed to flutter in the breeze, or look out on the courtyard below and its central Lakshmi shrine. A stunning gold window above the exterior main entrance depicts Vishnu and a heavenly host.

There's a great little **café** in the courtyard behind the museum, and a **gift shop** near the entrance.

The square

Starting at the newer – eighteenth-century – southern end of Durbar Square, the stone **Chyasin Dewal** in front of Sundari Chowk is the lesser of the square's two Krishna temples. Some say the octagonal temple was raised in memory of the eight wives that committed *sati* on a king's funeral pyre, although Krishna temples almost always have eight sides to commemorate Krishna's role as the eighth *avatar* (incarnation) of Vishnu. The cast-iron **Taleju Bell** was the first to be erected in the valley, in 1736; keen civic rivalry among the three valley capitals prompted Bhaktapur and Kathmandu to follow suit with their own bells. Nearby, a Victorian-looking statue is of a Rana prime minister's wife, erected in 1905 to commemorate the arrival of piped water in Patan.

North of here, the finely carved **Hari Shankar Mandir** is dedicated both to Vishnu (sometimes called Hari) and Shiva (alias Shankar), while the statue mounted on a pillar and praying to the Degu Talle depicts **Yoganarendra Malla**. An angry cobra rears up like a halo behind the king, and atop the cobra's head perches a gilded bird. Like all god-fearing rulers of the valley, Yoganarendra would have made sure to appease the *nag*, animist snake spirits who deliver or withhold the valley's rains. As for the bird, chroniclers state that the king, upon abdicating the throne to become a *sunyasan* (hermit) after the untimely death of his son, told his subjects that as long as the bird remained they would know he was still alive. To this day, the people of Patan keep a light burning and a bed ready for the absent king in an upper chamber of the palace.

If the two-tiered **Jagan Narayan**, built in 1565, is the oldest temple in the square, the most unusual one is the seventeenth-century **Krishna Mandir**. Its central structure, a Mughal-style *shikra*, is girdled by three levels of stone verandas, with detailed scenes from the great Hindu epics, the *Mahabharat* and *Ramayan*, carved along the lintels. An incarnation of Vishnu, Krishna is one of the best-loved characters of the *Mahabharat*: superhuman baby, mischievous lad, seducer of milkmaids and heroic slayer of the evil king Kamsa. The upstairs sanctum (closed to non-Hindus) displays images of the whole cast of the *Mahabharat*. *Bhajan* is sung here most nights, and devotees gather at the temple on Krishna's birthday in August or early September.

The **Bishwanath Mandir** contains a copy of the Shiva *linga* of the same name in Varanasi, India. The temple collapsed in 1990, but has been seamlessly restored. Last but not least, the seventeenth-century **Bhimsen Mandir** is dedicated to the ever-popular god of Nepali traders. Non-Hindus aren't allowed inside, but you can often see and hear *puja* being performed in the open upstairs sanctuary. Across the way, one of the valley's largest sunken public bathing tanks, **Manga Hiti**, has been operational since the sixth century.

North and west of Durbar Square

Some of Patan's most interesting sights – the Golden and Kumbeshwar temples and the ghats – lie north of Durbar Square, but there's also plenty of serendipitous exploring to be done among the back alleys west of the square.

Hiranyavarna Mahavihara (The Golden Temple)

The **Hiranyavarna Mahavihara** – that's Sanskrit for "Golden Monastery", but all the tour guides call it the **Golden Temple** – is the most opulent little temple in Nepal. The three-tiered pagoda occupies one side of the cramped courtyard of Kwa Bahal, a still-active twelfth-century Buddhist Newar monastery and the spiritual hub of old Patan. During early-morning *puja*, the *bahal* is a fascinating theatre of Nepali religion in all its perplexing glory. **Admission** is Rs25, and note that you're not allowed to bring anything made of leather inside.

The temple's gilt facade, embossed with images of Buddhas and Taras, is regarded as the pre-eminent example of large-scale repoussé **metalwork** in Nepal, while in the middle of the courtyard a small, lavishly ornamented shrine contains a priceless silver and gold Swayambhu *chaitya*. Both the shrine and the main temple are further decorated with what look like long metallic neckties: these *pataka* are supposed to provide a slide for the gods when they descend to answer the prayers of their worshippers. The *bahal* is so crammed with images, ornaments and fine details that a full account of all its wonders would fill a book. For descriptions of some of the main features, including the deities enshrined in alcoves around the courtyard, refer to the brochure that comes with the price of admission.

Sakyamuni Buddha is the temple's main image. According to **legend**, this image was made homeless in the twelfth century when the temple it formerly resided in collapsed. When King Bhaskardeva built it a new temple, the image informed him in a dream that it wished to move to a new place where *mice* chased *cats*. One day the king saw a golden mouse chasing a cat here at Kwa Bahal, and so he set about building a new, golden temple on the spot. Rats are said to be allowed to run free here in deference to the deity's wishes.

Though no longer a residential monastery, the *mahavihara* is an important centre of lay worship, following well-established Buddhist rituals and iconography that draw from both the Newar and Tibetan traditions. Its principal priest, a boy who must be no older than twelve, tends the main shrine. A Tibetan-style *gompa* upstairs on the northeastern side of the courtyard, which you can visit, is evidence of the spiritual ties forged between Patan and Tibet through centuries of trade.

One block to the east, the three-tiered **Radha Krishna Mandir** has been restored by the Kathmandu Valley Preservation Trust, an organization that has now moved on to saving several other derelict temples and residences in Patan. The lovers Krishna and Radha, to whom this temple is dedicated, are a favourite subject for sandalwood carvers.

Kumbeshwar Mahadev

The **Kumbeshwar Mahadev**, Patan's oldest temple and one of only two freestanding five-tiered pagodas in Nepal (the other is in Bhaktapur), was built as a two-roofed structure in 1392, and despite the addition of three more levels it remains well proportioned and to all appearances sturdy. Shiva is the honoured deity here: inside you can see a stone *linga* and a brass one with four faces; Nandi, Shiva's patient mount, waits outside. The temple apparently owes its name to an episode in which a pilgrim at Gosainkund, the sacred lake high in the mountains north of Kathmandu, dropped a pot (*kumbha*) into the water there. Much later, the same pot appeared in the water tank here, giving rise to the belief that the tank is fed by an underground channel from Gosainkund, and adding to Shiva's roll of titles that of Kumbeshwar – Lord of the Pots.

Thanks to this connection, Kumbeshwar's water tank is regarded as an alternative venue during Gosainkund's great annual **festival**, Janai Purnima. Falling on the full-moon day of late July or early August, Janai Purnima is the ceremony in which Brahmans and Chhetris formally change the sacred thread (*janai*) that distinguishes them as members of the "twice-born" castes. At Kumbeshwar, thousands come to pay respect to a *linga* erected in the middle of the tank, and a big part of the festivities is for bathers to see how much water they can splash at spectators.

Elsewhere in the temple courtyard stands the shrine of **Bangalamukhi**, the "heron-headed" form of Kali and a local manifestation of the popular Newar protectress Ajima, whose tiny idol is encased in an ornate silver frieze. Women queue here on Thursdays and Saturdays to pray for offspring and conjugal bliss.

Just north of the temple, the **Kumbeshwar Technical School** provides vocational and literacy training for poor women, orphans and other disadvantaged people, supported in part by sales from its small retail space (see "Shopping" on p.185).

The Northern Stupa and on to the ghats

Just northeast of the Kumbeshwar Mahadev, the **Northern Stupa** is the smallest and most central of the Ashokan mounds, and the only one that's been sealed over with plaster. Although it doesn't look wildly interesting for a 2200-year-old monument, you

Durbar Square, Kathmandu

Ganesh statue, Hanuman Ghat, Bhaktapur

Newar men with *nol*, Bhaktapur

AXIOM / JIM HOLMES

Woman doing *puja*, Kathmandu

DAVID REED

Near Rani Ghat

DAVID REED

Pashupatinath during Shiva Raatri

Swayambhu stupa

Dyokyapsi dancer, Syang, near Marpha, the Thak Khola

Carrying bamboo, Helambu trail

Terraced fields, the Central Hills

View from World Peace Pagoda, Pokhara

Trailside teahouse near Tansen

can let your imagination dwell on what treasures or relics Ashoka might have buried here – the contents are unlikely ever to see the light of day, since archeological digs are prohibited in the valley.

The stupa stands at the edge of the city. From here the road south plunges back between brick tenements and neglected temples to Durbar Square. Northwards, it wends through receding farmland towards Patan's **Sankhamul Ghat**, a half-kilometre-long embankment near the junction of the Manohara and Bagmati rivers. Confluences are regarded as auspicious locations, and Sankhamul Ghat serves as Patan's main cremation site and, during the festival of Magh Sankranti (usually January 14), an important spot for ritual bathing.

The ghat stretches on either side of a footbridge leading to the Naya Baneswar area of Kathmandu. Cremations are held to the west of the footbridge, where the putrid Bagmati still flows near the ghat. However, there's more to see east of the bridge. Flanked by sagging pilgrims' shelters and statues of Hanuman and Ganesh, a path leads under an arch and up to the exotic **Jagat Narayan** temple complex, named after its builder, the nineteenth-century prime minister Jagat Shamsher. The brick *shikra* shares a compound with monolithic stone statues of Garud, Hanuman and Ganesh, and a second gilt statue of Garud that makes Vishnu's man-bird vehicle look like a kendo warrior.

West to Pulchowk

From **Mangal Bazaar**, which these days sells mainly cloth and tourist odds and ends, central Patan's main drag heads out towards the Western Stupa. One of Patan's less touristed former monasteries, **Hakhu Bahal** (also known as Ratnakar Mahabihar), rises on the left after 300m. Its courtyard crowded with lotus pedestals, indicative of divinity, the *bahal* is the home of Patan's Kumari.

Though little more than a grassy mound beside a busy intersection, the **Western Stupa** comes alive on one day a year when it serves as the starting point of the great chariot procession of Rato Machhendranath (see p.180). A nearby shelter displays retired *ghama* – long, upward-curving chariot yokes – from past festivals. Chariot parts are considered sacred and may not be destroyed, so you'll often see them stowed next to temples or recycled into pillars or struts. Just to the right of the stupa, a whitewashed arch and a set of steps lead to the hilltop **Aksheshwar Mahabihar**, a working monastery that's not normally open to the public, though the views from the terrace in front are good.

Northwest to Patan Dhoka

The northwestern quarter of old Patan is a jumble of *bahal* – the lane leading from the Golden Temple west to Patan Dhoka takes you past quite a few. (*Patan Walkabout*, a booklet published by Patan's tourism development committee, provides a wealth of detail about the *bahal* and other sights in this area.) The next lane further south, which parallels the main road to the Western Stupa, skirts Patan's small fruit and vegetable **market** and eventually opens out into **Pim Bahal** and its large and less than glamorous *pokhari* (pond). An inscription in front of the Swayambhu-style stupa here says it was built in the fourteenth century and restored a few years later, after Muslim invaders damaged it.

A small bazaar area and bus park surrounding an unremarkable city gate, **Patan Dhoka** had its finest hour during the 1990 *jana andolan* (people's movement), when it stood on the front line of an all-out revolution. Nearly a month before the government's final capitulation Patan was declared "liberated", with ditches dug across every road into the city, and defiant residents vowing to kill any opponent of the *andolan* who dared enter. Several police cars and buses met their end at narrow Patan Dhoka – and throughout the uprising the banned Nepali Congress Party flag flew from the gate.

South and east of the square

South of Durbar Square you essentially have two choices. The southbound street passes the Machhendranath temple and other sights en route to the Lagankhel bus park, while the continuation of Mangal Bazaar leads southeastwards to Mahabuddha. The area directly east of Durbar Square, though short on specific sights, is an active artisans' quarter.

Bishwakarma Mandir and Ibaha Bahi

One of Patan's most charming streets runs parallel to Mangal Bazaar, a block to the south. This is an area of metalworkers and sellers of metal household wares, which perhaps accounts for the **Bishwakarma Mandir**'s facade of hammered gilt-copper and froggy copper lions standing guard. The name Bishwakarma refers both to the god of artisans and to members of the occupational caste of blacksmiths (more commonly known as Kami).

Patan's second-oldest monastery, **Ibaha Bahi**, stands one block further to the south. Founded in 1427, the *bahal* was recently restored with assistance from the Nippon Institute of Technology, and is supposed to be relaunched as a fully functional Buddhist centre and school.

RATO MACHHENDRANATH'S BIG RIDE

The Kathmandu Valley's oldest, lengthiest and most spectacular festival, the **Machhendranath Raath Jaatra**, begins the day after the full moon of Baisaakh (April–May), when priests ritually bathe Rato Machhendranath's sandalwood idol outdoors in Patan's Lagankhel square. Moved back to its temple at Ta Bahal, the idol then spends the next ten days undergoing the life-cycle rituals of Buddhist Newars, both male and female. Meanwhile, just south of the Western Stupa at Pulchowk, Machhendranath's **chariot** (*raath*) is assembled and its sixty-foot-high tower of poles and vegetation constructed; a smaller chariot to carry Minnath is built at its temple.

After a few more preliminaries, the idols are installed in their chariots and the great procession is ready to begin. It is an electrifying event. Scores of men heave at the ropes; Machhendranath's unwieldy vehicle rocks and teeters and suddenly lurches forward, its spire swaying and grazing buildings as it passes. The crowd roars, people leap out of the way, and the chariot comes to a stubborn stop until the pullers regroup and try to budge it again. It goes on like this, in stages, for four or more weeks, until the chariots reach Jawalakhel, a journey of about 4km. At three designated resting spots – Hakhu Bahal, Sundhara and Lagankel – neighbourhood residents celebrate the gods with offerings, music and other auspicious acts.

When the chariots reach Jawalakhel, the stage is set for the dramatic **Bhoto Jaatra**. At noon on a day ordained by the astrologers, a huge crowd assembles at Jawalakhel. The king and queen arrive in their limousine, and Patan's Kumari is carried by palanquin. At last a priest climbs aboard Machhendranath's chariot and holds aloft the god's magical jewelled vest, a relic of some ancient dispute. The king then pays homage to the gods and departs, after which the crowd charges the chariots for *prasad* (consecrated food offerings). Since the procession culminates during the showery pre-monsoon, Machhendranath usually obliges with rain: bring an umbrella.

Machhendranath's idol is then carried to Bungmati, 6km to the south (see p.195), where it is welcomed "home" with great fanfare – the cult of Rato Machhendranath is believed to have originated in Bungmati, accounting for the god's Newar name, Bunga Dyo ("God of Bunga"). The idol spends the summer months in Bungmati before being transported back to Ta Bahal, but once every twelve years it's kept in Bungmati all winter and the chariot procession begins and ends there. That will next happen in 2003.

Machhendranath Mandir

Outwardly, Patan's **Machhendranath Mandir** resembles many others: a huge seventeenth-century brick pagoda adorned with beautifully carved and gaudily painted struts and *torana*. It stands in an extra-large compound called Ta Bahal, about 300m south of Durbar Square, reached by following a narrow lane west from the main street and ducking under an arch next to a catering service.

What makes this temple extraordinary, however, is its idol, **Rato Machhendranath** ("Red Machhendranath"), a painted shingle of sandalwood which, for several weeks beginning in late April, is the object of one of Nepal's most extraordinary festivals (see box). Older than his white counterpart in Kathmandu, Rato Machhendranath is a god of many guises. To Newars he's Bunga Dyo, the androgynous god of agricultural prosperity and a manifestation of the great cult figure Karunamaya. To Buddhists of other ethnic groups he's Avalokiteshwara or Lokeshwar, the *bodhisattva* of compassion. As Machhendranath, the progenitor of the *nath* (lord) cult, he's the spirit of a seventh-century Hindu guru who once taught the Shah kings' beloved saint, Gorakhnath. Legend has it that Gorakhnath once visited the valley and, offended that he wasn't accorded a full reception, caused a drought by rounding up all the rain-bringing snakes. The locals sent a posse to Assam to fetch Machhendranath, who came to their rescue in the form of a bee. Wishing to pay tribute to his guru, Gorakhnath had to release the snakes, whereupon the rains returned and Machhendranath came to be revered as a rain-maker.

Minnath and on to the Southern Stupa

Set behind a *hiti* (sunken bathing tank) across the street, the smaller sixteenth-century **Minnath Mandir** is dedicated to yet another mythologized Indian saint. Historically supposed to have been Machhendranath's guru, Minnath has been transmuted by popular tradition into his sister, brother or even daughter, and his likeness follows Machhendranath in a smaller chariot of its own during the annual festival (see box).

South of here the main road widens to include a busy open-air bazaar and the chaotic **Lagankhel** minibus park, then jogs left; straight ahead lies an army base and a pair of overgrown water tanks that feed Patan's many *hiti*. It's not really worth travelling another kilometre south to visit the grassy **Southern Stupa** – the biggest of the four – although if you're going to the Patan Industrial Estate (see "Shopping" below) you'll pass right by it.

Southeast to Mahabuddha

Mangal Bazaar gets quieter and better for walking east of Durbar Square. After 300m it reaches **Sundhara**, a sunken bathing area with four golden (*sun*) spouts (*dhara*), which gives its name to a picturesque intersection with a number of rest shelters and temples used for evening *bhajan*. North of here is **Dupat**, whose close, dark alleys are brimming with atmosphere. To the south is **Oku Bahal**, Patan's main metalsmithing area and home of the famed Mahabuddha temple.

Nicknamed "Temple of a Thousand Buddhas", **Mahabuddha** is not your average Nepali temple. Constructed entirely of terracotta tiles – each one bearing the Buddha's image – this remarkable rococo structure mimics the famous Mahabodhi Temple of Bodhgaya in India, where its builder, an enthusiastic seventeenth-century Patan architect, had previously meditated for several years. Although the likeness is only approximate, the temple introduced to Nepal the Indian *shikra* form, which to this day remains prevalent around Patan. Reduced to rubble during the 1934 earthquake, it was put back together rather like Humpty Dumpty; the smaller temple beside it was built from the spare parts. So tightly is the temple hemmed in by residences, it's like a casket that's been up-ended to fit in a hole. For a better view, go up into one of the surrounding metal handicrafts sellers' buildings – looking is free, but of course they'll put the retail moves on you.

The name of this neighbourhood, Oku (or Uku) Bahal, comes from the former monastery at the next intersection to the south, which also goes by the name **Rudravarna Mahavihara** ("Red Monastery"). Though it's undergone a recent renovation, the now-defunct Buddhist monastery is believed to be Patan's oldest – the wooden struts on the north side of the courtyard date from the thirteenth century. Its ornate principal temple is surrounded by a small menagerie of bronze animals and mythological beasts.

Jawalakhel and around

The name **Jawalakhel** (pronounced *Jowl*-akel) is generally applied to a wide area around the big Jawalakhel Chowk roundabout and south from there down to the Ring Road. The southern part of it – often referred to as Ekantakuna ("Lonely Corner"), after a former Rana mansion now occupied by the Swiss development agency – is Patan's Tibetan ghetto.

Ekantakuna

The former Tibetan refugee camp at **Ekantakuna** is arguably the best place in the valley to watch carpets being made (see "Shopping", below). As a Tibetan cultural experience, though, it doesn't really compare with Boudha or Swayambhu: there's no big temple or power place here, only one small monastery, and except for the carpet-weaving centre and shops, very little commercial vitality.

Tibetans started pouring into the Kathmandu Valley immediately after the Chinese annexation of Tibet and the flight of the Dalai Lama in 1959. By 1960 their plight prompted the International Red Cross to set up a transit camp at Jawalakhel, later assigned to the Swiss Red Cross, which in turn formed the Swiss Association for Technical Assistance to help Tibetans on a long-term basis. SATA encouraged carpet-making and other cottage industries, and by 1964 the Jawalakhel "transit camp" was a registered company. A generation on, Jawalakhel's Tibetans are prospering from the booming carpet industry, and many have left the centre to establish businesses and live closer to the Buddhist holy places.

Those who remain, and a steady trickle of new arrivals, have created a small suburb of solid brick residences east of the sales centre. About the only sight worth seeing is a small **gompa** with a big prayer wheel right beside the main road; wander beyond it and someone will probably take you to their house and show you carpets or woollens, which will probably be more memorable than visiting a monastery. There's scant **food** in the immediate vicinity save *Bakena Batika* (see "Eating", below), but it's not far up the hill to the eateries of Jawalakhel Chowk.

The zoo

Nepal's only **zoo** (daily except Mon 10am–5pm; winter closes at 4pm; adults Rs60, children Rs30) – often rendered "jew" by Nepali-speakers – lies just south of Jawalakhel Chowk, on the way to the Tibetan area. It's probably the best attraction for kids in the entire Kathmandu Valley: besides looking at the animals, they can take elephant rides around the grounds (Rs100) and pedalo around the central lake. **Food** is available from a café and a couple of snack bars, and there are plenty of places for picnicking.

Most of the animal species kept here are indigenous to Nepal, and almost all have at least a South Asian connection. Many are hard to spot in the wild, though, so the zoo offers a chance to see them close up. Highlights include a tiger (a man-eater from Chitwan, now serving a life sentence here), rhinos, blackbuck antelope, gharial crocodiles, two species of bear, clouded leopards, an Asiatic lion and a bevy of big birds. (For background on Nepal's wildlife, see "Natural history" in Contexts.) Conditions for the animals aren't brilliant, but they've improved markedly since management of the zoo was handed over to the King Mahendra Trust for Nature Conservation, a non-governmental organization respected for its work in the Annapurna area and Nepal's lowland parks.

Kushunti Pancheshwar Mahadev Mandir

Kushunti, a suburb of Patan just south of the Ring Road, held little of interest until 1997, when it became the site of a latter-day miracle. Kalyani Thapa, a poor widow seized by a vision sent by Shiva, instructed villagers to start digging under a local dump. The excavation revealed a *linga* and images of an ox and snakes that devotees believe are emblems of Shiva. A modest brick-and-concrete temple, the **Pancheshwar Mahadev Mandir**, was quickly erected on the spot, and Mata Kalanyi (as she is now known) has become a local celebrity.

The temple receives a fair number of worshippers in the mornings and on Saturdays, and given the large amount of money being raised by Mata Kalanyi's followers, its fame seems certain to increase. To get to it, head south from Jawalakhel Chowk, make a left after the staff college, cross the Ring Road, and after 200m make a right on a road heading downhill.

Accommodation

While Patan welcomes day-trippers, it seems less keen on visitors staying overnight. There's a distinct lack of **accommodation** in the old part of city, and such as there is is generally priced higher than its Kathmandu equivalent. However, this situation is changing as more and more Thamel refugees find their way here. Arrive early and you should have no trouble getting a room.

Budget places

Only three of these **budget** places are in the old city (one of which barely qualifies for the budget category). The rest are less ideally situated in the Kumaripati and Man Bhawan areas, southwest of the centre, and are run mainly by ex-Gurkhas who've settled close to the brigade headquarters there.

Café de Patan, Mangal Bazaar (☎537599). Friendly, with well-maintained rooms, rooftop views and a highly regarded restaurant. Central location. ④/B⑤.

Hong Kong Guest House, Man Bhawan (☎523089). The better rooms are spacious and have TVs and phones, but the management isn't accustomed to dealing with foreigners. Snooker club, Newar restaurant. ③/B④.

Hostel for Ladies, Ekantakuna – off the map (☎523508). Undistinguished facilities, but attentive management. Short- and long-term stays in shared or private rooms, with two daily meals included in the price. ④.

Hungry Treat Home, Man Bhawan (☎534792). A cheaper version of the nearby *Hong Kong Guest House*, with clean rooms and a nice little terrace café. ③/B③.

Mahabuddha Guest House, Oku Bahal (☎540575, fax 535148). Great location just opposite the Mahabuddha temple. Very small (6 rooms), nice family, very clean rooms, small rooftop sitting area. ③.

Mahendra Youth Hostel, Jawalakhel (☎521003). Nepal's only HI-recognized establishment: lonely but quiet dorms (①); some private rooms (③).

Mountain View Guest House, Kumaripati (☎ & fax 538168). Average rooms, decent little rooftop garden, run by a colourful ex-serviceman. ③/B④.

Third World Guest House, Durbar Square (☎522187). Unbeatable location: all rooms look directly out on the square. ⑥/B⑦.

Moderate and expensive hotels

Aloha Inn, Jawalakhel Chowk (☎522796; *aloha@mos.com.np*). Small and functional. B⑦.

Bakena Batika, Ekantakuna, 100m south of the carpet-weaving centre – off the map (☎523998, fax

538246). A small, rusticated place with stylish Nepali decor and a good in-house restaurant, but rather inconveniently located. B⑦, including breakfast.

Hotel Clarion, Man Bhawan (☎524512). Small, with restaurant and gardens. B⑧.

Hotel Greenwich Village, Kopundol Heights (☎521780; *greenwich@wlink.com.np*). Located in the quiet northwestern part of town, with a pool and good views. AC⑨.

Hotel Himalaya, Kopundol (☎523900; *himalaya@lalitpur.mos.com.np*). Big, posh hotel with nice gardens, swimming pool, tennis courts, etc. AC⑨.

Hotel Narayani, Pulchowk (☎525015; *info@nbe.mos.com.np*). A somewhat less deluxe choice, also with a pool. ACi.

Summit Hotel, Kopundol Heights (☎524694; *summit@wlink.com.np*). Traditional Nepalese architecture, terrific view, beautiful grounds. ⑦/B⑨ (discounts in low season).

Hotel Zenith, Chakupat (☎522932; *amizenit@mos.com.np*). Pretty standard tourist-class accommodation, lacking in atmosphere. B⑧/AC⑧.

Eating

Finding a place to **eat** can be a problem at lunchtime, when places around Durbar Square get packed by day-trippers, but at night you'll feel like you've got the place to yourself. Sitting at a table overlooking the square on a balmy evening, with the temples lit from within, it can be magical.

Cafés and lunch places in the old city

Café de Patan, Mangal Bazaar (southwest of Durbar Square). Consistently good (tourist) food plus Newari dinner specials on weekends, phenomenal lassis, courtyard and roof terrace seating.

Café Pagode, northeast corner of Durbar Square. Serene courtyard and a sunny rooftop terrace that's literally a tourist trap, but understandably so.

Café du Temple, north side of Durbar Square. All-rounder menu, featuring good Indian food. Head for the roof for great views.

Patan Museum Café, in the Royal Palace. Superb snacks, lunches and daily specials in a peaceful back courtyard. You can eat here without paying to enter the museum.

Taleju Restaurant, south of Durbar Square. Western, Indian and Nepali food that's not worth the wait.

Third World Restaurant, west side of Durbar Square. Run-of-the-mill tourist food, but with the best views of Durbar Square.

Other tourist restaurants

Bakena Batika, Ekantakuna, 100m south of the carpet-weaving centre – off the map. Lovely garden restaurant specializing in Euro-Nepali wholefood dishes (it's one of the only restaurants in Nepal that serves brown rice). Expensive, by Patan standards.

Bakery Café, Jawalakhel Chowk. One of a chain of semi-fast-food restaurants, serving burgers, pizza, hot dogs, *momos*, etc. Employs hearing-impaired staff (no worries, just point at the menu).

Downtown Restaurant, Pulchowk. Trusty cheap Indian and Chinese food, packed at lunchtime by staff from the nearby UN complex.

Jwojalapa, Man Bhawan. An excellent place to try Newari food: it's authentic and cheap, but not as intimidating as *bhojanalaya* and *bhatti* (see below). Have someone take you through the menu before ordering.

Tama Restaurant, Pulchowk. Fairly authentic Japanese dishes and ambience; Indian food also available. Moderately expensive.

Bhojanalaya and bhatti

The old city is full of curtained **bhojanalaya** (diners), **bhatti** (taverns) and other local eateries. Many serve *woh*, a sort of fried lentil polenta that's particularly popular among Patan's Newars – perhaps the most famous place for it is located immediately west of the

Krishna Mandir on Durbar Square. Various other *momo* joints and fry stalls can be found in the lanes running north and west of the main vegetable market.

For a night out, Patan residents head for one of several (relatively) fancy *bhojanalaya* around Patan Dhoka or Jawalakhel Chowk – in the latter area you'll also find Nepali-style snack bars and tandoori takeaways. Places around Lagankhel are pretty dingy, but will suffice if you're waiting for a bus.

Bakeries and supermarkets
You could create a fine picnic out of the savoury rolls, breads and pastries sold at the Jawalakhel Chowk branch of the *Hot Breads* **bakery** chain. The *German Bakery*, just north of Jawalakhel Chowk, is the place that started the whole "German" bakery fad – it has only a limited range of items and is better for whole loaves. *Hermann Helmer's Bakery*, west of Pulchowk, is hard to find but is very popular with expats for its pastries and biscuits.

Central Patan's cold stores stock only the basics, but you can get whatever you want at the Namaste **Supermarket** and Gemini Grocer, both around Jawalakhel Chowk.

Shopping

Many of the handicrafts sold in Kathmandu and elsewhere are produced in Patan, so this is a good place to watch them being made and (maybe) to get a better price by buying from the source. Another unique feature of Patan is its many nonprofit shops, supported by the local aid community, which stock some excellent crafts made by disadvantaged workers.

In the old city: traditional handicrafts
Patan has always been renowned for its **metalsmiths**, who produce religious (mainly Buddhist) statues by the lost-wax and repoussé processes. Oku Bahal – the area around the Mahabuddha temple – is their traditional neighbourhood, and you'll find dozens of retail outlets-cum-workshops there. Pieces run the gamut of size and price, from crude little statuettes to magnificent large-scale works of art.

Shops in the area between Durbar Square and the Golden Temple sell a range of handicrafts, but the majority specialize in **thangka** or contemporary paintings of local scenes. Several galleries display *thangka*-influenced naive **landscape paintings** of Nepal and the Kathmandu Valley – they're mass-produced for the tourist market, but they still make nice souvenirs.

Woollens are available in a few shops, including the nonprofit Kumbeshwar Technical School Showroom, just north of the Kumbeshwar temple. Carpets are also sold there – the school is one of the few manufacturers of 100-percent Tibetan-wool carpets in Nepal. For **toys**, visit Educational Wooden Toys, a store and nearby factory outlet about 100m south of Durbar Square on the left. The Nepali-style toy trucks, jigsaw puzzles, doll houses and rocking horses are sold at many locations, but it's fun to see them being made here. A few stalls at the southwestern end of Durbar square specialize in *malla* (glass-bead **necklaces**) and *dhago* (red tassels for the hair).

Ekantakuna: carpets and wood
For **carpets**, the obvious place to start is Ekantakuna (Jawalakhel), Nepal's oldest and most famous carpet-weaving centre. You might as well start by paying an obligatory visit to the **Jawalakhel Handicraft Center** (daily except Sat 8am–noon & 1–8pm), where you can see workers spinning, dyeing and weaving. The complex includes a fixed-price sales showroom, where profits benefit elderly and poor Tibetans, and a couple of souvenir shops, one of which also sells Tibetan-related books. However, there are many more private shops out on the road leading back to Patan, and their prices are by and large quite a bit cheaper.

Also worth visiting in this area is the **Woodcarving Studio** (☎538528; *asianart@mos.com.np*), located just west and north of the main Ekantakuna intersection, up the hill from the Tibetan area. Visit on a Sunday afternoon (or other times by appointment) and proprietor Lee Birch will explain techniques, tools, designs and woods. The non-traditional Nepali-style furniture, mirror frames and windows sold in the showroom are exquisite (and priced to match).

(Mostly) Kopundol: contemporary crafts

The main drag from Kathmandu, where it passes through the Kopundol area, is known to English-speakers as "Fashion Row". Several boutiques along here specialize in Nepali-influenced **designer clothing**, but they're somewhat overshadowed these days by nonprofit outlets (and for-profit competitors) selling beautiful **contemporary crafts** and **home furnishings**.

Dhankuta Sisters, Kopundol. Small charity store that represents village women in the eastern hills, selling mainly *dhaka* clothes.

Dhukuti, Kopundol, north of *Hotel Himalaya*. Run by a village and low-income project marketing association, Patan's biggest nonprofit shop stocks a wide variety of cotton and quilted-cotton crafts, wool sweaters, dolls, copper vessels, basketry and leather.

Himalayan Leather Handicrafts, Man Bhawan, near *Hotel Clarion*. Outlet in aid of the Nepal Leprosy Trust. Excellent leather bags and other items, also batiks and textiles.

Mahaguthi, branches in Kopundol and inside the Royal Palace. Aided by Oxfam, this supports a home for destitute women, with a good selection of textiles, plus pine-needle crafts, toys and other items.

Mithila Show & Sales Room, Kopundol Heights, south of *Hotel Greenwich Village*. Retail outlet for the Janakpur Women's Development Centre, selling a good range of Mithila (eastern Tarai) folk art and crafts.

Sana Hastakala, Kopundol, opposite *Hotel Himalaya*. Good selection and display of woollens, *dhaka*, quilted cottons, ceramics, paper, Mithila art, toys and general gift items.

Women's Skills Development Project, Harihar Bhawan (west of the UN offices). The sales outlet for the Nepal Women's Organization (offices behind) specializes in block-printed cottons, with some quilted cotton items, woollens, toys and paper.

The Patan Industrial Estate: all sorts

Despite its forbidding name, the **Patan Industrial Estate** is industrious in the nicest possible way. Located just beyond the Southern Stupa, the laid-back "estate" includes (in addition to more mundane industries) a dozen or so handicraft factory showrooms. They're primarily pitched at tour groups, which means that independent travellers are generally left to mosey round the work areas without too much pressure.

The main reason to come here is to get educated about Nepali handicrafts and the processes used to make them – especially woodcarving and metalsmithing, and to a lesser extent rug-weaving and *thangka*-painting. It's also kind of handy to have such a wide selection of crafts gathered together in one place – a couple of the outlets are like handicraft department stores, selling everything from shawls to gemstones. This removes some of the hassle factor of shopping in the city, but also some of the fun. Prices are competitive, but not necessarily better than elsewhere. You can bargain, even in places with supposedly fixed prices.

The estate is within walking distance of old Patan, but along a dreadful corridor, so consider taking a taxi or tuk-tuk. Most shops are open daily except Saturday, 9am to 5pm.

Books and other items

Pilgrim's Book House has a branch in Kopundol, opposite *Hotel Himalaya*, with a broad range of nonfiction **books** on the Himalayan region and particularly good children's and antiquarian sections, plus an art gallery and a small café. Saraswati Book Centre,

THE CARPET INDUSTRY

If you've read the section on shopping in Basics, you'll know that there's not much Tibetan about so-called Tibetan carpets. Nonetheless, they do have their origin high up on the Tibetan plateau, where sheep are bred for their unusually long, high-tensile **wool**. Brought into Nepal by yak and mule train over passes in the far west, the Tibetan wool is blended with processed New Zealand wool and then carded and spun into yarn. Although **carding** machines are increasingly being used, **spinning** is still done exclusively by hand to produce a distinctive, slightly irregular look. The yarn is then taken to a **dyeing** plant, where it's dipped in vats of boiling dye (chemical dyes are used almost exclusively nowadays) and sun-dried before being rolled into balls, coded for colour and batch, and stored in warehouses. Weavers can then order up their colours by number, as instructed by a pattern or their carpet master.

As throughout Asia, weavers sit on benches in front of tall looms – but that's as far as the similarity goes. Tibetan-style carpets are produced by the **cut-loop method**, which bears little relation to the process employed by Middle Eastern and Chinese artisans. Rather than tying thousands of individual knots, the weaver loops the yarn in and out of the vertical warp threads and around a horizontally placed rod; when the row is finished, the weaver draws a knife across the loops, freeing the rod. The loops, cut in half, form the pile. This method enables relatively speedy production – one person can produce a 3 x 6-foot carpet in as little as seven working days – but it results in a rather low density of eighty to one hundred "knots" (cut loops) per square inch. Rather than **beating** each row down with an iron mallet, which in Middle Eastern carpets helps to create a tight weave, Tibetan-style weavers deliberately use wooden mallets for a looser, blanket-like feel.

The weaving done, carpets are taken off the looms and **trimmed** with shears to give an even finish. **Embossing**, an optional shearing stage, subtly separates the colours to highlight the design. Finally, carpets must be **washed** to remove dirt and excess dye, an industrial process which, in the absence of effective controls, pollutes local streams with chemicals that have been linked with birth defects.

Marketing is more sophisticated than it might at first appear. The carpets so haphazardly displayed in tourist shops represent only a tiny tip of the iceberg – most are in fact made to order for the export market and air-freighted to wholesalers in Frankfurt and London. A handful of export traders, led by the Carpet Trading Company, founded in 1966 with help from the Swiss Association for Technical Assistance (now the Swiss Agency for Development and Cooperation), handle international distribution.

In thirty years, carpet manufacture in Nepal has grown into a $200 million industry, accounting for two-thirds of the country's exports and **employing** (directly and indirectly) 300,000 people. Having long ago outstripped the Tibetan exile labour pool, it now provides work for members of every ethnic group, especially the poor and landless who might otherwise be forced into bonded labour or prostitution. It's an economist's dream – or at least it was, until the bubble began to burst in the mid-1990s.

Since then the industry has seen a worrying **decline in overseas sales**, generally attributed to poor quality control. Manufacturers now seem chastened and anxious to restore their reputations, but it's their employees who have paid the price in reduced hours and wages. Worse, carpet manufacture appears to be responsible for an alarming rise in **child labour** in Nepal, even as other carpet-producing countries are enacting laws to stop exploitation. And the carpet industry is far too concentrated in the Kathmandu Valley, which lacks the infrastructure to cope with it, resulting in water and air **pollution**, traffic, social dislocation and land speculation. Yet as long as carpets continue to bring in so much foreign exchange, the government is unlikely to take the industry to task over these issues.

further south near the *Downtown Restaurant*, has a reasonable selection of Nepal-related titles. A number of shops in the old city sell **CDs and tapes** – Himalayan Music Shop, at the northeastern corner of Durbar Square, is particularly good.

Film is sold near Durbar Square and Lagankhel, and there are quick photo-processing places east of Jawalakhel Chowk and north of Lagankhel.

Other practicalities

Patan has tourist sights, but not, as yet, tourist quarters. This means that facilities are comparatively limited, but you won't lack for anything – and if you do, Kathmandu is just a short ride away.

Official **moneychangers** near Durbar Square offer reasonably competitive rates. For full banking facilities, including credit-card cash advances, go to Nepal Grindlays, just east of Jawalakhel Chowk (Sun–Thurs 9.45am–3pm, Fri 9.45am–12.30pm). Several **email** and international **phone** services can be found in the same neighbourhood. The **post office** is at Patan Dhoka (Sun–Thurs 10am–5pm, Fri 10am–3pm), but you'd be better off using the one in Kathmandu or the private Everest Postal Care east of Jaulakhel Chowk.

For information on **health** and **emergencies**, see p.142 – two of Nepal's best hospitals in are located in Patan.

Kirtipur

Once-proud **KIRTIPUR** ("City of Glory") occupies a long, low battleship of a ridge 5km southwest of Kathmandu. An historic stronghold commanding a panoramic view of the valley, the well-preserved old town is vehicle-free and great for wandering. However, its unpaved, narrow lanes and mainly low-income families seem out of place so close to the prosperous capital, and in recent years it has been singled out by some tour companies as an example of picturesque poverty. It's the kind of place that may make you question your own motives for coming to Nepal.

Established as a western outpost of Patan in the twelfth century, Kirtipur had gained nominal independence by the time Prithvi Narayan Shah began his final conquest of the Kathmandu Valley in 1767. The Gorkha king, who had himself been born and raised in a hilltop fortress, considered Kirtipur the strategic linchpin of the valley and made its capture his first priority. After two separate attacks and a six-month siege, with no help forthcoming from Patan, Kirtipur surrendered on the understanding it would receive a total amnesty. Instead, in an **atrocity** intended to demoralize the remaining opposition in the valley, Prithvi Shah ordered his troops to cut off the noses and lips of every man and boy in Kirtipur. "This order was carried out in the most exact way," wrote the early twentieth-century traveller Percival Landon, "and it adds rather than detracts from the savagery of the conqueror that the only persons spared were men who were skilled in playing wind instruments. The grim statistic is added that the weight of the noses and lips that were brought to Prithvi Narayan in proof that his order had been obeyed amounted to no less than eighty pounds." The rest of the valley fell within a year. Kirtipur's residents haven't forgotten that episode, and to this day they don't allow the king and queen of Nepal to enter their town.

Kirtipur's hilltop position, once a strategic asset, has proved a serious handicap to development. The town has responded by shifting essentially all of its commerce to **Naya Bazaar** (New Market) at the southern base of the hill, which is why the upper town is so neglected. Many residents of the old town are Jyapus (members of the Newar farming subcaste), who work the fields below and in spring and autumn haul their sheaves up and thresh the grain in the narrow streets. Others, whose land was appropriated for the building of **Tribhuwan University** (Nepal's largest, with more than 5000 students), now commute to jobs in Kathmandu or produce handicrafts behind closed doors.

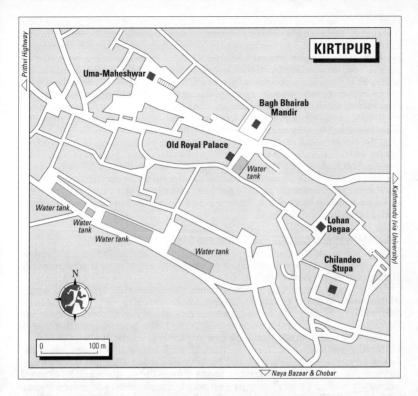

KIRTIPUR

Uma-Maheshwar

Bagh Bhairab Mandir

Old Royal Palace

Water tank

Water tank

Water tank

Water tank

Water tank

Lohan Degaa

Chilandeo Stupa

N

0   100 m

Prithvi Highway

Kathmandu (via University)

▽ *Naya Bazaar & Chobar*

Frequent **minibuses** run from the City Bus Park to a point just short of Naya Bazaar, from where it's a ten-minute walk up to the village. **Cycling** to Kirtipur is not a great experience, but a bike would be a good thing to have for exploring the more rural countryside beyond. The main way there is via Tribhuwan University, on the Dakshin Kali road (turn right at the red-brick gate and take the left fork another 1km later). Other paths lead to Kirtipur from the Prithvi (Kathmandu–Pokhara) Highway, the Ring Road and Chobar. For **food**, you can't expect much more than samosas or chow mein in Naya Bazaar.

Bagh Bhairab Mandir

The road from the university ascends to the saddle of Kirtipur's twin-humped ridge and deposits you in a weedy square outside the prodigious **Bagh Bhairab Mandir**, which serves double duty as a war memorial and a cathedral to Bhairab in his tiger (*bagh*) form.

Local legend relates that a shepherd, to pass the time, fashioned a tiger image out of burrs. The shepherd went off in search of a poinsettia leaf for the tongue, but when he returned he found his sheep gone – and the tiger's mouth dripping with blood. The people attributed the miracle to bloodthirsty Bhairab, and to honour him they enshrined in this temple a tongueless **Bhairab mask**, hidden behind the lattice screen to the left of the main door. Local musicians perform *bhajan* early in the morning and around dinnertime near the shrine, and on Tuesdays and Saturdays people sacrifice animals in front of it. In an upper chamber is kept a separate image of Indrayani, one of the Kathmandu Valley's eight mother goddesses (*ashta matrika*), who, according to one Cinderella-like legend, was bossed around by the other goddesses until she miraculously turned a pumpkin into gold. Kirtipur's biggest **festival** is in late November or early December, when Indrayani and Ganesh are paraded through town on palanquins and a pair of pigeons are ceremonially released. Mounted on the outside of the temple is a collection of rusty **weapons** captured during the siege of Kirtipur – either by the Gorkhalis or the defenders, depending on whom you ask. An unusually large number of gilt pinnacles top the temple, and faded murals depicting scenes from the *Mahabharat* can be seen on the upper walls of the ground floor.

At the southern end of the compound, between the two entrances, a small pagoda houses an ancient – possibly pre-Lichhavi (pre-fourth-century) – statue of a standing, armless **Shiva**, along with five tiny mother-goddess statues that are believed to be of the fifth century. Under a metallic umbrella in the northeast (far right) corner is a small statue of **Dhartimata**, an earth goddess, shown in a graphic state of giving birth – to what, no one seems to know. Women do *puja* to this statue to aid against problems during pregnancy and childbirth.

Uma-Maheshwar Mandir and Chilandeo Stupa

Kirtipur is a pleasantly confusing maze of stony alleys, and navigating isn't hard so long as you stick to the ridgeline. The northwestern end of town is predominantly Hindu, the southeastern Buddhist.

At the top of the northern, Hindu hump stands the elephant-guarded **Uma-Maheshwar Mandir**, mainly of interest for its sweeping view of Kathmandu, Swayambhu and the peaks behind. Kathmandu's quaint **aerial ropeway** runs just beyond the town's northwestern gate; built in the 1940s, before any roads connected the valley to the outside world, it's now idle but kept on standby.

Heading southeastwards from the Bagh Bhairab temple first brings you to the Lohan Degaa, a stone *shikra* shared by both Hindu and Buddhist worshippers. Beyond, the atmospheric **Chilandeo Stupa** crowns the southern hill, its exposed brickwork lending a hoary antiquity generally lacking in better-maintained stupas. Chilandeo (also known as Chilancho Bahal) is commonly believed to have been erected by Ashoka – though if Ashoka really built every stupa attributed to him he would have had little time for anything else. The ridge that rears up so impressively to the southwest is Champadevi (see box on p.192), one of the high points along the valley rim.

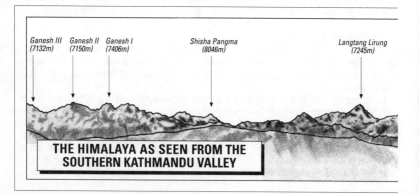

Ganesh III (7132m) Ganesh II (7150m) Ganesh I (7406m) Shisha Pangma (8046m) Langtang Lirung (7245m)

THE HIMALAYA AS SEEN FROM THE SOUTHERN KATHMANDU VALLEY

Naya Bazaar and the Theravada temple

Naya Bazaar's only attraction sits below the road where it rounds the southeast flank of the Kirtipur ridge. A Thai-style **Theravada temple**, the Nagara Mandapa Kirti Vihara was completed in 1989 with money donated by the Thai king and an array of the great and good of Thailand. In the minimalist Theravada tradition, the main sanctuary is unadorned except for an altar groaning with assorted gilded Buddhas and *bodhisattva*. A statue outside honours the Venerable Pragyananda Mahasthavir, the now-deceased patriarch of Nepali Theravada Buddhists, who lived in Patan. A separate image hall, brought to you by Thai Airways, supports on its roof replicas of the four holy sites of Buddhism: Lumbini, Bodh Gaya, Sarnath and Kushinagar.

The Dakshin Kali road

The longest and most varied of the valley's roads begins at the Ring Road southwest of Kathmandu and ends at the famous sacrificial shrine of Dakshin Kali, a distance of 18km. En route it passes several temples, some beautiful stretches of forest, pleasant rest stops and fine views as it rises more than 300m above the valley floor.

Buses and minibuses depart for Dakshin Kali from Kathmandu's City Bus Park roughly every hour, more often on Saturdays (although the latter are appallingly crowded). Kathmandu travel agents offer guided **tours** on Tuesday and Saturday mornings (about Rs250), or you could hire your own **taxi** (about Rs800 return to Dakshin Kali for a half day). For real independence, though, go by **mountain bike**, which takes at least two hours on the outward leg. Traffic eases up after Kirtipur, and is fairly light past the cement plant – except on Saturdays, when the road is busy with sacrificial traffic.

Chobar

CHOBAR, a former outpost of Patan, stands at the top of the deceptively tall hill over-looking the Bagmati River. A paved road marked by a "Welcome to Chobar" sign leads only partway up – if you're cycling, follow the road to the northwestern side of the hill, where a dirt track doubles back and eventually climbs to near the top. On foot, take the broad, stepped path under the arch, which leads straight to the central temple.

Chobar huddles around its idiosyncratic **Adinath Mandir**, the front of which is completely decorated with pots, pans and jugs. Various explanations are cited for the practice of offering kitchen utensils to Lokeshwar, the temple's deity: newlyweds will say it

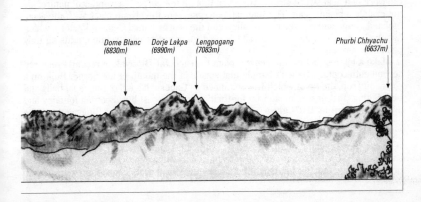

Dome Blanc
(6830m)

Dorje Lakpa
(6990m)

Lengpogang
(7083m)

Phurbi Chhyachu
(6637m)

HIKES TO CHAMPADEVI AND BHASMESUR

Champadevi and Bhasmesur are high points on the prominent ridge that forms the southwestern rim of the Kathmandu Valley. Champadevi is easier to get to, Bhasmesur is higher. The views of the Himalaya from both knolls are excellent.

Trails to **Champadevi** start from near Taudaha, Pikhel and Pharping. A hike up one and down another will take four to six hours, not including time spent at the top – bring plenty of food and water. The first trail begins where the road makes an abrupt bend beyond Taudaha, climbing steeply southwestwards to gain the ridge and then more gradually along it to the stupa-marked summit (2278m). From Pikhel, a dirt road heads north to the ridge, entering a splendid pine forest and passing the four-star *Haatiban Resort* (see below), then tracks northwest to join the first trail. The Pharping route (best taken going down if you intend to get a seat on the bus) follows a dirt road up a valley south of the ridge as far as a small pond, where it veers northwards straight up to the ridge.

Bhasmesur (2502m) is another hour's walk along the ridge, separated from Champadevi by a saddle. It can also be reached from Kirtipur: start by following the dirt road southwest from Naya Bazaar and then west to Machhegaun ("Fishville"), from where a trail switchbacks up to a saddle on the ridge just north of the summit. In Hindu myth, Bhasmesur was a demon who extracted a boon from Vishnu that everything he touched would turn to ash. Emboldened by his apparent invincibility, the demon proceeded to make a heavenly nuisance of himself until Vishnu, having taken the form of a fair maiden, seduced Bhasmesur into imitating a dance. Vishnu concluded the dance by touching his forehead, and Bhasmesur, following suit, incinerated himself. This mountain is reputed to be the pile of ashes left by the demon's demise.

ensures a happy union, others claim it's a necessary rite to send a recently departed loved one off to a prosperous next life. Like so many traditions, the act has become independent of its origins, and may hark back to a time when metal implements were new technology and decorating a temple with them was a way to keep it looking spiffy and up-to-date – just as other temples are often graced by European tiles and photographs. Lokeshwar is worshipped here in the form of a red mask, which bears a close resemblance to Patan's Rato Machhendranath.

Chobar Gorge

When Manjushri drained the Kathmandu Valley of its legendary lake, **Chobar Gorge** was one of the places he smote with his sword to release the waters. As the Bagmati River slices through a wrinkle in the valley floor south of Chobar, it really does look like the work of a neat sword stroke. However, though the gorge is a wonder of nature, it's not exactly a beauty spot. The Bagmati emerges from the chasm black with the accumulated gunge and sewage of the valley, and the nearby Himal Cement Factory, which has made possible much of the valley's modern concrete construction, adds an ugly pall to the air.

Make a left just before the cement plant to reach **Jal Binayak**, a recently restored seventeenth-century Ganesh temple that stands at the mouth of the gorge. Built on a rocky outcrop, the tip of which is worshipped as Ganesh, it's full of the usual bells and bell-ringing. Just upstream, an iron **footbridge**, custom-cast by a Scottish foundry and assembled here in 1907, gives a good view of the chasm and Jal Binayak (and the cement plant).

A path along the west bank scrambles up to the main entrance of **Chobar Gupha** (Chobar Cave), which Hindus associate with Shiva and Tibetan Buddhists with the saint Guru Padma Sambhava. A Czech team explored it in 1985 for at least 1.2km before pronouncing it the third-largest cave in South Asia. Locals claim it's connected to

Chobar's Adinath Mandir, the Shantipur temple at Swayambhu, or even Tibet or Varanasi. If you want to go inside, hire a guide locally and be prepared for a lot of stooping and crawling.

Taudaha and Shesh Narayan (Yanglesho)

Beyond the cement plant, the road begins climbing and after 2km passes **Taudaha**, a duck pond with a legend. The story goes that when Manjushri drained the Kathmandu Valley he left Taudaha as a home for the snakes, and the belief persists that the serpent king Karkatnag still lives at the bottom, coiled around a heap of treasure. Jang Bahadur Rana, prime minister in the middle of the last century, is said to have tried (unsuccessfully) to dredge the lake for booty. Nowadays Taudaha is considered sacred and is off-limits to hunters and fishermen; though choked with water hyacinths, it's a popular stopping place for migrant water birds in winter.

The road ascends steadily for another 6km to its highest point, a little beyond Pikhel. The villages of Khokana and Bungmati rest in tight whorls on the plateau across the river.

Cool, quiet and shady, **Shesh Narayan** crouches under a wooded hillside 2km beyond Pikhel and is regarded as a holy spot by both Hindus and Buddhists. Hindus worship Vishnu here as the mighty creator, who formed the universe out of the cosmic ocean; the snake Shesh (or Ananta), the "remainder" of the cosmic waters after Vishnu's creation, is symbolized by the four tranquil **pools** beside the road. A sculpture depicting Surya riding his twelve-horse chariot stands half-submerged in one of the pools. Steps from there lead to Narayan's **temple** at the base of a limestone overhang, whose serpentine stalactites are said by Vaishnavas to be the "milk", or blessing, of Shesh. A stone naturally eroded in the shape of a coiled snake, which was enshrined in the temple until its recent theft, provided a further association with Shesh. To the left of the temple is another hunk of eroded limestone known as Chaumunda – you're supposed to put your ear to it to hear the sound of running water.

To the right of the temple, a half-height wood latticed doorway conceals a cave that Buddhists call **Yanglesho**, where Guru Padma Sambhava, the eighth-century founder of the Nyingma-pa sect of Tibetan Buddhism, is supposed to have wrestled with a horde of *nag* and turned them to stone. This episode marked a turning-point in Padma Sambhava's career – allegorically, it probably refers to the saint's struggle to introduce his brand of tantric Buddhism from India – which accounts for the presence of a **gompa** next to the Shesh Narayan temple.

Pharping

A few hundred metres beyond Shesh Narayan, **PHARPING** is unexpectedly large and lively for this distant corner of the valley. It's divided between an unattractive modern commercial strip along the road and the more villagey original centre, reached by a side road where the main road swerves left. Nepal's first hydroelectric plant was built just downhill from Pharping, in 1911, but the power generated all went to light Singha Durbar.

A fifteen-minute walk uphill brings you to the golden-roofed **Pharping Bajra Jogini**, one of the valley's four tantric temples dedicated to the angry female aspect of Buddhahood. Foreigners usually aren't allowed to enter, but the upstairs sanctum contains two prancing images of Bajra Jogini, each holding a skull-cup and knife.

A staircase just to the left of the Bajra Jogini temple entrance leads further up the hill to a monastery sometimes used as a retreat by Buddhist Westerners. Introduce yourself and the monks will show you the **Padma Sambhava Cave** (also known as Asura Cave) in the courtyard; the irrepressible guru, whose image stands among butter candles, apparently meditated in this grotto as well as at Yanglesho. Buddhists say the handprint to the left of the cave entrance and the "footprints" in the centre of the courtyard are those of Padma Sambhava (Hindus claim they were left by Gorakhnath). The site has grown to be a major pilgrimage stop for Tibetan Buddhists, and has spawned several other nearby *gompa* of Padma Sambhava's Nyingma-pa sect, all connected by strings of prayer flags that from a distance make the hillside look like it's covered in a gigantic spider web. Red-robed monks are a common sight around Pharping.

A couple of small **restaurants**, the *Asura Cave* and the *Snowland*, cater to the monasteries' residents and visitors. They're located just downhill from the Bajra Jogini temple, so if you find them you'll know you're on the right track for the temple and cave.

Dakshin Kali

The best and worst aspect of **DAKSHIN KALI** is that everything happens out in the open. The famous sacrificial pit of Southern Kali – the last stop for hundreds of chickens, goats and pigs every week – lies at the bottom of a steep, forested ravine, affording an intimate view of Nepali religious rituals; unfortunately, the public bloodbath also attracts busloads of camera-toting tourists. For the full show in all its Technicolor gore, go on a Saturday or Tuesday morning, but get there *early* (before 8 if possible). If you're squeamish or wish to avoid the crush, try visiting in the afternoon or on another day. Whenever you go, respect the privacy of worshippers, especially if you're taking pictures.

Motorists and motorcyclists have to pay a small fee before the final switchback descent into the ravine, and then pay again to park. From the car park a path leads to a small bazaar of stalls selling food, drinks and sacrificial accessories. The **shrine** is directly below the bazaar, positioned at the auspicious confluence of two streams. Tiled like an abattoir (for easy hosing down) and covered with a gilt canopy, the sacred area consists of little more than a row of short statuettes, Kali being the heavily decorated one under the canopy. You can get a good view of the whole area from a secondary shrine on a promontory high above the far side of the ravine.

Dakshin Kali is as much a picnic area as a holy spot. The sacrifice done, families make for the pavilions that surround the shrine and merrily cook up the remains of their offerings. If you didn't sacrifice anything, you can get a good sit-down **meal** at the *Dakshinkali Village Inn* (see below), or fried snacks from the "fast food" restaurant across the way or from the stalls near the shrine.

A visit to Dakshin Kali can be combined with a few different **hikes** or **bike rides**. A trail heading south from the shrine area goes for miles into lush hill country. The road that continues straight past the *Daskhinkali Village Inn* makes a great downhill descent

---

A NOTE ON HINDU ANIMAL SACRIFICES

Hindu animal **sacrifice** is superficially similar to what the Old Testament patriarchs did, but Hindus don't kill animals to prove their loyalty to a deity so much as to propitiate it. Kali, the usual recipient, doesn't care about the personal sacrifice her worshipper has made in order to get an animal, all she wants is the blood. Nepalis lead their offerings to the slaughter tenderly, often whispering prayers in the animal's ear and sprinkling its head with water to encourage it to shrug in assent; they believe that the death of this "unfortunate brother" will give it the chance to be reborn as a higher life form. Only uncastrated males, preferably dark in colour, are used. At Dakshin Kali, men of a special caste slit the animals' throats and let the blood spray over the idols. Brahman priests (referred to as *baahun*, *pandit* or *pujari*) oversee the butchering and instruct worshippers in all the complex rituals that follow – the priests like to make things obscure to keep themselves in demand. However, you don't need to speak Nepali to get the gist of the explanations.

into the valley of the lower Bagmati. You can hike to Champadevi (see above), or follow other trails westwards from there all the way to the Kulekhani Reservoir and Daman (p.238).

Accommodation

There's no budget **accommodation** in this part of the valley (not as of this writing, anyway), but if you can swing the cost of one of the places listed below, it's well worth spending the night. The countryside in this part of the valley is beautiful, and you could easily spend a couple or three days hiking or biking around in it. Plus, staying overnight means you can visit Dakshin Kali first thing in the morning, and avoid the Saturday and Tuesday transport hassles by coming the day before.

Ashoka Resort, 200m before the Dakshin Kali gate (☎290657). An unsightly tower, but the rooms have excellent views and they're fairly well appointed. Bungalows also available. ⑨/B⑥.

Dakshinkali Village Inn, at the Dakshin Kali gate (☎290653, fax 330889). Cosy brick and thatch bungalows, lovely garden dining area, excellent location. B⑥.

Haatiban Resort, above Pikhel, on the way to Champadevi (☎370714; *nepal@intrek.wlink.com.np*). Perched 500m above the valley floor, it has clean air and great views. Pony rides and guided hikes to Champadevi. B⑨.

The Bungmati and Chapagaun roads

These two paved but minor roads take parallel courses southwards from Patan. The first leads to the delightful village of Bungmati, summer home of Rato Machhendranath. The second has no particularly interesting towns along it, but it goes much further south into attractive countryside.

The main reason you'd come this way is to do a **bike** circuit of the southern valley: these two roads aren't themselves that great for cycling, but they give access to smaller tracks and trails that are. **Buses** for Khokana/Bungmati depart from the Ring Road just south of the Ekantakuna area of Patan (hourly). Chapagaun buses depart from Patan's Lagankhel bus park (at least hourly).

Bungmati and Khokana

From a distance, you could almost mistake **BUNGMATI** for a well-preserved Tuscan village: scrunched together on a hillock, its tall, brick houses, with their tiled roofs sloping in different directions, look distinctly Romanesque. The bus stops along the road a short walk northeast of the town.

Close up, Bungmati is quintessentially Newar, and what at first looks like a tiny village quickly envelops you in its self-contained universe. All alleys eventually lead to the broad, teeming central plaza and the whitewashed *shikra* of **Machhendranath**, whose more ancient Newar name is Bunga Dyo ("God of Bunga"). According to legend, Bungmati marks the spot where Machhendranath, having arrived in the valley in the form of a bee to save it from drought, was "born" as the valley's protector-rainmaker. Each summer at the end of Patan's Rato Machhendranath festival, the god's red mask is brought to the Bungmati temple for a six-month residency, but every twelfth year it is kept here through the winter and then pulled by lumbering chariot all the way to Patan (see p.180).

One kilometre to the north, **KHOKANA** resembles Bungmati in many ways, but somehow lacks the character and magnetism of its neighbour. It's locally renowned for its mustard oil, and in season the presses run full tilt. Khokana's pagoda-style **Shekali Mai Mandir**, a massive three-tiered job, honours a local nature goddess. Midway between Khokana and Bungmati stands the poorly maintained **Karya Binayak**, another of the valley's four Ganesh temples.

Thecho and Chapagaun

THECHO, 8km south of Patan, is the largest town in this end of the valley, while **CHAPAGAUN**, 1km further south, is a smaller but similarly brick-built settlement. Thecho has a touch more atmosphere, Chapagaun more to eat.

More attractive than either town, the seventeenth-century **Bajra Barahi Mandir** is secreted in a small wood 500m east along a track from Chapagaun. Despite Shiva imagery, the temple is dedicated to a tantric manifestation of the goddess Kali: like the Bajra Joginis, Bajra Barahis represent the female, creative power of divinity. This goddess receives her share of worship and sacrifice on Saturdays, but most visitors come just to picnic in the park. The stone statue of Bajra Barahi kept in the sanctum is a

---

AGRICULTURE IN THE VALLEY

Agriculture employs two out of three residents of the Kathmandu Valley, the **farmers** a mixture of Newars, Baahuns, Chhetris and Tamangs (see p.95, p.227 and p.232 for background on these ethnic groups). Newar farmers, called Jyapus, dig their fields with two-handed spades called *kodaalo* (*ku* in Newari) – it's back-breaking work – and live in close, brick settlements on the valley floor, while the other groups tend to use bullock ploughs and build detached, mud-walled houses around the fringes. Many are tenant farmers and are expected to pay half their harvest as rent.

Low enough in elevation to support two or even three main crops a year, and endowed with a fertile, black clay – *kalimati*, a by-product of sediment from the prehistoric lake – the valley floor has been intensely cultivated and irrigated for centuries. **Rice** is seeded in special beds shortly before the first monsoon rains in June, and seedlings are transplanted into flooded terraces no later than the end of July. Normally women do this job, using their toes to bed each shoot in the mud. The stalks grow green and bushy during the summer, turning a golden brown and producing mature grain by October.

Harvest time is lazily anarchic: sheaves are spread out on paved roads for cars to loosen the kernels, and then run through portable hand cranked threshers or bashed against rocks. The grain is gathered in bamboo trays (*nanglo*) and tossed in the wind to winnow away the chaff, or, if there's no wind, *nanglo* can be used to fan away the chaff. Some sheaves are left in stacks to ferment for up to two weeks, producing a sort of baby food called *hakuja*, or "black" rice. The rice dealt with, terraces are then planted with **winter wheat**, which is harvested in a similar fashion in April or May. A third crop of pulses or maize can often be squeezed in after the wheat harvest, and vegetables are raised year-round at the edges of plots.

The lot of valley farmers has improved in the past generation. **Land reform** in the 1950s and 1960s, which didn't work too well in most parts of the country, was more diligently implemented near the capital, helping to get landlords and moneylenders off the backs of small farmers. However, the traditional Newar system of **inheritance**, in which family property is divided up among the sons, means that landholdings get smaller with each generation. That presents a contrasting problem: farms that are too small to make mechanical equipment worthwhile, necessitating labour-intensive methods and keeping productivity low.

Meanwhile, Kathmandu's **prosperity** is bringing problems. In the past decade, while the valley's population has nearly doubled to 1.2 million, housing (and the brick "factories" that make it possible) has been chewing up farmland at a speedy rate – a trend that threatens to accelerate, as ever more hill people flock to the valley for a piece of the action. At the same time, high land prices and the declining quality of life in the capital are only adding to the pressure on farmland. Those who can are fleeing the inner city, just as they have every other city in the world, and are rapidly creating a **suburban** commuter culture. In the absence of any greenbelt regulations, valley farmers and *guthi* (temple trusts) are steadily selling out, as their valuable farmland becomes even more valuable as real estate.

recent replacement for an ancient image that was stolen; the stolen image was later recovered and is now on display at the National Museum.

Tika Bhairab and Lele

The road, unpaved after Chapagaun, continues south for another 4km to **TIKA BHAIRAB**, a quarrying centre named after a locally famous abstract mural of the god Bhairab painted on a wall at the junction of two small streams. This stretch of road can be fairly unpleasant because of the heavy-vehicle traffic generated by stone quarrying in the area. A much better route is to go east from Chapagaun past the Bajra Barahi temple (this track eventually meets the paved Godavari road), then strike south on a smaller track that crosses a steep, forested ridge and enters the Lele valley several kilometres upstream of Tika Bhairab.

Once in the Lele valley, you can choose from a number of trails and small roads heading south into unspoiled and little-visited hill country. The road that fords the stream just south of Tika Bhairab ascends to an elevation of more than 2000m, and is bikable for many miles after that. About 1km east of Tika Bhairab is PIA Memorial Park, created in memory of an airliner that crashed near here in 1992.

There are two **places to stay** in this area. *Lobsay Guest House* (☎570051; B④), near the leprosy hospital just north of Tika Bhairab, is really just a self-catering house, but it might work for organized cycle groups. *Malla Alpine Resort* (☎410622, fax 418382; B⑨), on the road south of Tika Bhairab, is a deluxe sort of place with ethnic-style bungalows, pool and sauna – the location is beautiful and secluded, but it's a rough drive to get there.

The Godavari and Lubhu roads

The greenest, most pristine part of the valley is its southeastern edge, where you'll find something now all too rare in Nepal, or at least around the Kathmandu Valley: virgin forest. Once the dominant feature of the middle hills, it has come under increasing pressure in recent years from an exploding population desperate for fuel and farmland.

The principal starting point for day trips in this area is **Godavari** (pronounced Go-*daa*-vari), home of the Royal Botanical Garden, 10km southeast of Patan. On foot from Godavari you can hike to Phulchoki, the highest point on the valley rim and a full day's outing, or make a more leisurely low-elevation circuit via the curious shrine of Bishanku Narayan. On a mountain bike or motorcycle, you can do either of those, or you can connect up with the Chapagaun route (above) or with another road that reaches the valley's southeastern rim via **Lubhu** and the Lakuri Bhanjyang.

Local **buses** depart infrequently for the botanical garden from the City Bus Park in Kathmandu. From Patan's Lagankhel bus park, buses go to the St Xavier School in Godavari (hourly) and to Lubhu (also hourly).

Harisiddhi

The paved Godavari road starts rather inauspiciously, with heavy traffic fuelled in part by the many brick kilns around **HARISIDDHI**. Those bricks have built many a traditional Newar town, among them Harisiddhi itself. Despite its unimpressive appearance from the road, the village is actually a close-knit cluster of mostly old houses, a central temple, and a series of courtyards often occupied by local women spinning wool for Patan's carpet industry. It's reached by walking straight up a stepped path where the main road jogs left.

Harisiddhi's **Bal Kumari Mandir** received unwanted notoriety in 1997, when the *Sunday Telegraph* in London published an article implying that it was the centre of a child-sacrifice cult. The article was pure hack journalism, but it touched a nerve in Nepal because apparently human sacrifice *was* performed in the Kathmandu Valley not so very long ago. Though no historical proof exists, several nineteenth-century European visitors reported hearing of it, and some authorities claim the practice continued until the early twentieth century. Only a generation ago, parents in this part of the valley would jokingly warn their children to behave or they'd be sent to Harisiddhi.

Godavari and the Royal Botanical Garden

Somewhat quieter after Harisiddhi, the road climbs steadily past a number of plant nurseries to **GODAVARI**, worth a stop solely for its botanical garden. To reach the garden, follow the main road to the left of the Jesuits' St Xavier School for 1km, then turn left again just before a clump of local restaurants.

Despite its modest size, the **Royal Botanical Garden** (daily 10am–5pm; Rs2) contains some idyllic paths, streams and picnic areas; highlights are the orchid house and fern shed. If you're expecting well-labelled plants and trees you'll be disappointed, but a map of the garden and a general guide to Kathmandu Valley flora (available from the ticket booth) may be of some help in identifying species. The garden receives fairly enthusiastic support from the government – not surprising, perhaps, in a country where flowers play a major part in worship and medicine is largely based on plants. Moreover, the export of herbs, medicinal plants and essential oils is seen as a promising way to beef up Nepal's meagre foreign-exchange earnings. The spring-fed water tank of **Godavari Kunda**, just a couple of hundred metres north and then west of the car park, hosts a big *mela* every twelve years during July and August (the next will be in 2003).

The only **accommodation** in these parts is the pricey *Central Godavari Resort* (☎533675, fax 290777; B⑨), located about 2km northwest of Godavari. It has a nice rural setting and acres of gardens (plus a pool and health club), but it's not high enough for very good views. **Food** is available from the institutional *Tara Gaon Restaurant*, next to the entrance gate, and from the smaller eateries back at the intersection just before the car park.

Phulchoki

The road bearing straight ahead to the right of the St Xavier School switchbacks and spirals right to the top of **Phulchoki** – a 1200-metre ascent.

The only way to get to the top early enough to be sure of views is to go by **taxi** (about Rs1800, if you can find a driver willing to take his car up there) or **motorcycle**. The road is partly paved in the early going, but higher up the loose gravel is quite tricky. There's essentially no traffic, except on Saturdays. Given a lift to the top, you can **hike** down in three hours or less. You can also hike up and back – an all-day proposition – on a trail that starts behind the shrine to Phulchoki Mai, the mother goddess of these parts, 500m up the road and just opposite the entrance to an unsightly marble quarry. The trail crosses the road a few times, and can be very slippery. You'd have to be a very strong rider to make it up this steep, rough road on a **mountain bike**, and it would take you all day from Kathmandu.

Phulchoki means **"Place of Flowers"**, which is entirely apt. If you know what to look for, you'll see orchids, morning glories, corydalis and, of course, rhododendrons (March and April are best for catching them in bloom). The whole mountain is covered by tall, luxuriant **forest**, and as you climb from its subtropical base to its temperate summit you pass through mixed stands of oak, chestnut, walnut, bamboo, laurel and rhododendron. It's a great place for **birdwatching** – a trained eye is supposed to be able to spot a hundred or more species in a day – and also for **butterflies**, which are attracted to the flowers during spring.

If the **summit** (2762m) isn't wreathed in clouds, you'll have a magnificent view of a wide swathe of the Himalaya and practically the entire Kathmandu Valley (smog permitting). The effect is only slightly marred by the presence of a microwave relay station, erected with Canadian assistance, which is the only reason for the summit road's existence.

Bishanku Narayan
A bikable dirt track strikes north from the Godavari road just beyond the St Xavier School and contours around a lovely side valley drained by the Godavari Khola. If you're on foot you can access the valley more directly via a back road from the western side of the botanical garden.

Either way, it's about 5km to **Bishanku Narayan**, near a hilltop on the other (north-western) side of the valley. One of the valley's four main Narayan (Vishnu) sites, Bishanku is not a temple – rather, it's a small cave reached by a set of precarious steps. A chain-mail curtain protects the god's image inside the cave. If you're thin enough, you can descend through another narrow fissure; according to popular belief, those who manage to squeeze through it will be absolved of past sins. From Bishanku it's another 2.5km to the Godavari Road at Badegaun.

About 1km south of Badegaun, a quiet unpaved road leads westwards through farm country to the Bajra Barahi Mandir and Chapagaun (see above). The turning is impossible to miss because it's marked by a prominent sign for the *Central Godavari Resort* (see above).

Lubhu and Lakuri Bhanjyang
The 30-kilometre road connecting Patan with Panauti (see p.223) is a superb intermediate-level mountain-bike ride that can be done in either direction. From Patan, ride out of town on the road past Sundhara and the Eastern Stupa. The first section to **Lubhu**, a brickmaking and handloom centre 6km beyond the Ring Road, is busy and uninteresting, but things get better shortly thereafter. The road, now unpaved, climbs gradually at first and then commences a serious 500-metre switchback ascent through a woodcutters' area to **Lakuri Bhanjyang**. On a clear day, the view of the valley and mountains from here is splendid. The second half of the ride is a sweet descent through the close, rural valley of the Bebar Khola and its scattered Tamang, Chhetri and finally Newar settlements.

From Lakuri Bhanjyang, it's possible to descend to Godavari or Bishanku Narayan (see above) on a track that branches off to the left.

BHAKTAPUR AND THE EASTERN VALLEY

The valley's eastern arm maintains a discreet cultural, as well as geographical, distance from Kathmandu. Perhaps because it lay off the main India–Tibet trade route all those years, its Hinduism has scarcely been diluted by Buddhism. Creeping Westernization has been slower to take root here, too, and concrete has made fewer inroads against native brick. Fashions at this end of the valley remain conservative, especially among Jyapu women: most still wear the traditional black and red-trimmed *pataasi*, wrapped around the waist in tiers, giving the effect of a flamenco skirt. Hitched up in back, these often reveal tattoos above the ankles, believed to be necessary for a woman to enter heaven.

Bhaktapur makes an excellent base from which to explore this part of the valley. Roads and trails radiate from there in several directions, the temple complex of

Changu Narayan making an immensely rewarding excursion, particularly for fans of Nepali sculpture. Bhaktapur is also a staging post for Nagarkot, and can serve as a springboard for trips up the Arniko Highway to Dhulikhel and beyond (see Chapter Three).

Bhaktapur (Bhadgaun)

In the soft, dusty light of evening the old city of Bhaktapur, with its pagoda roofs and its harmonious blend of wood, mud-brick and copper, looked extraordinarily beautiful. It was as though a faded medieval tapestry were tacked on to the pale tea-rose sky. In the foreground a farmhouse was on fire, and orange flames licked like liquescent dragon's tongues across the thatched roof. One thought of Chaucer's England and Rabelais's France; of a world of intense, violent passions and brilliant colour, where sin was plentiful but so were grace and forgiveness . . .

Charlie Pye-Smith, *Travels in Nepal*

Kathmandu's field of gravity weakens somewhere east of the airport; beyond, you fall into the rich atmosphere of **BHAKTAPUR** (also known as **BHADGAUN**). A medieval world unto itself, Bhaktapur is Nepal's most perfectly preserved city. Well clear of the Ring Road, with no industrial zone, no diplomatic enclave and few suburbs, it feels more like a big village than a small city. Every turn of a corner brings a new wonder: a narrow alley, a neighbourhood shrine, a sudden vibrant courtyard, a red-and-gold-skirted pagoda. And everywhere the warm, salmon hue of bricks – streets paved with bricks in herringbone and parquet patterns, houses and temples built of bricks and carved wood – brick and wood, the essential media of Newar city-builders.

Bhaktapur's streets and alleys are all the more suited for wandering thanks to a long-term German-funded restoration and sanitation programme and, more recently, to the sometimes controversial policies of its communist municipal council. Say what you like about the city's entrance fee (see below), this is one Nepalese city that's got its act together. Much of it is pedestrianized or closed to commercial traffic at most times of day, temples and public shelters are being restored (without foreign aid), and new buildings are now required to follow traditional architectural styles. The city's effort to balance heritage and economic development appears to be as successful as any in the world today.

Bhaktapur is no utopia, but compared to other cities of the Kathmandu Valley it's relatively clean, prosperous and orderly. It's touristy, but only in spots, and only for a few hours during the day – after hours, it becomes utterly, authentically Nepali again. Although it's usually regarded as a day trip from Kathmandu, you really ought to spend at least one night to do the place justice. An increasing number of travellers are heading straight from Kathmandu airport to Bhaktapur.

Some history

The "City of Devotees" was probably founded in the ninth century, and by 1200 it was ruling Nepal. In that year Bhaktapur witnessed the launch of the Malla era when, according to the Nepalese chronicles, King Arideva, upon being called out of a wrestling bout to hear of the birth of a son, bestowed on the prince the hereditary title Malla ("wrestler"). To this day, beefy carved wrestlers are the city's trademark temple guardians. Bhaktapur ruled the valley until 1482, when Yaksha Malla divided the kingdom among his three sons, setting in train three centuries of continuous squabbling.

It was a Bhaktapur king who helped to bring the Malla era to a close in 1766 by inviting Prithvi Narayan Shah, the Gorkha leader, to aid him in a quarrel against

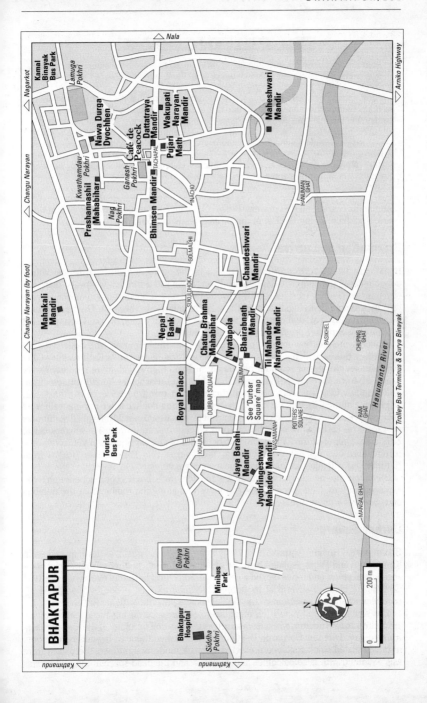

BHAKTAPUR

BHAKTAPUR'S ENTRANCE FEE

Foreigners are charged a one-time **fee** of Rs300 or $5 to enter Bhaktapur. If you intend to stay overnight, have your entrance ticket (sometimes actually referred to as a "visa") endorsed at the gate or by your guest house.

Many tourists complain that this fee is discriminatory or that it's too high, and some wonder whether the money is going into corrupt officials' pockets. The first two are certainly true, but that's the point: tourists cause impacts that locals don't, so Bhaktapur is charging money to regulate tourism and to offset its effects. There's a bit of a socialist soak-the-rich attitude behind the fee, but mostly it's elementary charge-what-the-market-will-bear capitalism. As for corruption, there may be some of that – corruption is a major feature of politics in Nepal – but recent public works projects show that at least some of the money is hitting the target.

Kathmandu. Seizing on this pretext, Prithvi Narayan conquered the valley within three years, Bhaktapur being the last of the three capitals to surrender.

Orientation and arrival

Bhaktapur drapes across an east–west fold in the valley, its southern fringe sliding down towards the sluggish Hanumante River. Owing to a gradual westward drift, the city has two centres (residents of the two halves stage a boisterous tug-of-war during the city's annual Bisket festival) and three main squares. In the west, **Durbar Square** and **Taumadhi Tol** dominate the post-fifteenth-century city, while **Tachapal Tol (Dattatreya Square)** presides over the older east end.

Probably the handiest form of public transport to Bhaktapur are the rattletrap electric **trolley buses**, which depart from the National Stadium south of Kathmandu's GPO every fifteen minutes or so and drop you on the main highway about ten minutes' walk south of town. Frequent Banepa-, Dhulikhel- and Barhabise-bound **buses** from Kathmandu's City Bus Park also stop there. Direct **minibus** services to Bhaktapur, originating at the City Bus Park, terminate near Siddha Pokhri, a five-minute walk west of Durbar Square. Local buses from Nagarkot terminate at Kamal Binayak, five minutes northeast of Tachapal; tourist buses from Nagarkot stop to drop passengers off at Kamal Binayak or at the "Tourist Bus Park" north of Durbar Square. If you come on a private tour bus you'll be deposited at the Tourist Bus Park. **Taxis** (Rs300 from Kathmandu) will take you only to the nearest city gate.

Bhaktapur has no rikshas and just a few resident taxis, but it's compact enough to be explored on foot. One-speed **bikes** can be rented along the road east of the minibus park (west of Durbar Square).

Durbar Square

Bhaktapur's **Durbar Square** hasn't got quite the same gusto as its namesakes in Kathmandu and Patan. Isolated near the old city's edge, it's neither a commercial nor a social focal point, and it has lacked a certain architectural harmony ever since the 1934 earthquake claimed several of its temples. Despite all that, it boasts one of Nepal's proudest artistic achievements – the Golden Gate – plus the National Art Gallery.

The square enjoyed one brief, magnificent renaissance during the shooting of the 1995 film **Little Buddha**, when it was used as the location for many of the ancient flashback scenes. Director Bernardo Bertolucci transformed the area beyond recognition: high, simulated brick walls were erected to block modern sightlines, the palace front was extended with false balconies and columns, and the dead space in the middle was

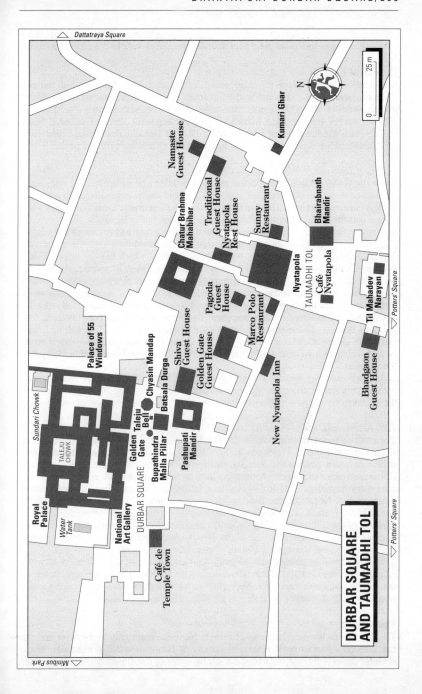

DURBAR SQUARE AND TAUMADHI TOL

Dattatraya Square

N

0 25 m

Kumari Ghar

Namaste Guest House

Bhairabnath Mandir

Chatur Brahma Mahabihar

Traditional Guest House

Nyatapola Rest House

Sunny Restaurant

Nyatapola

TAUMADHI TOL

Café Nyatapola

Pagoda Guest House

Marco Polo Restaurant

Palace of 55 Windows

Sundari Chowk

Chyasin Mandap

Shiva Guest House

Golden Gate Guest House

Til Mahadev Narayan

Golden Gate

Taleju Bell

Batsala Durga

Bupathindra Malla Pillar

Pashupati Mandir

TALEJU CHOWK

DURBAR SQUARE

New Nyatapola Inn

Bhadgaon Guest House

Potters' Square

Royal Palace

Water Tank

National Art Gallery

Café de Temple Town

Potters' Square

Minibus Park

taken up with a raised water tank. Residents won't soon forget that Hollywood facelift – nor the handsome fees Bertolucci paid them for the use of their houses and shopfronts.

The Royal Palace

Bhaktapur's **Royal Palace** originally stood further east, near Tachapal Tol, but was shifted westwards (like the city) in the fifteenth century; the present structure, dating from the eighteenth century, was renovated and greatly scaled down after 1934. Its superbly carved eastern wing, known as the **Panchapanna Jhyale Durbar** ("Palace of Fifty-Five Windows"), was raised around 1700 by Bupathindra Malla, Bhaktapur's great builder-king, whose *namaste*-ing figure kneels on a stone **pillar** opposite.

THE GOLDEN GATE AND TALEJU CHOWK

While the **Golden Gate** (Sun Dhoka) probably wouldn't be so famous if it were made of wood or stone – it is, in fact, gilt copper – its detail and sheer exuberance raise it to the level of a masterpiece. The *torana* above the door features a squat Garud and a ten-armed, four-headed Taleju, the Mallas' guardian deity, but to locals the most powerful figures are those of Bhairab and Kali, situated chest-high on either side of the gate.

Upon entry, you follow an outdoor passage around to another impressive doorway, depicting Taleju and her heavenly host in wood, beyond which lies the ornate **Taleju Chowk**. This temple is considered the original home of Taleju Bhawani in the valley: a south Indian goddess, she was brought here by the fourteenth-century king Harisinghadev, and was subsequently adopted also by the royal houses of Kathmandu and Patan. Taleju was never much worshipped by commoners, though, and since the dynasties that patronized her are long gone, her temples now hold more historical than religious interest. Those who worship her today equate her with Bhagwati or Durga. Only Hindus are allowed into the temple area, where a metal *kalash* (vessel) representing Taleju is kept, and only initiates may view the actual Taleju idol hidden inside the sanctum.

Another doorway nearby leads to **Sundari Chowk**, Bupathindra Malla's regal bathing tank fed by an ornate stone spout and protected by two gilt *nag* figures, once the centrepiece of a now-obliterated palace section.

THE NATIONAL ART GALLERY

The palace's western wing houses the excellent **National Art Gallery** (daily except Tues 10.15am–3.30pm, Fri closes 2.30pm; Rs20), displaying an extensive permanent exhibit of tantric *paubha* and *thangka*, plus a small number of oblong book covers and illuminated pages of religious texts going back as far as the eleventh century. There are some very important historical works here, including such paradigms of tantric art as a depiction of Nritaswor, the dancing, copulating union of Shiva and Shakti, and the *Sata Chakra Darsan*, a medical chart showing the location of the seven power points (*chakra*) of the human body. The collection also includes a few erotic miniatures and a number of stone images from the Malla dynasty. Stone friezes at the entrance portray Vishnu Varahi and Narasimha, Vishnu's boar and man-lion *avatar*.

English-speaking **guides** may be available for private tours, which are well worth joining to get the most out of this rich collection. Otherwise, ask for the brochure (they don't hand it out automatically). Keep your **entry ticket**, because it's good for admission to two other, smaller museums in Dattatreya Square (see below).

The square

The square itself won't detain you for long. Near the main gate at the west end you can admire a pair of multiple-armed statues of **Bhairab** and **Ugrachandi**, whose sculptor reportedly had his hands cut off by order of the Bhaktapur king to ensure that he wouldn't reproduce the images in Kathmandu or Patan. Among the clutch of minor temples opposite, a Shiva *shikra* showcases the often overlooked Newar art of brickwork.

In the entire square, only the fifteenth-century **Pashupati Mandir** at the busier, more touristy eastern end receives much in the way of reverence. The oldest structure extant here, the temple houses a copy of the exalted Pashupatinath *linga*, and its roof struts sport some wildly deviant erotic carvings. Next door stands the mid-eighteenth-century stone *shikra* of **Batsala Durga** and the obligatory **Taleju Bell**, plus a smaller replica known generally as the **"Bell of Barking Dogs"**, so called because its toll evidently inflicts ultrasonic agony on local canines.

Behind the bell rises the **Chyasin Mandap**, the Pavilion of the Eight Corners, erected in 1990 as an exact replica of an eighteenth-century structure destroyed in the 1934 earthquake. The restorers did a first-rate job of relocating original pillars and lintels and integrating them into a sturdy new structure – the steel reinforcing may clash a bit, but this pavilion is going to stay standing when the next quake hits. The upper floor makes a fine vantage point for observing the square. East of here are another fine stone *shikra* to Durga and the platforms of other demolished and half-heartedly rebuilt temples. This end of the square is slated for renovation, and in the long term may even see the construction of new temples.

Rare for predominantly Hindu Bhaktapur, the well-preserved **Chatur Brahma Mahabihar**, east of the square, attracts Buddhist as well as Hindu worshippers, and is a gathering place for neighbourhood metalsmiths in the evening; you might also hear languorous music performed on harmonium and tabla.

BISKET NEW YEAR, BHAKTAPUR STYLE

While many Nepali festivals have their origins in religious myth, Bhaktapur's high-spirited **Bisket** festival is based on a fairy tale. According to one version of the story, a Bhaktapur king wanted to marry off his daughter, but each time he made a match, the groom would turn up dead in the marital bed the next morning. Eligible bachelors were soon thin on the ground, and the people prayed for deliverance from the curse. One day a stranger came to town and learned of the situation from his host, whose son was due to be the next groom, and offered to take the son's place. Forcing himself to stay awake after doing the act with the princess, the stranger watched as two deadly serpents slithered out of her nostrils. The hero slew the snakes, broke the spell and won the undying gratitude of the people, who now celebrate his deed with an annual festival. The festival's Newari name, Biska, is a contraction of two words meaning "snake" and "death".

Bisket also differs from most Nepali festivals in that its date is reckoned by the solar calendar, not the lunar one, which means it always starts on April 9 or 10. It kicks off with a raucous **tug-of-war** in Taumadhi Tol, in which residents of the upper and lower halves of the city try to pull a creaky, three-storied chariot containing the image of Bhairab to their respective sides. On the fourth day – the day before Nawa Barsa (Nepali New Year) – Bhairab and another smaller chariot are pulled to the sloping open area above Chuping Ghat. When they're in place, men of the city struggle to raise a 25-metre-high **ceremonial pole** with a crossbeam to which are attached two banners representing the two slain snakes – an exciting and sometimes dangerous operation.

The pole stays up until the next afternoon, when residents again take up a tug-of-war, this time trying to pull the mighty pole down to their side. (This is an even more dangerous performance: on one or two occasions people have been killed by the falling pole.) The pole's plunge marks the official beginning of the **new year**. Bisket continues for another four days, with a wild *khat* (deity litter) parade in the eastern part of the city, a candlelight procession to Dattatreya Square, an all-city display of temple deities, and a final tug-of-war over Bhairab's chariot.

Taumadhi Tol

One hundred metres southeast of Durbar Square, **Taumadhi Tol** is a livelier place to linger, if only to admire the view from the balcony of one of the surrounding cafés. In mid-April this square serves as the assembly point for Bisket, Nepal's foremost New Year celebration (see box).

Dominating Taumadhi and all of Bhaktapur, the graceful, five-tiered **Nyatapola** is Nepal's tallest and most classically proportioned pagoda. So obscure is its deity, a tantric goddess named Siddhi Lakshmi, that she apparently has no devotees, and the sanctuary has been barred to all but priests ever since its completion in 1702. Perhaps that's why the temple is named not for a deity but, uniquely, for its architectural dimensions: in Newari, *nyata* means "five-stepped" and *pola* means "roof". The Nyatapola's five pairs of temple guardians – Malla wrestlers, elephants, lions, griffins and two minor goddesses, Baghini (Tigress) and Singhini (Lioness) – are as famous as the temple itself. Each pair is supposed to be ten times as strong as the pair below, with Siddhi Lakshmi herself, presumably, being ten times as strong as Baghini and Singhini. Bisket chariot components, including the solid wooden wheels, can be seen near here.

The heavy, thick-set **Bhairabnath Mandir** is as different from the slender Nyatapola as one pagoda could possibly be from another. The most peculiar thing about this hulk of a building, in fact, is the tiny Bhairab idol mounted on a sort of mantel on the front of the temple (several other figures are kept inside, including the larger mask that leads the Bisket parade). A story is told that Bhairab, travelling incognito, once came to Bhaktapur to watch the Bisket festivities. Divining the god's presence and hoping to extract a boon, the priests bound him with tantric spells, and when he tried to escape by sinking into the ground they chopped off his head. Now Bhairab, or at least his head, gets to ride in the Bisket parade every year – inside a locked box on board the chariot.

Hidden behind recent buildings southeast of the square, the seventeenth-century **Til Mahadev Narayan Mandir** displays all the iconography of a Vishnu (Narayan) temple: a gilded *sankha* (conch), *chakra* (wheel) and Garud are all hoisted on pillars out in front, in a manner clearly imitating the great temple of Changu Narayan, 5km north of Bhaktapur. The temple's name, it's said, derives from an incident involving a trader from Thimi who, upon unfolding his wares here, magically discovered the image of Narayan in a consignment of sesame seeds (*til*).

A block northeast of the Bhairabnath Mandir stands Bhaktapur's **Kumari Ghar**. An image of the goddess is kept upstairs and is only displayed publicly during Bisket. The living goddess herself resides in another building north of Tachapal Tol.

West to the Potters' Square

Like a brick canyon, Bhaktapur's main commercial thoroughfare runs from Taumadhi west to the city gate. Roughly 150m along, you'll reach a kind of playground of sculptures and shrines, and a *shikra* that rejoices in the name of **Jyotirlingeshwar Mahadev**, freely translatable as "Great God of the Resplendent Phallus" – a reference to a myth in which Shiva challenges Brahma and Vishnu to find the end of his organ (they never do). Further west, where the street's brick cobbles temporarily give way to flagstones, the **Jaya Barahi Mandir** commemorates the *shakti* (consort) of Vishnu the boar; you have to stand well back from this broad edifice to see its pagoda roofs. Non-Hindus aren't specifically barred from entering the upstairs sanctuary, but this intimate space wasn't designed for spectators.

Dark, damp alleys beckon on either side of the main road – north towards Durbar Square and south to the river. An obligatory destination in this area is Kumale Tol, the **Potters' Square**, a sloping open space southwest of Taumadhi Tol. Until recently,

Bhaktapur's potters (*kumal*) worked here fairly anonymously, cranking out simple water vessels, stovepipes, disposable yoghurt pots and the like. Nowadays the square has blossomed into quite a little tourist attraction, and as its output has shifted to tourist knickknacks, workaday pottery is increasingly being produced in other, smaller squares in the eastern part of the city.

Ironically, the tourist market gives these potters an incentive to stick to mostly traditional methods. You'll see them kneading their clay by hand, and a few still form their vessels on hand-powered wheels: using a pole to spin the wheel to a dervish pitch, the potter gets four or five minutes' working time before the wheel gradually winds down to a slow wobble and needs to be cranked up again. The finished creations are set out in soldierly rows to dry in the sun for a day or two before firing, which turns them from grey to brick red.

Tachapal Tol (Dattatraya Square)

From Taumadhi, the eastern segment of Bhaktapur's main artery snakes its way to the original and still-beating heart of the city, **Tachapal Tol** (or **Dattatraya Square**). Here again a pair of temples looms over the square, older than those of Taumadhi if not as eye-catching. More notably, though, Tachapal conceals Nepal's most celebrated masterpiece of woodcarving, the Pujari Math's Peacock Window, and a superb woodcarving museum. You'll also find the finest woodwork studios in Nepal here, which are well worth a browse, even if you haven't got room in your rucksack for an eight-foot, Rs100,000 peacock-window reproduction.

Just north of Tachapal, a second open space around Ganesh Pokhri is equally busy with *pasal* (shops) and street vendors. South of the square is also good for exploring, as Bhaktapur's medieval backstreets spill down the steep slope to the river like tributaries.

Dattatraya and Bhimsen temples

Rearing up behind an angelic pillar-statue of Garud, the **Dattatraya Mandir** (accent on the second syllable of Dattatraya) is Bhaktapur's oldest structure. The temple was raised in 1427 during the reign of Yaksha Malla, the last king to rule the valley from Bhaktapur, and like the Kasthamandap of Kathmandu, which it resembles, it was allegedly built from a single tree (the front portico was probably added later). Dattatraya, a sort of one-size-fits-all deity imported from southern India, epitomizes the religious "syncretism" (as anthropologists call it) that Nepal is famous for: to Vaishnavas Dattatraya is an incarnation of Vishnu, while Shaivas hail him as Shiva's guru and Buddhists even fit him into their pantheon as a *bodhisattva*.

The oblong temple at the opposite end of the square belongs to **Bhimsen**, the patron saint of Newar merchants, whose territory Tachapal is. As usual for a Bhimsen temple, the ground floor is open and the shrine is kept upstairs.

The Pujari Math

Behind and to the right of the Dattatraya temple stands the sumptuous eighteenth-century **Pujari Math**, one of a dozen priests' quarters (*math*) that once ringed Tachapal Tol. Similar to Buddhist *bahal*, these *math* typically sheltered communities of Hindu devotees loyal to a single leader or sect. Like *bahal*, most have now also been converted to other, secular uses. Given the nature of the caste system, it's not surprising that the grandest houses in the city traditionally belonged to priests. The Pujari Math's awesome windows can be seen on two sides; the often-imitated **Peacock Window**, overlooking a narrow lane on the building's far (east) side, has for two centuries been acclaimed as the zenith of Nepalese window-lattice carving.

The woodcarving and brass museums

Don't miss the small **Woodcarving Museum** (daily except Tues 10am–4pm, Fri closes 3pm) inside the Pujari Math. Well displayed and lit, it enables you to inspect a small collection of exquisite temple carvings that in their normal surroundings are often too high up to fully appreciate. Highlights of the collection are an alluring fifteenth-century Nartaki Devi, a large, waist-up Bhairava (Bhairab) of the seventeenth century, several magnificent steles and *torana*, and various abstractly weathered temple struts. The courtyard itself contains possibly the greatest concentration of woodcarving virtuosity in the country.

Somewhat misleadingly, the **Brass and Bronze Museum** (daily except Tues 10am–4pm, Fri closes 3pm) across the square contains none of the flamboyant religious art that one might expect, consisting instead of domestic and ritual vessels and implements. Still, by cataloguing the many esoteric forms of these items, the collection helps to suggest just how complex traditional Nepali culture is.

A single Rs20 **ticket** gives admission to both these museums and to the National Art Gallery in Durbar Square.

Nawa Durga Dyochhen and points east

North of Tachapal, the **Nawa Durga Dyochhen** looks like a haunted house, Nepali-style. A tantric temple only open to initiates, it honours the nine manifestations of Durga, who are especially feared and respected in Bhaktapur. According to legend, the Nawa Durga used to eat solitary travellers, turning the area east of Bhaktapur into a Bermuda triangle until a priest managed to cast a tantric spell on them. The Nawa Durga occupy a special place in Bhaktapur's spiritual landscape: the city is said to be delimited by symbolic Nawa Durga stones (*pith*), and most *tol* (neighbourhoods) have adopted one of the nine as their protector goddess.

Most famous of all are the **Nawa Durga dancers**, a troupe whose members are drawn from the caste of flower sellers. Each wears a painted clay mask which, empowered by tantric incantations, enables the wearer to become the very embodiment of the deity. Every September a new set of masks is moulded and painted, each with its own iconography – there are actually thirteen in all, the Nawa Durga plus four attendant deities. On Bijaya Dasami, the "victorious tenth day" of Dasain, the dancers and accompanying musicians gather at Brahmayani Pith, about 1km east of town, and dance all the way to the Golden Gate, where they re-enact the legend of Durga's victory over a buffalo demon. The troupe continues to perform at designated places on days determined by the lunar calendar throughout the winter and spring wedding and festival seasons. In the month of Bhadra (Aug–Sept) their masks are formally retired and burned, and the ashes saved to be added to clay to form the next year's masks.

West of the Nawa Durga Dyochhen, the **Prashannashil Mahabihar**, distinguished by its pagoda-style cupola, is another of Bhaktapur's few Buddhist institutions. East along the main road from Tachapal, the **Wakupati Narayan Mandir**, where local Jyapus worship Vishnu as a harvest god, displays no fewer than five Garuds mounted on pillars in a line.

Along the Hanumante Khola and beyond

The **Hanumante Khola** is Bhaktapur's humble tributary of the River Ganga, its name deriving from the monkey god Hanuman who, locals like to think, stopped here for a drink on his way back from the Himalaya after gathering medicinal herbs to heal Ram's brother in an episode of the *Ramayan*. Like all rivers in the valley, it's pretty disgusting, and doesn't exactly present Bhaktapur's best face, but several interesting bathing and cremation ghats flank the river as it curls along the city's southern edge. Unfortunately there's no riverside path connecting them.

The ghats

The most active site is **Hanuman Ghat**, located straight downhill from Tachapal Tol where two tributaries join to form the Hanumante. Morning *puja* and ablutions are a daily routine for many, while old-timers come here just to hang out. The area is reached by passing between two jumbo *shivalinga* hoisted on octagonal plinths. Behind the lefthand one is the Ram temple that gives the ghat its Hanuman association: a statue of the monkey god outside the sanctum pays tribute to his master sheltered within. Another Hanuman, painted orange, keeps watch over a clutter of small *linga* and other Shiva imagery scattered around the confluence area.

Downhill from Taumadhi Tol, **Chuping Ghat**'s temple complex has been partially restored and taken over by Kathmandu University's Department of Music, under joint Western–Nepali direction. If it's open you can go in – there's a lovely garden, and students may be heard practising their instruments. The long, sloping area above the ghat is the focal point on New Year's Day (Nawa Barsa) in April, when a 25-metre *linga* pole is ceremonially toppled by the throng. This area is inhabited mainly by members of the sweeper caste, so much of Bhaktapur's rubbish ends up nearby.

Ram Ghat, below Potters' Square, has little to offer beyond a run-of-the-mill Ram temple, though it's a good place to hear evening *bhajan*. **Mangal Ghat**, further downstream, boasts a more atmospheric selection of neglected artefacts, and by following the trail of *linga* across the river you'll end up at a forbidding Kali temple in one of Bhaktapur's satellite villages.

Surya Binayak

Once south of the Hanumante, you can ramble up to the forested ridge overlooking Bhaktapur, where **Surya Binayak** makes a worthy target. This most pleasantly situated of the valley's four main Ganesh shrines – catching the valley's first rays of sun – is reached by a steep, kilometre-long paved road from the trolley bus terminus. The temple itself is just an ordinary plaster *shikra*, surrounded by usual Ganesh trappings; smeared with red *sindur* paste, the god's image looks like a warm fire in an ornate Victorian hearth. Ganesh is regarded as a divine trouble-shooter, and this particular image specializes in curing children who are slow to walk or speak.

If you're on a bike, keep going: you can round the ridge either to the east or the west and noodle around a seldom-visited rural corner of the valley.

Accommodation

All Bhaktapur's **accommodation** falls into the guest-house category. Most places are small, friendly and exceptionally well located in the area around Taumadhi and Durbar Square. As a rule prices are somewhat higher than for comparable lodgings in Kathmandu, but Bhaktapur is worth it.

The city doesn't have that many beds, so book ahead in busy times, or arrive as early as possible in the day. Refer to the "Durbar Square and Taumadhi Tol" map for locations. You might also consider staying at Changu Narayan (see below).

Bhadgaon Guest House (☎610488, fax 610481). Rooms are ordinary, but a central garden and the super view from the three-level roof terrace really make this place. B⑥.

Golden Gate Guest House (☎610534, fax 611081). Relatively large place, secluded, with good views from the roof and upper (more expensive) rooms. ④/B⑤–⑥.

Namaste Guest House (☎610500, fax 225679). Newer building without much character, but the rooftop rooms are worth going for. ④/B⑤.

New Nyatapola Inn (☎611852; *dhaubdel@craft.mos.com.np*). Rather dark and lacking in atmosphere. B④–⑤.

Nyatapola Rest House (☎612415). A basic cheapie: just a few small, dark, ground-floor rooms, but there's room to spread out in the rooftop restaurant. ③.

Pagoda Guest House (☎613248, fax 612865). Rooms are cosy, especially the higher-priced ones, which come with phone, TV and heat. Overlooks the Nyatapola. ④/B⑤–⑦.

Shiva Guest House (☎613912, fax 610740). Clean and reasonably cheerful, with helpful management. Good location right on Durbar Square overlooking the Pashupati Mandir. ④/B⑥.

Traditional Guest House (☎611057, fax 612607). A laid-back, family-run place. Rooms are cramped but economical. B③.

Eating

Most of the guest houses have their own **restaurants** with standard tourist menus. Meanwhile, several cafés overlooking the various squares cater mainly to day-trippers – they're great places for watching the goings-on below, but the food is usually undistinguished and overpriced.

For something more authentically Nepali, there are plenty of cheap *bhojanalaya* west of Durbar Square and around the bus park, and Newar *bhatti* are found throughout the old city. If nothing else, you can always load up on thick, presweetened yoghurt (Bhaktapur's famed *juju dhau* – "king of curds"), available by the clay pot or glass from local stalls at a fraction of the price charged in tourist restaurants.

Café Nyatapola. A temple-turned-restaurant with a great location and middling food.

Café de Peacock. You can't beat the surroundings – the restaurant occupies a former *math* overlooking Dattatraya Square – but the food is run-of-the-mill tourist grub.

Café de Temple Town. Popular with day-trippers and tour groups. It's on the expensive side, but the food (especially the Indian) is quite good.

Marco Polo Restaurant. Enjoy the view over a cup of tea or a bowl of curd – but steer well clear of the food.

Sunny Restaurant. A cosy, hobbit-house of a place located in a low-ceilinged old building next to the Nyatapola. Great food, including decent Newari combo platters.

Shopping

Some of Bhaktapur's best buys are in **wood**: browse the workshops around the main squares to get a feel for different styles, woods and techniques, then haggle for bargains with the traders along the lane that contains the Peacock Window. See Basics for more on what's available.

Bhaktapur is also known for its Nawa Durga **puppets** and papier-mâché **masks**, which are associated with a local dance festival (see p.208). The puppets come in various sizes and with one, two or four faces. Masks also come in a range of sizes and in two qualities, but the selection is greater in Thimi (see below). Many of the **paper** products sold elsewhere in the valley are handmade here in Bhaktapur, at a UNICEF-supported factory near the Tourist Bus Park. And of course you can pick up cheap **pottery** at the Potters' Square: animal figures, planters, candlestick holders, ashtrays, piggy banks (called *kutrukke*, a word that imitates the sound of a coin being dropped in) and so on.

Nepalis recognize Bhaktapur for its traditional **textiles**, such as black-and-red *pataasi* material and black *Bhadgaonle topi*, formal headgear now worn mainly by traditionalists and government officials. Foreigners will be more attracted by the locally produced *dhaka* in original designs, as well as block-printed, quilted cotton items, woollens, *pashmina* shawls and Rajasthani-style tapestries.

Several shops around Taumadhi sell quality **thangka**, and artists can often be seen painting them. **Watercolours** of local scenes are popular. Some **metal** pieces, such as incense holders and traditional ritual objects, are produced here. Tea, incense and music CDs are also available.

Film is sold in many tourist shops. There's a film processing lab just west of the Durbar Square gate.

Other practicalities

Moneychangers can be found in each of the main tourist areas. Plenty of places offer international **telephone** services, and a few also do email. Take letters and postcards to the **post office**, just north of the minibus park, to have the stamps franked, or ask at your guest house if they'll do it. Some guest houses can make bookings on tourist **buses** and even on domestic flights, saving you a trip to Kathmandu.

Bhaktapur's **hospital** would not be a great place to have to go in an emergency. However, the **Bhaktapur International Homeopathic Clinic** (☎613197), with both Western and Nepali staff, is highly regarded throughout the valley. It's located up a lane going north from the Dattatreya temple; hours vary depending on individual staff schedules.

Changu Narayan

The beautiful, tranquil site of **CHANGU NARAYAN** is a must for everyone. Perched at the abrupt end of the ridge north of Bhaktapur, the ancient temple complex commands a fine view of the valley in three directions – especially in late afternoon, when the meandering Manohara River turns into a golden ribbon. A simple guest house offers the prospect of staying overnight here, and makes a potential stopover in a circuit to or from Nagarkot (see p.217).

The site

"One remembers all the wealth of carving of the rest of the Valley," wrote Percival Landon in 1928, ". . . but when all is recalled it is probably to the shrine of Changu Narayan that one offers the palm. Perhaps one drives back home from Bhatgaon more full of thought than from any other expedition to the many outlying places of this crowded centre of holiness and history and art." Protected by its remote location, Changu Narayan has changed little since Landon's day, with relatively few travellers, or even worshippers, making the effort to visit it. It is, on the face of it, just another pagoda, yet Changu Narayan's palpable age and its collection of the finest, oldest statues outside the National Museum seem to make it the archetypal Nepalese pagoda. Ideally, you should see it before you've burned out on the others.

The valley's **oldest Vaishnava site**, Changu Narayan's documented history goes back to the fifth century AD, and its sculptures attest to continuous worship here ever since. Some historians suspect an even greater antiquity, postulating that the Lichhavi temple was built atop a much older animist site.

The **main temple**, rebuilt around 1700, stands in a quiet quadrangle of rest houses and pilgrims' shelters. A measure of the temple's importance is the exaggerated size of the four traditional emblems of Vishnu – the wheel (*chakra*), conch (*sankha*), lotus (*padma*) and mace (*gada*) – mounted on pillars at its four corners. The repoussé work on the front (west side) of the building is as intricate as any you'll find in Nepal, as are the carved, painted struts supporting the roofs. The *torana* above the main door depicts Vishnu in his *sridhara* posture (see below), brandishing the four emblems in his four hands. The original fifth-century stone image of Vishnu, covered in a seventh-century gilt sheath, is allegedly kept inside the sanctuary, but only the temple priests are allowed to view it. From time to time, the statue is said to sweat miraculously, indicating that

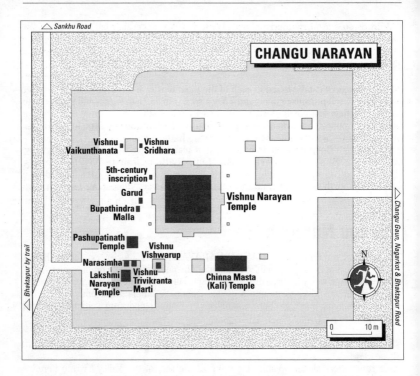

CHANGU NARAYAN

Sankhu Road

Vishnu Vaikunthanata
Vishnu Sridhara
5th-century inscription
Garud
Bupathindra Malla
Vishnu Narayan Temple
Pashupatinath Temple
Vishnu Vishwarup
Narasimha
Lakshmi Narayan Temple
Vishnu Trivikranta Marti
Chinna Masta (Kali) Temple
Bhaktapur by trail
Changu Gaun, Nagarkot & Bhaktapur Road
N
0   10 m

Vishnu is battling with the *nag* spirits, and the cloth used to wipe the god's brow is considered a charm against snake bites.

The base of the *chakra* pillar bears the **oldest inscription** in the valley. Dated 454 AD and attributed to the Lichhavi king Manadeva, it relates how Manadeva, upon the death of his father, dissuaded his mother from committing *sati* by promising to conquer his foes to the east.

Smaller temples in the compound are dedicated to **Chinna Masta** (a local version of Kali), Lakshmi (the goddess of wealth, Vishnu's consort) and Shiva. Some scholars speculate that Chinna Masta is the mother goddess who was worshipped at this site in prehistoric times. Her cult endures: a Chinna Masta Mai chariot procession is held here in the Nepali month of Baisakh (April–May).

The statues

The courtyard of Changu Narayan is an outdoor museum of priceless works of art, displayed in an almost offhand manner and all the more exciting for it. You'll find the oldest, famous statues grouped around the front of the temple (see map) plus loads of other, more recent (but still centuries-old) pieces in the vicinity. With few exceptions, they all pertain to Vishnu or his faithful carrier, Garud.

Probably dating from the sixth century, Changu Narayan's celebrated statue of **Garud** kneels before the temple, looking human but for a pair of wings and a cobra scarf (the face is believed to be a portrait of Manadeva). He used to be mounted on a pillar, the broken base of which is lying just to his right. Garud's association with snakes is legendary. It's said that when his mother was kidnapped by his stepmother,

Garud appealed to his serpentine stepbrothers to free her, which they did on condition that Garud brought them ambrosia from Indra's heaven. Although Indra later flew down and reclaimed his pot of nectar (leaving the snakes to split their tongues as they licked up the few drops spilt on the grass), Vishnu was so impressed that Garud hadn't been tempted to consume the ambrosia that he immediately hired him as his mount. The statues inside a screened cage next to Garud commemorate **King Bupathindra Malla** of Bhaktapur and his queen Bubana Lakshmi, who ruled during the late seventeenth and early eighteenth centuries.

Though damaged, the eighth-century image of **Vishnu Vishwarup** (Vishnu of the Universal Form) is an awesome example of Hindu psychedelia. The lower portion of this composite image shows Vishnu reclining on the snake of infinity in the ocean of existence, echoing the sleeping statues of Budhanilkantha and Balaju. Above, the god is portrayed rising from the waters before a heavenly host, his thousand heads and arms symbolizing sheer omnipotence. The latter image is borrowed from an episode in the *Mahabharat* in which the warrior Arjuna lost his nerve and Krishna (an incarnation of Vishnu) appeared in this universal form to dictate the entire Bhagavad Gita by way of encouragement.

Two notable statues rest on the platform of the Lakshmi Narayan temple. The eighth-century **Vishnu Trivikranta Murti**, Vishnu of the Three Strides, illustrates a much-loved story in which the god reclaimed the universe from the demon king Bali. Disguised as a dwarf (another of his ten incarnations), Vishnu petitioned Bali for a patch of ground where he could meditate, which need only be as far as the dwarf could cover in three strides; when Bali agreed, Vishnu grew to his full divine height and bounded over the earth, sky and heavens. (An even older version of this statue is held in the National Museum.) The adjacent eleventh- or twelfth-century image depicts Vishnu in yet another of his incarnations, that of the man-lion **Narasimha**.

At the northwest corner of the compound, the twelfth- or thirteenth-century **Vishnu Vaikunthanata** – reproduced on the Nepalese ten-rupee note – shows a purposeful Vishnu riding Garud like some sort of hip space traveller. Nearby stands a **Vishnu Sridhara** of the ninth or tenth century, an early example of what has since become a stereotypical Vishnu representation.

Getting there and back

You can approach the temple complex from Bhaktapur, the Sankhu road or Nagarkot – time permitting, the ideal itinerary is to walk from Nagarkot to Bhaktapur via Changu Narayan.

From Bhaktapur, an asphalted road forks off from the Nagarkot road about 200m east of the hilltop Mahakali shrine (see the main Bhaktapur map) and climbs directly up to Changu Gaun, the village immediately east of the temple. **Buses** make the journey approximately hourly, originating at the start of the Changu road. If you're **cycling** you'll need a mountain bike because the last 2km or so are very steep. Two other roads set off from the north side of Bhaktapur towards Changu Narayan, but they soon converge and eventually become a **trail** that passes through rural villages before a steep ascent to reach the temple after 5km.

The ten-kilometre **hike from Nagarkot** is described on p.221. The trail **from the Sankhu road** is only 2km long, but it's hard to find at its lower end and the bridge over the Manohara River is only seasonal. Descending is no problem, although when you reach the highway you'll have to flag down a minibus and probably stand all the way to Kathmandu.

Accommodation and eating

Accommodation is available at *Changu Narayan Hill Resort* (③), located about 500m east of the Changu Gaun gate, along the unpaved road to Nagarkot. Facilities are pretty minimal and arguably overpriced, but you pay for the solitude and views (Phurbi Chyachu is prominent from here). It's a little bit like Nagarkot was fifteen years ago, before it got put on the tourist map. Brace yourself for no hot water, however, and something of a language problem. Camping is also possible. A second, even more primitive option is a "bed and breakfast" (①) located along the trail heading straight down the hill west of the temple – ask for directions at the shops in front of the main temple entrance.

Even if you don't stay at the "resort", you can **eat** in the dining room – breakfast after a cycle up from Bhaktapur, perhaps, or lunch on the way down from Nagarkot. Snacks and drinks are also available in and around the temple area and at the Changu Gaun parking lot.

Thimi (Madhyapur) and around

THIMI, the valley's fourth-largest town, lies on a plateau 4km west of Bhaktapur. The name is said to be a corruption of *chhemi*, meaning "capable people", a bit of flattery offered by Bhaktapur to make up for the fact that the town used to get mauled every time Bhaktapur picked a fight with Kathmandu or Patan. Recently the town has revived its ancient name of **MADHYAPUR** ("Middle Place"),which recalls its midway location. Its mainly Newar inhabitants are indeed very capable craftspeople, and Thimi is the place to go for papier-mâché masks and pottery.

The Bhaktapur **trolley bus** will drop you off at the southern end of Thimi, but you'll get a far more favourable introduction by **cycling** in along the old road to Bhaktapur, which skirts the town to the north. **Minibuses** from Bhaktapur and Kathmandu also ply this back route.

Several handicrafts shops – Thimi's only real attraction – are located along the north road. The **papier-mâché masks** seen in tourist shops all over the Kathmandu Valley originated here, and Thimi's Chitrakar family, famed for generations as purveyors of fine festival masks, still produces them in a range of sizes and styles. Snarling Bhairab, kindly Kumari and elephant-headed Ganesh are most commonly represented by the masks, which are based on those worn by Bhaktapur's Nawa Durga dancers. Compared to those now produced in Bhaktapur and elsewhere, Thimi masks are cheaper, lighter, and have a duller, rougher finish. Lightness is an important feature in the larger festival masks worn by dancers, and cheapness makes the smaller ones the preferred choice for use in Nawa Durga puppets. Also available are hilarious salt and pepper shakers in the shape of the king and queen – though expensive, they make great, offbeat mementoes.

Pottery is an even older local speciality, and you can watch potters at work in alleys and courtyards at the north end of town. However, Thimi's potters have largely abandoned traditional hand-powered methods for electric wheels and kerosene-fired kilns, and with help from a German project they're shifting from cheap terracotta housewares for the local market to export-quality glazed products.

The remainder of Thimi is grotty and unglamorously primitive. Thimi's only temple of note is that of **Balkumari**, a sixteenth-century pagoda located near the southern end of the main north–south lane. Couples pray to the "Child Kumari" for babies, presenting her with coconuts as a symbol of fertility. Balkumari's vehicle is a peacock, which stands upon a nearby pillar. The temple is the focus of frenzied Bisket **festivities** in April, when dozens of deities are ferried around on palanquins and red powder (red being the colour of rejoicing) is thrown like confetti.

Bode

A small, tight-knit Newar community, **BODE** is built on a bluff overlooking the Manohara River, 1km north of Thimi. The village's main shrine, the **Mahalakshmi Mandir**, stands at the northwest corner of the village, a modest and not particularly well-maintained two-tiered pagoda. The goddess of wealth, Maha ("Great") Lakshmi is feted during a three-day festival beginning on New Year's Day (here called Baisaakh Sankranti, meaning the first day of Baisaakh – April 13 or 14). The highlight of the proceedings comes on the second day, when a volunteer has his tongue bored with a thin steel spike and, thus impaled and bearing a disc-shaped object with flaming torches mounted on it, accompanies the goddess as she's paraded around the village. Volunteers believe that they won't bleed if they've followed a prescribed three-day fast and have sufficient faith, and that by performing this act they'll go directly to heaven when they die.

CHAPTER THREE

THE CENTRAL HILLS

B
eyond the Kathmandu Valley, major roads head in three directions, and many
smaller roads branch off from them, making the **central hills** the most accessible – though not necessarily the most travelled – section of Nepal's jumbled,
700-kilometre band of foothills. To the northeast, the **Arniko Highway** follows
the old Kathmandu–Lhasa trade route through broad valleys and misty gorges to the
Tibet border; northwestwards, the **Trisuli Road** snakes its way down into a subtropical valley nearly 1000m lower than Kathmandu; and south, the **Tribhuwan Rajpath**,
Nepal's first highway, cuts a tortuous cross-section through the hills on its way to the
Tarai. If the scenery here is a shade less dramatic than what you'll encounter further
west, the land is nonetheless varied and rugged, only partially tamed by defiant terraces. It's only when you leave the Kathmandu Valley that you appreciate how atypical
it is of this hilly region.

The majority of places described here can be treated as easy overnights from anywhere in the Kathmandu Valley. The most popular are those that involve mountain
views and hill-walking or mountain-biking: **Nagarkot** and **Dhulikhel**, with well-devel-
oped lodgings, are acknowledged classics. **Kakani** is equally scenic, though short on
accommodation, and **Daman** is splendidly off the beaten track. These vantage points
can't compare with what you'll see on a trek, but they're worth visiting if you haven't
got time for a full-blown trek or you just want to get a quick dose of mountain views,

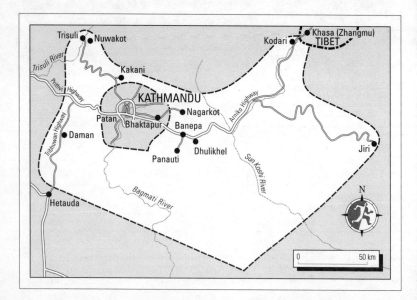

and they can also serve as springboards for longer explorations. The **Tibet border**
area, meanwhile, offers a whole range of activities, thanks to the opening of a new outdoor adventure centre. Although cultural attractions are relatively few outside the
Kathmandu Valley, **Panauti** and **Nuwakot** are among Nepal's most intriguing villages,
and all the more because they're so seldom visited.

To an extent, the boundaries of this chapter are dictated by travel formalities: towns
and **day hikes** are described here, while backcountry areas requiring a trekking permit are saved for Chapter Seven. Despite a relative abundance of roads, **buses** in the
central hills are slow and infrequent, and indeed few travellers brave them except to get
to the start of the Langtang/Helambu and Everest treks. All the more reason to go by
mountain bike or motorcycle, for the region contains some of Nepal's most popular and
rewarding **biking routes**.

Nagarkot

Like many of Nepal's best highways, the road to **NAGARKOT** serves mainly strategic,
not scenic, purposes: Nagarkot was originally developed as an army post, and tourist
facilities came later, with government encouragement. Set on a ridge northeast of
Bhaktapur, it commands a classic panorama of the Himalaya from Ganesh Himal to
Gauri Shankar, and on a good day you can see from Annapurna South to Everest.
Uniquely, you don't have to stay in an expensive hotel here to get a view right out of
your window.

The best thing about Nagarkot is its wealth of **hiking** and **biking** opportunities.
Since it's located at a high point and easily reached on a good road, many people choose
to get a lift up and then hike or bike down, though Nagarkot can also serve as a stop
on a mini-trek or cycle-trek around the Kathmandu Valley rim. At the very least you'll
want to spend the night to catch the sunrise over the peaks, either from your hotel or
from a view tower further along the ridge.

Getting there

In high season, two or three tourist **buses** depart each afternoon for Nagarkot from the
north end of Kantipath in Kathmandu and return the following morning. Book through
any ticket agent (the fare should be around Rs100 each way). The only public buses to
Nagarkot depart from Bhaktapur's Kamal Binayak area (hourly; Rs15). If you're coming from Kathmandu or anywhere else by public bus, you'll not only have to change in
Bhaktapur but also walk clear across town to make the connection: you might as well
spend the night in Bhaktapur. A **taxi** from Kathmandu will cost about $12. Free trans-
port should be provided if you're booked into one of the more expensive hotels.

The easiest **cycle** up is along the main road from Bhaktapur. It's consistently steep
for the last 12km – the vertical gain is 650m – but paved all the way and relatively free

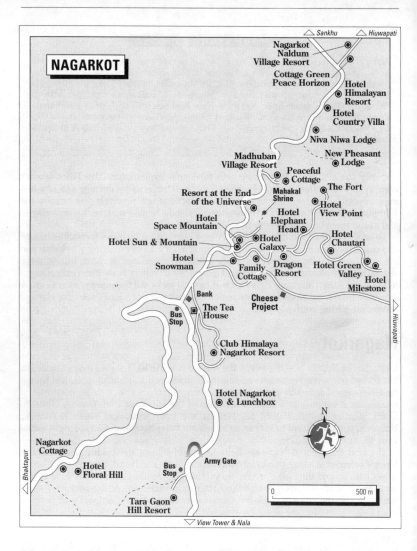

of traffic. Unpaved and generally steeper roads and tracks head up from Changu Narayan, Sankhu, Nala and other points – see the "Routes down from Nagarkot" section below. It's also possible to walk up any of these routes, but most people prefer to do that in reverse.

Being there

Erase from your mind any picture of a quaint hilltop village. Nagarkot is only a loose affiliation of guest houses and hotels stretching for 2km along an open ridgetop at around 1950m. Almost all the budget places are grouped around the plunging north end of the ridge, reached by a dirt road that forks off to the left at the public bus stop. Two landmarks in this vicinity are a tiny Mahakal shrine, at a high point of the ridge, and a small-scale cheese-making project, quite a bit downhill on the eastern side.

Most guest houses have good views of their own, but you'll get much better ones – and a greater sense of having earned them – if you walk or ride to the view tower at the highest southern point of the ridge (2164m). Follow the main paved (later dirt) road south for about 5km, which takes an hour to an hour and a half on foot from most guest houses. When you get to the tower you'll understand why Nagarkot has been the site of a fort (*kot*) since Rana times: this hilltop controlled the eastern entrance to the Kathmandu Valley and the vital trade route to Tibet. There's still an army base along the road to the tower, but nowadays the troops' primary responsibility is to regulate woodcutting in the area.

Many people set off before dawn to catch the sunrise at the tower and return to their lodgings in time to catch the midmorning tourist bus back to Kathmandu, but the programme is a lot more relaxed if you set aside the whole day. You can have your guest house pack you a lunch, or get Nepali food at a couple of *bhojanalaya* near the tower.

For further hiking and biking ideas, see "Routes down from Nagarkot", below. It's also possible to visit the view tower or tour area roads by jeep, hired out by some guest houses and hotels.

Accommodation

The arrival of electricity has turned Nagarkot's old trekking-standard lodges into Thamel-style guest houses and spurred the construction of a number of high-class hotels. In keeping with Nagarkot's image as a "resort", even many of the budget places have Kathmandu offices or agents and try to charge ridiculously inflated prices for pre-booked rooms. In high season it may be advisable to book ahead, since the lodgings are spread out and the better ones do fill up early, but you'll get a better rate if you call the guest house or hotel directly. (Nagarkot numbers, which are given below where available, begin with the prefix 290.) The price will be even lower if you just show up, but try to get there before the tourist bus arrives. Always ask for a "discount", which should amount to 50 to 75 percent off the published rate, depending on season.

The map shows all the lodgings existing or under construction at the time of writing, but don't be surprised to find a few more when you get there. Most are oriented towards the north–northeast to take advantage of the best mountain views, though some boast of sunrise views to the east or Kathmandu Valley views to the west. Only a few are positioned at the very top of the ridge where you can see in all directions. Views are apt to change as new places are built in front of older ones, though it's not necessarily such a bad thing to have to hike a little bit to see the mountains.

ROOM PRICE SCALES

Lodging prices change from season to season, so it would be misleading to quote exact prices in a guidebook. Instead, all guest houses and hotels have been price-graded according to the scale below, which is based on the price of the cheapest double room in high season. Codes prefixed by B denote the cost of the cheapest room with attached bathroom, and those prefixed by AC refer to air-conditioned rooms. See p.39 for a fuller explanation.

① Less than Rs140 ($2 if quoted in US$)
② Rs140–200 ($2–3)
③ Rs200–350 ($3–5)
④ Rs350–550 ($5–8)
⑤ $8–12
⑥ $12–20
⑦ $20–40
⑧ $40–75
⑨ Over $75

At the budget end, the single biggest determinant of price isn't views or room quality, but rather the availability of hot water: you'll pay the most for 24-hour (geyser) hot water, less for solar-heated water (which is hot only when the sun has been shining), and least for hot water by the bucket. Although quilts are provided, a sleeping bag might be worth bringing in winter; only the most deluxe places are heated. Bring a torch (flashlight) for walking between buildings after dark.

BUDGET

Family Cottage (☎610874). Very small outfit (supposedly expanding) with a partial view and bamboo huts. Cold water only. ②/B③.

Hotel Galaxy (☎290870). Clear views to east and west, but mountain views are obstructed. Operates its own tourist bus. Basic rooms with solar hot water (B④), more deluxe rooms with geyser (B⑤).

Hotel Green Valley (☎290878). Excellent mountain views, though you can't see the Kathmandu Valley from this side. Geyser hot water. ③/B④–⑤.

Madhuban Village Resort (☎290709). Excellent views. Dinky Robinson Crusoe-esque bamboo A-frames with common bath, or brick bungalows with attached baths. Hot water by the bucket. ②/B④.

Hotel Milestone (☎290888). Little brick huts with great views. Hot water by the bucket. ③/B③.

Hotel Nagarkot (☎256371). The only budget place south of the bus stop. Good but restricted views. Basic rooms with solar hot water. B③.

New Pheasant Lodge (☎417415). A few basic rooms, accessed by a great jungle trail. Hot water by the bucket. Electricity "coming soon". B②.

Resort at the End of the Universe (☎290709). Bamboo huts, a bank of other rooms and a cosy restaurant that shows nightly videos. At a high point of the ridge, though views from rooms are only partial. No hot water in the cheap rooms. B②–④.

MIDRANGE

Hotel Elephant Head (☎611825). Good views east and west, but blocked to the north (where it matters the most). B⑤ with solar hot water, B⑥ with geyser.

Nagarkot Naldum Village Resort (☎610963). Good views, average rooms. It can get lonely out at this end of the ridge. B⑤.

Peaceful Cottage (☎290877). Killer panorama of the mountains and the Kathmandu Valley from a high point on the ridge. Good restaurant. Hot water by the bucket in the common bath, attached baths have hot running water. ④/B⑤.

Tara Gaon Hill Resort (☎290861). Nagarkot's original government-run outfit is sadly run down and has befuddled service. Minimal views. B⑦, with discounts for longer stays.

Hotel View Point (☎417424). A big place with tidy brick bungalows and a smart glassed-in dining room (good food). Sits at a great high spot, but its view is somewhat marred by *The Fort*. B⑥.

EXPENSIVE

Club Himalaya Nagarkot Resort (☎290883). Luxurious fifty-room relative of Thamel's *Kathmandu Guest House*: indoor pool, sauna, gym, etc. Views are good, but not great. B⑨.

Hotel Chautari (☎290875). Medium-sized hotel. Most rooms are in semi-detached bungalows facing southeast (only partial views). Good restaurant. B⑧.

Hotel Country Villa (☎425305; *anima@wlink.com.np*). Nice rooms with east-facing balconies, but overpriced and faintly unsavoury. B⑧.

Hotel Floral Hill (☎290863). Undergoing renovation. Lush and secluded, but a 15-minute hike to views. B⑧.

The Fort (☎290869). Total views. Well-appointed rooms in the main building and also in cottages. Lovely gardens, traditional architecture, excellent restaurant. B⑧.

Nagarkot Farmhouse (☎272719; *nfh@mos.com.np*). Located nearly 2km north of the bus stop on the road to Sankhu (1km off the map). Run by the same folks who brought you the excellent *Hotel Vajra* in Kathmandu, this restful retreat places an emphasis on yoga and meditation. Lovely, secluded grounds with orchard. ⑦/B⑨.

Niva Niwa Lodge (☎259141). A stone castle with nice rooms and terrace, but overpriced. Mainly Japanese clientele. B⑨.

Eating and other practicalities
Food at the budget guest house dining rooms takes a long time to prepare and usually doesn't live up to expectations. But as in trekking lodges, mealtimes are lively social occasions with an intimate, we're-all-in-this-together energy.

You can always try seeing if the grass is any greener at other guest houses or hotels, though this is more convenient for breakfast or lunch – eating dinner out means returning in the dark. Some of the expensive hotels can offer some pretty fine dining, particularly the *Club Himalaya Nagarkot Resort*'s *Tea House* (located in a separate building above the public bus stop) and *The Fort*'s and *Niva Niwa Lodge*'s in-house restaurants. At the other end of the scale, you can get cheap, standard Nepali fare from any of several *bhojanalaya* in the small bazaar area around the bus stop.

For **changing money**, Himalayan Bank has an efficient branch near the bus stop (Sun–Fri 10am–3pm). There's no post office or any other tourist facilities to speak of.

Routes down from Nagarkot
Probably the most popular way down from Nagarkot goes **via Changu Narayan** (see p.211) to Bhaktapur, which can be reached in three or four hours on foot, or half that time on a mountain bike or motorcycle. The route follows the main road down to Phedi, where the road passes through a notch in the ridge (hikers can catch a bus to here). At Phedi, take the dirt road to the right and follow it generally along the wooded ridgeline to Changu Narayan. It's another 6km from Changu down to Bhaktapur.

The descent **to Sankhu** (p.167), which starts by following the road past Nagarkot's northern lodges, is favoured by mountain-bikers. The road forks not far past the *Nagarkot Farmhouse* (off the map): the lefthand route is steep, rutted and good fun (vehicles rarely use it); the righthand one is smoother and longer, contouring around the Kattike Daada, the next ridge north of Nagarkot, to enter Sankhu from the north.

A longer **mini-trek to the Shivapuri Watershed** (p.170) initially follows the latter route, then bears to the right (north) on a separate road to Bhotechaur. This trek can be done in numerous permutations, in either direction and on foot or by bike. Most hikers spend a night in a local teahouse in Bhotechaur or at the nicer *Banar Top Resort* (book through *Gauri Shankar Hotel*: ☎411605; B⑤) near the Jhule entry point to the watershed (Rs250 entry fee). From there it's another easy day's walk along a wood road to Sundarijal or Nagi Gompa, and an optional hard third day up to the summit of Shivapuri and back to Kathmandu via Budhanilkantha. It's not possible to ride a bike up to the summit, but cyclists can make it from Nagarkot to Nagi Gompa or further in a day, and to Kakani (p.235) in two days.

If you want to move on **to Nala** (see below), continue south from the view tower, from where it's a stiff 700-metre descent along any of three different routes. The road that bears right around the tower is the easiest for biking, providing a good intermediate-level ride for 7km to the Nala–Bhaktapur road. Two other hiking trails, via the villages of Tukucha and Ghimiregaun, descend from a track heading left from the tower. From Nala you can travel west to Bhaktapur or south to Banepa and Dhulikhel.

Yet another option is to descend eastwards **to Hiuwapati**, deep down in the valley of the Indrawati River. You can make this trip on either of two roads – one starting at the north end of the Nagarkot ridge, the other from near the bus stop – which join after only a couple of kilometres, or on the track that goes around the left (eastern) side of the view tower. If you walk, it'll take three to four hours and you should be able to catch a bus or some sort of vehicle from Hiuwapati to Panchkhal on the Arniko Highway, where there are connections to Dhulikhel and Kathmandu. On a bike it should be no trouble to reach Dhulikhel or return to Nagarkot via a different route in the same day.

A decent **map** will make route-finding on any of these excursions much easier. The best by far are the 1:25,000 sheets published by HMG/FINNIDA, but Himalayan Map House's "Nagarkot" (1:25,000) and "Kathmandu Valley" (1:50,000) will suffice.

Banepa, Nala and Panauti

Leaving the Kathmandu Valley through a gap at its eastern edge, Nepal's only road to the Tibet border is officially known as the **Arniko Rajmarg (Arniko Highway)**. Constructed by the Chinese in the mid-1960s – to India's great distress – the highway is a busy conduit for lorry-loads of Chinese goods by way of Lhasa, despite frequent blockages by landslides

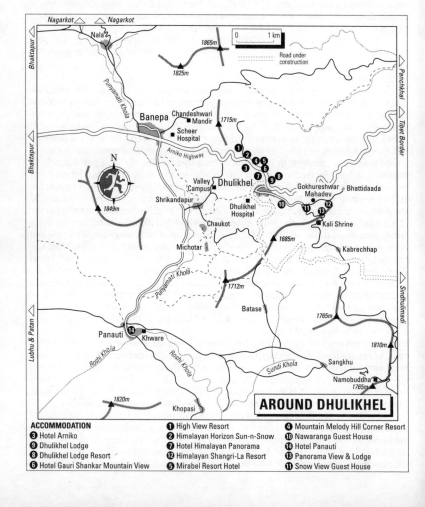

ACCOMMODATION
③ Hotel Arniko
⑨ Dhulikhel Lodge
⑧ Dhulikhel Lodge Resort
⑥ Hotel Gauri Shankar Mountain View

① High View Resort
② Himalayan Horizon Sun-n-Snow
⑦ Hotel Himalayan Panorama
⑫ Himalayan Shangri-La Resort
⑤ Mirabel Resort Hotel

④ Mountain Melody Hill Corner Resort
⑩ Nawaranga Guest House
⑭ Hotel Panauti
⑬ Panorama View & Lodge
⑪ Snow View Guest House

higher up. Appropriately, it's named after the thirteenth-century Nepali architect who led a delegation to Beijing and taught the Chinese how to build pagodas. The first stop along the highway is **Banepa**, which together with **Nala** and **Panauti** once comprised a short-lived independent kingdom east of the Kathmandu Valley.

Loads of **buses** and minibuses ply the Arniko Highway as far as Banepa. However, it's much prettier and less stressful to enter this area by **mountain bike** or motorcycle from Bhaktapur (entering Nala from the west along a dirt road) or Patan (via Lubhu and the Lakuri Bhanjyang – see p.199). Other biking and hiking routes are discussed in the Panauti and Dhulikhel sections below.

Banepa and Nala

BANEPA, 26km east of Kathmandu, was for centuries an important staging post to Tibet, and now – such is progress – it's an obligatory pitstop for buses heading up the Arniko Highway. The roadside buildup is pretty unattractive, and unfortunately there's not much left of the old bazaar: a fire burned most of it down in the 1960s, and earthquake damage has led to the replacement of many other old buildings. Cheap cotton cloth, woven here on semi-mechanized looms, is an important local industry. There are a few Nepali business-men's **lodges** around the main intersection, but they're all noisy, dirty and lacking in hot water – it's hard to think of a reason why you wouldn't stay in Dhulikhel or Panauti instead.

Beginning at the first roundabout north of the Arniko Highway, a road leading north-eastwards to Panchkhal (p.230) first passes by Scheer Memorial Hospital, established by the Seventh Day Adventists, and the **Chandeshwari Mandir**, overlooking a new set of cremation ghats beside a wooded ravine. The three-tiered temple, which is best known for the psychedelic fresco of Bhairab decorating its exterior, commemorates Bhagwati, who according to one of the *purana* (Hindu scriptures) slew a giant called Chand here, earning her the title Chandeshwari ("Lord of Chand"). The arch over the entrance to the temple compound depicts the scene. Chandeshwari's image is the object of a chariot festival here coinciding with Nepali New Year (April 13 or 14).

A second unpaved road heads 3km northwestwards to **NALA**, a quiet, parochial village near the head of the meandering Punyamati Valley. Fanning out at the base of a hill, the classically Newar houses look like a landslide of bricks, frozen in mid-tumble. Nala's main temple, a poorly maintained seventeenth-century pagoda dedicated to Bhagwati, is unusual for having four tiers – even numbers are usually avoided as they're considered unlucky. The weathered image of eighteen-armed Bhagwati is fer-ried around on a chariot on the third day of Indra Jaatra in August–September.

From Nala you can continue west along a wide dirt road, passing a Lokeshwar tem-ple on the outskirts of town, to reach Bhaktapur in 10km. Three lesser tracks branch-ing off from it ascend to Nagarkot via different routes (see above).

Panauti

PANAUTI leads a sleepy, self-sufficient existence in its own small valley 7km south of Banepa. Probably the best-preserved Newar town after Bhaktapur, it supports a large number of traditional brick extended-family dwellings, an important riverside holy site and plenty of miscellaneous architectural treasures. In the past few years, a French-aided restoration effort has greatly improved conditions in the old town by covering sewers, rebricking lanes and rehabilitating historic structures. Although most trav-ellers pass through Panauti only briefly on their way between Namo Buddha and Dhulikhel, accommodation is available, and it's an enchanting place to spend the night: wandering among the temples and bazaars by low-watt light is quite special.

The most pleasant way of **getting there** is by bike, either from Lubhu (p.199), Banepa (above) or Dhulikhel and Namo Buddha (below). The latter route is also feasible on foot. Another possibility is to walk from the summit of Phulchoki (p.198) – you'll need a good topo map and the whole day. Minibuses to Panauti depart from Kathmandu's City Bus Park approximately hourly, calling at Bhaktapur and Banepa en route.

The town

Wedged between the Punyamati and Roshi streams, Panauti forms the shape of a triangle, with a serpent (*nag*) idol standing at each of its three corners to protect against floods. Buses pull up at the newish northwest corner, but the oldest and most interesting sights are concentrated at the streams' confluence at the east end of town.

The shrine area at the sacred confluence, known as the **Khware** or **Tribeni Ghat**, is one of those tranquil spots that can waylay you for hours. The large *sattal* (pilgrims' house) here, a favourite hangout for local seniors, sports an eclectic range of frescoes depicting scenes from Hindu (and some Buddhist) mythology: Vishnu in cosmic sleep, Ram killing the ten-headed demon king Ravana, and even Krishna being chased up a tree by a pack of naked *gopi* (milkmaids). Krishna is the featured deity of the pagoda temple next door, too, where he's shown serenading his *gopi* groupies with a flute. Other small shrines dotted around the complex are dedicated to just about every deity known to Hinduism. Beside the river, the tombstone-shaped ramps set into the ghats are where dying people are laid out, allowing their feet to be immersed in the water at the moment of death. Cremations are held at the actual confluence. On the opposite bank, reached by a footbridge, stands the recently restored seventeenth-century Brahmayani Mandir; the goddess's *dyochhen* (god house) is located in Paumari Tol, in the heart of the old town.

The Khware has been regarded as a *tirtha*, a sacred power place, since ancient times, and on the first day of the month of Magh, which usually falls on January 14, it draws hundreds of people for ritual bathing. Every twelve years this date is celebrated with a full-scale *mela* (religious fair) – the last occurrence was in 1998. It's said that a third river, the mythical Padmati Khola, can be seen flowing here only during this *mela*.

Just west of the Khware, the massive, three-tiered **Indreshwar Mahadev Mandir** is dedicated to Shiva, the "Lord of Indra" in several myths, who is represented by a magnificent brass four-faced *linga*. Some authorities believe this to be the original temple (albeit restored since a 1988 earthquake) that was raised here in 1294, which would make it the oldest surviving pagoda in Nepal. The graceful and sensuous roof struts have been dated to the fourteenth century, although they may have been recycled; each carved from a single piece of wood, they predate the Malla style of carving the arms separately and then attaching them to the strut figures. Sharing the compound is a smaller, rectangular temple of Unmatta Bhairab, distinguished by three carved wooden figures occupying its upstairs windows. "Unmatta" refers to Bhairab's erotic form, in which he is depicted as a terrifying, red-bodied demon with a prominent hard-on.

Practicalities

Panauti's **accommodation** situation has gone up a notch with the opening of *Hotel Panauti* (☎259090; *nath@mos.com.np*; ③/B④), which has clean rooms, pleasant gardens, a decent rooftop restaurant and the only hot water in town. It's on the left about 200m along the main road south from the bus park – it's not in the old part of town, but then no lodgings are. In fact the only other alternatives are noisy, cold-water places in the immediate vicinity of the bus park, such as *Namaste Restaurant & Lodge* (①).

Food, if not taken at *Hotel Panauti*, is available at various *bhojanalaya* around town and a few *momo* joints near the bus park.

Dhulikhel

DHULIKHEL is justly famous as a well-preserved Newar town, mountain viewpoint, and hiking and biking hub, but its popularity is waning as **road-building and modernization** take their toll. Located 5km east of Banepa, just beyond the Kathmandu Valley rim, it sits in a saddle at the relatively low elevation of 1550m, which makes it warmer than Nagarkot. A number of resort hotels and guest houses are positioned along the highway to catch the best mountain views in the immediate vicinity, but the full vista can only be seen from a small summit above the town. Most visitors to Dhulikhel stay at least two nights, which allows time for a wander around the old town, a sunrise walk and a full-day circuit of the surrounding countryside and the cultural sites of Namobuddha and Panauti.

Unfortunately, the increasingly busy Arniko Highway passes just north of Dhulikhel and creates a less than idyllic barrier between most lodgings and the old town. On top of that, a major new highway to Sindhulimadi and the eastern Tarai is being built along the town's western and southern flanks. Donated by Japan, it's supposed to relieve pressure on the Prithvi (Pokhara) Highway by providing a second route into and out of the Kathmandu Valley, and its completion will turn Dhulikhel into one of Nepal's principal transport junctions, with all the revving and tooting that entails. Meanwhile, a flurry of secondary road-building in the area has taken a lot of the pleasure out of the standard Namobuddha–Panauti itinerary, although the destinations themselves remain as worthy as ever. Looking on the bright side, the new roads make possible more and still largely untested mountain-biking possibilities.

Dhulikhel is less well-served by tourist **buses** than is Nagarkot: at the time of writing, only Greenline Tours was driving there from Kathmandu (Rs150). Local buses (every half-hour from Kathmandu's City Bus Park or from Bhaktapur's trolley bus stop; Rs15) are exasperatingly slow. You can ask to be dropped off at any of the hotels along the highway, but for most of the cheap lodgings you'll want to stay on until the small bus park. On a **bike**, it's better to come one of the back ways – via Lubhu–Panauti, Bhaktapur–Nala or Nagarkot–Nala.

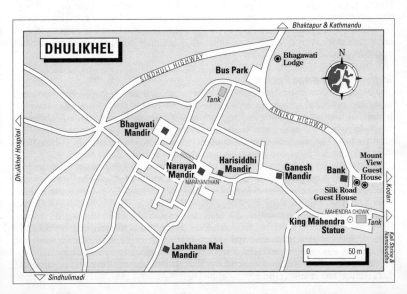

Old Dhulikhel

It's a short walk from the bus park along the highway to **Mahendra Chowk**, the main square at the new, east end of town – an unfortunately dismal introduction to Dhulikhel, but straightforward for orientation.

Old Dhulikhel starts immediately to the west. A close, traditional Newar settlement of remarkable architectural consistency, it's comprised almost exclusively of four- and five-storey brick mansions, many with ornate wooden lattices in place of glass windows, affecting a stern, almost Victorian elegance. These huge houses are extended-family dwellings: some Dhulikhel clans number fifty or more members. The older buildings, which are held together only by mud mortar, show some fairly serious cracks from the infamous 1934 earthquake; Dhulikhel also experienced some damage during the 1988 quake centred near Dharan in the eastern Tarai. Wandering around Dhulikhel is basically a matter of following your nose (and occasionally holding your nose), but highlights include the central square of **Narayanthan**, containing a temple to Narayan and a smaller one to Harisiddhi (both emanations of Vishnu), and the **Bhagwati Mandir**, set at the high point of the village with partial mountain views. Members of the Bhagwati temple association often do *bhajan* in the next-door building.

The sunrise walk

The done thing in Dhulikhel is to hike to the high point southeast of town in time for sunrise over the peaks. To get to the top, take the road leading east from Mahendra Chowk for about 1km, passing a big recreation area on the left, and then go right at the next fork. Cyclists will have to stay on this graded road, but hikers can take a more direct, gullied path that branches left almost immediately. On foot, allow about 45 minutes from Dhulikhel to the top. The summit (1715m) is marked by a small Kali shrine and, unfortunately, a small microwave tower. The peaks from Ganesh Himal to (supposedly) Everest are visible from here, and the sight of Dhulikhel's brick houses, salmon in the dawn light and perhaps wreathed in mist, is pretty wonderful, too.

On the way back down you can call in at a small, mossy temple complex, hidden down a flagstone path that angles off to the left just past the *Snow View Guest House*. The main temple, known as the Gokureshwar Mahadev Mandir, contains a large bronze *linga*. A couple of the adjacent Ram temple's marble statues have been lopped off at the ankles by temple-robbers – a persistent problem in Nepal, fuelled by demand from foreign collectors.

To Namobuddha and Panauti

The so-called "Namobuddha circuit" is not a terrific journey in itself – the roads are dusty and get some vehicle traffic, and the scenery is only so-so – but what makes it interesting are the stops along the way. Although it's usually hyped as a hike, it's better on a **bike**, which will enable you to zip through the less interesting sections and explore side routes. The road is graded (though sometimes uncomfortably cobbled) to Namobuddha and more of a jeep track after that, but bikable all the way.

If you **walk**, the advantage is that you can get onto some lesser trails in the latter half of the circuit. A full loop takes most of the day on foot, and *daal bhaat*, noodles and drinks are available at villages along the way. It's worth trying to combine Namobuddha with a sunrise walk to the Kali shrine, since the latter is on the way, although this requires a degree of organization that most people won't be able to manage first thing in the morning. Be advised that schoolchildren along the circuit delight in taunting foreigners, and will sometimes even spit or throw stones. It's a game you cannot win – just don't betray any exasperation, and if you know any Nepali, tease them back.

The route follows the road beyond the Kali shrine, passing through the village of Kabrechhap and crossing the new Sindhuli Highway after 2.5km, and contouring close

BAAHUNS, CHHETRIS AND OTHER HINDU CASTES

Nepal's human geography gets very confusing once you leave the Kathmandu Valley: over the course of millennia, waves of immigrants from Tibet and India have produced a complex overlay of cultures. Nearly half of all Nepalis are members of ethnic minorities and maintain distinct languages, customs and dress. The rest – the majority – are relative newcomers, descendants of Hindus who fled the Muslim conquest of northern India beginning in the twelfth century, or their converts. They are collectively referred to as **Parbatiyas** ("Hill-dwellers") or, more generically, **Hindu castes**. In India, Hindus are divided into four primary castes, but nearly all the Hindu migrants to Nepal were of the two highest orders, Brahmans and Kshatriyas, who had the most to lose from the advance of Islam. These are sometimes called the "twice-born" castes, because males are symbolically "reborn" through an initiation rite at the age of thirteen and thereafter wear a sacred thread (*janai*), changed annually during the festival of Janai Purnima. Though originally only a small minority themselves, the refugee Hindus' high birth fuelled them with the ambition necessary to subjugate the rest, and in the process provide the country with much of its cultural framework, including its *lingua franca*, Nepali.

Although **Baahuns** (Brahmans) belong to the highest, priestly caste, they're not necessarily the wealthiest members of society, nor are they all priests. Most are farmers. Some are landlords and moneylenders, earning a reputation for subjecting their borrowers to crippling interest rates and swift foreclosures. Priests, who generally follow their fathers into the vocation, make a living administering rites for fixed fees. Most Baahuns observe a range of rules to maintain the purity of their caste (certain foods and alcohol are prohibited), and orthodox Baahuns won't eat with lower castes or permit them to enter the house. Extra restrictions are placed on orthodox women, who, for example, have to keep strict seclusion during menstruation and for ten days after childbirth, when they're considered polluted.

The majority of Nepali Hindus are **Chhetris**, who correspond to Indian Kshatriyas, the caste of warriors and kings. While Baahuns usually claim pure bloodlines and exhibit the classic Aryan features of their caste, Chhetris are a more racially mixed lot and easily mistaken for members of other ethnic groups. Most of them are in fact the offspring of Hindus and the hill tribes they conquered, or of hill dwellers who converted to Hinduism and were made honorary Chhetris (in the early days, Baahuns were willing to bend the rules to gain allies). Those of pure Kshatriya blood – notably the aristocratic Thakuri subcaste of the far west, who are related to the king – can be as twitchy about caste regulations as Baahuns. Significantly, it was a Chhetri who unified Nepal and gave the country its abiding martial character, and the old warrior-caste mentality remains a key in understanding the politics of modern Nepal, for Chhetris occupy the palace and command the army to this day.

India's two lower castes, Vaisyas (traders and farmers) and Sudras (menials) aren't really acknowledged in hill Nepal: indigenous Nepalis who would have fallen into these categories saw no advantage in becoming part of the caste system, and simply retained their ethnic affiliations. Those whose professions would have branded them as untouchables – principally leather-workers (Sarki), blacksmiths (Kami) and tailors (Damai) – obviously did the same. To orthodox Hindus these **occupational castes** still carry the threat of ritual pollution, but untouchability of the kind seen in India isn't observed in Nepal's more open social order. Traditionally the importance of the work performed by these castes largely offset their lowly status, but nowadays their wares are increasingly being marginalized by mass-produced items. Typically landless and uneducated, many are turning to tenant farming, portering and day-labouring to make ends meet.

to the crest of a ridge for another 7km to an intersection at a small saddle. True off-the-beaten-path riding can be found down any of the tracks off to the left in this section, particularly the one at this last junction – see the HMG/FINNIDA map series for details. For Namobuddha, though, bear right.

Resting on a red-earth ledge near the top of a jungly ridge, **Namobuddha** (or **Namura**) is for Tibetans one of the three holiest pilgrimage sites south of the Himalaya. It's like a hick version of Swayambhu – smaller and pretty uneventful, except during the February–March pilgrimage season, when Tibetans and Bhotiyas arrive by the vanload to circumambulate it. The stupa celebrates an event in one of the legendary previous lives of the historical Buddha, in which he encountered a starving tigress about to devour a small child, and moved by compassion, offered his own flesh to her – a sacrifice that helped pave the way for his eventual enlightenment. The Tibetan name of the stupa, Takmo Lujin ("Tiger Body Gift"), links it explicitly to the well-known legend. According to one Tibetan scribe, the name Namobuddha ("Hail to the Buddha") came into popular usage in the seventeenth century, when the superstition took hold that the site's real name should not be uttered.

Among the houses and teashops surrounding the stupa is a scruffy little Tamang *gompa*, which you can enter. A steep path leads up to the prayer-flag-festooned ridge behind, and in a small shelter near the top is preserved a famous stone relief sculpture of the Buddha-precursor feeding his flesh to the tigress. A hole near the base of the shelter is said to be the tiger's lair. The large monastery occupying the ridgetop here is a retreat centre operated by the Trangu Tashi Choling Monastery in Boudha, which contains a big new meditation hall, a guest house for long-term retreat participants, several picturesque whitewashed *chaitya* and a larger-than-life Buddha statue. Access to the centre is from a drive starting at the junction above Namobuddha, but it's not really open to the public.

The road descends from Namobuddha to Sangkhu, where a right fork leads to Batase and eventually back to Dhulikhel along various roads or trails (refer to the "Around Dhulikhel" map). However, it's about the same distance – 9km – to Panauti (see above), and this is a preferable alternative if you have the time to spend the night there. From Panauti you can return to Dhulikhel a number of different ways by foot or bike, or by bus with a change at Banepa.

Accommodation

Dhulikhel used to get more independent travellers, but nowadays most of its **accommodation** is geared for tour groups. The closure of the old *Dhulikhel Lodge* has removed one of the main reasons to come here, and the few budget guest houses that remain are barely hanging on.

All other things being equal, it's not as nice staying in a place near the Arniko Highway, northwest of town. To get to anything of interest you have to deal with the highway, and even in the best-sheltered resorts you still hear distant honking and get the occasional whiff of exhaust fumes. For accommodation locations, refer to the "Dhulikhel" and "Around Dhulikhel" maps.

BUDGET

Mount View Guest House, on the highway at the entrance to town (☎011/64039). Good view, but being right on the highway spoils any enjoyment of it. A last resort, really. ③/B④.

Nawaranga Guest House, 300m east of Mahendra Chowk (☎011/61226). One of Dhulikhel's original guest houses: fairly primitive, but it has a cult following thanks to personable management, good food and rock-bottom prices. Partial view from the roof. ②.

Panorama View & Lodge, near the Kali temple (☎011/62085). Dynamite views, splendid isolation, though the place lacks atmosphere and it's a hassle to get to if you haven't got wheels. ③/B③.

MIDRANGE

Dhulikhel Lodge, on the highway (☎011/61753). The soulless successor to the now-defunct classic guest house that put Dhulikhel on the map. The only reason to mention this place is to warn you not to stay in it. B⑤.

Hotel Gauri Shankar Mountain View, on the highway (☎011/62079). Excellent views from the patio and the upstairs dining room, and nice gardens. ④/B⑤.

Snow View Guest House, 1km east of Mahendra Chowk (☎011/61229). Quiet, with an excellent garden, pretty good views from rooms, and good food by budget standards. No view, but it's relatively close to the Kali shrine viewpoint. ④/B⑥.

EXPENSIVE

Dhulikhel Lodge Resort, just off the highway (☎011/61114, fax 64001). Well-managed; tasteful architecture and grounds. All rooms with view. B⑧.

Dhulikhel Mountain Resort, on the highway 4km east of Dhulikhel – off the map (Kathmandu: ☎428774). Very scenic, private grounds with individual cottages, but nowhere near Dhulikhel. B⑨.

High View Resort, on a side road 600m off the highway (☎011/61966, fax 250364). Nice views overlooking the valley, well away from the highway, but facilities are overpriced. B⑧.

Himalayan Horizon Hotel Sun-N-Snow, on the highway (Kathmandu office: ☎225092; *bagmati@dmn.wlink.com.np*). Attractive Newar-style buildings, spectacular back terrace. The older (cheaper) building has a particularly nice, lived-in feel. B⑧.

Himalayan Mountain Resort, on the highway 4km east of Dhulikhel – off the map (☎011/61158). One of a couple of only slightly cheaper imitators of the nearby *Dhulikhel Mountain Resort*. B⑦.

Himalayan Shangri-La Resort, 1.5km east of Mahendra Chowk (Kathmandu: ☎427837; *himalayan@hsr.wlink.com.np*). The best views of Dhulikhel's resort hotels, very quiet and shaded. Rooms in Newar- and Gurung-style buildings. B⑨.

Mirabel Resort Hotel, just off the highway (☎011/61972; *sre@vishnu.ccsl.com.np*). An executive sort of place, with villa-style architecture. Good views, lovely grounds. B⑨.

Eating and other practicalities

Dhulikhel has no tourist **restaurants**, other than those attached to guest houses and hotels. Of the cheapies, *Nawaranga Guest House* does the best food (great custard pie). Both it and the *Snow View* have convenience going for them if you're looking for breakfast or lunch after a hard morning's mountain-viewing. Any of the hotel restaurants would be worth a splurge. For simple Nepali fast food, try the places around the bus park, or in the bazaar area east of the Nawaranga.

Apart from the postcards and primitive art for sale at the Nawaranga, there's nothing to buy in Dhulikhel. There are no banks or moneychangers either.

To the Tibet border and Jiri

Tour groups bound **for Tibet** follow the Arniko Highway to **Kodari**, the only official border crossing from Nepal, and a few individual travellers make the trip up to the border just to see it. Rafting parties also frequently pass this way en route to the Bhote Koshi and Sun Koshi rivers. Trekkers on their way to **Jiri**, the main trailhead for the Everest region, follow the Arniko Highway for most of its length before heading off on a spectacular side road.

There are no scheduled tourist **bus** services in this area, but express public buses ply both the Arniko Highway and the Jiri road. Note that these services depart from Kathmandu's City (Purano) Bus Park, not the main one at Gongabu; you can also get on at Bhaktapur or Dhulikhel, but don't expect to get a seat. Both these routes make excellent adventures on a **bike**.

To the border

Traffic drops off significantly beyond Dhulikhel, as do public transport options. About two **buses** an hour go as far as Dolalghat, but for Barhabise the services are only hourly, and only a couple of buses a day go all the way to Kodari.

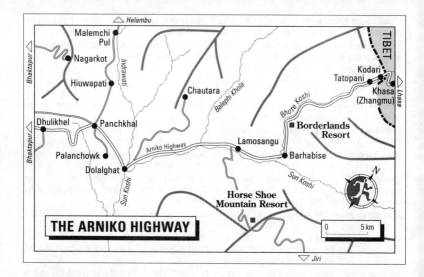

Dhulikhel to Dolalghat

From Dhulikhel, the Arniko Highway descends 600m into the broad Panchkhal Valley, a lush, irrigated plain cultivated with rice paddy, sugar cane and tropical fruits. The village of **Panchkhal** is a minor gateway to the Helambu trekking region: an unpaved road, served by local buses, heads north past Hiuwapati (see p.221) to the trailhead at Malemchi Pul. Just past Panchkhal another rough road to the south leads 9km to **Palanchowk**, home of the famous black-stone Palanchowk Bhagwati, which draws pilgrims seeking protection in time of need. The Nepalese contingent to the UN Peacekeeping Force trains nearby. *Sunkoshi Adventure Retreat* (Kathmandu: ☎223019; B⑦), located a few minutes' walk above the village, provides a base for exploring this rural area on foot, mountain bike, horse and raft.

The highway reaches its lowest (and hottest) point 29km beyond Dhulikhel at **Dolalghat** (634m), a small market town clumped at either end of the bridge across the impressively vast and braided Indrawati River. This is the put-in point for rafting trips on the Sun Koshi, which joins the Indrawati just around the corner. An initially paved side road forks left just beyond Dolalghat to reach **Chautara** (1400m), a workaday Newar bazaar and an obscure trailhead for Helambu treks, after 25km. The town is served by direct buses from Kathmandu, but has only bare-bones Nepali inns; a Bhimsen temple at a high point of the ridge 3km further up the road offers good views.

The Sun Koshi Valley

The scenery begins to change after Dolalghat, as the highway bends northeastwards up the deep, terraced **Sun Koshi Valley**. Nepal's terraces, while they're marvellous feats of engineering, are a sign of agricultural desperation: with so little flat land available and a growing number of mouths to feed, hill people have no choice but to farm ever steeper and less productive slopes. Terraces make good farming and environmental sense – they stabilize the topsoil and form a stopgap against erosion on deforested slopes – but maintaining them is a tremendously labour-intensive chore that detracts from the actual business of growing food, and building more terraces inevitably brings about further deforestation.

Having built the Arniko Highway, China has poured much of its aid to Nepal into infrastructure projects along the route. The first of these to come into view is a hydro-electric diversion, whose spillway and powerhouse are located just beyond the turning for Jiri (see below). Human impacts to the valley are much in evidence for the next couple of kilometres to **Lamosangu** (740m), which is distinguished by a magnesite processing plant, a ropeway and a big pile of castings.

Up the Bhote Koshi

A few kilometres upstream of Lamosangu, the highway proceeds up the larger of two tributaries, the **Bhote Koshi**, which it follows to its source in Tibet. **BARHABISE**, just beyond, is as far as most buses go; local buses and minibuses make sporadic runs from there to Tatopani, 23km further on. The highway and cross-border trade have turned Barhabise into an uncharismatic clutter of tall, slapdash buildings and shops selling mostly Chinese goods. However, it's still a traditional centre for the production of *lokta* paper, which is made from the bark of a type of shrub that's native to the hills above here; you can visit any of the local operations, which are easily recognized by their rows of frames tilted to dry in the sun. Several lodges in Barhabise let cold-water rooms and serve noodles and *daal bhaat* – *New Chandeswori Guest House* (③) and *Hotel Bhotekoshi* (②), at the north end of town, are perhaps a bit quieter than the rest.

The permanent pavement ends north of Barhabise, as it's virtually impossible to maintain a permanent surface in the face of annual monsoon **landslides**. The Chinese who engineered this highway put it in the most unstable zone near the bottom of the valley, which made it easier to build but harder to maintain – to be fair, given the terrain between here and Tibet, they may not have had any other options. If you're entering or exiting Tibet along this route during the monsoon, there may be blockages where you'll have to transfer to another vehicle waiting on the other side.

A few **rafting** companies run short but intense trips on this raging stretch of the Bhote Koshi. The put-in point is about 9km north of Barhabise, where Ultimate Descents has established the first traveller-friendly base in this part of Nepal, the **Borderland Resort** (Kathmandu: ☎425836; *resort@tibet-border.wlink.com.np*). Set at the bottom of the gorge at a relatively balmy 1100m, it's a very relaxing, social place with thatched-roof tents (on a four-person occupancy basis), an open-air dining pavilion and lovely gardens and lawns. It also functions as a sort of outdoor adventure centre, offering not only rafting but also **mountain-biking,** guided day **hikes** and overnight **treks,** and even **canyoning** in and around the waterfalls above camp. Packages including all activities and transportation from Kathmandu cost a flat $40 per person a day, or $25 for accommodation and food only. *Borderland* is likely to inspire competitors, and over time this area may develop into quite a little Mecca for outdoor sports.

The steep gradient to the border begins just beyond; in the autumn, Nepal's famed honey-hunters may sometimes be seen clinging to the cliffs below the road in pursuit of hives. Afternoon rain is common up here, even in the dry season, and despite a general scarcity of trees near the river, everything is intensely green, with waterfalls splashing down cliff faces at every turn. As the road approaches Tatopani the scenery is interrupted by the spillway and dam for a second Chinese-built hydroelectric plant, which is the first in a planned series of diversions that will eventually put an end to rafting on the Bhote Koshi. Just before Tatopani is a police checkpost, where you'll be expected to show your passport: from here up, the Bhote Koshi forms the border – Tibet is just across the river.

Tatopani

Until the mid-1980s, **TATOPANI** (1530m) enjoyed a small following among Westerners, who came to gaze into forbidden Tibet and soak in the village's hot springs

---

TAMANGS

Tamangs dominate Nepal's central hills between about 1500m and 2500m and constitute, numerically, the country's largest ethnic group: about one in every five Nepalis is a Tamang. The tribe is thought to have originated in Tibet and migrated south in prehistoric times, which accounts for their Mongoloid features but leaves the significance of their name, which means "horse trader" in Tibetan, unexplained. Tamangs follow a form of Buddhism virtually indistinguishable from Lamaism – religious texts are even written in Tibetan script – but they also worship clan deities, employ *jhankri* (shamans) and observe major Hindu festivals.

Despite their numbers, Tamangs are one of Nepal's most exploited peoples, and have been ever since the Gorkhali conquest of the late eighteenth century. Geography has been the Tamangs' downfall. The new rulers of Nepal, requiring land to grant to their victorious soldiers, arbitrarily appropriated much of the vast Tamang homeland surrounding the Kathmandu Valley. Displaced from their lands, Tamangs became tenant farmers or bonded labourers for their new masters, or freelanced as porters or woodcutters. Many drifted down to the Kathmandu Valley, to fetch and carry for the new aristocracy. So efficiently did the Tamangs carry out these menial functions that the government came to view them as a strategic asset and prohibited them from serving in the Gurkha regiments. More recently, Tamangs are being deprived of another source of income – woodcutting – due to deforestation and the closing off of the Shivapuri Watershed.

Lacking land and opportunities, the Tamangs remain at the bottom rung of the economic ladder. They are the porters, the riksha wallahs, the cart-pullers of Kathmandu. They comprise an estimated 75 percent of the carpet industry's work force, and create many of the *thangka* and other "Tibetan" crafts sold in Nepal – for contract wages, of course. Tamang boys are lured to the capital to work as *kanchha* (tea boys), and Tamang girls are prime targets for brokers in the Indian flesh trade. Surveys show a disproportionate number of prison inmates in Nepal are Tamangs. A silent underclass in their own homeland, Tamangs often compare themselves to another displaced group, the Tibetans – only nowadays even the Tibetans are the Tamangs' bosses.

(*taato paani* means "hot water"), but it's fallen out of fashion now that Tibet is open. It remains a quiet, relaxing place – probably too dull for most, but kind of nice if you're into offbeat locales.

The village stretches along the highway for almost a kilometre, in two parts. Tamangs are in the majority at this altitude, and they maintain a small **gompa** five minutes' walk above the southern bazaar. The building is modest, but it looks out on a fine view of the valley and, up at the head of it, the start of the Tibetan plateau. The signposted **hot springs** are at the northern end of the village, down steps towards the river. A hot tub it's not: the water splashes out of pipes into a concrete pool and is used strictly for washing. If you take the waters, remember that nudity offends in Nepal. You'll be expected to make a small donation.

Western menus have virtually disappeared from Tatopani, but a few **lodges** limp on from the good old days. *Maiti Lodge* (①), near the hot springs, is probably the best. Hints of China's nearness are everywhere: you'll see chopsticks and Thermos flasks in every kitchen, and some places even sell Chinese beer. **Buses** to Kathmandu originate at Kodari (see below) and so are often full by the time they reach Tatopani. To be sure of a seat, buy a ticket at the Kodari booking office the day before.

Kodari

Disabuse yourself of any visions of high, snowy passes into Tibet. The border village of **KODARI** (1640m), 3km on from Tatopani, sits at the bottom of a deep valley, with nary a yak in sight. The lowest point along the Nepal–Tibet border, Kodari has always been the preferred crossing for traders between Kathmandu and Lhasa. Its low elevation isn't as extraordinary as it might seem, though: the main Himalayan chain, which the border generally follows, is breached in several places by rivers that are older than the mountains themselves (the watershed, in fact, runs not along the highest peaks but as much as 100km to the north). In the case of Kodari, the border was actually shifted further south after an ill-advised war with Tibet in 1792.

Shared **taxis** ply between Tatopani and Kodari, and in good weather two **buses** a day make it up here from Kathmandu. The long, drawn-out roadside bazaar of Kodari is the Nepali equivalent of a service strip along a highway bypass, while old Kodari, a scattered village with a small gompa, perches on the ridge above. **Accommodation** is available at a few lodges along the road – you could do worse than the *Namgyal* or the *Lhasa* (both ②). Tatopani is the better bet, but if you're crossing into Tibet you might want to stay here to get an earlier start.

The border

The border is marked by the so-called **Friendship Bridge**, which spans the Bhote Koshi at the top end of town, guarded at either end by lackadaisical Nepali and Chinese soldiers. Up at the head of the valley, 600m higher than Kodari, the Chinese buildings of **Khasa** (or **Zhangmu**) cling to the side of a mountain – that's the extent of the view of Tibet from here. A steady stream of Nepalis and a few Chinese cross the bridge during daylight hours; you won't see any Tibetans crossing, of course, because those wanting to leave must do so secretly over remote mountain passes, and few are entering Tibet these days. Nepalis can travel as far as Khasa without travel papers, and are allowed to bring back small amounts of stipulated goods such as electronics, garments, wool and shoes duty-free. (Flour and ghee go in the opposite direction.)

Should you be **crossing the border**, the 9km between the Kodari and Khasa immigration posts is a no-man's-land which, when the road isn't washed out, will be traversed by some sort of shuttle vehicle. If the road is closed, you'll have to walk; you can hire a porter to carry your pack. Remember that Tibet is two hours and fifteen minutes ahead of Nepal, so you have to set off early to catch the bank in Khasa before it closes. Even if you've just come up to the border for a look, you stand a good chance of being allowed to cross and go up to Khasa if you leave your passport with the Chinese guards and promise to return in a couple of hours.

If you're **entering Nepal** from Tibet, set off from Khasa as early as possible, as it's a very full day's journey to Kathmandu. If you miss the direct Kodari–Kathmandu bus you'll probably have to take a taxi to Tatopani and then a bus to Barhabise, where there are more frequent connections. Better yet, don't go straight to Kathmandu: spend a night or two in Dhulikhel or Bhaktapur, which are much pleasanter places to wind down after China.

> You can't officially enter Tibet (China) from Nepal without a visa and Tibet entry endorsement, which must be obtained in Kathmandu. See p.149 for details.

To Jiri

The road **to Jiri** gives a marvellous foretaste of the immense country that's in store if you're on your way to Everest. It's very narrow and winding, with some unbelievable ups and downs, making it a gruelling **bus** journey of anywhere from ten to thirteen hours from Kathmandu. On a **mountain bike** it would be a marathon. On a **motorcycle**, though, it's an absolute magic-carpet ride – this has to be one of the world's great motorcycle journeys.

In the past this route has had a bad reputation for theft from the roofs of buses, but the bus companies seem to have quelled this scam and it's no longer necessary to book an extra seat for your bag. (But still be wary if someone insists on putting your bag on the roof.)

Along the Jiri road

Completed in 1985, the 110-kilometre-long **Jiri road** was financed by the Swiss government as part of its integrated development work at Jiri. It breaks off from the Arniko Highway at Khadichaur, 78km from Kathmandu, and immediately starts a merciless 1800m climb out of the Sun Koshi Valley. There's a delightful place to stay in **Mude**, 28km into the climb and not far from the top: *Horse Shoe Mountain Resort* (☎011/63174; B⑧), run by a former riding instructor to the Crown Prince, has rooms done up in Tamang style and a rusticated dining area. A path leads to a fine viewpoint.

The first high point (2540m), reached after 32km, brings views of Phurbi Chyachu and nearby peaks, though they're a bit despoiled by the operations of a soapstone quarry straddling the road. After contouring around two small basins, the road reaches the Newar pitstop of **Charikot**, just about at its midway point, where there are excellent views of Gauri Shankar and peaks to the east. A road to the left leads 5km to **Dolakha**, known for its temple to Bhimsen, the patron deity of merchants.

From Charikot the main road begins a long descent to the Tama Koshi (835m); downstream from this crossing, an important hydroelectric plant is being built on the Khimti Khola. Then it's another long pull up a rhododendron-forested ridge to the road's highest point (2555m), and finally a dip into the Jiri Valley, at 1900m.

Jiri

Most people come to **JIRI** for the Everest trek, and are too eager to hit the trail or get back to Kathmandu to spend more than a night here. That's a shame: an extra day is much better spent in Jiri than in Kathmandu. Set in a small, sloping valley, the bazaar features attractive whitewashed Sherpa-style buildings and is inhabited by a cosmopolitan mix of Jirels (the local indigenous group), Sherpas, Tamangs and Newars. It's a busy place, with lots of comings and goings as trucks drop off supply shipments and porters assemble to carry impossibly heavy loads out into the hinterland of Solu and Khumbu: you can learn a lot about the local economy just by observing the composition of porters' loads. Saturday is particularly colourful, as people from surrounding villages gather for the weekly market in the old bazaar, about 3km back up the road.

Charlie Pye-Smith, in his book *Travels in Nepal*, called Jiri "the half-caste offspring of an impoverished Nepalese mother and a wealthy Swiss father". In 1958 the Swiss established the **Jiri Multi-Purpose Development Project**, a ground-breaking scheme based on the now widely accepted view that development needs – health, agriculture, education and so on – are interrelated and can't be tackled separately. The programme established a hospital, technical school, experimental farm, managed forests and other facilities, most of which have now been handed over to HMG. But of all the improvements bequeathed by the Swiss, it was the road that brought the greatest material boost to Jiri, by making it the area's main commercial centre as well as the trailhead for Nepal's second most popular trekking region. (Ironically, the road is now being extended another 20km to access the Khimti hydroelectric project, and Jiri may soon lose its privileged status.)

At least a dozen trekker **lodges** are grouped around the western end of the bazaar – *Cherdung Lodge* (①) is comfortable enough, with a reasonable choice of food, but any one will do. Shops in the bazaar sell Nepali porter gear (small backpacks, jackets, socks, etc) in case you forgot anything. Lodge owners can arrange porters and guides. Be sure to book return bus tickets as soon as possible for the next day's departures, as seats go quickly.

The Trisuli road

One of Nepal's earliest forays into road-building, the **Trisuli road** was constructed in the mid-1960s as part of a hydroelectric project on the Trisuli River, northwest of Kathmandu. That's the official story, anyway, although the road probably owes its existence as much to historical nostalgia as progress: the route retraces the triumphal approach of Prithvi Narayan Shah, founding father of Nepal, from his fortress of Nuwakot to the Kathmandu Valley two centuries ago. It's since been extended north to a mining area in the Ganesh Himal. The majority of travellers passing this way are only concerned about getting to Dhunche, the usual starting point for treks to Langtang and Gosainkund, yet Nuwakot is sorely underrated as a stopover, and Kakani makes a serviceable destination in itself.

Nine **buses** a day go from Kathmandu's Gongabu Bus Park to Trisuli (4hr), and three to Dhunche (8hr). The road is slow and laborious by bus: its endless zigzagging, potholes, fords and light traffic are all better appreciated on a bike.

Kakani

KAKANI (*Kaa*-kuh-nee), the closest mountain viewpoint to Kathmandu, straddles the valley's northwestern rim at an elevation of 2070m. Like Nagarkot, Kakani is essentially a tourist invention, as opposed to a town, with mountain views and not much else. It's much less developed than Nagarkot, and the views are somewhat inferior, but it makes a nice halt along the Trisuli road, particularly if you're biking.

At least one Kathmandu company (Karnali Travel & Tours) operates a **tourist minibus** service to Kakani (1hr; Rs200). Trisuli-bound **public buses** drop you off at a gap in the valley rim, 24km from Kathmandu, from where it's 4km up a paved side road (there are shortcuts) that passes a large police training college en route. In the days of Prithvi Narayan Shah, the Kakani pass was the Kathmandu Valley's Achilles' heel – by controlling it, he was able to besiege the valley for two years – and this installation, like that of Nagarkot, is a vestige of the days of hand-to-hand combat, when hilltop positions provided military superiority.

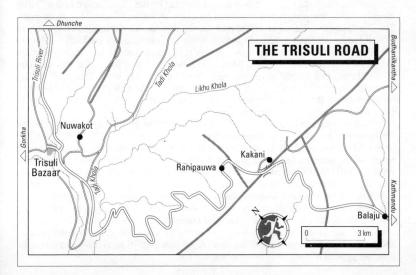

Limited **accommodation** makes Kakani a marginal destination. At the time of writing, the only halfway decent place to stay was the overpriced *Kakani Tara Gaon Resort* (☎290812; B⑦, discounts for stays of more than one night), just beyond the police college. It's fairly run-down and unwelcoming, but does feature a marvellous back lawn where you can lounge like a sahib, with the Ganesh and Langtang Himals splashed across the horizon and the Likhu Khola coursing through the valley 1000m below. If you're not choosy, you can stay much more cheaply (①) in one of the houses just below the *Tara Gaon*. Over the years a couple of other competitors to the *Tara Gaon* have tried to make a go of it in Kakani, but haven't lasted; perhaps the establishment of a tourist bus service will encourage others to start up. (Either that, or the lack of accommodation and visitors will put an end to tourist buses.) For **food**, the *Tara Gaon* serves palatable lunches.

Other than the mountains, Kakani is short on sights. The yellow building next door to the *Tara Gaon* is the former British Resident's bungalow, whose grounds once boasted a miniature golf course. During the Rana era, when Residents were prohibited from travelling outside the Kathmandu Valley, this was their window on the rest of Nepal; it's still owned by the British Embassy, and maintained for use by Gurkha officers. Occupying a high point further to the east, the well-tended Kakani Memorial Park honours those who died in a 1992 Thai airliner crash north of here.

From Kakani you can **walk back** to Balaju in three or four hours. Follow the dirt road east from Kakani past an agricultural station, then bear right and contour beneath the ridge before bending south and down along a spur. After passing a set of stupas, look for a fork to the left leading to Dharamthali and Balaju. **By mountain bike**, you can ride down to Budhanilkantha, a half-day descent requiring a good bike. Head east past the agricultural station and keep to the ridge: you'll have to carry your bike for about 2km before joining the Shivapuri Watershed road, which contours down to Budhanilkantha (see p.169). You'll have to pay Rs250 to enter the watershed.

Trisuli Bazaar

TRISULI BAZAAR (540m) is just 32km from Kathmandu as the crow flies, but 70km – and a good four hours – as the bus crawls. Curled at the bottom of a deep, subtropical (and once malarial) valley, it was put on the map by the construction of the Trisuli River hydroelectric project and flourished for a time as the trailhead for Langtang treks. The development bandwagon has moved on, and nowadays most trekkers don't stop in Trisuli for longer than it takes to swill a bottle of Coke and get back on the bus to Dhunche. Indeed, there's little to see in this ramshackle township, with the possible exception of the old, stair-stepped **bazaar** (reached through a passage at the west end of the bridge) and a small **stupa** perched above the opposite bank. That said, staying overnight at Trisuli permits a visit to nearby Nuwakot, which, if you find yourself with an extra day at the end of a trek, is a good deal more enjoyable than killing time in Dhunche or returning to Kathmandu early.

Trisuli also makes a good if spartan base for **mountain-biking**. Rural roads and tracks extend for miles in several directions: east to Nuwakot and beyond, south and then east up the Tadi Khola, west up the lovely Samari Khola towards Gorkha, and north to Dhunche and Somdang (the latter would be a good target in hot weather). The relevant HMG/FINNIDA **maps** of the area are invaluable in finding promising routes. You can also **trek** to Gorkha and Pokhara from here, starting up the Samri Khola.

Trisuli **buses** terminate in the main bazaar area on the west side of the bridge, and tickets for onward journeys are purchased there (Sajha services are marginally the fastest to and from Kathmandu). Dhunche-bound buses usually stop in Dhunge, the smaller bazaar on the other side, near the turning for Dhunche. All of Trisuli's **accommodation** is on the west side of the river: *Hotel Ranjit* (B③) is as downmarket as the rest, but at least it has rooms overlooking the river.

Nuwakot

One of Nepal's proudest historical monuments, Prithvi Narayan Shah's abandoned fortress looms like a forgotten shipwreck on a ridge above Trisuli, casting a poignant, almost romantic spell over the tiny village of **NUWAKOT** (accent on the second sylla-ble: Noo–*aa*–kote). The **walk** from Trisuli takes less than an hour, although the trail is a tad tricky to find: climb a flight of steps starting at the Dhunge (eastern) side of the Trisuli bridge until you reach the Dhunche road, walk up the road for about 150m and make a right at the first group of houses. The path becomes wide and eroded as it climbs through a spindly forest of *sal* trees – the trees are coppiced for animal fodder – and reaches Nuwakot on the crest of a ridge about 400m above the valley floor. To **cycle**, take the (initially) paved road that leaves the main road about 1km south of Dhunge.

The **fortress** stands to the right as you enter the village, consisting of three brick towers rising like Monopoly hotels within a walled compound. The tallest one is open to the public, though you'll have to track down the caretaker to unlock it for you. The views from the top-floor windows are stupendous, looking out on Ganesh Himal and the pastoral Trisuli and Tadi valleys.

It was from this command centre that **Prithvi Narayan Shah**, the unifier of Nepal, directed his dogged campaign on the Kathmandu Valley from 1744 to 1769, and gazing out through these windows you can gain some insight into the mind of this obsessive but brilliant military tactician. In his determination to conquer the valley, Prithvi Narayan had **three other towers** built in the name of the three valley capitals, perhaps hoping to bring about their downfall by a kind of voodoo; the Kathmandu and Patan towers share the main compound, while the crumbling Bhaktapur tower stands on a rise just outside. After Kathmandu's fall, Nuwakot had just one more moment in the limelight. In 1792, attempting to extend Nepal's territory into Tibet, Prithvi Narayan's successor pushed his luck too far and was driven all the way back to Betrawati, the next village north of Trisuli. In the resulting **peace treaty**, signed at Nuwakot, Nepal ceded to Tibet the lucrative trading posts of Kyirong (north of Trisuli) and Khasa (north of Kodari), accounting for two southward lunges in the border that remain to this day.

Nuwakot's old main street runs south from the fortress along the spine of the ridge and suddenly dead-ends, the land falling away to reveal a lovely panorama of the Tadi and Trisuli valleys. In the late eighteenth century, when Nuwakot enjoyed a brief flow-ering as the winter residence of the Kathmandu court, the houses along this boulevard must have looked considerably posher. Several ornate old brick-and-wood buildings remain, notably the two-tiered **Bhairabi Mandir**. During the annual Bhairabi festival here, held in the Nepali month of Chaitra (March–April), the priest, under the influence of divine powers, drinks the blood of an entire buffalo straight from its severed neck. He immediately vomits it back up; not so many years ago it was the custom for wor-shippers to drink the vomited blood as a sacrament.

To Dhunche and beyond

Beyond Trisuli the road is unpaved, steep and agonizingly slow, buses taking four hours to cover this 40km stretch. You may prefer to close your eyes as the bus negoti-ates some of the switchbacks. Foreigners must show **trekking permits** at a couple of different army posts above Trisuli.

The road has replaced what used to be the first two days of the Langtang trek, and **DHUNCHE**, an unmemorable administrative centre, has boomed since its completion. Dhunche's guest houses are clustered around the main drag just past the town gate and are all ① or B② – *Hotel Langtang View* has a good restaurant and hot water. To return to Kathmandu, make sure to book your seat as early as possible the day before.

Beyond Dhunche, the road angles down to cross the Trisuli River, then climbs con-tinuously to cross a ridge at around 3700m before descending slightly to the lead- and zinc-mining centre of **SOMDANG**, 34km northwest of Dhunche. Incredibly, there's a small hotel there, *Ganesh Himal Resort* (B⑦), but you can't book ahead because it has no telephone, and you have to bring all your own food.

The Tribhuwan Rajpath and Daman

Nepal's most magnificent and hair-raising highway, the **Tribhuwan Rajpath** (usually just called the Rajpath, which means "King's Way") heads west out of the Kathmandu Valley and then hurls itself, through an astounding series of switchbacks, straight over the Mahabharat Lek to the Tarai. En route it passes through lush stands of rhododendron and takes in superb views of the Himalaya. Mountain-bikers regard the road, and the culminating viewpoint of **Daman**, as something of a holy pilgrimage. The nearby **Kulekhani Reservoir** provides an interesting side trip.

Built by Indian engineers in the mid-1950s, the Rajpath was the first highway to link Kathmandu to the outside world – before that, VIPs were carried to the capital by palanquin, and the prime ministers' automobiles had to be portered from India, fully assembled, by 200-strong teams of coolies. History has proved the route chosen by the Indians to be completely idiotic*, however, and now even Nepalis avoid it, preferring to go the long way around via Narayanghat and Mugling. The road is therefore very poorly served by public transport, making it a perfect route for a mountain bike or motorcycle: challenging, varied, scenic and almost devoid of traffic. Whether by bike or by bus, it's easiest to get to Daman from Kathmandu and then continue on to Hetauda and the Tarai, rather than vice versa.

A good time to do this route is in April, when the **rhododendrons** are in bloom. The Rajpath is also famed for its many varieties of **orchids**, most of which bloom in March–June or in September–October.

Along the Rajpath

For its first 26km, the Rajpath follows the heavily used Prithvi Highway towards Pokhara. Leaving the Kathmandu Valley through its ugliest and most industrial corridor, it slips over a low point in the rim (good views here of Manaslu, Boudha, Ganesh and Langtang) and descends to **NAUBISE** (945m), near the bottom of the deep, wrinkled Mahesh Khola Valley. This first stretch is a real drag: traffic is heavy, there are often long waits to clear police checkposts, and the descent to Naubise is a slow crawl behind smoke-belching trucks (punctuated by adrenaline-pumping manoeuvres to overtake them between switchbacks). Nepali restaurants are plentiful in Naubise and a few places have rooms in the ①–② range.

At Naubise the Rajpath leaves the Prithvi Highway and forks off to the left, climbing relentlessly for 30km to Tistung (2030m) before descending into the **Palung Valley** and its tidy terraces (spinach – *paalung* – and potatoes are local specialities). The turning for Markhu and the Kulekhani Reservoir (see below) appears on the left 4km past Tistung, and the Newar village of Palung, at 1745m, is 5km beyond that. Very basic food and lodging can be had in **SHIKHARKOT**, 2km further on, but unless you're desperate it's worth toiling up the final, tough 10km to spend the night in Daman (below).

---

* The road is in fact a perfect example of politically distorted aid. At the time, India was on the brink of war with China and preferred to make any route through Nepal as inconvenient as possible to reduce the risk of invasion. King Tribhuwan, who owed his crown to India, agreed to allow the road to be built right over the highest ridge in the entire area, rationalizing it by saying it would help in the development of remote villages.

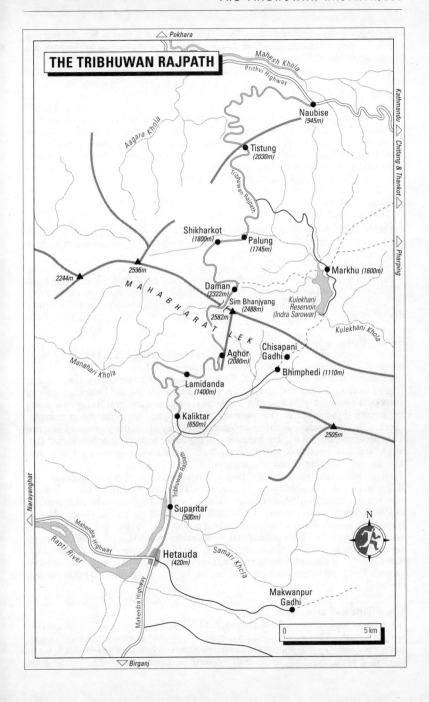

Three kilometres beyond Daman, the Rajpath crosses the pass of **Sim Bhanjyang** (2488m) – often icy in winter – where it enters a landscape of plunging hill country and begins a relentless, 2000-metre descent to the valley below. These south-facing upper slopes of the Mahabharat Lek are dramatically greener and wilder than those on the other side – they wring much of the moisture out of the prevailing winds, and are frequently wreathed in fog by afternoon.

The road passes through successive zones of mossy jungle, pine forest and finally terraced farmland until reaching the Bhimphedi turning (below), 40km from Sim Bhanjyang. The electric transformers seen near here relay power from the Kulekhani hydroelectric dam north of Bhimphedi, an important source of power for Nepal. The devices that look like ski lifts are ropeways, one bringing quarried limestone down to the big cement plant in Hetauda and the other, now disused, for ferrying raw materials up to Kathmandu. Hetauda (see p.346) is 10km further on.

Daman

DAMAN (2322m) is the most comprehensive of the Himalayan viewpoints surrounding Kathmandu, but it's also the most difficult to reach. The challenge of getting to it, and getting back down from it, is in fact one of its main attractions.

Sitting below the Rajpath's highest point, the hamlet overlooks the peaceful Palung Valley to a magnificent spread of peaks. However, the mountains will probably be in clouds when you arrive: an overnight stay is obligatory to see them in their best morning light. Bring a sleeping bag in winter, unless you've got reservations at the deluxe *Everest Panorama Resort*.

Getting there

The most useful and reliable (but unfortunately very local) **buses** to Daman are those operated by the Sajha cooperative. Plying the Rajpath in both directions, they depart simultaneously from Hetauda and Kathmandu (Bhimsen Tower) at 7am, arriving at Daman by around 10am and noon respectively. Book early the day before, as seats on these buses go quickly. At least two private bus companies also provide services along the Rajpath through Daman, but their schedules are sporadic and prone to change – check with ticket agents. Another problem is that they break the journey up into two days, departing around midday and overnighting either in Markhu or Shikharkot (see map), which means that if you're coming from Kathmandu you won't get to Daman until the next morning. A **taxi** will cost around $30.

All of which explains why it's best to come by **bike**. If you're cycling from Kathmandu, you'll definitely want to skip the Kathmandu–Naubise stretch – instead, take any bus bound for Pokhara or the Tarai and throw the bike on the roof. Naubise to Daman involves two separate climbs totalling 1700m of vertical gain – an exhilarating but (make no mistake about it) shattering all-day ride. Cycling up from Hetauda is an even more macho climb, gaining 2000m. An easier option is to take a taxi or bus up and pedal back down (but note that Sajha buses can't take bikes; coming from Kathmandu, take the bus to the Markhu turning or Shikharkot and pedal the final 500m ascent). Heads up for approaching vehicles, as the road is narrow and many corners are blind.

The village and around

A signboard announces you're in Daman, but blink and you'll miss it. The village consists of a loose gathering of houses, a couple of agricultural research facilities, a seismic station and – its one unmissable landmark – an enclosed **view tower** that looks as if it might have been built for air traffic control purposes. Operated by the adjacent

Daman Mountain Resort, the tower offers the best views in the village (admission Rs20 for non-guests). Tourism boosters claim you can see seven 8000-metre peaks from here, which may be stretching it, but certainly Annapurna, Manaslu, Shisha Pangma and the distant plume of Everest are visible, along with the closer and hence more prominent 7000-metre peaks of Himalchuli, Ganesh Himal and Langtang. A couple of high-powered telescopes give awesome close-ups of the peaks from this angle: the magnified view of Everest is almost identical to the one you get from Kala Pattar, ten days into the Everest trek. The view from the tower also gives you a good feel for the topography of the central hills and the Kathmandu Valley, from Phulchoki to the Trisuli Valley.

An even more sweeping (though unmagnified) vista can be had from the *Everest Panorama Resort*, a thirty-minute walk up the Rajpath, which also happens to be a fine spot for breakfast or lunch. One hairpin turn below the *Everest Panorama*, a signposted path winds through oak and rhododendron forest to a Buddhist **gompa** in another twenty minutes. Run by a Bhutanese lama, the monastery is small and unembellished, but the view from its meditation perch is awesome.

Practicalities

Daman lacks the facilities for travellers that other viewpoints such as Nagarkot and Dhulikhel have. For **accommodation**, there's not much choice, and all of it is expensive for what you get. At the budget end there's *Hotel Daman & Lodge* (③), a nightspot-cum-truckstop with a couple of very dark rooms and cold water, and *Hotel Sherpa & Hill Side* (③), which is little more than trekking digs. Not much English is spoken in either. At the pricier *Daman Mountain Resort* (Kathmandu: ☎247485, fax 247914; ⑥), accommodation is in safari-style tents – as tents go they're cushy, with beds, electricity, kerosene heaters and hot water, though you still have to go outside to use the bathroom. The "resort" also has a few rooms, but they're small and stark. If you really want to go in style, book into the *Everest Panorama Resort* (Kathmandu: ☎414644, fax 416029), 2.5km above Daman, where you can participate in organized activities ranging from hiking and mountain-biking to fishing and pony-riding. Rooms with central heating are B⑨, thatched-hut tents ⑦. In all likelihood, you'll **eat** wherever you're staying.

Moving on

Leaving Daman by public transport can be difficult, as **buses** passing through are standing room only, and standing on a bus on this road is no fun. Sometimes they're so full they don't even stop. Getting to Kathmandu is further complicated by the fact that only the Sajha bus goes directly there, the others overnighting in Markhu or Shikharkot. Infrequent trucks take on passengers, but nearly all of them are heading south to Hetauda after delivering their cargo to Kathmandu (fully laden vehicles bound for Kathmandu take the safer Prithvi Highway).

These transport peculiarities make a good case for **walking** or **biking** down instead. Departing from the Rajpath about 500m down from the view tower, a walking trail descends to the western shore of the Kulekhani Reservoir (see below) in three to four hours, and continues from there to the Kathmandu Valley. Biking down, you'll probably just take the Rajpath, but for a longer, more adventurous route to the Tarai you could backtrack to the road to Kulekhani and go up and over to Bhimphedi (below).

The Kulekhani Reservoir (Indra Sarowar) and Bhimphedi

Completed in 1982, Nepal's first major hydroelectric project dammed the Kulekhani Khola to form a sizeable lake east of Daman at an elevation of 1520m. The **Kulekhani Reservoir**, more commonly known as **Indra Sarowar**, is attractively nestled at the base of forested hills, and despite being a very deserving stopover on a couple of different itineraries from Daman, it remains completely undeveloped for tourism.

An unpaved but well-graded road leads 13km from the Rajpath to **MARKHU**, a small new village on the lake's northern shore settled by families displaced by the reservoir. Unfortunately, having been helped by an aid project to start a small-scale fishing industry here, their livelihood is now at risk: the Nepal Electricity Authority is threatening to ban fishing on the lake, after being ordered to pay compensation for a major fish kill apparently caused by its maintenance operations. You can get simple accommodation and food here, though there are no English-language signs.

Walking down from Daman, you'll arrive at the western shore, where you can take a boat across to Markhu. From Markhu you can either catch a bus to Kathmandu the next morning or walk another full day **to Pharping** in the Kathmandu Valley (see p.193). A second option from Markhu is a one- or two-day trek via Chitlang **to Thankot** on the Prithvi Highway, from where it's a quick bus ride to Kathmandu.

You can also continue on the road all the way around the lake's eastern shore to the **dam**, and then follow a trail up over the Mahabharat Lek to Bhimphedi via Chisapani Gadhi. Before the construction of the Rajpath, this was the main approach to Kathmandu from the Tarai – visiting dignitaries came this way by elephant and sedan chair – and there's a certain cachet to retracing the route. It's an easy day's trek on foot; it can be done on a bike, but requires some carrying. However, work has begun on a new sixteen-kilometre road that will soon supersede the trail and create a continuous motorable route between Markhu and Bhimphedi.

Perhaps the new road link will restore some prestige to **BHIMPHEDI**, which was an important regional centre until it was bypassed by the Rajpath. Connected to the Rajpath by an eleven-kilometre side road, it's a sleepy Newar bazaar whose only real contact with the outside world is two daily buses from Hetauda. A small **museum** of howdahs (elephant-riding platforms) highlights one aspect of Bhimphedi's heritage from its heyday. A few local lodges provide bed and *bhaat*.

CHAPTER FOUR

THE WESTERN HILLS

The **western hills** are Nepal at its most outstandingly typical: roaring gorges, precariously perched villages and terraced fields reaching to unsupportable heights, with some of the most graceful and accessible peaks of the Himalaya for a backdrop.

In this, Nepal's most populous hill region, people are the dominant feature of the landscape. Magars and Gurungs, the most visible **ethnic minorities**, live in their own villages or side by side with Tamangs, Hindu castes and the usual smattering of Newar merchants. Life is traditional and close to the earth, but relatively prosperous: the houses are tidy and spacious, and hill women are festooned with the family gold. The prosperity comes, indirectly, from an unlikely quarter, as the western hills were historically the most important recruiting area for **Gurkha soldiers**. It's an often-quoted statistic that Gurkha salaries and pensions were, up until the mid-1970s, Nepal's biggest foreign-exchange earner; in many villages here they still are, and they're arguably the major source of development financing as well. Ex-Gurkhas command the highest respect within their communities, and young men look up to them as role models. They also speak English, happily, and wherever you go there will probably be an ex-Gurkha to help you over the language barrier.

History, too, figures prominently here, for the foundations of modern Nepal were laid in the western hills. While the kings of the Kathmandu Valley were building temples, the princes of the hills built forts – many of which still stand – and it's the hillmen who rule Nepal today.

The chief destination here by far is **Pokhara**, a restful lakeside retreat as well as Nepal's major trekking hub. On the way there, you can detour to the magnificent hill-

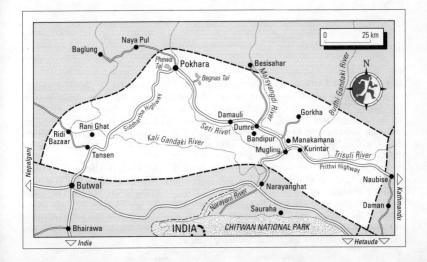

PUBLIC BUS SERVICES IN THE WESTERN HILLS

	Frequency (day)	Frequency (night)	Time (minimum)
To and from GORKHA			
Abu Khaireni	6		1hr
Birganj	2		7hr
Kathmandu	10#		6hr
Narayanghat	7		2hr 30min
Pokhara	2		5hr
Sonauli	1		7hr
To and from POKHARA			
Baglung	16		3hr
Begnas Tal	12		45min
Beni	4		3hr
Biratnagar		2	14hr
Birganj	6	2	9hr
Butwal	1	1	7h
Dhangadhi		1	18hr
Gorkha	2		5hr
Jagatpur	1		7hr
Janakpur		1	11hr
Kakarbhitta	2		16hr
Kathmandu	20*#	14#	7hr
Narayanghat		12	4hr
Nepalganj		2	15hr
Sauraha/Chitwan	*		
Sonauli	9*	3	9hr
Tansen	3		6hr
To and from TANSEN			
Butwal	30		2hr
Kakarbhitta		1	18hr
Kathmandu	2#	1	12hr
Pokhara	3		6hr
Ridi/Tamghas	6		2hr/6hr

* Tourist bus services also available – see p.275.
\# Sajha service available.
Note: **Internal flights** from Pokhara are listed on p.276.

top fortress of **Gorkha**, the pilgrimage site of **Manakamana** or the charmingly neglected backwater of **Bandipur**. Beyond Pokhara, on the road to the Indian border, lies laid-back **Tansen** and its picturesque countryside. All of these make excellent bases for **day hikes** – which can be almost as rewarding as trekking, without the commitment and red tape (treks are described in Chapter Seven). **Rafting** on the Trisuli, Kali Gandaki, Marsyangdi and Seti rivers also brings many travellers to the western hills (see Chapter Eight for river descriptions and advice).

Two main roads cut a swathe through the hills: the **Prithvi Highway** (Prithvi Rajmarg), running west from Kathmandu to Pokhara, and the **Siddhartha Highway** (Siddhartha Rajmarg), which carries on from Pokhara to the Indian border. These and three spur roads (to Gorkha, Narayanghat and Baglung) are literally the only paved roads in this region, and they're not always paved. Elsewhere, most journeys are made on foot – and you don't have to go far in this area to appreciate how blurred the distinction between "travelling" and "trekking" can be.

HEADING WEST:
THE PRITHVI HIGHWAY

Weaving through the heart of the hills, the **Prithvi Highway** (Prithvi Rajmarg) is most visitors' initiation into the pain and pleasure of Nepalese bus travel. You may find yourself on it several times, in fact, since besides linking Kathmandu and Pokhara it's also the first leg on most journeys between either city and the Tarai. Nepal's second trunk road when it was built with Chinese assistance in 1973, the Prithvi Highway has played a crucial role in modernizing the country, opening up the western hills and enabling Pokhara to develop into Nepal's second tourist city. More recently, the government and its foreign-aid bankers have rediscovered the highway's significance for industrial development, and have upgraded and widened it. It's now a fairly well-maintained road, though ironically this makes it more dangerous, since drivers are encouraged to go that much faster.

The road stays near the bottom of deep valleys for most of its 200km, providing only intermittent views. If you travel directly between Kathmandu and Pokhara you might think there's nothing worth stopping for, since there are few towns of any consequence along the way, but actually there's a lot to do here. Many **rafting** parties come this way to paddle Nepal's most popular river, the Trisuli, which the highway parallels for about 50km, or to put in on the Seti, which it crosses at Damauli. **Trekkers** going around Annapurna get off at Dumre.

In addition, three **cultural destinations** just off the highway – Manakamana, Bandipur and especially Gorkha – offer further reasons to break the journey. Not many people visit them, because it means giving up their seat on the tourist bus, although it's really not that bad continuing on by public bus. If you want to stick with tourist services, you can always buy a separate ticket for a later date and arrange to be picked up at the nearest town along the highway. Or go by mountain bike, motorcycle or hired car, which will allow you to stop wherever and whenever you like. (If cycling, put your bike on top of a bus for the first unpleasant leg to Naubise.)

Along the Prithvi Highway

After parting with the Tribhuwan Rajpath at Naubise (see p.238), the highway descends steadily along the south side of the Mahesh Khola, which soon joins the **Trisuli River** at Bhaireni, one of several rafting put-in points. Keep an eye out for magnificent, spidery suspension bridges and precarious ropeways spanning the river; you might also spot funeral pyres on the sandy banks, and rafting parties running the rapids. The high-water mark on the rocks shows how much the Trisuli, like all Himalayan rivers, swells and rages during the monsoon. The solid, three-storey farmhouses seen here generally belong to Baahuns and Chhetris, while the humbler mud-and-thatch huts are typical Tamang or Magar dwellings.

Malekhu and Kurintar

Most tourist buses make a mid-morning pitstop at **MALEKHU**, 70km from Kathmandu, which with its Westernized eateries feels like a miniature outpost of Thamel. Some services continue on to **KURINTAR** (102km), which is shaping up to be something of a tourism hub, thanks to its location within easy day-tripping range of Gorkha, Chitwan, Manakamana and raft trips on the Trisuli.

River Side Springs Resort (Kathmandu: ☎241408; *nangint@ccsl.com.np*; B⑧) provides the most luxurious **accommodation** here or indeed anywhere between

HILL CULTURE: GURUNGS AND MAGARS

Leavened with nothing but the water of God
Comes from Rumjatar the flour of millet pounded,
Gurungs have mastered the knowledge of God
And Brahmans are left astounded.

Nepali poet Jnandil (c.1821–83)

Hardy, self-sufficient peasant farmers, Gurungs and Magars are the "aboriginals" of the western hills. Both groups exhibit Mongoloid features and speak Tibeto-Burman dialects – signs that their ancestors probably migrated here from Tibet, though nobody's sure when. Together, they form the backbone of the Gurkha regiments (see p.283), and also account for a fair proportion of the Nepalese army.

Although **Gurungs** are a common sight around Pokhara, where many have invested their Gurkha pensions in guest houses and retirement homes, their homeland remains the middle elevations from Gorkha to the southern slopes of the Annapurna Himal. The majority who don't serve in the military herd sheep for their wool, driving them to pastures high on the flanks of the Himalaya, and raise wheat, maize, millet and potatoes. Gurungs were once active trans-Himalayan traders, but the Chinese occupation of Tibet ended that, while other traditional pursuits such as hunting and honey-gathering are being encroached upon by overpopulation.

Gurungs' unique form of **shamanism** is coming under pressure, too, as Hinduism advances from the south and Buddhism trickles down with Tibetan settlers from the north. Gurungs employ shamans to propitiate ghosts, reclaim possessed souls from the underworld, and guide dead souls to the land of their ancestors – rituals that contain clear echoes of "classic" Siberian shamanism and are believed to resemble those of the ancient Bon priests of pre-Buddhist Tibet. Some authorities see the ongoing power struggle between Tibetan lamas and Gurung shamans as a modern re-enactment of Buddhism's battle with Bon in seventh-century Tibet; in that instance, Buddhism won. (For an excellent introduction to Gurung shamanism, visit Pokhara's Tamu Kohibo Museum – see p.262.)

A somewhat less cohesive group, **Magars** are scattered throughout the lower elevations of the western hills (recently they've colonized parts of the eastern hills as well). A network of Magar kingdoms once controlled the entire region, but the arrival of Hindus in the fifteenth century brought swift political decline and steady cultural assimilation. Nowadays, after centuries of coexistence with Hindu castes, most employ Baahun (Brahman) priests and worship Hindu gods just like their Chhetri neighbours, differing only in that they're not allowed to wear the sacred thread of the "twice-born" castes. Similarly, with farming practices, housing and dress, Magars are an adaptable lot and not easily distinguished from surrounding groups – the velvet blouses, coin necklaces and *pote malla* (thin strands of glass beads) worn by many Magar women, for instance, are also common to Gurungs and Chhetris. Even the Magar language varies from place to place, consisting of at least three mutually unintelligible dialects (most Magars speak Nepali). Despite the lack of unifying traits, however, group identity is still strong, and will probably remain so as long as Magars keep marrying only within the clan.

Kathmandu and Pokhara. The bungalows and dining area are nice, but what really makes the place is its palatial pool and long, sandy Trisuli River frontage – if you're travelling with kids, this offers the closest thing to a beach holiday in Nepal. Across the river, *Brigands Bend* (Kathmandu: ☎536072; *brian@hilltrek.mos.com.np*; ⑦) is a tented camp with an even better beach and a more secluded location, although it lacks a pool. It's used mainly by rafting parties (two-day raft/overnight packages available), but others can stay overnight and hike around the nearby traditional villages; access is by raft or ropeway. A third outfit, *Manakamana Village Resort* (Kathmandu: ☎230287; *dinesh@crystal.wlink.com.np*; B⑨) represents a more affordable alternative, but it's rather close to the highway and more of a trek to the river.

The cable car to Manakamana (see below) starts 3km west of Kurintar.

Mugling

Public buses break for lunch at **MUGLING** (110km), a major crossroads at the junction of the Trisuli and Marsyangdi rivers. This is a much more Nepali sort of watering hole, where bad *daal bhaat* is the only item on the menu and the wood-fronted "hotels" look like something out of the wild west (indeed, many are brothels, servicing long-distance drivers). Wherever you stop, you can be sure your driver is getting a free meal. Mugling has a few legitimate guest houses – mostly cold-water bed-and-*bhaats* like *Naulo Hotel & Restaurant* and *Hotel New Bijay* (both ②) – but with buses coming and going 24 hours a day, it's surely one of the worst places in Nepal you could choose to spend the night. If for some reason you found yourself stuck here, it would be worth spending the extra money on *Motel du Mugling* (Kathmandu: ☎225242; B⑦), located across the bridge and commanding a view of the confluence.

At 280m, Mugling is the lowest point along the Prithvi Highway. Sugar cane is cultivated on a small scale around here, and you'll also see *simal*, a tall, angular Tarai tree that produces red flowers in February and pods of cotton-like seeds in May. Traffic bound for the Tarai turns left (south) at Mugling and continues along the Trisuli River, making the gradual 34-kilometre descent to Narayanghat (see p.313).

To Dumre

Most of the second half of the journey to Pokhara is a gradual ascent, initially up the valley of the Marsyangdi and then, after crossing a low divide, up the Seti. Just past Mugling, the Prithvi Highway crosses the Trisuli and heads upstream along the Marsyangdi, passing the massive **Marsyangdi Hydroelectric Project** powerhouse 2km later. The dam and reservoir are 12km further on; water is diverted through a tunnel to the powerhouse and then channelled down to the turbines, leaving this stretch of river all but dry outside of the monsoon. Completed in 1990, the project was at the time the single most expensive thing ever built in Nepal, costing $210 million of German, Saudi and World Bank money, and it generates nearly 30 percent of the country's electricity. (See "Development dilemmas" in Contexts for a discussion of the problems surrounding hydroelectric development schemes.) The mountain views are excellent after the powerhouse: the closest peaks seen from here are Boudha and Himalchuli of the Manaslu Himal. The spur road to Gorkha (see below) leaves the highway at **Abu Khaireni**, 7km west of Mugling and home to a big rubber factory.

Marking the point where the highway leaves the Marsyangdi, 11km past Abu Khaireni, **DUMRE** (450m) is a drab roadside bazaar that's really only of interest as the turning for two side roads: one north to Besisahar, the starting point of the Annapurna Circuit (see p.397), and one south to Bandipur (below). If you're cycling between Kathmandu and Pokhara, Dumre would be a marginally quieter place to stay than Mugling, but still pretty dire. *Mustang Hotel & Lodge* and *Hotel Chhim Keshori* (both ①) are two of many trekkers' inns left over from Dumre's heyday as a trailhead, before the construction of the Besisahar road.

Damauli

West of Dumre, the hills get gentler and more heavily cultivated. It's 8km uphill and another 8km down from Dumre to **DAMAULI** (350m), a nondescript administrative town overlooking the confluence of the Madi and Seti rivers.

This confluence, like so many others in Nepal, is highly venerated, and the large complex of shrines that has built up around it is one of those weird and wonderful places that you find only in the Indian subcontinent. To get there, follow the main street that runs perpendicular to the highway for about 500m, pass through an arch, bear left and descend a broad set of steps to the river. To the left is **Byas Gupha**, a cave where Byas (or Vyasa), the sage of the *Mahabharat*, is supposed to have been born and lived. It's really only a rock overhang with a concrete room containing a statue of Byas attached to it, but the attending priest will give you a *tika* and point you in the direction of an enclosed park area that's bursting with shrines, statues, rest houses and pilgrims.

After crossing the Madi, the Prithvi Highway rises and then descends gradually to rejoin the broad Seti Valley, finally reaching Pokhara 54km from Damauli. Begnas and Rupa lakes, off to the right of the highway on the approach to Pokhara, are described in the later "Pokhara Valley" section.

Manakamana

Just about every Nepali has either been to **MANAKAMANA** (Ma-na-*kaa*-ma-na) or hopes one day to go. Located on a prominent ridge high above the confluence of the Trisuli and Marsyangdi rivers, the attractive village is home to Nepal's most famous "wish-fulfilling" temple. Each year a half-million people make the journey, and the recent inauguration of cable car service is expected to double that number. The place goes into overdrive on Saturday mornings, when the vast majority of pilgrims come to perform animal sacrifices; the festivals of Dasain (in September–October) and Nag Panchami (in July–August) bring even greater numbers of celebrants. Visiting Manakamana is a very Nepali thing to do, and even if you don't sacrifice an animal you'll feel like you've received an initiation into the society.

Getting there

A visit to Manakamana, which used to be an all-day or even an overnight commitment, can now be done in as little as an hour, thanks to an impressive new **cable car** service (daily 9am–5pm; $8 one way, $10 return; children under 3ft tall ride for half price). Manufactured by Austrian company Doppelmayr, the gondolas are just like those found in international ski resorts, with seating for six and plenty of windows for 360-degree views; the ride is smooth, silent and comfortable, and it takes just ten minutes to ascend the 2.8-kilometre-long line. Any bus will drop you off at the turning for the base station, which is marked by a big brick archway just off the Prithvi Highway about halfway between Kurintar and Mugling. Be prepared for long queues on Saturday mornings.

Completed in 1998 at a cost of $7.5 million, the Manakamana cable car line is one of the most ambitious tourist developments in Nepal, and one of the few targeted squarely at *Nepali* tourists. It's proving to be wildly successful. Though business will probably drop off somewhat after the novelty has worn off, the line has given a huge boost to domestic tourism and has become the main attraction of the Kurintar–Manakamana–Gorkha area. As a result, Manakamana is no longer a once-in-a-lifetime religious pilgrimage – now it's an easy stopover for anyone just wanting a change of scenery or a breath of cooler air. (The cable car also promises to make possible new tourist activities, such as lift-served paragliding.)

Of course the cable car has taken a toll on the old **walking route**: few pilgrims go by foot nowadays, and the teashops along the trail are suffering. However, the hike is still very much worth doing, since it's really the most meaningful part of a pilgrimage to Manakamana. The trail begins in Abu Khaireni, about 1km up the Gorkha road on the right, slipping through a gap in the bazaar and immediately crossing the Marsyangdi by footbridge. It's a steep hike and involves a vertical gain of 1000m – allow two or three hours to get to the top.

FARMING IN THE HILLS

Most Nepalis live in countryside like that seen along this stretch of the Prithvi Highway, and the **farming** methods practised here are fairly representative of those employed throughout the hills. The land is used intensively but sustainably: trees and bamboo are pruned for fodder; livestock, fed on fodder, pull ploughs and provide milk and manure; and manure, in turn, is dolloped onto the fields as fertilizer (and used as fuel at higher elevations). Goats, chickens and pigs recycle scraps into meat and eggs, and even pariah dogs are tolerated because they eat garbage and faeces.

Nepali hill farmers have a harder go of it than their Tarai counterparts (see p.314): the average hill family's half-hectare holding is fragmented into several plots located at different elevations, often a half-hour or more apart. The typical household owns only simple hand tools – its only beast of burden a buffalo or ox – and grows just 70 percent of the food it needs each year. Most farmers barter surplus grain for odd essentials such as salt, sugar, pots and pans, and have little to do with the cash economy, though growing numbers near the highway are starting to raise vegetables for sale. Several research stations in this area are experimenting with improved seeds, but tractors and chemical fertilizers will probably never be appropriate for the vast majority of farms in Nepal's hills.

The village and around

The trail from Abu Khaireni enters Manakamana from the west. Whitewashed Newar houses and Mediterranean-style cafés line the route as it makes its final approach to the famous **Bhagwati Mandir**, set in a square near the top of the village. The cable car summit station is situated just south of the temple; it's about five minutes' walk up an obvious path and steps from there. Tradition has it that the goddess Bhagwati rewards those who make the pilgrimage to her shrine by making their wishes come true; she's especially popular with Newar newlyweds, who come to pray for sons. Animal sacrifices are an essential part of the ritual, and locals raise goats, chickens and pigeons specifically for the sacrificial market.

Manakamana is also famous for its oranges, which come into season in November and December, and for its mountain views: from high points around the village you can see a limited panorama from Annapurna II and Lamjung Himal across to Peak 29 and Baudha of the Manaslu Himal. If you're game for more, you can continue 45 minutes further up the ridge to another temple, the **Bakeshwar Mahadev Mandir**, and then another fifteen minutes to **Lakhan Thapa Gupha**, a holy cave near the highest point of the ridge, where the views are tremendous. From there, the path bends north along the ridge and eventually meets the Gorkha road, reaching Gorkha in three to four hours' walking time from Manakamana.

Manakamana is a far more pleasant and entertaining place to **spend the night** than, say, Mugling or Abu Khaireni. Dozens of cheap lodges vie for pilgrims' business, and you're unlikely to have any trouble finding a room, though on a Friday or Saturday night should stake your claim early. Options include *Malla Hotel* (②), *Manakamana Lodge* (②/B④, but still only cold water) and many others not advertised in English. For a deluxe experience, try *Manakamana Resort* (Kathmandu: ☎434656; *manaresort@wlink.com.np*; B⑦), about ten minutes' walk west of the temple and cable car station. Perched on a small promontory in the midst of an orange grove, it boasts nice views, fancy tented accommodation and dining pavilion, pony treks and weekend music programmes (reservations essential on weekends).

Moving on from Manakamana, board any local bus plying the Prithvi Highway, either at the cable car turning or at the main Abu Khaireni junction. Buses sometimes originate at these locations; your chances of getting a seat are best in the morning, when many people will be getting off for Manakamana.

Gorkha and around

Despite being midway between Kathmandu and Pokhara, **GORKHA** (Gor-*khaa*) remains strangely untouristed, probably because of the former difficulty of getting there. That's no longer the case, however, as the 24-kilometre paved road up from Abu Khaireni makes it a relatively painless half-day's ride from Pokhara, Kathmandu or Chitwan, and the new Manakamana cable car takes most of the sweat out of hiking here. The government is devoting a large chunk of its tourism budget to sprucing up Gorkha's monuments, and there seems to be some vague notion of putting the town on the tourist map. But for the time being, at least, Gorkha is suspended in a happy halfway state, with just enough basic facilities to get by, yet still primitive enough to keep the crowds away.

Cradle of a nation and the ancestral home of the Nepalese royal family, Gorkha occupies a central place in Nepalese history. The village itself is minuscule, but hunched on the hilltop above is its link with that splendid past, the **Gorkha Durbar**, an architectural tour de force worthy of the flamboyant Gorkha kings and the dynasty they founded. Unless you're setting straight off on a trek or just finishing one (the old Pokhara–Trisuli

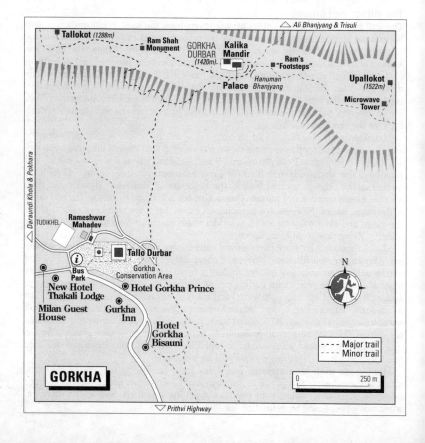

trail passes through Gorkha), you'll have to spend the night here. Think about staying longer: the Durbar and environs could easily soak up a day, and hikes around the area could keep you busy for another day or two. The hill climate is agreeable, the pace is easy and, for the moment at least, there's not an apple pie or pizza in sight.

Direct **bus** services connect Gorkha with Kathmandu, Pokhara, Narayanghat, Sonauli and Birganj (see p.244 for frequencies and journey times). Depending on where you're coming from, though, it might be easier to take a tourist bus for Pokhara or Kathmandu to Abu Khaireni and ride a local bus from there. All buses terminate at Gorkha's modest bus park at the lower edge of the village. If you're pedalling, bear in mind it's a 900-metre ascent from Abu Khaireni to Gorkha, and it gets steeper as you go.

Note that the countryside around Gorkha is one of the strongholds of Nepal's **Maoist insurgents**, and Gorkha, being a district headquarters, has experienced some acts of violence. At the time of writing, police were strictly enforcing a 10pm curfew.

Some history

In a sense, Gorkha's history is not its own. A petty hill state in medieval times, it was occupied and transformed into a sort of Himalayan Sparta by outsiders who used it as a base for a dogged campaign against Kathmandu and then, having won their prize, restored Gorkha to obscurity. Yet during those two centuries of occupation, it raised the nation's most famous son, **Prithvi Narayan Shah**, and somehow bred in him the audacity to conquer all of Nepal.

Prithvi Narayan's ancestors came to Gorkha in the mid-sixteenth century, having been driven into the hills from their native Rajasthan by the Muslim horde, and they soon gained a reputation as a single-mindedly martial lot. His father launched the first unsuccessful raid on the Kathmandu Valley in the early eighteenth century, and when Prithvi Narayan himself ascended to the throne in 1743, at the age of twenty, he already had his father's obsession fixed in his mind*. Within a year, he was leading Gorkha in a war of expansion that was eventually to unify all of present-day Nepal, plus parts of India and Tibet. Looking at the tiny village and meagre terraces of Gorkha today, you can imagine what a drain it must have been to keep a standing army fed and supplied for 27 years of continuous campaigning. The hardy peasants of Gorkha got little more than a handshake for their efforts. After conquering the valley in 1769, Prithvi Narayan moved his capital to the bright lights of Kathmandu, relegating Gorkha to a mere garrison from which the later western campaign was directed. By the early nineteenth century, Gorkha had been all but forgotten, even as an alternative spelling of the name – Gurkha – was becoming a household name around the world.

In and around the village

Nestled on a shelf beneath a steep ridge, most of the village stretches along a single main lane, with buildings huddled close together to save space for farming. To get there from the bus park you'll first walk past or through the **Gorkha Conservation Area Project**, a newly developed zone consisting of gardens, walkways, monuments,

---

* An odd legend confirms Prithvi Narayan's destiny, but also puts the scale of his accomplishment into perspective. When still a prince he was approached by an old man, who took the boy's hand and spat in it. The spittle turned to yoghurt and the man ordered Prithvi to eat it; the prince, not unreasonably, flung the curd on the ground at his feet. At that, the old man revealed himself to be Gorakhnath, the demigod protector of the Shah kings, and pronounced that Prithvi Narayan would go on to rule wherever he placed his feet – but had he eaten the curd, he would have ruled the world.

an information centre and other as-yet-unbuilt facilities. The one historic building actually conserved by the project is the old **Tallo Durbar** (Lower Palace). Built in around 1750, this imposing Newar-style edifice served as the kingdom's administrative headquarters, while the upper Durbar housed king and court. Seen from above, Tallo Durbar indeed looks like a mini-Pentagon. Its fine brick and woodwork is getting a slow facelift, and the building is eventually supposed to be opened up as a museum of Gorkha history spanning the generations of Shahs leading up to Prithvi Narayan.

The main road into the village leads past Gorkha's modest Tudikhel (parade ground) and a small temple precinct. The gilded figure kneeling atop a pillar facing the onion-domed **Rameshwar Mahadev Mandir** is Prithvi Pati Shah; grandfather of Prithvi Narayan Shah, he established most of the temples and shrines still in use around the town, including the Kalika temple in the upper Durbar.

The Gorkha Durbar

It's a brisk, 250-metre ascent to the **Gorkha Durbar** along the main trail from Pokharithok, the junction just east of Tallo Durbar (figure on half an hour). At the top of this route – once the royal approach to the palace – you can marvel at the former grand staircase that's one of the Durbar's most distinctive features, despite its recent conversion into a retaining wall. Pure ostentation or cheeky bluff, either way it must have cowed visiting vassals into submission – a neat trick for a tinpot realm that could barely muster 150 soldiers at the time of Prithvi Narayan's first campaign. Entrance to the Durbar is now through a doorway on its western side, reached by a path to the left of the retaining wall. No leather is allowed in the compound, and photography is prohibited.

Conceived as a dwelling for kings and gods, the fortress remains a religious place, and first stop in any visit is the **Kalika Mandir**, probably the most revered shrine this side of Kathmandu. Occupying the left (western) half of the Durbar building, its interior is closed to all but priests and the king of Nepal (others would die upon beholding Kali's terrible image, say the priests). Plenty of action takes place outside, though: sacrifices are made in the alcove in front of the entrance, and after the twice-monthly observance of Astami, which is celebrated with special gusto in Gorkha, the paving stones are sticky with blood. Most worshippers arrive cradling a trembling goat or chicken and leave swinging a headless carcass. Chaitra Dasain, Gorkha's biggest annual **festival**, brings processions and more bloodletting in late March or early April, as does the tenth day of Dasain in October.

The east wing of the Durbar is the historic **palace**, site of **Prithvi Narayan's birthplace** and, by extension, the ancestral shrine of the Shah kings. This accounts for King Birendra's regular visits (his helipad is just west of the complex) and the government's spare-no-expense renovation of the Durbar's exceptional eighteenth-century brick- and woodwork. Though predating the Gorkhali conquest of Kathmandu, the palace bears the unmistakable stamp of Newar craftsmanship: the Gorkhalis, who never pretended to have any art or architecture of their own, imported workmen from Kathmandu. The building is open only on the tenth day of Dasain, but if you look through a lattice window on the east side you can see what is claimed to be Prithvi Narayan's **throne**.

The remaining space within the fortress walls is fairly littered with other Hindu shrines. By the main entrance is a small temple built around the holy **cave of Gorakhnath**, the centre for worship of the shadowy Indian guru who gave Gorkha its name and is regarded as a kind of guardian angel by the Shah kings. Sadhus of the Gorakhnath cult are known as *kaanphata* ("split-ears"), after an initiation ceremony in which they insert sticks in their earlobes – which is a walk in the park compared to some of the other things they get up to in the name of their guru. *Kaanphata* priests sometimes administer ashen *tika* from the shelter above the cave.

Viewpoints and forts

The views are good from the Durbar, but carry on for much better ones. Exit the compound through a door to the east and descend to **Hanuman Bhanjyang** (Hanuman Pass), a small notch in the ridge named after the valiant monkey king whose image guards the popular shady rest stop. Cross the main trail (a branch of the Pokhara–Trisuli porter route) and follow a steep, stone-paved path up for just a couple of minutes to an awesome vantage point where you can stand in the stone **"footsteps"** of Ram, hero of the *Ramayan* and Hanuman's best buddy, and snap a postcard picture of the Durbar and the mountains to the north. From this angle, the Durbar looks like Nepal's answer to Mad Ludwig's castle. The Himalaya seen from here stretch from the Annapurnas (and even Dhaulagiri, which from this angle is to the right of Annapurna I and Machhapuchhre) to Ganesh Himal, with the pyramids of Baudha and Himalchuli occupying centre stage. If you can manage it, come early to catch the sunrise.

From Hanuman Bhanjyang it's another half-hour hike to **Upallokot** (Upper Fort), a 1520-metre eyrie at the highest, easternmost point of the ridge. To get to it you have to walk through a fenced microwave relay facility, and views are unfortunately restricted by vegetation. Upallokot itself is more a hut than a fort, its thatched roof long gone. The small walled pen contains a grinding-wheel-shaped *yoni* and a set of stones laid out in the shape of a reclining human figure – obscure icons of Kali and Bhairab.

At the other end of the ridge stands **Tallokot**, another watch post with limited views. You can easily stroll there from the Durbar, passing a small Ganesh shrine and a new monument to **Ram Shah**, the seventh-generation ancestor of Prithvi Narayan Shah who is reckoned by some to have been the progenitor of the Shah title. The views from this monument are also excellent. A rough track descends directly from Tallokot to Gorkha, tripping down terraces past small clusters of farmhouses and the odd communal spring.

Longer walks

If that circuit whets your appetite for longer walks, there are three main options. One with a unique cultural dimension is the route **to Manakamana** (see above), which

---

CHAUTAARA

A uniquely Nepali institution, the **chautaara** is more than just a resting place – it serves important social and religious functions as well. Every hill village has its *chautaara*, and you'll find them at appropriate intervals along any reasonably busy trail. The standard design consists of a rectangular flagstoned platform, built at just the right height for porters easily to set down their *doko*, and sometimes a smaller platform atop that. Two trees planted in the earthen centre provide shade for all who gather underneath: passing strangers, old friends, couples, village assemblies.

Chautaara are erected and maintained by individuals as an act of public service, often to earn religious merit or in memory of a deceased parent. Commonly they'll be found on sites associated with animist deities, indicated by *sindur*-coloured stones. The trees, too, are considered sacred. Invariably, one will be a **pipal**, whose Latin name (*Ficus religiosa*) recalls its role as the *bodhi* tree under which the Buddha attained enlightenment. Nepalis regard the pipal, with its heart-shaped leaves, as a female symbol, and women will sometimes fast and pray before one for children, or for success for the children they already have. Its male counterpart is the **banyan** (*bar* in Nepali), another member of the fig genus that sends down Tarzan-vine-like aerial roots which, if not pruned, will eventually take root and establish satellite trunks. A *chautaara* is incomplete without the pair; occasionally you'll see one with a single tree, but sooner or later someone will get around to planting the other.

starts on an unpaved side road off the main Gorkha road about 4km down from the town, and takes three to four hours. You would probably want to spend the night in Manakamana and carry on down to Abu Khaireni the following morning.

The high road through Hanuman Bhanjyang gives access to the country east of the Durbar, descending gently for about an hour and a half to Ali Bhanjyang (shops), then ascending along a ridge with fabulous views **to Khanchok Bhanjyang** after about two and a half hours. This would be about the limit for a day hike, but given an early start you could continue down to the subtropical banks of the Budhi Gandaki at Arughat, a long day's 20km from Gorkha, and find basic lodging there – at this point you'd be a third of the way to Trisuli. Other, less distinct trails from Upallokot and the Ram Shah monument take roundabout routes to Ali Bhanjyang.

Alternatively, follow the main trail west out of Gorkha village, which reaches the untrammelled **Daraundi Khola valley** after an hour and a half. You could continue on for another three hours to Khoplang, a beautiful hill village with lodgings. You could even do a two-day loop: Gorkha to Khanchok Bhanjyang, from there down to the Daraundi at Ulte, head downstream to Chorkate, and then back up to Gorkha. For trekking from here, see Chapter Seven.

Practicalities

Accommodation in Gorkha is expensive for what you get. The best in town is *Gurkha Inn* (☎ & fax 064/20206; Kathmandu: ☎412953; B⑦), which is fairly new and clean, and has decent food and a nice garden. *Hotel Gorkha Bisauni* (☎ & fax 064/20107; ⑥/B⑦, dorm beds ①) is similar, but is more run-down and has less reliable hot water. Both of these places will usually go way lower on their prices if you press them, since they're hardly ever full and they both know that you can take your business to the other. (Another midrange option may be in the offing, as the Gorkha Conservation Area Project's master plan calls for the construction of a "tourist lodge complex" near the Tudikhel.) *Hotel Gorkha Prince* (☎064/20131; ②/B③) is a cheaper, dingier option with hot water but no greenery. The rest are the most basic sort of cold-water lodgings – try *New Hotel Thakali Lodge* or *Milan Guest House* (both ①), which are at least at the quieter end of town, beyond the bus park.

Gorkha also has a more luxurious "resort", but it's not in town: *Gorkha Hill Resort* (☎064/20325; Kathmandu: ☎419798, fax 419260; B⑧) is located 4km down the road, on the way to Manakamana.

For **food**, the choice is fairly limited. *Gurkha Inn*'s and *Gorkha Bisauni*'s restaurants do reasonably good Western fare, including seasonal fresh vegetable soups. Plenty of places near the bus park serve up the usual *momo*, *thukpa* or all-you-can-eat *bhaat*.

There's a bank up in the village, but no **foreign exchange** facilities as yet.

Bandipur

Each new edition of this book spotlights one or two amazing but hitherto overlooked destinations (Nepal is full of such places). This edition's featured newcomer is **BANDIPUR**, a fantastically neglected little town on a ridge above Dumre that has history, architecture, incredible views, caves, countryside and more. Its downfall is that it has only the most spartan facilities – except in one upmarket tented camp, it's all cold water and *daal bhaat* here – although a few town boosters seem to be trying hard to change that. In any case, innkeepers seem genuinely keen to have foreign guests (even if they don't know quite what to do with them), and that makes Bandipur a potential base for exploring a beautiful, untouristed part of Nepal.

If you happen to be coming from Narayanghat, you can catch the daily direct **bus** to Bandipur. From anywhere else, take any bus heading along the Prithvi Highway and get off at Dumre. The historic **trail** to Bandipur – immortalized in a poem by the late King Mahendra – starts 500m east of the main Dumre intersection and climbs through shady forest punctuated by very civilized rest shelters and waterspouts. The walk takes two to three hours, so it shouldn't be a problem getting there by dark. Alternatively, you could wait in Dumre for the bus from Narayanghat, which should pass through around 3 or 4pm. It may also be possible to hire a vehicle in Dumre. If travelling by **bike**, you'll take the initially paved (but not for long) road that starts 1km west of Dumre.

The town and around

Bandipur has a derelict, old-world atmosphere that feels almost Mediterranean. The town was once a prosperous **trading centre**, and its substantial buildings, with their Neoclassical facades and shuttered windows, bespeak past glories. Originally a simple Magar village, it was colonized in the early nineteenth century by Newars from Bhaktapur, who took advantage of its malaria-free location to develop it into an important stop along the India–Tibet trade route. Bandipur hit its heyday in Rana times, when, as a measure of its power and prestige, it was granted special permission to have its own library (which is still going). However, the town began to lose its edge in the 1950s, when the eradication of malaria in the Tarai made travel easier there. In the 1960s, the district headquarters was moved from Bandipur to Damauli, and the completion of the Prithvi Highway in 1973 shifted commerce to Dumre, leaving Bandipur a semi-ghost town.

Sitting in a saddle at 1000m beneath dramatic limestone hills, Bandipur's quiet main **bazaar** is oriented from southwest to northeast. Vehicles enter at the southwestern end. Hiking up, you approach the bazaar from the northwest, first passing the **Tudikhel**, which is certainly one of the most dramatic in Nepal. Perched exhilaratingly on a rock outcrop with a sheer dropoff to the east, it looks like the perfect place to put a prison for really bad criminals that you want to make sure never escape; but this being Nepal, it's used as a school playground. The view to the north is stunning: basically, you're looking at a map of the first half of the Annapurna Circuit, with the Marsyangdi valley straight ahead and the Annapurna and Manaslu ranges behind. It's best visited at sunrise and sunset, in part because that's when the kids aren't using it.

Bandipur has several temples, though none are very much to look at. The main **Khadga Devi Mandir**, reached by bearing left up the steps at the north end of the bazaar, looks like a one-room schoolhouse; it houses a holy sword (*khadga*) supposedly given to a local king by Lord Shiva himself, which is displayed on the seventh day of Dasain. The shrine of **Thani Mai**, Khadga Devi's "sister", is of more interest for its awesome views – it's at the top of Gurungche Daada, the limestone hill southwest of the bazaar.

Day hikes around Bandipur could fill up several days. The obligatory destination is **Siddha Gupha** (Rs10), Nepal's biggest cave, which incredibly was discovered only in 1987. It's 10m wide, 400m long and full of stalactites, not to mention a sizeable bat population. You'll need to bring your own torch/flashlight. It takes about an hour and a half to walk to the cave from Bandipur. A trail also leads up to it from the Prithvi Highway at Bimalnagar, 1km east of Dumre, and there are plans to build a road to it. A hike to Siddha Gupha can be combined with a visit to another cave, **Patale Dwar** ("Portal to the Underworld"), which is supposed to be a geologic wonder. Other, longer hikes go through pretty, cultivated hills and traditional Magar villages, and are worth considering as alternatives to leaving Bandipur by bus. You can walk **to Damauli** via the Chabda Barahi Mandir in about four hours, the last part of it on a motorable road. Given an early start and all day, it's reportedly possible to walk south **to the Seti River** and then downstream to its confluence with the Trisuli, where there's a bridge across to the highway not far north of Narayanghat.

Practicalities

Bandipur's numerous **guest houses** are right in the main bazaar, and they're all ①. There's not much to choose between them, though *Pradhan Service Paying Guest Accommodation*'s proprietor speaks excellent English, and *Bandipur Guest House* wins the prize for the most picturesquely ruinous building. None has a phone, but there's no need to call ahead because hardly any tourists go to Bandipur so it's inconceivable that any of these places wouldn't have a room. If you can afford it, **Bandipur Mountain Resort** (☎220162; *island@mos.com.np*; B⑨), located at the beautiful north end of the Tudikhel, offers very comfortable tented-camp accommodation and serviceable food, and can also arrange nature treks from here down to Chitwan National Park.

Bandipur is perhaps most easily fitted into a journey between Pokhara and Chitwan, since when it's time to **leave** you'll be assured of a seat on the direct bus to Narayanghat. You could also try getting on a tourist bus in Dumre, since trekkers getting off there usually free up a few seats.

POKHARA

The Himalaya form the highest, sheerest rise from subtropical base to icy peaks of any mountain range on earth, and nowhere is the contrast more marked than at **POKHARA** (pronounced *Poke*-ruh). Sited at just 800m above sea level, it boasts a nearly unobstructed view of the 8000-metre-plus Annapurna and Manaslu *himal*, just 25km to north. Dominating the skyline, in beauty if not in height, is the double-finned summit of Machhapuchhre ("Fish-Tailed") – so named for its twin-peaked summit, though only one is visible from Pokhara.

Basking in the view, Nepal's main resort area lolls beside the shore of **Phewa Tal** (Phewa Lake), well outside the actual town of Pokhara. This is Nepal's little budget paradise: carefree and culturally undemanding, though extremely touristy, with a steaks-and-cakes scene rivalling Kathmandu's. Whatever you're looking for, it's a buyer's market here – everything comes so easily, the main challenge is sifting through the growing multitude of possibilities. New businesses pop up like mushrooms after each monsoon, and disappear just as quickly; cheap places have a habit of going upmarket, great

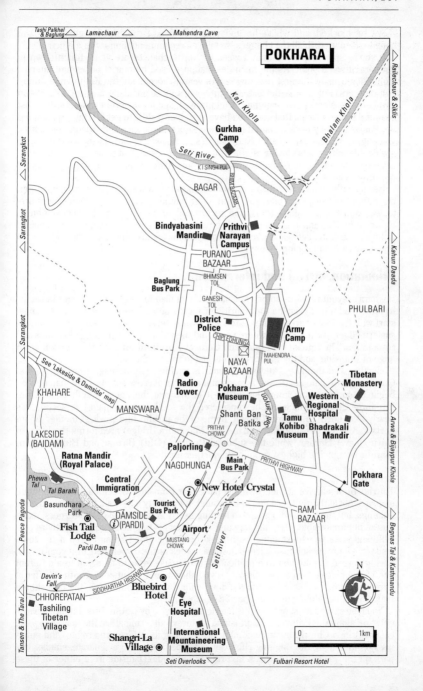

POKHARA

Tashi Palkhel & Baglung △ — Lamachaur △ — △ Mahendra Cave

Railechaur & Siklis

Kali Khola

Bhalam Khola

Gurkha Camp

Seti River

K I SINGH PUL

BAGAR

Sarangkot

Sarangkot

Sarangkot

Bindyabasini Mandir

Prithvi Narayan Campus

PURANO BAZAAR

BHIMSEN TOL

Baglung Bus Park

GANESH TOL

District Police

CHIPLEDHUNGA

NAYA BAZAAR

MAHENDRA PUL

PHULBARI

Kahun Daada

Army Camp

See 'Lakeside & Damside' map

KHAHARE

MANSWARA

Radio Tower

Pokhara Museum

Shanti Ban Batika

Tamu Kohibo Museum

Western Regional Hospital

Bhadrakali Mandir

Tibetan Monastery

Arwa & Bijaypur Khola

LAKESIDE (BAIDAM)

Ratna Mandir (Royal Palace)

Phewa Tal

Tal Barahi

Basundhara Park

Fish Tail Lodge

Pardi Dam

Peace Pagoda

Paljorling

NAGDHUNGA

Central Immigration

DAMSIDE (PARDI)

Tourist Bus Park

PRITHVI CHOWK

Main Bus Park

PRITHVI HIGHWAY

New Hotel Crystal

Airport

MUSTANG CHOWK

Seti River

RAM BAZAAR

Pokhara Gate

Begnas Tal & Kathmandu

Devin's Fall

SIDDHARTHA HIGHWAY

CHHOREPATAN

Tashiling Tibetan Village

Bluebird Hotel

Eye Hospital

Shangri-La Village

International Mountaineering Museum

Tansen & The Tarai

N

0 — 1km

Seti Overlooks ▽ — ▽ Fulbari Resort Hotel

views get blocked, and what's hot today may be dead tomorrow. No guidebook can hope to keep up with all the changes, so take all recommendations with a pinch of salt.

If you're spending more than a week in Nepal, chances are you'll touch down in Pokhara at some point. As the main destination served by tourist buses and internal flights, it's usually the first place travellers venture to outside the Kathmandu Valley. For trekkers, Pokhara is the gateway to Nepal's most popular trails; for rafters and kayakers, it's Nepal's river-running headquarters; and for everyone else, it's the most beautiful place in Nepal that you *don't* have to trek or paddle to get to. Day trips around the Pokhara Valley beckon, and if the area is short on temples and twisting old alleys, you might find that a relief after Kathmandu's profusion. Despite its shallow hedonism – which definitely gets cloying after a while – Pokhara is a great place to recharge your batteries, especially after a trek or a time in India. By comparison, Kathmandu seems downright claustrophobic.

Because it's 500m lower than the capital, Pokhara is a warmer place to be in winter, but rather hot from April onwards. With lower foothills to the south, it's also less protected from the prevailing rains, and receives about twice as much precipitation as Kathmandu. Touring the valley, you'll be struck by the active, shaping presence of water everywhere: lakes and rivers are conspicuous features here, and the paddies are traced by canals of roiling mountain water.

Orientation, arrival and information

Pokhara's layout requires some explanation if you plan to do any sightseeing (an activity which, admittedly, isn't a top priority for most visitors here). To get your bearings, start with the tourist areas of **Lakeside** and **Damside**, set along the eastern and southeastern edges of **Phewa Tal**, where you'll find the vast majority of budget lodgings and restaurants. The **tourist bus park** and **Central Immigration** both lie at the northern edge of Damside, and the **airport** begins just to the northeast.

Northeast of the lake, **Pokhara Bazaar** is maddeningly diffuse, sprawling a good 6km along two main north–south roads and a ladder of cross streets – the map doesn't begin to suggest how interminably far it is to cycle the entire length of it. From **Mustang Chowk**, which can be considered the southernmost main intersection, it's nearly 2km north to **Prithvi Chowk**, home of the **public bus park**. A further 1.5km northwards, the bustling **Mahendra Pul** (Mahendra Bridge) area forms the heart of **Naya (New) Bazaar**, while the subdued **Purano (Old) Bazaar** and **Bindyabasini Mandir** occupy the highest ground still further north.

Arrival

Tourist buses arrive at their own bus park near Damside (Greenline buses continue on to a depot at the southern end of Lakeside). It's a pretty easy walk from there to most lodgings, but the touts, who go into a feeding frenzy at the arrival of Westerners, make this all but impossible. The only way to escape intact is to grab a taxi as quickly as possible and state your destination with great certitude. Don't be surprised if the touts insist that your guest house burned down last week or the owner died, or if your driver, having agreed to take you to a particular guest house, tries to take you to a different one where he can earn a commission. If you allow a tout to entice you with an offer of a free taxi ride, expect to be charged double for the room; otherwise, the fare should be Rs25–75, depending on your specific destination.

You'll be spared most or all of this hassle if you arrive by **public bus**. Public services entering along the Prithvi and Siddhartha highways all terminate at the main bus park, east of Prithvi Chowk. If you're coming off a trek in the Annapurna region and entering Pokhara along the Baglung Highway, you'll be dropped at a separate, smaller bus park on the west side of town. A taxi ride to Lakeside/Damside from either of these should cost about Rs100. It's also possible to **trek directly to Lakeside**, in which case you'll enter it from the north via the Bangladi and Khahare areas.

Flying to Pokhara from Kathmandu cuts out some of the hardships of the journey (see p.276 for airline info). The mountain views from aloft are stupendous; take the earliest flight available, before clouds obscure the peaks, and book early for a seat on the righthand side of the plane. At the time of writing, taxi fares from the airport were fixed at Rs60 for Damside and Rs90 for central Lakeside.

Information

A shiny new **tourist office** is supposed to open "soon" in Damside, though at the time of writing it was not looking anywhere near completion. In the meantime, staff at the old office, opposite the airport, can answer simple, specific questions (Sun–Thurs 10am–5pm, 4pm in winter, Fri 10am–3pm). The Kathmandu Environmental Education Project (KEEP) has plans to open a Lakeside branch, but nothing had been fixed at the time of going to press.

However, all the information you really need is contained in the standard tourist **map** of Pokhara, sold in most bookstores. Even better, though more expensive, are Karto Atelier's "Pokhara Town & Valley" and the very detailed series of 1:25,000 sheets published by HMG/FINNIDA (the latter may be hard to find in Pokhara).

Getting around

Poor local transport makes getting around Pokhara time-consuming, widening the divide between lake and bazaar and making it that much harder to tear yourself away from the tourist fleshpots. A crosstown journey on one of Pokhara's **local buses** takes the better part of an hour. Four main routes, all starting or ending at the Prithvi Narayan Campus near the north end of the bazaar, go to Lakeside (via Mahendra Pul), Damside (via Chipledhunga), Chhorepatan (via Mustang Chowk) and Mahendra Cave. Catch buses in Damside near the *German Bakery* and at various points in Lakeside.

Taxis wait at several spots in Lakeside and Damside, but it's usually easier to have your innkeeper call one for you. Some taxis are metered, but drivers are very reluctant to use them – expect to bargain if you're going to any standard tourist destination. For day trips around the valley it might make sense to hire a taxi for the day, which should cost about $20 including petrol (more for overnights or longer journeys) – again, let someone at your guest house do the negotiations. Older, more beat-up **shared taxis** ply fixed routes between major points in the bazaar the same way that tempos do in Kathmandu; they cost just a few rupees per person.

A **bicycle**, rentable all over Lakeside and Damside, multiplies your mobility and flexibility tremendously. One-speed bikes go for about Rs50 a day. A **mountain bike** with gears is more practical for exploring the valley, which has a lot of slopes to it, although the ones for rent on the street aren't very good – for better quality, try Himalayan Mountain Bikes For speedier zipping around the valley, consider renting a **motorcycle**, available from many Lakeside outlets for about Rs300 a day (not including fuel).

Phewa Tal (Phewa Lake)

Visitors to Pokhara typically spend most of their time within arm's reach of apple pie, which means staying close to **Phewa Tal**. This is not fertile territory for cultural interaction, but a number of activities on the lake will at least help you to work off the calories. According to a local **legend**, the lake covers the area of a once-prosperous valley,

---

The telephone code for Pokhara is ☎061..

NAUTICAL PURSUITS

Boating (or just floating) on Phewa Tal is the easiest way to get away from the business of getting away from it all. Oversized **rowing boats** (*dungaa*), which hold six easily, can be rented all along the eastern shore. Prices are supposed to be fixed at Rs130 per hour or Rs350 per day, but "discounts" are possible, especially at Damside. If you've got a specific destination in mind, it might work out better to hire a boatman to take you there for a fixed price. Fibreglass **sailboats**, available from *Hotel Fewa* and from a couple of freelances nearby, cost Rs250 per hour or Rs1200 per day; wooden ones are somewhat less. At least one operator rents pedalos (Rs200 per hour), and some rafting companies (see p.273) rent out **kayaks** for Rs500–800 a day. Motorized boats aren't allowed on the lake – the tourist industry, to its credit, has reached a fairly firm consensus on that.

Swimming is best done from a boat, as much of the shore is muddy and choked with water hyacinths, and bacteria counts are sometimes unhealthy due to sewage seeping from a couple of prominent Lakeside hotels and from the police camp just south of Basundhara Park. That said, Phewa Tal's water is fairly clean for a subtropical lake, largely because the monsoon rains flush it out each year. The stuff floating on the surface at certain times of year is pollen, not sewage (which it resembles when the wind balls it up).

Stay away from the dam area, as the **current** is deceptively strong – an Irish woman drowned in 1996 when her boat capsized near the dam and she was sucked over the edge. The shore around the Royal Palace is off-limits, and if you see gesticulating security guards, you're too close.

An obvious first destination is **Tal Barahi**, the island shrine located a few hundred metres offshore from the palace. While the temple itself is modern and not much to look at, it's a busy spot on Saturdays, when the lake goddess exacts a steady tribute of blood sacrifices. If that doesn't put you off your lunch, the island makes a fine place for a picnic. During the spring wedding months you might find yourself caught up in a flotilla of merrymakers headed for the island, where music, dancing and *raksi*-drinking go on until all hours.

From the island it's about the same distance again to the far shore which, with dense jungle, manic monkeys and few places to put ashore, is most easily observed from the water. If you want to walk around on the other side, make for **Anadu**, the diffuse Gurung village that covers the hillside directly opposite Lakeside, twenty to thirty minutes' row from the palace. Food is available from a few lakeside establishments. For some real exercise, you could row to the farthest (northwest) end of the lake and up the meandering Harpan Khola.

whose inhabitants one day scorned a wandering beggar. Finding only one sympathetic woman, the beggar warned her of an impending flood: as the woman and her family fled to higher ground, a torrent roared down from the mountains and submerged the town – the "beggar" having been none other than the goddess Barahi Bhagwati. The woman's descendants settled beside the new lake and erected the island shrine of **Tal Barahi**; for local innkeepers and restaurateurs, who've done rather well out of the lake, a few alms at her shrine still don't go amiss.

The other, geological explanation is that the entire Pokhara Valley, like the Kathmandu Valley, was submerged about 200,000 years ago when the fast-rising Mahabharat Lek dammed up the Seti River. Over time, the Seti eroded an ever-deeper outlet, lowering the water level and leaving Phewa Tal and several smaller lakes as remnants. Phewa was further enlarged by the installation of **Pardi Dam** in 1967, which brought electricity and irrigation to the valley, and gave Damside its name.

Like most Himalayan features, Phewa Tal is geologically very young and fast-changing, and may prove to be a short-lived phenomenon. Its watershed is steep and highly prone to erosion (a process that's hastened by agriculture and deforestation), so the streams that feed it carry massive quantities of suspended **sediments**. When the sediments reach the lake, they settle out: the Harpan Khola, the lake's main tributary, has already deposited a "delta" that covers the western third of the lake's former surface. Year by year, farmers who lost land to the dam are reclaiming it as rice paddy. Their gain will eventually be Lakeside's loss, for some experts are predicting that siltation will fill up the lake in as little as thirty years.

Lakeside (Baidam)

Next to eating, promenading along **Lakeside**'s pipal-shaded main drag is the favourite pastime in Pokhara. It's a pleasant enough stroll in parts, but new construction in this area (known locally as **Baidam**) has largely spoiled its former rural character: they've literally paved paradise here. Shops and restaurants now crowd together so closely on the main strip that they effectively block off any lake views between the Royal Palace and the campground. It's actually illegal to build commercial structures along the lake side of the road, and these buildings are all theoretically under a demolition order, but the government has never shown the political will to enforce the law, and the buildings are now so numerous and valuable that it's hard to imagine the order ever being carried out.

Basundhara Park, Lakeside's biggest patch of open space, is the venue for the annual **Annapurna Festival** (usually held in April), a cultural event featuring music, dance and food, and for occasional other commercial expos. At other times it's quiet and not very interesting, though it has extensive shoreline. The main reason to enter it is to get to the **rope ferry** that leads across this narrow neck of the lake to *Fish Tail Lodge*. You don't have to be staying there to go across and have a look.

Further north at **Gauri Ghat**, where the Lakeside strip passes at its closest to the lake, a set of steps leads from a leafy *chautaara* down to a rocky outcrop marked by a *linga* shrine. Midway along the strip sits Ratna Mandir, the winter **Royal Palace**, a definite no-go area during the king's residence each winter or early spring. (Hima Griya, further south, is an annex of the palace reserved for guests and lesser royals.) At the palace's northern edge, a road leads down to the lake at a shady spot known as **Barahi Tol**, where Nepalis and visiting Indians often go to escape the Western-dominated strip, and the main launching site for boats to Tal Barahi.

Numerous other lanes head back away from the lake into what was until recently lush farmland. The farmers have now all sold out to developers and speculators, although many of the family-run guest houses retain their traditional vegetable plots, sugar-loaf haystacks and banana-palm borders. Traditional thatched oval houses – designed to be warm in winter and cool in summer – have almost all been replaced by rectangular concrete ones. North of Lakeside in the area known as **Khahare**, the lake again becomes visible from the main road, which reverts to a dirt track that can be followed along the less developed northern shore. Side trails lead up to Sarangkot (p.277) from there.

Damside (Pardi)

In **Damside** (**Pardi**), go for mountain views – the classic scene, captured in a ubiquitous Ministry of Tourism poster, can be viewed from a small Vishnu shrine in the triangle of land between the spillway and the lake.

Pardi Dam is of no intrinsic interest, and unfortunately you can't walk across it, but from the footbridge that crosses the Pardi Khola, downstream, trails lead south to Devin's Fall (see p.285) or up the ridge to the west for phenomenal views. A pukka but sometimes smelly path connects Damside with Lakeside, going from the new tourist information centre to Basundhara Park – it's not really a walk you'd do for pleasure, but it chops a bit of the distance off getting to Lakeside restaurants.

Pokhara Bazaar

Until being linked to the outside world by the Prithvi Highway in 1973, **Pokhara Bazaar** was a small Newar market town along the trade route from Butwal to Mustang.

The original bazaar has now grown into a city of 100,000, with traffic, pollution and all the rest, yet it still rests lightly on the land – natural wonders are always near to hand.

The northern bazaar

Most of Pokhara was destroyed in a fire in 1949, but remnants of the original Newar quarter can still be seen in the **Purano Bazaar**, which runs from Bhimsen Tol up to Bag Bazaar. Perched on a hillock in the middle of this area you'll find the **Bindyabasini Mandir**, Pokhara's main cultural attraction, a quiet temple complex more noteworthy for its sweeping mountain views than its collection of shrines. The featured deity, Bindyabasini, is an incarnation of Kali, the mother goddess in her bloodthirsty aspect, who is carved from a *shaligram* stone (see p.290). Animal sacrifices are common at this temple, particularly on Saturdays and the ninth day of Dasain in October. Bindyabasini has a reputation as a bit of a prima donna: in one celebrated incident, her stone image began to sweat mysteriously, causing such a panic that the late King Tribhuwan had to order special rites to pacify the goddess. The 1949 fire allegedly started here, when an offering burned out of control.

Tucked away in one corner of the Prithvi Narayan Campus at the northeastern part of town, the **Annapurna Regional Museum** (daily except Sat 9am–12.30pm & 1.30–4pm; free) offers a feeble treatment of Nepal's natural history that's really meant for local schoolkids. The display of Himalayan butterflies is genuinely interesting, though, and useful for identifying some of the many species seen in the Pokhara area. An adjacent **information centre**, maintained by the Annapurna Conservation Area Project, contains some enlightening exhibits about geology and culture in the ACAP area – it's a pity it's way out here.

Along the Seti River

Immediately east of town lies the dramatic, sometimes almost invisibly narrow **Seti River gorge**, where the abrasive torrent has cut like acid though the valley's soft sediments. One of the best places to see it, amazingly, is just north of the ugly main bus park. Walk north past Shanti Ban Batika, a park/picnic spot that's slowly reverting to jungle, then make a right down a path. The river emerges from its narrow confines for about 1km here to produce a sizable canyon, incongruously close to the bazaar, from which sand and gravel are extracted and carried up by porters for use in local construction. From here you can walk upstream to where the Seti's churning waters emerge from a dark, mossy, inaccessible ravine, or downstream to where they plunge back into another similar chasm (certain death if you slip). Several of Pokhara's bridges (*pul*), including Mahendra Pul, K. I. Singh Pul and the footbridge east of the airport, provide top-down views of some of the narrowest parts of the gorge.

Two nearby museums are definitely worth visiting if you're in the area. The **Pokhara Museum** (daily except Tues 10am–5pm, Friday closes at 3pm; Rs5), located south of Mahendra Pul, is small but quite well done, with informative displays and commentary on Nepalese ethnic groups, rites, customs, crafts, trade and costumes. The similarly small **Tamu Kohibo Museum** (irregular hours; Rs20), dedicated to Gurung culture and shamanic traditions, gives an intriguing introduction to a potentially esoteric subject without overloading the visitor. Its distinctive building, which looks like a garlic bulb split into four equal cloves, overlooks the Seti canyon on its east side, and is easily spotted from just about anywhere in the canyon area.

Other sights

Just west of Prithvi Chowk hides the smallest and least interesting of Pokhara's three former Tibetan refugee camps (see p.280). **Paljorling**, shown on some maps as the **Tibetan Handicrafts Centre**, is now not so much a community as a factory with on-site housing. The emphasis is on retail sales, and its inhabitants work over any for-

Longer day trips and overnights from Pokhara are covered in "The Pokhara Valley", p.276..

eigners who inadvertently fall into their web. There's little reason to actually enter the compound, as handicrafts are sold in shops along the main road outside.

When it's completed, the **International Mountaineering Museum** should make a worthwhile destination in the extreme southern end of the bazaar. It's supposed to house models of famous peaks, mannequins of famous climbers, an historical exhibit of mountaineering equipment, and information on the geology, flora and fauna of the Himalaya and other ranges. It's an ambitious project, and there is some doubt as to whether the Nepal Mountaineering Association can pull it off.

Accommodation

Pokhara is glutted with cheap and moderately priced **accommodation**. Scores of small lodges have been built in recent years by ex-Gurkhas and Thakalis (the enterprising innkeepers of the trekking region north of Pokhara), but things are getting way out of hand. At any given time there seem to be a dozen concrete behemoths in the pipeline, and every small lodge owner has a scheme to replace his perfectly nice building with an ugly new one. Even the places that don't redevelop often have to share the noise and dust of nearby construction, and then get their views blocked by taller neighbours. The result is that the homely establishments that brought travellers here in the first place are being steadily edged out, and the lakeside accommodation districts are going the way of Goa and Ko Samui. You have to wonder where it's all going to end. A shake-out seems inevitable: the desperation of the touts at the bus park shows how bad it's already got, and sad to say, it won't get any better until guest houses start going under.

But looking on the bright side, you'll never have any trouble finding a room. And given the oversupply in the low and middle price ranges, you'll seldom have to pay the published rate, even in high season. Indeed, Pokhara offers the cheapest hot-water lodgings in Nepal, as well as some of the friendliest – most **budget guest houses** are small and family-run, and some are still like little farmhouses. The more **expensive hotels** are a bit riskier, because if you're not careful you can end up in a real clunker. They're usually comfortable enough, but are often big and soulless, and lack the personal touch of the smaller places.

Just about all independent travellers stay in **Lakeside** or **Damside**. Far removed from the din of the bazaar, overlooking the lake and peaks, and awash with Western food and comforts, both areas certainly offer a numbingly easy existence. If you're looking to get away from other tourists, however, consider staying in **Bangladi** or **Anadu**, or in one of the outlying destinations described later, such as Begnas Tal or Sarangkot.

ROOM PRICE SCALES

Lodging prices change from season to season, so it would be misleading to quote exact prices in a guidebook. Instead, all guest houses and hotels have been price-graded according to the scale below, which is based on the price of the cheapest double room in high season. Codes prefixed by B denote the cost of the cheapest room with attached bathroom, and those prefixed by AC refer to air-conditioned rooms. See p.39 for a fuller explanation.

① Less than Rs140   ⑤ $8–12
   ($2 if quoted in US$) ⑥ $12–20
② Rs140–200 ($2–3)   ⑦ $20–40
③ Rs200–350 ($3–5)   ⑧ $40–75
④ Rs350–550 ($5–8)   ⑨ Over $75

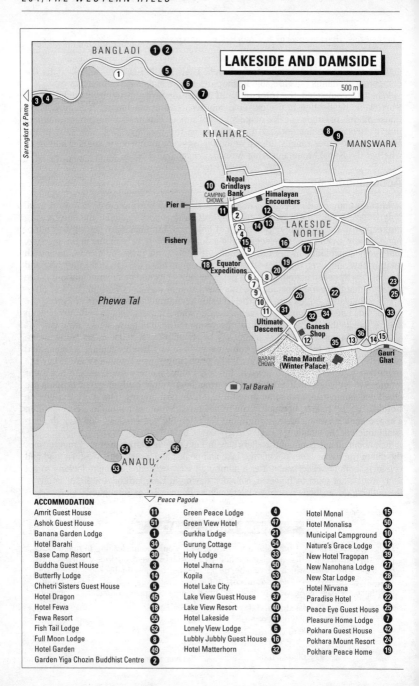

LAKESIDE AND DAMSIDE

0 ——————— 500 m

BANGLADI

KHAHARE

MANSWARA

Sarangkot & Pame

Nepal Grindlays Bank

CAMPING CHOWK

Himalayan Encounters

Pier

LAKESIDE NORTH

Fishery

Phewa Tal

Equator Expeditions

Ultimate Descents

Ganesh Shop

BARAHI CHOWK

Ratna Mandir (Winter Palace)

Gauri Ghat

Tal Barahi

ANADU

Peace Pagoda

ACCOMMODATION

Amrit Guest House	⑪	Green Peace Lodge ④
Ashok Guest House	㊿①	Green View Hotel ㊼
Banana Garden Lodge	①	Gurkha Lodge ㉑
Hotel Barahi	㉞	Gurung Cottage ㊴
Base Camp Resort	㉚	Holy Lodge ㉝
Buddha Guest House	③	Hotel Jharna ㊿
Butterfly Lodge	⑭	Kopila ㊾③
Chhetri Sisters Guest House	⑤	Hotel Lake City ㊹
Hotel Dragon	㊺	Lake View Guest House ㊲
Hotel Fewa	⑱	Lake View Resort ㊵
Fewa Resort	㊽⑤	Hotel Lakeside ㊶
Fish Tail Lodge	㊼②	Lonely View Lodge ⑥
Full Moon Lodge	⑧	Lubbly Jubbly Guest House ⑯
Hotel Garden	㊾	Hotel Matterhorn ㉜
Garden Yiga Chozin Buddhist Centre	②	

Hotel Monal	⑮
Hotel Monalisa	㊿
Municipal Campground	⑩
Nature's Grace Lodge	⑫
New Hotel Tragopan	㊴
New Nanohana Lodge	㉗
New Star Lodge	㉘
Hotel Nirvana	㊱
Paradise Hotel	㉒
Peace Eye Guest House	㉕
Pleasure Home Lodge	⑦
Pokhara Guest House	㊷
Pokhara Mount Resort	㉔
Pokhara Peace Home	⑲

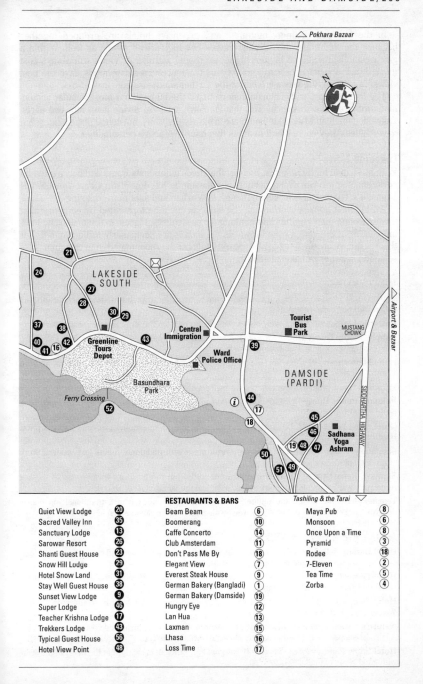

Pokhara Bazaar

LAKESIDE
SOUTH

Tourist
Bus
Park

MUSTANG
CHOWK

Central
Immigration

Greenline
Tours
Depot

Ward
Police Office

DAMSIDE
(PARDI)

Basundhara
Park

Ferry Crossing

Sadhana
Yoga
Ashram

Airport & Bazaar

SIDDHARTHA HIGHWAY

Tashiling & the Tarai

Quiet View Lodge	20	**RESTAURANTS & BARS**	
Sacred Valley Inn	35	Beam Beam	6
Sanctuary Lodge	13	Boomerang	10
Sarowar Resort	26	Caffe Concerto	14
Shanti Guest House	23	Club Amsterdam	11
Snow Hill Lodge	29	Don't Pass Me By	18
Hotel Snow Land	31	Elegant View	7
Stay Well Guest House	38	Everest Steak House	9
Sunset View Lodge	9	German Bakery (Bangladi)	1
Super Lodge	46	German Bakery (Damside)	19
Teacher Krishna Lodge	17	Hungry Eye	12
Trekkers Lodge	43	Lan Hua	13
Typical Guest House	56	Laxman	15
Hotel View Point	48	Lhasa	16
		Loss Time	17

Maya Pub	8
Monsoon	6
Once Upon a Time	8
Pyramid	3
Rodee	18
7-Eleven	2
Tea Time	5
Zorba	4

In the following listings, midrange and expensive hotels are grouped together because the midrange ones usually have a few high-priced rooms as well. Within a given establishment, the bigger, higher-up rooms with better views will always cost more; but it doesn't necessarily follow that the more expensive hotels have the best views. In general, the views are better the further south you go.

The listings start with Lakeside, since that's the biggest and most popular accommodation area. It's so big, in fact, that it makes sense to divide it up into two parts. Lakeside North and Lakeside South are arbitrary divisions, not actual place names, but nevertheless they correspond to areas that have distinctive personalities.

Lakeside North

With its strip of high-rise guest houses, thatched-roofed restaurants and corrugated-tin curio shacks, the **northern** portion of Lakeside is like Robinson Crusoe meets Las Vegas. It's Thamel all over again, though less urban and a lot more relaxing.

Avoid guest houses overlooking the strip, as you'll be tormented by early-morning buses revving their engines and honking for passengers. Places on the main road leading east from the campground towards the bazaar are particularly to be avoided. For this reason, relatively few higher-priced hotels can be recommended in this area – the selection is better in Lakeside South.

INEXPENSIVE

Amrit Guest House (☎24401). If you really want to be on the strip, this is a relatively cheap, quiet option with big, clean rooms. B④.

Butterfly Lodge (☎22892). Lovely big garden, sheltered from the strip. Simple rooms. ③/B④.

Lubbly Jubbly Guest House (☎22881). A small but shady banana garden and a little café make this place quite sociable. Good value. ③/B④.

Hotel Matterhorn (☎26734). Sort of unfinished-looking, but not bad, and the price is right for such a central location. ②.

Paradise Hotel (☎26983). Decent rooms, small garden seating area, views. ③/B③.

Pokhara Peace Home (☎23205). Quiet, restful grounds and big rooms on a less developed back lane. ③/B④.

Quiet View Lodge (☎22612). Very small, traditional place – simple, but you can't beat the price. Handy location for nightlife. ②.

Sanctuary Lodge (no phone). Tiny family-run place with traditional rooms and gardens. Very cheap for a place so close to the strip. ②.

Sarowar Resort (☎23037). Undistinguished facilities, but the premises include one of the last remaining oval Baahun farmhouses in Lakeside, and the family is nice. ③/B④.

Teacher Krishna Lodge (no phone). Farmhouse accommodation in a traditional old house: delightful but spartan, and it probably won't withstand modernization much longer. ①.

MIDRANGE AND EXPENSIVE

Hotel Barahi (☎21879, fax 22659). Gorgeous grounds, surprisingly peaceful for such a central location. Tennis on a rather uneven court. B⑦/AC⑧.

Hotel Fewa (☎20151). Gorgeous setting right on the lake, nice screened veranda with views, great restaurant (*Mike's*); rooms are only so-so for the price. B⑦.

Hotel Monal (☎21459, fax 23265). Good facilities, adequately set back from the strip. Nepali-Western management. B⑥.

Nature's Grace Lodge (☎20793; *cws@mos.com.np*). Cosy, nicely furnished rooms; in-house pub. All profits support a charity that sets up childcare facilities. ④/B⑤.

Hotel Snow Land (☎20384; *Snowland@mos.com.np*). Efficient place right in the heart of the strip, with good views of the lake. B⑦/AC⑧.

Lakeside South

Things get quieter and less Disneyesque **south** of the Royal Palace. You can actually see the lake from the strip, and the mountain views are better, too. The flip side of all this is that the choice of restaurants, bars and shops isn't as great, so you may find yourself trekking up to Lakeside North a couple of times a day.

INEXPENSIVE

Holy Lodge (☎22094). Big, leafy garden, thatch seating area with fireplace in winter. Clean rooms; the cheap ones are in a rustic old building. ①/B③.

Hotel Lakeside (☎20073; *travel@magnific.mos.com.np*). Nice location and leafy, secluded grounds. Facilities are declining a bit, but that's reflected in the price. B④–⑥.

Lake View Guest House (☎23980). Basic rooms, wee garden, decent views from roof. B③.

New Star Lodge (☎22478). Older building with simple rooms in a relatively uncommercialized area. ①.

Hotel Nirvana (☎23332, fax 23736). Huge, very clean rooms and spacious balconies in a rather palatial building. Nepali-Western management. ③/B④–⑥.

Peace Eye Guest House (no phone). Funky, family-run place with a shady garden. B③.

Sacred Valley Inn (☎23384). Very clean, nice balconies with views, optional home-cooked dinners with family. Nepali-Western management. ③/B④–⑥.

Shanti Guest House (☎22687). Small garden, modest facilities, friendly. Good little library. ②/B④.

Snow Hill Lodge (☎22685). Pleasant sanctuary in a quiet part of the strip. B④–⑤.

Stay Well Guest House (☎22624). Small, friendly and quiet, with a view from the roof. Cute little castle of a building. B④–⑥.

MIDRANGE AND EXPENSIVE

Base Camp Resort (☎21226; *basecamp@bcr.mos.com.np*). For this price there ought to be better grounds, but the rooms are quite swish. AC⑧–⑨.

Fish Tail Lodge (Kathmandu office: ☎221711; *fishtail@lodge.mos.com.np*). Lakeside's original deluxe hotel has gone a little downhill, but it still has fabulous grounds and an unrivalled view of the lake and the classic profile of the mountains behind. Access by rope ferry. B⑨.

Gurkha Lodge (☎20798). Gardening buffs will love this place, tucked down a long Baidam lane, run by an ex-Gurkha and his English wife. Rustic stone thatched bungalows. B⑥.

Lake View Resort (☎23254; *Lakeview@Resort.mos.com.np*). Nice grounds, great location right across from the lake, but a tad run-down. ⑥/B⑧.

New Nanohana Lodge (☎22478). Spotless rooms, pleasant big balconies. Friendly management. B④–⑥.

Pokhara Guest House (☎21228). Beautiful big rooms, attentive service, views from roof. B⑥.

Pokhara Mount Resort (☎ & fax 22465). Modest place with pleasant small grounds. Not a great location, but good value for air-conditioned rooms. B⑦/AC⑦.

Trekkers Lodge (☎21458). Decent facilities and pleasant garden at the quiet southern end of Lakeside. B⑤.

Khahare, Bangladi and beyond

The area north of Camping Chowk (the main crossroads near the municipal campground) is well-known to long-termers, hippies, Israelis and other bargain-hunters. It's also convenient if you're trekking directly into Lakeside, since it's the first lodging area you'll come to. **Khahare**, the more southerly part of this area, is sort of a suburb of Lakeside – quieter and less commercialized, but still within its sphere of influence. **Bangladi**, further north, preserves some of the undeveloped ambience of old, with simpler facilities and mostly unmolested views of the lake. A few lodges in the farm country beyond Bangladi provide even more rural settings.

Taxis can get reasonably close to any of the guest houses listed below, but they'll charge more than the standard fare to Lakeside.

INEXPENSIVE

Banana Garden Lodge (☎21880). Lovely gardens and outside seating, though the place is losing its views to new construction. Very popular, hence often full. Located above the last pick-up point for tourist buses. ②.

Buddha Guest House (no phone). Small family operation with tidy rooms and magnificent views of the lake and surrounding countryside. Hot water by the bucket only. ②.

Chhetri Sisters Guest House (☎24066; *sisters3@cnet.wlink.com.np*). The eponymous sisters run a happening little guest house (often full) that is command central for everything to do with trekking for women. No garden, but nice views of the lake from a small restaurant. ③/B④.

Garden Yiga Chozin Buddhist Centre (☎22923; *gyc@mos.com.np*). This is the natural place to stay if you're interested in doing a meditation course (see p.274), but you don't have to be participating to take a room in this peaceful retreat centre. ③.

Green Peace Lodge (no phone). Basic but very friendly, right by the lake. Not to be confused with *Hotel Green Peace*, which is further south in the main part of Lakeside. ②.

Lonely View Lodge (☎26994). A nice combination of rural location and proximity to town. Beautiful garden/orchard, excellent views, friendly family, cool atmosphere. ②.

Maya Devi Village (no phone). The last word in seclusion: located at the extreme northern end of the lake, it's 3km beyond Camping Chowk (way off the map). Delightful little thatched bungalows, no electricity, set meals. Nepali-Western management. ③.

Pleasure Home Lodge (no phone). Big rooms, lake views, small garden and the aptly named *Mellow Fellow* restaurant. ②.

Sunset View Lodge (☎23025). Basic rooms (hot water by the bucket), lush location with great views overlooking Baidam and the lake. It's a bit of a hike to food or drink. ②.

MIDRANGE

Full Moon Lodge (☎21511). A unique place in an above-it-all location (access by a steep set of steps). The garden area is littered with Hindu shrines, statues and unusual touches. Good-sized rooms. ④/B⑦.

Damside

Closer to the bazaar and the highway, **Damside** feels more urban than Lakeside. The mountain views are better, but it's questionable whether they compensate for the ugly foreground and lack of greenery. There's also less tourist razzmatazz than in Lakeside, making the streets quieter and the neighbourhood more residential, but the choice of restaurants and shops is correspondingly limited. For some reason, Damside is very popular with Japanese tourists, which is an interesting cultural feature in itself.

INEXPENSIVE

Ashok Guest House (☎20374). Garden seating, and a good view of the lake and mountains from the roof. There are only a few of the cheap rooms. ②/B⑤.

Hotel Garden (☎20870). Spacious, with a good location, greenery and view. ②/B④–⑤.

Green View Hotel (☎21844). Well-managed place, with a secluded, very flowery garden and a roof view. The cheap rooms are in an older wing. ①/B③.

Hotel Lake City (☎21341; *lakecity@rolake.mos.com.np*). Clean, with well-laid-out grounds, lawn seating and a good view from the roof. Good in-house restaurant. Nepali-Western management. Profits go to a Dutch charity doing education work in Nepal. B③–⑤.

Super Lodge (☎21861). Pretty basic, but cheap. There's a view, but it's hemmed in by new construction. ①/B③.

Hotel View Point (☎21787). Standard facilities, but a good view from roof. B③.

MIDRANGE AND EXPENSIVE

Hotel Dragon (☎22630; *dragon@mos.com.np*). Pretty garden with good views. Air-conditioned rooms with Tibetan furnishings. AC⑧.

Hotel Jharna (☎21925). Ideal location: overlooking the lake with the mountains behind. The lakeside rooms are the more expensive ones, of course, but the views from them are just stunning. B④–⑤.

Hotel Monalisa (☎ & fax 20863). Equally good location, but a bit more upmarket than the *Jharna*. B⑤–⑦.

New Hotel Tragopan (☎21708, fax 23027). Ugly location, but rooms come with air-conditioning and TV, and there's a small pool. AC⑦.

Across the lake: Anadu

Anadu, directly across the lake from Lakeside, is not one of Nepal's friendliest or best-kept villages, but there's a certain bohemian attraction to staying in a place that can only be reached by boat. (Actually, you can walk to Anadu from the highway on the other side of the ridge behind, but let's not spoil the illusion.) It's also an extremely peaceful place, well outside of the Lakeside mainstream yet not completely divorced from it. Furthermore, the views from here are better than they are from anywhere in Lakeside, the water is clean, and there's a great hike (to the Peace Pagoda) right out your back door.

If you're thinking of staying in one of the cheap places here, rent a boat and scout things out first, as new places may have sprung up. The nearest of the places listed here, the *Typical*, can be reached in about twenty minutes' rowing from the palace area of Lakeside.

Fewa Resort (☎27952, fax 24881; Kathmandu: ☎254123). Green, quiet and roomy, with a fair restaurant and excellent views. Free boat service. ⑤/B⑦.

Gurung Cottage (no phone). Awfully primitive (cold water and *daal bhaat* only), but certainly secluded. ①.

Kopila (☎28369). This is the clear winner among budget places here. awesome views, lovely shady grounds, good (though terribly slow) restaurant, hot water. Known for its full-moon parties, which sometimes get out of hand. Free boat service. B③.

Typical Guest House (☎26978). Kind of dark and dingy, though not bad for food. Cold water only. Boat service available on demand (small charge). ②.

In the bazaar

Pokhara Bazaar has little going for it, and its lodgings, catering mainly to Nepali and Indian businessmen, charge more for less. Realistically, you'd have to be either really stuck or really antisocial to stay here. That said, the **Mahendra Pul** area, Pokhara's main commercial centre, certainly has got spark, and you can get almost anything you need here. A messier, more organic locale, **Prithvi Chowk** seethes with a tumultuous melange of Nepalis, Indians and Tibetans; it happens to have a couple of new and rather posh guest houses, but otherwise it's grotty and takes its cues from the nearby bus park. If need be, you can find plenty of cheaper places than the ones listed here.

Hotel Anand, Prithvi Chowk (☎20029). Rooftop garden and TV. B⑤.

Hotel Kailash, Mahendra Pul (☎21726). Clean, with a roof garden. ②/B③–⑤.

New Palace Hotel, Prithvi Chowk (☎22859). An Indian businessman's dream. ②/B③.

Other hotels

Several of Pokhara's older hotels are rather unhappily situated opposite the airport, relics of the days when the only way to get here was by air. The three newest, poshest ones are located south of the airport. See also the "Begnas Tal and Rupa Tal" section, p.283.

Bluebird Hotel, south of the airport (Kathmandu: ☎228833; *hotel@bluebird.mos.com.np*). Large five-star hotel affiliated with *Bluestar Hotel* in Kathmandu. Swimming pool. AC⑨.

Fulbari Resort Hotel, way south of the airport (Kathmandu: ☎527588; *dosm@fulbari.com*). Humongous complex overlooking the Seti gorge, with a nine-hole golf course, heated pool, six restaurants, etc. AC⑨.

New Hotel Crystal, opposite the airport (Kathmandu: ☎228561; *ajsthapit@mos.com.np*). Medium-sized hotel rather too close to the airport. Mediocre grounds, small pool. B⑦/AC⑨.

Rani Ban Retreat, on ridge across from Lakeside (☎22219; Kathmandu: ☎413873; *raniban@cnet.wlink.com.np*). Unparalleled views from the ridge west of the Peace Pagoda. Only four rooms, plus luxury tents. Reached by a half-hour walk from Devin's Fall. B⑧.

Shangri-La Village, south of the airport (☎22122; *hosangp@village.mos.com*). Deluxe bungalows, very nice grounds, pool and conference centre. AC⑨.

Camping

Pokhara's **municipal campground** is right by the lake and not half bad, and popular with overland groups. Charges are Rs20–40 per vehicle (depending on size), Rs40 per tent, Rs40 for a hot shower, and Rs40 to use the kitchen facilities. However, you'd probably be better off working out a deal with one of the guest houses along the back lanes of Lakeside.

Eating

Restaurants are everywhere in Pokhara, and food is a major preoccupation. Lakeside North, in particular, is one long trough of feeding opportunities. Eating also sets the social agenda: there's not much nightlife after around 10.30pm, but the congenial restaurants and cafés around the lake are easy places to make friends and find trekking partners. Candlelight (often imposed by load-shedding) adds to the romance. Most tourist restaurants boast a more or less standard menu, featuring an implausible selection of improvised **non-Nepali** dishes and local fish prepared umpteen different ways. The recipes are very formulaic, since Nepali cooks all receive the same training and copy each other shamelessly; the better restaurants, sad to say, are generally run by Westerners. Still, even if what you get doesn't bear much resemblance to what you ordered, it'll probably taste pretty good – especially after a couple of weeks on the trail.

If pseudo-Western food gets you down, many restaurants do set **Nepali** meals and some pretty good **Indian** dishes. For something much cheaper, try one of the myriad **momo** shacks, where locals eat. Watch out for the **juice** sellers, though: they'll charge whatever they think they can get, and dilute the juice with (unsafe) water and sugar behind a curtain.

Prices are comparable to those in Kathmandu's Thamel area. Restaurants described here as cheap will charge less than Rs150 per person for a full dinner, not including alcohol (proportionately less for breakfast or lunch). Inexpensive restaurants will run to Rs150–250, moderately priced ones Rs250–500.

Lakeside North

Boomerang. Great for breakfast or an afternoon snack: seating under umbrellas and thatched pavilions on a vast lawn sloping down to the lake. Children's playground. Inexpensive.

Elegant View. Very comfortable for outdoor seating, but also nice indoors after dark. Good for breakfasts, bakery items and Indian food. Inexpensive.

Everest Steak House. Lively rooftop place serving beef in every conceivable form; the huge garden is pleasant for daytime seating. Inexpensive.

Hungry Eye. A pricier, tour-group version of the other standard-menu restaurants on the strip, with a nightly culture show. Reliable food, good desserts and ice cream. Moderate.

Little Tibetan Tea Garden. A good range of Tibetan food, along with the usual Western stuff, in a lovely little bamboo grove next to Himalayan Encounters. Cheap.

Maya Pub. Popular mainstream restaurant/bar serving good soups, pastas, sizzlers and vegetarian dishes. Inexpensive to moderate.

Mike's. The ultimate tranquil spot, literally right beside the lake at the *Hotel Fewa*. Like the related Kathmandu restaurant of the same name, it's best for breakfast or lunch: it serves authentic American-style *huevos*, waffles, eggs benedict, etc. Good margaritas, too. Moderate.

Monsoon. Excellent Indian, Nepali and Continental dishes, sophisticated atmosphere. Moderate.

Moondance. The epicentre of Lakeside eating, at the Ganesh Shop, with reliable food (especially pizza), a great atmosphere, and of course location, location, location. Inexpensive to moderate.

Once Upon a Time. Another formulaic but very popular establishment with a fun, island-castaway decor. The food is interchangeable with that of the neighbouring *Maya Pub*. Inexpensive to moderate.

Pyramid. All-rounder specializing in thin-crust pizza and crepes. Inexpensive.

Snow Land. At the *Hotel Snow Leopard*. Decent Indian food, but not much atmosphere. Inexpensive.

Tea Time. One of Lakeside's original bamboo joints, good for daytime people-watching, drinks and snacks. Inexpensive.

Zorba. Makes a welcome change from the bamboo warehouses: a mellower, more mature atmosphere and Swiss/Austrian specialities that avoid the sameness of so many of Lakeside's restaurants. Moderate.

Lakeside South

Caffe Concerto. Authentic pizza, lasagne, gnocchi and other Italian dishes (their *tiramisu* is the real McCoy), tolerable wine. Mellow atmosphere. Videos banished to a back room. Inexpensive to moderate.

Lan Hua. Barely adequate Chinese food, although the tofu is quite good. Inexpensive.

Laxman. Large indoor/outdoor hangout, one of the pioneers of the cosy-wicker decor now so prevalent around Lakeside. Steaks, pastas, serious cakes. Pool and snooker tables. Inexpensive.

Lhasa. Good range of Tibetan specialities, also excellent Indian food. Monotonous music. Inexpensive.

Khahare and Bangladi

German Bakery. Spectacular setting for breakfast: seating under thatch pavilions overlooking the lake on two sides. Cheap.

Damside

Damside's guest houses tend to have their own self-contained restaurants, so there are fewer separate eating places to recommend.

Don't Pass Me By. Really lovely patio seating right beside the lake. Competent all-round food, excellent for breakfast. Cheap to inexpensive.

German Bakery. Tolerable croissants and wholegrain bread, and Damside's premier cake display. Cheap.

New Hotel Tragopan. Decent North Indian food in a vaguely upscale setting. Inexpensive to moderately priced.

Loss Time. Passable all-rounder, better for Indian food. Cheap to inexpensive.

Rodee. Next door to *Don't Pass Me By*, and just as nice. Cheap to inexpensive.

Rose. Great garden seating (unusual for Damside), nightly menu featuring Continental (especially Dutch) specialities. Shares premises with *Hotel Lake City*. Inexpensive to moderate.

Pokhara Bazaar

Indian traders have moved in on Pokhara Bazaar, as they have wherever there's commercial potential, and Indian restaurants are a welcome result of their presence. You'll find several serviceable eateries around the northwest corner of Prithvi Chowk (west of the public bus park), and a few others in Mahendra Pul and Chipledhunga. One or two greasy spoons near the Paljorling entrance do Tibetan food.

Nightlife

While nightlife around Pokhara usually just means a second helping of pie, a good way to break the routine is to catch a **culture show**. The *Hungry Eye* and a few other tourist restaurants put on free dinner music performances by local folk troupes. *Hotel Dragon* and *Fish Tail Lodge* host more elaborate music and dance programmes nightly in the high season. Tickets cost Rs100–200 and are available through agents.

Lakeside's **bars** regularly push back the usual 10pm bedtime barrier, at least during the high season. Their turnover rate is high, but the following were still raving as this book went to press.

Beam Beam. Laid-back inside/outside affair with a nice belly-up bar. Occasional live music.

Club Amsterdam. Well-stocked bar, pool table, satellite TV above the bar…all the trappings of a college-town bar back home.

Moondance Pub. A lively pub with eclectic music that centres around pool tables, darts and carom boards. The restaurant is good for quieter after-dinner drinks.

7-Eleven. Cheesy lounge with authentic *ghazal* entertainment, popular with local Nepalis and visiting Indians.

Shopping

Shopping is still a mainly outdoor activity in Lakeside and Damside, where laid-back curio stalls make a welcome change from the hard-driving salesmen of Kathmandu, even if their prices and selection don't quite compare. Local specialities include **batiks**, wooden **flasks**, **dolls** in ethnic dress and fossil-bearing **shaligram** stones from the Kali Gandaki. Hand-stitched **wall hangings** in simple Tibetan designs have been produced for the tourist market, but are attractive nonetheless. Persuasive Tibetans peddle their wares in Lakeside's cafés, but these aren't produced locally, and **carpets** are best purchased at the Tibetan villages. Hand-knitted **woollen** sweaters, socks and such aren't of very good quality here, but may fit the bill for trekking. Kashmiris have colonized Lakeside, as they have Thamel, with boutiques touting "Asian" art: mainly high-priced carpets and cheap **papier-mâché** and soapstone widgets. Other than that, you'll find the usual range of tourist bait, most of it imported from Kathmandu: ritual masks, *thangka*, embroidered T-shirts (wear that trek!), cloth bags and hippie clothes. Stalls along the strip opposite the palace are extremely competitive.

The **bookshops** and stalls around Lakeside and Damside are individually small, but collectively they can muster a good selection. Pokhara's second-hand market is very good.

Activities

Pokhara has emerged as the outdoor-recreation capital of Nepal. Something like 80 percent of all trekking permits are issued for the Annapurna region, and an increasing number of travellers are coming here for rafting, kayaking and mountain-biking. Pokhara is also a nice setting for meditation or yoga studies, though the options here are more limited than in the Kathmandu Valley.

Trekking

There are any number of ways to get to the start of a **trek** out of Pokhara. Most people, being in a hurry to get up into the mountains, take a taxi to **Suikhet (Phedi)**, **Naya Pul** or **Beni**. The fare to Naya Pul – the most popular gateway – should be about Rs500. Cheaper (but much slower and more dangerous) local buses depart hourly from the Baglung bus park. You can also enter the region by hiking straight in from Lakeside, via **Sarangkot** (see p.277), or by hiring someone to row you across the lake and upriver to a point below Naudaada. Those trekking the Annapurna Circuit typically start at Besisahar, reached by taking a bus to **Dumre** (on the way to Kathmandu), from where trucks shuttle the rest of the way; an alternative trailhead is **Begnas Tal**, reached by taxi or local bus from Chipledhunga in the bazaar.

Recommending **trekking agencies** in Pokhara is even riskier than in Kathmandu. Anyhow, you don't need an agency to trek the Annapurna region unless you're doing something unorthodox – one company that organizes Annapurna-area treks off the teahouse routes is Wayfarers, with an office in Damside (☎24052; *wayfarer@mos.com.np*). Trekking **guides** and **porters** can be hired through almost any trekking agency, guest house or equipment shop. Three Sisters Adventure Trekking, operating out of the *Chhetri Sisters Guest House* (☎24066; *sisters3@cnet.wlink.com.np*), can arrange female guides and porters. See "Listings", below, for information on the local Central Immigration office, and Chapter Seven for full details on trekking preparations and routes. To find a **trekking partner** you could put up messages at any of the Lakeside restaurant notice boards, but don't worry too much if you don't hook up with anyone before you leave – you'll meet tons of people as soon as you start walking.

Pokhara's selection of rental **trekking equipment** pales beside Kathmandu's, but you'll pay for fewer days by renting locally. Sleeping bags, packs and parkas are easily obtainable (about Rs20–30 per day per item, depending on quality).

Rafting and kayaking

Pokhara is within striking distance of no fewer than four **rafting** rivers – the Kali Gandaki, Trisuli, Seti and Marsyangdi. The Kali is probably the most popular trip out of Pokhara; the Trisuli is better done out of Kathmandu, since the starting point is closer to there and the river flows towards Pokhara. The Seti is best known as the venue for **kayak** clinics, which are organized by several companies; kayaks can be rented from most of the places listed below ($10–20 a day). See Chapter Eight for more detail about rivers, rafting and kayaking. See "Nautical pursuits" (p.260) for information on **boating** on Phewa Tal.

Many **river operators** have offices in Lakeside, but as in Kathmandu, most don't have enough of a track record to be worthy of recommendation. Some are merely agents. The following are the more reputable companies.

Equator Expeditions (☎20688; *equator@mos.com.np*). Rafting trips with kayak support, also four-day kayak courses on the Seti. Experienced Western and Nepali guides, good equipment.

Ganesh Shop (☎22657). If you're in Nepal to kayak independently, this should be your first stop. The shop has a wide variety of kayaks and associated gear for rent, as well as hydrospeeds. Runs Seti kayak clinics.

Himalayan Encounters, (☎22682; *raftnepl@himenco.wlink.com.np*). Nepal's longest-serving rafting operator, with experienced Nepali guides.

Ultimate Descents (☎23240; *rivers@ultimate.wlink.com.np*). Nepal's biggest river operator, with good rafts and kayaks, mainly Western guides; also does Seti kayak clinics.

Other outdoor activities

Local **mountain-biking** possibilities are highlighted where appropriate in the "Pokhara Valley" section, p.276. General advice on biking, equipment and routes is given in Chapter Nine. Himalayan Mountain Bikes and Dawn Till Dusk, both with offices in Lakeside, run organized day trips and longer tours out of Pokhara, and also rent out decent bikes for $10–15 per day. Experienced **paragliders** have been unofficially launching from Sarangkot, the hill north of Lakeside, for years. By the time you read this, Sunrise Trekking in Barahi Chowk (near the *Hungry Eye* in Lakeside) should have received official sanction to offer instruction and accompanied flights for beginners. Avia Club Nepal (☎25192; *aviaclub@ccsl.com.np*) does short piloted trips around the valley in **ultralight** aircraft, which carry one passenger at a time. The price is $45 for a fifteen-minute flight, $170 for an hour.

Kids and their parents will get the most out of **pony-riding**. Many outfits run short rides beside the lake, half-day rides around the north shore to Pame, and full-day treks up to Sarangkot. Prices are around Rs300 per hour or Rs1500 per day; book through any agent.

If the season is right, you can play **tennis** at the *Hotel Barahi* in Lakeside, **swim** at the *Shangri-La Village* or *Bluebird Hotel*, or play **golf** at the *Fulbari Resort Hotel*'s nine-hole course (non-guests are charged a fee to use the facilities, obviously). The once-popular **Pokhara Triathlon** has unfortunately gone dormant due to lack of sponsorship, but you never know, it might be revived – to find out, contact *karto@wlink.com.np*.

Meditation and yoga

Many spiritual centres last only a season or two in Pokhara. One that appears to be permanent is **Garden Yiga Chozin Buddhist Centre** (☎22923; *gyc@mos.com.np*), a very peaceful facility a short walk north of Lakeside, where regular residential courses and daily teachings are designed for mainly Western participants. Inquire about three-day retreats (Rs2600, all inclusive) and daily yoga, taichi and reiki sessions in high season (around Rs100). The centre's meditation hall and library are open to the public for free.

Sadhana Yoga Ashram (☎25891), operating out of *Hotel Orion Legend* in Damside, offers one-day yogic cleansing and hatha yoga sessions ($10) and longer residential courses ($10–15 per day, depending on standard of accommodation).

Other courses are organized by centres in Kathmandu (see p.139), but you may be able to join up on the spot – check the noticeboards around Lakeside/Damside.

Listings

Banks and moneychangers Nepal Grindlays in Lakeside handles foreign exchange and Mastercard/Visa cash advances, Sun–Thurs 9.45am–4.15pm, Fri 9.45am–1.15pm. Many registered moneychangers operate in Lakeside and Damside and at the airport, generally 8am–7pm. Some hotels will change money as well.

Central Immigration A short walk north of Damside, it issues trekking permits (Annapurna and Rara treks only) and visa extensions. Application hours are Sun–Thurs 10.30am–1pm (12.30pm in winter), Fri 10am–noon; permits and visas are ready later the same day. For most trekking permits, an additional Annapurna Conservation Area fee is payable. Trekking or travel agents can handle the paperwork for a fee (about Rs300). Passport photos are available in minutes from studios near the office (about Rs200 for four).

Email/Internet Typical rates (which are negotiable to some extent) are Rs10 per minute of online access, Rs2–3 per minute to compose messages offline, and Rs15 per kilobyte to send. Most places will allow you to receive email – two established ones are Office Depot Communication & Travels (*odc@mos.com.np*) and Global Net Communication Service (*globenet@chet.com.np*).

Film and processing Films are available at roughly Kathmandu prices. A few places in Lakeside and Pokhara Bazaar do same-day processing, and other tourist shops can send film out.

Haircutting Pokhara has a preponderance of barbers, who do not only haircuts but also shaves and massages (see "Massage", below). Establish the price and exact extent of services beforehand.

Health Several pharmas in Lakeside/Damside do stool tests, though incorrect diagnoses are common. One or two also offer ayurvedic medicine. In an emergency head for the Western Regional Hospital (☎20066), also known as the Gandaki Hospital – its ER looks terrible, but quite a few Western-trained doctors work there. Have your hotel phone ahead to make sure a doctor is on duty.

Laundry Most lodges take laundry for a few rupees per item. The places calling themselves "dry cleaners" return your clothes dry, but wash as wet as the others.

Massage Sanja Lama at Natural Health Clinic, opposite *Hotel Snow Land* in Lakeside, can be recommended for many types of massage and physical therapy (Rs800 for a one-hour full-body massage). Many other uncertified masseurs charge less (typically around Rs300 per hour) – they're probably OK for ironing out post-trek kinks, but not for professional therapy. The neck-cracking that barbers do may be appropriate for some, but can result in temporary stiffness for others.

Media International newspapers and magazines are available in bookshops, usually one or two days late. The English-language Nepali papers arrive around mid-afternoon (they're delivered by the buses from Kathmandu).

Post Tourist book- and postcard shops sell stamps. Some shops and many hotels and guest houses will take mail to the post office for franking, but you'll have to decide whether you think they're trustworthy. The main post office, in Mahendra Pul, is open Sun–Thurs 10am–5pm (4pm in winter), Fri 10am–3pm. They've got a tiny poste restante department, but it may not be as reliable as the one in Kathmandu – don't have anything of value sent to you here (and for that matter don't post anything of value *from* here).

Provisions Mini-supermarkets along the Lakeside strip anticipate your every need. Basically, everything you can get in Kathmandu, you can get in Lakeside/Damside: chocolate, tinned food, bread, cheese, wine, spirits, toiletries, batteries, etc.

Telephone calls As in Kathmandu, you'll find plenty of ISD/IDD businesses (most open 7am–11pm), plus many guest houses have international dialling facilities. International calls are charged at around Rs170–200 per minute, depending on country (shop around), trunk calls to Kathmandu about Rs15 per minute. Callback (receiving an incoming call) costs Rs5–10 per minute.

Moving on

Buses link Pokhara with Kathmandu via the Prithvi Highway, and with the Tarai and India via the Siddhartha Highway. All the major domestic airlines connect Pokhara with Kathmandu.

Buses

As many as a dozen companies operate **tourist buses** and minibuses from Pokhara to Kathmandu. The fare is around Rs200–300 (minibuses are more expensive), which is about twice the price of public buses, but the tourist services are more comfortable and somewhat faster and safer, and they pick up passengers in Lakeside and Damside. One company, Greenline Tours, operates more expensive (Rs600) luxury coaches. A couple of companies also run tourist buses to Sauraha (for Chitwan National Park). Buses to the Indian border at Sonauli aren't technically tourist services, but they do pick up passengers in Lakeside/Damside. See the box on p.244 for a summary of **public bus** services from Pokhara.

All tourist buses and some public buses can be booked through ticket agents, but shop around since not every agent represents every bus company, and prices vary quite a bit. The agent's fee for obtaining a public bus ticket may be more than the ticket itself, but it's well worth it to avoid an extra encounter with the bus park. However, some buses aren't bookable in advance, in which case you're on your own. Buses serving the Prithvi and Siddhartha highways depart from the **main bus park**, and tickets are sold from the booking hall at the top of the steps on the west side. For services along the Baglung Highway (including those to various Annapurna region trailheads), you need to buy tickets from the separate **Baglung bus park**, located on the western side of the bazaar. However, Baglung buses are very local and have a reputation for reckless driving and fatalities, so it's far preferable to take a taxi to the start of a trek.

If you're heading **to India**, read the section on ticket agents in Basics (p.31) first.

Private vehicles

Long-distance travel by **private vehicle** works out to be more expensive than the usual daily rental rate, since you have to pay for the car and driver to return to Pokhara even if you're travelling only one way. However, it's more comfortable and flexible than going by bus, and cheaper than flying, especially if there are two or more of you. For most

INTERNAL FLIGHTS FROM POKHARA			
	Frequency	**Time**	**Fare ($)**
Jomosom	5–6/day	25min	50
Kathmandu	10–20/day	35min	61
Manang	0–3/week	25min	61
Mountain flight	0–2/day	30min	60

journeys the most economical option will be a taxi; jeeps and vans can also be arranged. Standard rates for a taxi or similar are $60 to Kathmandu, $45 to Chitwan, $75 to Lumbini/Sonauli. Travel agencies can arrange rentals, but it's easier and probably more satisfactory all around to have your hotel or guest house do it.

Flights

It's easier to use a travel agent to book **internal flights**, but here's a list of airlines that operate out of Pokhara. See the box for frequencies and fares. Many agents can also book or reconfirm **international flights** by phone to Kathmandu.

Buddha Air (☎21429). Kathmandu, Mountain flight.

Cosmic Air (☎21846). Kathmandu, Jomosom.

Gorkha Airlines (☎25971). Kathmandu.

Lumbini Airways (Kathmandu: ☎483381). Kathmandu, Jomosom.

Necon Air (☎26011). Kathmandu.

RNAC (☎21021). Kathmandu, Jomosom, Manang (seasonal).

Yeti Airways (☎20027). Kathmandu, Jomosom.

THE POKHARA VALLEY

Day trips around the **Pokhara Valley** make excellent training for a trek, and serve as an effective antidote to lakeside idleness. Excursions generally entail a healthy amount of cycling or hiking, often both. Start early to make the most of the views before the clouds move in and the heat builds – it can get really sticky here in all but the winter months – and bring lunch and a full water bottle. If you're feeling adventurous (or running behind schedule), you can **stay overnight** at Sarangkot, Tashi Palkhel or Begnas Tal.

Many of the **ethnic groups** that make treks north of Pokhara so popular – Gurungs, Magars, and Baahun and Chhetri Hindu castes – are equally well represented around the valley, and less touched by tourism here. In addition, the **Tibetan settlements** in the area are less commercial, and in their own way more instructive about Tibetan culture, than those in the Kathmandu Valley.

There are worthwhile things to see in just about every direction from Pokhara. To put them into some semblance of order, this section covers the sights in a generally clockwise manner, starting in the southeast.

The World Peace Pagoda

The newly constructed **World Peace Pagoda**, which crowns the ridge across the lake at an elevation of 1113m, provides one of the most satisfying short hikes in the Pokhara area. The views from the top are phenomenal, and since there are several routes up and back, you can work this into a loop that includes boating on the lake and/or visiting

Devin's Fall and the Tibetan settlement of Tashiling (described later in this section). A basic up-and-back trip can be done in as little as two hours, so you can leave after breakfast and be back in time for lunch.

The easiest approach is by trail **from Damside**. Cross the river on a footbridge just downstream of the dam, then follow the path as it bears left and passes a small shrine before beginning a gradual ascent up the back (south) side of the ridge. The way is somewhat obscure and littered at first, but soon becomes a fine wide path through chestnut forest until the final, steeper ascent. The climb is steeper and damper **from Anadu**, the village across the lake (reached by boat from Lakeside). A signposted trail starts at the *Typical Guest House*, though all trails heading up from the various put-ashore points eventually join this one. If descending this way, you should have no trouble getting a canoe back to Lakeside – you may even be intercepted by a boatman before you reach the lake. There's also a signposted trail ascending straight up **from the Siddhartha Highway** at Chhorepatan, about 1km past Devin's Fall, but this is probably a better route for descending and continuing on to the falls and Tashling. To make an even longer loop you can keep walking along the ridgeline past *Rani Ban Retreat* to the village of Bhumdi, where a rough road descends to the highway and a trail curves around the lake and down to the Harpan Khola (see below). Drinks and biscuits are sold near the pagoda, and more substantial food is available at Anadu and Chhorepatan.

Standing more than 40m tall, the so-called **pagoda** looks more like a cross between a stupa and a lighthouse. It seems rather grandiose for a religious shrine, but if it helps achieve its stated aim (world peace) then more power to it. The Japanese Buddhist organization that funded the monument maintains an adjacent monastery with a small meditation hall and monks' quarters. The **view** from here is just about the best wide-angle panorama you can get of this part of the Himalaya, and certainly the only one with Phewa Tal and Pokhara in the foreground. Over on the far left there's the towering hump of Dhaulagiri and its more westerly sisters, in the middle rises the Annapurna Himal and the graceful pyramid of Machhapuchhre, and off to the right are Manaslu, Himalchuli and Baudha.

Sarangkot and beyond

Sarangkot, a high point (1590m) on the ridge north of Phewa Tal, is by far the most popular of the mountain viewpoints around Pokhara. The peaks appear even closer from here than from the Peace Pagoda, though not quite as many of them are visible. Sarangkot's popularity stems mainly from the fact that it's been on the tourist map a lot longer than the Peace Pagoda has, and perhaps also because it has a substantial little village near the top that can provide lodging – many people hike up in the afternoon, spend the night and then catch the views first thing the next morning. As with the hike to the Peace Pagoda, there are various routes to the top and at least one route further along the ridge once you're up there, so a number of different itineraries are possible. You can also cycle up, potentially making this the first stop on a longer cycle trek through the country north of Pokhara.

Getting there

There are two principal **hiking routes** up Sarangkot, a hard one and an easier one. The first entails walking straight up **from Lakeside**, which is quite a long, steep climb with no mountain views until the very top – if you're running late you might miss them altogether. Follow the road north from Lakeside as it bends around the lake, goes up and down a small hill and traverses a large cultivated area. Two kilometres beyond Camping Chowk the trail, marked by a painted stone, forks off to the right; when in doubt, stay on the flagstoned path and keep heading generally towards the summit. You'll be doing well to make it from the trailhead to the top in less than two and a half hours. The easier route starts near the **Bindyabasini temple** in the bazaar, a Rs80 taxi

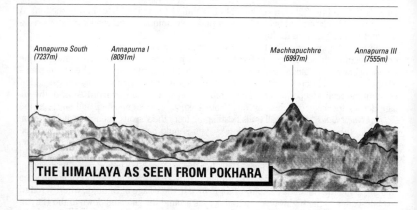

THE HIMALAYA AS SEEN FROM POKHARA

Annapurna South (7237m) Annapurna I (8091m) Machhapuchhre (6997m) Annapurna III (7555m)

ride from Lakeside. A paved road goes from there to within a half-hour's hike of the top, so if you want to make this a really easy route you can have the **taxi** take you all the way to the end of the road (Rs350 one way). Otherwise, walk westwards from the temple along the signposted road and then take the obvious shortcuts, which stick to the spine of the ridge and avoid the road for much of the way. Compared to the Lakeside approach this is a gentler ascent, and the scenery – both mountains and lake – gets better and better as you go. That said, it's also far more commercialized, with offers of cold drinks, curios and guide services all along the upper stretch. There are apparently other trails to the top, including one that starts about 200m north of the radio tower southwest of the main bazaar.

It takes a good **mountain bike** to get to Sarangkot and back down again in one piece. Follow the road from the Bindyabasini temple to where the pavement gives out, after about 5km; this is as far as most vehicles go, but on a bike you can keep going up the road, which doubles back and becomes steep and rough here. The road angles generally westwards for 3km until it reaches a junction: Sarangkot is another 3km along the road to the right, while the lefthand fork leads to Kaskikot and Naudaada (see below). Most people will find the 850-metre ascent to Sarangkot quite enough for one day, though given an early start a strong rider could make it to Naudaada and back. For a longer, more gradual ascent to Sarangkot, you cycle up the Baglung Highway to Naudaada first. All of these roads are also negotiable on a **motorcycle**.

The village and summit

The **village** of **SARANGKOT**, nestled just below the summit, has tea shops, handicrafts sellers and something like a dozen **lodges**. All have electricity and most can provide hot washing water by the bucket. Names change often here, but *Lake View Lodge* (☎29363; ①) and *Hotel Mountain Prince* (no phone; ①/B②) seem fairly well established. Several simple restaurants line the path up to the top, some with excellent views.

For the **summit**, continue another ten minutes up to a walled compound, where the local council will hit you for a donation for any of various projects. *Kot* means "fort" in Nepali, and this is the remains of one. (You'll find that just about every hilltop in this region, which was once divided among many warring principalities, is called Something-kot.) If you've hiked up from Lakeside, the sudden view here will come as a staggering revelation. The peaks seem to levitate above their blue flanks, the gathering clouds add a quality of raw grandeur, while to the south, Phewa Tal shimmers in the

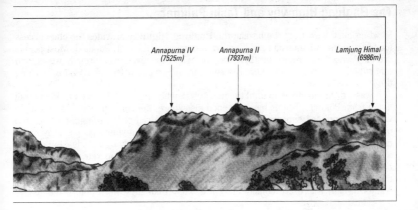

Annapurna IV (7525m)   Annapurna II (7937m)   Lamjung Himal (6986m)

hazy arc of the valley. If you hadn't been planning on trekking, this is where you might change your mind.

Routes beyond Sarangkot

An unpaved road now connects Sarangkot with Naudaada, about 10km further west on the Baglung Highway, making possible all sorts of longer trips beyond Sarangkot. Contouring along the south side of the ridge, the road lets you make good time on foot or bike. A few villages are located along the way, notably Maula, the starting point of a flagstoned path up to **Kaskikot**, seat of the kingdom that once ruled the Pokhara Valley, perched on a craggy brow of the ridge with views as big as Sarangkot's. (Maula is therefore sometimes referred to as Kotmuni – "Below the Fort".) A stone enclosure and a house-like Kali temple are all that remain of the citadel of the Kaski kings, which fell to the Gorkhalis without a fight in 1781. **NAUDAADA** (or Nagdaada), the first place from which Machhapuchhre's true fishtail profile can be seen, is another 4.5km west of Maula. Two or three nice little lodges offer trekking-style accommodation along the road between Maula and Naudaada.

On foot, you'll probably catch a bus from Naudaada back to Pokhara. However, other interesting variations are possible, including walking down from Maula to Pame or west along the main road from Naudaada and then south to Pachaase Daada (see below) – for such hikes you'll need a good map, though. On a bike, you can either continue deeper into the hills on the Baglung Highway (below) or return to Pokhara, an easy 32-kilometre coast via Tashi Palkhel (below).

Around Phewa Tal

The road along the north shore of Phewa Tal, past the trail to Sarangkot, serves as the gateway to various low-key hiking routes that don't require a trekking permit. The first 7km of road borders the lake and then follows the sluggish **Harpan Khola** past marshes and paddy to **Pame**. From near Pame you can head off to the left and up the ridge to Bhumdi and around to the Peace Pagoda (above) for a one-day circumnavigation of Phewa Tal (however, route-finding is easier going in the other direction), or make a longer circuit via **Pachaase Daada** (2509m), the prominent ridge west of Phewa, with supreme views. The latter trip requires an overnight in Pachaase Bhanjyang, from where trails lead north to Bhadaure and the Baglung Highway and south to Bhumdi by way of Ramche Daada. Very few foreigners venture into this area, so again, a good map or knowledgeable guide is recommended.

The Baglung Highway and Tashi Palkhel

Heading northwest from the bazaar, the **Baglung Highway** provides the chief access for treks in the Annapurna region and rafting trips on the Kali Gandaki. Most people are only whizzing through on their way to their respective adventures, however, and other than a few mountain-bikers returning from Sarangkot (see above), towns along the road see few foreign faces.

It was a different story up until the mid-1980s, when this was the main trekking trail north from Pokhara. But as has happened elsewhere, the construction of a new highway has introduced enormous changes to the local social order, bringing wealth and prosperity to a few – mostly outside developers – and luring young people away to the cities. The Yamdi Khola valley has been transformed, not only by vehicles, but also by a hydroelectric project and a roadside smattering of modern concrete dwellings emanating like a comet's tail from Pokhara Bazaar. The old walking route has fallen into disuse, since trekkers and locals alike seldom walk when they can ride a bus. Bazaars like Naudaada and Kaare are considerably less busy than they were before the road –

TIBETANS IN EXILE

Thirty years ago, Dervla Murphy worked as a volunteer among **Tibetan refugees in Pokhara**, and called the account she wrote about her experiences *The Waiting Land*. Pokhara's Tibetans are still waiting: three former **refugee camps**, now self-governing and largely self-sufficient, have settled into a pattern of permanent transience. Because Pokhara (unlike Kathmandu) has no Buddhist holy places, most Tibetans have remained in the camps, regarding them as havens where they can keep their culture and language alive. Many plainly don't see the point of moving out and setting up permanent homes in Nepal when all they really want is to return to their former homes in Tibet.

The settlements – Tashi Palkhel, Tashiling and Paljorling – are open to the public, and a wander around one is an experience of workaday reality that contrasts with the otherworldliness of, say, Boudha or Swayambhu. You'll get a lot more out of a visit if you can get someone to show you around – and if the tour inevitably finishes with a sales pitch back at your guide's one-room home, so much the better.

At the time of the **Chinese invasion** of Tibet in 1950, the Tibetans now living in Pokhara were mainly peasants and nomads inhabiting the border areas of western Tibet. The political changes in faraway Lhasa left them initially unaffected, but after the Dalai Lama fled Tibet in 1959 and the Chinese occupation turned genocidal, thousands streamed south through the Himalaya to safety. They gathered first at Jomosom, where the terrain and climate were at least reminiscent of Tibet, but the area soon became overcrowded and conditions desperate. Under the direction of the Swiss Red Cross, three **transit camps** were established around low-lying Pokhara and about two thousand refugees were moved down.

The first five years were hard times in the camps, marked by food rationing, chronic sickness and general unemployment. Relief came in the late 1960s, when the construction of Pardi Dam and the Prithvi and Siddhartha highways provided welcome work. A second wave of refugees began around the same time, after the United States' detente with China ended a covert CIA operation supporting Tibetan freedom-fighters based in Mustang. Since then, the fortunes of Pokhara's Tibetans have risen with the local **tourism** industry, and carpet-weaving and handicraft sales have become the main source of income, especially for women. Many of the men work seasonally as trekking porters or guides, where they can make better money than in the camps. A small but visible minority have become smooth-talking curio salespeople, plying the cafés of Lakeside and Damside, but whereas Tibetans have by now set up substantial businesses in Kathmandu, opportunities are fewer in Pokhara, and prosperity has come more slowly. See p.456 for more on the lives of Tibetan exiles.

they've lost not only trekkers' business but also much of their former market in house-hold provisions, since local residents can now easily do their shopping in Pokhara, pre-viously a day or two's walk away.

Tashi Palkhel (Hyangja)

With nine hundred residents – eighty of them monks – **Tashi Palkhel** (also known as **Hyangja**, after the village 3km beyond) is the largest and also the least commercial of Pokhara's Tibetan settlements. The entrance is clearly marked, about 4km northwest of the north end of Pokhara Bazaar on the Baglung Highway. Get there by bike, taxi or a bus from the Baglung bus park. If you're doing the Siklis trek you can hit the trail not far from here.

A path past curio sellers draws you naturally to the community's large and growing **gompa** (monastery), where resident monks usually gather for chanting at 6.30am and 4pm. The *gompa* is of the Kagyu-pa sect, and portraits either side of the Buddha statue inside the hall depict the Dalai Lama and the late Kagyu leader, the sixteenth Karma Lama; smaller figures behind represent the one thousand Buddhas believed to exist during the present age. A long **weaving hall** is the focal point of Tashi Palkhel's carpet industry, and forming the other sides of a quadrangle are wool dyeing and drying areas. The community also has a school, an old people's home (many of the original refugees are now getting on in years), a clinic and community hall.

If you decide to stay overnight, Tashi Palkhel's co-operative **guest house** can supply rooms (②); hot showers are sometimes available, and camping is possible. Get **food** at the guest house or at one of the smoky, buttery holes-in-the-wall nearby. **Handicrafts** can be purchased at the cooperative shop in the guest house compound, whose profits support community projects, as well as from private shops and freelance vendors.

To Beni

The Baglung Highway is smoothly asphalted as far as Baglung, a zonal headquarters 72km from Pokhara, and roughed in to Beni, 10km further on. It grows a little longer each year, and there are plans to extend it all the way up the Thak Khola to Jomosom.

Combined with a visit to Sarangkot (above), the highway makes for an enjoyable two-plus-day bike ride or motorcycle cruise. It ascends seriously past Naudaada (above) to its high point near **Kaare** (1770m), then descends into the valley of the Modi Khola, where you can overnight in **Naya Pul** or in one of the nice lodges at **Birethanti** (off the highway, at the boundary of the Annapurna Conservation Area). The downhill ends at **Kusma**, where the road leaves the Modi and bends upstream along the Kali Gandaki. Most rafting trips on the Kali start at **Baglung**, but at certain times of year some companies put in farther up near **Beni**.

Mahendra Gupha (Cave) and the Kali Khola

While it just about scrapes a description as a geological wonder, **Mahendra Gupha** (Mahendra Cave; Rs15) is probably best thought of as a base from which to explore the snug hills and side valleys north of Pokhara. To get there by bike, cross K. I. Singh* Pul (Bridge) at the top end of Pokhara and head north past the Gurkha camp, turn right up a paved road 600m beyond the bridge, and follow it for about 3km to the end. The climb is relentless and if you're on a one-speed bike you'll have to push some of the way (the reward comes on the way back). A taxi will charge about Rs300 return. Some city buses come up this way (change at Prithvi Narayan Campus).

---

*A cross between Che Guevara and Houdini, K. I. Singh led the western insurgents in the 1951 overthrow of the Rana regime, twice being imprisoned and twice escaping. He later briefly served as prime minister.

Water percolating through the valley's limestone sediments has created a honey-comb of caves extending up to 2km from the main entrance, though a guided tour of the illuminated part only takes about ten to fifteen minutes. Mahendra Cave used to be well known for its stalactites, but these have unfortunately been ransacked by vandals; a few surviving **stalagmites** are daubed with red *sindur* and revered as *shivalinga* because of their resemblance to phalluses. A café near the entrance serves food in a pleasant garden setting.

If caves are your cup of tea, then ask one of the guides to take you to **Chamere Gupha** ("Bat Cave"; Rs15 plus something for the guide), about ten minutes' walk away. It's a bit of a scramble down into the main chamber, a big, dripping, sweating space with thousands of bats hanging from the ceiling – only in Nepal could you go into such a place with a stranger and not be worried about being bludgeoned to death. Bring your own torch/flashlight, or rent one from the ticket seller.

Eastwards from Mahendra Cave, a trail beckons up the **Kali Khola**, a minor tribu-tary of the Seti, to the village of Armala. Adventurous types might want to forge on. Scrambling up the cultivated slopes on either side of the valley might make for some interesting encounters and good views. By traversing the ridge to the south, you should theoretically be able to return to Pokhara the same day via the Bhalam Khola.

About 1km south of Mahendra Cave, the road from Pokhara passes through **BATULECHAUR**, a village locally famous for its **gaaine**. Wandering minstrels of the old school, *gaaine* are still found throughout the hills, earning their crust by singing ballads to the accompaniment of the *sarangi*, a four-stringed, hand-hewn fiddle: "I have no rice to eat/let the strings of the *sarangi* set to," runs the *gaaine*'s traditional opening couplet. These days, many find they can make better money down at Lakeside sere-nading tourists, spawning legions of inept imitators.

To vary the route on the way back, take a left onto a paved road just before K. I. Singh Pul and then look for a pathway off to the left. From there you can cross the Kali and Bhalam rivers by footbridges (you'll have to carry your bike a bit) to get to the Kahun Daada area (see below).

Kahun Daada and the Bhalam Khola

If the view from **Kahun Daada**, the hill east of Pokhara, is a shade less magnificent than Sarangkot's, a lookout tower near the top gives you a better crack at it, and trails up to it are totally uncommercialized. The easiest and most interesting starting point is the **Tibetan monastery** 2km east of Mahendra Pul. At the top of a breathless couple of hun-dred steps at the southern base of Kahun Daada, the Karma Dhubgyu Chhokhorling Nyeshang Korti Monastery occupies a breezy spot – always good for keeping the prayer flags flapping – with valley views east and west. Around thirty monks and monklets inhab-it the monastery, which is modern and contains all the usual Vajrayana paraphernalia.

The trail to the lookout tower starts at the bottom of the steps, initially following a road that hugs the western base of the ridge for about 1km, and then climbs through several lazy settlements collectively known as **Phulbari**. Keep heading towards the tower (1444m), which is visible most of the way and can be reached in about an hour and a half from the monastery. From the half-finished concrete platform, you can con-template the tremendous force of the Seti River and its tributaries, which tumble out of the Annapurna Himal clouded with dissolved limestone (*seti* means white) and, merg-ing at the foot of the Kahun Daada, split the valley floor in a bleached chasm. Descending back to the monastery, paths bearing to the left may suggest a longer cir-cuit via the valley and villages on the east side of the ridge.

Also eminently worth exploring is the tidily terraced side valley of the **Bhalam Khola**, immediately north of Kahun Daada. To get there directly from the tower involves some nasty bushwhacking, so it's better to backtrack towards the monastery

THE GURKHAS

. As I write these last words, my thoughts return to you who were my comrades: the stubborn and indomitable peasants of Nepal. Once more I hear the laughter with which you greeted every hardship. Once more I see you in your bivouacs or about your fires, on forced march or in the trenches, now shivering with wet and cold, now scorched by a pitiless and burning sun. Uncomplaining, you endure hunger and thirst and wounds; and at the last, your unwavering lines disappear into the smoke and wrath of battle. Bravest of the brave, most generous of the generous, never had a country more faithful friends than you.

Ralph Lilley Turner, *Dictionary of the Nepali Language* (1931)

Comprising an elite Nepalese corps within the British and Indian armies for over 180 years, the **Gurkha regiments** have been rated among the finest fighting units in the world. Ironically, the regiments were born out of the 1814–16 war between Nepal and Britain's East India Company: so impressed were the British by the men of "Goorkha" (Gorkha, the ancestral home of Nepal's rulers) that they began recruiting Nepalis into the Indian Army before the peace was even signed.

In the century that followed, Gurkhas fought in every major British military operation, including the 1857 **Indian Mutiny** and campaigns in Afghanistan, the North-West Frontier and Somaliland. More than 200,000 Gurkhas served in the two world wars, and, despite being earmarked for "high-wastage" roles, earned universal respect for their bravery: ten of the one hundred **Victoria Crosses** awarded in World War II went to Gurkhas. Following India's independence after the war, Britain took four of the ten Gurkha regiments and India retained the rest. More recently, Gurkhas have distinguished themselves in Sarawak, Cyprus and the Falklands.

Gurkhas hail mainly from the Magar, Gurung, Rai and Limbu hill tribes (growing up in the Nepal hills is ideal preparation for the army). Most boys from these groups have traditionally dreamt of making it into the Gurkhas, not only for the money – the annual salary of £5000 is about fifty times the Nepalese average – but also for a rare chance to see the world and return with prestige and a comfortable pension. However, the Gurkhas' long and faithful service to Britain is winding down. With Hong Kong (the Gurkhas' former headquarters) having been handed over to China and the Sultan of Brunei's contract for Gurkha protection now expired, Britain's need for military forces in Asia has declined. Anticipating this, the main Gurkha recruiting and training centre in Dharan was handed over to civilian use in 1989, and all remaining operations are now carried out at the smaller facility in Pokhara. Would-be recruits can still try out for places in the lower-paid Indian regiments – which is what most who failed to make the cut for the British Gurkhas used to do anyway – but the gradual loss of salaries and pensions is apt to take the steam out of many Nepali hill communities.

until you pick up the first main northbound trail. It's also accessible by a rough (bikeable) track heading northwards on the east side of the Seti River. The power of erosion can readily be seen from this route as it passes the confluence of the Bhalam, Seti and Kali rivers, where they undercut old gravel beds, leaving sheer, mossy cliffs. The track continues at least another 3km to the village of Railechaur, and trails go further up the valley from there. This route can be linked with the one to Mahendra Cave (see above) by crossing two footbridges over the Bhalam and Kali rivers, but it's easier to visit the cave first.

Begnas Tal and Rupa Tal

With Lakeside and Damside now so overdeveloped, **Begnas Tal** and **Rupa Tal**, twin lakes 15km east of Pokhara, look destined to be the next big tourist discoveries. Begnas

Tal, the bigger and better-known of the two, is framed by meticulously engineered paddy terraces marching right down to its shore, while Rupa, on the other side of an intervening ridge, remains pristinely hidden in a bushy, steep-sided valley. Come prepared to spend the night: several lodges can put you up, and roads and trails open up a wealth of outstanding walking opportunities.

A **taxi** to Begnas costs about Rs200 one way. **Local buses**, departing every hour or so from New Road just south of Chipledhunga, take 45 minutes and tend to be crowded. The **bike** ride from Pokhara is getting rather grotty, although it's great to have a mountain bike or motorcycle once you get there. After the first (mostly downhill) 10km along the Prithvi Highway, turn left at the sign onto a straight, paved road, and from there it's 3km to the end of the line at the dumpy hamlet of **BEGNAS**: typical of so many roadhead towns, it seems to exist only as a conduit for corrugated roofing, bags of cement and other tools of progress for the surrounding hills.

But Begnas Tal is just around the corner, up the road to the left immediately before the cul-de-sac where the buses stop. It's not even five minutes' walk along here to the dam at the south end of the lake, below which the Ministry of Agriculture has built a big **fish farm**, consisting of concrete holding tanks fed by water from the lake. Fish farming is getting to be big business here, with Chinese carp and native *sahar* and *mahseer* being raised for restaurants in Pokhara and Kathmandu. Phewa-style **boats** are rented out beside the lake just beyond the dam; with tent-shaped Annapurna II for a backdrop, the paddling here is at least as scenic as at Phewa Tal, and you'll practically have the lake to yourself. A good destination is the wooded peninsula at the north side of the lake, which is a **bird sanctuary**.

A better introduction to the lakes, although it involves a fair amount of up and down, is the trail along **Panchbhaiya Daada**, the ridge that separates them. Starting at the bus turnaround, follow a graded dirt road north for about twenty minutes, then take the trail to the left, which ascends steadily along the ridge (bikers, stay on the road). Begnas is visible first, on the left, and then Rupa comes into view after the highest point is passed, about 45 minutes from the bus stop. Local belief has it that the lakes are husband and wife, and that an object thrown into one lake will eventually appear in the other. The things that look like fences peeping above the water of both lakes are more fish farms – Rupa Tal is said to be particularly rich in nutrients. In another ten minutes or so the trail rejoins the road and then a few minutes later reaches the half-dozen shops of **SUNDARI DAADA**, the jumping-off point for just about all explorations in this area.

From Sundari Daada, a trail to the left descends to the lake and *Begnas Lake Resort*, where you should be able to get a boat back to the dam area. A bit further along the road, a trail leading off to the right, signposted "Karputar", descends to the north end of Rupa Tal and the village of Talbesi – this route makes an attractive alternative way into the Annapurna Circuit, and offers the possibility of a steep side trip to the hilltop viewpoint of **Rupakot**. Another 1km down the road, a trail to the left leads up to another village called Begnas and then to **Begnaskot**, an even better viewpoint of the Annapurnas and lake from the grassy crest of the ridge; this trail is part of the Royal Trek (see p.399). The road itself swings around to Talbesi and Shyauli (13km), and is eventually supposed to be pushed all the way through to Besisahar, the starting point of the Annapurna Circuit. When buses are able to negotiate this route, expect it to vie in popularity with the one from Dumre – but also to kill off the walking route.

Practicalities

Several **guest houses** are clumped near the dam, an easy walk from the bus stop – the location is good for access to the lake, but otherwise lacklustre. Of these, *Hotel Daybreak*, which has nice views from its gardens and the uglier *New Begnas Lodge* (both ①/B③) have a slight edge on comfort. A couple of places along the Panchbhaiya Daada trail are harder to get to and on the whole more primitive, but are indescribably peaceful and definitely have better views. *Hotel Himalayan Range* (①), reached first, is absolutely idyllic but you really have to be prepared to rough it, while *Dinesh's House* (②), higher up, is less traditional but more modern (well, it has electricity) and boasts great views of both lakes.

One **luxury hotel**, *Begnas Lake Resort and Villas* (Kathmandu: ☎249619; *sales@blr.mos.com.np*; B⑧), overlooks the lake from its forested southeastern shore, with great views and serious seclusion. Another even fancier outfit run by the Tiger Tops people, *Tiger Mountain Pokhara Lodge* (Kathmandu: ☎411225; *tiger@mtn.mos.com.np*; B⑨), is located along the Royal Trek on a ridge to the northwest of Begnas Tal, and offers naturalist-led treks.

Obviously, the **food** served by the cheap guest houses here is pretty unexciting compared to what's on offer in Pokhara, although it probably won't be long before tourist menus make their appearance. Apart from the guest houses and hotels, the only other eateries are a couple of *bhojanalaya* near the bus stop, serving typical Nepali food.

Tashiling, Devin's Fall and Seti canyon overlooks

The most accessible of Pokhara's Tibetan settlements, **Tashiling** lies just south of the Siddhartha Highway in Chhorepatan, about 2km west of Damside. On a bicycle you can be there in ten or fifteen minutes. With some 750 residents, Tashiling is smaller than Tashi Palkhel, but laid out on much the same lines. The entrance road takes you first past a *gompa*, a primary school, several rows of distinctly Tibetan barracks-style stone houses (the windows trimmed with characteristic orange and white skirts) and, in a separate compound on the left, a school for Tibetan orphans from all over Nepal. Next comes a central open area that supports a semi-permanent bazaar of curio stalls and shops, whose salespeople call out from the sidelines like sirens – this is where those Lakeside *didis* learned their skills! Still, if you're planning to make any purchases while in Pokhara, it's worth at least checking out the offerings here first. Walk all the way to the far end of the compound to reach the community's small carpet-weaving hall and wool-dyeing shed; a short walk beyond brings you to an abrupt drop and a glorious panorama of the valley of the Phusre Khola, a Seti tributary.

On the opposite side of the highway, **Devin's Fall** (entrance Rs5) marks the spot where the Pardi Khola – the stream that drains Phewa Tal – enters a grottoed channel and sinks underground in a sudden rush of foam and fury. Given a good monsoon runoff in the autumn it can be damned impressive, as the green water corkscrews and thunders into the earth, forcing up a continuous plume of mist; in the spring it's a washout. The spot is perhaps more interesting as a source of pop mythology: known to locals as **Patale Chhango** (roughly, "Waterfall to the Underworld"), the sinkhole is said to have acquired its Western-sounding nickname when a "female European" was drowned while skinny-dipping with her boyfriend. An alternate spelling, David's Fall, suggests it may have been the boyfriend who perished. The sign at the entrance reads "Devi's Fall", illustrating the Nepali propensity to deify everything that moves (*devi* means goddess). The whole story sounds like a fabrication to warn local youth to shun promiscuous Western ways.

If you're in this neighbourhood on a bike, set aside at least a little time to check out the dramatic **Seti canyon** south of Pokhara. There's an access point to the river near the mountaineering museum, and the road following the river southeastwards from there makes an excellent jaunt – you can ride for miles, though don't forget that you're going downhill and you'll eventually have to climb back up.

SOUTH OF POKHARA

The only through road beyond Pokhara, the **Siddhartha Highway** (Siddhartha Rajmarg), points south: a slow, uncomfortable, but occasionally rewarding journey to the Tarai. In 160km the highway traverses four major river drainages, negotiates countless twists and turns, crosses many landslide paths, and often claims a tyre or an axle. Six hours would be a fast run. Although it's the most direct route between Pokhara and the Indian border, give some thought to going via Chitwan if you're travelling by bus. Cyclists, however, will enjoy the variety and light traffic.

From Pokhara, the road labours 800m up to a divide before descending to **Naudaada**, a little-used alternative starting point for treks into the Kali Gandaki/Annapurna region (minibuses from Chipledhunga in Pokhara shuttle up here every half-hour or so). An old Kaski fortress guards the pass from the hill just to the east. Entering the Amdhi Khola watershed, the highway wriggles tortuously across the side of the valley, purposely avoiding the flat, straight valley floor – in a country so reliant on agriculture, you don't put a road through the best farmland. After the bazaar of **Syangja**, the valley draws in and the hills rear up spectacularly in places. Signs of erosion are evident everywhere here: these hills are geologically very unstable, and slough their topsoil like a thin skin.

Public buses stop at **Waling**, a nondescript wayside that owes its existence to busloads of hungry travellers. Beyond, the highway ascends gradually and then begins its descent to the Kali Gandaki, first passing the access road to the huge new **Kali Gandaki "A" Project**. The $450-million, 144-megawatt hydroelectric diversion, due for completion in 2001, is the largest and most expensive project ever undertaken in Nepal – and like it or not, it's now the finishing point for rafting trips on the river. The Siddhartha Highway crosses the river at **Ramdi Ghat**, the site of many caves, before climbing almost 1000m to its highest point. A few kilometres beyond is the turning for **Tansen** (below), the only town of note in this area. From there it's an hour's descent to Butwal and the Tarai (covered in Chapter Five). This last forty-kilometre stretch is particularly prone to landslides and so is often in dreadful shape.

Tansen and around

TANSEN is sold as is, unvarnished for tourist sensibilities. Once the seat of a powerful kingdom and now a lowly district headquarters, it makes no attempt to be anything but a typical market town in the heartland of the western hills. Yet slowly, almost reluctantly, Tansen yields its secrets: clacking *dhaka* looms glimpsed though doorways; the potters of Ghorabanda; the view from Srinagar Hill. Above all, it makes a superb base for day hikes and bikes in the surrounding countryside. As long as you're passing by on the Siddhartha Highway it's well worth breaking the journey here – especially if you're coming from India, for Tansen makes a more authentic introduction to Nepal than Pokhara.

Tansen's **history** goes back to the early sixteenth century, when it was known as Palpa, and when the Sen clan of princes, already established at Butwal, chose it as a safer base from which to expand family holdings that soon covered the length of the lower hills, almost to Sikkim. Makunda Sen, Palpa's legendary second king, allegedly raided Kathmandu and carried off two sacred Bhairab masks, only to be cut down by a plague sent by the Pashupatinath *linga*. Chastened by the king's death, his successors settled for forming a strategic alliance with Gorkha, which bought them breathing space when the latter began conquering territory in the mid-eighteenth century. Aided by a friendly Indian rajah, Palpa staved off the inevitable until 1806, when it became the

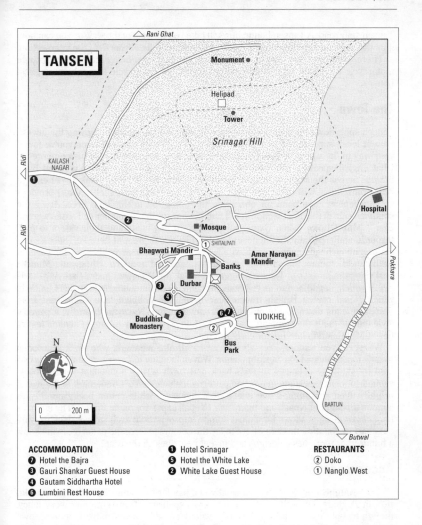

TANSEN

△ Rani Ghat

Monument

Helipad

Tower

Srinagar Hill

KAILASH NAGAR

◁ Ridi

◁ Ridi

❶

❷

▣ Mosque

SHITALPATI ①

Bhagwati Mandir

Banks

Amar Narayan Mandir

Durbar

❸

❹

❺

Buddhist Monastery

❻❼

② TUDIKHEL

Bus Park

Hospital

▷ Pokhara

SIDDHARTHA HIGHWAY

BARTUN

N

0   200 m

▽ Butwal

ACCOMMODATION
❼ Hotel the Bajra
❸ Gauri Shankar Guest House
❹ Gautam Siddhartha Hotel
❻ Lumbini Rest House

❶ Hotel Srinagar
❺ Hotel the White Lake
❷ White Lake Guest House

RESTAURANTS
② Doko
① Nanglo West

last territory to be annexed to modern Nepal. Tansen remains the headquarters of Palpa District, and many still refer to the town as Palpa. You might also hear it called Tansing, which was its original Magar name – the hills here are Magar country, although the town is now predominantly Newar.

Getting there

Public **buses** serve Tansen from Pokhara, Butwal, Kathmandu and Kakarbhitta (see p.244 for frequencies and times); from other points in the Tarai, change at Butwal. Coming from Pokhara or Sonauli you've also got the option of taking a faster and more comfortable quasi-tourist bus. However, these buses don't leave the Siddhartha Highway, so you have to get off at Bartun, the village at the start of the three-kilometre

Tansen spur road. A Tansen-bound bus will take you the rest of the way, or you can hoof it up the steep one-kilometre short cut that starts immediately north of the intersection.

There are no taxis or rikshas in Tansen, although the better hotels can arrange motorcycle or vehicle hire. It may be possible to rent a bicycle through some guest houses.

The Town

Tansen spills down the flank of Srinagar Hill, with the **bus park** occupying the lowest, newest level, surrounded by a tacky bazaar area. Things improve once you've found your way to the **upper town**. The direct footpath up from *Hotel the Bajra* emerges at what English-speakers call Bank Street, home of a modest bazaar and a Nepal Bank branch; across the street is the prosaic twentieth-century Durbar. Bank Street ends at **Shitalpati**, the hub of the upper town, where a new public rest shelter (*pati*) provides an excellent vantage point for observing the goings-on in this busy area. Along the southern side of this intersection you'll find the only visible reminder of Tansen's grand past – **Mul Dhoka** (Main Gate), tall enough for elephants and their riders to pass through, and reputedly the biggest of its kind in Nepal. West of here lie Tansen's oldest neighbourhoods, whose cobbled alleys and brick houses could pass for parts of Kathmandu, minus the crowds. An undistinguished modern **Bhagwati Mandir** enshrines the hostess of Tansen's biggest festival, the Bhagwati Jaatra (late Aug–early Sept), which, in addition to its religious function, also commemorates an 1814 battle in which Nepal routed British troops near here. The cobbled lane going east from Shitalpati leads down to the nineteenth-century **Amar Narayan Mandir**, a pagoda-style temple that's the stopping place for sadhus on their way to Janai Purnima festivities at Muktinath in late July or early August.

Wherever you wander, keep an eye out for **dhaka weavers**, who work at wooden treadle looms shaped like upright pianos. Woven in many hill areas, *dhaka* fabric is created by shuttling coloured threads back and forth across a constant vertical background to form repeating, geometric patterns. Palpali *dhaka*'s trademark is the use of brightly dyed *pashmina*, a fine goat's wool, against a white cotton background – it's famous throughout Nepal, and many *topi* (Nepali caps) are made from it. The simplicity of *dhaka* designs allows for almost infinite improvisation: each weaver decides without chart or counting threads where to lay the colours to form the patterns; many know a hundred or more basic designs and invent new ones all the time.

Accommodation

You pay roughly double in Tansen what you'd pay for the same class of **accommodation** in Pokhara. Oh well – it's still not very expensive. There's nothing very fancy, though two places try. Hot water and electricity are always intermittent, and the town is under a permanent water shortage. Don't settle for the lodges near the bus park, which are noisy and a steep slog from the centre.

Gauri Shankar Guest House (☎075/20150). A dreary place in a noisy, depressing location; the rooms are big and tolerably clean, but overpriced. ②/B③.

Gautam Siddhartha Guest House (☎075/20280). A fairly primitive Nepali lodge in a relatively quiet but uninteresting neighbourhood. ②.

Lumbini Rest House (no phone). A cheaper, cold-water place next door to the *Bajra*. ①.

Hotel Srinagar (☎075/20045, fax 20467). It's difficult to understand how this place keeps afloat. The location is great – it's the only lodging in Tansen with views nearby – but the facilities and service are poor for the price. It's a long way above town, so call ahead to arrange transport. B②.

Hotel the Bajra (☎075/20443). A big place with decent rooms and hot water, just far enough from the bus park to provide some seclusion. ②/B③.

Hotel the White Lake (☎075/20291). Compared to *Hotel Srinagar* (its only competitor), it's way better managed, though the in-town location makes it somewhat noisier and you have to walk to views. Decent restaurant. B⑤–⑥.

White Lake Guest House (book through *Hotel the White Lake*). Tansen's premier budget choice: a comfortable establishment in a very quiet location, with lovely grounds and a fine view of the town below. It's a long walk from the bus park, but a pickup service is available. ③.

Eating and other practicalities

Nanglo West, a branch of a Kathmandu-based **restaurant** chain, provides a welcome culinary oasis in Tansen. Overlooking Shitalpati, it has comfy indoor and outdoor tables, and serves excellent Nepali and Newar food (the European food is only so-so). Some of the guest houses boast rudimentary menus with Western items, but only *Hotel the White Lake* and *Hotel Srinagar* are serious contenders in the tourist food department. *Doko Restaurant* serves a good range of *momo* and other Newari dishes, and loads of nameless *bhojanalaya* and *mithai pasal* around the bus park and in the old part of town do *daal bhaat*, road snacks and sweets.

Shopping is easy in Tansen because the choice of handicrafts is mercifully limited to just a couple of local specialities. *Dhaka* (see above) is the main item – many shops in the bazaar sell nothing but *dhaka*. A good-quality Palpali weave will set you back Rs400 a metre, although you can get lesser quality for as little as Rs100. Tansen is also known for its *karuwa* – heavy, bulbous brass water vessels, which cost Rs200–2000 depending on size.

One of the two **banks** on Bank Street, Rastriya Banijya or Nepal Bank (Sun–Thurs 10am–2pm, Fri 10am–noon), should be able to change US dollar travellers' cheques, but it's doubtful they can cope with anything else. There are **telephone** services all over, and at least one place just uphill of Shitalpati does **email**.

Around Tansen: Srinagar Hill and beyond

The best thing about Tansen is getting out of it and exploring the outlying hill country and unaffected Magar villages. People on the trail will likely greet you with delighted smiles and the full palms-together *namaste* – a sign of gratitude for the assistance provided by foreign doctors at the nearby United Mission Hospital, which they will tend to assume you work for.

First stop on most excursions is **Srinagar Hill** (Srinagar Daada), north of town. The most direct route, which takes about half an hour on foot, starts from a small Ganesh temple above Shitalpati, but you have to zigzag a bit to get to the temple. From *Hotel Srinagar* it's an easy twenty-minute walk east along the ridge. The top (1525m) is planted with thick pine forest – catch the view from the helipad or the open area west of *Hotel Srinagar*. The peaks appear smaller and hazier from here than they do from Pokhara, but the Dhaulagiri and Annapurna ranges are still impressive; Machhapuchhre is less dominant, but its true "fishtail" profile is visible from this angle. On the other side, beyond Tansen, lies the luxuriant Madi Valley, which on winter mornings is filled with a silver fog. The area north of the helipad, just below the summit, has been turned into a large municipal park.

Besides the three described below, other hikes are possible from Tansen – ask your innkeeper or consult the HMG/FINNIDA maps for the area.

Rani Ghat

For walks beyond Srinagar there are at least two strong options, the first being the fourteen-kilometre round-trip to **RANI GHAT**, site of a fantastically derelict palace along the Kali Gandaki. The trail begins 200m east of *Hotel Srinagar* (locals call this intersection Kailash Nagar) and descends through an immensely satisfying landscape of farmland, trailside hamlets and, finally, a jungly gorge with impressive waterfalls. The walk itself takes at least four or five hours, but you'll want to set aside the whole day (it's quite an uphill climb on the way back). A road is eventually supposed to be built between Tansen and Rani Ghat, but it shouldn't interfere with the trail.

Set in a tranquil spot beside the turquoise Kali Gandaki, Rani Ghat is the site of occasional cremations. But the main attraction here is the spooky old **palace**, which was built in the late nineteenth century by a former government minister who, according to the custom of the day, was exiled to Palpa after a failed palace coup. Perched atop an outcrop directly overlooking the river, it was abandoned to the elements for many years but is now in the process of being renovated. You get a great view of it from the suspension bridge that crosses the river here.

Rani Ghat itself isn't really a village, just a couple of *chiya pasal* that offer only very limited food and emergency shelter. Bring a lunch and picnic on the tranquil, sandy beach.

To Ridi Bazaar

RIDI BAZAAR makes an equally eventful all-day outing, either on foot (13km one way, with the option of bussing back) or by bike (60km round-trip). From *Hotel Srinagar*, walk west to a fork at a police checkpost, bear right and in half an hour you'll reach Chandi Bhanjyang; turn left here and descend through a handsome canyon before rejoining the unpaved road for the last 7km. On a bike, stay on the main road all the way.

Set on the banks of the Kali Gandaki, Ridi is considered sacred because of the wealth of **shaligrams** – fossil-bearing stones associated with Vishnu – found in the river here. It used to be said that if a person were cremated at Ridi and his ashes sprinkled into the river, they would congeal to form a *shaligram*, and if the stone were then made into a likeness of Vishnu, the devotee would be one with his god. The spiral-shaped ammonite fossils typically found in *shaligram* are 150–200 million years old, dating from a time when the entire Himalayan region was submerged under a shallow sea.

Ridi has declined in importance over the years, but remains an occasional cremation ground and, during the **festival** of Magh Sankranti (January 14 or 15), a pilgrimage site for ritual bathing. Celebrations of the *ekadashi* of Khattik (the eleventh day of the bright fortnight of October–November) include processions and dancing. The colourful commercial end of town lies across a stream that joins the Kali Gandaki here, while the magical eighteenth-century **Rishikesh Mandir** is south of the stream, just above the bus stop. According to legend, the idol inside the squat temple, a form of Vishnu, was fished out of the river and originally bore the likeness of a young boy, but over the course of years has matured into adult form.

Several **buses** a day head back to Tansen, taking two hours. You can stay overnight if you get stuck. The return journey can be combined with a visit to **Palpa Bhairab**, up a short path from the pretty Newar village of Bhairabsthan, 8km before Tansen. So many animal sacrifices are performed at this temple, especially on Saturdays and Tuesdays, that it's often compared with that of Dakshin Kali in the Kathmandu Valley. Its much-feared Bhairab image is kept in a small chamber at the far corner of the compound; the gilded *trisul* here is claimed to be the biggest in Asia, and pilgrims have left a large number of smaller replicas at its base.

Ghorabanda

The most interesting of the villages east of Tansen, **GHORABANDA** is locally famous for its **potters**. It's just off the Siddhartha Highway, 3km north of the Tansen turning, but without your own wheels you'll have to walk. Take the dirt road from the Amar

Narayan temple towards the United Mission Hospital, bear right onto a trail after about 500m, descend and then contour through extensive paddy – if you've done it right, you'll drop down to the highway after about 2km, with Ghorabanda another 1km further along the road. Ghorabanda's potters, members of the Kumal caste, throw their almost spherical water jugs on heavy clay flywheels, shaping them and adding a stipple pattern with a wooden paddle, then sun-drying and finally kiln-firing them. The farmhouses and potteries of Ghorabanda spread down the hill from the highway.

CHAPTER FIVE

THE WESTERN TARAI

I n a country best known for its mountains, the lowland **Tarai** often gets short shrift. A narrow strip of flatland extending along the entire length of Nepal's southern border – including several *dun* (inner Tarai) valleys north of the first range of hills – the Tarai was originally covered in thick, malarial jungle. In the 1950s, however, the government identified the fertile southern plains as a major growth area to relieve population pressure in the hills, and, with the help of liberal quantities of DDT, brought malaria under control. Since then the jungle has been methodically cleared and the Tarai has emerged as Nepal's most productive agricultural and industrial region, representing 70 percent of the country's arable land, accounting for more than half its GDP and supporting about half its population. The barrier that had once insulated Nepal from Indian influences as effectively as the Himalaya had guarded the north, making possible the development of a uniquely Nepali culture, has been replaced by the geographic and political equivalent of a welcome mat. An unmistakable quality of Indianness now pervades the Tarai, as evidenced by the avid mercantilism of the border bazaars, the wearing of *lungyi* and chewing of betel, Muslim mosques and orthodox Brahmanism, the heat and dust, the jute mills and sugar refineries, and the many roads and irrigation projects built with Indian aid.

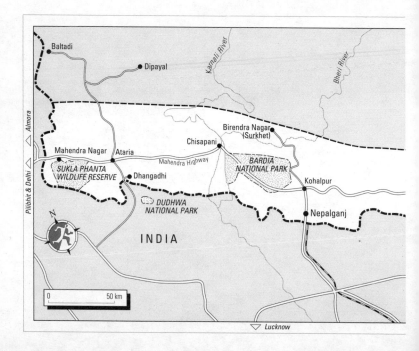

Fortunately, the government has set aside sizeable chunks of the **western Tarai** in the form of national parks and reserves, which remain as some of the finest **wildlife** and bird havens on the subcontinent. Dense riverine forest provides cover for predators like tigers and leopards; swampy grasslands make the perfect habitat for rhinoceros; and vast, tall stands of *sal*, the Tarai's most common tree, throng with what at times seems to be the entire cast of *Bambi*. You'll probably only have the time to visit one national park. **Chitwan**, the richest in game and the most accessible, is deservedly popular, but if crowds bother you and you're willing to invest some extra effort, check out **Bardia** or **Sukla Phanta**.

The region's other claim to fame is historical: the Buddha was born 2500 years ago at **Lumbini**, and his birthplace – one of the four holiest pilgrimage sites for Buddhists – is an appropriately serene place. Important archeological discoveries have been made in Lumbini, at nearby **Tilaurakot** and at several other outlying sites.

Four **border crossings** in the western Tarai are open to foreigners. **Sonauli** is the most heavily used because it's on the most direct route between Kathmandu and Varanasi, and fits in well with visits to Lumbini and Chitwan, but it's horrible. **Mahendra Nagar**, at the far western frontier, makes an adventurous backdoor route between Kathmandu and Delhi, and takes you right past Bardia and Sukla Phanta. For a really obscure international experience, you can cross at points south of **Nepalganj** or **Dhangadhi**.

Bus connections to the Tarai from Kathmandu and Pokhara are well developed via Narayanghat. The Tarai itself is traversed by a single main road, the **Mahendra Highway** (the Mahendra Rajmarg in Nepali, also known as the **East–West Highway**), now paved all the way to the far western border. Traffic drops off dramatically west of Butwal, which makes for great **cycling** but potentially long waits for bus connections.

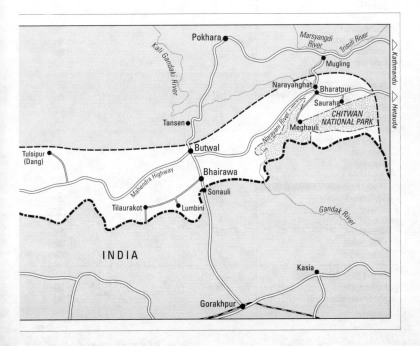

PUBLIC BUS SERVICES IN THE WESTERN TARAI

	Frequency (day)	Frequency (night)	Time (minimum)
To and from BHAIRAWA			
Biratnagar		5	14hr
Birganj	4	3	7hr
Butwal	24		1hr
Janakpur	1		10hr
Kakarbhitta		3	16hr
Kathmandu	8#	10#	8hr
Lumbini	18		1hr
Taulihawa	2		3hr
To and from BUTWAL			
Bhairawa/Sonauli	24		1hr
Birganj	4	3	6hr
Dhangadhi		2	10hr
Janakpur		3	9hr
Kathmandu	5	17	8hr
Mahendra Nagar	1	1	12hr
Nepalganj	2		6hr
Pokhara	1	1	7hr
Tansen	30		2hr 30min
To and from DHANGADHI			
Baitadi		1	12hr
Butwal		2	10hr
Dipayal	2	1	8hr
Kathmandu		2	18hr
Mahendra Nagar	12		3hr
Nepalganj	3		8hr
Pokhara		1	18hr
To and from JAGATPUR			
Kathmandu	2#		7hr
Narayanghat	10		2hr
Pokhara	1		7hr
To and from LUMBINI			
Bhairawa	18		1hr
Kathmandu	2	2	10hr
To and from MAHENDRA NAGAR			
Banbasa (border)	20		30min
Birganj		1	16hr
Butwal	1	1	12hr
Dhangadhi	12		3hr
Kathmandu		3	20hr
Nepalganj	3		7hr
To and from MEGHAULI			
Kathmandu	2#		7hr
Narayanghat	7		2hr

	Frequency (day)	Frequency (night)	Time (minimum)
To and from NARAYANGHAT**			
Bandipur	1		5hr
Devghat	12		30min
Gorkha	7		3hr
Jagatpur	10		2hr
Kakarbhitta		2	12hr
Kathmandu	9#		5hr
Meghauli	7		2hr
Nepalganj		2	8hr
Pokhara	12		5hr
Tadi Bazaar	20		45min
To and from NEPALGANJ			
Birendra Nagar (Surkhet)	12		5hr
Butwal	2		6hr
Dhangadhi	3		8hr
Janakpur		2	14hr
Mahendra Nagar	3		7hr
Narayanghat		2	8hr
Kathmandu	1#	4	12hr
Pokhara		2	12hr
Thakurdwara	2		4hr
To and from SAURAHA (CHITRASARI)			
Kathmandu	*		
Pokhara	*		
To and from SONAULI			
Butwal	24		2hr
Gorkha	1		7hr
Kathmandu	7	8	9hr
Pokhara	9*	3	9hr
To and from TADI BAZAAR**			
Kathmandu	2#		6hr
Narayanghat	20		45min
To and from TAULIHAWA			
Bhairawa	2		3hr
Kathmandu	1#	1	12hr
To and from THAKURDWARA			
Nepalganj	2		4hr

* Tourist bus services also available – see the respective sections for details.
** Many other buses pass through (in the case of Bhairawa, many originate in Sonauli).
# Sajha service available.

Internal **flights**, while expensive and not always reliable, can save a lot of time; Nepalganj is the air hub for western Nepal, and there are potentially useful airstrips in Meghauli and Bhairawa.

The **weather** in the Tarai is at its best from October to January – the days are more pleasantly mild during the latter half of this period, though the nights and mornings can be surprisingly chilly and damp. However, the wildlife viewing gets much better after the thatch has been cut, from late January on, by which time the temperatures are starting to warm up again. It gets really hot (especially in the far west) in April, May and June. The monsoon brings not only rain but mosquitoes, malaria and leeches, and many roads become impassable at this time

CHITWAN AND AROUND

Chitwan is the name not only of Nepal's most visited **national park** but also of the surrounding *dun* valley and administrative district. The name means "Heart of the Jungle" – a description that, sadly, now holds true only for the lands protected within the park and a few designated community forests. Yet the rest of the **valley**, though it's been reduced to a flat, furrowed plain, still provides fascinating vignettes of a rural lifestyle that's different again from the hill-clinging existence of upland Nepal. Really ugly development is confined to the wayside conurbation of **Narayanghat/Bharatpur** – and even this has left the nearby holy site of **Devghat** unscathed.

Chitwan National Park

The best and worst aspects of **CHITWAN NATIONAL PARK** are that it can be done on the cheap and it's relatively easy to get to. In recent years the park has risen meteorically on the list of Things to Do in Nepal, so that these days, unless you go during the steamy season, you'll have to share your experience with a lot of other people. If you want to avoid crowds, go to Bardia or Sukla Phanta, described later in this chapter.

You're forgiven if you thought **Sauraha** is the only place for budget tourists to stay in Chitwan. For all intents and purposes, it is. In the late 1970s some genius had the idea of setting up a little thatched-roof lodge just outside the Sauraha park entrance, and the place has basically had a monopoly ever since. But package trips have taken a lot of the spontaneity out of Sauraha, and in autumn, with the inhabitants of forty-odd lodges all converging on the same finite patch of park, the area can get uncomfortably crowded. If you don't mind roughing it a little, try **Ghatgain** or **Meghauli** instead. Or, if you've got the money – usually at least $100 a night per person, all-in – go for pampered seclusion at any one of half a dozen luxury lodges and tented camps **inside the park**.

Promises of "safari adventure" at Chitwan are misleading. While the park's **wildlife** is astoundingly concentrated, remember that the dense vegetation doesn't allow the easy sightings you get in the savannahs of Africa (especially in autumn, when the grass is high). But go with realistic expectations, don't buy into the package-tour mentality, and it's still possible to enjoy yourself. **Elephant rides**, **jeep tours**, **canoe trips** and just plain **walks** each give a different slant on the luxuriant, teeming forest.

Park entry permits are valid for two consecutive days, which tends to dictate the length of most travellers' stays. Rushed as it is, this can work out quite reasonably, but don't be led into thinking that you can "do" Chitwan in two nights and three days. Keep flexible or you might regret not being able to stay longer.

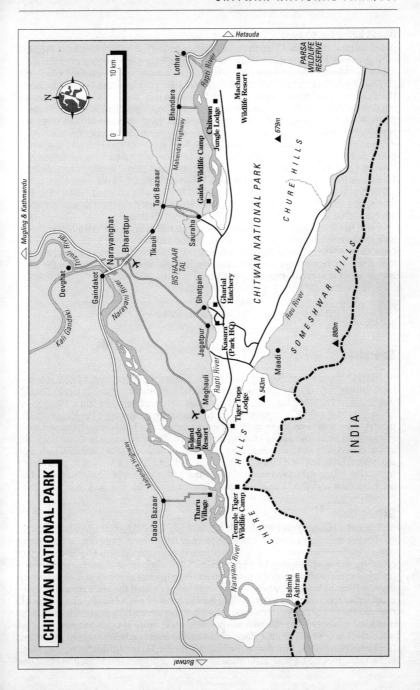

About budget packages

Avoid them! A three-day Chitwan "safari" **package** booked in Kathmandu or Pokhara only gives you a day and a half in the park, and you'll have little control over the if-it's-8am-it-must-be-time-for-the-bird-walk programme of activities. You'll be locked into staying at a lodge that has little incentive to work for your business (and every incentive to cut corners, since it has to give the booking agent 50 percent), you'll be served inferior set meals, and you probably won't get to choose your guide either. Finally, a package costs somewhat more than doing the same thing on your own, and saves you hardly any trouble, since Chitwan is incredibly easy to visit independently.

If you must be bound by an itinerary, at least book it directly through the lodge's own office in Kathmandu or Pokhara, which will be more accountable for arrangements than an agent will be. You can get office addresses and phone numbers by collecting brochures from agents. A typical package will **cost** around $50 per person for a two-night stay in a budget lodge with common bath ($60 with attached bath), including meals, bus transport from Kathmandu or Pokhara, park entry permit and activities. (Doing the same thing independently will cost about $5 less.)

A visit to Chitwan can also be combined with a **raft trip** on the Trisuli River, bookable through rafting operators in Kathmandu and Pokhara, but it's still a bad idea to book the Chitwan stay as part of the raft trip. And while rafting can cut out some of the long drive, no matter what the salesman says, it won't take you all the way to the park: Narayanghat is normally the end of the line.

> The telephone code for Sauraha and Chitwan District is ☎056.

Sauraha

SAURAHA (pronounced *So*-ruh-hah), Chitwan's original budget safari village, is one of those unstoppably successful destinations at which Nepal seems to excel. In fact it's the spitting image of Pokhara's Lakeside a decade or so ago: quiet, unpaved lanes, folksy guest houses, a small cluster of restaurants (many spuriously named after Pokhara establishments), a few provisions shops and bakeries, a smattering of bikes for rent, the odd bookshop and ticketing office, and a growing number of concrete eyesores. In recent years, the arrival of electricity and the paving of the road from the Mahendra Highway have increased the general noise level and hustle factor, and are fuelling a speculative rush to build luxury hotels. The village still retains much of its intimacy and its unhurried, almost soporific character, but each year, like Lakeside, it loses a little more of what once made it so enjoyable.

Getting there

Daily **tourist buses** serve Sauraha from Kathmandu and Pokhara; the fare is Rs150–200 (minibuses are more expensive) and the journey takes about six hours. At the time of writing the buses weren't actually going all the way to Sauraha, due to an unspanned river crossing, and were stopping at a place called Chitrasari, about 2km short of town. A bridge is in the works, so by the time you get there the bus may take you all the way to the new Sauraha bus park, where the touts will have prepared the usual ambush for you. If not, cross the footbridge to the waiting fleet of battered guest-house **jeeps**, which will take you the rest of the way for a fixed price (Rs30 per person). Each guest house has its own jeep, so whoever you ride with will probably make every effort to win your business – you don't have to stay at their place, of course, but count on being dropped off there.

The nearest **public bus** stop is Tadi Bazaar on the Mahendra Highway, 6km north of Sauraha. Tadi isn't a final destination for most long-distance services (the exception

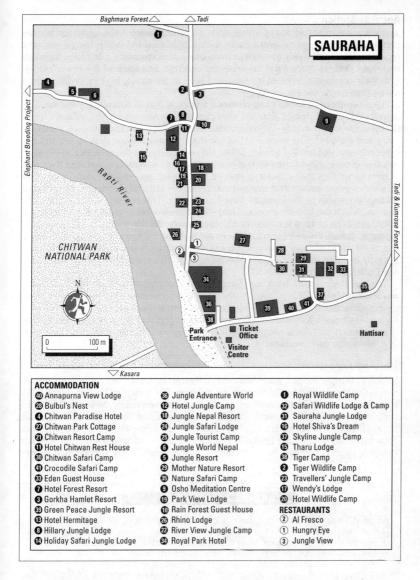

SAURAHA

Baghmara Forest △   △ Tadi

Elephant Breeding Project

Rapti River

CHITWAN NATIONAL PARK

Tadi & Kumrose Forest △

N

0   100 m

△ Kasara

Park Entrance

Ticket Office

Visitor Centre

Hattisar

ACCOMMODATION

⑳ Annapurna View Lodge	㊱ Jungle Adventure World	❶ Royal Wildlife Camp
㉘ Bulbul's Nest	⑫ Hotel Jungle Camp	㉜ Safari Wildlife Lodge & Camp
❹ Chitwan Paradise Hotel	⑱ Jungle Nepal Resort	㉛ Sauraha Jungle Lodge
㉗ Chitwan Park Cottage	㉔ Jungle Safari Lodge	⑯ Hotel Shiva's Dream
㉑ Chitwan Resort Camp	㉕ Jungle Tourist Camp	㊲ Skyline Jungle Camp
⑪ Hotel Chitwan Rest House	❻ Jungle World Nepal	⑮ Tharu Lodge
㉚ Chitwan Safari Camp	❺ Jungle Resort	㊳ Tiger Camp
㊶ Crocodile Safari Camp	㉙ Mother Nature Resort	❷ Tiger Wildlife Camp
㉝ Eden Guest House	㉟ Nature Safari Camp	㉓ Travellers' Jungle Camp
❼ Hotel Forest Resort	❾ Osho Meditation Centre	⑰ Wendy's Lodge
❸ Gorkha Hamlet Resort	⑲ Park View Lodge	⑳ Hotel Wildlife Camp
㊴ Green Peace Jungle Resort	⑩ Rain Forest Guest House	**RESTAURANTS**
⑬ Hotel Hermitage	㉖ Rhino Lodge	② Al Fresco
❽ Hillary Jungle Lodge	㉒ River View Jungle Camp	① Hungry Eye
⑭ Holiday Safari Jungle Lodge	㉞ Royal Park Hotel	③ Jungle View

being Sajha from Kathmandu), but any bus passing by Tadi along the Mahendra Highway will let you off there. If you arrive at Tadi by midday your chances of meeting up with a guest house jeep are pretty good (again, Rs30). Otherwise, catch a cycle rik-sha to Chitrasari, or if you think you can pedal with a pack on, rent a bike in Tadi and have your guest house return it later.

It's also possible to **fly** to Bharatpur, about 15km west of Tadi Bazaar – see p.313.

Accommodation

Sauraha has a great tradition of "camp"-style **accommodation** – the best guest houses here are like rustic little country clubs, with simple mud-and-thatch bungalows, airy dining pavilions and shady gardens or open lawns. Unfortunately, many have forsaken traditional designs and natural materials for concrete, and some of the newer places, with their regimental rows of bunkers and little or no shade, look more like prison camps than jungle camps.

Often the deciding factor when choosing a place to stay in Sauraha is **location**. The largest share of lodgings line up shoulder to shoulder along the village's main north–south strip – handy for restaurants and the park entrance, though relatively noisy and crowded. The ones overlooking the river avoid those drawbacks, and are especially peaceful around sunset. Other places scattered in the area east of the park entrance provide a good combination of seclusion and convenience, and what they lack in river views they make up for in mature landscaping and shade. Finally, a growing number of guest houses and more upmarket hotels are materializing along the road leading westwards to the Elephant Breeding Project. This is a very quiet and solitary location, which can be both good and bad – it's more trouble to eat out if you're staying there, and it can be hard to connect with other people. It's also a long trudge to the park entrance, though the more upscale lodges out that way will ferry you to and fro by jeep, and to return to cheaper lodgings you can exit the park more directly and adventurously by crossing the river. On the plus side, you're that much closer to the Baghmara and Buffer Zone forests (see p.309).

You can theoretically book any Sauraha accommodation through the local **hotel association** (☎056/29363), though the people who answer the phone there don't always speak much English. Booking ahead may also weaken your bargaining position; if you call a lodge's Kathmandu office you'll almost certainly be quoted a package rate.

A reminder: Sauraha is not the only place to stay – see the later "Alternative bases" and "Inside the park" sections.

BUDGET LODGES

Sauraha's **budget lodges**, which outnumber the rest by a wide margin, are the ones so aggressively promoted by the touts at the bus stop. The archetypal budget lodge has a row of cheap (②–③) mud-and-thatch huts with a common toilet/shower facility, and a separate block of bigger concrete bungalows with attached bathrooms (B④). The latter usually have ceiling fans; mosquito netting should come with either type of room. Solar hot-water systems are gradually replacing crude wood-fired boilers, but in either case hot water is typically only available at certain times of day. Competition is very

---

ROOM PRICE SCALES

All guest houses and hotels have been price-graded according to the scale below, which is based on the price of the cheapest double room in high season. Codes prefixed by B denote the cost of the cheapest room with attached bathroom, and those prefixed by AC refer to air-conditioned rooms. See p.39 for a fuller explanation.

① Less than Rs140 ($2 if quoted in US$)	⑤ $8–12
	⑥ $12–20
② Rs140–200 ($2–3)	⑦ $20–40
③ Rs200–350 ($3–5)	⑧ $40–75
④ Rs350–550 ($5–8)	⑨ Over $75

keen in the budget category, so prices will often drop dramatically when occupancy is low, and discounts for singles can generally be negotiated.

The lodgings are too spread out, and it's usually too hot, to do much comparison-shopping in Sauraha. The best strategy is to decide on a guest house in advance and try to get a ride with a jeep that's going directly there. The following list is short but selective. Most of the others shown on the map are perfectly adequate, but one or two (notably *Tharu Lodge* and *Safari Wildlife Lodge*) seem to generate consistently bad reports, so keep an ear out for both negative and positive word of mouth. Also, be aware that budget guest houses change hands frequently in Sauraha: if a name has changed from what's shown on the map, that's a likely sign that it's being run by new people who may not uphold the same standards.

Annapurna View Lodge (no phone). Nice location and grounds, with a short, shady walk to the park boundary. ③/B④.

Chitwan Paradise Hotel (☎60069). A dressed-up version of the standard Sauraha lodge, with spacious rooms and a big lawn. Managed by a Tharu NGO, it donates 60 percent of profits to projects aiding the local community. ③/B⑤.

Chitwan Resort Camp (Kathmandu: ☎227711; *mandala@ccsl.com.np*). Close to the village but reasonably insulated from it. Sun and shade, with a *machaan* that's great for sitting. B④–⑤.

Hotel Forest Resort (no phone). Small, shady, mellow and cheap. ①/B③.

Green Peace Jungle Resort (Kathmandu: ☎423744). Lush grounds and a great location, although the rooms, which are in four-room blocks, aren't quite up to snuff. ②/B④.

Island Tented Camp (no phone). A splendidly primitive outfit located on the way to the Elephant Breeding Project (2km off the map), with just a couple of *machaan* beside the river that offer a good chance of seeing – or at least hearing – animals at night. ④.

Mother Nature Resort (no phone). A well-kept place in a fairly good location. Nepali–Western management. ③/B④.

Rhino Lodge (☎29365, fax 60161). Unbeatable river views, though the facilities are a bit dreary. B④.

River View Jungle Camp (☎60164). It isn't actually on the river, but it's close enough. Pricier than most, but with pleasant, leafy grounds. ④/B⑤.

MODERATE AND EXPENSIVE LODGES

Price is not necessarily an indicator of quality in Sauraha. Some lodges charge deluxe prices for budget facilities, on the theory that package tourists will never know the difference. However, the ones listed here are a cut or two above the budget pack: you should be able to count on superior location or grounds, good (or at least better) food, reliable hot water and perhaps air coolers in the rooms, a jeep in good working order, experienced guides, and small touches like a library, slide shows and enough binoculars to go around.

These lodges get by mainly on package business, but they'll usually take you on an accommodation-only basis if you just show up, enabling you to save quite a bit of money by paying for activities à la carte.

Baghmara Wildlife Resort, northwest of Sauraha near the Baghmara Community Forest – off the map (☎60250; Kathmandu: ☎222180, fax 226392). A strange, desolate place, though it does have a swimming pool and air conditioning. B⑧/AC⑨.

Hotel Jungle Camp (Kathmandu office: ☎240669; *jungle@camp.mos.com.np*). Extensive forested grounds, nifty bamboo bungalows, restaurant and bar. B⑧.

Jungle Adventure World (☎29364; Kathmandu: ☎434380). Forested compound, decent bungalows in an excellent location near the river, park entrance and village. B⑥.

Osho Camp (☎29367, fax 60235). Huge, shady and very peaceful grounds, but it's actually a Rajneesh retreat centre, so you probably wouldn't want to stay here unless you plan to participate in the daily sessions. ⑤.

Royal Park Hotel (☎29361; Kathmandu: ☎412987). Nicely furnished bungalows scattered throughout spacious grounds. Good restaurant and bakery. B⑦.

Tiger Camp (☎60189; Kathmandu: ☎224318; *sundar@boodles.mos.com.np*). Arguably the best location in Sauraha, overlooking the river right at the park entrance – the garden seating area is great for watching elephant-bathing and other river activity. Good restaurant. Disappointing rooms (bit of a rodent problem), though there's a marvellous *machaan*-like hut. ⑥/B⑦.

Eating and drinking

Guest house dining rooms are okay for breakfast and hobnobbing with guides and fellow travellers, but their main meals are by and large not very appetizing. The **restaurants** in Sauraha's burgeoning little dining quarter, while nowhere near as sophisticated as those in Nepal's other tourist hotspots, at least offer the chance to break free from the guest-house routine and put a little variety in your diet. Most cover all the standard bases – sizzlers, pastas, cutlets, noodles, local fish – and a few advertise "special" lassis made with *bhang* (pounded marijuana, which produces a hell of a kick). The slick *Al Fresco Café & Pub* serves excellent Indian, Chinese and Continental dishes under an open pavilion, while the *Jungle View*, *Hungry Eye* and *KC's* (next door to the *Hungry Eye*) offer great river views from their upstairs tables and passable food. You could also visit one of the classier guest houses for a nice meal – *Tiger Camp* can be recommended – or go for really cheap local fare at one of the *bhatti* east of the *Hungry Eye* or around *Nature Safari Camp*.

A couple of transient **"pubs"** have taken root on the beach north of Tiger Camp, which is a heavenly place to hang out during the late afternoon and around sunset. Some of the rooftop restaurants advertise "happy hours" and are good for evening drinks, but nothing stays open very late. In any case, you'll want to make your way back to lodgings before 10pm or so to avoid unplanned encounters with wildlife.

Entertainment

Sauraha's trademark entertainment is the **Tharu stick dance**, a mock battle in which participants parry each other's sticks with graceful, split-second timing. The original purpose of the dance, it's said, was simply to make a lot of racket to keep the wild animals away at night. It still forms a traditional part of Tharu celebrations of Faagun Purnima (the full moon of February–March), but the version you're likely to see is a more contrived tourist show put on for package groups at Sauraha lodges. Performances are held every evening in high season at one or more venues (your lodge should know who's performing where), and anyone is welcome to watch; *Tiger Camp* also hosts regular sunset shows for guests and diners.

Tharu Cultural Program Hall, at the north end of the village, puts on nightly **culture shows** featuring regional music and dance for tourist consumption (Rs50). In addition, some lodges host informal folk-dancing sessions, where audience participation is expected, if not coerced.

Park practicalities

Park **entry permits** (Rs650 for 2 days; children under 10 free) are purchased at the ranger's office (hours vary seasonally, but generally daily 6–9am & 1.30–4pm) to the left of the visitor centre. A separate fee may be required to enter certain forested areas outside the park – see p.309. The permit queue can be slow around opening time, so get there early, or have someone from your lodge wait for you (a surcharge may be payable). Elephant rides can be booked at the same time. Ask to see the ticket before setting off, as guides sometimes try to sneak their clients into the park with invalid tickets, or take them to forested areas outside the park where a permit isn't necessary. There's no formal park **entrance**; you enter by canoe or by wading across the river.

The **visitors' centre** (daily 6am–6pm) has a modest but informative display on the ecology of the park. Chitwan **maps** sold in Sauraha are helpful if you're planning to do any non-standard explorations in the park or unguided excursions outside it.

Guides

For safety reasons (see box), visitors are not allowed to enter the park on foot without a certified **guide**. In fact, at the time of writing officials were requiring that every group entering the park be accompanied by *two* guides, although this is likely to be a short-lived policy.

Sauraha's guides are for the most part keen and personable, both on and off the job, and their knowledge of species (especially birds) can be encyclopedic. They're **certified** by the King Mahendra Trust as "junior" or "senior", and should be able to show their credentials. However, certification level isn't a very good indicator of **experience**, because it doesn't take much to reach senior status – the question you need to ask prospective guides is how many *years* they've been guiding in Chitwan. Unfortunately, leading tourists through a jungle full of two-ton horned animals is a hazardous occupation, and anyone with any sense gets out of it as soon as they can, so it may be hard to find a guide with more than three or four years' experience. Note that less experienced guides are also apt to speak less English, so it's harder for them to impart what information they do know, and there's more risk of miscommunication in a dangerous situation. (If your guide yells *look*, that means "hide" in Nepali!)

Every lodge has its own **in-house guides**, but you can also hire one through a number of freelance **guide services**. The biggest of these is United Jungle Guide Service, a syndicate of ex-lodge guides who've joined forces and purport to maintain high standards; most other services are just one-man outfits. Freelance guides tend to have more experience, but there are some excellent in-house guides, too – ask other travellers if they've found someone they can recommend. Another possible reason to go with one

---

STAYING ALIVE IN CHITWAN

Lodge owners and guides often play down the risks associated with tracking wildlife, so as not to scare off business. In fact, **safety** is a serious issue in Chitwan. A year doesn't go by without one or two fatalities in the park; those killed are usually locals during the January thatch-gathering, or guides protecting their clients. There are no emergency medical facilities in or near the park – the closest hospital is in Bharatpur, a minimum two-hour evacuation when you add up all the stages, which means if there's major bleeding the patient is essentially out of luck.

The greatest danger comes from **rhinos**, who have poor eyesight, a keen sense of smell and a tendency to charge at anything they perceive to be a threat. If a rhino is about to charge it will lower its head and take a step back; if it does, try to run in a zigzag path and throw off a piece of clothing (the rhino will stop to smell it), or better yet, climb the nearest big tree. **Sloth bears** can also be dangerous if surprised. Fortunately, **tigers** rarely attack humans. (A tiger will occasionally turn "man-eater", but only when age has weakened the animal to the point that it can no longer chase its accustomed prey, and even then it will probably prefer livestock to people.) If a bear or tiger charges, climb a *small* tree. Don't get anywhere near a mother with young ones of any of these species.

The best safety tip is not to go into the jungle without a **guide**, but even a guide can't guarantee your personal safety. Most guides are young and gung-ho, and in their eagerness to please will sometimes encourage tourists to venture too close to animals. And no matter how competent, a guide can't know where all the animals are, nor can he, in an emergency, assist more than one person at a time. For this reason most reputable guides will limit **group size** to four clients – it's in your interest to support them in doing so.

of your lodge's guides is that it will probably be easier to put together a group of four, which lowers the per-person cost. Guide **fees** depend on the activity, and are detailed in the relevant sections below.

Other practicalities

Sauraha's fast-changing strip has all the same conveniences as Lakeside and Thamel, albeit on a smaller scale. Small **shops**, stalls and "German" bakeries stock basic food and other items (bottled water, film, batteries, toilet paper, postcards and so on). You can even buy and sell books. Curio shops sell mainly geographically inappropriate items, but if you search around you can find some locally produced Tharu handicrafts such as woven-grass baskets and hats – try the community shop near the visitors' centre.

A couple of **moneychangers** have offices on the strip, though their rates are a couple of percent lower than what you can get in a real bank (the nearest bank is in Tadi).

CHITWAN IN THE BALANCE

It's an open question whether Chitwan has been blessed or cursed by its own riches. Its big game couldn't escape the notice of trigger-happy maharajas for long: when Jang Bahadur Rana overthrew the Shah dynasty in 1846, one of his first actions was to make Chitwan a private hunting preserve for rulers and visiting dignitaries. The following century saw some truly hideous **hunts** – King George V, during an eleven-day shoot in 1911, killed 39 tigers and 18 rhinos. In those days the technique, if you could call it that, was to send *shikari* (trackers) into the forest to locate a tiger and set out a buffalo calf as bait. The sahibs were then alerted, loaded onto elephants and, joined by other huntsmen, the whole party of as many as 600 elephants and riders would approach the spot from all directions. As the circle closed, helpers would spread white sheets between the advancing elephants to keep the tiger from breaking through. High up in their howdahs, the sahibs could get off shots at point-blank range.

Still, the Ranas' patronage afforded Chitwan a certain degree of protection. So did malaria. That all changed in the early 1950s, when the Ranas were thrown out, the monarchy was restored, and the new government launched its malaria-control programme. Settlers poured in and **poaching** went unpoliced – rhinos, whose horns were (and still are) valued for Chinese medicine and Yemeni knife handles, were especially hard-hit. By 1960, the human population of the valley had trebled to 100,000, and the number of rhinos had plummeted from 1000 to 200. With the Asian one-horned rhino on the verge of extinction, Nepal emerged as an unlikely hero in one of conservation's finest hours. Chitwan was set aside in 1962 as a **rhino sanctuary** (it became Nepal's first national park in 1973) and, despite the endless hype about tigers, rhinos are Chitwan's biggest attraction and its greatest triumph.

Chitwan now boasts more than 500 **rhinos** – a quarter of the species total – and numbers are growing healthily. Poaching isn't nearly the problem here that it is in India, no doubt thanks to the deployment of an entire army battalion in the park, although killings do still occur, especially along the park's southern border. The latest tiger census counted 107 **tigers** in Chitwan and another twelve in adjacent Parsa Wildlife Reserve. These numbers appear to be very stable, which is encouraging news in the light of dwindling tiger populations almost everywhere else in South Asia. Chitwan also supports at least 400 **gaur** (Indian bison), found mainly in the drier upland areas, and provides a part-time home to as many as 45 wild **elephants** that roam between here and India. Altogether, 51 mammalian species are found in the park, including sloth bear, leopard, langur and four kinds of deer. Chitwan is also Nepal's most important sanctuary for **birds**, with more than 520 species recorded, as well as two varieties of **crocodile**. (For more detail on Tarai wildlife, see "Natural history" in Contexts.)

But Chitwan's seesaw battle for survival continues. While its forest ecosystem is healthy for the time being, **pollution** by upstream industries is endangering the rivers flowing into it: gangetic dolphins have now disappeared from the Narayani, and gharial

International **telephone** and **email** services are available, but again, charges here are significantly higher than in Kathmandu or Pokhara. The **post office** is at the intersection east of Osho Camp (off the map), but have your guest house take letters there for franking, or better yet wait till you get to someplace bigger.

Bikes can be rented from a few operators in the village for about Rs100 a day, and some guest houses have their own. **Motorcycle** rental is quite expensive (Rs800 per day, not including fuel) but the price ought to come down as the bikes get trashed.

Moving on

Leaving Sauraha is easy **by tourist bus**. Your guest house or an agent in the village can arrange the ticket to Kathmandu or Pokhara, and a guest house jeep will get you to the departure point in time. Fares quoted include whatever commission the seller thinks he can take you for, so are negotiable; book as far in advance as possible to be sure of a seat.

---

crocodiles are only hanging on thanks to human intervention (see p.310). Human **population** growth represents an even graver danger in the long term. With more than 300,000 people now inhabiting the Chitwan Valley, conservationists wonder how much longer residents will tolerate the setting aside of such fertile land, not to mention the destruction of their crops by the rhinos and elephants that are protected there. **Tourism** has undoubtedly helped make animals and trees worth more alive than dead, but only to those few in the tourist industry – for everyone else, tourism is another potential cause for resentment, since while the government is telling them to stay out of the park, it's actually *encouraging* foreigners to enter. At any rate, tourism causes impacts of its own. (Park officials are finally recognizing that the Sauraha area is overused, and have started making the first tentative steps to disperse tourists to other entrance areas.)

The key to safeguarding Chitwan, everyone agrees, is to win the support of local people, and there's some indication that this is beginning to happen. The much-touted open season on **thatch-gathering** in the park each January was an early attempt to offer some compensation to those inconvenienced by the park. More recently, the establishment of a **buffer zone** around the park has paved the way for a much more far-reaching series of actions. Many villages in this critical and heavily populated strip have been encouraged to set up **community forests**, which reduce residents' need to go into the park by giving them their own areas for gathering wood, thatch and other resources. Some of these community forests are nearly as rich in flora and fauna as the park itself, and communities near Sauraha have found it's in their interest to manage their forests like unofficial national parks (see p.309). The prospect of collecting hefty entrance fees is turning local people into zealous guardians of the environment, and is thankfully reducing the role played by the so-called **Rhino Patrol**, the corrupt and ineffective force originally set up to prevent poaching and illegal woodcutting in the buffer zone.

Two initiatives deserve particular credit for improving the lot of local people, which indirectly benefits the park. One is the **Parks and People Project**, funded mainly by the UN Development Programme, which is active in Chitwan as well as the other Tarai parks and wildlife reserves. Working from the grassroots up, the project organizes income-generating schemes and small-scale infrastructure improvements in buffer-zone communities. The **King Mahendra Trust for Nature Conservation**, funded by the World Wildlife Fund and others, has been instrumental in helping set up community forests and is active in general community-development efforts such as building schools, health posts, water taps, roads and appropriate technology facilities. These and other projects have received a huge boost from the 1995 **Buffer Zone Act**, which has recently started allocating 50 percent of park entrance fees for local use. As whenever there are big pots of cash like this, there's always the potential for corruption, but whatever money does get through should prove to be a bonanza for buffer-zone communities. Such measures stand to give local people a real stake in the park's continued protection; without them, even an army battalion won't be enough.

Difficulties may arise if your next destination isn't along a tourist bus route. First, the agent will probably be unable to get you a confirmed seat on a **public bus** from Tadi (the nearest stop), since almost all originate elsewhere. Second, there may not be any jeeps going to Tadi when you want to go. This second point will cease to be a problem if and when taxis start serving Sauraha, but in the meantime the best solution is to get a ride in your guest house's jeep to Tadi whenever it's going (probably in the early morning), and from there catch any bus heading in your direction. Your guest house should be able to advise on the timings of relevant services. You could also ride a local bus to Narayanghat, the nearest transport hub, where there will be a greater selection of onward services.

Agents in Sauraha can also arrange **air tickets** from Bharatpur to Kathmandu (4 daily; $55).

Alternative bases

It's becoming increasingly easy (though still not very popular) to stay in other villages near the park that are much less touristed than Sauraha. Two areas along the park's northern boundary – Ghatgain and Meghauli – have guest houses, guides, elephants and entry checkposts, and others may soon follow suit. These places are by definition off the beaten track, so unless you're staying in one of the upmarket package-only places there, don't expect highly developed services or lots of fellow travellers. If you're not sure that's what you want, go to Sauraha first and consider doing a jungle trek (see p.311) from there to Ghatgain or Meghauli.

Ghatgain and Jagatpur

Several lodges are located along or near the Rapti River at **GHATGAIN** and **JAGAT-PUR**, respectively 16km and 20km west of Sauraha. All are within easy reach of the Kasara park headquarters, the gharial crocodile breeding project, two interesting lakes (Lami Tal and Tamar Tal) and a good patch of jungle. Currently only a couple of elephants are quartered in this area, but park officials are said to be planning to move more of Sauraha's animals here and establishing some sort of permanent entrance station near Jagatpur.

Most likely you'll come here on a jungle trek **with a guide** from Sauraha, but once here you might want to stay more than one night. Alternatively, you can take a **jeep** tour to Kasara and walk from there, although you might have trouble finding these lodges on your own. Daily express buses connect Jagatpur with Kathmandu and Pokhara, and local **buses** trundle to Jagatpur from Narayanghat every 45 minutes in the morning, less frequently in the afternoon. For Ghatgain lodges, ask to be let off at Patihani (if that doesn't ring a bell, ask for *Safari Narayani*), from where it's a 1.5-kilometre walk south on a side road – they're all very close together.

The park starts on the other side of Rapti River: cross by dugout canoe from Ghatgain or Jagatpur and pay your entry fee (if you haven't already got a ticket) to one of the soldiers on the other side.

Ghumtee Riviera Lodge, Ghatgain (no phone). Brick-and-mud bungalows, shady grounds and an awesome river overlook. Cold water. ②.

Nature Darai Village, 1.5km west of Jagatpur (no phone). This lodge is right on the road that continues westwards from Jagatpur, and nowhere near the river. It's inferior to the Ghatgain places, but it might be better located for certain jungle trek itineraries. ②.

Riverview Lodge, Ghatgain (☎29347). Simple rooms in a cottagey longhouse with a great view of the river. Hot water by the bucket. ②.

Safari Narayani Lodge, Ghatgain (☎20130; Kathmandu: ☎525015; *info@nbe.pc.mos.com.np*). Deluxe package-only outfit with comfy rooms, fine food and its own elephants and jeeps. It's affiliated with the *Narayani Safari Hotel* in Narayanghat. B⑨.

Sunset View Lodge, Ghatgain (no phone). A slightly more humble version of the *Riverview*, with the same view. Cold water. ①.

Meghauli

MEGHAULI, 15km west of Jagatpur, is home to the **airstrip** used by guests visiting *Tiger Tops*, which all but owns this part of the park (daily flights from Kathmandu; $72). Consequently the village sees daily herds of upmarket tourists migrating back and forth on planes and jeeps, but has very little to do with them. Few independent travellers make it here either, as it's a two-day trek from Sauraha, or about two hours by local **bus** from Narayanghat (hourly in the morning, less frequent after 10am). There are also daily express buses between Kathmandu and Meghauli.

Though Meghauli has only one guest house now, it has the ingredients to become a serious competitor to Sauraha. Bhimle, the area of park just across the Rapti River, boasts superb **rhino** and **tiger** habitat – *Tiger Tops* wouldn't be here otherwise, would they? – and it's also universally hailed as the best **bird-watching** site in Chitwan. The countryside and traditional Tharu and Baahun **villages** surrounding Meghauli make for great outside-the-park exploring. And to top it all off, for several days in early December Meghauli hosts one of Nepal's most absurdly enjoyable events, the **World Elephant Polo Championships**, which is definitely worth adjusting your schedule to see – the action is surprisingly fast-paced and sporting.

Buses stop at the newest, easternmost end of the village, known as Parsadhap Bazaar. Several separate settlements, all considered part of Meghauli, are dotted along the dirt road that leads westwards past the airstrip (which begins about 1.5km from the bus stop) and on to the Rapti River crossing (another 2km). Dugouts ferry *Tiger Tops* guests across here, but the boatmen are told not to assist independent travellers, so *bakshish* may be necessary. The Bhimle guard post, where you have to show your park permit or pay an entrance fee, is another 3km beyond.

Meghauli's sole place to **stay**, *Chital Lodge* (no phone; ③), is set in a shady grove south and east of the airstrip. It's primitive, but in a really pleasant way, with rustic little huts on stilts, friendly management and good (Nepali) food. The owner is a bird expert who speaks good English and can arrange just about anything his counterparts in Sauraha can – elephant and jeep rides, guided walks, and onward bus or plane tickets.

Inside the park: luxury lodges and tented camps

Accommodation **inside the park** includes the most expensive lodgings in Nepal. They pay the government massive fees to stake out exclusive concession areas, with the result that you really feel like you've got the park all to yourself. Some are lavish **lodges** with permanent facilities, others are more remote **tented camps** – camping in the softest sense, with fluffy mattresses, solar-heated showers and fully stocked bars – and some are both. The prices quoted below, which are per person based on double occupancy, include all activities and meals (taxes extra). **Book ahead** for these places, either through an agent or by calling directly. They'll arrange your travel there and back by private vehicle, plane or raft, which in most cases costs extra.

Chitwan Jungle Lodge (Kathmandu: ☎228918). The biggest operator in the park, with 32 rooms. $260 per person for 2-night, 3-day package (includes transport).

Gaida Wildlife Camp (Kathmandu: ☎220940). Lodge situated uncomfortably close to Sauraha, though it's acknowledged to have the best rhino habitat. $351 for 2 nights; jungle camp 8km south at base of hills, $130 per night.

Island Jungle Resort (Kathmandu: ☎220162). Often overcrowded lodge and tented camp on an island in the middle of the Narayani River. $220 for 2 nights at the lodge, $190 at the tented camp.

Machan Wildlife Resort (Kathmandu: ☎225001; *wildlife@machan.mos.com.np*). Lodge with the only swimming pool in the park. $225 for 2 nights.

Temple Tiger Wildlife Camp (Kathmandu: ☎221585). Lodge and tented camp at the west end of the park. $463 for 2 nights.

Tharu Village (Kathmandu: ☎411225; *tiger@mtn.mos.com.np*). A relative of *Tiger Tops* where cultural activities outside the park are as much a part of the mix as wildlife inside the park. $112 per night.

Tiger Tops (Kathmandu: ☎411225; *tiger@mtn.mos.com.np*). The first and still the most fashionable, with an excellent location for wildlife and renowned service. Perched on stilts, the lodge is pure jungle Gothic: $692 for 2 nights. Tented camp costs $168 per night.

Park activities

The following **activities** are most commonly done inside Chitwan National Park. Most can also be done in nearby community forests outside the park, but some sort of entrance fee will usually still be payable (see box). All can, and in most cases should, be arranged through your lodge or a guide service. For certain popular activities (eg, elephant rides) it's essential to book the night before, or even earlier during the cut-throat months of October, November and March. All prices quoted are in addition to entry fees (most activities are half price for children under 10).

Jungle and bird walks

Walking is the best way to observe the park's prolific **bird** life. The region is an important stopover spot for migratory species in December and March, as well as being home to many year-round residents – look for parakeets, Indian rollers, paradise flycatchers, kingfishers, hornbills, ospreys and literally hundreds of others. (The Bird Education Society, headquartered near the main Sauraha intersection, is a good source of local information, and sells a checklist that's indispensable for any serious birder. Tour du Tarai, just across the street, is a guide service that specializes in bird-watching tours.)

By walking you'll also be able to appreciate the smaller attractions of the jungle at your own pace: orchids, strangler figs, towering termite mounds, tiger scratchings, rhino droppings piled up like cannon balls. Experienced jungle-walkers say they get their best animal sightings on foot, although that usually doesn't apply when they've got four flat-footed neophytes in tow. Throw away that shopping list of animals; you have to be content with what's on offer. You are virtually guaranteed a **rhino** (probably several), and deer and monkeys are easy to spot, but tiger sightings are rare – maybe one or two a week.

The best **season** for walking is spring, when the grass is shorter, though at other times of year you can compensate by spending more time in the forest. In cool weather some guides lead walks in the Chure Hills, where you may see gaur in addition to deer, monkeys and birds. No matter when you go, bring lots of water. The **cost** for a morning's walk is Rs250–400 per person (depending on the guide's certification level and the number of clients), and Rs400–700 for a full day. An all-day walk doesn't necessarily increase your chances of seeing game – most of the rhinos hang out close to Sauraha – but it gets you further into the park where you aren't running into other parties every two minutes.

Elephant rides

In terms of cost per hour the jeep's a better deal, but how often do you get to ride an **elephant**? The park keeps a dozen rideable animals and sends them out on one-hour-plus trips in shifts in the early morning and again in the afternoon. The **cost** is Rs650, not including the Rs50–100 fee for your lodge to arrange the trip for you. During slack times you can sign yourself up at the ranger's office at 6am for one of that day's rides,

OUTSIDE THE PARK: BAGHMARA, KUMROSE AND BIS HAJAAR TAL

Large patches of jungle still exist outside the park, albeit in a less pristine state. Part of Chitwan's buffer zone (see p.305), these areas are managed primarily for human use but are still fairly abundant in wildlife – especially during the January thatch-gathering, when animals in the park are disturbed and flee to outlying forests. They're often touted as cheaper alternatives to the park, but since you'll almost certainly be buying a two-day park permit anyway, these areas are probably best visited either on your first afternoon or after your park permit has expired.

Two community forests on either side of Sauraha are specifically marketed as outside-the-park destinations for elephant rides, guided walks and (uniquely) camping. **Baghmara Community Forest** is the closer and more popular of the two, and a visit to it can lead on to the Bis Hajaar Tal area (below), which it borders, or the Elephant Breeding Project (p.311), just to its south. Its main entrance is 1km west of Sauraha, at the end of the road past *Royal Wildlife Camp*. **Kumrose Community Forest**, 2km east of Sauraha, is further away from most lodges, though the route to it is itself partially forested. To get there, follow the road past *Nature Safari Camp*, then make your first right and keep heading east (don't take the first righthand fork, which leads to *Gaida Wildlife Camp*). These community forests don't yet seem to have settled on a permanent fee structure, but at the time of writing they were charging foreigners Rs100 to enter on foot; there's no charge if you enter by elephant, but you must have a valid park permit. Both Baghmara and Kumrose have concrete *machaan* (observation towers) where you can **spend the night** for Rs600 per person – good for nocturnal viewing if the moon is out. As in the park, a guide is required to enter either of the community forests on foot.

Far larger than either community forest, the **Bis Hajaar Tal** ("Twenty-Thousand Lakes") area provides an important corridor for animals migrating between the Tarai and hills, and is said to be Nepal's second-biggest natural wetland. The name refers to a maze of marshy oxbow lakes, many of them already filled in, well hidden among mature *sal* trees. The forest starts just west of the Baghmara forest and the Elephant Breeding Project and reaches its marshy climax about 5km northwest of there. To explore this area, have a guide lead you in on foot from the breeding project, and allow a full day. Without a guide, you'd be wise to take the long way round to avoid getting lost: cycle to Tadi Bazaar, follow the main highway 3km west to a signposted turning on the left (the village here is called Tikauli), then go southwest on a gravel road beside a canal for about 2km until you begin to see the lakes. The road initially passes through a thin strip of community forest, which charges a small fee (Rs20) to pass through. This road continues along the canal for another 8km or so to Gita Nagar, on the Bharatpur–Jagatpur road. The government has yet to establish a clear policy on whether or not to allow tourists into Bis Hajaar Tal, and if so how much they should pay. Until it does, you can enter for free, but expect this to change – get an update from your guest house.

but if you do this you're apt to get second-class treatment at the boarding platform. Rides in community forests last longer and cost less, but that's because there's more plodding on roads to get to the actual forests; these rides are on private elephants and should be booked through agents. Note that elephants don't work on major holidays, such as the eighth and ninth days of Dasain, and Lakshmi Puja.

The elephant's stately gait takes you back to a time, as recently as the early 1950s, when this was the way foreign delegations entered Nepal. The *phanit* (driver) sits astride the animal's neck, giving it commands with his toes and periodically walloping its huge skull, and attentively fending branches out of passengers' way. An elephant is the safest way to get around in the grasslands – especially in summer and autumn, when the grass towers 8m high – and it's the best way to observe **rhinos** and possibly wild boar or sloth bear without scaring them off, since the elephant's scent masks your own.

Jeep rides ... and gharial crocodiles

A **jeep ride** is the closest thing to a tour of Chitwan, as it also takes in the park's two permanent sights, the gharial crocodile breeding project and Kasara Durbar, both at the park headquarters about 20km west of Sauraha. For big game, however, you're limited to what you can see through the dusty wake of a Russian army surplus vehicle in the midmorning or afternoon (not the best time for wildlife viewing), which pretty much means **deer**. The whole trip takes three or four hours and **costs** Rs600, plus Rs15 to see the gharials. Most lodges have their own jeep; the park only allows four or five in at a time, but as long as you book early enough your lodge will get you a seat on whichever vehicle is going. The **best months** are from February to April, after the grass has been cut and the new shoots attract the deer. Note that jeeps can't cross the river after the monsoon until late November or early December; during that time shorter, lamer, cheaper trips may be run outside the park.

The longest of the world's crocodiles – adults can grow to more than 7m from nose to tail – the **gharial** is an awesome fishing machine. Its slender, broom-like snout, which bristles with a fine mesh of teeth, snaps shut on its prey like a spring-loaded trap. Unfortunately for the gharial, its eggs are regarded as a delicacy, and males are hunted for their bulb-like snouts (*gharial* means bulb), which are believed to have medicinal powers. In the mid-1970s, the world suddenly realized there were only 1300 gharials left. Chitwan's **breeding project** was set up in 1977 to incubate eggs under controlled conditions, upping the survival rate, which is only 1 percent in the wild, to as high as 75 percent. The majority of hatchlings are released back into the wild after three years, when they reach 1.2m in length; more than 500 have been released so far into the Narayani, Koshi, Karnali and Babai rivers. Having been given this head start, however, the hatchlings must then survive a growing list of dangers, which now include not only hunters but also untreated effluents from upstream industries (Narayanghat's Bhrikuti Paper Mill and Gorkha Brewery are named as the main culprits) and a lack of food caused by the lack of fish ladders on a dam downstream in India. Recent counts indicate that captive-raised gharials now outnumber wild ones on the Narayani, which suggests that without constant artificial augmentation of their numbers they would soon become extinct.

Kasara Durbar, constructed in 1939 as a royal hunting lodge, has now been rebuilt in concrete and serves as the park's administrative headquarters. Inside is a **museum** (daily except Sat), with a meagre collection of animal skulls, a small display of butterflies and various pickled reptiles. Baby rhinos, orphaned by the work of poachers, can often be seen roaming freely and begging for food near here pending relocation. The lovely safari camp opposite the headquarters is kept ready for use by HM and his retinue for a few days each spring. (The king used to come here to hunt tigers, but has apparently given it up as bad PR.)

Lami Tal ("Long Lake"), a marshy oxbow lake about 1km to the east, is a prime spot for watching **birds** and **mugger crocodiles**. There's a rickety view tower about midway along. This would be a good place to wait for tigers or rhinos very early in the morning, but on a jeep trip you'll blow by in the heat of the day.

Canoe trips

A float down either of two rivers in the Sauraha area by dugout **canoe** gives you your best shot at seeing **mugger crocodiles** (which, unlike the pointier-snouted gharials, prefer such marshy areas), and is also a relaxing way to watch birds and look for occasional wildlife on the shore. It's best done in winter, when the water's cool and the muggers sun themselves on the gravel banks; ruddy shelducks may be seen in profusion. In hot weather the outing is less rewarding, though you'll be assured of plenty of birds.

The standard itinerary is to depart from near the Baghmara Community Forest and float down the **Budhi Rapti** (Old Rapti) River for about half an hour to the Elephant

Breeding Project (see below), then walk or jeep back to your lodging. The time spent on the water is brief, and if you're not in the first couple of canoes that morning or afternoon you may not see much. Somewhat longer trips on the main **Rapti** River are subject to arcane negotiations between canoe operators and park officials; when such trips are permitted, you can return either through the park along a heavily used trail (the animals know better to hang out there) or outside the park via the Elephant Breeding Centre.

The canoe ride **costs** about Rs200 per person, plus the usual rate for a guided walk or jeep ride back. A park permit is required for trips on either river.

Jungle treks

To get well clear of the Sauraha crowds you need to walk for two or more days, overnighting en route – think of it as a **jungle trek**. Staying with the trekking analogy, there's one "teahouse" route in the park, plus any number of other possibilities for those willing to stay in private homes.

The teahouse route follows the forest road from **Sauraha to Kasara** and on to **Meghauli**, or vice versa. It takes two days of roughly equal length, or you could just do one half or the other. The Sauraha–Kasara leg is more commonly trekked, and is also the route taken by jeep tours out of Sauraha. There are of course no teahouses inside the park, but you can spend nights at Meghauli and Gaighat/Jagatpur (see p.306). It's possible to get another park permit at Bhimle (near Meghauli) and carry on trekking for a further two days, overnighting at **Maadi** (in a beautiful valley along the park's southern boundary) and then returning to Sauraha. This permits you to get to less-visited parts of the park's interior, such as Tamar Tal, which is excellent for bird-watching. You can return to Sauraha by local buses or arrange to have a jeep take you back. Go with a guide who's done this trek before – most haven't. The **cost** of doing a jungle trek is simply the guide's daily rate, plus his food and lodging.

Jungle trek itineraries are limited by the fact that **camping** is currently not allowed inside the park, though this policy could change (ask at guide services). In the meantime, the next-best thing to camping in the park is to spend a night in an observation tower in the Baghmara or Kumrose community forests (see box, p.309).

Activities outside the park

After you've had your two days in the park, you might be reluctant to shell out for another permit. Here are a some admission-free options.

The hattisar (elephant stables) and Elephant Breeding Project

The majority of Chitwan's elephant workforce is housed at the government **hattisar** (elephant stables), on the southeastern edge of Sauraha. The best time to catch them is mid-afternoon, when they're sure to be around for feeding time. In hot weather they're taken down to the river for a bath at midday – immensely photogenic. To the west of here, the **Nepal Conservation Research and Training Centre** functions as the base for animal research and monitoring, naturalist training and sustainable development programmes supported by the King Mahendra Trust for Nature Conservation.

Sauraha lodges offer jeep tours out to the **Elephant Breeding Project** (Rs15), 4km west of the village, where baby elephants are the main attraction. You can visit the project independently either on foot or bicycle, though you have to cross the Budhi Rapti just before you get there. Come with a guide, who can explain the goings-on and then take you on to Bis Hajaar Tal (see p.309). Until the mid-1970s, the parks department commonly bought its elephants from India, where they were captured in the wild and trained in captivity. As the wild population shrank this procedure became increasingly

ASIAN ELEPHANTS

In Nepal and throughout southern Asia, **elephants** have been used as ceremonial transportation and beasts of burden for thousands of years, earning them a cherished place in the culture – witness the popularity of elephant-headed Ganesh, the darling of the Hindu pantheon. Thanks to this symbiosis with man, Asian elephants (unlike their African cousins) survive mainly as a domesticated species, even as their wild habitat has all but vanished.

With brains four times the size of humans', elephants are reckoned to be as **intelligent** as dolphins; recent research suggests they may communicate subsonically. What we see as a herd is in fact a complex social structure, consisting of bonded pairs and a fluid hierarchy. In the wild, herds typically consist of fifteen to thirty females and one old bull, and are usually led by a senior female; other bulls live singly or in bachelor herds. Though they appear docile, elephants have strongly individual personalities and moods. They can learn dozens of commands, but they won't obey just anyone – as any handler will tell you, you can't make an elephant do what it doesn't want to do. That they submit to such apparently cruel head-thumping by drivers seems to have more to do with thick skulls than obedience.

Asian elephants are smaller than those of the African species, but their statistics are still formidable. A bull can grow up to 3m high and weigh four tons, although larger individuals are known to exist. An average day's intake is 200 litres of water and 225kg of fodder – and if you think that's impressive, wait till you see it come back out again. All that eating wears down teeth fast, which is why an average elephant goes through six sets in its lifetime, each one more durable than the last. The trunk is controlled by an estimated 40,000 muscles, enabling its owner to eat, drink, cuddle and even manipulate simple tools (such as a stick for scratching). Though up to 2.5cm thick, an elephant's skin is still very sensitive, and it will often take mud or dust baths to protect against insects. Life expectancy is about 75 years and, much the same as with humans, an elephant's working life can be expected to run from its mid-teens to its mid-fifties; training begins at about age five.

unaffordable, so the government began breeding and training its own elephants, first at the old *hattisar* and then, in 1988, establishing this separate facility, where elephants can mate in peace and mothers and babies can receive special attention. At any given time the project is home to a couple of breeding bulls and ten to fifteen cows, and usually a couple of calves. The young elephants need to spend as much time as possible with their mothers to become socialized into elephant society. Come here in early morning or late afternoon – in the middle of the day they're usually off on educational trips to the river and the jungle.

Tharu villages and bike rides

Guided Tharu village walks out of Sauraha usually mean a loiter through the houses and villages nearest to Sauraha. It's all rather voyeuristic, especially when you consider how many tourists have trooped through before you, and the way guides point at residents and pick up their tools without asking is not something that should be encouraged. For cultural tours with more sensitivity, try Tour du Tarai (*web@mos.com.np*) near the *Jungle View Restaurant*.

You'll learn a lot more about real Tarai village life by hopping on a bike and just getting lost on the back roads to the east and west of Sauraha. In November, when the **rice** is harvested, you'll be able to watch Tharu and Baahun villagers cutting the stems, tying them into sheaves and threshing them – or, since it's such a busy time of year, piling them in big stacks to await threshing. January is **thatch-gathering** time, when you'll see people bringing huge bundles out of the park, to be put by until a slack time before the monsoon when they can repair their roofs. In early March, the **mustard**, **lentils** and **wheat** that was planted after the rice crop is ready; **maize** is then planted, to be harvested in July for animal fodder, flour and meal. Rice is seeded in dense starter plots in March, to be transplanted into separate paddy fields in April. During each of these harvest seasons you'll hear the rhythmic toot-toot of local mills, hulling or polishing grain, or pressing oil.

From Sauraha, the most fertile country for exploration lies to the east: heading towards Tadi along the eastern side of the village, turn right (east) at the intersection marked by the King Mahendra Trust health post and you can follow that road all the way to **Parsa**, 8km away on the Mahendra Highway, with many side roads to villages en route. Given a full day and a good bike or motorcycle, you could continue eastwards from Parsa along the highway for another 10km, and just before Bhandaara turn left onto a track leading to **Baireni**, a particularly well-preserved Tharu village. Another 10km east of Bhandaara lies **Lothar**, where by following a trail upstream you'll reach the waterfalls on the Lothar Khola, a contemplative spot with a healthy measure of birdlife.

For a short ride west of Sauraha, head north for 3km and take the first left after the river crossing, which brings you to the authentic Tharu villages of **Baghmara** and **Hardi**. If you're game for a longer journey, pedal to Tadi and west along the Mahendra Highway to Tikauli. From there the canal road through Bis Hajaar Tal leads about 10km through beautiful forest to **Gita Nagar**, where you join the Bharatpur–Jagatpur road, with almost unlimited possibilities from there. Also don't overlook the possibility of an outing to Devghat (see below).

Narayanghat, Bharatpur and Devghat

It's hard to travel very far in Nepal without at least passing through **NARAYANGHAT**: the construction of the Mugling–Narayanghat highway has made it the gateway to the Tarai and the busiest crossroads in the country. What was once a far-flung intersection is now a 500-metre strip of diesel and *daal bhaat*, and it's said that real estate changes hands here for almost as high stakes as in Kathmandu. **BHARATPUR**, its sister city to the east and the headquarters of Chitwan District, boasts a large regional college, a couple of breweries and an airstrip. Unflattering as all that may sound, you may have occasion to stay, or at least eat, in the area. The side trip to Devghat may provide an incentive.

Buses to Pokhara, Gorkha and Devghat have their own bus park at the north end of Narayanghat on the road to Mugling. All other express buses stop at the fast-food parade just east of Pulchowk (the intersection of the Mugling and Mahendra highways). There are two additional bus parks for local services: buses and minibuses to Tadi Bazaar and eastern Chitwan District start from Sahid Chowk, about 500m east of Pulchowk; minibuses to Meghauli and Jagatpur start from just north of Sahid Chowk – walk north for 50m, take the first right down a small lane and it's on the left after 200m. Bharatpur's **airstrip** is just south of the Mahendra Highway. Cosmic Air (☎24218), Gorkha Airlines (☎21093), Lumbini Airways (Kathmandu: ☎221523) and RNAC (☎20326) all fly daily to Bharatpur from Kathmandu ($50), and their offices are all along the highway near the airstrip.

Rikshas should take you anywhere within the two towns for Rs10 or less.

Narayanghat and Bharatpur accommodation

A few resort-style **hotels** near the Bharatpur airstrip are meant to serve as crash pads for the first night of a package tour of Chitwan, but the concept doesn't really make sense – why waste a night here when you could be spending it in Chitwan? Nevertheless, the rates for walk-ins (exclusive of activities) at these places are reason-

TARAI CULTURE: THARUS AND NEWCOMERS

Two mysteries surround Nepal's second-biggest ethnic minority, the Tarai-dwelling **Tharus**: where they came from, and how they came to be resistant to malaria. Some anthropologists speculate that the tribe migrated from India's eastern hills, filtering across the Tarai over the course of millennia. This would account for their Mongoloid features and Hindu-animist beliefs, but it doesn't fully explain the radically different dialects, dress and customs of different Tharu groups. Isolated by malarial jungle for thousands of years, bands of migrants certainly could have developed their own cultures – but why, given such linguistic and cultural evolution, would the name "Tharu" survive with such consistency? Confusing the issue are the Rana Tharus of the far west, who claim to be descended from high-caste Rajput women who were sent north by their husbands during the Muslim invasions and, when the men never returned for them, married their servants. (There's some circumstantial evidence to support this, as Rana Tharu women are given extraordinary autonomy in marriage and household affairs.)

As to the matter of **malaria resistance**, red blood cells seem to play a role – the fact that Tharus are prone to sickle-cell anaemia might be significant – but very little research has been done. At least as significant, Tharus boost their natural resistance with a few common-sense precautions, such as building houses with tiny windows to keep smoke in and mosquitoes (and ghosts) out.

As **hunter-gatherers**, Tharus are skilled at snaring pigs and other small animals, fishing, and using plants for myriad medicinal and practical purposes. Modern times have forced them to become **farmers** and livestock raisers, clearing patches in the forest and warding off wild animals from flimsy watchtowers called *machaan*. Their whirling stick dance evokes their uneasy but respectful relationship with the spirits of the forest, as do the raised animal emblems that decorate their doorways. **Fishing** remains an important

able for what you get. Budget travellers would do better to head for Narayanghat, which has numerous inexpensive **guest houses**. (See also Devghat below.)

INEXPENSIVE

Quality Guest House, Pulchowk, Narayanghat (☎20939). A bit better than your basic Nepali lodge, with solar hot water. ②/B③.

Hotel River View, behind the Pokhara bus park, Narayanghat (☎21151). The best-situated budget option – it really does have a river view and makes the best base for visiting Devghat. ②/B③.

Royal Rest House, Pulchowk, Narayanghat (☎21442). The largest of several inns here, cavernous and noisy but with good food. The rooms with attached baths are quite a bit better and come with air coolers. ②/B⑤.

Uncle's Lodge, west of Narayani bridge, Narayanghat (☎22502). Small garden, close to the river, friendly. B④.

MIDRANGE AND EXPENSIVE

Hotel Chitwan Keyman, Bharatpur (☎20200). Air conditioning, restaurant, underwhelming facilities. AC⑧.

Island Jungle Resort Bharatpur Heights, Bharatpur (Kathmandu: ☎220162). Quite leafy and set back from the highway, but it's still very noisy beyond the compound walls. B⑦.

Safari Narayani Hotel, Bharatpur (☎20130; *info@nbe.pc.mos.com.np*). Pleasant grounds with a pool and tennis courts, good restaurant, but again, the location is intrinsically bad. AC⑦.

Narayanghat and Bharatpur eating

Food, plentiful but not wildly exciting, can be found all around Pulchowk. Standing out slightly from the greasy spoons and whisky shacks are *Royal Rest House*'s restaurant activity – given the Tarai's high water table, it's easy enough to scoop out a pond and stock it – and you're likely to see fisherwomen wielding hand-held nets between crossed poles, or carrying their catch home in wicker boxes.

Tharu **houses** are made of mud and dung plastered over wood-and-reed frames, giving them a distinctive ribbed effect. Traditionally, western Tharus built communal **longhouses**, big enough for a half a dozen families or more and partitioned by huge vial-shaped grain urns, but most have now moved up to detached models. While **clothing** varies tremendously by area, Tharu women often wear thick silver bracelets above the elbow; tattooing of the forearms and lower legs is common among older women but is falling out of fashion with the younger generation.

The Tarai has long been viewed as Nepal's frontier and the Tharus dismissed as primitive aboriginals. Since the early twentieth century – when, as a preliminary step to abolishing slavery, the government encouraged **slaves** to homestead in the Tarai – it's been seen as a place where a settler can clear the land and start a new life. The government's malaria-control programme accelerated the process, and several million gung-ho **immigrants** from the hills and India (the border is highly porous) have now cleared, tamed and transformed the Tarai into the breadbasket of Nepal, felling much of the valuable timber in the process. The migration is far from over – the Tarai's population is doubling every twenty years (some urban areas are doubling twice as fast). Prosperity has probably peaked, however, and since productivity isn't keeping up with population, the Tarai's agricultural surplus is steadily declining.

In one generation, the Tharus have been outflanked, outfarmed and in many cases bought out and reduced to sharecropping. Traditional culture is still strong in the far west, particularly among the Dangauria and Rana groups, but in other areas it's been all but drowned by a tide of hill, Indian and Western tendencies. Like indigenous peoples the world over, Tharus know more about their own environment than anyone, but they're not being listened to.

and, further east and across the street, *Fish Tail Restaurant*, with English menus and Indian/Chinese/"Continental" (ie everything with chips) food. *Safari Narayani Hotel*'s dining room does superb meals for not too much more money.

Devghat

DEVGHAT (or Deoghat), 5km northwest of Narayanghat, is a lot of people's idea of a great place to die. An astonishingly tranquil spot, it stands where the wooded hills meet the shimmering plains, and the Trisuli and the Kali Gandaki merge to form the Narayani, one of the major tributaries of the Ganga (Ganges). Some say Sita, the heroine of the *Ramayan*, died here. The ashes of King Mahendra, the present king's father, were sprinkled at this sacred *tribeni* (a confluence of three rivers: wherever two rivers meet, a third, spiritual one is believed to join them), and scores of *sunyasan*, those who have renounced the world, patiently live out their last days here hoping to achieve an equally auspicious death and rebirth. Many have retired to Devghat to avoid being a burden to their children, to escape ungrateful children, or because they have no children to look after them in their old age and to perform the necessary rites when they die. *Pujari* (priests) also practise here – their professional signs are the only advertising you'll see – and often take in young candidates for the priesthood as resident students.

Hourly **buses** shuttle between Narayanghat and Devghat, taking about half an hour, but it's quite pleasant to **walk**. Head north from the Pokhara bus park along the main highway to Mugling and after 1km turn left on a paved road under an arch – Devghat is at the end of the road, about 5km through forest. Either way, you come to the Trisuli and cross it by a footbridge (immortalized in the Nepali film *Kanchhi*, in which a heartbroken lover attempts suicide here), then bear left to the village. You can also cross the river further downstream by **dugout canoe** – for the return trip, the ferryman, if he thinks he can be spared from his duties, might consent to take you all the way back to Narayanghat for Rs50 or so.

Dozens of small shrines lie dotted around the village, but you come here more for the atmosphere than the sights. Vaishnavas (followers of Vishnu) congregate at Devghat's largest and newest temple, the central *shikra*-style **Harihar Mandir**, founded in 1998 by the famed guru Shaktya Prakash Ananda of Haridwar. Shaivas (followers of Shiva) dominate the area overlooking the confluence at the western edge of the village. **Galeshwar Ashram**, on your right as you walk down the steps to the confluence, and **Aghori Ashram**, further downhill on the right, are named after two recently deceased holy men. A follower of the outrageous Aghori tradition (see p.157), the one-armed Aghori Baba, who was often referred to as the "Crazy Baba", claimed to have cut off his own arm after being instructed to do so in a dream. Various paths lead upstream of the confluence, eventually arriving at **Sita Gupha**, a sacred cave that is closed except on Makar Sankranti, and **Chakrabarti Mandir**, a shady temple area housing a famous *shaligram* that locals say is growing.

A huge **pilgrimage** is held at Devghat on Makar Sankranti (Jan 14 or 15), and Shiva Raatri, falling on the new moon of February–March, brings many Indian devotees. At other times, sadhus and pilgrims do *puja* at the point where the rivers meet – cremations are also held here – and old-timers meditate outside their huts in the sun. Be sensitive to the residents, and don't disturb them or touch anything that might be holy: many are orthodox Baahuns and your touch would be polluting.

A couple of teahouses near the Trisuli bridge on the Devghat side can provide really bare-bones **lodging**, but frankly Devghat is the sort of place that visitors should leave in peace after the sun goes down. For a nearby base, try *Lovely River Resort* (☎056/22699; Kathmandu: ☎425041), a peaceful riverside retreat reached by a separate access road from the main highway about 4km north (upstream) of the Devghat turning. The resort has standard rooms and deluxe tents, and charges a package rate of $55 per person per night, which includes all meals and various cultural activities.

LUMBINI TARAI

Hordes of travellers hurry through this ancient part of the Tarai, west of Chitwan; few take the time to look around. It's best known, unfairly, for **Sonauli**, the main tourist border crossing between Nepal and India. Yet only 20km away is one of Nepal's premier destinations, **Lumbini**, birthplace of the Buddha and the site of ruins going back almost three thousand years.

Two main highways – the Siddhartha and the Mahendra – connect the region with Pokhara and the rest of the Tarai, and buses to Sonauli are frequent. The journey to Lumbini is a bit taxing, but well worth the extra effort. Accommodation and food here, as in most other parts of the Tarai, are readily available but usually very simple.

Butwal to Sonauli

Westwards from Narayanghat the Mahendra Highway runs across a washboard of cultivated fields, briefly climbs over a jungle-cloaked spur of the Chure Hills, and passes long stretches of heavily used but seemingly healthy forest. It's a relatively painless 110km to Butwal.

Butwal

Crouching uninvitingly at the mouth of a canyon, **BUTWAL** is the hub of the Lumbini administrative zone: north lies Pokhara; south is Sonauli and the Indian border; and to the west, the Mahendra Highway barrels along towards Nepalganj and Nepal's western border.

Placed at the start of an important trade route to Tibet as well as the pilgrim trail to Muktinath, the **tax post** at Butwal was for centuries a tidy little earner for Palpa (Tansen) and then Kathmandu. Much later, it came to be a staging post for Nepal's most lucrative export: Gurkha soldiers, bound for the recruiting office at Gorakhpur in India. In the early nineteenth century, Nepal and the East India Company fell into a dispute over the territory around Butwal, and the murder of some British police here touched off a two-year **war with Britain**. Nepal scored several improbable early victories here and elsewhere but, outnumbered four to one, was eventually forced to surrender. Under the terms of the resulting treaty, the Tarai territories from Butwal west had to be ceded to the British (Nepal struck a deal to get the disputed land around Butwal back the same year). Any reminders of the past are, however, conspicuously absent in modern Butwal.

Many **buses** originate or terminate at this busy crossroads – see p.294 for routes and frequencies. Most express services stop at "Traphik Chowk", a bazaar area on the Siddhartha Highway as it skirts the east side of town. Local buses use the bus park four blocks to the west, a few hundred metres south of the bridge over the Tinau River.

Accommodation and eating

If you're looking for a comfortable **room** with a TV and air cooler, you'll find it at a very reasonable price in Butwal. Unfortunately, most of the good hotels are around Traphik Chowk, which is horrendously noisy – it's actually quieter in the bazaar, further west. The more expensive hotels are your best bet for Indian and Western-ish **food**. A few *bhojanalaya* around Traphik Chowk serve decent Nepali fare, and you can get *sekuwa*, noodles and coffee from nearby street vendors.

Hotel Kandara, Traphik Chowk (☎071/40175). Clean place with hot water, a small garden, and restaurant. Most rooms with TV and air cooler. B④/AC⑤.

Santosh Guest House, two blocks west of Traphik Chowk (no phone). The most palatable budget option: basic, but in a relatively quiet part of town. ②, dorm beds ①.

Hotel Siddhartha, Traphik Chowk (☎071/40380). Large, well-appointed outfit, with hot water and a good restaurant. B④/AC⑤.

Hotel Sindoor, just south of the local bus park (☎071/40189). An older place that has river views and is pretty well insulated from the awful neighbourhood that's grown up around it. The rooms are shabby for the price, though. B⑤.

Bhairawa (Siddhartha Nagar)

Half an hour south by bus, **BHAIRAWA** (officially, the name has been changed to **SIDDHARTHA NAGAR**, but it's not catching on) is a virtual rerun of Butwal. The bazaar, west of the main roundabout on the Siddhartha Highway, supports a sizeable minority of Muslim traders and, like so many border towns, exists primarily to peddle imported goods to acquisitive Indians. Its only recommendation is that it's better than Sonauli.

For **orientation** purposes, think of Bhairawa's three main streets forming an upright triangle: the eastern side is the highway to the border, Bank Street runs along the south, and Narayanpath along the west. The latter two comprise the bazaar. Buses stop on the border highway near the *Hotel Yeti* (a handy landmark), which stands at the southeastern apex of the triangle; rikshas and shared jeeps bound for Sonauli also wait here. The road to Lumbini leaves the border highway about 1km north of the *Hotel Yeti*, just north of the triangle's northern apex.

Accommodation and eating

As in many Tarai cities, Bhairawa's **accommodation** is all either cheap in a very Nepali way or upscale in a more Indian style; there's not much middle ground. *Hotel Yeti*s dining room does competent Indian and Chinese **meals**, and *Kasturi Restaurant*, near the intersection of Bank Street and Narayan Path, is good for vegetarian Indian food.

INEXPENSIVE

City Guest House, Bank Street (no phone). Standard cold-water lodge in a lively but noisy part of the bazaar. The nearby *Hotel Sayapatri* is equivalent. ②/B③.

Hotel Durga & Guest House, on the border road 500m south of Bank Street (no phone). Its distance from the bazaar makes it relatively quiet but also somewhat inconvenient; facilities are very basic. ③.

Hotel Shambhala, Bank Street (no phone). Perhaps the cleanest of the bazaar guest houses, though not by much, and still no hot water. ③/B④.

MIDRANGE AND EXPENSIVE

Hotel Lumbini Pagoda, on the border highway 500m south of Bank Street (☎071/21837). Air-cooled rooms and Bhairawa's quietest garden, but it's not really a full-service hotel: you have to walk to the main intersection to get decent food or make any arrangements. B⑤.

Hotel Nirvana, Paklihawa Road, 2km southwest of the bazaar (☎071/20837; *nirva@ccsl.com.np*). Deluxe hotel catering mainly to Japanese tour groups, with facilities that include a pool and an authentic Japanese-style bathhouse. AC⑨.

Hotel Shantanu, on the border road 500m north of Bank Street (☎071/21545). Bright and spacious, but not very geared up for Western guests. B⑥/AC⑦.

Hotel Yeti, corner of the border highway and Bank Street (☎071/20551). Central and professional, and the staff have long experience helping travellers get to Lumbini or at least out of Bhairawa. B⑦/AC⑧.

Moving on

Cars and **jeeps** can be rented by the day (Rs1500 plus fuel) or for the journey to Lumbini (Rs300 one way) or Tilaurakot (Rs500) – arrange through the better hotels or any travel agent around the main intersection near *Hotel Yeti*. You might be able to rent a **bike** or **motorcycle** informally through your guest house.

For onward **bus** tickets, the private and Sajha offices are located at the main intersection. Most long-distance buses originate at Sonauli, but getting a seat from Bhairawa is no problem as long as you book it the day before. See the box on p.294 for frequencies and times. Travel agents can also book internal **flights** from Bhairawa to Kathmandu (on Buddha, Lumbini, Necon or RNAC; $72); the airstrip is 10km north of town.

Sonauli (Belahiya) and the border

Four kilometres south of Bhairawa, **SONAULI** (Soo-*no*-li) is a thoroughly disagreeable place – an unflattering introduction to Nepal if you're just arriving, and a rude send-off if you're leaving. Trucks backed up waiting to cross the border and buses trying to enter and leave the bus park produce appalling traffic jams on the Nepal side (locally referred to as **BELAHIYA**). The lodgings are universally awful. The general mood among travellers finding themselves in this hell is despair, or in the case of those who discover upon arrival that they were cheated by the travel agent in Gorakhpur and that there is no "air-conditioned tourist bus" to Kathmandu, rage.

Nevertheless, Sonauli is by far the most popular border crossing between Nepal and India, and most bus and train package deals to or from India involve an overnight here.

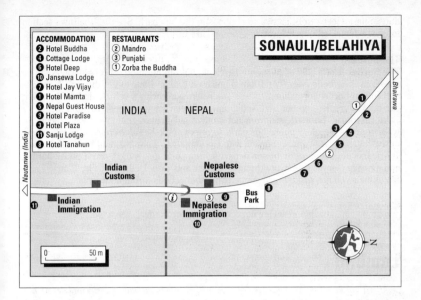

ACCOMMODATION
② Hotel Buddha
④ Cottage Lodge
⑥ Hotel Deep
⑩ Jansewa Lodge
⑦ Hotel Jay Vijay
① Hotel Mamta
⑤ Nepal Guest House
⑨ Hotel Paradise
③ Hotel Plaza
⑪ Sanju Lodge
⑧ Hotel Tanahun

RESTAURANTS
② Mandro
③ Punjabi
① Zorba the Buddha

SONAULI/BELAHIYA

INDIA   NEPAL

Nautanwa (India)

Bhairawa

Indian Customs

Nepalese Customs

Indian Immigration

Nepalese Immigration

Bus Park

N

0   50 m

If you ignored the warning about these packages in Basics then you'll have no choice but to stay in Sonauli and take whatever **accommodation** is assigned to you, where the facilities will probably be filthy and the service indifferent, since the proprietor doesn't have to do anything to win your business. If you're arriving here independently, your options still aren't great, but at least you can choose to stay in Bhairawa (see above), which is slightly more liveable, or given more time and effort, Lumbini (below), which is infinitely better. It would be an exercise in futility to recommend lodgings in Sonauli, as standards rise and fall (mostly fall) so rapidly. The half-dozen guest houses are close enough together so you can shop around to see which one's been remodelled most recently. They're all around ②/B③, and should be able to provide hot water by the bucket. (In case you're thinking of trying your luck on the Indian side, the choice there is clearer: the only place worth crossing the border for is *Hotel Niranjana*, a stark but fairly quiet Government of UP hostel with air-cooled rooms at B④.)

At least the **food** in Sonauli's guest houses and local restaurants isn't bad – whichever way you're heading, the menus give a taste of what's in store further on. *Zorba the Buddha*, run by refreshingly cheerful Rajneesh people, provides a vegetarian alternative.

Government-registered **moneychangers** in Sonauli keep long hours, so there's no problem exchanging money, and the rates are the same as elsewhere in Nepal. If changing Nepali into Indian rupees, make sure the moneychanger hasn't offloaded torn notes on you, which are hard to pass in India. Indian currency is readily accepted in Sonauli but not beyond. International **telephoning** is possible from here (about Rs160 per minute).

As a funnel for traffic from India, Sonauli is well served by **buses** (see the box on p.294 for a rundown of services), but be sure to book ahead, since an empty seat in Sonauli might be spoken for in Bhairawa. Each guest house has its own man-and-a-desk "travel agency" that can book onward tickets (for a small commission) and provide general advice. They can also arrange **jeeps** to Lumbini (Rs300 one way) or other destinations. Shared jeeps to Bhairawa start opposite the bus park. See the Bhairawa section for more advice on onward travel.

The border

The **border** is officially open round the clock, but immigration officers are likely to be asleep in their beds after 9 or 10pm. Figure on half an hour to get through Nepalese and Indian border formalities, unless you're crossing with a vehicle, in which case it can take hours. Remember that Nepal time is fifteen minutes ahead of India.

Indian **tourist buses** depart from just south of Indian immigration – an easy 200-metre walk from the Nepalese public bus park, so offers of riksha rides aren't to be taken seriously. Tourist buses connect Sonauli with Gorakhpur (6 daily; 3hr) and Varanasi (1 daily; 10hr). Indian **government buses** depart from a point nearly 1km south of the border, and provide services to Gorakhpur, Varanasi and also Delhi (6 daily; 22hr). From Gorakhpur you can make broad-gauge **train** connections throughout India.

Indian visas are not obtainable at the border – see p.148.

Lumbini

After I am no more, Ananda! Men of belief will visit with faithful curiosity and devotion to the four places – where I was born . . . attained enlightenment . . . gave the first sermons . . . and passed into Nirvana.

The Buddha (c.543–463 BC)

For the world's one billion Buddhists, **LUMBINI**, 22km west of Bhairawa, is where it all began. **The Buddha's birthplace** is arguably the single most important historical site in Nepal – not only the source of one of the world's great religions but also the centre of Nepal's most significant **archeological finds**, dating from the third century BC. With only modest ruins but powerful associations, it's the kind of place you could whizz round in two hours or soak up for days.

The Buddha has long been a prophet without much honour in his own country: the area around Lumbini is now predominantly Muslim, while the main local **festival** is a Hindu one, commemorating the Buddha as the ninth incarnation of Vishnu – it's held on the full moon of the Nepali month of Baisaakh (April–May). Celebrations of **Buddha Jayanti** (the Buddha's birthday) are comparatively meagre because, as the local monks will tell you with visible disgust, Buddhists from the high country think Lumbini is too hot in May. Until recently, poor access and a lack of tourist facilities put off most pilgrims, who instead stuck to the more developed Indian sites of Bodh Gaya, Sarnath and Kushinagar.

But Lumbini is changing. In the 1970s the government, with the backing of the United Nations, set aside land and authorized a hugely ambitious **master plan** for a five-square-kilometre **religious park** consisting of monasteries, cultural facilities, gardens, fountains and a tourist village. After a very slow start, the plan is finally starting to take shape under the direction of (or perhaps in spite of) the Lumbini Development Trust. Several national temples and monasteries have been built or are under construction, 600,000 trees have been planted, and Japanese tour groups have begun to add Lumbini to their whirlwind tours of the Buddhist holy sites. An international airport has even been mooted. Of course there is ample cause for scepticism, yet if the remaining plans come off, Lumbini could grow to be quite a cosmopolitan religious site – the only one of its kind in the world.

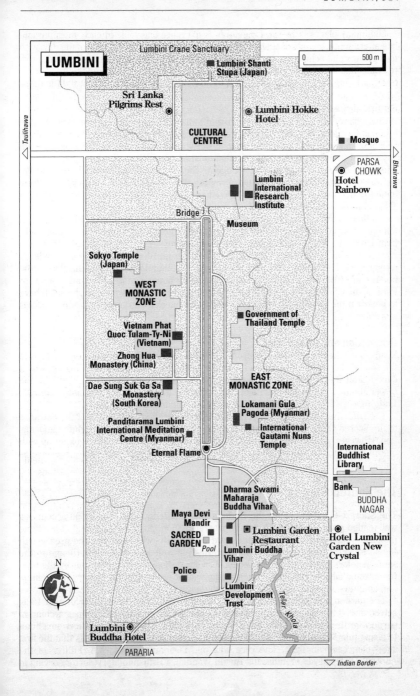

LUMBINI

Lumbini Crane Sanctuary

Lumbini Shanti Stupa (Japan)

0   500 m

Taulihawa

Sri Lanka Pilgrims Rest

Lumbini Hokke Hotel

CULTURAL CENTRE

Mosque

PARSA CHOWK

Hotel Rainbow

Bhairawa

Lumbini International Research Institute

Bridge

Museum

Sokyo Temple (Japan)

WEST MONASTIC ZONE

Government of Thailand Temple

Vietnam Phat Quoc Tulam-Ty-Ni (Vietnam)

Zhong Hua Monastery (China)

EAST MONASTIC ZONE

Dae Sung Suk Ga Sa Monastery (South Korea)

Lokamani Gula Pagoda (Myanmar)

Panditarama Lumbini International Meditation Centre (Myanmar)

International Gautami Nuns Temple

Eternal Flame

International Buddhist Library

Bank

BUDDHA NAGAR

Dharma Swami Maharaja Buddha Vihar

Maya Devi Mandir

SACRED GARDEN

Pool

Lumbini Garden Restaurant

Lumbini Buddha Vihar

Hotel Lumbini Garden New Crystal

Police

Lumbini Development Trust

Telar Khola

N

Lumbini Buddha Hotel

PARARIA

Indian Border

Like many places in Nepal, Lumbini is much more enjoyable in early morning and late afternoon, when it's cool and peaceful. If you only see it in the heat of the day, with tour groups and school parties trooping around and the sounds of construction activity emanating from the temples, you'll probably be disappointed. For this reason it's highly recommended to stay overnight in Lumbini, despite some logistical difficulties.

Getting there

If you're travelling between Kathmandu and India via Sonauli, it's relatively easy to stop in Lumbini along the way. Public express **buses** drive daily from Kathmandu to Lumbini – a long ten-hour journey, but no worse than the one to Sonauli. Coming from anywhere other than Kathmandu, first go to Bhairawa or Sonauli, where you can book a **jeep** to Lumbini through any travel agent. The fare should be Rs300 one way, Rs400 for a return trip with an hour or two's waiting time (you'll have to negotiate anything longer than that). As long as you're hiring a vehicle, consider having it take you first to Tilaurakot (see below) and then drop you in Lumbini on the way back.

Another option – if it's not too hot – is to go by **bike**: head west out of Bhairawa, turn left onto a paved side road after 20km, and turn right at the obvious intersection about 2km later. The bike will come in handy for getting around Lumbini's sights, which cover a wide area. The decrepit local **minibuses** from Bhairawa should be considered a last resort. They depart from the start of the westbound road to Lumbini, clear at the north end of Bhairawa, and take an interminable hour or more. Most are bound for Pararia, the village immediately south of the master plan area, which means you'll have to get off at the Buddha Nagar intersection, near the east entrance; the last bus back is at 5.30pm.

Orientation and information

Roads enter the master plan area from several directions, but the **main entrance** is at the southeastern edge. A road leads straight from there to the **Sacred Garden**, which contains all the archeological treasures associated with the Buddha's birth. All the newer temples lie to the north of the Sacred Garden in two **"monastic zones"**. **Lodgings** are scattered both inside and outside the master plan area.

The **information booth** temporarily erected near the parking area at the entrance to the Sacred Garden is distinguished by an abject lack of any sort of printed information. However, guide service may be available there – it's well worth hooking up with one of the Lumbini Development Trust's archeologists, who sometimes freelance as guides.

The Sacred Garden

The **Sacred Garden**, where the Buddha was reputedly born, was by all accounts a well-tended grove in his day. It was consecrated soon after his death, and at least one monastery was attached to it by the third century BC when Ashoka, the great north Indian emperor and Buddhist evangelist, made a well-documented pilgrimage to the spot. Ashoka's patronage established a thriving religious community, but by the time the intrepid Chinese traveller Hiuen Tsang visited in the seventh century it was limping, and must have died out after the tenth century.

The garden was lost for at least six hundred years, and its **rediscovery**, in 1896, solved one of the last great mysteries of the Orient. Europeans had been searching in earnest for the site since 1830, but it wasn't until 1893, when a Nepali officer on a hunting expedition found a related Ashokan relic some miles to the northwest, that the first solid clue came to light. The race was on. Two main rivals, A.A. Führer of the Archeological Survey of India, and Austin Waddell, a British military doctor serving in

FFOTOGRAFF / TOBY SMEDLEY

Asian one-horned rhino, Bardia
National Park

DAVID REED

Eternal flame, Lumbini

DAVID REED

Chitwan National Park

JERRY DENNIS

Woman combing wool, Annapurna
region

DAVID REED

On the banks of the Kali Gandaki,
Devghat

Tharu fisherwomen, Western Tarai

Janaki Mandir, Janakpur

Yak train, Gokyo Lakes, Everest region

Everest (left) and Nuptse (centre)

DAVID REED

A porter testing his load, Jiri

DAVID REED

Kayaker, Bhote Koshi

JERRY DENNIS

Ghorapani, near Poon Hill, Annapurna region

THE BUDDHA: A LIFE

The year of the Buddha's **birth** is disputed – it was probably 543 BC – but it's generally accepted that it happened at Lumbini while his mother, Maya Devi, was on her way to her maternal home for the delivery. He was born Siddhartha Gautam ("he who has accomplished his aim"), the son of a king and a member of the Shakya clan, who ruled the central Tarai from their capital at Tilaurakot (see below). Brought up in his father's palace, Prince Siddhartha lived a sheltered life until, at the age of 29, he made a fateful trip into town where, according to legend, he encountered an old man, a sick man, a corpse and a hermit: old age, sickness and death were the end of life, he realized, and contemplation seemed the only way to understand the nature of suffering.

Siddhartha fled the palace and spent five years as an ascetic before concluding that self-denial brought him no closer to the truth than self-indulgence. Under the famous *bodhi* tree of Bodh Gaya in India, he vowed to keep meditating until he attained **enlighten- ment**. This he did after 49 days, at which time Siddhartha became the Buddha, released from the cycle of birth and death. He made his way to Sarnath (near Varanasi in India) and preached his **first sermon**, setting in motion, Buddhists believe, *dharma*, the wheel of the truth. Although he's said to have returned to Kapilvastu to convert his family, and according to some stories he even put in an appearance in the Kathmandu Valley, the Buddha spent most of the rest of his life preaching in northern India. He **died** at the age of 80 in Kushinagar, about 100km southeast of Lumbini. For a fuller account of Buddhism, see "Religion" in Contexts.

Calcutta, each pursued various trails based on their interpretations of the writings of Hiuen Tsang and other early pilgrims to Lumbini. In the end, the site was found by pure chance. In a last-minute change of plans, Führer's Nepali escort, General Khadga Shamsher Jung Bahadur Rana, suggested a rendezvous in Pararia. While awaiting Führer's arrival, the general learned of an ancient pillar nearby and had his peons begin excavating it. Führer, who immediately recognized the pillar as the one described by the early travellers, claimed credit for the find in his reports, and though he was later stripped of his credentials for his falsifications, he continues to be known as the dis- coverer of Lumbini.

The Maya Devi Mandir and sculpture

Centrepiece of the Sacred Garden, the **Maya Devi Mandir** contains brickwork dating back to 300 BC, making it the oldest known structure in Nepal. Unfortunately, a major restoration project has reduced it to a jumble of bricks cordoned off under an ugly tin roof, spoiling the harmony of the entire garden. The plan is to put everything back together again with portions of each layer left exposed to illustrate the original struc- ture's 800-year architectural evolution, but this being Nepal it probably won't happen for years.

Excavations done in the course of the restoration confirmed earlier speculation that the known Gupta-period (fourth to sixth centuries AD) temple sat atop foundations from the earlier Kushana and Maurya periods. In fact, the lowest foundation seems to indicate a **pre-stupa structure** of a kind that existed at the time of the Buddha, sug- gesting that the site was venerated well before Ashoka's visit and adding further weight to Lumbini's claim as the Buddha's birthplace. Near the lowest level, archeologists also found a reddish-brown, 70-centimetre-long stone that some believe is the **"marker stone"** that Ashoka is reputed to have placed at the precise location of the Buddha's birth.

The excavation and restoration of the Maya Devi Mandir has been something of a botched chapter in the annals of archeology. The project, launched in 1990, was origi- nally conceived as a simple "renovation", which was supposed to mean trimming back a large **pipal tree** whose roots had for many years been interfering with the temple. But with little oversight or public consultation the Japan Buddhist Federation, the organization leading the effort, launched a full-scale excavation and cut down the tree, which had been regarded by many as a living link with the Buddha's day. The archeologists in charge of the excavations have come under further criticism for shoddy work, and for leaving the artefacts exposed to the elements for so long. Having bankrolled the excavation, the Japan Buddhist Federation is now pressuring the Nepalese government for permission to build its own temple and congregation hall at the Sacred Garden, dismaying those who feel that the Buddha's birthplace should remain free of any associations with specific sects or nationalities.

The temple derives its name from Maya Devi, the Buddha's mother, for until its restoration it housed a famous bas-relief **sculpture** depicting her and the newborn Buddha in the Mathura style (second or third century AD). The sculpture is now on view at a nearby building. So worn are the features, due to the flaky quality of the sedimentary stone, that archeologists at first dismissed the temple as Hindu because locals were worshipping the image as the wish-fulfilling goddess Rumindei (believed to be a corruption of "Lumbini Devi"). A recent replica reconstructs the tableau: Maya Devi grasping a tree branch for support, a tiny Buddha standing fully formed at her feet, and (ecumenical, this) the Hindu gods Indra and Brahma looking on. The sculpture illustrates an elaborate Buddhist nativity story, according to which the baby Buddha leapt out of the womb, took seven steps and proclaimed his world-saving destiny.

The Ashokan pillar and other remains

West of the temple, the **Ashokan pillar** is the oldest monument in Nepal. It's not much to look at – it looks like a smokestack – but the inscription (also Nepal's oldest), recording Ashoka's visit in 249 BC, is the best available evidence that the Buddha was born here. Split by lightning sometime before the seventh century, its two halves are held together by metal bands. Pillars were a sort of trademark of Ashoka, serving the dual purpose of spreading the faith and marking the boundaries of his empire: this one announces that the king granted Lumbini tax-free status in honour of the Buddha's birth. The carved capital to this pillar, which early pilgrims such as Hiuen Tsang describe as being in the shape of a horse, has never been found; the weathered stone lying on the ground beside the pillar is the lotus- or bell-shaped "bracket" upon which it would have rested.

The square, cement-lined **pool** just south of the Ashokan pillar is supposed to be where Maya Devi bathed before giving birth to the Buddha. Heavily restored **brick foundations** of buildings and stupas around the site, dating from the second century BC to the ninth century AD, chart the rise and fall of Lumbini's early monastic community. The two mounds north and south of the garden aren't ancient – they're archeological debris removed during amateur excavations in the 1930s led by Field Marshal Kesar Shamsher Rana.

The Tibetan and Theravada monasteries

Two active monasteries face the Sacred Garden and are open to the public; neither is tremendously old, and like all buildings not sanctioned by the master plan they're slated for eventual demolition (it's looking increasingly unlikely that anyone will enforce this, though). The **Dharma Swami Maharaja Buddha Vihar**, a Tibetan monastery established by the well-known lama Chogye Trichen Rinpoche and financed by the king of Mustang, displays a typical array of prematurely aged frescoes and gilded Buddhas and *bodhisattva* in glass cabinets. It provides a winter residence for up to fifty monks from Chogye Trichen's monastery in Boudha, who can be heard chanting in the early morning and mid-afternoon; only a skeleton crew stays on during the hot months.

The Theravada **Lumbini Buddha Vihar** offers less to look at, but its solitary gold-robed monk, the Venerable Vimalananda, speaks good English and is interesting to talk to. Built by the government of Nepal, the monastery has the feel of something designed by an international committee, with an eclectic mix of Newar woodwork, Burmese and Thai images and Tibetan-style paintings.

Around the master plan area

A walk northwards from the Sacred Garden, pleasant for its own sake in the cool of an evening, hits the highlights of the slowly unfurling master plan. An elevated path passes through what's supposed to be a reflecting pool encircling the Sacred Garden, and beyond burns an **eternal flame**, a symbolic remembrance of the "Light of Asia".

From here you can follow the kilometre-long central canal past the **East and West Monastic Zones**, where 41 plots have been set aside for temples and monasteries representing each of Buddhism's major sects and national styles of worship. At least half a dozen have already been built, some of them quite impressive – the **Myanmar (Burmese) pagoda**, done in the style of Rangoon's famous Shwedagon temple, and the **Chinese monastery**, a sort of mini-Forbidden City featuring a big Buddha statue, are highlights. There seems to be more than a bit of religious one-upmanship going on here, and the area may someday turn into a Buddhist Disneyland, but it's still interesting to see so many different manifestations of Buddhism assembled in one place.

The canal ends at what is being billed as Lumbini's **Cultural Centre**, which at the time of writing was decidedly lacking in culture, or for that matter, any sign of life at all. The tubular buildings of the Japanese-built **Lumbini International Research Institute** and an Indian-funded **museum** were in place, but forlornly vacant, while a planned auditorium, restaurants and shops remained stubbornly on paper. Altogether more than $50 million worth of improvements are envisioned by the master plan, but the Nepalese government has essentially no money for such projects and must await donations from foreign sponsors, which have not been forthcoming for some time.

North of the Cultural Centre, the massive **Lumbini Shanti Stupa** is slowly taking shape; when completed it will rise more than 40m from its base. Beyond, the **Lumbini Crane Sanctuary** provides habitat for the endangered sarus crane, the world's tallest flying bird. About 30 of Nepal's 200–300 sarus cranes reside here, along with storks, egrets and other arboreal birds. The Lumbini master plan area is itself something of a bird sanctuary, thanks to its wetlands and forests, with 165 species recorded.

Practicalities

Lumbini's **accommodation** is spread thinly over a wide area. Ideally you want to stay as close as possible to the Sacred Garden, but the only options there are the adjacent **monasteries**, which shelter pilgrims informally for a modest donation but are sorely lacking in things like bedding (bring your own). The Theravada monastery has a tranquil *dharmsala* set in a mango garden, while, outside of the busy winter months, the Tibetan monastery can put visitors up in its monks' quarters. Further afield, and a bit more comfortable, dorm lodging is available at the Dae Sun Suk Gu Sa Monastery's guest wing, where you may be invited to join the monks and nuns for Korean food at mealtimes; again, payment is a donation. Other monasteries may in time start allowing travellers to stay on this basis.

The only officially sanctioned **budget** accommodation in the master plan area is *Sri Lanka Pilgrims Rest* (☎071/80109; ⑤), way the heck at the northern end and a good half-hour's walk from the Sacred Garden. It's a huge, 188-bed hostel that looks a bit like a minimum-security prison, though it does have hot water, a cafeteria and lots of shade.

Hotel Rainbow (☎071/80169; B⑤) is an overpriced, shadeless little place in a bad location right on the highway, but the air-cooled rooms might be worth considering if it's really hot. In the past there have been other, cheaper lodges in the village of Buddha Nagar, which is a better location; at the time of writing there was nothing, but there might be again in the future, so look for signs at that intersection on your way in.

Lumbini Buddha Hotel (Kathmandu: ☎423618; *asainadv@mos.com.np*; B⑦, dorm beds ⑤), in a shady grove not too far southwest of the Sacred Garden, represents a reasonable **midrange** option; it has air-cooled rooms, geyser hot water and a small restaurant. At the **top end**, *Lumbini Hokke Hotel* (☎ & fax 071/80236; AC⑨) has Japanese- and European-style rooms, a Japanese bath and a fancy restaurant. *Hotel Lumbini Garden New Crystal* (Pokhara: ☎061/20035), under construction at the time of writing, is supposed to have a swimming pool, health club and meditation centre.

The only sources of **food** around the Sacred Garden area are *Lumbini Garden Restaurant*, which charges rather a lot for unexceptional tourist and Indian dishes, and a grass-shack eatery in the Theravada monastery compound, which serves much simpler, cheaper fare. Nepal-Bank of Ceylon, located in Buddha Nagar on the corner of the main road, has **foreign exchange** facilities (Sun–Thurs 10am–2.30pm, Fri 10am–12.30pm).

Tilaurakot and around

The ruins of **TILAURAKOT**, 24km west of Lumbini, are believed to be the remains of ancient **Kapilvastu**, seat of the ancient Shakya kingdom and the childhood home of Prince Siddhartha Gautam. It gets far fewer visitors than Lumbini, yet its ruins are at least as interesting, and shaded by mango, *kusum* and *karma* trees, they have a serenity that Lumbini has begun to lose.

Admission to the **excavation** site is free, and the lonely guards will probably be happy to give you a tour around the shaded grounds (donation expected). Among the visible remains are a couple of stupa bases, thick fortress walls and four gates – the **eastern gate** being of great metaphorical significance to Buddhists, as it was the start of the Buddha's journey in search of enlightenment. It's doubtful that this is literally the ruins of the palace of King Suddhodana, the Buddha's father, for the style of bricks used aren't thought to have been developed until the third century BC, but it may well have been built on top of it; assuming the earlier structure was made of wood, no trace of it would remain. (Another site near Piprahawa, just across the border in India, also makes a credible claim to being Suddhodana's palace.)

A small **museum** (daily except Tues 10am–5pm, Fri closes 3pm; Rs5), opposite the start of the side road to the Tilaurakot site, displays some of the three thousand coins found in the area (including one bearing the Shakya name), together with Lumbini and Kapilvastu pottery spanning three distinct periods and a thousand years. Even older pottery discovered in caves near Jomosom, high in the Himalaya, is for some reason also displayed here.

Practicalities

The easiest way to get to Tilaurakot is by **jeep** from Sonauli or Bhairawa (Rs500 and up, depending on waiting time), which enables you to hit Lumbini en route. Don't get locked into a rushed half-day tour of Lumbini and Tilaurakot, though – negotiate plenty of waiting time, and consider staying over at Lumbini on the way back. Getting there by public transport, you're stuck with the two morning **minibuses** which make their way from Bhairawa to **Taulihawa**, 22km beyond Lumbini on the same road; you could try flagging these down from Lumbini at the Parsa Chowk intersection near the *Hotel Rainbow*, but don't expect to get a seat. From the centre of Taulihawa, go 3km along the main (paved) northbound road to an obvious intersection where the museum is on the left and a paved road on the right leads 400m to the site. If you've got a bicycle you could pedal on the paved road from Lumbini to Tilaurakot in less than two hours.

Basic **food** is available at Taulihawa. If you get stuck, you can **stay** at *New Siddhartha Guest House* (①) or a couple of other Nepali inns a short distance north of the town centre along the road to Tilaurakot. A luxury hotel is supposed to be in the works.

Other archeological sites

Tilaurakot is only one of several archeological sites dating to the time of the Buddha scattered in the countryside surrounding Taulihawa. Some Buddhists make a pilgrimage circuit of the whole lot, but this is only practical in a vehicle rented in Bhairawa (driven by someone who knows the way to all the sites). **Niglihawa**, 10km northeast of Taulihawa, is the location of a broken Ashokan pillar associated with one of the mythical Buddhas of a previous age. **Sagarhawa**, 5km further to the northwest, contains an ancient water tank identified as the site of a notorious Shakya massacre. The Ashokan pillar and brick stupa at **Gotihawa**, 6km south of Taulihawa, commemorate another previous Buddha, while the *pokhari* at **Kudan**, 2km southwest of Taulihawa, is said to be where the Buddha returned after his enlightenment to preach the *dharma* to his father and young son.

THE FAR WEST

Until recently, the sheer misery of travelling the Mahendra Highway was enough to deter all but the most dedicated from entering Nepal's remote **far west**. Now, with the highway all but completed, this once-neglected quarter of the country looks poised to open its doors to travellers. It's still a hell of a haul to get here, but the new highway makes this an up-and-coming route to or from Delhi (which is just ten hours by bus from the far western border crossing).

As word gets out, expect the sights described in this section to grow in popularity and sophistication. Two in particular, **Bardia National Park** and **Sukla Phanta Wildlife Reserve**, may someday become serious rivals to Chitwan National Park.

Nepalganj and Birendra Nagar

The Mahendra Highway makes good time to Nepalganj, 250km west of Butwal, crossing the Duduwa Hills (350m ascent) and following the green and pleasant valley of the Rapti River (no relation to the river of the same name in Chitwan). North of here lies Dang, home of the white-clad Dangaura Tharus and fine cycling country. The last 40km to Kohalpur, the turning for Nepalganj and Birendra Nagar, passes through the Kusum–Ilaka forest, which is being eyed as a potential extension area of Bardia National Park.

Nepalganj

Industrial and transport hub of the far west – for what little industry and transport there is in the far west – **NEPALGANJ** is, more interestingly, Nepal's most Muslim city. The presence of Muslims in the Tarai is hardly surprising, of course, since the border with India, where Muslims comprise a significant minority, was only determined in the nineteenth century. Until just prior to the 1814–16 war with the British, this part of the Tarai belonged to the Nawab of Oudh, one of India's biggest landowners; after Nepal's defeat it was ceded to the East India Company and only returned to Nepal as a goodwill gesture

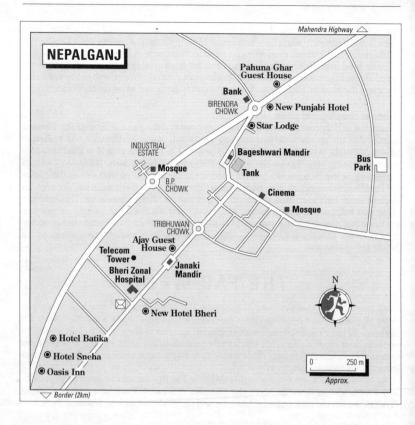

for services rendered during the Indian Mutiny of 1857. A fair few Muslims fled to Nepalganj during the revolt – Lucknow, where the most violent incidents occurred, is due south of here – and others filtered in during the Rana years, seeing chances for cross-border trade. The result is a permanent Muslim community, self-contained but maintaining business and family links with India. Indeed, the entire city feels overwhelmingly Indian, with its cheap neo-Mughal architecture and frenetically mundane bazaar.

Nepalganj sprawls more than a city of 50,000 should, thanks in part to an influx of labourers and project managers working on the Mahendra Highway in the early 1990s. Its heart is **Tribhuwan Chowk**, the lively but dilapidated intersection of the city's two main shopping thoroughfares, south of which rikshas wait beneath an Indian-style Janaki Mandir that sits in the middle of the road like a toll booth. The **Muslim quarter** lies northeast of Tribhuwan Chowk – "picturesque" is probably too strong a word, but one canopy-shaded section is almost like a North African souk, with bearded traders wearing crocheted caps and pyjama-like clothes, and transactions conducted on wooden benches in the street. The mosques in this area are disappointingly modern, and at any rate out of bounds to nonbelievers. Hindu worship and trade is centred around the nondescript but active **Bageshwari Mandir**; behind the temple is a large pool with a jaunty statue of Mahadev (Shiva) in the middle – marvellously kitsch. Shrines across the lane from the Bageshwari entrance are to Shiva and Bhairab.

Practicalities

Hardly anybody sets out to see Nepalganj, but a few people heading further west end up spending an unintended night here. If you're flying to any of the far-western airstrips there'll be a change in Nepalganj and, all too often, some problem or other with the onward flight. Nepalganj's **airport**, the country's fourth busiest, is 6km north of town by shared tempo, riksha or *tonga* (horse-drawn cart); see below for flight details. The **bus park** has been inconveniently banished to the extreme north end of the city, and it might be a good idea to buy an onward ticket when you arrive to avoid the extra trip later on.

Nepalganj's best **hotels** are *Hotel Batika* (☎081/21360, fax 22318; B⑦/AC⑦) and *Hotel Sneha* (☎081/20119; B⑦/AC⑦), side by side on the highway well south of the main part of town. Both have beautiful, secluded grounds and offer decent though musty rooms, some with air conditioning. The *Batika* has a small pool, which is intermittently operational, but the *Sneha* is more experienced at dealing with foreigners. Just beyond the *Sneha* is *Oasis Inn* (☎081/20827; AC⑦), a copycat place that doesn't really have its act together.

At the **budget** end, *New Punjabi Hotel* (☎081/20818; ③/B④) and *Pahuna Ghar Guest House* (☎081/22358; ②/B③) offer the best value. They're both fairly efficient and clean, and have reasonably priced "deluxe" rooms with air coolers and hot water; the *Punjabi*'s are bigger. Their only drawback is that they're located on the ugly main road and are noisy – the *Punjabi* a bit less so thanks to an insulating row of shops. *New Hotel Bheri* (☎081/20213, fax 21618; B⑤/AC⑥) is a bit more expensive, but it's in a much quieter, cleaner location and has a garden with a bit of greenery. Nepalganj's cheapest places, of which there are many, are all cold-water, betel-stained, smelly and noisy: at least *Ajay Guest House* (☎081/21986; ①/B①) and *Star Lodge* (☎081/22257; B②) are in the bazaar, which is more interesting than being out on the highway.

Nepalganj has an amazing number of roadside **restaurants**, and they do some great food. The busiest eating area is around Birendra Chowk, where scores of *dhaba* keep curries simmering in pots, cafeteria-style – just ask them to lift lids to see what's on the go. *New Punjabi Hotel*'s excellent little restaurant is basically a formalized version of the same, with a printed menu and colder beer. Along Garwari Tol, the lane leading to the Bageshwari temple, several places run by displaced Sherpas and Humla Bhotiyas do terrific *momo*, but that's all they do. In this area and around Tribhuwan Chowk you'll also find many places serving basic *daal bhaat* as well as a few sweet shops. In the evenings, street vendors in the bazaar dish up curd and *raabri*, a local speciality made from sweetened cream flavoured with cardamom and saffron. For tourist food, try the *Sneha* or *Batika*.

Change money at Nepal Rastra Bank at Birendra Chowk (Sun–Thurs 10am–2.30pm, Fri 10am–noon).

Moving on from Nepalganj

Bus services out of Nepalganj are patchy (see p.294 for a rundown of routes). Only a handful of buses a day head west, and of these only the Thakurdwara and Mahendra Nagar ones are likely to be much help. These services depart from the main road north of the bus park. Eastbound, the only day buses are to Butwal and Kathmandu – the rest travel at night because of the long distances involved. The Kathmandu run is a Sajha service, which you'll have to book first thing the day before to have any hope of getting a seat.

If you're moving west, consider renting a vehicle or flying. **Vehicles** can be arranged through any of the better hotels or directly from where they wait on the main road southwest of B. P. Chowk. A basic jeep – an old, ratty, canvas-sided job with room for three or four passengers plus luggage – will cost Rs1600 per day plus fuel. Newer and more comfortable Land Rovers and similar are available for somewhat more money.

FLIGHTS FROM NEPALGANJ			
	Frequency	**Time**	**Fare ($)**
Bajhang (Chainpur)	1/week	45min	77
Bajura	3/week	45min	72
Birendra Nagar (Surkhet)	3/week	20min	33
Chaurjhari (Jajarkot)	2/week	25min	39
Dhangadhi (via Bajhang)	2/week	2hr	55
Dolpo (Dunai)	1–2/day	45min	77
Jumla	1–2/day	45min	57
Kathmandu	2–3/day	1hr 10min*	99
Rukum	2/week	20min	39
Sanfebagar	2/week	35min	61
Simikot	3/week	50min	88
* Indirect flights will take longer.			

Establish up front if fuel is included, whether or not you intend to go on rough roads, and where the driver will sleep and eat and at whose expense. **Motorcycles** can also be rented for about Rs400 per day.

Far western Nepal is where domestic **flights** really come into their own, and Nepalganj is the hub for all air services in the region. If you're planning to trek around Jumla, Simikot or Dolpo, flying from here saves a good deal of money over flying from Kathmandu (see box). Buddha Air (☎081/20745) and Necon Air (☎081/20307) fly the Kathmandu–Nepalganj route daily, RNAC (☎081/20239) most days of the week; RNAC and Lumbini Airways (Kathmandu: ☎221523) serve the mountain airstrips. All the airlines have offices around Birendra Chowk or B. P. Chowk, but there's no need to go to them – have your hotel make the booking.

The **border crossing** of Jamunaha, 5km south of Birendra Chowk, is open to tourists; get there by cycle riksha. There's nothing at the border besides immigration and customs offices. Buses connect Rupaidia, the town on the Indian side of the border, with Lucknow (7hr).

Birendra Nagar (Surkhet)

A hundred kilometres northwest of Nepalganj – way, way off the beaten track – **BIREN-DRA NAGAR** (as often as not called by its old name, **SURKHET**) comes as a pleasant surprise. Placed in the middle of an undulating *dun* valley, it's neither as hot, flat nor Indian as towns closer to the border. It's also managed to escape the usual shabby fate of Tarai boomtowns, thanks, surprisingly, to government planning: HMG has transferred its western regional headquarters from Nepalganj to here, a move that has created plenty of jobs and trade. A good deal of development effort is going into the valley, too, as evidenced by the gaggle of American, British, Japanese and other volunteers.

You might find yourself in Birendra Nagar for the start or end of a trek – from here it's a week to Rara Lake – or to raft the Karnali River, the put-in point for which is a day's trek to the north. By **bus**, it's a rugged five-hour trip from Nepalganj, though the road is gradually improving. No one seems to have tried it yet, but this route would make an excellent two-day ride on a **mountain bike** – and once here, the bike would come in handy for getting around the valley and exploring northwards on the main road, which is being extended all the way to Jumla (trekking permit required).

While in Birendra Nagar, you might as well see **Karki Bihar**, 2km out of town on a wooded knoll in the middle of the valley, which houses the remains of an ancient Buddhist temple. In town, the only real attraction is **Bulbule Tal**, a new but agreeably cool and shady park that's good for bird-watching. **Food** and **lodging** in Birendra Nagar are of the most basic sort, with plenty of Nepali inns in the bazaar.

Bardia National Park

With Chitwan becoming increasingly mass-market, **BARDIA NATIONAL PARK**, northwest of Nepalganj, beckons as an unspoiled alternative. Hard to get to and still barely developed, it's the largest area of undisturbed wilderness left in the Tarai. Budget lodging is available, but there's nothing like the commercialism of Sauraha here. Indeed, if this section oversells the comparisons with Chitwan, it's because Bardia has everything Chitwan has – except Sauraha.* As the word gets out about Bardia, transport connections may get easier and facilities cushier, but its distance from Kathmandu should shield it from the masses for many years to come.

Ecologically, Bardia spans an even greater range of habitats than Chitwan, from thick riverine forest and *sal* stands to *phanta* (isolated pockets of savannah) and dry upland slopes. The **Geruwa**, a branch of the awesome **Karnali River**, forms the park's western boundary and major watering hole, and the density of wildlife and birds along this western edge is as great as anywhere in Asia. The less accessible eastern portion of the park is drained by the **Babai River**, which forms a sanctuary-like *dun* valley teeming with game.

Like Chitwan, Bardia is widely hailed as a conservation success story. **Rhinos**, hunted to extinction here earlier this century, were reintroduced in the mid-1980s and now number about 45 individuals – still not nearly as many as in Chitwan, but enough for most visitors to see one. **Tigers** are also on the increase: 42 are known to inhabit the park, but officials think the actual number is closer to 70. Because of Bardia's remoteness and minimal human disturbance, tiger experts regard it as the most promising place in Nepal in which to maintain a viable breeding population, and to that end the World Wildlife Fund has recommended extending the park westwards to increase its area by 60 percent, which would make it the biggest tiger reserve in the world. For the same reasons, Bardia has also become an important sanctuary for migratory **wild elephants** of western Nepal and adjacent portions of India, and as many as sixty animals spend at least part of the year here. One of them, a docile tusker known to locals as Raja Gaj, stands 11 feet 3 inches (3.4m) at the shoulder and is believed to be the biggest Asian elephant alive.

The Karnali/Geruwa is probably the best place in Nepal to get a peep at rare **gangetic dolphins**, which favour the river's deep channels, and to fish for huge **mahseer**. Mugger (and, increasingly, gharial) **crocodiles** can also be spotted in winter. Five species of **deer** – spotted, sambar, hog, barking and swamp – can be seen in abundance, along with **langurs** and **wild pig**. **Nilgai** ("blue bull"), bovine-looking members of the antelope family, roam the drier upland areas, while graceful, corkscrew-horned **blackbuck** (featured on the back of Nepal's ten-rupee note) graze an area south of the park. More elusive are sloth bear, leopard and other nocturnal creatures, as well as the endangered hispid hare, which survives in Bardia's grasslands. The park is also home to nearly 400 bird species, three of which – the Bengal florican, the lesser florican and the sarus crane – are endangered. The commonest sight of all around Bardia are the **termite mounds**, looking like sand-coloured volcanoes, which reach their greatest height – up to 2.5m – in the *sal* forest here.

---

*And tourists: in 1996–97 (the most recent year for which figures are available), 96,000 people visited Chitwan National Park, while just 1600 visited Bardia.

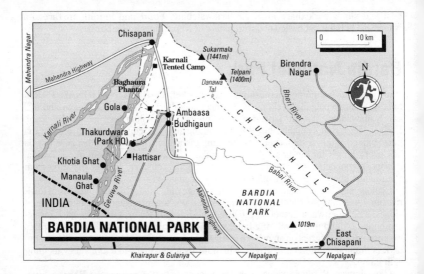

Thakurdwara

Virtually all of Bardia's lodgings are within walking distance of the park headquarters at **THAKURDWARA**, 12km off the highway in a game-rich corner of the park near the Geruwa River. A sleepy Tharu farming settlement, Thakurdwara is archetypal Tarai. It has no centre, unless you count the cluster of mud houses just south of the HQ, or the microscopic bazaar where the bus stops, at the edge of the clearing another 1km to the east. It supports no tourist facilities other than its guest houses, and precious few even for locals. Electricity still hasn't arrived here, though it's rumoured to be coming. A small temple near the bus stop serves as the focus of activities for a modest *mela* (religious fair) held on Magh Sankranti (January 14 or 15). A few other park-related points of interest are scattered in and around the village, notably the leafy headquarters compound, but most of the action is inside the park. In short, it's a lot like Sauraha was in the good old days: quiet, remote and adventurous.

Tourism will inevitably change Thakurdwara, but conservationists are already taking steps to ensure it doesn't repeat Sauraha's mistakes. Efforts are under way to create regulations to pre-empt inappropriate growth, and the Parks and People project (see "Chitwan in the balance", p.304) is working on ways to help local people literally make money from the park.

Getting there

From Kathmandu, the quickest and easiest way to get to Bardia is to **fly** to Nepalganj and travel the rest of the way by jeep (3hr). This is standard procedure for the more expensive package tours of Bardia, but you can do the same thing independently. Even if you don't want to spend the money on the flight, consider renting a **jeep** in Nepalganj (p.327) or Mahendra Nagar (p.339). Besides making for a more comfortable journey and greater flexibility, the vehicle will enable you to explore the park more fully (see "Jeep rides", below). It'll cost Rs1000 to drive into the park, on top of the Rs1600-plus daily rental charge plus fuel, but split between four people it works out to not much more than the cost of an elephant ride.

The next-quickest, but by no means easiest, way to get to Bardia from Kathmandu or Pokhara is to take a **night bus** bound for Dhangadhi or Mahendra Nagar, getting off at Ambaasa, the turning for Thakurdwara. This is a hell of a way to come – aside from the usual miseries of night travel, you'll have the extra worry of making sure not to miss your stop in the dark, since night buses pass Ambaasa between 3 and 6am. At least you won't have to worry about the final 12km to Thakurdwara, though, since guest-house jeeps wait at Ambaasa specifically for the arrival of prospective pre-dawn guests.

To travel to Bardia by day you'll have to start from at least as far west as Butwal. **Day buses** from Butwal, Nepalganj, Dhangadhi and Mahendra Nagar pass Ambaasa on their way to other destinations, and direct local services to Thakurdwara originate in Nepalganj (see box, p.294). Night buses heading eastwards from Mahendra Nagar or Dhangadhi should also get you to Ambaasa before dark. Guest-house jeeps don't normally wait at Ambaasa in the afternoon, but you can call ahead to request a ride. At present there's no phone at Ambaasa – it's just a couple of tea shacks – but you can call from Budhigaun, 5km east of Ambaasa, and wait to be picked up there. A requested jeep ride is "free" if you stay at the guest house that's providing it, though as usual this will translate into a higher room price. Alternatively, catch one of the local buses to Thakurdwara as they pass through at around 4 and 7pm. The Thakurdwara bus stop is a long walk from lodgings, though, and if it's after dark you'll probably have no choice but to let yourself be guided by a guest-house tout. A stream crossing between Ambaasa and Thakurdwara may be impassable during and immediately after heavy

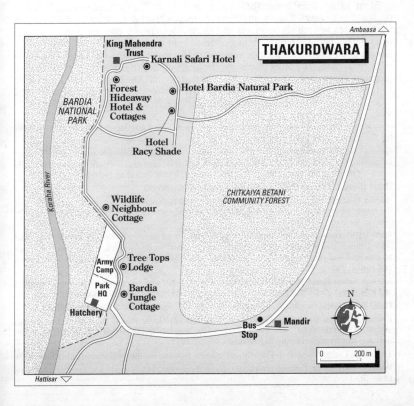

rain, but if so, your guest house will get you across somehow if they know you're coming.

Without a doubt the most enjoyable way to get to Bardia is by **raft** down the Karnali River (see p.422). Most commercial trips on the Karnali include the option of finishing up with two or more nights at a Bardia lodge.

Accommodation

Until a few years ago, the only way to experience Bardia was to stay in an exclusive safari resort costing upwards of $350 for a two-night package. That's all changed with the opening of several budget operations in and around Thakurdwara, offering simple alternative lodging for a tiny fraction of the price.

BUDGET LODGES

Thakurdwara's **budget lodges** are spread out along the park boundary north and south of the HQ (refer to the Thakurdwara map for locations). They're all very similar, being based on the formula pioneered in (and steadily disappearing from) Sauraha: mud-and-thatch huts, a simple dining pavilion, a separate toilet/shower block and, in a few cases, solar hot water. The food is simple: mainly *daal bhaat* and crude approximations of Western dishes. Rates are a bit steep by Chitwan standards, but you're paying for an elite experience, and in any case accommodation makes up only a small part of the cost of visiting Nepal's wildlife parks.

Of the lodges listed below, three stand out as providing the best service, food and guides. *Bardia Jungle Cottage* and *Forest Hideaway Hotel & Cottages* have the longest track records and are also the most popular, which increases your chances of meeting other people but also means it's more advisable to book ahead. *Karnali Safari Hotel*, though geared more for package tourists, is also excellent and its walk-in prices are quite reasonable. The other places are cheaper, but they're not as good at catering to travellers' needs, and they get so few guests that they may well have folded by the time you get there. Most lodges will heat water for showers on demand or at scheduled times, but this is done by burning wood or garbage, so try to minimize your hot-water use.

Many of these places offer **packages**, but as in Chitwan, these provide little benefit for their added cost (see p.298).

Bardia Jungle Cottage (☎084/29714; Kathmandu: ☎258327). Thakurdwara's original budget lodge, run by a former assistant park warden. Unbeatable location near the park HQ, lovely grounds and a big dining area. Jeep, rental cycles, fishing rods. ③/B④, including breakfast.

Hotel Bardia Natural Park (no phone). Small and primitive. ③.

Bardia Wildlife Paradise (☎084/29715). On the road to the *hattisar*, 1km south of park HQ (off the map). A very small place, somewhat lacking in shade and rather far from the HQ, though it's close to the river. ③/B③.

Forest Hideaway Hotel & Cottages (☎084/29716; *forest.hideaway@geo.wlink.com.np*). Excellent leafy grounds and two classes of accommodation. Under Nepali–Western management, staff are professional and speak good English. Probably the best food in Tharkurdwara. Jeep, rental bikes and a small library. ④, including breakfast.

Karnali Safari Hotel (☎084/29721; Kathmandu: ☎427124). In a big compound with good gardens and a nice dining hall/bar. Jeep, raft. ③/B⑤, plus ① beds in a cool little attic-like dorm room.

Hotel Racy Shade (no phone). Not much shade, actually. Small place with modest facilities. Jeep. ③.

Rhino Lodge Bardia (☎084/29720; *rhinotvl@ccsl.com.np*). On the road to the *hattisar*, 2.5km south of park HQ (off the map). Concrete bunkers, no shade or landscaping – this is the sort of place that only survives by suckering package tourists. Jeep. B④.

Tree Tops Lodge (no phone). Friendly and in a nice location, but the facilities are rather lifeless. ③.

Wildlife Neighbour Cottage (no phone). Small, family-run, lots of shade and greenery, but very basic. ③.

EXPENSIVE LODGES

Three lodgings in and around Bardia are considerably more **expensive** than the above, but only two are really worth it, and they're nowhere near Thakurdwara. The only official concession inside the park, *Tiger Tops Karnali Tented Camp* (Kathmandu: ☎411225; *tiger@mtn.mos.com.np*; ⑨) overlooks the Geruwa River at a point 15km north of Thakurdwara, and provides a good old-fashioned luxury safari experience with the full range of activities led by experienced guides. Two nights at the tented camp and a third at the affiliated *Karnali Lodge*, just outside the park on its southern edge, costs $534 (flights and ground transportation extra). *Dolphins Manor* (Kathmandu: ☎420308), located 1km south of the park HQ on the road to the *hattisar*, surpasses Thakurdwara's budget lodges only in its pretensions: accommodation is in deluxe tents or stone bungalows, and meals are eaten in a huge banquet hall that's completely out of keeping with local architecture.

Other practicalities

There are no restaurants in Thakurdwara, and only basic provisions stalls near the bus stop. Guest houses can **change money** informally. A few local people, supported by the King Mahendra Trust, make and sell **handicrafts** out of their homes. **International calls** can be made from any guest house with a phone, though charges are relatively expensive. There's a local **health post** near the bus stop, but no pharmacy, so it's advisable to come equipped with a first-aid kit. The nearest hospital is in Nepalganj.

Park **entry permits** cost Rs650 and are valid for three consecutive days. Buy them from the **ticket office** inside the headquarters compound, or have your guest house do it for you. The same goes for elephant-ride tickets and vehicle and fishing permits (see below). Park brochure/maps may be available from the nearby **warden's office**, but don't count on it. While you're at the HQ, stop by the park's reptile **hatchery**, a small, zoo-like facility where gharial and mugger crocodiles are raised from eggs. Like a similar effort at Chitwan (see p.310), this project greatly ups the chances of these endangered and sensitive species living to maturity, at which point they're released into local waters.

Although the rhino danger is somewhat lower here than in Chitwan, it would still be extremely foolish to enter the park without a **guide**. Hire one informally through your guest house; the price will be Rs250–300 for a half day, twice that for a full day. Although guides here generally speak less English and are less well trained than those at Chitwan, they know the territory and can keep you out of harm's way.

See "Staying alive in Chitwan" (p.303) for jungle safety tips.

Moving on

Bus services in the far west are improving all the time, so the following advice may be superseded by better ways of moving on – check with your lodge for the most up-to-date information. Again, night **buses** are an option if you're in a hurry to get to Kathmandu or Pokhara. Have your lodge book you a seat on the bus originating at Chisapani, which will pick you up at Ambaasa in the afternoon (other night buses aren't bookable from Thakurdwara). If you prefer to travel by day, catch one of the morning local buses to Nepalganj, which leave Thakurdwara at around 8 and 10am. If you're heading east, take the earliest bus and get off at Kohalpur, where you ought to be able to book a confirmed seat on a day express out of Nepalganj bound for Butwal. Heading west, get off at Ambaasa and flag down any bus that's going. You should be able to get to Mahendra Nagar before dark, though you may end up having to change buses at Chisapani or Atariya (the turning for Dhangadhi). Your lodge may also be able to book **plane** tickets out of Nepalganj.

Activities

Bardia's menu of activities is similar to Chitwan's; you'll find lengthier descriptions of walks and elephant rides in that section. All access to the park is via the main headquarters entrance, crossing the Koraha River from there.

Walks

As in Chitwan, tall grass restricts visibility and makes jungle **walks** more dangerous before the thatch is cut in mid-January. Most walks entail wading through some streams, so bring flipflops or sandals as well as walking shoes.

Your guide will be able to suggest routes tailored to your interests. Most walks inside the park take a northerly bearing from Thakurdwara, roughly paralleling the Geruwa River through mixed grassland and jungle. Some of the park's best rhino habitat, as well as areas favoured by wild elephants, are found in the riverine corridor between Thakurdwara and **Gola**. Tigers, bears, boars, nilgai and (in the river) dolphins may be sighted, and you're assured of seeing deer, monkeys and all manner of birds. The track to **Baghaura Phanta**, about 7km northeast of Thakurdwara, is a prime bird-watching route.

To watch Bardia's hardest-working employees enjoying some down time, visit the government **hattisar** (elephant stable), outside the park about forty minutes' walk south of the HQ. Although it's not set up as a breeding centre, this *hattisar* usually has a baby elephant or two in residence, thanks to the nocturnal visits of wild bulls. Remaining outside the park, the road continues southwards along the river past **Manaula Ghat** and **Khotia Ghat**, two of the best places to look for dolphins.

Camping isn't allowed inside the park, which limits the scope for longer hikes. However, guides have developed a two-day trek from Ambaasa to **Danawa Tal** and then up to **Telpani** (1400m), a high point along the crest of the ridge that forms the park's northern boundary, where you can spend the night in a teahouse and then return via Chisapani the next day. The way is mostly through *sal* forest (monkeys and deer), with some possibility of seeing rhinos or elephants at Danawa Tal; the view of the Surkhet valley from Telpani is great. This walk is best done in the winter months.

Elephant rides

Arrange **elephant rides** at the HQ ticket office, or have your guest house do it. The charge is Rs650 per hour, up to three hours – longer rides take you deeper into the park and provide more chances to see animals. Rides must be reserved the day before. It may be advisable to book two days in advance if there are many other tourists in the village, as only eight rideable elephants are kept here, and not all of them may be on duty on any given day. Departures are in the early morning and late afternoon from a platform at the far end of the HQ compound. The usual route heads west and north from the HQ into mixed jungle and grassland, where you could see (in approximate order of likelihood) deer, langurs, boar, rhinos, bear and tiger.

Jeep rides

A **jeep** might or might not increase your chances of surprising game, but it will certainly enable you to penetrate remoter parts of the park where the game isn't as wary of humans. Most lodges either have their own jeeps or plan to get one; whether your lodge has one or not, they'll book you on whichever vehicle is going into the park that day. The price depends on the number of paying clients, so can be anything from Rs600 to Rs1000 per person for a half-day ride. If you've brought your own hired jeep to Bardia, you'll need to obtain a special permit from park HQ to enter the park with it (Rs1000 per day).

Most trips are confined to the network of tracks in the park's western sector, which takes you through *sal* forest and the grasslands of **Baghaura Phanta** (where there's a view tower) and gives access to pristine stretches of river and rich wildlife habitat. Given more time you could continue north to Chisapani to look for gharials and dolphins. Note, however, that vehicles can't cross the Koraha River to access this area until mid- or late November. From Ambaasa, you can follow a track eastwards to **Danawa Tal**, a wetland at the base of the foothills where rhinos and elephants are sometimes spotted. The road continues from there into the idyllic Babai valley, where most of Bardia's elephants live, but entrance to this area is currently restricted (it's worth asking, though).

Nepal's only herd of blackbuck antelope congregates around a big *phanta* well south of the park at **Khairapur**, 45km from Thakurdwara by road and most easily reached by vehicle. From Thakurdwara drive north to Ambaasa, then 3km south along the Mahendra Highway to Budhigaun, and then take the road south from there; look for the herd on your left as you approach Gulariya. Blackbuck were actually thought to be extinct until three were sighted here in 1973; careful management brought their number up to 100–150 by the mid-1980s, and it has remained stable since then. The government is attempting to create a separate wildlife reserve here to protect the herd.

River trips

A few **rafting** companies do week-long trips down the Karnali, pulling out at Chisapani, but those trips are all organized out of Kathmandu or Pokhara. Once you get to Bardia your options are limited to day trips on the Geruwa. *Karnali Safari Hotel* has a raft, and other lodges can rent it if it's available: for Rs2000 per person you can do a one-day float from Chisapani to the *hattisar*. Another option offered by some lodges is a **dugout canoe** ride from the southern boundary of the park down to the Indian border, costing Rs1000–2000 per person depending on the number of clients.

Once on the river, you've got a good chance of seeing dolphins, muggers, monkeys and birds, and some people have seen elephants and even tigers from the water. It's also a great way to fish.

BARDIA'S HUMAN FACTOR

Nepal's wildlife parks never sit easily with the inhabitants of nearby villages, who not only are barred from their former woodcutting areas but also must cope with marauding animals. In the case of Bardia National Park the potential for resentment is especially high, because the government has actually reintroduced rhinos to the area, giving local farmers a headache they thought they'd gotten rid of. It's estimated that half the crops in fields adjoining Bardia are damaged by wildlife (primarily rhinos and elephants).

The work being done by nonprofit organizations to assist communities in Bardia's buffer zone is therefore especially important: as in Chitwan (see p.304), the long-term viability of the park depends as much on human factors as ecological ones. Operating in Bardia as it does in all the Tarai parks and wildlife reserves, the Parks and People Project is helping local people develop alternative skills and sources of income, and is also improving watering holes and grazing areas inside the park so that animals aren't so tempted to leave it. The King Mahendra Trust for Nature Conservation has backed a number of similar efforts, including the establishment of home handicrafts businesses. The Bardia Integrated Development Programme, supported by the Danish government, is active in community development and forestry, while CARE Nepal has helped set up the Chitkaiya Betani Community Forest, giving residents in the Thakurdwara area an alternative source of wood.

Fishing

The Karnali/Geruwa is renowned for its **mahseer**, a sporting fish related to carp that can weigh up to 40kg. If you catch one, release it: the *mahseer* population is declining due to pollution, dams, barriers and a general lack of headwaters protection. The Babai is superb for *mahseer* and *goonch*, another huge fish. Be alert for crocodiles.

Fishing is allowed everywhere on the Karnali and Geruwa rivers, but on the Babai is restricted to the waters below the dam (the Mahendra Highway crossing). You'll need a fishing **permit**, which costs Rs300 per day and can be obtained from the ticket office at park HQ. *Bardia Jungle Cottage* rents fishing gear, but if you're at all interested in angling you'll want to bring your own – and strong tackle.

Bike rides and Tharu villages

Some guest houses in Thakurdwara rent **bicycles**, which opens up a host of possibilities for exploring the surrounding countryside. Two roads head south from Thakurdwara and take you through numerous traditional Tharu villages. The one past the *hattisar* and on to Khotia Ghat (see above) gets far more tourist traffic, and the kids along it are definitely switched on to the bye-bye-one-rupee chorus. Cycling north along the road to Ambaasa is also a possibility. Given more time and a packed lunch, you could conceivably cycle to Chisapani or some of the other spots normally only reached by jeep (see above).

It might be worth joining a guided "village walk" to learn more about local Tharu culture, if you can get past the human-zoo aspect of it.

West of the Karnali

When it's finally completed, the Mahendra Highway from Nepalganj to the far western border post of Mahendra Nagar will be, for Nepal, something of an engineering marvel. Laying down 215km of asphalt was easy; building bridges over the countless streams that dice the route (not to mention spanning the Karnali) has been the real challenge. At the time of writing, the bus ride from Nepalganj to Mahendra Nagar took at least seven hours, but when all the bridges are passable that time should drop to six.

The Karnali Bridge and Chisapani

The Mahendra Highway emerges from Bardia National Park to vault the mighty **Karnali River**, surging out of a gap in the rugged foothills, on what is reputed to be the longest single-tower suspension **bridge** in the world. Before the completion of the bridge, in 1993, the Karnali effectively formed the western border of Nepal: those living on the other side maintained stronger links with Delhi than with Kathmandu. The World Bank-funded bridge hasn't automatically brought the far west back under Kathmandu's sway – Delhi is still closer – but together with a smooth new highway it should bring more trade and industry to this undeveloped part of the country.

As for the bridge's exotic design, it appears to have been dictated mainly by the foreign contractors' need for a showcase project. Alas, after crossing this gleaming, state-of-the-art span, the paved highway promptly reverts to a four-wheel-drive track, illustrating the politically sensitive nature of development in Nepal. China was contracted to build this section of the Mahendra Highway, but in 1994, with the work nearing completion, India became nervous about the presence of Chinese so close to its border and offered to buy out the contract. Nepal agreed and sent the Chinese home, but due to various political upheavals and basic inattention, work stopped for nearly five years. At the time of writing, work had resumed but there remained a jarring six-kilometre gap just west of the Karnali, followed by several temporary river crossings between there and the Dhangadhi turn-off.

An even bigger showcase project may be in the works for the Karnali. Reviving an idea that's been kicking around for decades, an American company has proposed building a mammoth dam upstream of the bridge. The 10.8-gigawatt **Karnali-Chisapani Project** would be one of the largest hydroelectric installations in the world, costing as much as $8 billion. (See p.467 for more on hydroelectric megaprojects in Nepal.)

Overlooking the forested west bank of the Karnali, the shacks of **CHISAPANI** look like they were erected yesterday in the expectation that they'd be dismantled tomorrow. Booms and busts have marked Chisapani's recent history, as bridge and road construction projects have swollen its population with itinerant labourers. But despite its temporary appearance, this polyglot little bazaar has long been an important trading centre for shoppers throughout the hills to the north, some of whom walk a week or more to buy basic provisions here. If you're stuck, there are a few makeshift bunkhouses at the north end of the bazaar. This would be a very adventurous place to be stranded – savour the experience!

On to Dhangadhi

West of Chisapani the highway passes through alternating forest and farmland. Hidden in one forested area just north of the road about 30km beyond Chisapani is **Ghodagodhi Tal**, a lake famed for its kingfishers, lapwings and waterfowl; it's being studied as a potential national wildlife refuge. The four-way junction of **Ataria**, 80km west of Chisapani, is the only town of note in this section. If by this point you're getting sick of bus travel, just be glad you're not riding to Baitadi or Dipayal, which lie an abominable twelve hours' journey north of here in Nepal's disadvantaged far-western hills.

From Ataria a paved spur road leads 12km south to the indescribably boring border town of **DHANGADHI**. Unless you're heading for India's Dudhwa National Park (which is just south of the border) or, God forbid, catching a bus to Dipayal, there's no reason to come this way. The **bus park** is about 1km east of the main roundabout, and the breezeblock bazaar extends for more than 1km east of that. The **airstrip** ($149 to Kathmandu) lies 10km north of town on the way back to the highway – rikshas are plentiful – and the **RNAC office** (☎091/21205) is in the bazaar.

The Indian **border**, 1km south of the roundabout, is open to foreigners. Local buses on the Indian side go to Palia Kala, 35km distant, where there are long-distance connections. Dudhwa National Park is about 20km south of the border, reachable by bus or jeep.

Lodgings are for the most part cheap and modest. *Annapurna Guest House* (☎091/23336; ②/B③), at the main roundabout at the west entrance to town, is a competent place with air coolers and TVs in the better rooms and a popular restaurant. The nearby *Sangam Lodge* (☎091/21880; ①/B②) also has some air-cooled rooms, but its cheaper rooms are actually less dank. *Hotel Afno Ghar* (☎091/22959; B④) has scruffy air-cooled rooms, hot water and an attempt at a garden. It's in a quiet location, but hard to find: head north from the main east–west road just beyond the bus park, then take a left at the fork after about 400m. A half-dozen other places in the bazaar and around the bus park offer cold-water facilities. Plenty of places serve Indian, Nepali and even Tibetan **food**. Nepal Rastra Bank in Hasanpur, the aid enclave 1km east of the bus park, does **foreign exchange** (Sun–Thurs 10am–2pm, Fri 10am–noon).

Mahendra Nagar

The end of the line is **MAHENDRA NAGAR**, another border town but with a good deal of spark, thanks to day-tripping shoppers from India. The town is laid out in an unusually logical grid south of the highway, with the **bus park** at the northwestern end. Walk south from the bus park for 500m and you come to the first intersection of the grid: to the left (east) is the main shopping street, and to the right (west) is the road to the **airstrip** (3.5km) and Sukla Phanta Wildlife Reserve (see below). RNAC discontinued its weekly flights to Mahendra Nagar in 1998, but may in time resume them.

From the intersection walk east on the main shopping street and you'll count four lanes heading off to the right (south). **Lodgings** are grouped mainly on the second and third lanes. *Hotel New Anand* (☎099/21693; B③), in the second lane, is a smart, central establishment with a range of rooms, some with hot running water, air coolers and TVs, and a good in-house restaurant. *Hotel Alpine* (☎099/21165; ②/B③), a long way down the third lane in a quieter, duller part of the bazaar, offers good value for a comparable range of rooms if you're not bothered about hot water. *Royal Guest House* (☎099/21906; ②), on the main east–west street near the entrance to town, is friendly, and its front-facing rooms are big and have nice balconies. Mahendra Nagar's best accommodation, *Hotel Sweet Dream* (☎099/22313; B④/AC⑤), sits out on the highway east of the bus park – all its rooms are either air-cooled or air-conditioned and it has a passable tourist restaurant, but it suffers from early-morning noise from the highway.

Several *dhaba*, concentrated mainly along the first lane, do a fair range of Nepali and Indian **food**. They all look the same on the outside, with their tandoori ovens and pots of pre-made curries, but each has its own specialities. If you want alcohol you'll have to drink it discreetly. Kanchanpur, the district of which Mahandra Nagar is the headquarters, is a dry district, thanks to a successful 1995 campaign led by local women fed up with their husbands drinking their wages. However, it's unclear whether the women's goal has been achieved: alcohol is still easily obtainable, but at a higher price, and smugglers and police are said to be equally happy with the arrangement.

Any of the guest houses mentioned above can fix you up with a **jeep** for exploring Sukla Phanta or Bardia (Rs1200 per day plus fuel). Rastriya Banijya Bank, opposite Hotel Alpine, can **change** Indian rupees and US dollars, but other currencies may be beyond its abilities (Sun–Thurs 10am–2pm, Fri 10am–noon). IC is readily accepted and unofficially exchanged everywhere in Mahendra Nagar.

Mahendra Nagar's bustle is only a border aberration, for the outlying region is one of the more traditional parts of the Tarai. Rana Tharu sharecroppers work the fields, maintaining an apparently happy symbiosis with their old-money landlords, and their **villages**, scattered along dirt tracks north of the Mahendra Highway, still consist of traditional communal longhouses.

The border

The **border** begins 6km west of Mahendra Nagar, reached by shared tempo or (slower) *tonga* or bus. A rough road traverses the one-kilometre no-man's land between the Nepalese and Indian immigration posts. From Indian immigration you can catch a cycle riksha (Rs40 NC) across the wide Mahakali River along the top of a huge flood-control/irrigation barrage and then a further 4km to Banbaasa, the first Indian town. The road across the barrage is only one lane wide, which is why the border is open to vehicles only at certain times in each direction; for pedestrians it's open from 6am to 7pm. Accommodation in Banbaasa is poor, and since crossing the border is fairly time-consuming, you'll want to make an early start from Mahendra Nagar to avoid being stuck there. Buses connect Banbaasa to Bareli (the nearest broad-gauge rail station; 2hr 30min), Almora (6hr), Naini Tal (7hr), Haridwar (9hr) and Delhi (10hr). Narrow-gauge trains from Banbaasa are slow and infrequent, so you're better off taking a bus.

If you're **entering Nepal**, refer to the box on p.294 for onward bus information. There are direct night buses from Mahendra Nagar to Kathmandu, but unless you're on urgent business you'd do better to make the journey in stages: Sukla Phanta Wildlife Reserve, Bardia National Park and Lumbini all make worthwhile stopovers.

Sukla Phanta Wildlife Reserve

In Nepal's extreme southwest, a different feature appears on the land: *phanta*, great swathes of natural grassland that could almost be mistaken, albeit on a smaller scale, for the savannahs of East Africa. **SUKLA PHANTA WILDLIFE RESERVE**, south of Mahendra Nagar, is dotted with them, and touring it is, for once, really like being on safari. The reserve is home to the world's largest population of swamp deer – sightings of 1000 at a time are common – as well as a good concentration of tigers. It's also astonishingly rich in birds, with 470 species having been counted here, one of the highest concentrations in Nepal. Seeing Sukla Phanta independently is relatively expensive, as it entails renting a vehicle, but you'll have the satisfaction of going where few have gone before. It's also possible to visit the reserve on a luxury package tour.

Several four-wheel-drive tracks crisscross the reserve, making itineraries flexible, but first stop is bound to be *the* **Sukla Phanta** at the southwestern end, a rippling sea of grass that turns silvery-white in October (*sukila* means white in the local Tharu dialect). You're guaranteed **swamp deer** here, and in quantity – make for the view

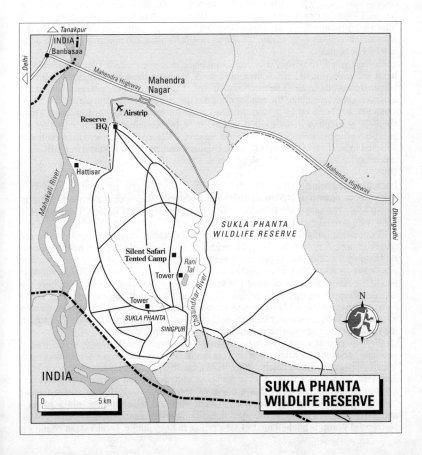

tower in the middle and scan for them with binoculars. As *barasingha* ("twelve points"), the swamp deer was one of Kipling's beloved *Jungle Book* animals – "that big deer which is like our red deer, but stronger" – and common throughout the plains and hills. Today it's an endangered species, finding safety in numbers in the *phanta* and particularly the boggy parts where seasonal fires don't burn off the grasses. The species' high density in Sukla Phanta assures plenty of prey for the reserve's thirty-odd **tigers**, which for the time being seem healthy. However, a question mark hangs over their long-term survival, as habitat outside the reserve is steadily disappearing, and Sukla Phanta alone isn't large enough to support an independent breeding population. The riparian area along the Chaundhar River from **Singpur** northwards supports the reserve's greatest concentration of tigers.

Having seen your obligatory *phanta*, make a beeline for **Rani Tal** (Queen's Lake), near the centre of the reserve. Surrounded by riotous, screeching forest, the lake – a lagoon, really – is like a prehistoric time capsule, with trees leaning out over the shore, deer wading shoulder-deep around the edges and crocodiles occasionally peering out of the water-hyacinth-choked water. The **birdlife** is like nothing you've ever seen, a dazzling display of cranes, cormorants, eagles and scores of others. You can watch all the comings and goings from a tower by the western shore. Nearby is an overgrown **brick circle**, 1500m in circumference, which locals say was the fort of Singpal, an ancient Tharu king (Rani Tal is said to have been his queen's favourite spot). The fact that the remains have never been excavated shows how little historical research has been done in western Nepal.

Though you'd think they'd be hard to miss, chances are Sukla Phanta's **elephant herd** will give you the slip – they now seem to spend most of their time in Bardia National Park and India's Corbett National Park. Evidence of their passage is abundant, however, especially along the road south from the entrance, where in places the forest looks like it's been hit by a tornado. The dominant male of this herd, dubbed Thula Hatti ("Big Elephant"), was killed in 1993 by a homemade mine, planted either by poachers or by a farmer trying to protect his crops. Before his demise, Thula Hatti was believed to be the world's biggest Asian elephant, and was even featured in a BBC documentary.

Park practicalities

The reserve **entrance** is 5km southwest of Mahendra Nagar, not far from the airstrip (see p.340). The **entry fee** is Rs650 (plus a vehicle entry fee of Rs100). The reserve is open from around 8am to sunset.

The nearest budget lodgings are in Mahendra Nagar, which seriously blunts the reserve's appeal as well as adding considerably to the cost of visiting it **independently**. The only feasible way to enter the reserve – and certainly the best way to track game across the *phanta* – is by jeep, rentable in Mahendra Nagar. Although rikshas will take you to the reserve entrance, you won't be allowed to enter alone on foot, and there are no English-speaking guides. Elephant rides are available, but the starting point, at the *hattisar* 8km southwest of the reserve headquarters, is miles from the best game area so you're unlikely to see much. You could cycle in, but note that it's about 25km from the entrance to the game-rich areas along the Chaundhar River.

There is another way to visit Sukla Phanta, but it involves more money – still, even if you hate the idea of a **luxury safari**, this might be the place to do one. An unpretentious family outfit, Silent Safari (☎099/21230, fax ☎099/22220; Kathmandu: ☎520523), runs customized trips in the reserve for about $140 per person per night, and can also arrange Tharu village treks. It's a one-man operation – Col. Hikmat Bisht, former hunter, retired military attaché, patrician landowner and self-styled man of the forest – and a trip with him is one of the most delightfully idiosyncratic experiences in Nepal. His **tented camp** is pitched next to a waterhole in deep jungle – real Tarzan country –

and there's also the unique opportunity to spend a night or two in a *machaan* (tree-top blind) for nocturnal sights and sounds. He is considering building a more moderately priced lodge just outside the reserve's southern boundary, with rooms in the $20 range.

CHAPTER SIX

THE EASTERN TARAI AND HILLS

A s with the west, the **eastern Tarai** – the portion east of Chitwan – is where Nepal dovetails with India. It's lusher and more tropical than the west, but also less wild, more populous and more industrial. It's also, if anything, more Indian. Although the foothills are usually within sight, the main east–west highway sticks to the plains, where the way of life is essentially identical to that of Bihar and West Bengal just across the border; in many parts of this region, Nepali is the second or even third language, after Maithili, Bhojpuri or other north Indian dialects.

Most travellers only flit through here on their way to the border crossings of **Birganj** (for Patna) and **Kakarbhitta** (for Darjeeling), and outside these places you won't find

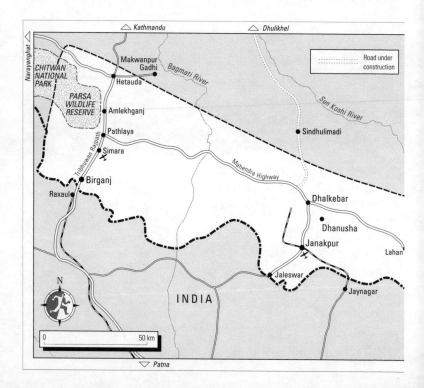

a speck of tourist hype. The cities are admittedly awful, but with one outstanding exception: **Janakpur**, a pilgrimage centre that's immensely famous among Hindus but seldom visited by Westerners, which provides all the exoticism of India without the attendant hassles. Although large tracts of jungle are less common east of Chitwan, bird-watchers can check out **Koshi Tappu Wildlife Reserve**, straddling the alluvial plain of the mighty Sapt Koshi River.

What few visitors the **eastern hills** get tend to be trekkers bound for the Everest or Kanchenjunga massifs, which rear up like goalposts on the northern horizon, or rafters running the Sun Koshi. But while the prospect of travelling twenty-plus hours by bus from Kathmandu puts most people off, this isn't a problem if you're already in the eastern Tarai. By turns riotously forested and fastidiously terraced, the hills are great for day-hiking, even if you've vowed not to trek (but get a permit anyway, just in case you change your mind). Two all-weather roads extend into the hills, one serving the lovely Newar town of **Dhankuta** and rowdier **Hile**, and the other **Ilam**, Nepal's tea-growing capital.

Buses make good time through the eastern Tarai on the Mahendra Highway, and the completion of the Dhulikhel–Sindhuli Highway will soon (perhaps as early as 2001) make getting to the east even easier. However, most of the places described in this chapter are located on side roads, thus requiring various degrees of extra toil to get to. Also, **tourist facilities** in this region are minimal to nonexistent, adding to the difficulty (or adventure) of travelling here. You won't find much Western cuisine, but the Indian and Nepali food is wonderful. If you're cycling, many of the small bazaars en

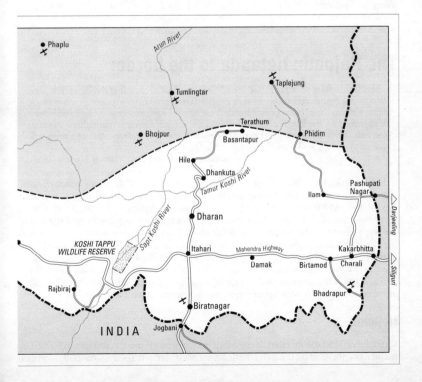

ROOM PRICE SCALES

All guest houses and hotels have been price-graded according to the scale below, which is based on the price of the cheapest double room in high season. Codes prefixed by B denote the cost of the cheapest room with attached bathroom, and those prefixed by AC refer to air-conditioned rooms. See p.39 for a fuller explanation.

① Less than Rs140   ⑤ $8–12
($2 if quoted in US$)   ⑥ $12–20
② Rs140–200 ($2–3)   ⑦ $20–40
③ Rs200–350 ($3–5)   ⑧ $40–75
④ Rs350–550 ($5–8)   ⑨ Over $75

---

route can provide basic food and, at a pinch, lodging. A phenomenon specific to eastern Nepal is the **haat bazaar**, or weekly market, and it's worth trying to coincide with one or two of these pan-cultural extravaganzas.

THE EASTERN TARAI

For travellers coming by road from other parts of Nepal, Hetauda is the gateway to the eastern Tarai: from Narayanghat (Chitwan) it's an easy two-hour bus ride to Hetauda along the **Mahendra Highway**, hugging the hills as it follows the attractive *dun* (inner Tarai valley) of the Rapti River; the **Tribhuwan Rajpath** (see p.238) enters the town from the north and continues south to the Indian border at Birganj.

The Rajpath: Hetauda to the border

There is something peculiarly sinister and ominous about the jungle of the Tarai. You have that feeling that danger in one form or another lurks around every corner . . . Over everything a strange, oppressive silence broods . . . A big gray ape chatters at us maliciously from his perch on an overhanging rock. A leopard, camouflaged almost to invisibility by his spotted hide, steals on stealthy feet across the road. There is a sudden crash of underbrush behind the jungle wall – an elephant or a tiger perhaps.
E Alexander Powell, *The Last Home of Mystery* (1929)

For centuries the only developed corridor through the Tarai, this route was, before air travel, every foreigner's introduction to Nepal. A narrow-gauge railway used to run from Raxaul, the last Indian station, as far as Amlekhganj; dignitaries were transported from there by elephant over the first band of hills to Hetauda before being carried the rest of the way to Kathmandu by donkey or sedan chair. Those few who made the journey during Nepal's isolation years before 1951, such as our Mr Powell, did so only by invitation of the prime minister or king. The construction of the **Rajpath** in the 1950s eliminated the need for elephants and sedan chairs, but the railway wasn't decommissioned until the 1970s. If you're driving your own vehicle in from India, the Rajpath makes an exhilarating introduction to Nepal, with an overnight stay in Daman (see p.240).

Hetauda

Clumped around the junction of the Mahendra Highway and the Rajpath, **HETAUDA** is still a staging-post on the India–Kathmandu route, but whatever romance it may once have had has long gone. Indian trucks rumble through with fuel and bulk goods for Kathmandu, while buses stop here at all hours: it's a restless, transient place. Prostitution is common, helping make the city a link in the transmission of AIDS from India to Nepal. Among Nepalis, Hetauda is probably most famous for its cement plant, whose output has built many of the Tarai's factories and concrete bazaars, and its industrial estate, responsible for much of Nepal's prodigious beer production. In fairness, though, Hetauda isn't all industry and ugliness. The local council has tidied up the central crossroads area a bit, and as part of a general beautification drive has even banned the use of plastic bags in the city. Tributaries of the Rapti River run peacefully along the town's southern and western edges (bearing Hetauda's industrial effluents to Chitwan, unfortunately), and much of the surrounding area is dominated by *sal* forest.

The centre of Hetauda is **Mahendra Chowk**, a four-way intersection with the Mahendra Highway coming in from the west, the Rajpath from the north, and the two of them merging for a time along the highway heading south. The intersection's eastern spoke is at present only a local road to Makwanpur Gadhi, 17km distant, but it's eventually supposed to be extended all the way to Tika Bhairab in the Kathmandu Valley. When (or if) that happens, Hetauda will become an even more important junction, and its industries will get a lift by gaining better access to the capital.

Practicalities

Hetauda's **bus park** is located southwest of Mahendra Chowk; the main entrance to it is from the north. Many buses pass through here bound for destinations to the east and west. If you're trying to get to Daman or Kathmandu, only one daily Sajha bus travels the Rajpath in each direction (two other private buses also serve this route, but their services are irregular and they overnight in Markhu and Shikharkot respectively – see p.240).

Cyclists will probably **spend the night** here, as there are no other worthwhile places to stay between Daman and the border or Chitwan. Fortunately, *Motel Avocado* (☎057/20429, fax 20611; B④/AC⑦) more than compensates for Hetauda's shortcomings. Located in a quiet, shady compound 500m north of Mahendra Chowk, the grounds include an orchid garden and a small grove of avocado trees planted by displaced Californians when this was the USAID guest house. In late autumn practically everything on the menu has avocado in it. Running a distant second is *Hotel Rapti* (☎057/20882; B④), south of Mahendra Chowk, which is the only place in the bazaar with a little sound-deadening space around it. Rooms there have TVs and (unpredictable) hot water. There are several cheaper choices north of Mahendra Chowk (such as *Neelam Lodge*; ①) or west of it (*Hetauda Rest House*; ①). North is quieter.

Food outside the guest houses is unexceptional, but you'll find a number of tea stalls and *sekuwa* vendors near *Neelam Lodge*.

South to Birganj

Heading south over the low **Chure Hills**, the Rajpath, merged with the Mahendra Highway here, enters a strange landscape of stunted trees, wide gravel washes and steeply eroded pinnacles. These hills are the newest wrinkle in the Himalayan chain, heaved up as the 30-million-year-long collision between the Indian and Asian continental plates ripples southwards – less than half a million years old, they're so young that the surface sediments haven't yet been eroded to expose bedrock.

Leaving the hills once and for all, the road passes Amlekhganj, the former rail terminus (now Nepal's main fuel depot), and 4km further on, the entrance to **Parsa Wildlife Reserve**. An annex of Chitwan National Park, providing secondary habitat for many of its sub-adult tigers, the reserve isn't developed for tourism. No food or lodg-

PUBLIC BUS SERVICES IN THE EASTERN TARAI AND HILLS

	Frequency (day)	Frequency (night)	Time (minimum)
To and from BASANTAPUR			
Dharan**	20		5hr
To and from BIRATNAGAR			
Basantapur	2		6hr
Bhairawa		5	14hr
Birganj	5	2	8hr
Dhankuta	2		4hr
Dharan	20		1hr 30min
Janakpur	5		6hr
Kakarbhitta	24		3hr
Kathmandu		6	14hr
Pokhara		2	14hr
To and from BIRGANJ			
Bhairawa	4	3	7hr
Biratnagar	5	2	8hr
Butwal	4	3	6hr
Dharan	4		8hr
Gorkha	2		7hr
Janakpur	5		5hr
Kakarbhitta	1	1	9hr
Kathmandu	2#	10#	9hr
Mahendra Nagar		1	16hr
Pokhara	6	2	9hr
To and from BIRTAMOD			
Bhadrapur**	6		1hr
Ilam**	5		4hr
Kakarbhitta	24		30min
Phidim**	2		10hr
To and from DHANKUTA			
Basantapur**	20		2hr
Biratnagar	2		4hr
Dharan**	20		3hr
Hile**	20		30min
Kathmandu		1	17hr
To and from DHARAN			
Basantapur**	20		5hr
Biratnagar	20		1hr 30min
Birganj	4		8hr
Dhankuta**	20		3hr
Hile**	20		3hr 30min

ings are available, though the warden might let you stay in the government guest house if there's room (nominal charge). Visitors aren't allowed in on foot without a guide (who may also be unavailable). Accompanied by a guide brought from Sauraha (see p.298), you could do day trips from Birganj and have the run of the whole place, but you'd need a vehicle to get into interesting habitat. The entrance fee is Rs650.

The Mahendra Highway branches off to the east at **Pathlaya**, 3km south of the Parsa entrance, and **Simara**, another 3km south, heralds a dreary succession of factories and fields that continues all the way to Birganj. For obscure reasons of national security,

	Frequency (day)	Frequency (night)	Time (minimum)
Kakarbhitta	24		3hr
Kathmandu		6	14hr
To and from HETAUDA*			
Kathmandu (via Daman)	1–3#		8hr
Kathmandu (via Narayanghat)	12		7hr
To and from HILE			
Basantapur**	20		1hr 30min
Dhankuta**	20		30min
Dharan**	20		3hr
Kakarbhitta	2		6hr
Kathmandu		1	18hr
To and from ILAM			
Birtamod**	5		4hr
Kathmandu		1	20hr
Phidim**	2		6hr
To and from JANAKPUR			
Bhairawa		1	10hr
Biratnagar	5		6hr
Birganj	5		5hr
Butwal		3	9hr
Jaleswar	10		30min
Kakarbhitta	2	2	7hr
Kathmandu	2#	7#	11hr
Nepalganj		2	14hr
Pokhara		1	11hr
To and from KAKARBHITTA			
Bhairawa		3	16hr
Biratnagar	24		3hr
Birganj	1	1	10hr
Birtamod	24		30min
Dharan	24		3hr
Hile	2		6hr
Janakpur	2	2	7hr
Kathmandu		10	16hr
Narayanghat		2	12hr
Pokhara		2	16hr
Tansen		1	18hr

* Many other buses pass through.
** Shared Land Rovers also ply this route.
# Sajha service available.

Nepal passed a law in the mid-1980s requiring that all new factories must be built at least 10km from the Indian border, which is causing the major border cities to flare northwards. Simara has an **airstrip** (daily flights to Kathmandu, $44).

Birganj and the border

BIRGANJ isn't one of the best places to spend time in Nepal, but it sure beats Raxaul, its evil twin across the border. Nepal's busiest port of entry, Birganj has seen explosive growth in the past decade – its population has probably doubled since the 69,000 counted in the 1991 census – and has prospered from a corresponding boom in cross-border trade. Fortunately, it had the good sense to build a highway bypass and a new bus park, making the commercial core south of the prominent clocktower vastly more liveable. (Raxaul has done nothing to manage its traffic, and is all but paralyzed.)

There's no conceivable reason you'd come here except to cross the border to or from Varanasi, Calcutta or other points in northeast India. Even then, you're more likely to use Sonauli (see p.318) because of its better connections within Nepal, although if you're visiting Nepal as part of a bigger tour of the subcontinent then travelling this route could save some backtracking. **Buses** connect Birganj with Kathmandu, Pokhara and a few major Tarai cities (see box on p.348). The new bus park is located almost 1km east of the clocktower, beyond the bypass and off the map. Rikshas and shared tongas (horse carts) provide transport from there.

If you're stranded in Birganj, you could probably kill a few hours in the old-ish market area around **Maisthan**, a mother-goddess temple just off the main drag. Beyond

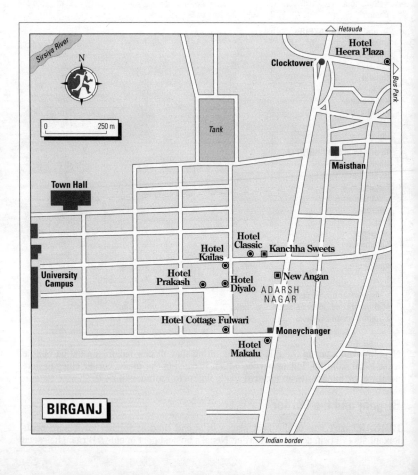

that, though, the city has little to offer: **Adarsh Nagar** is a fairly humdrum market area that's unlikely to appeal to anyone except Indian consumers, and the new west side of town is devoid of interest.

Practicalities

You can manage quite comfortably for food and **lodging** in Birganj. Hotels and guest houses are grouped mainly in Adarsh Nagar and along the road going out to the bus park – all things considered, Adarsh Nagar has more going for it. At the top end, *Hotel Makalu* (☎051/23054; hmakalu@mos.com.np; B⑤/AC⑥ –⑦) and *Hotel Heera Plaza* (☎051/23988, fax 23916; B⑤/AC⑥) are relatively swanky expense-account places, while *Hotel Samjhana* (☎051/22122; B⑤/AC⑦) is a rather run-down establishment that nevertheless boasts Birganj's best gardens and only swimming pool. The latter is in a strange location, 1km north of the clocktower (off the map), but that's not necessarily a bad thing. The best of the midrange choices, *Hotel Cottage Fulwari* (☎051/21103; B④/AC⑤), *Hotel Classic* (☎ & fax 051/27137; B③/AC⑤) and the older *Hotel Kailas* (☎051/23084, fax 22410; ③/B④/AC⑥) all have good restaurants. *Hotel Prakash* (☎051/22351; ②/B③) and *A-One Guest House* (②/B③), near the bus park, are about as cheap as guest houses get in Birganj; *Prakash* is marginally the better of the two, again because of its better in-town location.

THE ETHNIC SCENE

There seems to be an unwritten rule in Nepal that all migrations have to be from west to east, with the result that contingents of almost every Nepalese ethnic group now jostle together in the eastern quarter of the country.

The original inhabitants of the eastern hills were the **Kirantis** (or Kiratas), a warlike tribe mentioned in the *Mahabharat* who may well have been the same Kiratas who ruled the Kathmandu Valley in semi-mythological times. The Kiranti nation long ago fragmented into several tribes, the most important ones being the **Rais** and **Limbus**. Like the Magars and Gurungs of the west, members of these dauntless hill groups make up a significant portion of the Gurkha regiments; similarly, they follow their own form of shamanism, but increasingly embrace Hindu or Buddhist practices, depending on their location. Unusually, the Kiranti clans bury their dead (cremation is the usual practice throughout the subcontinent), and Limbus erect distinctive rectangular, whitewashed grave markers. Rais, who have a reputation as a staunchly independent people, traditionally occupy the middle-elevation hills west of the Arun River, while Limbuwan, as the Limbu homeland is sometimes still called, is centred around the lower slopes of the Tamur Koshi Valley, further east.

Rais and Limbus had the hills virtually to themselves until a spate of migrations, beginning in the late eighteenth century, completely transformed the ethnic map of eastern Nepal. The Gorkhali army marched in and annexed the region in 1776; in their wake, **Baahuns** and **Chhetris** began infiltrating the Arun basin and **Newars** took over the trading crossroads. At about the same time, **Sherpas** and **Tamangs** were steadily elbowing the Rais out of Solu, and more recently, **Magars** and **Gurungs** have hopped across from their traditional homelands in the west. Little wonder, then, that when the Rais and Limbus were recruited by the British in the last century to pluck tea in Darjeeling, they too headed east.

Even more than in western Nepal, the clearing of the eastern Tarai during the past three decades has spurred a feverish new land rush, as hill people in turn displace native **Tharus** (see p.314), **Danuwars** (a related group, whose women wear their homespun saris like togas) and the Maithili-speaking **Hindus** who predominate between Janakpur and Biratnagar. Meanwhile, **Biharis** and **Bengalis** keep arriving in droves from India. Bouncing along the Mahendra Highway, where housing and dress styles change from one village to the next, you almost feel as if you're watching the migration in motion.

All the better hotels – notably the *Kailas* and the neighbouring *Diyalo* – have fine tandoori **restaurants**, while the nearby *Kanchha Sweets* and *New Angan* serve up tempting assortments of Indian goodies. You'll also find *sekuwa*, *momo*, fried fish and other street food in stalls around the town centre.

Cross-border commerce supports several **banks** in Birganj, but they're not very good at foreign exchange – it's easier to use the moneychanger across the street from *Hotel Makalu*. Nearly all businesses in Birganj accept Indian rupees at the official rate. You can make international **phone calls** from all but the cheapest hotels and from a few ISD places in Adarsh Nagar. Birganj's poorly equipped and overtaxed **hospital** is south of the city (off the map), just past the cigarette factory.

The border

The **border** is 2km south of Birganj, and **Raxaul**, the first Indian town, sprawls for another 2km south of the border. Horrendous traffic jams are a regular occurrence here – if you're driving it can take hours to get through physically, leaving aside the paperwork. Rikshas charge about Rs40 to ferry passengers from Birganj to Raxaul (make sure the price quoted is in Nepalese rupees). Shared tempos are cheaper, but they only go as far as the border. The border is open 24 hours, but if you arrive between 7pm and 5am you'll probably have to search around for someone. If you're entering Nepal and you don't already have a visa, make sure you have the correct change in cash (dollars).

Raxaul is the terminus of a metre-gauge rail line and has daily direct train service to Calcutta (24hr), departing in mid-morning; for other destinations, change at Patna (5hr). Buses also depart for Patna several times a day.

Indian visas are not obtainable at the border – see p.148.

Along the Mahendra Highway

Resuming its eastward journey at Pathlaya, the **Mahendra Highway** initially cuts through extensive forest alternating with farmland. Timber and sugar are important exports of this area. Sugar cane, which is harvested in winter with the help of Indian migrant labourers, is processed by numerous small factories and a couple of big ones visible from the road. After 55km the highway crosses the **Bagmati River**, its volume here about ten times bigger (and cleaner, thanks to dilution) than in the Kathmandu Valley. This section of the Mahendra Highway was originally constructed with Soviet assistance, which explains the monumental road signs and bus shelters.

East of the turn-off for Janakpur (see below) at Dhalkebar, the highway enters more settled country, and things become increasingly Indian. For a long stretch after Lahan, a nondescript market town, there's very little to remind you that you're in Nepal. Cyclists passing through here often complain of being stared at by locals.

The landscape changes markedly at the **Sapt Koshi**, Nepal's biggest river. Crossing the **Koshi Barrage** – not a dam, but a network of dykes and flood-control gates – you can look in amazement at the immense body of water that squeezes through here before fanning out again into the shimmering haze of India. Reaching the far side, the highway bends north and runs parallel to a disused railway: keep an eye out for the rusty old rolling stock which, until the railway tracks were severed in a 1988 earthquake, hauled rubble to build up the seven- to ten-metre embankments that keep the Sapt Koshi in check during the monsoon.

The landscape is particularly flat and featureless east of the Sapt Koshi to **Itahari**, a major junction town and the turning for Biratnagar and Dharan (described later in this chapter). For its final and smoothest leg, to the border at Kakarbhitta (p.364), the Mahendra Highway traverses the more picturesque districts of **Morang** and **Jhapa**. Once renowned for its virulent malaria, Morang's forest has now been almost entirely cleared and the land homesteaded by immigrants from the hills; the half-timbered houses are the work of transplanted Limbus. Jhapa, further east, has had a somewhat longer history of settlement, and is known for tea cultivation: its shaded plantations are a reminder that Darjeeling is barely 50km away as the crow flies, and Ilam (p.372), Nepal's prize tea-growing region, sits in the hills just north of here. Though the roadside bazaars are monotonously similar in this area, the countryside is idyllic: banana trees and thatched-roof houses on stilts (one strategy for dealing with heavy monsoon rains) give it a classically Asian look.

Janakpur and around

JANAKPUR, 165km east of Birganj, is indisputably the Tarai's most fascinating city. Also known as **Janakpurdham** (*dham* denoting a sacred place), it's a holy site of the first order, and its central temple, the ornate Janaki Mandir, is an obligatory stop on the Hindu pilgrimage circuit. Although Indian in every respect except politically, the city is, by Indian standards, small and manageable: motorized traffic is all but banned from the centre, tourist hustle is largely absent, the poverty isn't oppressive, and the surrounding countryside is delightful. To top it all, Janakpur's railway, the only one still operating in Nepal, makes an entertaining excursion in itself. There's so much going on, both in and around Janakpur, that it's worth setting aside a few days to absorb it all – though bear in mind that there are no tourist-style lodgings, restaurants or other facilities.

Hindu mythology identifies Janakpur as the capital of the ancient kingdom of **Mithila**, which controlled a large part of northern India between the tenth and third centuries BC. The city features prominently in the *Ramayan*, for it was in Janakpur that **Ram** – the god Vishnu in mortal form – wed **Sita**, daughter of the Mithila King Janak. Recounting the divine couple's later separation and heroic reunion, the *Ramayan* holds Ram and Sita up as models of the virtuous husband and chaste wife; in Janakpur, where the two command almost cult status, the chant of "Sita Ram, Sita Ram" is repeated like a Hindu Hail Mary, and sadhus commonly wear the tuning-fork-shaped *tika* of Vishnu. Mithila came under the control of the Mauryan empire around the third century BC, then languished for two millennia until Guru Ramananda, the seventeenth-century founder of the sect of Sita that dominates Janakpur, revived the city as a major religious centre.

Despite the absence of ancient monuments to confirm its mythic past – no building is much more than a century old – Janakpur remains a strangely attractive city. Religious fervour seems to lend an aura to everything; the skyline leaves a lasting impression of palm trees and the onion domes and pyramid roofs of local shrines. Most of these distinctively shaped buildings are associated with **kuti** – self-contained pilgrimage centres and hostels for sadhus – some five hundred of which are scattered throughout the Janakpur area. Janakpur's other distinguishing feature is its dozens of **sacred ponds** (*sagar* or *sar*), which here take the place of river ghats for ritual bathing and *dhobi*-ing. Clearly man-made, the roughly rectangular tanks might, as locals claim, go back to Ram's day, although it's more likely that they've been dredged over the centuries by wealthy merit-seekers.

Janakpur is a long haul from Kathmandu – eleven hours by **bus** – and only a couple of services ply the route during the daytime. The rest are night buses. The new Dhulikhel–Sindhuli Highway (completion in 2001 or 2002) is expected to bring the travel time down to eight or nine hours, making Janakpur a lot more accessible. In

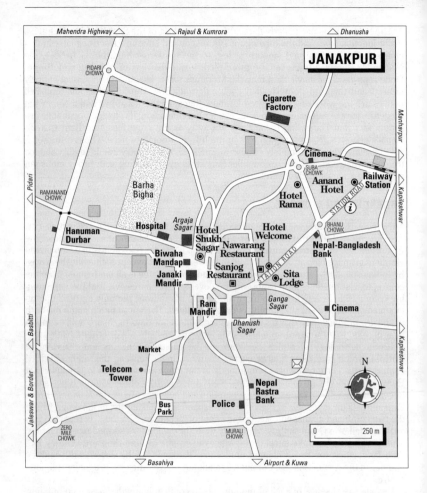

the meantime, your only other options are to break the journey in Hetauda or Birganj (the latter is better for getting a seat on to Janakpur) or fly. Necon Air and Royal Nepal both **fly** from Kathmandu to Janakpur ($55), Necon's service being the more reliable.

Arrival and information

Janakpur lies 25km south of the Mahendra Highway. It's a small city arranged in a classic concentric fashion, with a few main roads extending outwards from a compact core. **Station Road**, which runs from near the **Ram Mandir** northeastwards to the train station, is the nearest thing to a commercial thoroughfare, and it also happens to contain virtually all of Janakpur's lodgings and restaurants. Another important road zigzags northwestwards past the main **Janaki Mandir** to **Ramanand Chowk**, which is turning into something of a main entrance to the city. Sajha buses drop passengers off at Ramanand Chowk, while other services terminate at the main **bus park** southwest of the centre; it's an easy riksha ride to lodgings from either. The **airstrip**, 2km further to the south, is a longer, more tedious ride.

Staff at the **tourist office** (Sun–Thurs 10am–4pm, Fri 10am–3pm) don't speak much English, but that's forgivable considering that the vast majority of the people they deal with speak Hindi, Maithili or Nepali. Nevertheless, the office may be useful for learning about upcoming festivals (see box below). It's on Station Road, east of Bhanu Chowk (named after Bhanu Bhakta Acharya, a much-loved Nepali poet, whose statue graces the intersection).

The City

Central Janakpur is remarkably car-free, thanks partly to a prohibition on commercial traffic entering the core but also to a general dearth of private vehicles. It's a joy to get around here – just watch out for all the cyclists. Though the city is easy enough to navigate on foot, **rikshas** are a terrific deal; they wait in efficient ranks all over town and are supposed to stick to a fixed-price structure, though it may be hard for a foreigner to get them to abide by it. You may be able to rent a **bicycle** informally through your hotel.

THE JANAKI MANDIR

A palatial confection of a building in the Mughal style, the **Janaki Mandir** (pronounced *Jaa*-nuh-kee) is supposed to mark the spot where a golden image of Sita was discovered in 1657 and, presumably, where the virtuous princess actually lived. The present plaster and marble structure, erected in 1911 by an Indian queen, is already looking a little mouldy. The outer building encloses a courtyard and inner sanctum, where at least twice a day (generally 8am and 4pm) priests draw back a curtain to reveal an intricate silver shrine and perform various rituals for attending worshippers; non-Hindus are allowed to watch, and the priests even seem willing to bestow blessings on unbelievers. It's an enchanting place at night and early in the morning, when the devout gather in lamplit huddles and murmur haunting hymns. The temple is also a traditional place for boys to undergo the ritual of *chhewar* (the first shaving of the head), and male dancers in drag (*natuwa* in Nepali), who are often hired to perform at the ceremony, may sometimes be seen here.

JANAKPUR'S FESTIVALS

At any time of year, Janakpur's atmosphere is charged with an intense devotional zeal. New shrines are forever being inaugurated and idols installed, while *kuti* loudspeakers broadcast religious discourses and the mesmerizing drone of *bhajan*. Pilgrimage is a year-round industry, marked by several highlights in the **festival** calendar:

Parikrama As many as 100,000 people join the annual one-day circumambulation of the city on the day of the full moon of February–March, many performing prostrations along the entire eight-kilometre route. The pilgrimage coincides with the festival of Holi, when coloured water is thrown everywhere and on everyone.

Ram Navami Ram's birthday, celebrated on the ninth day after the full moon of March–April, attracts thousands of sadhus, who receive free room and board at the city's temples.

Chhath Women bathe in Janakpur's ponds and line them with elaborate offerings to the sun god Surya at dawn on the third day of Diwali (Tihaar). Women in the villages surrounding Janakpur paint murals on the walls of their houses.

Biwaha Panchami The culmination of this five-day event – Janakpur's most important festival – is a re-enactment of Ram and Sita's wedding at the Janaki Mandir, which draws hundreds of thousands of pilgrims on the fifth day after the new moon of November–December.

Climb the stairs to the roof of the outer building for a view of the central courtyard and the dense, brick-laned Muslim village butting right up against the temple's rear wall: one of Janakpur's most extraordinary aspects is the way rural life can be seen almost in the heart of the city. North of the temple, the modern, Nepali pagoda-style **Ram Janaki Biwaha Mandap** (Ram Sita Wedding Pavilion) houses a turgid tableau of the celebrated event.

OTHER SIGHTS

The city's oldest, closest quarter lies to the south and east of the Janaki Mandir – making your way through this area, with its sweet shops, *puja* stalls and quick-photo studios, you begin to appreciate that Janakpur is as geared up for Indian tourists as Kathmandu is for Western ones. The main landmark here, the pagoda-style **Ram Mandir**, isn't wildly exciting except during festivals. Immediately to the east, **Dhanush Sagar** and **Ganga Sagar** are considered the holiest of Janakpur's ponds. The sight of Hindus performing ritual ablutions in the fog at sunrise here is profoundly moving, and during festivals the scene is on a par with Varanasi's famed ghats in India.

Walk westwards from the Janaki Mandir to the highway and you reach **Ramanand Chowk**, the nucleus of many of Janakpur's *kuti* and a major sadhu gathering place during festivals. A four-way arch bearing a statue of Guru Ramananda, the saint responsible for Janakpur's modern fame, is gradually being constructed over the intersection that bears his name. Two well-known establishments, Ramanand Ashram and Ratnasagar Kuti – the latter, rising grandly in the midst of farmland, looking uncannily like a Russian Orthodox church – are located west of here, but like most *kuti*, they are closed to non-Hindus, whose presence would necessitate all sorts of ritual cleansing.

If by this time you're tiring of the serious side of Hinduism, head to **Hanuman Durbar**, a small *kuti* 150m south of Ramanand Chowk on the west side, which until 1998 was home to the world's biggest (well, fattest) rhesus monkey. Bauwa Hanuman is much missed by local shopkeepers, for he was the area's major attraction. Priests still proudly display photos of the late great monkey, and they seem to be fattening up another one as his replacement.

Around Janakpur

The Tarai is full of great little villages, and Janakpur makes a particularly good base for visiting them. The holy city's traditionalism extends into the surrounding countryside, which is inhabited by Hindu castes and members of the Tharu and Danuwar ethnic groups, and features some of the most meticulously kept farmland you'll see anywhere. You can ride the narrow-gauge railway east or west, or bike along several roads radiating out from the city. (Needless to say, winter is a much more comfortable time for biking.)

THE JANAKPUR RAILWAY

If you've already had dealings with Indian trains, Janakpur's **narrow-gauge railway** will be less of a thrill, but it's still an excellent way to get out into the country. On a misty winter's morning, the ride past sleepy villages and minor temples is nothing short of magical. Built in the 1940s to transport timber to India from the now-depleted forest west of Janakpur, the railway these days operates primarily as a passenger service.

Janakpur is the terminus for two separate lines, each about 30km long: one eastbound to **Jaynagar**, just over the border in India, and the other westbound to **Bijalpura**. Departure times vary seasonally, but in general the Jaynagar service runs three times a day and takes about two hours one way. The Bijalpura service runs only once a day, departing Janakpur in the late afternoon and returning the next morning (and at the time of writing it wasn't even running all the way to Bijalpura due to a washed-out bridge). That makes the Jaynagar line the more feasible for a day trip: you could ride all the way to Khajuri (last stop before the border) and then catch the train as it passes through on the way back, or get off somewhere earlier and walk or cycle around that area until the train returns.

The **fare** to Jaynagar is Rs13 in second class or Rs35 in first, the latter being far from luxurious but perhaps a shade less crowded. Arrive early for a seat; on the way back you'll probably end up riding on the roof.

THE JANAKPUR WOMEN'S DEVELOPMENT CENTER
Hindu women of the deeply conservative villages around Janakpur are rarely spared from their household duties, and, once married, are expected to remain veiled and silent before all males but their husbands. Fortunately, their rich tradition of folk art (see below) offers them an escape from this isolated existence. The non-profit

MAITHILI PAINTING

For three thousand years, Hindu women of the region once known as Mithila have maintained an unbroken tradition of **painting**, using techniques and ritual motifs passed down from mother to daughter. The colourful, almost psychedelic images can be viewed as fertility charms, meditation aids or a form of storytelling, but on a deeper level they represent, in the words of one critic, "the manifestation of a collective mind, embodying millennia of traditional knowledge".

From an early age Brahman girls practise drawing complex symbols derived from Hindu myths and folk tales, which over the course of generations have been reduced to *mandala*-like abstractions. By the time she is in her teens, a girl will be presenting simple paintings to her arranged fiancé, perhaps using them to wrap gifts; the courtship culminates with the painting of a **kohbar**, an elaborate fresco on the wall of the bride's bedroom, where the newlyweds will spend their first four nights. Depicting a stylized stalk of bamboo surrounded by lotus leaves (symbols of male and female sexuality), the *kohbar* is a powerful celebration of life, creation and everything. Other motifs include footprints and fishes (both representing Vishnu), parrots (symbolic of a happy union), Krishna cavorting with his milkmaids, and Surabhi, "the Cow of Plenty, who inflames the desire of those who milk her". Perhaps the most striking aspect of the *kohbar* is that, almost by definition, it's ephemeral: even the most amazing mural will be washed off within a week or two. Painting is seen as a form of prayer or meditation; once completed, the work has achieved its end.

Women of all castes create simpler **wall decorations** during the autumn festival of Diwali (Tihaar). In the weeks leading up to the festival they apply a new coat of mud mixed with dung and rice chaff to their houses and add relief designs. Just before Lakshmi Puja, the climactic third day of Diwali, many paint images of peacocks, pregnant elephants and other symbols of prosperity to attract a visit from the goddess of wealth. Until Nepali New Year celebrations in April, when the decorations are covered over with a new layer of mud, they're easily viewable in villages around Janakpur.

Paintings **on paper**, which traditionally play only a minor part in the culture, have grown to become the most celebrated form of Maithili art – or Madhubani art, as it's known in India, where a community-development project began turning it into a marketable commodity in the 1960s. More recently, the Janakpur Women's Development Center (see overleaf) has helped do the same in Nepal, making Maithili paintings a staple of Kathmandu tourist gift shops. When working on paper, the artist first outlines the intended design in black, then adds a border and embellishes every remaining space with fantastic detail, and finally illuminates it with brilliant, poster-paint colours. Many artists concentrate on traditional religious motifs, but a growing number are depicting people – mainly women and children in domestic scenes, always shown in characteristic doe-eyed profile.

Janakpur Women's Development Center (Sun–Thurs 10am–5pm/4pm in winter; free), 3km south of Janakpur provides a space for women from nearby villages to develop personally and artistically. Founded in 1989, with assistance from several international aid organizations, the artists' cooperative helps its fifty-odd members turn their skills into income – and the fact that some have gone on to start their own companies is a sure sign of the project's success. But more importantly, the centre empowers women through training in literacy and business skills, and support sessions in which they can share their feelings and discuss their roles in family and society.

Initially specializing in Maithili paper art, the centre has since branched into other media and now has separate buildings for sewing, screen printing, ceramics and painting. Visitors are welcome to tour the beautiful, mango-shaded facility, and to meet the artists and learn about their work and traditions. A gift shop sells crafts made on the premises, as well as the JWDC's own booklet, *Master Artists of Janakpur*, a sensitive treatment not only of Maithili art but also of the women who make it here.

The centre is a fifteen-minute bike or riksha ride from Janakpur. Head south towards the airport and make a left turn about 1km after Murali Chowk (look for the big painted arch and signs). Bear right after about 200m, passing through the well-kept village of **Kuwa**. The centre, in a walled compound, appears on the right after about 500m. If in doubt, ask for Nari Bikas Kendra. Or just have a riksha wallah take you – they all know the way.

OTHER VILLAGES

Dozens of villages dot the land around Janakpur at regular intervals, each with its own mango grove and a *sagar* or two. Subsistence farming – livestock, grains, vegetables and fish – is virtually the only occupation here: you'll rarely see even the smallest shop.

From Kuwa and the Janakpur Women's Development Center, a road heads east to Lohana and then **south** to Bahuarwa, Devdiha and, about 10km from Janakpur, larger and more prosperous **Nagarain**. There are two other ways to get between Janakpur and Nagarain, so you can make a loop – the better (less travelled) of the two is the road heading south from the bus park, which passes through Basahiya, Donauli and Bishnupur, and eventually wends its way eastwards to Nagarain via Phulgama (this entails a stream crossing). The third way to Nagarain is simply the main road south past Kuwa and the airport. This rather shadeless road, which is served by infrequent, claptrap buses, continues to the Indian border, 3km beyond Nagarain.

Westwards from Ramanand Chowk, you can follow a dirt lane through the huts of Pidari, over the train tracks and through some nice shady groves, and finally to **Khurta**, a substantial community with grain mills and a Friday-afternoon market. A separate track heads west from near "Zero Mile" to Basbitti and Bhramarpura.

North from Suba Chowk, the road to Dhanusha has been rendered a bit less interesting by being upgraded, but you can make a couple of nice detours where it bypasses the villages of Bhenga and Thumana. **Dhanusha** (Dhanushadham), 18km from Janakpur, is an important pilgrimage site. According to the *Ramayan*, it was here that King Janak staged an Arthurian contest for the hand of his daughter, Sita, declaring that the successful suitor would have to prove himself by lifting an impossibly heavy bow. After all others had given up, Ram picked up the bow with ease, and broke it in two for good measure. Villagers can point you to a walled compound encircling a volcanic rock that's said to be a piece of the bow.

There are also several picturesque villages on either side of the main road that connects Janakpur to the Mahendra Highway. Loveliest is **Kumrora**, on the right about 4km north of Pidari Chowk, a tidy Brahman settlement of one- and two-storey houses and particularly expressive wall murals. To avoid the worst of the roadside grunge around Pidari Chowk, take a back way just to the east, via Rajaul, which joins the main road halfway.

Other roads heading **east** go to the villages of Kapileshwar and Manharpur, but the options in this direction are limited by a major stream that's crossed only by the railway and a road running parallel to it. You might as well take the train.

Janakpur accommodation

Janakpur's few **lodgings** cater mainly to Indian pilgrims, so consequently are not too well versed in what Westerners want: they're all of the crummy, concrete variety. Bus and truck noise isn't a problem, for once, but the *kuti* around the Janaki Mandir manage to create a hell of a racket over their loudspeakers. While the scarcity of accommodation normally doesn't present a problem, you need to book well ahead during the big festival times. Refer to the map for locations.

Aanand Hotel (☎041/22145, fax 20196). A perpetually half-completed building with the rudiments of a garden seating area, located in a lively part of town. Hot water is available in the more expensive rooms. ②/B③.

Hotel Rama (☎041/20059). Quiet, though it's rather far from the sights. The more expensive upstairs rooms are quite spacious and have hot water and air conditioning. B③/AC④–⑤.

Hotel Shukh Sagar (☎041/20488). Great (but noisy) location overlooking the Janaki Mandir. Reasonably clean. Good sweet shop/vegetarian restaurant downstairs. ②/B③–④.

Sita Lodge (no phone). Cheap and dingy. A few comparable places with or without English signs can be found nearby. ①/B②.

Hotel Welcome (☎041/20646, fax 20922). The most experienced at dealing with foreigners, but in a state of decline. ①/B③/AC⑥–⑦.

Eating and other practicalities

If you enjoy Indian **food**, you'll eat like a rajah in Janakpur. *Hotel Welcome*'s and *Hotel Rama*'s restaurants and the *Sanjog*, at the western end of Station Road, all do beautiful veg and non-veg meals, while various places around the Janaki Mandir do pure vegetarian food. For Nepali fare, the *Nawarang* (sign in Nepali only), around the corner from *Hotel Welcome*, is the ticket. For Indian sweets or *chiura dahi* (beaten rice and curd), take your pick from a host of *mithai pasal* near the Janaki and Ram temples. To sample the local brew, ask for *sophi* or *dudhiya*, fennel- and aniseed-flavoured spirits that are just about drinkable when mixed with soft drinks.

The **bank** (Nepal Rastra Bank) at the southern end of town exchanges some foreign currencies (Sun–Thurs 10am–2pm, Fri 10am–noon). Nepal Bangladesh Bank, at Bhanu Chowk, can change cash but not travellers' cheques. Many shops along Station Road offer international and trunk **telephone** services, and a couple of them have **email**. Janakpur has a **hospital**, but hope you never need it; pharmacies and private doctors' practices can be found along the street in front of the hospital.

Moving on

For **bus** frequencies and travel times from Janakpur, see p.353. Note that Sajha tickets are purchased at Ramanand Chowk, not at the bus park, and the Sajha bus to Kathmandu originates there (another Sajha service, originating in Jaleswar, also stops there). Tickets for night buses to Kathmandu are also sold from desks along Station Road near the *Aanand Hotel*, but for a better seat assignment go to the bus park. Two **airlines** – RNAC (☎20185) and Necon Air (☎21900) – fly from Janakpur to Kathmandu most days of the week ($55), and both have offices near Bhanu Chowk in town.

There is a small-time **border crossing** about 20km east of town at Jaleswar, and another at Jaynagar (reached by railway), but neither of these is officially open to foreigners.

Koshi Tappu Wildlife Reserve

Straddling a floodplain of shifting grassland and sandbanks north of the Koshi Barrage, **Koshi Tappu Wildlife Reserve** is the smallest and most low-key of the Tarai's parks. It's not bound to appeal to most travellers – there are no tigers or rhinos, nor even any jungle – but **bird-watchers** can have a field day here. Koshi Tappu is one of the subcontinent's most important wetlands, and thanks to its location just downstream from one of the few breaches in the Himalayan barrier, it's an internationally important residing, staging and wintering area for waterfowl and waders. Some 350 bird species, many of them endangered, have been counted here. Flocks of up to 50,000 ducks may be seen at Koshi Tappu in winter and spring (especially mid-February to early April), and most of Nepal's egrets, storks, ibises, terns and gulls are also represented.

The reserve was established to protect one of the subcontinent's last surviving herds of **wild buffalo** (*arnaa*), believed to number 150 animals. However, wildlife experts are concerned about the number of domestic buffalo getting into the reserve and mating with the wild ones: if this is allowed to continue, the result could be a semi-domestic herd whose continued protection would be hard to justify. In addition, eighty **gharial crocodiles** from the Chitwan hatchery have been relocated here from Chitwan – at last count, only four or five were known to have survived – and about a dozen **gangetic dolphins** are trapped upstream of the barrage. The latter will probably disappear altogether from Koshi Tappu in the next few years, as one by one they're killed by local

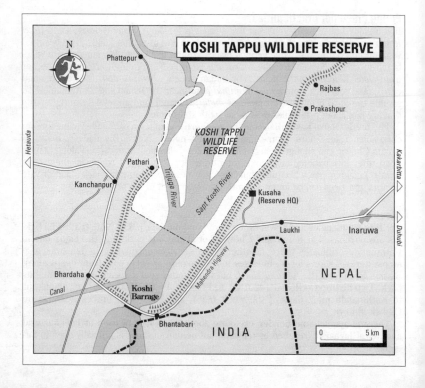

fishermen for their oil or are sent downstream during flood-control releases. Also inhabiting the reserve are blue bull (*nilgai*), wild boar, langur and spotted deer (*chital*).

With no rhinos or large carnivores, Koshi Tappu is comparatively safe for entering **on foot**, but you'll need a guide. **Elephant** and **canoe rides** can also be arranged. Two rivers join at the reserve: the Trijuga generally hugs the western embankment, while the Sapt Koshi has formed two main channels, along the east side and down the middle, and tends to shift from one to the other every couple of monsoons. Between these three channels lie a number of semi-permanent islands of scrub forest and grassland that are the main stomping ground for blue bull. (*Tappu* means "island" in Nepali, which is an accurate description of this floodplain in the wet summer months.) Birds and buffalo are best viewed along the Sapt Koshi, but given the way the rivers change course it's impossible to give specific advice on where to look. It may be necessary to cross one or more channels to reach the current hot area, which can be done by canoe. Stalking the wild cousins of common water buffalo is sometimes hard to take seriously – especially when they moo – yet these are big animals with very big horns, and they make a thunderous noise when frightened. And while they normally run away at the first scent of humans, you have to make sure not to block their escape route.

Park practicalities

The reserve is marked by a yellow sign beside the Mahendra Highway about 12km east of the barrage – or, if you're coming from the other direction, 3km west of Laukhi – and from here an access road leads 3km north to the **reserve headquarters** (generally known as the *warden ophis*). An **entry permit** costs Rs650 and is valid for two days.

Only about 500 foreigners visit Koshi Tappu annually. Of those, most come on fairly expensive **package tours**, flying in and out of Biratnagar, 55km to the southeast, and staying in one of two small tented camps. The more comfortable and better shaded of the two, *Koshi Tappu Wildlife Camp* (☎01/247078; *explore@pramok.wlink.com.np*; ⑨), is located just outside the northeastern corner of the reserve, near the village of Prakashpur, and is reached via a separate road. *Aqua Birds Unlimited Camp* (☎01/429515; *aquabird@ccsl.com.np*; ⑨), is just a few minutes' walk from the reserve headquarters. Both provide accommodation in deluxe twin-bedded tents with solar hot-water showers, serve decent food and have experienced guides. All meals, activities and transportation to and from Biratnagar are included in the price.

A new **budget lodge**, *Koshi Tappu Village Rest House* (☎025/21488; ⑥), was still under construction at the time of writing, so its facilities can't be vouched for. Located immediately northeast of the reserve HQ, it's supposed to consist of a few rustic sleeping huts and a dining room. The two owners know the reserve well but are perhaps not as strong on birds as the guides at the deluxe places. The price includes all meals, but activities are extra. It's also possible to camp at the headquarters (Rs300 per night).

Biratnagar

About 200km east of the Janakpur turn-off, **BIRATNAGAR** is Nepal's industrial capital and its second-biggest city, with more than 200,000 residents. Its nearness to the port of Calcutta enabled it to become a major exporter of jute (used in rope and sacks) early on in the country's industrial development, and it has since diversified into steel, textiles, vegetable ghee, soap and plastics. It's also famous (in Nepal) for being a political hotbed, having produced four prime ministers in the past fifty years. However, Biratnagar's future is in doubt. Jute is in decline, its other industries can't compete with their bigger Indian rivals, Birganj is muscling in on trade with Calcutta, and the 1995 cancellation of a $1 billion hydroelectricity project in the hills to the north has turned a speculative boom into a bust.

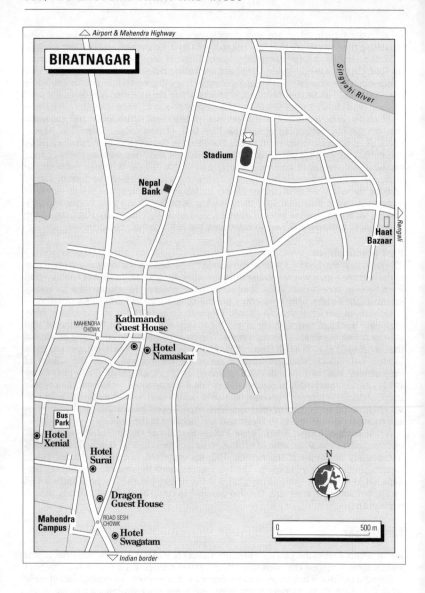

There are actually two Biratnagars – the downtown trading centre and the sprawling industrial belt along the highway to the north of the city – neither of which is remotely interesting. Frankly, the only reason to come here would be to make a flight or bus connection to somewhere else. That said, the city centre is relatively laid-back and traffic-free. There are few sights, but if you're here on a Wednesday you could at least visit Biratnagar's **haat bazaar**, held east of town, where you can count on a colourful assembly of Tharus, Danuwars, Rais, Limbus and various Indian castes. In the countryside surrounding Biratnagar, Tharus and Danuwars are indigenous: to sample **village life**, head out on the road past the *haat bazaar* towards Rangali, east of town, and head north or south after crossing the canal. The Jogbani **border crossing**, 5km south of town, is closed to foreigners (officially, anyway).

Practicalities

Kathmandu–Kakarbhitta buses don't go through Biratnagar, but stop at **Itahari**, a crossroads bazaar on the Mahendra Highway; Biratnagar is 23km south, and Dharan (covered later in this chapter) lies to the north. Direct buses to Biratnagar let you off at the dismal **bus park** southwest of the city centre. The **airport** is 4km north of town (Rs150 by taxi).

Biratnagar's finest **accommodation** is *Hotel Xenial* (☎021/27303; *xenial@ccsl.com.np*; AC⑧), which has all air-con rooms, a small pool, business facilities and a terrific restaurant. Midrange options include *Hotel Swagatam* (☎021/24450, fax 22299; B⑤/AC⑥), which is clean and friendly but gets a lot of highway noise; *Hotel Namaskar* (☎021/21199, fax 23499; B④/AC⑥), in a better location but more run-down and with indifferent service; and *Hotel Surai* (☎021/26178; B④), with dark rooms and a forlorn attempt at a garden. It would be nice to be able to recommend more of a choice at the budget end, but it just doesn't exist. *Kathmandu Guest House* (☎021/21657; B②) is the best, or at least the biggest, of several relatively cheap cold-water places grouped around the central intersection east of Mahendra Chowk. *Dragon Guest House* (☎021/27129; B③) might be worth considering because the management claims to supply hot water for washing by the bucket.

Even if you're not staying there, *Hotel Xenial*'s **restaurant** is worth the riksha ride for its superb Indian food. The *Swagatam* and *Namaskar* also have good restaurants. For cheap local fare, make for one of the rough-and-ready eateries north of Mahendra Chowk, which do tasty *sekuwa* and *maachhaa masaala* (local carp fried in a spicy tomato sauce); try also *dudhiya*, the local aniseed-flavoured *raksi*. The main shopping street running north from the *Namaskaar* contains a couple of fine *mithai pasal* (sweet shops).

Nepal Bank does **foreign exchange** (Sun–Thurs 10am–2pm, Fri 10am–noon), but you really have to hunt around for the right person. The better hotels will change money for their guests.

Moving on

Biratnagar being the air hub of eastern Nepal, you will have to pass through here to **fly** to Taplejung (for Kanchenjunga). Flights to other hill airstrips and Kathmandu may be of interest – see the box below. Buddha, Necon and RNAC all run flights out of

FLIGHTS FROM BIRATNAGAR			
	Frequency	**Time**	**Fare ($)**
Bhojpur	3/week	25min	39
Calcutta	3/week	1hr 15min	100
Kathmandu	6–7/day	50min	77
Lamidanda	3/week	30min	50
Phaplu	1–2/week	35min	66
Rumjatar	1/week	30min	55
Taplejung	3–5/week	30min	60
Tumlingtar	4–6/week	30min	43

Biratnagar; book through travel agents along the road going east from Mahendra Chowk.

Jeeps/Land Rovers can be hired by the day (Rs1500 plus petrol) through hotels or directly – they wait on the main road north of Mahendra Chowk. Onward **bus** connections from Biratnagar are fairly limited (see p.348).

Kakarbhitta and the border

KAKARBHITTA is one of the more laid-back crossings on the Nepal–India border, since it's mainly a gateway for people, not goods. Most of those using it are Indians, hopping over from Darjeeling for some quick shopping or heading to Biratnagar for business; the presence of nearly 90,000 Bhutanese refugees in camps west of here (see box opposite) probably contributes to the flow as well. A recently negotiated transit treaty between Nepal and Bangladesh may eventually increase the commercial traffic through here, but for the time being Kakarbhitta feels very much like a back-door entry whose only apparent link with the rest of the world is the fleet of night buses that roars in from Kathmandu every morning and roars out again every afternoon.

You won't want to stay in Kakarbhitta any longer than necessary, but if you have some time on your hands you could take a stroll in any direction into the surrounding countryside. The **Satighata tea estate** is just ten minutes' walk south of town, and a Buddhist monastery run by Tamangs can be visited on the way. A walk along the banks of the Mechi River, just east of town, is nice at sunset or sunrise.

All of Kakarbhitta's **accommodation** is within spitting distance of the bus park, so it's easy to shop around – you can judge these books by their covers. Two better places that have stood the test of time are *Hotel Rajat* (☎023/62033; ②/B⑤) and *Hotel Kanchan* (☎023/62015; B③–④), side by side at the north end of the bus park. The *Rajat*, which is run by very professional Newars from Kathmandu, has hot water and TVs in its more expensive rooms (some are supposed to get air conditioning as well), a restaurant and a small garden/parking area. The *Kanchan* is further down the luxury scale, but the owners are friendly and supply hot water by the bucket. At the bottom

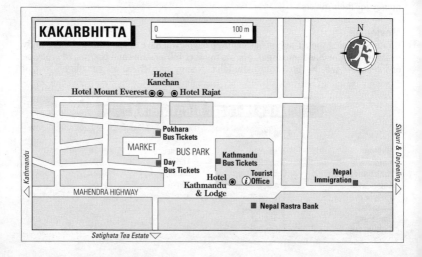

KAKARBHITTA

0   100 m

N

Hotel Kanchan
Hotel Mount Everest   Hotel Rajat

Pokhara Bus Tickets

MARKET   BUS PARK   Kathmandu Bus Tickets

Kathmandu

Day Bus Tickets   Hotel Kathmandu & Lodge   Tourist ⓘOffice   Nepal Immigration

Siliguri & Darjeeling

MAHENDRA HIGHWAY

Nepal Rastra Bank

Satighata Tea Estate

LHOTSHAMPAS: NEPAL'S OTHER REFUGEES

Every visitor to Nepal knows about its Tibetan refugees. But few have heard of its **Bhutanese refugees**, who far outnumber Tibetans in Nepal and are much worse off. Some 95,000 ethnic Nepalis, forcibly expelled from Bhutan in 1991–92, are interned in eastern Nepal, pawns in an obscure political stalemate.

Members of Nepali hill groups began migrating into Bhutan in significant numbers as long ago as the mid-nineteenth century, eventually accounting for at least a third of Bhutan's population and earning the designation **Lhotshampas** (southerners), after the southern hill areas where they came to predominate. Right up to the early 1980s, multicultural government policies encouraged their integration with Bhutan's ruling **Drukpas**. However, during the mid-1980s, the continued influx of ethnic Nepalis and a rise in Nepali militancy in neighbouring Darjeeling and Sikkim gave rise to a wave of Drukpa nationalism. The Drukpas, believing their language and unique culture to be under threat, were quick to make scapegoats of the Lhotshampas – who, not coincidentally, controlled lands that were emerging as the economic powerhouse of Bhutan.

In 1986, King Singye Wangchuk instituted the **Drig Lam Namzha** code of cultural correctness, which among other things required all residents of Bhutan to wear traditional heavy wool garments that were neither natural nor practical for the southerners. In 1988, after a national **census** was taken, the government began a process of systematic discrimination against anyone who couldn't provide written proof of residency in Bhutan in 1958. A campaign of ethnic cleansing gathered momentum, culminating in 1991 when "illegal" families were forced to sign "**voluntary leaving certificates**" and evicted from their lands with little or no compensation, while those identified as "anti-nationals" (and their families) were harassed, imprisoned, tortured and raped.

The refugees fled initially to India, but receiving little encouragement there, most continued on to their ethnic homeland, Nepal. As their numbers swelled, the Nepalese government, wanting to keep the problem out of sight, established **refugee camps** at Timai and Goldhap (south of Birtamod), Pathari (southeast of Itahari) and, biggest by far, Beldangi I, II and II (north of Damak). Since then, a number of international and Nepali non-governmental organizations have built housing, schools, health posts and other essential facilities in the camps under the direction of the UN High Commission on Refugees (UNHCR). Conditions in the camps are fairly liveable, but residents are desperately poor and utterly dependent on aid since they're prohibited from seeking employment.

The crisis shows no signs of being resolved anytime soon. Diplomatic and human-rights observers all agree that **repatriation** of the refugees to Bhutan is the only permanent solution, but talks between the Nepalese and Bhutanese governments have gone nowhere. Nepal, with its constant changes of government, has lacked a clear negotiating position and has failed to take its case to the international community. Bhutan has continued to insist that it expelled only a small number of illegal immigrants, and that the vast majority of those who left did so of their own free will. India has remained silent, not wanting to take sides in a dispute between two of its buffer states. Other countries have taken weak or noncommittal positions, mainly because they've got bigger human-rights tragedies on their plates, but also because they have a hard time believing that happy little Bhutan could do any wrong. Preparing for a long haul, aid agencies have shifted their focus from relief work to **income-generation projects** that will give the refugees some economic independence.

end, *Hotel Kathmandu & Lodge* (②/B④) and *Hotel Mount Everest* (②/B③) can't exactly be recommended, but they at least aren't too dire.

Most guest houses have their own **restaurants**, but assuming you're only going to be eating one hot meal in Kakarbhitta, you might as well eat it at *Hotel Rajat*. Moneychangers and lodges will swap Nepalese and Indian rupees at the market rate, but to change hard currency you'll have to use the **bank** (Nepal Rastra Bank, the pink building on the south side of the highway signposted only in Nepali; daily 8am–6pm). International and long-distance **phone calls** are possible from the better guest houses and various ISD shops.

Bus tickets for travel within Nepal can be purchased from various desks around the bus park (see map). Roving ticket touts won't save you much effort for their added commission, and can't be entirely trusted. Night buses to Kathmandu and Pokhara leave Kakarbhitta in staggered intervals between 3 and 5pm, but book at least a couple of hours ahead to be sure of a good seat. That said, you'll be much happier sticking to day buses: Dharan and Janakpur make good intermediate destinations from here (see p.349 for a rundown of services). Travel agents in Kakarbhitta can book **flights** to Kathmandu from Bhadrapur ($99) or Biratnagar ($50). Bhadrapur is much closer, but hard to get to (rent a jeep), and its airstrip can accommodate only very small planes; Biratnagar is three hours away by bus, but has more frequent and reliable flights.

The guy at the **tourist office** (Sun–Thurs 10am–5pm, Fri 10am–2pm) speaks some English and may be able to provide some impartial advice on onward travel. The manager of *Hotel Rajat* is also a useful source of information.

The border

The wide Mechi River forms **the border**, about 500m east of town. Formalities are pleasantly relaxed, even with a vehicle. Nepalese immigration is open 24 hours a day, though it may be hard to find anyone after dark. Obtaining a Nepalese **visa** here is expedited by having the correct amount in US dollars cash – if you have anything else they'll make you go to the bank (after hours you're out of luck). Nepalese immigration here is also able to issue **trekking permits** for eastern Nepal, including the Everest region – worth doing if you know for sure you're going to be trekking there, since getting the permit in Kathmandu is a much bigger hassle. Getting a permit upon entry here also makes it possible to do a trek in the eastern hills (see below) on your way to Kathmandu.

If you're **entering India** here, chances are you're heading for Darjeeling, Sikkim or Calcutta. For any of these destinations, you'll probably be best off taking one of the shared jeeps that start just opposite Nepalese immigration. Most of these jeeps shuttle **to Siliguri** (Indian Rs30 per person), where the Toy Train to Darjeeling and bus services to Gangtok and Kalimpong all originate. A few go straight through to Darjeeling (Rs120 per person). It's also possible to take a riksha or walk the 2km to the first Indian settlement, Raniganj, and take a local bus from there to Siliguri, but that's a lot of extra work to save a few rupees. From Siliguri it's 4km by taxi or riksha **to New Jalpaiguri** (NJP), the broad-gauge rail station with train services to Calcutta, and the **Bagdogra** airport, with flights to Calcutta and Delhi.

> **Indian visas** are not obtainable at the border – see p.148.

THE EASTERN HILLS

Two main roads link the Tarai with the hills east of the Sapt Koshi – the **Dhankuta road**, leaving the Mahendra Highway at Itahari, and the **Ilam road**, beginning at Charali. **Bus** services are more fickle on these than along the Mahendra Highway, but this is made up for by the availability of **shared Land Rovers**, which are faster than buses and don't cost much more.

This section describes short hikes in the area, but realise that you won't be able to go too far before you start getting into what His Majesty's Government considers a trek, requiring a special permit obtainable only in Kathmandu or Kakarbhitta.

The Dhankuta road

Call it development or call it colonialism by another name, but the big donor nations have staked out distinct spheres of influence in Nepal, and nowhere is this more apparent than in the British bailiwick around **Dhankuta**. Britain's interest in this area has not been without ulterior motives: roughly half the recruits for the Gurkha regiments have traditionally come from the eastern hills, and the biggest Gurkha training camp was, until 1989, in Dharan. In the 1970s, no doubt pricked by a sense of obligation to the people of the area, Britain initiated a series of projects based in Dhankuta under the auspices of the **British Aid Project Support Office (BAPSO)**. Agriculture, forestry, health and cottage industries have all been funded by British aid through this programme, recently transferred to HMG, but the biggest and most obvious undertaking has been the **road** to Dharan, Dhankuta, Hile and Basantapur. Constructed with £50 million of British taxpayers' money, it's almost absurdly luxurious for a hill region with minimal traffic, though in fairness it must be seen in the context of the entire integrated development programme. It's now in the process of being extended still further into the hills.

Dharan and around

From the Mahendra Highway, the Dhankuta road winds languidly through forest as it ascends the Bhabar, the sloping alluvial zone between the Tarai and the foothills. **DHARAN**, 16km north of the highway, sits a slightly cooler 300m above the plain.

Dharan hit world headlines in 1988 when a powerful **earthquake** killed 700 people and flattened most of the town. Disaster struck a second time at the end of 1989 when the **British Army**, foreseeing forces reductions, pulled out of Dharan and handed its Gurkha Camp back to HMG. The withdrawal dealt a blow to would-be recruits here, who must now travel all the way to Pokhara to compete for even fewer places in the regiments (for more on the Gurkhas, see p.283). Fortunately, Dharan has bounced back smartly. Earthquake-damaged areas have now been almost entirely rebuilt, the city's western half has actually grown into quite a neat little enclave of retired Gurkhas' bungalows, and the former Gurkha Camp has been reincarnated as a fancy medical institute.

Dharan's **bazaar** remains as earthily Nepali as ever, though. For many people throughout the eastern hills this is still the proverbial Bright Lights, where they come to sell oranges by the sackload and spend their profits on pots and pans, radios, watches, clothing, haircuts and bottles of Urvashi from well-stocked spirits stalls. In the area northeast of the central Bhanu Chowk, you'll see hill women investing the family fortune in gold ornaments – the age-old safe haven – and shops selling silver coins to be strung into necklaces. If you happen to be in the market for a cauldron, check out the brass-workers' quarter further east.

A Rs25 riksha or tempo ride west of the bus park, the **British Gurkha Camp** (as it's sometimes still called) is now officially the home of the **B. P. Koirala Health Science Institute**, which runs an extensive medical teaching facility and, rolling in Indian aid, is throwing up new buildings all over the place. You can wander freely around the grounds now, which you wouldn't have been allowed to do when the Gurkhas occupied it, and although there's not much to see, the long, tree-lined lanes are blessedly quiet – it's like a university campus during summer break. The southeastern portion of the camp used to be occupied by the Dharan Country Club, complete with a nine-hole golf course, but this appears not to have survived the handover from BAPSO to the institute.

The modest **Dantakali Mandir** occupies a low ridge just east of the bazaar, and is accessed by an easy path that continues on to two other temples to Buddhasubbha and

Bindyabasini. **Chatara**, 15km west of Dharan, is the finishing point for rafting trips on the Sun Koshi. Walk an hour north of Chatara and you'll reach the sacred confluence of **Barahakshetra**, site of a temple to Vishnu incarnated as a boar (Barahi) and an annual pilgrimage on the day of the full moon of October–November.

Practicalities

Accommodation in Dharan is generally poor, and made worse by bus-park noise – it can be hard to get a good night's sleep. Two reasonably quiet places are *Hotel Aangan* (☎025/20640; ③/B④) and *Shristi Guest House* (no phone; ②/B③). *Aangan* has the better facilities, with clean, nicely furnished rooms, geyser hot water and TVs in some rooms; *Shristi* is strictly a cold-water proposition. *Hotel Saanjh* (☎025/22010; B④) is the only other establishment with hot water, and is comparable to the *Aangan* but has only a few rooms and is noisier. Of several lodges around the bus park, *Hotel Family Inn* (☎025/20848; B③) seems to be the cleanest and quietest, but that's not saying much. Little English is spoken at any of these places.

Several **restaurants** do quite tasty Nepali, Indian and even Continental dishes ("chicken sizzler" has somehow made it all the way to Dharan). The restaurants at the *Aangan* and *Saanjh* hotels can be recommended, as can the one in *Hotel Nawa Yug* (next door to *Hotel Family Inn*) and the upstairs cabin-style *Chimal Restaurant*. *Centre Point* is a smaller version of the *Chimal* located further up the bazaar that's handy if you're staying in *Shristi Guest House*. Other, more local-oriented *bhojanalaya* just west of Chatta Chowk serve *daal bhaat*, *sekuwa* and *sokuti*. Street vendors around Bhanu Chowk sell some weird and wonderful fried morsels.

Moving on
Buses run from Dharan to Biratnagar and Kakarbhitta every half hour during the day, less frequently to Birganj (see p.348 for route details). To reach other Tarai destinations, change at Itahari or Biratnagar. If you want to go straight to Kathmandu, you'll have to book ahead on one of the night buses that leave in mid-afternoon. Buses to Dhankuta and points north are basically local and chronically overcrowded, and it can be a real ordeal getting a seat. Faster and more comfortable **Land Rovers** depart from the eastern side of Bhannu Chowk – they usually operate on a "reserve" basis (ie, you have to hire the whole vehicle), but it may be possible to share a ride for not much more than the cost of a bus ticket.

Dhankuta and around

From Dharan the road switchbacks abruptly over a 1420-metre saddle at Bhedetar, with dramatic views and some competent roadside restaurants, then descends to cross the Tamur Koshi at Mulghat (280m) before climbing once again to **DHANKUTA**, stretched out on a ridge at 1150m. Though you'd never guess it by looking at it, Dhankuta is the administrative headquarters for eastern Nepal. There are of course bigger, more developed cities in the eastern Tarai, but Nepal is after all a hill country run by hill people, and so the job of administering the region must fall to a hill town. This political promotion, and the road that came with it, has decisively shifted Dhankuta's economic base from trade to bureaucracy: bypassed by the road, the bazaar has lost much of its commercial importance, while a whole new suburb of government and aid agency offices has sprung up along the road above town.

But for travellers who make it this far, Dhankuta is an easygoing, predominantly Newar town, with pedestrian-only streets, smartly whitewashed houses and shady *chautaara*. The main **bazaar** runs from south to north, starting just up from the bus park. The lower half of the bazaar, up to the police station, is paved and reasonably active; the flagstoned upper half is quieter but also picturesque. The outlying area is populated by Rais, Magars and Hindu castes, who make Dhankuta's **haat bazaar**, on Thursday, a tremendously vivid affair. The **Dhankuta Museum** (daily except Sat, 10am–5pm; Rs10), located near the top of the bazaar, displays ethnic and archeological artefacts of eastern Nepal. To get to it, walk up the flagstoned bazaar to the four-way intersection of Bhim Narayan Chowk (statue), follow the paved road to the right around and down for 250m – the museum is a whitewashed building above the road on the left, signposted only in Nepali.

Although you can't see the Himalaya from here, the area makes fine **walking** country, and you're bound to run into chatty aid workers or ex-Gurkhas on the trail. In **Santang**, a Rai village about 45 minutes southeast of town, women can be seen embroidering beautiful shawls and weaving *dhaka*, which is as much a speciality of the eastern hills as it is in the west (see p.56). You can walk to Hile in about two hours by taking short cuts off the main road: stick to the ridge and within sight of the electric power line.

Practicalities
Dhankuta's most salubrious **place to stay**, the *BAPSO Guest House* (☎026/20354; B⑤), was at the time of writing facing imminent closure, but it's still worth a phone call or brief detour just in case it's still going. Located 200m south of the bus park, it features

a garden, solar hot water, real furniture, a sitting room, and stodgy Western fare. Cheapies in the bazaar are cold-water, trekking-standard outfits with minimal command of English. *Hotel Parichaya* (①), near the police station, is friendly and clean; the nearby *Hotel Sunrise* and *Upama Hotel & Lodge* are comparable. Plenty of **eateries** in the bazaar do *daal bhaat*, *pakauda* and the like, and one or two can rustle up *momo*, *thukpa* and curries.

Hile and around

If you're here to start (or finish) a trek to Everest or Makalu – and you'd be crazy to come all this way and *not* trek – **HILE** (pronounced *Hee*-lay) might seem anticlimactic. Yet this spirited little settlement would merit a stay even if it weren't a trailhead. One of the most important staging areas in eastern Nepal, Hile is a melting pot of ethnic groups and commercial interests, and, in a sense, a microcosm of Nepal.

Most buses to Dhankuta continue as far as Hile. Seemingly teetering over the deep, often fog-shrouded Arun Valley, the village huddles along the main road, 15km beyond Dhankuta and 750m higher up along the same ridge. A straggling strip of shops, a few hotels and a couple of one-room *gompa* just about sum up the **bazaar**; you can walk the length of it in five minutes. The shops bristle with commodities like plastic containers, readymade clothes, metal pots and salt, all bound for the hinterland: porters gather in Hile by the dozens, and the trail to Tumlingtar, three days up the Arun Valley, is like a *doko* highway.

Local Rais, Newar merchants and Indian entrepreneurs have all established commercial presences in Hile, but its most visible minority are Bhotiyas (see p.396) from the highlands near Kanchenjunga. Undoubtedly one of the most exotic things you can do in Nepal is to spend an evening in a flickering Bhotiya kitchen sipping hot millet grog from an authentic **tongba**: unique to this area, these miniature wooden steins with brass hoops and fitted tops look like they were designed for Genghis Khan. Hile's **haat bazaar**, on Thursday, is lively, but not as big as Dhankuta's.

Magnificent **views** (even by trekking standards) can be had just a half-hour's hike from Hile. Walk to the north end of the bazaar, bear left up a dirt lane and after 250m go up a set of steps to join the Hattikharka trail, which contours around the hill, skirts an army base and finally reaches a grassy plateau. The panorama spreads out before you like a trekking map: to the northwest, the Makalu Himal floats above the awesome canyon of the Arun (though Everest is hidden behind the crest, you can see its characteristic plume); the ridges of the Milke Daada zigzag to the north; and part of the Kanchenjunga massif pokes up in the northeast. It's heaven – pity about the army base, though. The trail to Tumlingtar angles to the left near the north end of the bazaar, passing the British-funded agricultural research station at Pakhribas en route.

Encouraged by a recently liberalized market, some landowners in this area have begun to cultivate tea, which is already big business to the east of here in Ilam (see below). You can visit the **Guranse tea estate**, whose main entrance is just down the road from the bazaar.

Practicalities

Hile's **lodges** are pretty savvy about catering to foreigners, though innkeepers don't speak much English. Top of the line is *Kanjirowa Resort* (☎026/20665; B③), in a quiet location well south (downhill) of the bazaar. Run by the mayor of Dhankuta, it's done up in Tamang style with big but basic rooms, hot water, and spacious, grassy grounds; culture programmes and horse-riding are supposedly planned. Of places in the bazaar, *Hotel Gajur*'s rooms are clean (①), and its kitchen is legendary for *momo*, *sokuti* and *tongba* (there's also a small garden seating area). The rooms are somewhat bigger at *Hotel Himali* (①), but the walls are thinner and the dining area isn't so cosy. Both of these places provide hot washing water by the bucket; *Hotel Hill Stone* (①) has solar-heated showers, but its building has less character than the others. In addition to the guest houses, many stalls at either end of the bazaar do Nepali/Tibetan **food** such as *momo, sokuti* and chow mein.

When it's time to **move on**, you can get a night bus direct to Kathmandu if you're in a hurry, but it's a brutal eighteen-hour ride. If possible, break the journey into two or more days, with stops in Janakpur and/or Chitwan. Buses leave Hile every half hour for Dharan, where you can pick up onward connections.

Basantapur and beyond

Most buses rumble on as far as **BASANTAPUR**, a dusty 21km from Hile. You get tremendous views of the Makalu massif for much of the way, and Kanchenjunga pops into view near the end.

Basantapur's dank, muddy, almost Elizabethan bazaar sits in a saddle at 2400m – it's exotic or godforsaken, depending on how you cock your head. This, for the moment, is where the frontier has moved to. Besides being a major supply line for the entire north-east corner of Nepal, Basantapur plays host to trekking groups bound for Kanchenjunga and the Milke Daada. Several **lodges** offer basic accommodation, *Hotel Yak* (①) being the most proficient in the food and hot-water departments.

Scurvy as Basantapur is, the hills above it are a delight for **walking**: mixed pasture and dense mossy forest, rhododendrons, orchids, jasmine, and friendly villages. Likely targets are Tinjure (lodging available), situated at a high point on the ridge (great views) two to three hours above Basantapur, and Chauki, an hour further on. Anything beyond that is a trek.

Three rough roads continue deeper into the hills from Basantapur. The Hile–Basantapur road has been extended **to Terathum**, 25km to the east and 700m lower, and is plied by shared Land Rovers. A second route is being gradually pushed through **to Chainpur**, Khandbari and Tumlingtar, beautiful Newar towns in the trekking country to the northwest. The third, part of a road that was to have served the now-shelved Arun III hydroelectric project, goes only about 10km northwards in the direction of **Gupha Pokhari**, and is eventually supposed to reach Taplejung to connect with the Ilam road.

The Ilam road

Like the Dhankuta road, the **Ilam road** keeps getting longer: originally engineered by the Koreans to connect the tea estates of Kanyam and Ilam with the Tarai, it now goes all the way to Taplejung, the most common starting point for Kanchenjunga treks (however, nobody in their right mind would go to Taplejung by road when they can fly). The road is paved and in excellent shape as far as Ilam, but it's extremely steep and entails a couple of monster ascents totalling 2300-metre elevation gain.

Buses to Ilam start at Birtamod, located on the Mahendra Highway 8km west of the actual start of the road at Charali – they tend to be very crowded, and the last one leaves at 10am or 11am. The 78-kilometre journey takes about four hours by bus; shared **jeeps**, also departing from Birtamod, are somewhat faster and more comfort-able. Be sure to catch the bus or jeep in Birtamod, as you won't get a seat if you try to board in Charali.

After traversing lush lowlands, the road begins a laborious 1600-metre ascent to Kanyam and its undulating monoculture of tea. At Phikal, a few kilometres further on, a paved side road leads steeply up for 10km to **Pashupati Nagar**, a small bazaar at 2200m just below the ridge that separates Nepal and India here. Some diplomatic kerfuffle has so far prevented this border crossing from being opened to all foreigners, but it's very popular with Nepalis and Indians, since it's only 35km by sealed road from there to Darjeeling. Beyond Phikal the road descends 1200m in a series of tight switchbacks to cross the Mai Khola before climbing another 700m to Ilam (1200m).

Ilam and around

To Nepalis, **ILAM** (Ee-*laam*) means tea: cool and moist for much of the year, the hills of Ilam district (like those of Darjeeling, just across the border) are perfect for it. Ilam town, headquarters of the district, sits right on the edge of a tea estate, which gives it almost a wine-country atmosphere. Unfortunately, the bazaar itself is rather dumpy, though it contains some nice old wooden buildings, and there are no mountain views from anywhere very close by. It's unlikely that you'd travel all this way just for some tea, though there is some very good **bird-watching** in the area.

Settled by Newars, Rais and Marwaris (a business-minded Indian group with interests in tea), Ilam was at one time eastern Nepal's main centre of commerce. While hill towns like Ilam have lost much of their trading importance to the Tarai in recent years, its Thursday *haat bazaar* still draws shoppers from a wide radius, and of course tea cultivation provides an anchor for the local economy.

Unaccustomed to dealing with foreign travellers, **accommodation** here is on the spartan side. *Green View Guest House* (☎027/20103; ③/B④) is at least clean and has geyser hot water, and some of its rooms have balconies overlooking the tea gardens. The next step down from there would be *Danfe Guest House* (②), your basic trekking inn in a quiet location amidst the tea. All the rest are too depressing to mention.

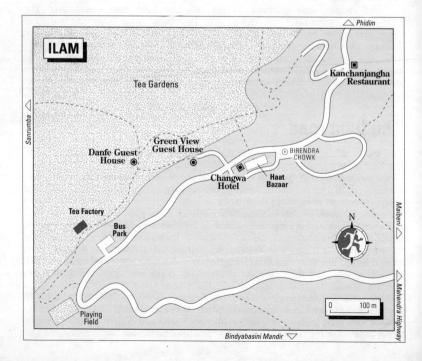

Simple **meals** are available at loads of eateries along the main drag – *daal bhaat* is generally very good in Ilam. Two places that can be recommended are *Changwa Hotel*, about midway along the bazaar, and *Kanchanjhangha Restaurant*, near the top end.

The tea gardens and factory

Ilam's **tea gardens** carpet the ridge above town and tumble down its steep far side; between April and November you can watch the pluckers at work, and at other times it's just a relaxing place to be. Nepal's first tea estate, it was established in 1864 by a relative of the prime minister after a visit to Darjeeling, where tea cultivation was just becoming big business. Marwaris, who had already cornered the cardamom trade here, soon assumed control of the plantation on a contract basis, an arrangement that lasted until the 1960s, when the government nationalized this and six other hill estates under the direction of the Nepal Tea Development Corporation (NTDC). One look at the Ilam facility will show that this is a classically inefficient state-owned enterprise that really ought to be re-privatized. Tea experts say Nepal's plantations could be twice as productive if they were more professionally managed, and economists note the sad irony that Nepal is the world's only tea-producing nation that's a net importer of tea. In fact the government has been promising for years to sell off NTDC, but politics keep getting in the way, though the liberalization of tax laws has at least encouraged the development of some new private tea estates.

You can visit the **tea factory** just above town and see how the world's most popular beverage is produced. The process begins with the plucked leaves being loaded into "withering chutes" upstairs, where fans remove about half their moisture content. They're then transferred to big rolling machines to break the cell walls and release their juices, and placed on fermentation beds to bring out their characteristic flavour and colour. Finally, most of the remaining moisture is removed in a wood-fired drying machine and the leaves are sorted into grades ranging from the coveted TGFOP (Tippy Golden Flower Orange Pekoe, "tippy" referring to the tenderest new leaves) to the lowly PD (Pekoe Dust). Ilam's TGFOP compares favourably with the best of Darjeeling, and indeed most of it is exported to Germany to be blended into "Darjeeling" teas. The best Ilam tea here costs much less than the comparable grade in Darjeeling, though it's still too expensive for most Nepalis, who typically brew their *chiya* from tea dust processed by Tarai plantations.

Beyond Ilam: walks and bird-watching

The Ilam area is noted for its greenness – higher up, the jungle is profuse and exuberant, and even the terraced slopes are teemingly fertile. Keep an eye out for **cardamom**, which grows in moist ravines and has become an important cash crop here. This black cardamom (*sukumel*), which is an inferior form of the tropical green variety (*elaichi*) grown in Kerala, is shipped through India to Singapore where it's sold on the world market. Another common cash crop cultivated in this area is **broom grass** (*amliso*), which is used to make traditional Nepali whisks. Local farmers also produce a surplus of milk here, which you'll see being transported in canisters on horseback to local **cheese** factories. Rais make up the majority of villagers, followed by Baahuns, Chhetris and Limbus.

Rewarding **walks** set off in at least three directions. From the tea gardens, you can contour westwards and cross the Puwamai Khola, ascending the other side to Sanrumba, site of a Tuesday market (there are supposed to be views of Kanchenjunga from further along this ridge). A trail heading east from Ilam descends to cross the Mai Khola, where the annual Beni Mela attracts thousands of Hindus on the first day of Magh (January 14 or 15), and continues on to Naya Bazaar. A sacred pond atop a wooded ridge north of Ilam, Mai Pokhri can be reached by walking or hitching along the road towards Phidim and making a right at Bipliati, from where it's another two or three hours' ascent. If you're looking for a quick leg-stretch, check out the small but attractively sited Bindyabasini Mandir, about 1km down the main road from the bus park.

The **Mai Valley**, which Ilam overlooks, is renowned for its **birds**: its dense, wet habitat and abundant undergrowth provide cover for some 450 species. However, the valley spans a large range of elevations, so to see anywhere near that number of species you have to move around a lot, and you'll need a guide brought from Kathmandu, Chitwan or Koshi Tappu. Lowland species such as drongos, bulbuls and flycatchers (as well as the more exotic Asian fairy bluebird, blue-eared barbet and pale-headed woodpecker) are best observed in the Sukarni forest southwest of Ilam, below the Soktim tea estate. Temperate birds (tits, finches, warblers, barwings, minlas and many others) inhabit the oak-rhododendron forest of the upper Mai Valley to the northeast of Ilam, from Mabu up to Sandakpur on the Indian border, at elevations of 2000m to 3000m.

Buses ply the road north of Ilam to **Phidim** and **Taplejung**, but you're supposed to have a trekking permit to travel beyond here.

PART THREE

OUTDOOR PURSUITS

Route of Trekking:-

Trishuli, Dhunche, Gosaikund, Langtang, Ganjal,
Helambu, Patibhanjyang, Sundarijal.

NEPAL IMMIGRATION

(TREKKING)

T.P.No. 126269

Machhapuchhare
Base Camp

MACHHA

Mardi Himal

Immigration Officer
Code No.

CHAPTER SEVEN

TREKKING

A hundred divine epochs would not suffice to describe all the marvels of the Himalaya.

Hindu proverb

Rearing up over the subcontinent like an immense, whitecapped tidal wave, the **Himalaya** (Hi-*maal*-aya) are, to many travellers' minds, the whole reason for visiting Nepal. Containing eight of the world's ten highest peaks – including, of course, Everest – Nepal's 800-kilometre link in the Himalayan chain puts all other attractions in the shade. More than just majestic scenery, though, the "Abode of Snow" is also the home of Sherpas, yaks, yetis and snow leopards, and has always exerted a powerful spiritual pull: in Hindu mythology the mountains are where gods meditate and make sacrifices, while the Sherpas hold certain peaks to be the very embodiment of deities; mountaineers are often hardly less mystical.

Nepal's **trekking regions**, as defined by the government, take in all parts of the country more than about a day's walk from a main road – a huge area covering nearly the entire northern half of Nepal, and including not only the Himalaya but also large sections of the hills. These regions span an incredible diversity of terrain and cultures, but one thing they all have in common is that you need a **trekking permit** to travel there.

Trekking needn't be expensive nor agonizingly difficult. Most treks follow established routes where you can eat and sleep in simple inns for less money than you'd spend in Kathmandu. Trails are often steep, to be sure, but you walk at your own pace, and no standard trek goes higher than about 5500m (the *starting* elevation for most climbing expeditions). That said, trekking is not for everybody – it's demanding, sometimes uncomfortable, and it does involve an element of risk. This chapter is organized to help you decide if you want to trek, and if so, how and where you might like to do it. The first section covers things you need to know about trekking in general, and the second gives overviews of the most popular, and a few of the more notable out-of-the-way, treks. It is *not*, however, intended to take the place of a trekking guidebook.

Seasonal considerations

Where you go and how you do it will depend to a great extent on the time of year. **Autumn** (October–November) is normally dry, stable and very clear, although bear in mind that bad weather can strike in any season (in recent years dozens of trekkers and porters have died in weather-related avalanches and landslides, most in the autumn). Temperatures are moderate, making it a good time for any trek. It can be cold at night higher up, but not as cold as it gets later on, and the daytime temperatures are pleasantly cool for walking. At low elevations it may still be quite hot during the day. Of course this is also the most popular season for trekking, so queues at the permit offices will be long, porters will charge top dollar, and all standard routes – especially Annapurna and Everest – will be maxed. Don't expect solitude.

Winter (December–January) is for the most part dry and settled, albeit colder. When precipitation does fall, the snow line may drop to 2500m and sometimes even lower. Passes over 4000m may be blocked by snow and ice, and some settlements

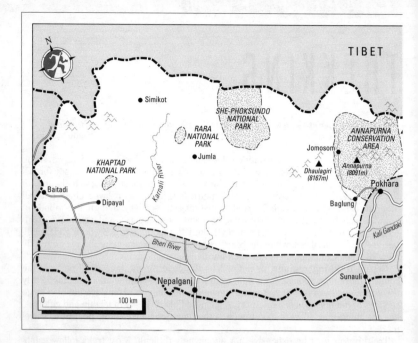

described in trekking guidebooks may be uninhabited. High-altitude treks, such as Everest, require good gear and experience in cold-weather conditions during this period. Below 2000m, temperatures can be quite spring-like, though valleys are often filled with fog or haze. The teahouses that remain open are much quieter than in the autumn, and proprietors have more time to chat.

Temperatures and the snow line rise steadily during **spring** (February–April), while the likelihood of precipitation increases. The warmer weather brings more trekkers, though not as many as in autumn. The main factor that keeps the numbers down is a disappointing haze that creeps up in elevation during this period. By April, you probably won't get good views until you reach 4000m or so. The most colourful rhododendrons bloom in April between 2000m and 3000m.

It gets that much hotter, hazier and unsettled in May and early June. The warming Asian landmass has begun drawing air up from the south, ushering in the **pre-monsoon** – a period of erratic afternoon clouds and occasional squalls as hot, dry air from India is forced up over the mountains. The trails and teahouses again begin to empty out. This is a time for going high, but be prepared for rain, especially in traditionally wet areas such as Annapurna and eastern Nepal.

Few foreigners trek during the **monsoon** (June–September) because of the rain, mud, leeches, travel difficulties and general lack of mountain views. (The leeches along the mid-elevation trails are not for the squeamish!) However, treks in the Himalayan rain shadow and in Nepal's far west are largely sheltered from the monsoon. Even in wet areas, gaps in the clouds occasionally reveal dramatic, mist-wreathed peaks, and wildflowers and butterflies can be seen in abundance. Note that the monsoon isn't consistently rainy – it builds up to a peak in July and August, then tapers off again.

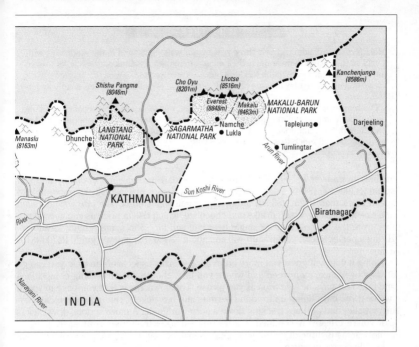

TREKKING BASICS

This section runs through the different **styles** of trekking, **preparations** you'll have to make before setting off, **health** matters to be mindful of, and other factors of **life on the trail**. It's designed to complement the information given in standard trekking guides, with particular emphasis on the nuts and bolts of independent trekking.

Trekking styles

How you choose to trek will depend on your budget, your time frame, and what sort of experience you're after. Trekking independently saves money and gives you a more individualized experience, but is more limiting. Joining an organized trek minimizes hassles and enables you to reach remote backcountry areas, but you pay dearly for it.

Trekking independently

Trekking independently means making all your own arrangements instead of going through a trekking company. Most budget travellers trek this way, carrying their own packs and staying in teahouses, simply because it's cheaper.

The **cost** of lodging is negligible, and there's very little else to spend your money on besides food. Even in the Annapurna and Everest regions, where trekker menus may tempt you to order relatively expensive items, the average tab for three meals a day is

WHY TREK?

Most Nepalis will admit to only three reasons for walking around in the mountains with a load on their back: to go home to their village, to make a religious pilgrimage, or to earn money portering. Those in the trekking business are used to the idea that foreigners will spend huge sums to play the part of a lowly porter, but even they don't necessarily understand *why*.

The reason, of course, is that trekking is the best way to experience Nepal's incredible beauty, both natural and man-made. Explaining this to Nepalis, when appropriate, will not only help them to understand you better, it will also remind them that they have much to be proud of, and much that is worth preserving.

unlikely to go over Rs500 ($7). Along other standard routes you'll probably find you spend Rs300–450 ($4–6) a day, and off the beaten track it may actually be impossible to spend more than Rs250 ($3.50) a day. These guidelines don't take into account such non-essentials as beer, soft drinks and chocolate, which rise in price as you ascend further from the nearest road (a single beer can sell for $5 in some remote locations). Hiring a porter to carry your stuff will add about Rs350 ($5) a day, a guide Rs700 ($10) a day.

Doing it yourself gives you more **control** over many aspects of the trek: you can go at your own pace, stop when and where you like, choose your travelling companions and take rest days or side trips as you please. The downside is that you have to spend two or three days lining up trekking permits and bus tickets, renting equipment, buying supplies and perhaps tracking down a porter or guide. A more serious drawback is that you're effectively confined to a few mass-market **teahouse routes**; trekking to remote areas is difficult unless you speak Nepali or you're prepared to deal with considerable porter logistics.

Life on the trail is described later, but suffice it to say that an independent trek is **less comfortable** than one arranged through an agency. Lodges can be noisy and lacking in privacy, while the food is often fairly uninteresting. The active teahouse **social scene** goes some way to compensating for this, however – even if you start out alone, you'll quickly meet up with potential trekking companions.

By not being part of a group, you're better placed to learn from Nepali ways rather than forcing Nepalis to adapt to yours. Equally important, a high proportion of the money you spend goes directly to the local economy (whereas most of the money paid to trekking agencies goes no further than Kathmandu, and often finds its way overseas). However, as an independent trekker you must guard against contributing to **deforestation**. If you stay in teahouses and order meals cooked over wood fires, you encourage innkeepers to cut down more trees, and if you bring along a guide or porter,

A FEW BAD APPLES

This is an advisory notice for women contemplating trekking alone with a male guide: reports in the past few years suggest that two or three Kathmandu-based guides make a practice of raping their female clients. These men have not been brought to trial – perhaps because of bribes, perhaps because their victims have been unable or unwilling to remain in Nepal long enough to bring legal action. In the absence of convictions, this book cannot name names. The vast majority of Nepali guides are good as gold, but women should be aware that there are a few bad apples. The best way to avoid them is to hire your guide on the recommendation of someone you trust, and bring along a trekking partner. Consider hiring a female guide – see p.273.

so do they. Fortunately, kerosene is replacing wood in the most popular areas. See the box on p.390 for tips on minimizing your environmental impact.

Hiring porters and guides

Porters are an important part of the Himalayan economy and there's no shame in hiring one. With a porter taking most of your gear, you only have to carry a small pack containing the things you need during the day; this can be a great relief at high elevations, and it's essential when trekking off established routes, where tents, food and cooking equipment have to be brought in. As porters rarely speak much English, you might want to pay more for a **guide** who does. In the Annapurna area many are willing to carry gear as well, but this isn't always the case: ask. Guides are really only necessary on esoteric routes, but any trek will be enlivened by the company and local knowledge of a guide, who may well take you on unusual side trips to visit the homes of family and friends.

Hiring a porter or guide is simple enough – just ask your guest house, or try any trekking agency or equipment-rental shop. Trekking agencies are more professional and have better contacts, but they mark up porters' fees by up to 100 percent; guest houses have an incentive to make sure you're well looked after because they want you to come back and stay with them. The hiring process is very informal and not always reputable, so shop around and interview more than one candidate if necessary. A bad guide can be worse than useless. A guide who's actually from the area you plan to trek in is vastly preferable to one who's not, because he or she will have family and friends along the way and will be respected by the local people. If you're not sure you need a porter, or you think you'll only need one for a few tough days of a trek, you can usually hire someone on the spot at Namche, Jomosom or other major towns along the established routes.

Be clear whether or not the agreed **wage** includes food – a porter can run up a huge bill if you're paying – and don't pay too much of it up front (50 percent is pretty standard). Expect also to give your guide or porter a **tip** equivalent to about one day's extra pay for each week worked, assuming the work was well done. Some of this might be given in the form of gear or clothing.

However, the **responsibilities** of employing a porter or guide cannot be overstated. Several porters die needlessly each year, typically because their sahib (pronounced "sahb") thought they were superhuman and didn't mind sleeping outside in a blizzard. You *must* make sure your employees are adequately clothed for the journey – on high-altitude treks, this will mean buying or renting them good shoes, a parka, sunglasses, mittens and a sleeping bag. Establish beforehand if something is a loan. If they get sick, it's up to you to look after them, and since most porters hired in Kathmandu and Pokhara are clueless about altitude-related problems, it's your responsibility to educate them. Don't let a porter carry a double load, even if he volunteers, and don't hire anyone who looks underage.

If you've never trekked before, don't try to organize a trek off the teahouse routes. Finding a guide familiar with a particular area will be hard, and transporting him with a crew of porters and supplies to the trailhead a major (and expensive) logistical exercise. Getting a trekking agency to do it might not cost much more.

Organized trekking

Organized treks are for people who haven't got the time or inclination to make their own arrangements, or who want to tackle ambitious routes that can't be done independently. They **cost** from $15 to $150 a day, depending on the standard of service, size of the group, remoteness of the route, and whether you book the trip in your home country or in Kathmandu. The price should always include a guide, porters, food and shelter, although cheap outfits often charge extra for trekking permits, national park fees and transport, and may cut other corners as well. The cheaper the price, the more wary you need to be.

A trek is hard work however you do it, but a good company will help you along with a few **creature comforts**: you can expect appetizing food, "bed tea" and hot "washing water" on cold mornings, camp chairs and a latrine tent with toilet paper. Depending on the size of your party, a guide, *sirdar* (guide foreman) or "Western trek leader" (native-English-speaking guide) will be able to answer questions and cope with problems. Trekking groups usually sleep in **tents**, which, while quieter than teahouses, may be colder and are certainly more cramped. The daily routine of eating as a group can get monotonous, and gives you **less contact** with local people. There's something to be said for safety in numbers, but trekking with a group imposes a somewhat **inflexible itinerary** on you, and if you don't like the people in your group, you're stuck.

In theory, organized treks are more **environmentally sound**, at least in the Everest and Annapurna areas, where trekkers' meals are supposed to be cooked with kerosene. Sometimes, however, cooks use wood so they can sell the kerosene at the end of the trek – and, worse still, for each trekker eating a kerosene-cooked meal, there may be two or three porters and other staff cooking their *bhaat* over a wood fire.

But the main advantage of organized trekking is it enables you to get **off the beaten track**: there's little point in using an agency to do a teahouse trek. The more crowded and commercialized the teahouse routes become, the more rewarding it is to get away from them. A number of companies now offer "wilderness" treks, which forsake the traditional village-to-village valley routes for obscure trails along uninhabited ridgelines. Shop around and you'll also find special-interest treks based around Tibetan Buddhism, shamanism, bird-watching, rhododendron-viewing, medicine, even trail construction and trash cleanup. Many companies also run trips that combine trekking with rafting, cycling and wildlife-viewing.

Budget operators

Small **budget operators** in Kathmandu and Pokhara, charging $15–25 a day, are notoriously hard to recommend: most are fly-by-night operations offering mainly customized treks, but they're rarely competent to handle anything off the mass-market routes. Many represent themselves to be trekking operators when in fact they're merely agents, taking a commission and providing very little service for it. Names change and standards rise and fall – if you hear of a good one by word of mouth, try it. A few of the more established budget companies run scheduled treks, but again, usually only to the most popular areas.

Bigger operators

Kathmandu's **big operators** mainly package treks on behalf of overseas agencies, but they may allow "walk-ins" to join at a reduced price, and some offer cheaper treks specifically for the local market (typically $30–60 a day). A list of recommended companies is given on p.137. Request brochures to make sure your schedule coincides with theirs; for customized treks to exotic areas, contact them several months in advance, or be prepared to wait up to a week in Kathmandu while arrangements are being made.

Overseas agencies

Booking through an **overseas agency** lets you arrange everything before you leave home, but expect to pay £50–100/$80–160 per day. Some agencies have their own Nepali subsidiaries in Kathmandu, others use independent outfitters like those listed on p.137. The overseas agency will look after all your arrangements up till the time you leave your home country, and will also play a part in maintaining quality control in

---

QUESTIONS TO ASK TREKKING COMPANIES

Trekking companies in Nepal speak the green lingo as fluently as anyone, but in many cases their walk doesn't match their talk. Here are some specific questions to put to them to find out what they're actually doing to minimize their impact on the environment. You probably won't find a company able to answer every question satisfactorily, but the exercise should help establish which outfits are genuinely concerned.

• Do they carry enough kerosene to cook all meals for all members of the party, including porters?

• What equipment do they provide to porters – tents, proper clothing, shoes, UV sunglasses?

• Do they separate trash and carry out all non-burnable/non-biodegradable waste?

• How many of their staff have attended the Kathmandu Environmental Education Project's annual Ecotrek workshop on responsible trekking? (Attendees will be able to show a certificate.)

• Do staff have wilderness first-aid training?

Nepal. Some may allow you to join up in Kathmandu at a reduced price. See p.60 for names and addresses.

Trekking peaks and mountaineering

The Nepal Mountaineering Association has designated eighteen lesser summits, ranging in elevation from 5587m to 6654m, as **trekking peaks**. These peaks offer a compromise between a standard trek and a full-on mountaineering expedition, ranging in difficulty from moderately steep glacier walks to technical, multi-day rock and ice climbs. Previous climbing experience isn't strictly necessary, but you need to be especially fit and able to cope with very cold and potentially stormy conditions.

Climbing a trekking peak takes more time (at least three to four weeks) than a standard trek, and the **cost** per day is comparable to that of a high-end organized trek. That's because trekking peak expeditions must be organized by a registered trekking company, and must be accompanied by a certified climbing guide/*sirdar*. A special permit ($150–300 per party) is also required. The guide/*sirdar* will handle all the logistics and can advise on what extra equipment to bring or obtain in Kathmandu. Bill O'Connor's *The Trekking Peaks of Nepal* (Crowood Press, UK) is the standard guidebook. Further information is available from the Nepal Mountaineering Association (☎434525; *peaks@nma.wlink.com.np*).

Equator Expeditions, Thamel Northwest (☎415782; *equator@mos.com.np*), runs a **mountaineering** school for beginners in the Everest region. Sessions, held in April and October–November, cost $1800 for three weeks or $2000 for four weeks (inclusive of accommodation in Kathmandu). A cheaper option is to trek to the Everest region independently and join up with Equator for a six-day course on Lobuje East. At $700 a person, this actually works out cheaper than organizing the climb of this trekking peak yourself, plus you get instruction. This course is held only a couple of times a year, so check with Equator for dates.

Preparations

Arranging a trek is like anything else in Nepal: complications arise, things inevitably take longer than planned, but it's unquestionably worth it in the end. Obviously, trekking independently involves more preparation than joining an organized group. The remainder of this chapter is geared specifically to independent trekkers, although most of the information will apply to groups as well.

Permits and other formalities

A **trekking permit** is required for entry into any of the areas described in this chapter. Apply at the Central Immigration offices in Kathmandu or Pokhara (details on p.142 and p.274). Pokhara is generally easier to deal with than Kathmandu, but both are frantic during October – especially just before and after the week-long Dasain holiday. Note that Pokhara issues permits only for treks in the Annapurna region and western Nepal. Application forms are colour-coded by region, so be sure to fill in the correct one. Two passport-sized photos are required with your application, but you can get these from nearby fast-photo studios.

For the most popular trekking areas, permits cost **$5** per person per week (payable in rupee equivalent) for the first four weeks, $10 per week thereafter. Some other areas are restricted, which means trekkers must pay a higher permit fee (up to $100 per day, depending on the area) and go with a registered agency; trekking peaks (see above) are also considered restricted. If your trek goes through any of the national parks or conservation areas, you'll have to purchase a separate entry ticket (Rs650 or Rs1000 for most areas) either at the time of application or when you enter the park. Children under ten receive free trekking permits and park admission.

Before setting off on any trek, **register with your embassy** in Kathmandu, as this will speed things up should you need rescuing. You can have the Kathmandu Environmental Education Project or Himalayan Rescue Association (see below) forward the details to your embassy. It's also advisable to be **insured** for trekking – note that travel-insurance companies may add a surcharge to their rates to cover "hazardous sports" such as trekking.

Information, maps and books

The best sources of current trekking **information** are the Kathmandu Environmental Education Project (☎259567), Himalayan Explorers Club (☎259275) and Himalayan Rescue Association (☎262746), all with offices in the same building on Jyatha Thamel in Kathmandu. (By the time you read this, KEEP should have a second branch in Pokhara Lakeside.) These are nonprofit organizations that rely on membership dues and donations to do their work. All keep logbooks full of comments from returning trekkers – invaluable for tips on routes and trekking agencies – and can advise on trail conditions and equipment. All have small libraries, and KEEP also sells books, iodine tablets and other trekking-related items. KEEP doesn't take a position on independent versus agency trekking, but encourages trekkers to use their clout as consumers to effect changes in the trekking industry; exhibits in the office give a primer on trekkers' impact on the environment and culture. HRA provides information on altitude sickness, health posts and weather. Noticeboards outside these offices are good for finding **trekking partners** and used equipment.

Nepal's trekking regions are fairly well **mapped**, although the rule, as always, is you get what you pay for. The locally produced Himalayan Map House, Mandala and Nepa series include colour maps of the most popular routes; generally these work fine if you stick to the main trails, but they can't really be trusted for off-the-beaten-track route-finding. Better, though pricier, are the Geo-Buch ("Schneider") maps of the Everest and Langtang/Helambu areas and the ACAP map of Annapurna, all of which are available in the bigger tourist bookshops. For more obscure treks that aren't well depicted by the standard series, try the HMG/FINNIDA maps, produced by His Majesty's Government in cooperation with the Finnish aid agency – they're superb and not too expensive, though they're not designed specifically for trekking.

Trekking **guidebooks** and general books on the Himalaya are listed in Contexts (p.487); all can easily be bought in Kathmandu or Pokhara. All-Nepal guidebooks, such as Stephen Bezruchka's *Trekking in Nepal: A Traveler's Guide* and Stan Armington's *Trekking in the Nepal Himalaya*, give a broad perspective that's useful when doing ini-

EQUIPMENT CHECKLIST

Items marked (*) can be purchased in Nepal and those marked (**) can also be
rented, but if you want to be absolutely sure of having it, bring it with you.

ESSENTIALS
Backpack* – one with an internal frame
and hip belt is best.
Sleeping bag* – a three-season bag is
adequate for hill treks; above 4000m, or
in winter, you'll need a four-season bag
and possibly a liner.
Medical kit – see p.387.
Water bottle*
Iodine* and/or **water-purification sys-
tem** – see p.387.
Toiletries*
Toilet paper* – see "Conservation tips",
p.390.
Towel*
Flashlight (torch)* – remember that
batteries run down faster in the cold.
Pocket knife*
Matches*
Sunglasses* – a good UV-protective pair,
ideally with side shields if you expect to
be in snow.
Sunscreen/lip balm* – at altitude you'll
need a high protection factor or zinc
oxide.

FOOTWEAR
Hiking boots* – leather or Gore-Tex
boots are best if wet or snowy conditions
are expected.
Trainers* – okay for most low-elevation
trails, handy for evenings.
Flipflops* or **sport sandals** – may be
useful for evenings at low elevations.

CLOTHES
Shirts/T-shirts*
Trousers* – baggy (to leave room for
thermal underwear) and with plenty of
pockets; separate lightweight pair for
warm days.
Skirt/dress* – mid-calf length is best.
Shorts – not recommended on off-the-
beaten-track routes.
Sweat pants – can be worn over shorts
in the morning; also good for evenings.
Socks* – several thin cotton/blend and
thick woollen pairs.

Underwear – thermal underwear essen-
tial for high-altitude or winter treks.
Sun hat* – helpful at low elevations.
Wool sweater* or **fleece jacket***.
Bandana – to use as a handkerchief,
sweatband or scarf.
Parka* – preferably filled with down or
lightweight fibre.
Wool hat* – one that covers the ears is
best.
Wool mittens* – ski gloves are warmer,
but bulkier.
Rain shell/poncho* – breathable water-
proof material (such as Gore-Tex) is best.
An umbrella* will suffice at lower eleva-
tions, and can also function as a parasol.

HIGH-ALTITUDE GEAR – OPTIONAL
Gaiters* – worth having for passes
where snow is likely.
Gloves – thermal liners and waterproof
outer shell.
Down pants* and **booties** – welcome
luxuries on cold evenings.
Ski poles* – may be useful for keeping
your balance in snow or for descents.
Ice axe* – may be needed for icy pass-
es in winter.
Crampons* – ditto.

OTHER USEFUL ITEMS
Day pack*
Foam mat* – optional for teahouse
treks on the main routes.
Camera equipment*
Sewing kit
Stuff sacks – handy for separating
things in your pack and for creating a pil-
low when filled with clothes.
Plastic bag* – to put over your pack in
the rain.
Candles*
Emergency snack food* – biscuits and
chocolate can be bought along the way
on teahouse routes.
Entertainment* – book, cards, musical
instrument, juggling balls, etc.

tial research, but on the trail you might prefer to carry one of the slimmer, trek-specific guides.

What to bring

Having the right **equipment** on a trek is obviously important, though when you see how little porters get by with you'll realize that high-tech gear isn't essential – bring what you need to be comfortable, but keep weight to a minimum. The equipment list given here is intended mainly for independent trekkers staying in teahouses. If you're planning to camp, you'll need quite a few more things, and if you're trekking with an agency you won't need so much.

By **renting** bulky or specialized items in Nepal, you'll avoid having to lug them around during the rest of your travels. Kathmandu has dozens of rental shops, and Pokhara a somewhat more limited selection; if you're trekking in the Everest region, you can rent high-altitude gear in Namche. However, you might have trouble finding good gear during the busy autumn trekking season. You'll be expected to leave a deposit of money or an international air ticket. Inspect sleeping bags and parkas carefully for fleas (or worse) – if there's time before setting off, have them cleaned – and make sure zippers are in working order. You can also **buy** equipment quite cheaply (see p.135). If you buy or rent boots, obviously make sure they fit properly, and break them in before hitting the trail.

Clothes must be lightweight and versatile, especially on long treks where conditions vary from subtropical to arctic. Many first-time trekkers underestimate the potential for extremes in temperature. What you bring will depend on the trek and time of year, but in most cases you should be prepared for sun, rain, snow and very chilly mornings; dress in layers for maximum flexibility. As explained in "Cultural hints" in Basics, Nepalis have innately conservative attitudes about dress: in warm areas, women should wear calf-length dresses or skirts with demure tops; men should wear a shirt and long pants (not shorts) wherever possible, and both sexes should wear at least a swimsuit when bathing.

For **footwear**, running shoes will suffice for most trekking situations, and serve as a good backup for evenings. However, hiking boots, by providing better traction, ankle support and protection, will take you through a greater range of the sort of conditions you're likely to encounter. Leather boots are heavier than synthetic ones, but, being sturdier and more easily waterproofed, are recommended for treks at high elevations or during the winter or monsoon. Bring plenty of socks, because you'll be changing them often.

Bringing **camera** equipment involves a trade-off between weight and performance – a pocket-size point-and-shoot model might be a good compromise. An SLR body with long and short zoom lenses will produce much better results, especially with a tripod and polarizing filters, but it's heavy and obtrusive. You'll find more general tips on photography in Basics.

Health and emergencies

Guidebook writers tend to go overboard about the **health** hazards of trekking, particularly altitude sickness. Don't be put off – the vast majority of trekkers never experience anything worse than a mild headache. That said, health is of paramount concern when doing any strenuous physical activity, and all the more so when trekking, which routinely takes you a week or more from the nearest medical facilities. Stomach troubles can spoil a trek, while injuries or altitude sickness, if untreated, could prove fatal. It's best to err on the side of caution.

Children, seniors and people with disabilities have all trekked successfully, but a minimum **fitness** level is required. Needless to say, the better prepared you are physi-

FIRST AID CHECKLIST

Most of the following items can be purchased in Kathmandu or Pokhara for much less then they cost back home. This is a minimum first-aid kit – trekking guidebooks usually give much longer lists. See p.23 for tips on self-diagnosis, and use antibiotics advisedly.

FOR INJURIES

Plasters/Band-Aids – large and small sizes.

Gauze pads

Sterile dressing

Surgical tape

Moleskin or **"Second Skin"** – synthetic adhesive padding for blisters.

Elastic support bandages – for knee strains, ankle sprains.

Antiseptic cream – for scrapes, blisters, insect bites.

Tweezers

Scissors

Thermometer – one that also reads low temperatures, in case of hypothermia.

FOR ILLNESSES

Aspirin/Paracetamol

Cold medicine

Throat lozenges – sore throats are common at high elevations.

Diarrhoea tablets

Oral rehydration formula – for diarrhoea.

Allergy tablets – if you need them (especially in spring).

Tinidazole – an anti-protozoan, for giardia.

Antibiotic – Ciprofloxacin, Norfloxacin or Cephalosporin for intestinal bacteria, Erythromycin for throat/bronchial infections. Other drugs may also be used – consult a doctor or trekking guidebook.

Diamox – for treatment of mild AMS symptoms (see below).

cally, the more you'll enjoy the trek. Don't allow yourself to be talked into biting off more than you can chew – choose a trek that's appropriate to your abilities or you'll have no fun and could conceivably get into trouble. If you're in any doubt about your ability to cope with strenuous walking, see your doctor. It's also worth seeking advice if you have any allergies, especially to antibiotics.

Stomach troubles

The risk of **stomach troubles** is particularly high while trekking, and water is the usual culprit: you need to drink lots of fluids on the trail. Innkeepers normally boil water and tea, but not always for long enough, and at high altitudes the boiling point of water is so low that germs might not be killed. All running water should be assumed to be contaminated – wherever you go, there will be people, or at least animals, upstream.

   Treating the water is not only the best line of defence against illness, it also reduces your reliance on boiled or bottled water. Iodine is the safest method, either in tablet or crystal form or, more commonly, as a two-percent liquid solution (known as Lugol's solution): use two to five drops per litre, depending on the cloudiness of the water, and wait at least twenty minutes before drinking. You might want to cover up the taste with powdered fruit drink. Chlorine-based tablets may not be effective against amoebas and giardia. Ceramic filter pumps produce pure water without the aftertaste, although they're expensive and take up space.

   See p.24 for tips on treating stomach upsets.

Minor injuries

Most minor injuries occur while walking downhill; **knee strains** are common, especially among trekkers carrying their own packs. If you know your knees are weak, bind them up with crepe (ace) bandages as a preventative measure, or hire a porter. Good, supportive boots reduce the risk of **ankle sprains** or twists, but the best prevention is just to pay careful attention to where you put your feet: don't try to admire the scenery and walk at the same time. A walking stick or ski pole(s) can help.

It's hard to avoid getting **blisters**, but make sure your boots are well broken in and always wear two pairs of socks, changing them regularly (especially if they get wet). Apply protective padding (eg moleskin) to hotspots as soon as they develop, making sure to clean and cover blisters so they can heal as quickly as possible.

Acute mountain sickness

Barraged by medical advice and horror stories, trekkers all too often develop altitude paranoia. The fact is that just about everyone who treks over 4000m experiences some mild symptoms of **acute mountain sickness (AMS)**, but serious cases are very rare, and the simple cure – descent – almost always brings immediate recovery.

At high elevations there is not only less oxygen but also lower atmospheric pressure, which can have all sorts of weird effects on the body: it can cause the brain to swell, fill the lungs with fluid, or suppress appetite and cause muscle tissue to waste away. The syndrome varies from one person to the next, and strikes without regard for fitness – in fact, young people seem to be more susceptible, possibly because they're more hung up about admitting they feel rotten.

PREVENTION

Most people are capable of acclimatizing to quite high elevations, but the process takes time and must be done in stages. The golden rule is **don't go too high too fast**. Above 3000m, the daily net elevation gain should be no more than 500m; take mandatory acclimatization days at around 3500m and 4500m – more if you're feeling unwell – and try to spend these days day-hiking higher. These are only guidelines, and you'll have to regulate your ascent according to how you feel. Trekkers who fly directly to high airstrips have to be especially careful to acclimatize.

Drink plenty of **liquids** at altitude, since the body tends to retain water, and the air is incredibly dry. The usual adage is that you're not drinking enough unless you pee clear. Keeping warm, eating well, getting plenty of sleep and avoiding alcohol will also help reduce the chances of developing AMS.

Acetazolamide (better known under the brand name **Diamox**) has been shown to improve respiration at altitude, which can accelerate acclimatization. Some doctors recommend a preventive dose (125mg twice a day) for people trekking at high elevations, though note that the Himalayan Rescue Association does not advocate the use of Diamox for trekkers. Diamox is a diuretic, so it's all the more important to keep hydrated while taking it; some people also experience minor side effects such as numbness and tingling sensations.

SYMPTOMS

AMS usually gives plenty of warning before it becomes life-threatening. Mild **symptoms** include headaches, dizziness, insomnia, nausea, loss of appetite, shortness of breath and swelling of the hands and feet; one or two of these shouldn't be cause for panic, but they're a sign that your body hasn't yet adjusted to the elevation. You shouldn't ascend further until you start feeling better, or, if you do keep going, you should be prepared to beat a hasty retreat if the condition gets worse. Serious symptoms (persistent vomiting, delirium, loss of coordination, bubbly breathing and bloody sputum, rapid heart rate or breathlessness at rest, blueness of face and lips) can develop within hours, and if ignored can result in death.

CURE

The only effective cure for advanced AMS is **descent**. Anyone showing serious symptoms should be taken downhill immediately, regardless of the time of day or night –

hire a porter or pack animal to carry the sufferer if necessary. Recovery is usually dramatic, often after a descent of only a few hundred vertical metres.

Diamox may be taken to relieve mild AMS symptoms, although it has to be stressed that it does nothing to treat the underlying cause of AMS. For further advice on AMS, visit the Himalayan Rescue Association's aid posts at Manang (on the Annapurna Circuit) and Pheriche (on the Everest trek).

Other dangers

Other altitude-related dangers such as hypothermia and frostbite are encountered less often by trekkers, but can pose real threats on high, exposed passes or in bad weather.

The symptoms of **hypothermia** are similar to those of AMS: slurred speech, fatigue, irrational behaviour and loss of coordination. Low body temperature is the surest sign. The treatment, in a word, is heat. Get the victim out of the cold, put him or her in a good sleeping bag (with another person, if necessary) and ply with warm food and drink.

Frostbite appears initially as small white patches on exposed skin, caused by local freezing. The skin will feel cold and numb. To treat, apply warmth (*not* snow!). Avoid refreezing, which can lead to permanent damage.

Common-sense **precautions** bear repeating: wear or carry adequate clothing; keep dry; cover exposed extremities in severe weather; eat lots and carry emergency snacks; and make for shelter if conditions get bad.

Avalanches can be a serious hazard in certain areas such as the Annapurna Sanctuary and the Thorung La. If you don't know how to recognize avalanche zones or gauge avalanche danger, ask for a crash course at one of the HRA posts.

Snowblindness shouldn't be a worry as long as you're equipped with a good pair of sunglasses. On snowy surfaces you'll need proper glacier glasses with side shields.

Emergencies

Ninety-nine percent of the time, trekking in Nepal is a piece of cake and it's hard to imagine something going wrong. But while few trekkers ever have to deal with **emergencies** – illness, AMS, storms, missteps, landslides and avalanches are the main causes – they can happen to anyone.

Bezruchka's *Trekking in Nepal* gives full advice on emergency **procedures** and a rundown of hospitals, aid posts, airstrips and radio transmitters found near the main trekking routes. In non-urgent cases, your best bet is to be carried by porter or pack animal to the nearest **airstrip** or **hospital**, although bear in mind that medical facilities outside Kathmandu and a few other major cities are very rudimentary. Where the situation is more serious, send word to the nearest village equipped with a radio to request a **helicopter rescue**. A typical rescue costs upwards of $1200, and they won't come for you until they're satisfied you'll be able to pay; being registered with your embassy will speed the process of contacting relatives who can vouch for you.

Trekking life

A trek, it's often said, is not a wilderness experience. Unlike most other mountain ranges, the Himalaya are comparatively well settled, farmed and grazed – much of their beauty, in fact, is man-made – and the trails support a steady stream of local traffic. If you're trekking independently, you'll probably be sleeping and eating in teahouses and making equal contact with locals and other foreigners. You'll need a good deal of adaptability to different living situations, but the payback comes in cultural insights, unforgettable encounters, and of course breathtaking scenery.

The trailhead is typically reached at the end of a long, bumpy bus ride, and **getting there** is an integral part of the experience. This is also a big factor in deciding where

CONSERVATION TIPS

The main environmental problem in the Himalaya is **deforestation**, and trekking puts an additional strain on local wood supplies: it's been estimated that one trekker consumes, directly and indirectly, between five and ten times more wood per day than a Nepali. In addition, trekkers leave **litter**, strain local **sanitation** systems and contribute to water **pollution**. The following are suggestions on how to minimize your impact on the fragile Himalayan environment.

• Where the choice exists, eat at tea-houses that cook with kerosene, electricity or propane instead of wood.

• Bring plenty of warm clothes so you (and your porter) are less reliant on wood fires to keep warm.

• Try to time your meals and coordinate your orders with other trekkers; cooking food in big batches is a more efficient use of fuel.

• If trekking with an agency, see that all meals are cooked with kerosene or propane, and complain if they aren't.

• Decline offers of hot showers except in inns where the water is heated by electricity, solar panels or fuel-efficient "back boilers".

• Treat your own drinking water (see p.387) rather than relying on bottled or boiled water. Plastic water bottles can't be recycled in Nepal and pose a serious litter problem in trekking areas. Water sterilized by boiling uses precious wood or other fuel.

• Use latrines wherever possible. Where there's no facility, go well away from water sources, bury your faeces and burn your toilet paper. Better yet, don't use toilet paper at all – use water, as Nepalis do.

• Use phosphate-free soap and shampoo, and don't rinse directly in streams.

• Deposit litter in designated rubbish bins, where they exist. Elsewhere, carry all non-burnable litter back out – that includes tins, plastic bottles and especially batteries.

to trek, as the going and returning can eat up two days (or more) and, in the case of far-flung treks reached by air, can represent the single biggest expense. See Basics for general information on bus and air travel.

Trails

Trekking in the Himalaya is no stroll in the park. If you're not an experienced outdoors person, prepare yourself for serious, strenuous **walking**. Most trekkers take it in easy stages, from one glass of *chiya* to the next – there's no race to the top. It's best to set off early each morning to make the most of the clear weather, as clouds usually roll in around midday. Pad your schedule for rest days, weather and contingencies, and make time for at least one unusual side trip – that's when things get really interesting.

Trails are often steep and rough, and bridges precarious. You may occasionally **get lost**, but not for long: stopping to chat and ask directions is part of the fun, and a good opportunity to learn some Nepali. Don't **trek alone**, or at least stay within sight of other people and spend nights in the company of others, as they can help you if you get hurt and can detect signs of AMS or hypothermia. Nepalis think all lone travellers are a bit odd, so you might find it worthwhile teaming up with others just to avoid the constant question, *Eklai?* ("Alone?"). Be sure to read "Cultural hints" in Basics; again, *don't* give pens or rupees to children, whether they ask or not – if you do, every trekker that comes after you will be hounded for handouts.

Teahouses

Teahouses along the major trekking routes are efficient little operations, with English signs, menus and usually an English-speaking proprietor. Although they cater exclusively to trekkers and their porters, most of these tourist inns still follow the Nepali tradition of providing practically free lodging (usually Rs75 or less per bed) to dinner customers. Private rooms are available along the most popular routes, but elsewhere it may be necessary to take dormitory accommodation. The beds will normally have some sort of padding, but a foam mat may come in handy, and a sleeping bag is obligatory. Many places have wood stoves or kerosene heaters, and a growing number have electricity.

You'll find fewer comforts on **less-trekked trails**, however, where lodgings are likely to be private kitchens and meals are eaten by the fire amid eye-watering smoke, and you may have to sleep on the floor. Such places rarely advertise themselves, but once you've spent a little time off the beaten track you'll start realizing that almost every trailside house with an open front is potential shelter.

Recommending specific trekking lodgings is beyond the scope of this book. At any rate, they come and go so quickly that your best recommendations will be from trekkers coming the other way.

Food and drink

Trekking cuisine is a world unto itself. Although teahouses' plastic-coated cardboard menus promise tempting international delicacies, items often turn out to be permanently *paindaina* (unavailable), and you'll notice that the "spring roll" wrappings, "enchilada" tortillas, "pizza" crusts and "pancakes" all bear more than a passing resemblance to chapatis. But at any rate, eggs, porridge, custard and even apple pie are all reassuringly familiar, and goodies like chocolate and muesli are available on the main trails.

However, many trekkers order "Western" food simply because it's there, not because it's good, and indeed it costs much more than **local food**. In highland areas you'll be able to eat such Tibetan dishes as *momo*, *thukpa* and *riki kur*, and instead of porridge you might be served *dhedo* or *tsampa* (see "Eating and drinking" in Basics). At lower elevations, *daal bhaat*, chow mein, packet noodles and seasonal vegetables are the standard offerings. A further advantage of eating local fare is that it's almost always quicker: there are usually unlimited quantities of *daal bhaat* steaming away on the back burner, whereas foreign food has to be made specially. On less-travelled routes, where *daal bhaat* and potatoes are often the only food available, you'll have to force yourself to eat large amounts to get enough calories and protein (you might also want to bring vitamin tablets).

When **ordering**, bear in mind that the cook can only make one or two things at a time, and there may be many others ahead of you: simplify the process by coordinating your order with other trekkers. Most innkeepers expect dinner orders to be placed several hours in advance, and there's usually a dog-eared notepad floating around on which you're meant to keep a tally of everything you've eaten. Pay when you leave, and be sure to bring plenty of small money on the trek, since innkeepers often have trouble changing anything over Rs100.

Tea and "hot lemon" are the main **drinks** on the trail. Bottled soft drinks, water and even beer are common along the popular routes, but the price of each bottle rises by Rs15–25 for each extra day it has to be portered from the nearest road. Don't miss trying *chhang*, *raksi* and *tongba* – again, see Basics for fuller explanations of these alcoholic specialities.

Sanitation

Washing and toilet facilities, where they exist, range from primitive to modern. Off the established routes or at higher elevations, you'll have to bathe and do laundry under makeshift outdoor taps in freezing cold water (which explains why hot springs are such major attractions). Most teahouses in the Annapurna and Everest regions have solar or electric-heated showers. Others will offer washing water that has been heated on a wood fire, but this is an environmentally dubious practice. Most teahouses provide outdoor latrines (*chaarpi*), and a few even have indoor flush toilets, but don't be surprised if you're pointed to a half-covered privy hanging over a stream, or simply to a paddock.

THE TREKS

Nepal's mountains can be divided into five regions, the first three being most suitable for first-time independent trekkers. On a limited budget and schedule, you'll be restricted to the **Annapurna** and **Helambu–Langtang** regions, north of Pokhara and Kathmandu respectively. Given more time or money, you'll be able to tackle **Everest** or some of the longer Annapurna routes. With experience, or a sense of adventure, you should consider treks in the more remote regions of **eastern** and **far western Nepal**.

The sections below give overviews of the areas and describe the major trekking possibilities within them, but for a step-by-step route description you'll need a full-blown trekking guidebook. The box on the next page summarizes the major teahouse treks.

North of Pokhara: Annapurna

Nearly 60 percent of all trekking permits are issued for the **Annapurna** region north of Pokhara. The popularity is well deserved, since nowhere else do you get such a rich feast of spectacular scenery and varied hill culture. Compared to most other regions, **logistics** are simple: treks all start or finish close to Pokhara, and transportation to trailheads is well developed; with great views just two days up the trail, short treks are par-

ANNAPURNA TRAVEL CONNECTIONS				
	Buses		**Flights**	
	Frequency	Time	Frequency	Time
To and from POKHARA				
Baglung	1/hr	3hr		
Begnas Tal	1/hr	45min		
Naya Pul	1/hr	2hr		
Dumre/Besisahar *				
Gorkha	2/day	5hr		
Jomosom			5–6/day	25min
Manang			0–3/wk	25min
Phedi/Surkhet	1/hr	1hr		
Tansen	3/day	6hr		
To and from KATHMANDU				
Besisahar	5/day	8hr		
Gorkha	10/day	6hr		
Pokhara	30/day	7hr	10–20/day	35min
	(6–12/day)#	7hr		
Trisuli	9/day	4hr		

* No direct buses: take any eastbound bus from Pokhara, get off at Dumre (2hr), from where buses and jeeps run to Besisahar (another 3hr).

Number in parentheses refers to tourist buses.

TEAHOUSE TREKS AT A GLANCE

Trek	Days*	Best Months	Elevation (m)	Difficulty	Comments
Helambu	3–10	Oct–April	800–3600	Moderate	Easy access, uncrowded, varied; only modest views.
Gosainkund	4–7	Oct–Dec, Feb–May	1950–4380	Strenuous	Sacred lakes; festival in July–August.
Poon Hill	4–6	Oct–April	1100–3200	Moderate	Easy access, excellent views; very commercial.
Siklis	4–7	Oct–April	1100–2200	Moderate	Easy access; need 2 days' supplies.
Rara	6–8	Oct–Nov, April–June	2400–3500	Moderate	Fly in; must be prepared to camp; pristine lake and forest.
Pokhara – Trisuli	6–10	Nov–March	400–1450	Easy	Pleasant hill walk, snow-free in winter, basic teahouses; for a shorter trek you can do just half the route.
Dolpo	7–14	April–Sept	2100–5110	Strenuous	Fly in, possibility of walking out; remote and rugged, simple teahouses.
Langtang	7–12	Oct–May	1700–3750	Moderate	Beautiful alpine valley close to Kathmandu.
Lower Kali Gandaki	7–9	Nov–March	900–3200	Moderate	Longer version of Poon Hill, returning a less commercial way.
Annapurna Sanctuary	8–10	Oct–Dec, Feb–April	1100–4130	Moderate/Strenuous	Spectacular scenery, easy access; acclimatization necessary.
Dhorpatan circuit	10–14	Oct–April	470–3400	Moderate	May need guide, shelter and food.
Jomosom/ Muktinath	10–12	Oct–April	1100–3800	Moderate	Spectacular; varied; very commercial.
Everest (Lukla fly-in)	14–18	Oct–Nov, March–May	2800–5550	Strenuous	Superb scenery; flights a problem; acclimatization necessary.
Annapurna circuit	16–21	Oct–Dec, March–April	450–5380	Strenuous	Incredible diversity and scenery; high pass requires care and acclimatization.
Everest (Jiri walk-in)	26+	Oct–Nov, March–April	1500–5550	Very strenuous	Wonderful mix of hill and high-elevation walking, but with a lot of up and down.
Everest (E. approach)	28+	Nov, March	300–5550	Very strenuous	Similar, but with an even greater net vertical gain.

* Not including transport to and from the trailhead.

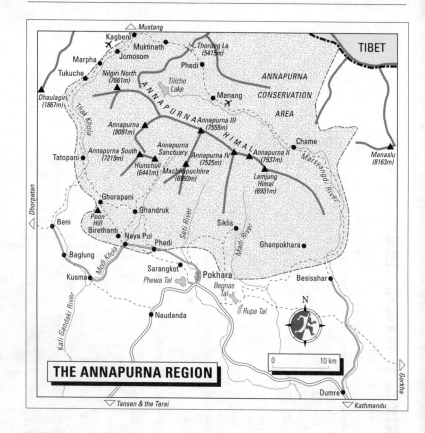

THE ANNAPURNA REGION

ticularly feasible. Pokhara is the only place outside Kathmandu with a Central Immigration office that issues **trekking permits**, and the Pokhara office is if anything saner than Kathmandu's. If your trek starts and ends in Pokhara, you'll be able to store excess luggage and **rent equipment** there as well.

That said, the popular treks in the Annapurna region have become highly **commercialized** and culturally rather tame – this is the Costa del Trekking. To be fair, most trekkers regard familiar food, mattresses, English signs and Western company as pluses, but if you're looking to get away from it all, look elsewhere. Also note that there are frequent reports of **theft** and sometimes even violence against trekkers in this region, so do not trek alone in remote or forested areas.

The **Annapurna Himal** faces Pokhara like an enormous sofa, 40km across and numbering nine peaks over 7000m, with Annapurna I above all at 8091m. It's an area of stunning diversity, ranging from the sodden bamboo forests of the southern slopes (Lumle, northwest of Pokhara, is the wettest village in Nepal) to windswept desert (Jomosom, in the northern rain shadow, is the driest).

The *himal* and adjacent hill areas are protected within the **Annapurna Conservation Area Project** (ACAP), for which you have to pay a Rs1000 **entry fee**. The money goes to a good cause. A quasi-park administered by a non-governmental trust, ACAP has won high praise for its holistic approach to tourism management. Its twofold aims are to protect the area's natural and cultural heritage, while at the same time ensuring sustainable economic and social benefit for local people. To take the pressure off local forests, the project has set up kerosene depots and installed micro-hydroelectric generators to provide alternative fuels, and has supported the creation of tree nurseries and reforestation efforts. Lodge owners benefit from small-business training and low-interest loans, enabling them to invest in things like solar water heaters and efficient stoves, while rubbish pits, latrines, health posts and a telephone service have been established with ACAP entry fees.

The Jomosom trek

JOMOSOM TREK is an acknowledged classic: an ideal sampler of Himalayan scenery and culture, and, not surprisingly, the most developed stretch of trail in Nepal. A guide definitely isn't necessary. **Food and lodging** are of a relatively high standard: most lodges have electricity and hot showers, and some look like they've been imported wholesale from Thamel. All have English menus and outdo each other with the Westernness of their cuisine.

The full Jomosom trek takes ten to twelve days, but the trail network is extensive, so shorter and longer variations are possible. The first half of the trek, which can be done on its own, is described first. The usual **starting point** is Naya Pul, reached by bus or taxi from Pokhara; it's also possible to start from Lakeside, Suikhet/Phedi or Beni (see p.272 for transport advice).

To Poon Hill

If you haven't time to do the full Jomosom trek, you can get a taster of it by turning the first half into a circuit of four to six days. The route ambles through steep, lush hill country, taking in some lovely Gurung villages and, weather permitting, rewarding you with outstanding views of the Annapurnas and Machhapuchhre. The **trails** are wide and well maintained, though steep in places. The highest point reached is 3200m, which shouldn't present any altitude problems, but it's high enough that you'll need **warm clothes** at night. Rain gear is also advisable.

Poon Hill, a day and a half northwest of Naya Pul and 2000m higher, is literally the high point of this instant-gratification route: watching the mountains at sunrise from here is probably the single most done thing in the trekking universe. If clouds block your view, as they often do, it's well worth hanging on for an extra day. You can vary the return trip by heading east through magnificent stands of giant rhododendrons dripping with orchids to the pretty Gurung town of **Ghandruk**, headquarters of the ACAP, with a visitor centre and museum. From Ghandruk, trails head up to the Annapurna Sanctuary and down to Naya Pul and Phedi (Suikhet).

The Thak Khola

North of Poon Hill, the trail drops into the valley of the Kali Gandaki (locally called the **Thak Khola**) and the fun really begins: as you follow the course of the world's deepest gorge – the 8000-metre hulks of Dhaulagiri and Annapurna tower on either side – the scenery changes by the mile. The valley is also famous for its ethnic diversity, Thakalis being the dominant group. Make way for their jingling donkey trains, which feature so prominently in this area.

The walking actually gets easier after Poon Hill (and by this time you should be in better shape), and the trail stays below 3000m until the last day's climb to Muktinath at 3800m. There's essentially only one route through the Thak Khola, so unless you carry on up over the Thorung La (described in "The Annapurna Circuit", below) or fly back from Jomosom, some **backtracking** is unavoidable; but by the same token, you can

BHOTIYAS AND THAKALIS

Bhotiya is the Nepali term for all northern border peoples of Tibetan descent. Unfortunately, Bhotiyas themselves have tended to resent the label ever since an 1854 government edict, intended to find places for all minority groups in the Hindu caste system, placed them in the lowly category of "enslavable alcohol-drinkers" because they ate yak meat (which Hindus regarded as being almost as bad as eating beef). Most prefer to identify with a specific regional group, of which there are at least a dozen in Nepal; Sherpas, the best-known Bhotiya group, are highlighted in the Everest section later in this chapter.

In most ways, Bhotiyas are indistinguishable from Tibetans. Except in certain areas in the far west, where some have been influenced by Hinduism, they are exclusively **Buddhist**, and their *chorten* (stupa-like cremation monuments), *mani* walls (consisting of slates inscribed with the mantra *Om mani padme hum*), *gompa* (monasteries) and prayer flags (*lung ta*: literally, "wind horse") are the most memorable man-made features of the Himalaya. Farmers, herders and trans-Himalayan traders, they always settle higher and further north than other ethnic groups. The climate there is harsh, and life is a constant struggle to eke out a living. Bhotiya villages vary in appearance, but those in the Annapurna region are strongly Tibetan, with houses stacked up slopes so that the flat roof of one serves as the grain-drying terrace of the next. Like Tibetans, they like their tea flavoured with salt and yak butter, and married women wear trademark rainbow aprons (*pangden*) and wrap-around dresses (*chuba*).

Unencumbered by caste, Bhotiyas are noticeably less tradition-bound than Hindus, and **women** are better off for it: they play a more nearly equal role in household affairs, speak their minds openly, are able to tease and mingle with men publicly, and can divorce without stigma. (Having said that, even Bhotiyas tend to consider a female birth to be the result of bad karma, and during death rites lamas customarily urge the deceased to be reincarnated as a male.)

A hill group with influence far beyond their small numbers, **Thakalis** are the ingenious traders, innkeepers and pony-handlers of the Thak Khola, the valley followed by the Jomosom trek. Their entrepreneurial flair goes back at least to the mid-nineteenth century, when the government awarded them a regional monopoly in the salt trade. When Nepal opened to the outside world, many branched out into more exotic forms of commerce such as importing electronics from Singapore and Hong Kong, while others set up efficient inns in many parts of the western hills. Similarly, the **Manangis** of the upper Marsyangdi built early trading privileges into a reputation for international smuggling and other shady activities. Women have traditionally run most of the trekking lodges in both of these valleys, while their well-travelled husbands spent most of their time away on business. In recent years, however, the relaxation of import restrictions and currency controls has deprived these groups of their special status, and many traders have returned to their home villages.

walk as far as you like and head back when you need to. The round trip from Pokhara to Muktinath takes ten to twelve days. If you **fly** from Pokhara to Jomosom, or vice versa, you cut the time in half; there are up to six scheduled flights a day in the high season ($50), weather permitting.

The towns of the Thak Khola are worthy destinations in their own right. **Tatopani** is renowned for its Western food, videos (cringe) and **hot springs** (*taato paani* means "hot water"). Further up, the trail passes through thick, monkey-infested forest to Tukche, once the main Thakali trading centre, and **Marpha**, a tidy, stone-clad village surrounded by apple and apricot orchards. **Day hikes** and overnight trips up from the valley floor are the best way to appreciate the incredible dimensions of the Thak Khola and the peaks around it: little-trekked trails lead to North Annapurna Base Camp, the Dhaulagiri Icefall and Dhampus Pass. Above Tukche, the vegetation dies out as you begin to enter the

Himalayan rain shadow, and a savage, sand-blasting wind from the south makes it unpleasant to trek after midday. **Jomosom**, though it gives its name to the trek, is no place to linger unless you've got business at the airstrip – far more romantic is the fortress town of **Kagbeni**, only a couple of hours further on, with its medieval ruins and terracotta Buddhist figures. Geographically speaking, you're on the edge of the Tibetan plateau here, with the main Himalaya chain looming magnificently to the south.

Finally, it's a 1000-metre climb up a side valley – out of the wind, thankfully – to poplar-lined **Muktinath**, one of the most important religious sites in the Nepal Himalaya. The *Mahabharat* mentions Muktinath as the source of mystic *shaligram* fossils (see p.290); a priest will show you around the Newar-style temple and its wall of 108 water spouts, while further down the trail you'll find a Buddhist shrine that shelters two miraculous perpetual flames. Yartung, a madly exotic **festival** of horse-riding, is held at Muktinath around the full moon of August–September.

The lower Kali Gandaki

On the return journey, if you don't feel like slogging back up the ridge south of Tatopani, you can keep following the Kali Gandaki River south from Tatopani, a low-key **valley walk** with occasionally impressive views; since there's little up and down, it's possible to make good time. This route sees far fewer trekkers than the main Jomosom trail, so **accommodation** and **food** are cheap but rudimentary. At this low elevation the weather is balmy in winter, but in spring and early autumn the heat and mosquitoes are unpleasant. The trail passes through cultivated land and villages, where Magars and Gurungs are the dominant **ethnic groups**, as well as the big Newar bazaars of Beni and Baglung.

The Pokhara–Baglung Highway is being extended northwards, bound eventually for Jomosom, but progress is slow. At the time of writing the end of the road was Beni, with regular buses to Pokhara departing from Baglung.

The Annapurna Sanctuary

The aptly named **ANNAPURNA SANCTUARY** is the most intensely scenic short trek in Nepal. From Ghandruk on the Jomosom route, the trail bears singlemindedly north into the very heart of the Annapurna range: following the short, steep Modi Khola, it soon leaves all permanent settlements behind, climbs through dense bamboo jungle and finally, rising above the vegetation line, makes for a narrow notch between the sheer lower flanks of Machhapuchhre and Hiunchuli. Once past this sanctuary "gate", it stumbles across moraines to a cluster of huts (often still called "Machhapuchhre Base Camp") and, further on, to the so-called **Annapurna Base Camp**. Wherever you stand in the sanctuary, the 360-degree views are unspeakably beautiful, and although clouds roll in early, the curtain often parts at sunset to reveal radiant, molten peaks. The altitude is 4100m: bring warm gear.

The sanctuary can be treated as a side trip from the Jomosom trek, adding five to seven days, or an eight- to ten-day round trip from Pokhara, accessed from Naya Pul or Suikhet (Phedi). The actual distance covered isn't great, but **altitude**, **weather** and **trail conditions** all tend to slow you down – the trail gains more than 2000m from Ghandruk to the sanctuary, so unless you're already well acclimatized you'd be wise to spread the climb over four days. Frequent precipitation makes the trail extremely slippery at the best of times, and in winter it can be impassable due to snow or avalanche danger.

The Annapurna Circuit

The **ANNAPURNA CIRCUIT** is a challenging but rewarding three-week trek with excellent views, plenty of cultural contact and the greatest net vertical gain of all the popular routes. Starting in subtropical paddy at about 500m, the trail ascends steadily to the 5415-metre **Thorung La** (Thorung Pass) before returning along the previously described Jomosom route. A minimum of sixteen days is required, but a few extra days should be set aside for digressions, acclimatization and other contingencies. The trek is strenuous, and you'll need boots, gloves and very warm clothes for the pass, and a good four-season bag for a night spent at 4400m.

Although the eastern half of the circuit is less developed for trekkers than the Jomosom side, **food and lodging** are always available, and somewhat cheaper. A guide isn't necessary. The full circuit is best done between mid-October and mid-December – crossing the Thorung La is iffy from late December till March, though not out of the question, while the lower parts of the trek are uncomfortably warm from April onwards. Snow can block the pass at any time of year, so be prepared to wait it out or go back down the way you came. You may be able to **fly** in or out of Manang (seasonal; $61 from Pokhara), saving a week of walking.

Nearly everyone goes around the circuit anticlockwise, the only reason being that the Thorung La makes a longer climb from the Jomosom side, requiring an extra acclimatization day above Muktinath. The upshot of this is that if you go anticlockwise you'll be in step with the same people for the entire trek, whereas if you go clockwise you'll be constantly passing people coming the other way. The usual **starting point** is Besisahar, reachable by direct public bus from Kathmandu or (probably better) by tourist bus to Dumre on the Prithvi Highway and then by jeep or local bus from there; if all goes well, you can leave Kathmandu in the morning and be in Besisahar that night. If you're coming from Pokhara, you can avoid Dumre and instead follow the Pokhara–Trisuli trek (see below) to Besisahar in two days.

The circuit follows the Marsyangdi Valley north and then west all the way to the pass. The first few days are a long preamble through terraced farmland and frequent villages, with only fleeting views to whet your appetite, but then, in the course of two days, the valley constricts and the trail climbs steeply, leaving the paddy behind and passing through successive climatic zones: temperate forest, coniferous forest, alpine meadows and finally the arid steppes of the rain shadow. The walk from Chame to **Manang** is spectacular and shouldn't be rushed. The sight of the huge, glacier-dolloped Annapurnas towering almost 5000m above the valley will stay with you forever. Manang's architecture, like that of all the older villages here, is strongly Tibetan; *gompa* at Manang and Braga are well worth visiting. Manang also has an airstrip and a **Himalayan Rescue Association post**, where they give daily talks on AMS. If you're going for the Thorung La, the next night will probably be spent at **Phedi**, a grotty place where you'll be woken up at 3am by trekkers who've been told (wrongly) that they have to clear the pass by 8am. The climb up the pass, and the knee-killing 1600-metre descent down the other side to Muktinath, is a tough but exhilarating day. The remainder of the circuit follows the Jomosom trek (see above).

Other Annapurna treks

Aside from the fact that they share some of the same trails, the following treks have nothing in common with the razzle-dazzle teahouse trails in the Annapurna area. You'll typically find only Nepali food and lodging along these trails, and except for the Pokhara–Trisuli and Siklis routes, you'll need to be equipped to camp or be willing to stay in people's homes. If you're not trekking with an agency, you'll probably want to go with a **guide**.

Pokhara–Trisuli

The old **POKHARA–TRISULI** trail is little trekked now that it's been superseded by the Prithvi Highway, and that's its chief recommendation. A gentle, low-altitude trek, it wanders through typical hill country and dozens of laid-back ethnic villages, with Annapurna, Manaslu and Ganesh Himal popping up often enough to keep things ticking over scenically. This is the only serious trek that's guaranteed to be snow-free all year, making it a good choice for winter.

The trek can be done in six days, but allow eight or ten; many trekkers start or finish at Gorkha, the midway point, for an easy outing of four to five days. There are any number of ways to get started from Pokhara, but to bypass a lot of road-walking, take a bus to Begnas Tal and take any trail heading east and north towards Besisahar on the Annapurna Circuit – try to go by way of **Ghanpokhara**, a lovely Gurung village – finally reaching **Gorkha** in a minimum of three days (more like five via Ghanpokhara). From there it's another four days or so of undulating between subtropical valleys and scenic ridges to Trisuli, which is linked by road with Kathmandu.

The Siklis trek

An alternative to other short treks in the region, the **SIKLIS TREK** probes an uncrowded corner of the Annapurna Conservation Area under the shadows of Lamjung Himal and Annapurnas II and IV. The main teahouse itinerary takes about a week, starting at Begnas Tal and heading north to the Madi Khola, then following the river's west bank up to well-preserved **Siklis** (1980m), Nepal's biggest Gurung village. From here you strike westwards over the thickly forested ridge that separates the Madi and Seti drainages and then descend via Ghachok, another Gurung settlement, to reach the Pokhara–Baglung Highway. Many other variations are possible. As part of an effort to develop this into a model ecotrekking route, ACAP has funded the construction of a small museum and cultural facility in Silkis.

The Royal trek

Although this is the shortest, easiest and lowest trek described in this chapter, it's rarely attempted by independent trekkers because of the lack of teahouse accommodation en route. On the other hand, it's fairly popular with groups and families. It's been known as the **ROYAL TREK** ever since Prince Charles took a rally-the-troops swing along it in 1980 to visit the villages of Gurkha recruits. Taking just three or four days, it starts (or ends) at the Bijalpur Khola, just east of Pokhara Bazaar. From there it heads westwards, ascending a ridge to Kalikasthan (another possible starting point, reached by rough road from Pokhara), and follows the ridgeline eastwards past Thulakot and Begnaskot (good views) to Syaglung, then bends back westwards to Begnas Tal via Sundari Daada. The route goes no higher than 1420m, making it suitable for winter. No trekking permit is required, but there is some talk of charging royal trekkers the Rs1000 ACAP entrance fee.

The Dhorpatan circuit

The **DHORPATAN CIRCUIT** breaks away from the Kali Gandaki River at Beni and wanders westwards up into high, open hill country with commanding views of the Dhaulagiri Himal. The trail crosses a tough but beautiful 3400-metre pass and reaches the broad Dhorpatan Valley in about four days, where the attraction isn't the valley itself but the opportunities for exploring the huge **Dhorpatan Hunting Reserve** to its north. In a day, you can get up onto the 4100-metre summit immediately north of the valley for dynamite views; if you're prepared for a few nights out you can continue into the rugged Dhaulagiri area, check out mountaineering base camps and maybe even see some **blue sheep** or **tahr**. Leaving Dhorpatan, two lower, less dramatic routes complete the circuit, one returning to Baglung and the other finishing at Tansen.

Two weeks would be a realistic time frame for Dhorpatan. The circuit is fairly demanding, taking you a long way from conventional tourist places. Lodging is available throughout, but you'll have greater flexibility if you **bring your own equipment**. Anytime between October and April is fine for Dhorpatan, although in winter the high route may be blocked by snow.

Around Manaslu

It takes three weeks to trek **AROUND MANASLU**, a challenging circuit east of the Annapurna area that ventures into extremely remote country and over a 5200-metre pass. Government restrictions on travel in this area mean you need a special trekking permit ($75 per week; $90 in Sept–Nov), plus you must be self-sufficient for a full week of the trip. The trek usually starts in Gorkha, first heading east and then north up the valley of the Budhi Gandaki, finally rounding behind Manaslu (8163m) over the Larkya La (5213m). From there it's two days down to Bagarchap on the Marsyangi River. The rest of the trek follows the Annapurna Circuit in reverse to Besisahar.

Mustang

Since 1991 trekkers have been allowed in limited numbers into **MUSTANG**, the high desert region north of Jomosom that still has its own nominal king. ACAP has taken over the management of the area for tourism purposes, but it's expensive to visit ($700 for the first ten days, $70 per day thereafter). The starting point is Jomosom – groups usually fly in and out – and the trip takes a minimum of ten days, following the Thak Khola north to two walled cities before doubling back on the same trail.

North of Kathmandu:
Helambu, Langtang and Gosainkund

Trekking **north of Kathmandu** is curiously underrated and uncrowded. The most accessible of all the trekking regions, it's well suited to one- or two-week itineraries, which is handy if you're trying to cram a trek into a short stay in Nepal or you don't want to stray far from Kathmandu. What it lacks in superlatives – there are no 8000-metre peaks in the vicinity (unless you count Shisha Pangma, across the border in Tibet) – it makes up for in base-to-peak rises that are as dramatic as anywhere. Langtang, in particular, delivers more amazing views in a short time than any other walk-in trek in Nepal, with the possible exception of the Annapurna Sanctuary.

Two distinct basins and an intervening *lek* (ridge) lend their names to the major treks here; each stands on its own, but given enough time and good weather you can mix and match them. **Helambu** is closest to Kathmandu, comprising the rugged north–south valleys and ridges that lie just beyond the northeast rim of the Kathmandu Valley. North of Helambu, running east–west and tantalizingly close to the Tibet border, lies the high, alpine **Langtang Valley**, which in its upper reaches burrows spec-

NORTH OF KATHMANDU BUS CONNECTIONS		
To and from Kathmandu	Frequency	Time
Dhunche	3/day	8hr
Malemchi Pul*		
Sundarijal	4/day	1hr
Trisuli	9/day	4hr

* No direct buses: take any bus up the Arniko Highway to Panchkal (3hr), from where buses run to Malemchi Pul (another 2hr).

GANESH
HIMAL

Trisuli River

Langtang Lirung
(7245m)
Langtang II
(6672m)
LANGTANG HIMAL
Yala Peak
Langtang (5033m)
Kyanjin

Pemthang
Karpo Ri
(6830m)

TIBET

Khangjung

LANGTANG VALLEY

Dhunche
Syabru
Sing Gompa

GOSAINKUND

LANGTANG
NATIONAL PARK

Ganja La
(5122m)

Dorje Lakpa
(6990m)

JUGAL
HIMAL

Ramche

Tharepati
Malemchi Gaun
Tarke Ghyang

Panch
Pokhari

Trisuli River

Gorkha

Trisuli Bazaar
Nuwakot

Tadi Khola

HELAMBU

Shermathang

Balephi Khola

Likhu Khola

Talamarang

Malemchi Khola

Indrawati Khola

Kakani

SHIVAPURI
WATERSHED

Pati Bhanjyang

N

Malemchi
Pul

Chautara

Sundarijal
Sankhu

0   10 km

KATHMANDU

**HELAMBU, LANGTANG
AND GOSAINKUND**

Tibet border

Dolalghat

tacularly between Langtang and Jugal Himals. **Gosainkund** comprises a chain of sacred lakes nestled in a rugged intermediate range northwest of Helambu. One practical inconvenience is that the connections between these three treks aren't reliable – winter snow may block the passes between Helambu and the other two – and done on their own, the Langtang and Gosainkund treks require you to retrace your steps for much of the return journey.

Food and lodging here is less luxurious than in the Annapurna and Everest regions, but never a problem on the usual routes.

Helambu

HELAMBU (or Helmu) is great for short treks: access from Kathmandu is easy, and an extensive trail network enables you to tailor a circuit to your schedule. The area spans a wide elevation range – there's a lot of up and down – but the highest point reached is only 2700–3200m (depending on route), so acclimatization is rarely a problem. Winter treks are particularly feasible. The peaks of Langtang Himal are often visible, but the views aren't as close-up as those in other areas. Helambu was once considered a hidden, sacred domain, and its misty ridges and fertile valleys are still comparatively isolated; relatively few people trek here, and with so many trails to choose from, they tend to spread themselves out. Helambu's Bhotiyas call themselves **Sherpa**, although they're only distant cousins of the Solu-Khumbu stock (see p.405): their ancestors probably migrated from Kyirong, the area just north of the Kodari border crossing. Tamangs are also numerous, while the valley bottoms are farmed mainly by Hindu castes.

Sundarijal, a local bus or taxi ride from Kathmandu, is the most common **starting point**, but alternative trailheads include Budhanilkantha, Sankhu, Kakani, Nagarkot and Malemchi Pul. However you go, first impressions are somewhat dispiriting – the Kathmandu Valley approaches are heavily populated, and the route from Malemchi Pul involves a rather tedious local bus ride from Panchkhal on the Arniko Highway – but things quickly improve as you get up onto the ridges. Entering the region from the Kathmandu Valley takes you through the Shivapuri Watershed (entry fee Rs250). Most trekkers make a loop around two main ridges and the valley of the Malemchi Khola, trying to stay as high as possible and taking in the villages of **Malemchi Gaun**, **Tarke Ghyang** and **Shermathang**. The walk between the second two is especially rewarding, passing picturesque monasteries and contouring through forests of oak, rhododendron and *lokta*, whose bark is used to make traditional paper. Countless other trails strike west and east to villages that see few trekkers.

Other variations on Helambu are more challenging. Gosainkund can be reached by a long, rugged day's walk from Tharepati, via a 4600-metre pass, but an overnight stop at Gopte or Phedi to acclimatize is advisable. The route to Langtang heads north from Tarke Ghyang over the 5122-metre **Ganja La**, a very tough three-day hike for which you'll need a tent, food, crampons and ice axe (it may be impassable Dec–March). From Tarke Ghyang, lesser trails lead to **Panch Pokhri** (3800m), a set of lakes two or three days to the east, and from there you could continue east or south to the Arniko Highway. All these routes take you into **Langtang National Park** (entry fee Rs650).

Langtang and Gosainkund

In contrast with Helambu, the Langtang and Gosainkund treks make straight for specific destinations, gaining elevation quickly and then leaving you to explore at your own pace. To return, a certain amount of backtracking is unavoidable, unless you cross into Helambu. Culture is not a big part of either, except during Janai Purnima, a massive Hindu **pilgrimage** held at Gosainkund during the full moon of July–August.

Both treks **start** at Dhunche (see p.237), about eight hours by bus from Kathmandu, and fall within **Langtang National Park** (entry fee Rs650).

Langtang

The **LANGTANG TREK** can be done in as little as a week, but day hikes in the upper valley are sure to detain you for at least another two or three days, and given more time you'll want to add Gosainkund to the itinerary. It takes about a day to get interesting, first following the continuation of the Dhunche road (a spectacularly destructive feat of engineering, built to reach a lead and zinc mine in the Ganesh Himal) up the unpromising side of the Bhote Koshi before leaving the road and rounding a bend to Syabru in the Langtang Valley. The next two days are spent climbing briskly up the gorge-like lower valley, where oaks and rhododendron give way to peaceful hemlock and larch forest; after ascending an old moraine, snowy peaks suddenly loom ahead and the gorge opens into a U-shaped glacial valley. Springtime is excellent for flowers here, and in autumn the berberis bushes turn a deep rust colour.

Two Bhotiya villages occupy the upper valley: **Langtang** (3300m), the bigger of the two, makes a good place to spend a night and acclimatize, while **Kyangjin** (3750m) boasts a small *gompa*, a cheese "factory" (fabulous yoghurt) and an attractive chalet-lodge. The Langtang Glacier is a full day's walk further up the valley. You'll want to spend at least a couple of nights in the upper valley to explore the glaciers and ascend **Tsergo Ri** (5033m), from which you can view an awesome white wilderness of peaks, including 8013-metre Shisha Pangma.

You can **return** by crossing into Helambu over the Ganja La (see above), but most people go back down the valley, varying the trip by going via Khangjung, high up on the grassy northern side, and Syabrubensi, site of a Tibetan resettlement project. To link up with Gosainkund, you have to backtrack to Syabru.

Gosainkund

GOSAINKUND can be trekked on its own in as little as four days, but because of its rapid ascent to high elevation – 4380m – it's best done after acclimatizing in Langtang or Helambu. Combined with either of these, it adds three or four days; a grand tour of all three areas takes sixteen or more days.

From either Dhunche or Syabru, trails ascend steeply through mossy rhododendron forest to the monastery and cheese factory of **Sing Gompa** at 3250m (the climb from Dhunche is particularly brutal). Above here, the trail climbs through tall fir stands before emerging above the tree line for increasingly panoramic views of the high peaks (Laurebinayak is a great place to stop) and finally entering the barren upper reaches of the Trisuli River, where glacial moraines and rockslides have left a string of half a dozen **lakes** (*kund*). Several lodges sit by the shore of **Gosainkund**, the most sacred of the lakes and renowned among Nepali Hindus. A famous legend recounts how Shiva, having saved the world by drinking a dangerous poison, struck this mountainside with his *trisul* to create the lake and cool his burning throat. In good weather you can climb a nearby summit (5144m) for superb views.

Everest (Solu-Khumbu)

Everest – or to give it its proper Nepali name, **Sagarmatha** ("Brow of the Ocean"), or its even more proper Sherpa name, **Chomolungma** ("Mother Goddess of the World") – is more a pilgrimage than a trek. As with all pilgrimages, it is a tough personal challenge with a clear goal at the end. Lasting images, however, are of the revelations along the way: remote monasteries, irrepressible Sherpas, and peaks with almost human moods and personalities. Prior experience isn't strictly necessary, but treks in this region require extra effort.

The Everest region is the main trekking destination east of Kathmandu, and in terms of popularity it runs second to Annapurna. It divides into two distinct areas, the lower, greener and more populous country to the south known as **Solu** – if you're not flying in, you'll probably begin at Jiri and spend the first week of your trek walking eastwards across Solu's deep canyons and tall ridges – and **Khumbu**, wedged between Solu and the Tibetan border, comprising the spectacular, harsh landscape of Everest and the surrounding peaks and glaciated valleys.

The challenge of **getting there** puts many people off. The choice is between **flying** into Lukla, at 2800m on the doorstep of Khumbu ($83 from Kathmandu; note the wrecked planes beside the runway), and taking the **bus** to Jiri in Solu (which adds 5–7 days' walking each way). In an ideal world, you would walk in from Jiri to get acclimatized and fly out of Lukla to avoid backtracking, but it seldom works out that way, as high-season flights may be booked up by organized trekking parties or grounded due to bad weather. Largely for this reason, more than half the people who trek Everest go with a group.

The walking in Solu is very strenuous, while in Khumbu, **altitude** is the overriding factor: to get a good look at Everest, you'll have to spend at least four nights above 4000m and at least one at around 5000m. There is a risk of developing acute mountain

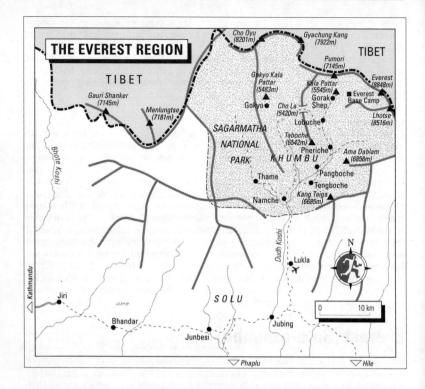

sickness (AMS) and you must know the signs. Not only is this the highest of the standard treks, it's also the **coldest**, so you'll need a good four-season bag, several layers of warm clothes, and sturdy boots that will keep out mud and snow. A great help on this front are the rental shops of Namche, in Khumbu, where you can stock up on high-altitude gear and return it on the way back down. Because of weather, the **trekking "window"** is especially short in Khumbu – early October to mid-November, and late March to late April – and this, in turn, creates a seasonal stampede on the trails and at the Lukla airstrip. Winter isn't out of the question, but it's just that much colder.

While Everest isn't as heavily trekked as Annapurna, its high-altitude **environment** is even more fragile. Khumbu, with only four thousand inhabitants, receives more than nine thousand trekkers a year (plus probably twice as many porters). Locals spend three times longer collecting firewood than they did a decade ago, and the demand for wood is now estimated to be three times the regeneration capacity of the area. Even some trek leaders privately admit that the best thing for Khumbu would be to give it a rest from trekking for a few years. Most of Khumbu is protected within **Sagarmatha National Park**, which is helping to preserve the remaining forest, but it can't be said often enough: have as little to do with wood-burning as possible.

The popular trails through Solu-Khumbu are all equipped with **teahouses**. The main Jiri–Lukla–Namche–Base Camp route is very straightforward, but a **guide** is advisable if you're planning to do anything unusual. Solu-Khumbu is the easiest area in Nepal to hire a **woman porter** – a Sherpani – although few speak enough English to serve as guides.

EVEREST REGION TRAVEL CONNECTIONS

To and from Kathmandu	Buses		Flights	
	Frequency	Time	Frequency	Time
Jiri	4/day	10hr		
Lamidanda			1/day	35min
Lukla			up to 10/day	40min
Phaplu			1–2/day	25min

Solu: the Jiri walk-in

The **JIRI WALK-IN** is the most popular Everest approach, as Jiri (see p.234) is connected by bus to Kathmandu, and innkeepers along the trail are reasonably accustomed to serving Westerners (other approaches are described later in the "Eastern Nepal" section). The **bus** is no picnic though, taking anywhere from ten to thirteen hours – experienced climbers often joke that they'd scale Everest tomorrow but they'll never take the bus to Jiri again. It's also possible to **fly** to Phaplu, four days east of Jiri, though it's not much cheaper ($77) than flying all the way to Lukla, three days further on.

Cutting across the lay of the land, the trail bobs between valleys as low as 1500m and passes as high as 3500m: the ups and downs can be disheartening, but the fitness and acclimatization gained come in handy later on. A few glimpses of peaks – notably Gauri Shankar (7145m) – urge you along during the first five or six days, although Solu's last-

THE SHERPAS

Nepal's most famous ethnic group, the **Sherpas** probably migrated to Solu-Khumbu four or five centuries ago from eastern Tibet; their name means "People from the East". They were originally nomads, driving their yaks to pasture in Tibet and wintering in Nepal, until change came from an unlikely quarter: the introduction of the potato in the 1830s is believed to have been the catalyst that caused Sherpas to settle in villages, and the extra wealth brought by this simple innovation financed the building of most monasteries visible today.

Sherpas maintain the highest permanent settlements in the world – up to 4700m – which accounts for their legendary hardiness at altitude. Their mountaineering talents were discovered as early as 1907, and by the 1920s hundreds of Sherpas were signing on as **porters** with expeditions to Everest and other Himalayan peaks – from the Tibet side, ironically, as Nepal was closed to foreigners at the time. When mountaineering expeditions were finally allowed into Nepal in 1949, Sherpas took over the lion's share of the portering work, and four years later **Tenzing Norgay** reached the top of Everest, clinching Sherpas' worldwide fame. The break couldn't have come at a better time, for trans-Himalayan trade, once an important source of income, was cut short by the Chinese occupation of Tibet in 1959. Since then, Sherpas have deftly diversified into tourism, starting their own trekking and mountaineering agencies, opening lodges and selling souvenirs. Conveniently, the trekking season doesn't conflict with summer farming duties.

Like Tibetans and other Bhotiya groups, Sherpas are devout Buddhists, and most villages of note support a *gompa* and a few monks (or nuns). But in a throwback to animism that's perfectly permissible in Lamaist Buddhism, they revere **Khumbila**, a sacred peak just north of Namche, as a sort of tribal totem, and regard fire as a deity (it's disrespectful to throw rubbish into a Sherpa hearth). Sherpas eat meat, of course, but in deference to the *dharma* they draw the line at slaughtering it – they hire Tibetans to do that.

ing images are of tumbling gorges, rhododendron forests and terraced fields hewn out of steep hillsides. Solu has benefited from several projects funded by **Edmund Hillary's Himalayan Trust**; groups of children may accompany you on their way to one of the "Hillary" schools in the area.

The route passes through some important Sherpa villages, notably **Bhandar** and **Junbesi**, the latter with an active monastery and a "village tourism" programme. Most trekkers are understandably impatient to get up to Everest or back to Kathmandu, but side trips to the cheese "factory" at **Thodung** and **Thubten Chholing Gompa** north of Junbesi are fascinating. From **Jubing**, a Rai village five days in, the trail finally bends north towards Everest, following the valley of the Dudh Koshi. Two days later, it side-steps **Lukla** and joins the well-trodden route to Khumbu.

The bulk of traffic through Solu consists of porters humping in gear for trekking groups and expeditions flying into Lukla, and this is reflected in the no-frills **food and lodging** available.

Khumbu: the Everest trek

The trail north from Lukla is the trunk route of the **EVEREST TREK**: everyone walks it at least once, and all but a few backtrack along it as well. Most trekkers follow it to the end at Kala Pattar (the classic viewpoint of Everest) and Everest Base Camp, both about eight days northeast of Lukla; quite a few combine this with a trip to the beautiful Gokyo Lakes, about the same distance north of Lukla.

Khumbu **lodges** are heavily geared for trekkers, and you should have no trouble getting a bunk and a good meal wherever you go along the busier trails. Prices aren't unreasonable, considering the distance supplies have to be carried, but they do rise steadily as you go up. An additional expense is the Rs650 entry fee for **Sagarmatha National Park**.

Lukla to Everest Base Camp and Kala Pattar

From Lukla the trail meanders north along the Dudh Koshi before bounding up to **Namche** (3450m), where Khumbu and the serious scenery start. Nestled handsomely in a horseshoe bowl, the Sherpa "capital" has done very well out of mountaineering and trekking over the years. Besides trekking equipment, Namche's shops sell absolutely anything a trekker could desire – film, maps, batteries, Mars bars from around the world, a dozen styles of Swiss Army knife, albeit all at inflated prices. There's also a bank, post office and even Internet access. Try to make your trip coincide with the pan-cultural **Saturday market**, or visit the national park **visitors' centre**, perched on the ridge east of town, which contains an informative museum.

Beyond Namche, the trail veers northeast into a tributary valley and climbs to **Tengboche**, surrounded by protected juniper forest and commanding a show-stealing view of everybody's favourite peak, Ama Dablam (6828m). Tengboche's much-photographed monastery, which burned down in 1989 when its newly installed electrical wiring malfunctioned (is there a lesson in this?), has now been rebuilt. Mani Rimdu, the Sherpa dance-drama **festival**, is held here on the full moon of November–December. The trail continues to **Pangboche**, containing Khumbu's oldest *gompa*, where for a donation the lama will show you some yeti relics, and on to **Pheriche** (4250m), site of a **Himalayan Rescue Association post** (AMS talks every afternoon during the trekking season). From here up, settlements are strictly seasonal, and their stone enclosures and slate-roofed huts are reminiscent of Scottish crofts.

From Pheriche the route bends north again, ascending the moraine of the Khumbu Glacier and passing a series of monuments to Sherpas killed on Everest, to reach **Lobuche** (4930m). Another day's march along the glacier's lateral moraine brings you

EVEREST

In 1849, while taking routine measurements from the plains, members of the Survey of India logged a previously unnoted summit which they labelled simply Peak XV. Three years later, computations revealed it to be the world's highest mountain, and the British subsequently named it after **Sir George Everest**, head of the Survey of India from 1823 to 1843. Politically off-limits until the early twentieth century, the climb to the summit was first attempted from the Tibetan side in 1922 by a British party that included **George Mallory**, who coined the famous "because it is there" phrase. Two years later, Mallory and Andrew Irvine reached at least 8500m – without oxygen – before disappearing into a cloud; their bodies were never found, but some believe that they reached the summit. Several more attempts were made until World War II suspended activities, and climbs were further hampered by the Chinese invasion of Tibet in 1950, which closed the northern approach to mountaineers.

With the opening of Nepal in 1951, however, attention turned to southern approaches and a race between the Swiss and the British was on. The mountain was finally scaled, using a route via the South Col, by New Zealander **Edmund Hillary** and Sherpa **Tenzing Norgay** in a British-led expedition in 1953. On the morning of May 29, Hillary planted the Union Jack, the Nepalese and United Nations flags on the summit; Tenzing left an offering of sweets and biscuits to the mountain's gods.

Throughout the next two decades, increasingly big expeditions put men and women on the top by various routes, and sometimes got carried away in their bids for lucrative sponsorship – in 1970 a Japanese, **Yuiichi Miura**, attempted to ski down the mountain, but made it only 1500 vertical metres before falling and almost disappearing down a crevasse (others have since skied and also snowboarded further). In the mid-1970s the trend shifted from large-scale assaults to small, quick "alpine-style" ascents. Dominating the field for more than a decade, **Reinhold Messner** was one of two climbers to reach the summit without oxygen in 1978, and in 1980 he made the first successful solo ascent of Everest.

Other records continue to fall. Briton **Allison Hargreaves** became the first woman to reach the summit without oxygen in 1995 (tragically, she died on K2 later the same year). In 1998, **Kazi Sherpa** achieved the fastest ascent from Base Camp – 20 hours, 24 minutes – via the southeast ridge. Meanwhile, **Ang Rita Sherpa** notched up his tenth successful climb of Everest in 1998, while his younger compatriot **Appa Sherpa** reached the top for a ninth time.

One record that can only be broken is the number of people who have reached the summit. At the time of writing, more than 700 climbers had successfully ascended Everest, and with "commercial" Everest expeditions opening up the mountain to less experienced climbers (who pay as much as $65,000 for a place) the number is rising rapidly. So, too, is Everest's **death toll**. At the time of writing, nearly 150 people had died on the mountain (eight of them in the much-publicized guided-climb fiasco chronicled in Jon Krakauer's *Into Thin Air*); historically, three out of every hundred climbers ascending above Base Camp have perished.

to **Gorak Shep** (5180m), the last huddle of teahouses – and a cold, probably sleepless night. The payoff comes when you climb up the grassy mound of **Kala Pattar** (5545m): the extra height provides an unbelievable panorama, not only of **Everest** (8848m) but also of its neighbours Lhotse (Nepal's third-highest peak, at 8516m) and Nuptse (7861m), as well as the sugarloaf of Pumori (7165m). A separate day trip can be made across the amazing Khumbu Glacier to **Everest Base Camp**. In spring you may encounter a half-dozen or more expedition parties here, constantly ferrying supplies up the dangerous Khumbu Icefall to higher camps; the climbers may be happy to have well-wishers, but if they seem wary of trekkers you can't blame them.

Gokyo Lakes

The scenery is every bit as good at **Gokyo Lakes**, in the next valley to the west, and other trekkers are noticeably fewer. If you're equipped to cross a snowy pass and are good at route-finding, you can be there in two days from Gorak Shep, crossing the strenuous **Cho La** (5420m) west of Lobuche and descending a treacherous scree slope. Otherwise, you'll have to backtrack almost to Tengboche, and then follow the Dudh Koshi north for two days to Gokyo, set beside the immense Ngozumba Glacier (the biggest in Nepal). Several brilliant blue lakes, dammed up by the glacier's lateral moraine, dot the west side of the valley above and below Gokyo. The high point of Gokyo is an overlook called, again, **Kala Pattar**, surveying a clutter of blue teeth – Cho Oyu, Everest and Lhotse are just the ones over 8000m – and the long grey tongue of the Ngozumba Glacier. You can also scramble north beside the glacier as far as Cho Oyu Base Camp.

Eastern Nepal

Treks in **eastern Nepal** are hampered by a fundamental problem of access: Hile, the principal trailhead, is an eighteen-hour bus journey from Kathmandu. However, it's possible to enter (or leave) this region by way of Everest, which cuts out the long ride in one direction. Flights are also good value for money here – the one from Kathmandu to Tumlingtar costs only $57. **Food and lodging** is patchy, though, and seldom geared for trekkers.

Ethnically, eastern Nepal is even more diverse than the Annapurna region: Rais and Limbus are dominant in the hills, Gurungs and Magars are found in smaller numbers, while Sherpas, Tamangs and other Bhotiyas inhabit the high country and Hindu castes

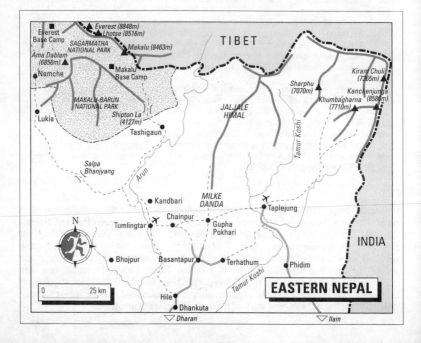

the valleys. Makalu and Kanchenjunga provide stunning **views** from most high points. Flora and fauna are also of great interest to specialists, especially the **butterflies** and other insects of the upper Arun Valley, and the **rhododendrons** of the Milke Daada.

The Everest eastern approach

While still not nearly as developed as the Jiri walk-in, the **EASTERN APPROACH** to Everest is becoming more popular and facilities along it are expanding yearly. It's usually treated as an "escape route" from Everest by trekkers who want to avoid the long backtrack to Jiri; there's no reason why the itinerary can't be done in reverse, except perhaps that it's better to gain some confidence on the more developed Everest trails before tackling this less-trekked region. Another factor to consider is the **season**: try to do the lower section of the trek when it's cooler.

The **route** leaves the Jiri walk-in at **Kharte**, about a day south of Lukla, and heads southeastwards to reach Tumlingtar five to seven days later. Part of this stretch traverses the Makalu-Barun Conservation Area (see below), and an entrance fee may be required. The first half of the trek passes through tangled hills inhabited mainly by Rais; after reaching a high point at the lush Salpa Bhanjyang (3350m), it descends steadily to the deep, hot and predominantly Hindu Arun Valley. **Tumlingtar** is a busy bazaar overlooking the Arun; RNAC flies from there to Kathmandu about four times a week ($57). If you're returning to Kathmandu by bus, carry on to Hile (see p.370), two days south and 1400m higher. The route is equipped with **teahouses** and a guide isn't needed, but don't expect English signs or fancy food. You'd be wise to bring a few provisions just in case.

For more adventure, you could carry on walking from Tumlingtar **to Phidim** (see p.374) by way of Chainpur, a tidy village renowned for its brassware, and the Milke Daada (see below). Another route aims roughly due south from Lukla **to Lamidanda** (daily to Kathmandu; $66). If you can't get on a flight there, trails continue south to the Tarai or east to Hile via Bhojpur, Nepal's most famous *khukuri*-making centre.

THE YETI

The **yeti** ("man of the rocky places") has been a staple of Sherpa and Tibetan folklore for centuries, but stories of hairy, ape-like creatures roaming the snowy heights first came to the attention of the outside world during the early days of British rule in India. Explorers in Tibet reported seeing mysterious moving figures and large, unidentified footprints in the snow – captivated by the reports, an imaginative Fleet Street hack coined the term "abominable snowman" – but it wasn't until 1951, during the first British Everest expedition from the Nepal side, that climber Eric Shipton took clear photographs of yeti tracks. Since then, several highly publicized yeti-hunts, including one led by Sir Edmund Hillary in 1960, have brought back a wealth of circumstantial evidence but not one authenticated sighting.

Sceptics dismiss the yeti as a straightforward myth, of course, arguing that the hairy creatures in question are more likely bears, and that the oversized footprints could be any animal's tracks, melted and enlarged by the sun. Meanwhile, relics kept at the *gompa* of Pangboche and Khumjung have failed to provide scientific proof of the yeti's existence. The "skulls" have been examined by experts and deemed to be made of serow (Himalayan wild goat) skins, while the skeletal hand at Pangboche is presumed to be human. Yet yaks continue to be mauled, and Sherpas insist the yeti isn't a hoax. Perhaps the most significant aspect of the yeti is humans' reaction to it: we want it to exist, like the Loch Ness Monster – some secret part of the world that mankind hasn't yet discovered and explained – yet in our endless curiosity we want to find and dissect it. Thankfully, it has eluded us so far.

<table>
<tr><td colspan="5">EASTERN NEPAL TRAVEL CONNECTIONS</td></tr>
</table>

	Buses		Flights	
	Frequency	Time	Frequency	Time
To and from Kathmandu				
Basantapur	*			
Hile	1/night	18hr		
Ilam/Phidim	**			
Taplejung	**		3–5/wk	2hr#
Tumlingtar			3–4/wk	55min

* No direct buses: change at Dharan or Hile.
** No direct buses: change at Birtamod.
# Via Biratnagar.

Other treks in eastern Nepal

Many hill treks north of Hile and Ilam are probably feasible without supplies. Development workers in the area rave about a circuit from Phidim to Basantapur via Taplejung. Bhojpur, Chainpur and Khadbari, quintessential Newar hill towns within two or three days' walk of Hile, also make great targets. This is fine country for adventurous trekkers who like exploring places that aren't written up in guidebooks, and this book isn't going to spoil that pleasure by writing about them.

However, here are three more conventional treks which, though they would be difficult to do independently, are finding their way into agency brochures.

The Milke Daada

A long north–south ridge famed for its rhododendrons, the **MILKE DAADA** can be linked up with a visit to Chainpur for a seven- to ten-day trek that combines spectacular flora with one of Nepal's best bazaars. The route goes no higher than 3500m, but takes in plenty of mountain views. From Basantapur (see p.371) the route heads north, initially following the main porter trail to Taplejung and then continuing north through the lush cloud forest of the Milke Daada. Various trails to **Chainpur** branch off to the west; from there you can continue to the airstrip at Tumlingtar ($57 to Kathmandu) or return to Hile. Alternatively, you could head east from Gupha Pokhari to Taplejung ($137 to Kathmandu, via Biratnagar).

Basic **food and lodging** can be found along most of this route, but the absence of teahouses north of Gupha Pokhari limits an independent trekker's ability to explore the Milke Daada. Groups with porter support can continue north into the Jaljale Himal.

Makalu Base Camp

MAKALU BASE CAMP, a three-week trek from Hile up the Arun Valley and over the Shipton La (4127m), requires a tent and food for ten days; the last teahouse is at Tashi Gaun, less than a day beyond where the trail leaves the Arun. Much of this trek passes through the wild and remote **Makalu-Barun National Park** and the contiguous **Makalu-Barun Conservation Area** (Rs1000 entry fee), which forms a protective buffer zone in the inhabited area to the south and east. Established in 1992, the park is intended to stem the growing human pressure around the base-camp area and preserve what is regarded as one of the most biologically diverse areas in the Himalaya. The conservation area, meanwhile, is supposed to be modelled on the Annapurna Conservation Area Project and operate on similar principles of involving locals in conservation.

Kanchenjunga

The most incredible trek in this part of Nepal is to the foot of **KANCHENJUNGA**, at 8586m the third-highest peak in the world. Kanchenjunga is an expensive trek because it's restricted to agency-organized groups. Because of its remote location in the extreme northeastern corner of the country, most groups fly in and out of Taplejung ($137 from Kathmandu), which requires a plane change in Biratnagar. To save money and take in some pretty hill country, you could walk to Taplejung from Basantapur (see p.371) in three days, but you'd still have to have a couple of porters toting two weeks' worth of supplies. Two separate routes head northeastwards from Taplejung, one to the so-called North Base Camp and Pang Pema, the other to the South Base Camp and the Yalung Glacier; these routes can be combined into a circuit.

Far western Nepal

West of Dhaulagiri, the Himalaya subside somewhat and retreat north into Tibet, and the band of foothills flares out to become an almost impenetrable jumble. The northern third of the region, left in the rain shadow of the foothills, receives little monsoon moisture – in every way but politically, this highland strip is part of Tibet. Jagged Himalayan grandeur isn't so much in evidence, but there's a wildness and a vastness here, and the feeling of isolation is thrilling. The **far west** is the deep end of trekking in Nepal, and the treks here are well off the beaten track: they're a chore to get to, they require a lot of preparation and, with the exception of Rara Lake, you'll find that very few Westerners have gone before you. All that might appeal if you're an experienced trekker looking for new challenges, but if you're a first-timer without agency support, forget it.

Logistics make or break a trek in the far west. Given the distances involved, you'll need to fly to the starting point, but **flights** from Kathmandu all go by way of Nepalganj; they're often delayed, and Nepalganj isn't a great place to be stuck waiting for a plane.

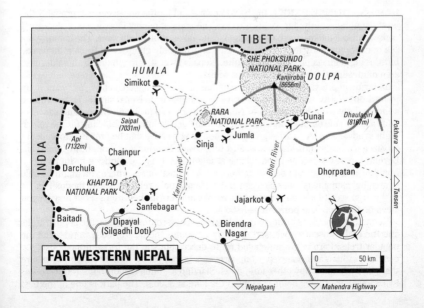

WESTERN NEPAL TRAVEL CONNECTIONS

To reach any of the trailheads in this region from either Kathmandu or Pokhara, it's necessary first to travel to Nepalganj or Dhangadhi. Onward connections from there are detailed in the boxes on p.294 and p.330.

	Buses		**Flights**	
	Frequency	Time	Frequency	Time
To and from Kathmandu				
Dhangadhi	2	18hr	1–2/week	1hr 50min*
Nepalganj	5	12hr	4–5/day	1hr 10min*
To and from Pokhara				
Dhangadhi	1	18hr		
Nepalganj	2	12hr		
* Indirect flights will take longer.				

Food and lodging are in uncomfortably short supply, so you'll need to bring a tent, cooking utensils and at least some provisions. You should be prepared to carry it all yourself, because **porters** here are a fickle lot and often can't be spared from their farmwork. **Guides** are also scarce, so you shouldn't venture out without a reasonable command of Nepali. If you go on an **organized trek** you may not be entirely insulated from these inconveniences, and for this reason agencies may try to steer you towards more easterly destinations.

As roads gradually penetrate into the far west, trekking might become easier. In the meantime, the four treks described below are the most realistic possibilities. Three require a standard trekking permit; the fourth, Dolpo, requires a special permit.

Rara National Park

RARA NATIONAL PARK is the best known – and for the non-specialist, probably the least daunting – of the far western treks. The usual itinerary is a loop that starts and ends at Jumla, 150km north of Nepalganj, and takes about eight days. The country is a sea of choppy, mostly forested mountains, offering only glimpses of Himalayan peaks, but the highlight is pristine **Rara Lake**, Nepal's largest, surrounded by a wilderness area of meadows, forest and abundant wildlife.

In terms of practicalities, the Rara trek has always been a challenge. You want to **fly in and out**. RNAC and Lumbini Airways fly to Jumla from Nepalganj ($57), but getting a timely flight from Kathmandu to Nepalganj ($99) is a problem. Delays and cancellations are the rule on the Jumla leg, and you can't get a confirmed booking for the return flight in advance – try to arrange this as soon as you arrive, but be prepared to walk out to Birendra Nagar (Surkhet), a week's hike away. **Food** can be bought in Jumla, but beyond the bazaar is often unavailable at any price. There are **lodges** in Jumla and a bunkhouse at the lake; in between, there are a few teahouses where you might be able to stay, but camping is more pleasant and certainly more reliable. The orthodox Hindus of the area aren't keen on having outcaste Westerners in their homes, but may let you sleep on the roof. The **park fee** is Rs650.

Technical difficulties aside, Rara makes a fair compromise between the popular treks and the really obscure ones, and in a way combines the best of both worlds: like the popular treks, Rara is given detailed route descriptions in the trekking books so you can do it without an organized group or even a guide, yet it's remote enough to ensure that you'll see few if any other foreigners. Starting at Jumla (2400m), the route crosses two 3500-metre ridges before reaching the lake at 3000m. The park is one of the best places in Nepal to see mountain **wildlife**, including Himalayan black bear, tahr, goral, musk deer and the rare red (lesser) panda. Autumn and spring are the **best seasons**, and Rara is particularly worth considering in May and June, when the weather elsewhere is getting too hot or unpredictable. A day and a half south of the lake is **Sinja**, where the ruins of the capital of the twelfth- to fourteenth-century Khasa dynasty (see "The historical framework" in Contexts) can be viewed across the river.

Dolpo (She-Phoksundo National Park)

DOLPO (sometimes written Dolpa) is an enormous, isolated district northwest of Dhaulagiri and bordering Tibet, the western half of which has been set aside as **SHE-PHOKSUNDO NATIONAL PARK**, Nepal's biggest. The park, established in 1984, protects an awe-inspiring region of deep valleys, unclimbed peaks, remote monasteries and rare fauna. Dolpo was the setting of Peter Matthiessen's *The Snow Leopard* (see "Books" in Contexts), and until recently the book was as close as most foreigners were allowed to get to it. Southern ("Lower") Dolpo is now open to independent trekkers and is gaining in popularity; the permit costs $10 per week. (Northern, or "Upper", Dolpo is also open, but only to groups, and is much more expensive – $700 for the first ten days, $70 per day thereafter.) There are teahouses, but it's a food-deficit area so you'll need to bring several days' worth of provisions. Guides and porters, pretty well essential here, can be hired in Dunai. The climate is continental and only slightly affected by the monsoon, so the **best time to go** is May to September.

Dolpo lies between Dhorpatan and Rara, and two of these treks, or even all three, could be combined into a single tour from Pokhara to Jumla – this would take a minimum of four weeks. Dolpo on its own takes one to two weeks, assuming you fly in and out of **Dunai** ($77 each way from Nepalganj). Everyone heads north from there, entering the park after about a day (Rs650 **entry fee**) and reaching Ringmo and the stunningly blue **Phoksundo Tal** after another two days. There are plenty of day-hiking opportunities around the lake. From there you can retrace your route to Dunai or, given an extra week, take a much longer, harder route westwards over the Kagmara La (5114m), returning eastwards over the Balangra La (3837m). It's also possible to continue walking south from Dunai to Jajarkot, where there's a road and buses.

Other treks in far western Nepal

These last two treks are fairly obscure: most agencies don't do the first, and those that do charge a lot of money; the second is open to independent trekking, but you'd have to be very independent indeed to tackle it.

Humla and treks to Tibet

Tucked away in the extreme northwest corner of Nepal, **HUMLA** is high, dry and strongly Tibetan. Snowcapped peaks hem the district in on three sides and shut out most outside influences, including the monsoon. It's open only to organized groups, and the permit costs $90 for the first week, $15 per day thereafter (treks into Tibet carry additional fees of at least $500). This area is prone to food shortages and in recent years has experienced serious spring and early-summer famines, so it's essential to bring all the food you'll need and then some.

RNAC **flies** from Nepalganj to **Simikot** (Humla's district headquarters) about every other day ($88). The most popular trek from there goes straight north to the **Tibet** border at the Nara La (3426m), about five days' walking, from where a jeep will take you to the starting point for the three-day-plus circumambulation of sacred **Mount Kailas**. Staying in Nepal, the standard itinerary is a seven- to nine-day walk to Jumla, stopping at Rara Lake along the way. Doing it vice versa – going towards the mountains – would seem more natural, but bear in mind that Jumla is easier to get out of than Simikot. The trail involves a good deal of up and down, but goes no higher than 3600m. In May–June, which is the **best time** to go, the wildflowers are out of this world.

Khaptad National Park

Set on a plateau in the middle of the foothills, **KHAPTAD NATIONAL PARK** is, for lack of a better term, a spiritual park. A five-square-kilometre core area has been set aside for "meditation and tranquillity", comprising a pilgrimage spot of Hindu shrines and sacred streams. Hovering at about 3000m, the plateau consists of rolling, open grassland and forest, with views of Saipal (7031m) and Api (7132m), the far west's tallest peaks. The main attractions are a sacred confluence, site of the Ganga Deshara **festival** in May–June, and the hut of the late **Khaptad Baba**, a famous mountaintop guru who was until his recent death literally the centrepiece of the park.

Two year-round **airstrips** – at Bajhang/Chainpur ($77 from Nepalganj) and Sanfebagar ($61 from Nepalganj) – are within one or two days' walk of the park, making it possible to do this trek in as little as a week. **Food and lodging** are available at the airstrip towns, the southern park entrance and the park HQ. The food is poor and you'll want to bring as much of your own as possible, but you should be able to get by without a porter. The park **entry fee** is Rs650.

CHAPTER EIGHT

RAFTING AND KAYAKING

I n recent years **rafting** and **kayaking** have really boomed in Nepal, with many visitors coming to the country specifically for river running. The reason? Big mountains mean big, exciting, scenic rivers. Nepal has some of the best whitewater in the world – a few of the longer trips are world classics, offering the experience of a lifetime – and rafting in Nepal is incredible value for money when compared to other countries. So if you ever thought you might like to try rafting or kayaking, then this might be the place to do it.

A river trip is a wonderful way to experience Nepal. You actually see more of the traditional countryside while rafting than you do on one of the apple-pie treks, and in fact some of the remoter trips entail mini-treks through little-visited areas just to get to the put-in point. Then there's the sheer escapism of life on the river: camping on white sand beaches, campfires under the stars, warm water (most rivers in Nepal are at lower, semi-tropical elevations), green jungle-clad slopes, wildlife and birds (bring your binoculars), and the tranquillity of being away from towns and roads. And of course there are the thrills, laughter and companionship that come from shooting rapids. It's also worth mentioning that almost all rivers in Nepal are clean, and there are almost no nasty biting insects on the beaches (mosquitoes are very rare).

When to go
Time of year makes an enormous difference to water volumes: flows during the height of the monsoon (July and August) are ten or more times greater than in February and March. The major rivers are off-limits to all but experts during the monsoon, and if you're a beginner you probably won't want to try rafting until mid-October, when things have calmed down.

The water is more manageably exciting in late October through November, which is the peak rafting season, and becomes mellower (but colder) from December through to April or May, when snowmelt begins to add to flows again. Winter isn't as chilly as you might think, since most raftable river sections are below 500m elevation, but it's a slow time for tourism generally in Nepal, so many river operators don't run trips then. March and April are the best months for long, warm days and excellent bird-watching.

However, different rivers are at their best at different times of the year – for example, the Sun Koshi is actually quite good starting in late September – so which river you go on will depend to a large extent on when you're in Nepal. Also note that a given trip will take less time in high water than when the water is running more slowly.

Rafting operators and agents
A fairly sophisticated river-running industry exists in Nepal, with dozens of Nepali and Western-run **rafting operators** offering both scheduled and customized trips. Unless

you're an experienced kayaker (see below) or are on some sort of a self-organized expedition, you'll go with one of these companies. The standards of most operators are high and exceed international guidelines, but as with most things in life, you get what you pay for. Trip prices and quality vary enormously, so if you buy the cheapest trip from a budget operator you may have a thoroughly miserable and dangerous experience.

A few of the more reputable Nepal-based operators are listed in the Kathmandu and Pokhara sections (pp.137 & 273). These deal with bookings from overseas, but they'll also take walk-in clients, and if you can muster up a few friends you can arrange your own customized departure. Booking with an agency in your own country (see list, p.60) is more expensive, of course, but it guarantees arrangements ahead of time – in high season the best trips are fully booked weeks in advance.

Some of the cut-price outfits in Kathmandu and Pokhara aren't bad, but making recommendations would be misleading – companies come and go, and standards rise and fall from one season to the next. Shop around, and press operators hard on the criteria given below. Only use a company belonging to the Nepal Association of Rafting Agents, a trade body that sets safety standards, requires its members to employ only trained and licensed guides, and handles complaints.

Many places advertising rafting trips are merely **agents**, who usually don't know what they're talking about and who will add their own commission (low or high) to the operator's price, so you're strongly advised to **book directly with the rafting operator**. Another reason for dealing directly with the operator is that you can find out who else is booked on the trip, which might well influence your enjoyment.

Costs and red tape

Trips booked in Nepal **cost** from $15 to $75 a day, depending on the river, number of people in the party, and standard of service. For trips on the Trisuli and Kali Gandaki (the most popular rafting rivers), upmarket companies typically charge $30–40 a day to a walk-in customer, which should include transport to and from the river by private van and good, hygienic meals. Budget outfits offer these trips for around $20 a day, but at that price you can expect to travel by regular bus and be served pretty unappetizing food; anyone charging less than $20 is likely to make you buy your own bus tickets and meals. (Other more remote rivers cost $10–20 a day extra.) These prices assume full rafts, which hold up to seven paying passengers each.

Your rafting company is responsible for arranging the rafting **permit**, which costs around $10 per person and is normally included in the package (one passport photo required). Budget operators may collect permit fees and pocket the money.

Be sure to check that your travel **insurance** policy covers for your proposed activity. If you're going to be away from main roads then helicopter rescue may be needed, and no helicopter will take off without cash in hand or the assurance of repayment by an insurance company. Leave a copy of your travel policy with the operator, highlighting the telephone number they should contact in case of an emergency.

Equipment

Most companies use **paddle rafts**, in which everyone paddles and the guide steers from the rear – lots of fun and group participation. On less exciting oar trips, the guide does all the work, giving the clients the chance to sit back and enjoy the scenery.

Your rafting company will advise you what to **bring**, but you'll definitely need a swimsuit, sunglasses, plenty of suntan lotion, rubber-soled shoes or sport sandals, a change of clothes and shoes for camp, a towel, a head torch/flashlight and spare batteries. Cotton T-shirts and shorts are standard river wear, but if the weather is likely to be cold and/or wet bring thermal tops and trousers, since cotton provides no warmth when wet; the better companies furnish wetsuits, thermal tops and paddling jackets. Tents, foam mattresses and waterproof bags are normally supplied, but you need to bring your own sleeping bag (rentable in Nepal). Some companies provide special waterproof boxes or barrels for cameras, but a better idea may be to buy a disposable waterproof camera.

Safety and the environment

By and large, rafting is a reasonably safe activity with a much better accident rate than, say, mountain-biking or skiing (or for that matter trekking). However, **safety** is a perennial worry because there are few government controls on Nepal's low-end operators. In recent years there have been a couple of fatalities of Western clients – the first in two decades, mind you – and it's probably no coincidence that these involved low-budget operators.

Make sure the company supplies lifejackets, helmets and a full first-aid kit, and satisfy yourself that the rafts are in good running order and that there will be a safety demonstration before entering the river. There must be a minimum of **two rafts**, in case one capsizes. In high-water conditions or on more difficult rivers, the rafts should be self-bailing and there should be **safety kayakers** to rescue "swimmers". (A few companies provide safety kayaks on all trips as a matter of course.) Most important of all, **guides** must be trained, certified, have experience guiding on the stretch of river in question, and speak adequate English (there should be an opportunity to meet guides before departure).

Rafters have the same responsibilities to **the environment** as trekkers, particularly regarding firewood, sanitation and litter – see the tips on p.390.

Kayaking and other river sports

In the last few years Nepal has taken off as one of the world's leading destinations for recreational **kayaking**, and is now recognized as the best country in the world for whitewater multi-day trips. The old myths of Nepal's rivers being only for macho expeditions have now largely been exploded, and the message has got out that they're easily accessible and suitable for all abilities, including beginners.

Most visiting kayakers start by booking on a rafting trip for a warm-up – often on the Sun Koshi or Kali Gandaki rivers. If you book on as a kayaker, the rafting company will normally provide you free use of a kayak as part of the deal, or give you a discount of around $10 a day if you bring your own boat. There is a wide selection of modern kayaks available for **rent** at around $15 a day in both Kathmandu and Pokhara – the latter has become quite a thriving centre for kayakers, with an excellent rental outlet (Ganesh Shop). It's worth bringing all your own personal kayaking gear with you, but this also is available for rent if necessary. Many people bring their own boats as well, but some have ended up paying high excess-baggage charges on the way back, so if you're considering doing this you should talk to other kayakers who have visited Nepal recently, and search for up-to-date advice through the Internet.

Kayak schools are a recent development in Nepal as travellers – often people who've got a taste for it through a rafting trip – have begun to realize that Nepal is a perfect place to learn to kayak. Most clinics start with a half-day introduction on Phewa Tal in Pokhara, then proceed to the nearby Seti River for another four days' practice and paddling with rafting support. The Seti is warmed by geothermal springs, making it a very pleasant place to practise rolling. Typical price for a five-day course is around $300, which includes tuition, gear, food, transport, raft support and camping. That's great value, with the added attraction of being able to casually mention that you learned to kayak in the Himalayas.

Yet another conveyance for enjoying Nepal's whitewater is the **hydrospeed**, a sort of boogie board for swimming down rivers. Pokhara's Ganesh Shop rents out hydrospeeds with wetsuits and helmets for $15 a day. It also rents out inflatable canoes (known as "**duckies**") and **catarafts** for those planning a do-it-yourself trip.

The rivers

Your choice of where to raft will be largely dictated by what the rafting companies are running when you're in Nepal. But within that context, consider what you're after in a river trip – thrills, scenery, culture, relaxation – as well as how much time and money you're willing to invest. For more information on these and other rivers of Nepal, you'll definitely want to get yourself a copy of *White Water Nepal* or *Rafting Nepal* (see "Books" in Contexts).

Note that the building of new roads and dams is putting the status of Nepal's rafting rivers in a state of flux. A number of proposed or planned hydroelectric dams and diversions – an important part of the country's development strategy – may eventually shorten or eliminate some popular rafting trips, and put more pressure on the remaining ones. But on the other hand, roads – which are supposedly being extended to every district headquarters as part of another strategic policy, and are sometimes also built to access new dams – can open up previously unrunnable river sections by creating new put-in and take-out points.

The descriptions that follow are given roughly in order of most to least popular/accessible.

The Trisuli

Perhaps seventy percent of all raft trips are done on the **Trisuli**, west of Kathmandu, and this is an obvious choice if your time is limited and you're looking for a short introduction to rafting at the cheapest possible price. Most itineraries are two or three days. The Trisuli has some rapids of medium difficulty (Class 3+) and good scenery, though it's hardly wilderness – the main road to Kathmandu follows it the entire way, and campsites can be noisy. In October and November you'll have to share the river with many other parties and perhaps compete for beaches. Some operators have their own campsites and boast of "road support", meaning the overnight gear is kept in a van, which precludes camping on the river's less crowded and usually quieter north side.

Ask where the put-in point is: anything starting at Kuringhat or Mugling will mainly be a relaxing float trip. The best whitewater section is upstream of Mugling, from Charoundi to Kuringhat, and this can be done as a full-on half day's trip (perhaps as a break in the journey from Kathmandu to Pokhara).

RIVER CLASSIFICATIONS

Here's a summary of the international classification system of rafting river difficulty.

Class 1. Easy. Moving water with occasional small rapids. Few or no obstacles.

Class 2. Moderate. Small rapids with regular waves. Some manoeuvring required but easy to navigate.

Class 3. Difficult. Rapids with irregular waves and hazards that need avoiding. More difficult manoeuvring required but routes are normally obvious. Scouting from the shore is occasionally necessary.

Class 4. Very difficult. Large rapids that require careful manoeuvring. Dangerous hazards. Scouting from the shore is often necessary and rescue is usually difficult. Kayakers should be able to roll. Turbulent water and large irregular waves may flip rafts. In the event of a mishap, there is significant risk of loss, damage and/or injury.

Class 5. Extremely difficult. Long and very violent rapids with severe hazards. Continuous, powerful, confused water makes route-finding difficult and scouting from the shore is essential. Precise manoeuvring is critical and for kayakers, rolling ability needs to be 100 percent. Rescue is very difficult or impossible and in the event of a mishap there is a significant hazard to life.

Class 6. Nearly impossible. Difficulties of class 5 carried to the extreme of navigability. Might possibly (but not probably) be run by a team of experts at the right water level, in the right conditions, with all possible safety precautions, but still with considerable hazard to life.

The Trisuli lies en route between Pokhara, Kathmandu and Chitwan National Park, so it makes sense to incorporate your raft trip into your travel schedule to cut down on time in buses. Your rafting company will normally be able to help you plan the logistics and look after your luggage. However, rafting all the way to Chitwan isn't allowed, so you'll have to travel from Narayanghat to the park by vehicle.

The upper Kali Gandaki

The **upper Kali Gandaki** is Nepal's second most popular rafting river and provides an exciting three- or four-day itinerary out of Pokhara. Serious whitewater (Class 4) starts soon after the put-in point near Baglung and continues the whole trip to the take-out at the new dam at the confluence with the Andi Khola. This trip is away from roads and civilization, and offers excellent upriver views of the Annapurnas and Dhaulagiri. However, it's a popular stretch of river, and campsites are well used and may be a little squalid. There have been quite a few accidents on this river, so choose your operator carefully.

The upper Kali Gandaki is probably at its best for rafting at low and medium flows: mid-October to mid-December and March to April. It's a good idea to think about adding this raft trip onto the end of a trek in the Annapurna region. Several travellers have recommended flying to Jomosom, trekking down the Kali Gadaki to Baglung, and then continuing down the river on a rafting trip – a journey from the highest mountains on earth to the jungle lowlands.

The Marsyangdi

Recently opened to commercial rafting, the **Marsyangdi** is a magnificent blue whitewater river with a spectacular mountain backdrop. Kayakers rave about it. It's a full-on, continuously technical river, like a large nonstop slalom, needing self-bailing rafts and shore support. It's normally run from near Kudi (along the Annapurna Circuit trek) down to the Kathmandu–Pokhara highway as a four-day trip. It's especially worth combining

NEPAL'S RIVERS AT A GLANCE

River	Class	Volume	Total Days	River days	Scenery/Wildlife rating	Overall rating	Elevation (start/finish)
Trisuli	2/3+	Big	1–4	1–4	*	**	330m/170m
Upper Kali Gandaki	4-	Med	4	3	**	***	750m/500m
Marsyangdi	4+	Med	6	4	***	**	850m/370m
Sun Koshi	4-	Huge	10	8	**	***	615m/105m
Bhote Koshi	4+	Med	2	1–2	**	***	960m/700m
Seti	2	Small	3	2	**	**	345m/190m
Lower Kali Gandaki	2	Med	5	4	**	**	370m/170m
Karnali	4	Huge	10	8	***	***	560m/195m
Tamur	4	Med	11	6	**	***	635m/105m
Bheri	3+	Med	8–10	6–8	***	**	770m/195m
Arun	4-	Big	4	3	**	*	290m/115m

Notes.

Relative volumes are given because the actual flows vary so enormously according to season.

Total days = days from Kathmandu or Pokhara and back.

The overall rating is a somewhat subjective score of the river as a rafting trip, taking into account whitewater, scenery, logistics and cost:
*** = highly recommended,
** = recommended,
* = specialist interest.

with a scenic three-day trek from Begnas Tal (near Pokhara) to Kudi. The river is likely to be dammed in the next few years, so run it while you can. It's particularly beautiful in November – levels are reasonably low and the mountain views are usually clear.

The Sun Koshi

Described as one of the ten best rafting trips in the world, the **Sun Koshi** is an excellent choice for most people and especially for those doing their first river trip in Nepal. It's the most popular of several longer trips in Nepal, and logistics are fairly easy, making it one of the cheapest in terms of cost per day. It's an eight-day run beginning at Dolalghat, three hours east of Kathmandu, and ending at Chatara, near Dharan in the eastern Tarai. If you're planning to go on from Nepal to Darjeeling, this raft trip cuts out most of the twenty-hour bus ride to the eastern border.

Fewer companies do scheduled trips on the Sun Koshi, so you're less likely to see other parties and the camping is great. It traverses a remote part of the country, flowing through a varied landscape of jungle-clad canyons, arid, open valleys and sparse settlements. Unlike most rivers, which start out rough and get tamer as they descend, this one starts gently, affording a chance to build up experience and confidence prior to a steady diet of increasingly exciting whitewater (Class 3–4). It's at its best for rafting at medium to high flows – from mid-September to late October and in May and early June. Note that a new main highway is being built down the top 40km of the Sun Koshi, which when completed will allow shorter six-day trips on the river and will also probably halve the return time from the take-out.

The Bhote Koshi

The **Bhote Koshi**, which runs alongside the road to the Tibetan border northeast of Kathmandu, is probably the steepest and hardest commercial rafting river in Nepal. In low water it's like a pinball machine (and you're the ball); in medium flows it's more like being flushed down the U-bend of a toilet. A few companies specialize in this deviant experience, offering it as a two-day trip out of Kathmandu using road support and empty rafts. If you have previous rafting experience or are just looking for an adrenaline rush, then this is the one for you. It's a cold river, so you'll want to run it in the window between high water and winter – normally November, March and April are the best months.

Note that Ultimate Descents has an exclusive deal with the *Borderland* resort, near the put-in point, which means that you stay overnight in a rather comfortable safari camp. Other companies may soon be offering similar fixed camps.

The Seti

Another river most easily reached from Pokhara, the **Seti** offers an easier alternative to the upper Kali Gandaki. It's a fairly tame (Class 3-) but very picturesque river, taking three days from Damauli to near Narayanghat. This is a better choice than a similar trip starting on the Trisuli, as it takes you away from the road, and has a fine green jungle corridor and beautiful white beaches for camping. It's a popular choice for birdwatching groups who often schedule it into their itinerary from Pokhara to Chitwan. The water temperature is incredibly warm, making it a popular choice for winter trips and also for kayak clinics.

The lower Kali Gandaki

The **lower** section of the **Kali Gandaki**, starting from Ramdi Ghat on the Siddhartha Highway, offers a longer alternative to the Seti. It's a medium-volume and relatively easy river, with the same beautiful scenery as the Seti, and it flows in a completely unspoilt and untouristy valley of pretty villages, small gorges and jungle-backed beaches. Although the river is easily accessible, it's surprisingly unfashionable as a raft trip. Several kayakers have recommended this as the perfect river for a relaxed, romantic, away-from-it-all break with your partner. Like the Seti, this is probably a good choice for a do-it-yourself "duckie" trip.

The Karnali

Nepal's biggest and longest river, the **Karnali** is perhaps the finest trip of its kind in the world. Way out in the remote far west of Nepal, it requires a long bus ride to Surkhet (it's possible to fly) and a one-day trek to get to the start, and then there are eight days of challenging, big-water rapids, superb canyons, pristine wilderness and plentiful wildlife. The biggest rapids (Class 4) come in the first couple of days, with the river gradually mellowing after that. The trip finishes at Bardia National Park, a more off-the-beaten-track alternative to Chitwan, so many parties take the opportunity to spend a few extra days watching wildlife there.

The Karnali is best run at low to medium levels – it's a particularly good choice in March and April, though the nature of the channel makes it lively at all times outside of high water. It's also renowned as Nepal's premier fishing river, with giant *mahseer* (a freshwater perch) and catfish.

The Tamur

Only recently opened to rafting, the **Tamur** offers six days of fabulous and challenging whitewater in a remote and scenic valley in eastern Nepal, coupled with a highly scenic trek. The river is at its best in medium flows (it would be a nightmare at high levels) with the optimum time after a normal monsoon being the end of October to early November. Note that the last day of the Tamur from Mulghat (where a highway crosses the river) can be added as an exciting extra day's climax to a Sun Koshi trip.

The logistics of getting to the put-in point are a bit involved, starting with a twenty-hour bus ride to Basantapur. However, the four-day walk in from there, along a high ridge with wide panoramas of Kanchenjunga and the Everest peaks, is often described as one of the most beautiful treks in Nepal. Alternatively, you can fly from Kathmandu to Taplejung ($137; 2+hr via Biratnagar), a couple of hours' hike from the put-in point at Dobhan.

The Bheri

The **Bheri** offers a shorter and easier alternative to the Karnali, of which it's a tributary. It's one of the most scenic rivers in Nepal, with golden cliffs, green jungle, crystal-clear green water; white beaches, excellent fishing, good bird watching; coupled with a powerful current and sparkling rapids of moderate difficulty. Access is from the Nepalganj–Birendra Nagar road, a total of about fifteen hours of bus travel from Kathmandu (via Nepalganj). Few companies raft the Bheri at the moment but improved roads mean that it is likely to become deservedly more popular in the future.

The Arun

A powerful and famous river that dominates eastern Nepal, the **Arun** offers a shorter and easier alternative to the Sun Koshi, with big rapids of moderate difficulty and a fine jungle corridor. A few companies offer trips on this little-travelled river, but the necessity of flying in to Tumlingtar ($57), near the put-in point, makes it relatively expensive for such a short trip.

Peter Knowles and David Reed
Peter Knowles is the author of White Water Nepal, *and has spent sixteen years exploring the rivers of the Himalayas from Pakistan to Bhutan, leading many expeditions and first descents.*

CHAPTER NINE

MOUNTAIN-BIKING

It's long been conventional wisdom that the best way to get around Nepal, with its huge trail network and terrible roads, is to walk. Nowadays, thanks to the increasing availability of rental mountain bikes, route information and organized tours, you'll do just as well to *ride*. **Mountain-biking** provides a more intimate experience of the land and its people than you'll get through the smudged windscreen of a speeding jeep or bus. Like trekking, it enables you to get to places vehicles can't, but at a much faster and more exciting pace.

The sense of what's possible on a mountain bike in Nepal is expanding all the time. Much of the country has yet to be explored on wheels: tour operators and bike-shop gurus are continually pioneering new off-road rides. Meanwhile, rapid road construction is creating new routes and giving access to many others, making loops possible and producing an exponential increase in the biking possibilities. On the down side, however, new and upgraded roads bring more traffic, which is becoming a serious problem in certain parts of the country, especially in Kathmandu. The rapid pace of change also makes it hard for any guidebook to keep up: what's fun now might be unpleasant by the time you get there, but by the same token what's unridable now might be fantastic. Seek the latest information locally.

A few hardy people come to Nepal specifically to tour the country – or the subcontinent – by bike. Others join organized tours in which cycling is the main event, or is an important mode of travel between other activities such as trekking, rafting and wildlife-watching. But most people who mountain-bike in Nepal do it only casually, pedalling around temples and villages on their own or perhaps taking a more challenging guided off-road ride. Many try mountain-biking for the first time in Nepal.

Despite Nepal's Himalayan mystique, it's not all steep: the Kathmandu Valley's slopes are generally easy, and the Tarai is just plain flat. There are rides to suit all abilities. The longer and more scenic rides do tend to require a high level of fitness, and there are monster ascents for those who relish that sort of thing, but there are also plenty of relaxed village-to-village rambles and downhill rides. No special paperwork is required unless you plan to cycle in one of the designated trekking areas, in which case you'll need a trekking permit.

It should be stressed that biking in Nepal almost always means *mountain*–biking. A road bike is not recommended, even for the lowlands, because of the generally rough or at best unpredictable surfaces of the roads.

Seasonal considerations

While mountain-biking is a year-round activity in Nepal, some **seasons** are better than others, and when you go will influence where and how you ride.

If you have a choice then go for October to December, when there's little chance of rain and the visibility is as good as it gets. During this period temperatures get gradually cooler and the comfort zone shifts down in elevation. Not that it ever gets very cold in the hills – in fact, even in December and January the days are pleasantly cool for cycling anywhere up to about 3000m; it's just that it's frosty at night, and snow may be encountered as low as 2000m. These also happen to be the most comfortable months for cycling in Pokhara and the Tarai, which are hot at other times of year. The shortening days are also a factor, and by December you'll need to be off the roads or trails by 4.30pm or so.

From January to March the story is the same in reverse, with the days lengthening and growing warmer. This too is a good time for biking, as fewer tourists are around and hotels are fairly quiet, though the visibility isn't as good as in the autumn. In April, May and the first part of June, the weather just keeps getting hotter and hazier, so sunscreen and an extra water bottle become essential. On the plus side, you can take advantage of long daylight hours.

The monsoon (mid-June to late Sept) is generally not the best season for cycling in Nepal, since the air is hot and damp, the mountains are usually hidden by clouds, and the trails are muddy. However, this is prime riding time in Tibet and Ladakh, which are shielded from the rains by the Himalaya.

Information and maps

The bike shops in Kathmandu and Pokhara are your best sources of up-to-date **information** on trails, roads, equipment and servicing. Go easy on the questions, though, because they're in business mainly to sell tours, and won't want to divulge all their secret routes.

To date, no one has written a **guidebook** to mountain-biking in Nepal, although James Giambrione's *Kathmandu Valley Bikes & Hikes* (Insight Guides, 1994) gives excellent coverage of its more limited area. That makes it all the more important to go armed with a good **map**. The series of maps produced jointly by His Majesty's Government and FINNIDA, the Finnish aid agency, are extremely accurate and come in a scale (1:25,000) ideal for day rides, although you may find you need more than one to cover the area you're planning to ride; other trekking series may prove useful for certain rides. HMG's 1:500,000 country map, which comes in three sheets, is the best road map for long-distance touring, even though it's now somewhat out of date. Maps for specific areas are recommended in the relevant sections of other chapters. Note, however, that even the most accurate maps soon go out of date in fast-changing Nepal.

Organized versus independent biking

Like trekking, mountain-biking can be done independently or as part of an organized tour. With mountain-biking, the specialized equipment involved and the difficulty of route-finding make additional cases for joining a tour, but at the end of the day it comes down mainly to how you prefer to travel and what you can afford.

Organized tours

There are two main reasons for joining an organized bike **tour**, the first being ease of logistics. Good bikes and all the necessary gear are provided, and guides take care of bike maintenance and ensure that the bikes are safe at night. On longer tours, a "sag wagon" will tote heavy gear, provide emergency backup, and whisk you past the busier or less interesting stretches of road to ensure that you spend as much time as possible hitting the highlights. Basically, the operator does everything but pedal the bike for you – and if you don't want to pedal very much, they'll even drive you to the top of a hill and let you cycle down.

Secondly, if you're into single-track riding, a tour guide will show you trails you'd never find on your own. And, like trekking guides, biking guides can interpret the culture and answer any questions.

Of course joining a tour is quite a bit more expensive than doing it yourself. A one-day trip will typically **cost** $20–25, while longer trips work out to $40 or more per day because of the extra expenses of vehicle support and accommodation (the standard of the latter has a big effect on price). The "Adventure travel operators and agents" box on p.60 includes some overseas companies that offer mountain-bike tours. However, almost all tours booked through these companies are organized by a few **operators** in Kathmandu (see p.139), and you can save money by booking directly with them. These companies usually require a minimum of four people for vehicle-supported tours, but may be able to organize shorter customized trips for just two people. Contact operators in advance to see if they've got any trips already scheduled for the time you're planning to be in Nepal.

If you want to cycle to **Tibet** from Nepal (or vice versa) you'll have to take a tour, for the reasons explained on p.13. You don't necessarily have to take a bike tour– it may be possible to fly or drive to Lhasa with a conventional tour and then cycle back to Nepal independently. However you do it, be sure to go with the proper documentation or you risk having your bike confiscated by the Chinese authorities.

Cycling independently

Cycling independently, you can do just about everything a tour group can do, and more cheaply and flexibly, but it takes a certain pioneering spirit and a greater tolerance for discomfort. It will be up to you to rent or bring your own equipment and to arrange food and (on overnight trips) accommodation; if starting from Kathmandu, you'll need to organize transport out of the city or else put up with some ugly traffic in the early going. You'll have to find your own way, which may mean getting lost and doing some unnecessary backtracking or carrying. A few Nepali phrases and a positive attitude will help.

Day trips in the Kathmandu and Pokhara valleys are the easiest ones to do on your own – though you probably won't find the obscure trails that a tour company would take you on, you'll no doubt stumble upon others and have adventures of your own making. Riding long-distance without vehicle support, you'll have to tote your own gear and will probably find yourself spending many nights in very primitive lodges where little English is spoken and foreigners are considered the evening's entertainment. This will be par for the course if you're on a long tour of the subcontinent, though, and in fact you'll probably find the going much easier in Nepal than in India: the roads are for the most part less busy, and there's less staring, hassling and risk of theft.

Equipment

The main dilemma facing the independent cyclist is what, if any, **equipment** to bring to Nepal. Since good (and not-so-good) bikes can be rented there, you'll probably be better off not bringing a bike from home unless you plan to do a lot of riding. However, certain clothing and accessories are worth bringing, especially if you think you'll make use of them while doing other activities such as trekking or rafting.

Renting or buying a bike in Nepal

Rental bikes fall into two categories in Nepal. Those of the first type – cheap **Indian-made bikes**, available from streetside vendors for Rs150–200 per day – really only qualify under the loosest definition of the term "mountain bike". Superficially they look the part – some even have full suspension – but they're heavy and uncomfortable to ride, their components are incredibly flimsy, little attention is paid to maintenance, and they rarely come with a helmet. You wouldn't want to take one of these bikes on trails or rough roads, where a malfunction could spell disaster. They're mainly intended for around-town use, though you could probably chance taking one on easy there-and-back day rides and perhaps on a modest overnight loop on paved or graded unpaved roads. Rule of thumb: don't ride one of these bikes any further than you're prepared to walk back with it.

For any sort of hard or long-distance riding you'll need a **real mountain bike**, which can be rented from only a few specialist bike shops/tour operators in Kathmandu and Pokhara. These bikes are good but not top of the line – they're usually fairly new or at least reasonably well maintained, and feature decent components though not necessarily shocks. A helmet should come with the bike. The daily rate will be Rs500–1000, depending on quality and features; you'll be expected to leave a passport or something of value as security. Be sure to reserve these bikes as far ahead as possible, especially during busy times, because the choice is very limited.

Whichever kind of bike you rent, it's your responsibility to make sure all is to your liking before setting off. **Check** brakes and brake pads, test spoke tension (they should all be taut), ensure that tyres have sufficient tread and are properly inflated (check inflation while sitting on the bike), test the chain for tautness, and work the bike through its gears to see that the derailleurs function smoothly. And make sure the bike has a bell – you'll be using it a lot. You'll be responsible to cover loss or damage to the bike.

Since mountain bikes are currently only rentable in Kathmandu and Pokhara, and you'll have to return the bike to where you rented it, you'll probably end up just doing excursions from those places. However, there are a number of other fine mountain-biking bases around the country, so you might consider lugging a rental bike along by bus.

You may be able to **buy** a decent used bike from a departing traveller, especially toward the end of the autumn or spring seasons – check notice boards in Kathmandu or Pokhara. The only new bikes for sale in Nepal are the cheesy Indian-made ones, which cost Rs6000 and up with gears.

Bringing a bike from home

Bringing a **bike from home** avoids the vagaries of renting, and depending on how much time you plan to spend in the saddle, can save a significant amount of money. You may also feel safer or more comfortable on your own bike, especially if it has full suspension or other features you cherish. For any long-distance tour, especially one that involves India as well as Nepal, you'll obviously want to bring your own bike. However, don't bring a bike unless you have the time, energy and commitment to use it a lot of the time – otherwise it will just be a millstone that you have to lug everywhere and keep safe.

Airlines (both international and domestic) will accept a bicycle as baggage at no extra charge, so long as it doesn't put you over the weight limit. No special container is needed, but you'll be expected to deflate the tyres and swivel the handlebars to be parallel with the frame. Nepalese customs will want some sort of assurance that the bike will be returning with you when you leave the country, but this shouldn't be a problem and should not cost money.

Clothes and other equipment

Other than a helmet and water bottle, no special gear is necessary for simple day trips. But if you're planning a long-distance ride, especially an independent one, you'll need to give a lot of thought to what to bring.

EQUIPMENT CHECKLIST

You won't need everything on this list. Items marked by (*) can be
purchased in Nepal, and those marked by (**) can also be rented.

Lightweight breathable waterproof shell (eg Gore-Tex)	Energy bars and electrolyte powder
Windbreaker*	Sunscreen*
Cycling top and shorts	Sunglasses*
Fleece top*	Torch/flashlight*
Warm hat and gloves*	Waist- or backpack*
Cycling gloves	Panniers**
Helmet**	Security cable/lock
Pollution mask*	Shock cords (bungie cords)*
Stiff-soled shoes suitable for biking	Puncture repair kit & spare inner tube
Water bottles or backpack water holder (eg Camelbak)	Pump
	Tool set
Iodine tablets*, crystals or solution*	Bike bell*
First-aid kit* (see p.387)	Spare parts
	Bike lube

Cycling **clothing**, shoes and gloves aren't easily obtainable in Nepal, nor is good waterproof/windproof outerwear. Note that tight-fitting Lycra clothing, while functional, is embarrassing and potentially offensive to many Nepalis, especially when worn by women. To avoid causing offence, wear a pair of comfortable shorts and a T-shirt over your body-hugging bike gear. As for warm clothes, you'll probably only need one layer, maybe two in winter at higher elevations, which can be purchased in Nepal.

A **helmet** and water bottle will come with a better rental bike. If renting a cheaper one, you may be able to buy a helmet in one of the Kathmandu department stores, and you can always make do with a mineral water bottle. Be sure to have iodine for water purification – more specifics on this on p.387. If you're attached to your saddle/seat or pedals, bring them along and have them fitted to your rental bike. **Panniers** and racks can be rented from the better bike shops, and camping equipment (sleeping bags, mats, tents) from trekking shops. Locally made daypacks and waist-packs are sold all over tourist areas, and you can pick up bungie cords in motorcycle accessory shops. If you do much riding in Kathmandu you'll do well to wear a face mask – good (expensive) ones are sold in Kathmandu department stores, and pharmacies sell cheaper surgical masks.

A bike – especially a fancy one brought from home – can go missing at the blink of an eye, so a good **lock** and cable are essential. Lock the bike to something permanent, and bring it inside at night, or you could find yourself lonely and walking. Puncture-repair places are everywhere on the roads, but it's still advisable to come with your own **patch kit**, inner tube(s), pump and basic tool kit, especially if riding off-road. If you bring your own bike you'll of course want to bring more tools, spare parts and lube.

Repairs and service

At least two of the Kathmandu tour operators (Himalayan Mountain Bikes and Dawn Till Dusk) have **workshops** with trained bike mechanics, a full range of tools and even a stock of spare parts. These are good places to go for servicing if you've been cycling around the subcontinent for weeks or months.

> Many of the same environmental do's and don'ts for trekking also apply to you when
> mountain-biking, especially if you're camping. See p.390.

Local bike **repair shops**, found in every town and crossroads, are equipped mainly
to fix Indian-made models, but they can patch any sort of flat ("puncture") and are often
remarkably adept at figuring out mountain bikes and performing improvised repairs
and mini-tuneups. Just be sure to ask the price first: a puncture repair should only cost
about Rs10.

Riding conditions

A number of different experiences are possible on a mountain bike in Nepal, ranging
from one-day trail rides to months-long tours of the subcontinent. The country itself is
incredibly varied: a ride in the hills is naturally going to be more strenuous and challenging than a ride through the flat Tarai or one confined to the undulating floor of the
Kathmandu Valley. It's hard to generalize, but this section describes the various riding
conditions you're likely to encounter.

Highways

You can count Nepal's long-distance **highways** on one hand. That's not good news
for cyclists, because it means that all heavy-vehicle traffic converges on those few
lanes and makes them more congested and polluted than one might expect in a
fabled Himalayan kingdom. The situation on Kathmandu's city streets is downright
awful (see p.88). Still, the unpleasant stretches of road are limited mainly to central
Nepal (principally on the Kathmandu–Pokhara and Mugling–Birganj routes).
Although highway cycling always entails a certain amount of dust and exhaust
fumes, the traffic diminishes noticeably as you get further from Kathmandu; the
eastern and particularly the far-western portions of the Mahendra Highway are
delightfully rural.

Bear in mind that you don't have to pedal all the way from A to B. If you want to skip
a busy section or a steep climb, or avoid backtracking, take a **bus** or a **taxi**. The latter
come in especially handy in the Kathmandu Valley, where all it takes is a comparatively short lift to get past the urban blight and out into fine cycling country. And in a mountainous country like Nepal, there's a lot to be said for getting a lift to a high point and
then riding down. It's usually no problem to load your bike on the roof of a bus for an
extra charge of Rs40–80, depending on the distance and your negotiating skills. Lay the
bike down flat and tie it down securely (bungie cords are useful for this), and make sure
that other luggage isn't loaded on top of it.

Lesser roads and trails

Nepal has a surprising number of paved and unpaved secondary **roads**, most of which
see very little traffic. Many other primitive, half-completed or half-washed-out roads can
also be found – a good map will help you locate them. If you're adventurous, the possibilities for exploring off the beaten track, especially in the Tarai, are almost unlimited.

Off-road riding in Nepal is probably not like what you're used to back home.
Although there are zillions of **trails**, most aren't suitable for mountain-biking because
they're too steep, stepped and heavily used by humans and animals. A few bikers have
"ridden" trekking trails to Everest Base Camp and elsewhere, but have ended up carrying their bikes between fifty and eighty percent of the way (for most people, carrying even twenty percent of the way would be too tedious).

There are some excellent single-track rides, but it takes a lot of exploring to find them (this is a good reason to go with a tour). If you do go off-road, give other people and livestock **priority** on the trail. Local people won't be expecting anything to come through at anything faster than a walking pace, so slow down around all signs of habitation, and signal your approach by ringing your bell or yelling *"Saikal aiyo!"* ("Cycle coming!"). It will often be necessary to dismount. Maintain a watchful eye for children, who like to grab hold of the back of bikes and run alongside. Be careful around buffalo and other livestock because it's easy to send them stampeding down a narrow trail, obliging their owners to chase after them.

Pedestrians and other hazards

Pedestrians in Nepal will frequently walk right into oncoming traffic without so much as looking left or right. There's an inherent attitude of "let others watch out for me": once the pedestrian sees an oncoming vehicle he or she has the responsibility to avoid it, so it's better not to look. This also helps explain the widespread use of horns and bells, the sounding of which sends the message, "I'm here, so don't say I didn't warn you." The result is a constant chain reaction of swerving cars, buses, tempos, motorcycles and bikes, all honking like crazy.

On a bicycle, you're near the bottom of the pecking order. Cars and buses will squeeze you off the road, motorbikes will approach you head-on, taxis will suddenly veer around obstacles without any apparent regard for your presence. You'll quickly see there are no road rules, that police have little control, and if you hit someone you'll almost surely be asked to pay compensation, whether it was your fault or not. Add to this cud-chewing cows in the middle of major intersections, children blithely playing beside highways and bus drivers sharing their seats with two others and this is what you need to be ready for on the roads. Still, it's a lot better than taking the bus.

The single saving grace is the slow speed at which most vehicles travel in Nepal. However, fancy new cars and smooth new highway surfaces are tempting many to go faster.

Route-finding

Little English is spoken in the village areas that are best for riding. Asking directions will be a whole lot easier if you have a few basic phrases in Nepali. The most important piece of information to communicate is the name of the next destination or village on your route. Don't point when asking directions, as most people out of courtesy will say yes, even if they don't know – it's better to put your hands in your pockets and ask "Which way to…" Do this several times in a short distance to be sure you've got the right answer. Numerous trail intersections can make it difficult to provide accurate directions, and unfortunately one wrong turn may leave you carrying your bike for hours to reconnect with the right path.

Don't ask how far it is to a given destination, ask how long it takes to get there. The answer will be the walking time in hours; you'll somehow have to convert that to riding time. Distances on the map bear little relation to actual difficulty, since a day's ride may entail an ascent and/or descent of 1000 or more vertical metres. The most realistic benchmark is "hours riding per day", and most people will find a six- to seven-hour day, including lunch break, to be sufficient. Plan to arrive at your destination three or four hours before dark, which provides for a balanced day and time for some sightseeing, repairs, washing and relaxing on arrival.

This chapter was revised and expanded for this edition with help from Peter Stewart, owner of Himalayan Mountain Bikes in Kathmandu and Pokhara.

MOUNTAIN-BIKING ITINERARIES AT A GLANCE

There are so many potential cycling itineraries in Nepal that it's hard to catalogue them systematically, but here's an attempt. The routes are all described in greater detail in the respective sections of the guide.

DAY RIDES AND OVERNIGHTS IN AND AROUND THE KATHMANDU VALLEY

A list of suggested itineraries in and around the Kathmandu Valley is given on p.151, and more advice on riding in the Shivapuri Watershed on p.170. Here's a rundown of places to base yourself (or places to stop along the way).

Kathmandu The most popular base, thanks to the availability of lodging, food and good bikes, but traffic and pollution make it a poor starting point for rides. Take a taxi to the outskirts, from where you can pedal to Ichangu Narayan, Nagarjun Ban, Kakani, the Shivapuri Watershed, Sankhu or many other places via Patan or Bhaktapur.

Patan A springboard for the southern Kathmandu Valley, including Dakshin Kali, Godavari/Bishanku Narayan, Phulchoki, the Lele Valley, and the Lakuri Bhanjyang (Lakuri Pass) to Panauti.

Bhaktapur Ideally situated in the very ridable eastern Kathmandu Valley, with excursions to Changu Narayan, Nagarkot, Nala, Dhulikhel, Panauti and beyond.

Nagarkot A hilltop viewpoint 700m above the valley floor: all routes lead downhill, either to Changu Narayan, Nala, the Shivapuri Watershed or the Indrawati Valley.

Dhulikhel A very popular base for exploring the Kathmandu Valley's eastern rim area, especially Namobuddha and Panauti; other tracks also lead further east into less-travelled country.

Panauti Possibly a more attractive alternative to Dhulikhel, given the increasing amount of traffic and urbanization around the latter.

Kakani A fine destination in itself, it gives access to the scenic Trisuli Road and, with a bit of carrying, to the Shivapuri Watershed and across to Nagarkot.

Daman Like Nagarkot, this is a high point that you'll probably cycle down from only once – either back to Kathmandu by road, to Pharping via the Kulekhani Reservoir, or down to the Tarai.

DAY RIDES AND OVERNIGHTS IN AND AROUND POKHARA

In Pokhara, base yourself in Lakeside/Damside and make for these destinations, which are all described in more detail in "The Pokhara Valley" starting on p.276.

Sarangkot Ride up from the bazaar to this hilltop viewpoint, where lodging is available; a bikable road continues along the ridge to the Baglung Highway.

Baglung Highway A 70-kilometre paved road leads to Baglung, a trekking trailhead alongside the Kali Gandaki River.

Begnas and Rupa Tal A dirt road follows a ridge between these beautiful lakes and deep into the hills; overnight accommodation available.

Seti Canyon Unpaved roads head south along the Seti, with dramatic canyon overlooks.

LONG-DISTANCE RIDES

If you're planning a long-distance trip then you'll probably combine Nepal with India or Tibet – those routes are summarized in "Cycling into Nepal" (p.13). Here are a few other possible itineraries within Nepal:

Kathmandu–Tibet border An adventurous 1000-metre climb on a mostly good road, with hot springs, a deep gorge and an outdoor-adventure resort where you can join up with a rafting trip on the Bhote Koshi (4–5 days, round trip).

Kathmandu–Trisuli Continuing past Kakani on the valley rim, it's a long (1500m) descent to a subtropical valley with a nearby historic fort (4 days, round trip); experts might want to continue to Dhunche and Somdang.

Kathmandu–Chitwan A classic, challenging ride along the spectacular and little-used Tribhuwan Rajpath, gaining 1800m as it ascends to Daman and over the Mahabharat Lek before descending 2000m to Hetauda and Chitwan National Park (2–4 days, one way).

Kathmandu–Pokhara This road is rather busy and not necessarily recommended for cycling, but if you do ride it you can make side trips to Gorkha, Manakamana and Bandipur (2+ days, one way).

Pokhara–Tansen–Lumbini A strenuous ride along a winding, scenic highway through the hills, spending at least one night in Tansen (a base for excellent day rides) and then continuing to the Buddha's birthplace in the Tarai (3+ days, one way).

Lumbini–Bardia – A diverse, sometimes hilly ride from the Buddha's birthplace to a remote wildlife park, traversing a beautiful *dun* valley with lots of scope for side trips into the hills to the north (4 days, one way).

PART FOUR

THE
CONTEXTS

THE HISTORICAL FRAMEWORK

For a tiny Himalayan backwater, Nepal has played a surprisingly pivotal role in Asian history. In its early days it reared the Buddha and hosted the great Indian emperor Ashoka; much later, its remarkable conquests led it into wars with Tibet and Britain, and during the past three decades it has come to be regarded as a vital buffer state by both India and China. Its name and recorded history go back nearly 3000 years, although it has existed as a nation for barely 200: before 1769, "Nepal" referred only to a kingdom based in the Kathmandu Valley.

BEGINNINGS

Neolithic tools found in the Kathmandu Valley indicate that humans have inhabited parts of Nepal for tens of thousands of years – and the fact that the shrines of Swayambhu and Changu Narayan are located on hilltops suggests that ancient animists may have lived and worshipped there as much as 200,000 years ago, while the valley floor was submerged under a primordial lake. The Newar creation myth, which tells of the *bodhisattva* Manjushri releasing the waters and establishing Swayambhu, perhaps preserves a dim racial memory of that prehistoric era.

Nepal's early semi-mythological genealogies aren't borne out by any archeological evidence, but at some points they tally with other sources. The **Kirata** (or Kiranti) tribe pops up in several Hindu texts – and even in Ptolemy – although the term might well have applied to all hill people in the first millennium BC. Significantly, the Kirata were often described as a warlike people known for carrying deadly knives. Whoever they were, by the sixth or seventh century BC the Kirata appear to have divided into two distinct groups, one controlling the eastern hills and the other the Kathmandu Valley.

Hindus were by this time encroaching on the less malarial parts of the Tarai and founding the city-states of **Mithila** (modern Janakpur), the scene of many of the events in the *Ramayan* epic, and **Kapilvastu** (now Tilaurakot), where the Buddha spent his pre-enlightenment years during the sixth century BC. North India was unified under the **Mauryan empire** (321–184 BC), whose most famous ruler, Ashoka, was responsible for spreading Buddhism throughout the subcontinent, including Nepal. Following the fall of Maurya, north India was again divided among a number of states and Hinduism began a slow but inexorable comeback in the Tarai.

EARLY DYNASTIES

Nepal's history comes into sharper focus with the arrival of the **Lichhavis**, a north Indian clan who overthrew the Kiratas around 200 AD and established their capital at Deopatan (modern Pashupatinath). Exploiting Nepal's position as a trading entrepôt between India and Tibet, the Lichhavis founded a strong, stable and culturally sophisticated dynasty. No buildings from the period survive, but contemporary accounts by Chinese travellers describe "multi-storeyed temples so tall one would take them for a crown of clouds" – perhaps a reference to the pagoda style that was to become a Nepali trademark. Under Lichhavi sponsorship, artisans ushered in a classical age of stone sculpture and produced Nepal's most acclaimed pieces, many of which still casually litter the Kathmandu Valley. Although Hindus, the Lichhavis endowed both Hindu and Buddhist temples – Pashupatinath and Swayambhu were built, or at least expanded, during their rule – and established a policy of religious tolerance that has been maintained to the present day.

Much of what we know about the Lichhavis comes from a handful of stone inscriptions whose authors were probably more intent on self-praise than historical accuracy. The earliest inscription, dated 464 AD and still on view at Changu Narayan, extols **Manadeva**, the legendary builder of the Boudha stupa. The greatest of the Lichhavi line, **Amsuvarman** (605–621) is said to have composed the first Sanskrit grammar and built a splendid palace believed to have been located at present-day Naksal in Kathmandu. "Down to the reign of this monarch the gods showed themselves plainly in bodily shape," intone the Nepalese chronicles, "but after this they became invisible." By this time Nepal had become a vassal of Tibet, and Amsuvarman's daughter Bhrikuti, who was carried off by the Tibetan king, is popularly credited with introducing Buddhism to Tibet.

The Lichhavi era came to a close in 879, and the three centuries that followed are sometimes referred to as Nepal's "Dark Ages". The Nepalese chronicles record a long list of **Thakuri kings**, although the title was probably a Hindu honorific and not the name of an hereditary dynasty; these kings may well have been puppets installed by one or more of the powers controlling the Tarai at the time. Nonetheless, learning and the arts continued to thrive, and from the eleventh century onwards the valley became an important centre of tantric studies (see "Religion", p.443).

THE KHASAS AND MALLAS

While the Thakuris were ruling central Nepal, yet another Hindu clan, the **Khasas**, were migrating up from the plains and carving out a small fiefdom in western Tibet. In the early twelfth century a Khasa king, Nagaraja, moved his capital down to Sinja in the Karnali basin and established a powerful dynasty which at its height controlled a broad sector of the Himalaya from Kashmir to present-day Pokhara. The history of the Khasas is little understood, for they left few written records and only minor ruins at Sinja (now Hatsinja) and Dullu, south of Jumla.

Nepal entered a new and much better documented period of its history when the Thakuri king of Bhaktapur, Arideva, took the title **Malla**, probably in the year 1200. Malla was, in fact, a popular form of royal address in India at the time – the Khasa kings also called themselves

Mallas – but the name has come to be associated with at least three separate dynasties, lasting more than five centuries, that presided over the renaissance of Nepali culture during which most of the temples and palaces still on display in the Kathmandu Valley were built.

The early Malla era was marked by great instability: the Khasas mounted several raids on the valley, although they were never able to gain a ruling foothold, and in 1349 Muslims swept up from Bengal and pillaged both Hindu and Buddhist holy sites in a brief spree of destruction and violence. Despite these disruptions, trade flourished, many of the valley's smaller cities were founded, and Arniko, the great Nepali architect, was dispatched to the Ming court to instruct the Chinese in the art of building pagodas. **Jayasthiti Malla** (1354–95) inaugurated a period of strong central rule from Bhaktapur, but his most lasting contribution was to dragoon his Buddhist subjects into the Hindu hierarchy by dividing them into 64 occupational castes – a system which remained enshrined in Nepali law until 1964. Malla power reached its zenith under **Yaksha Malla** (1428–82), who extended his domain westwards to Gorkha and eastwards as far as present-day Biratnagar. Upon his death, the kingdom was divided among three sons, and for nearly three centuries the independent city states of Kathmandu, Patan and Bhaktapur (and occasionally others) feuded over lucrative trade arrangements with Tibet. Judging by the opulent durbars built during this period, there must have been enough to go around, and the intense rivalry seems to have been good for both art and business.

The Khasa kings didn't fare so well, and by the late fourteenth century their empire had fragmented into a collection of petty provinces. The Muslim conquest of north India during the early part of the century figured indirectly in Khasa's downfall: a steady stream of princes from Rajasthan, which had borne the brunt of the invasion, limped into the Khasa hills in search of consolation prizes, and rapidly wheedled their way into positions of power. Those who took the reins of the Khasa provinces came to be known as the **Baaisi Raja** (Twenty-two Princes), while others who subjugated Magar and Gurung states to the east became the **Chaubisi** (Twenty-four).

UNIFICATION

For three centuries the Chaubisi and Baaisi confederacies were able to maintain an uneasy status quo, forming numerous defensive alliances to ensure that no one state could gain control over the rest. Divided, they were small, weak and culturally backward. **Gorkha**, the most easterly territory, was no different from the rest, except that it was that much closer to the Kathmandu Valley and that much more jealous of the Mallas' wealth. Under the inspired, obsessive leadership of **Prithvi Narayan Shah** (1722–75), Gorkha launched a campaign that was to take 27 years to conquer the valley, and as long again to unite all of modern Nepal.

At the time of Prithvi Narayan's rise to the throne, in 1743, rivalry between the three Malla kings had reached an all-time high. Still, Gorkha wasn't nearly strong enough to invade Nepal outright; Prithvi Narayan first captured Nuwakot, a day's march northwest of Kathmandu, and from there directed a ruthless twenty-year **war of attrition**. By 1764 he was able to enforce a total blockade, starving the valley and at the same time replenishing Gorkha's coffers with Tibetan trade. Kirtipur was targeted for the first major battle, and surrendered after a six-month siege. Answering a plea from the Kathmandu king, Jaya Prakash Malla, the East India Company sent in 2400 soldiers against the Gorkhalis, who proceeded to cut them to shreds; only 800 returned. On the eve of Indra Jaatra in 1768, Jaya Prakash, by now rumoured to be insane, let down the city's defences and **Kathmandu fell** to the Gorkhalis without a fight. They took Patan two days later, and Bhaktapur the following year, and by 1774 had marched eastwards all the way to Sikkim.

Suspicious of Britain's growing influence in India, Prithvi Narayan adopted a closed-door policy that was to remain in force until the 1950s. Missionaries were thrown out forthwith: "First the Bible, then the trading station, then the cannon," he warned. The bloody **battle for succession** that followed Prithvi Narayan's death set the pattern for Nepali politics well into the twentieth century. Yet when they weren't stabbing each other in the back, his successors managed to subdue Gorkha's old Chaubisi and Baaisi rivals in the west, so that by

1790 Nepal stretched far beyond its present eastern and western borders. Lured on by promises of land grants – every hillman's dream – the Nepali army became a seemingly unstoppable fighting machine, with Kashmir in its sights.

Westward progress was interrupted, however, by a brief but chastening **war with Tibet**. Troubles had been brewing for some time over trade relations, and the Tibetans were growing alarmed by Nepal's encroachments on their ally, Sikkim. In 1788 and again in 1791, Nepal invaded, plundered a few monasteries and exacted tribute from Tibet, but in 1792 the Tibetans launched a counterattack, penetrating as far as Nuwakot and forcing Nepal to accept harsh terms.

Nepal's further adventures in the west brought it into increasing **conflict with Britain**'s East India Company, which by now controlled India, and open hostilities broke out in 1814 when Nepal annexed the Butwal sector of the Tarai. For the British, the dispute provided a perfect pretext to "open up" Nepal, which had been so tantalizingly closed to them, and thus to muscle in on trade with Tibet. Britain attacked with a force of 50,000 men against Nepal's 12,000, expecting an easy victory; in the event it took two years and heavy losses before Nepal was finally brought to heel. The **Treaty of Segauli** forced Nepal to accept its present eastern and western boundaries and surrender much of the Tarai, and worst of all, to admit an official British "resident" in Kathmandu. Yet so impressed were the British by "our valiant opponent" – as a plaque at an Indian battle site still proclaims – that they began recruiting Nepalis into the Indian Army before the treaty had even been signed. These companies formed the basis for the famed **Gurkha regiments** (see p.283). Britain restored Nepal's Tarai lands in return for its help in quelling the Indian Mutiny of 1857.

THE RANA YEARS

The Kathmandu court was practically paralysed by intrigue and assassinations during the first half of the nineteenth century, culminating in the ghastly **Kot massacre** of 1846, in which more than fifty courtiers were butchered in a courtyard off Kathmandu's Durbar Square. In the ensuing upheaval, a shrewd young general, **Jang Bahadur**, seized power, took the title **Rana** and proclaimed himself prime minister* for life, an office which he later made hereditary by establishing a complicated roll of succession. For the next century, the kings of Nepal were nothing more than puppets, while Ranas ruled like shoguns and packed the palace with their ever-increasing offspring. Authoritarian and blatantly exploitative, they built grandiose palaces while putting virtually no money into public works, suppressed education for fear it would awaken opposition, and remained firmly isolationist to avoid losing control to the British. (Ironically, an impoverished Nepal suited Britain, since it assured a steady supply of willing Gurkha cannon fodder.) Only a handful of foreign dignitaries were allowed to enter – usually only as far as Chitwan – and even the British resident wasn't allowed to venture beyond the Kathmandu Valley. To survey Nepal and Tibet, Britain had to send in Indian spies disguised as Buddhist monks.

Yet Jang Bahadur knew the value of staying on good terms with the British Raj, now at its zenith; in 1850 he broke with tradition and travelled to England, where he met Queen Victoria and by all accounts cut a dashing figure. He returned with several Western affectations, including a fondness for Neoclassical architecture and epaulettes; soon after, to his credit, he abolished the practice of *sati*.

Other Ranas continued in the same vein. **Chandra Shamsher Rana**, who came to power in 1901 by deposing his brother, is best known for building the thousand-roomed Singha Durbar and (belatedly) abolishing slavery. He also made some feeble attempts at modernization, including the construction of Nepal's first college, railway, hydroelectric plant and paved roads. By 1940, underground resistance against the regime was developing, and **Juddha Shamsher Rana** had four plotters executed; after the fall of the Ranas these men were declared martyrs and a monument south of Kathmandu's Tudikhel was erected in their honour.

---

*Though the "Rana" title has generally been equated with that of a prime minister, technically it conferred a grade of kingship. The holder's full title was Shri Tin Maharaja (short for Shri Shri Shri Maharaja; "Shri" is an honorific prefix). The king's was, and still is, Shri Paanch (Five Shri) Maharajdhiraj.

THE MONARCHY RESTORED

The Ranas' anachronistic regime wasn't able to survive long after World War II, from which over 200,000 soldiers returned with dangerous ideas of freedom and justice. In 1947 the British quit India, and with them went the Ranas' chief support. The new Indian government mistrusted the Ranas, and became genuinely worried about Nepal's weakness as a buffer state after the Communist takeover of China in 1949. Seeking stability, India signed a far-reaching **"peace and friendship" treaty** with Nepal in 1950 which, despite the upheavals that were to follow, remains the basis for all relations between the two countries.

Later the same year the strategic balance shifted again as a result of the Chinese invasion of Tibet, and the **Nepali Congress Party**, recently formed in Calcutta, called for an armed struggle against the Ranas. Within a month, King Tribhuwan had requested asylum at the Indian embassy and was smuggled away to Delhi; the next morning, the Nepali Congress Party launched simultaneous assaults on Birganj and Biratnagar. Sporadic fighting continued for two months until the Ranas, internationally discredited, reluctantly agreed to enter into negotiations. Brokered by India, the so-called **Delhi Compromise** arranged for Ranas and the Congress Party to share power under the king's rule, with Nepalis given the right to vote in the parliamentary-style democracy.

The compromise was short-lived. **Tribhuwan**, a previously retiring figure, emerged as a "hero of the revolution" and an adroit politician, and before the end of 1951 he had dismissed the Rana prime minister. This was an end to the Rana regime, but not Rana influence: by an agreement that has never been made public, the Shah royal family continues to appoint Ranas to most key military posts, and the families are inseparably tied by marriage (the queen is a Rana, and two of her sisters are married to two of the king's brothers). In his four years as king, however, Tribhuwan neither consolidated his power nor delivered the elections he promised. Unaccountable to the voters, the party bosses who controlled the interim government weren't much of an improvement over the Ranas.

PANCHAAYAT POLITICS

Crowned in 1955, **King Mahendra** lost no time in offsetting the parties' power by developing his own grassroots network of village leaders, forcing the parties to do likewise. They demanded elections; the king stalled, but finally agreed to a vote in 1959. Amazingly, the Nepali Congress Party swept seventy percent of the seats, and under Prime Minister **B. P. Koirala** began bypassing palace control and creating a party machine very much like India's. Mahendra was none too pleased with this **"experiment with democracy"**, as it came to be called – the following year he sacked the cabinet, banned political parties and threw the leaders in jail. For the rest of his reign he relied on heavy police measures to quell dissent.

In place of democracy, Mahendra offered the **"partyless" panchaayat system**, a uniquely Nepali form of government that grew out of the king's old-boy village network. Village councils (*panchaayat*) were established to look after local affairs; these were to send one representative on to a district council, which in turn elected members to a national assembly. The king chose the prime minister and cabinet and appointed one-fifth of the national assembly, which served as a rubber stamp for his policies. "Partylessness" meant, of course, one party – the king's. The *panchaayat* system conveniently preserved an illusion of democracy while silencing opposition and ensuring loyalty to the king: in other words, it was a new and improved version of absolute monarchy. Corruption was the same as before, only now more decentralized, as every village *panchaayat* wallah had a tiny piece of the pie.

India was unhappy with the changes, but Mahendra, unlike his father, didn't owe his crown to India, and sought wider international support. He threw open Nepal's doors to **foreign aid**, which endeared him to the major powers, enriched the state's coffers and swelled the bureaucracy (see "Development dilemmas"). After the 1962 Sino-Indian border war, Mahendra was able to exploit Nepal's buffer position with particular skill, alternately playing off the two powers against each other to obtain economic and military aid; no sooner had India completed the Rajpath, Nepal's first highway from the plains to Kathmandu, for example, than Mahendra persuaded the

Chinese to extend the road to Tibet, much to India's horror. The **"China card"** became an important unofficial strand of foreign policy, but ultimately it was to help bring about the downfall of the *panchaayat* system.

The present king, **Birendra**, assumed power after Mahendra's death in 1972, although for astrological reasons wasn't actually crowned until 1975. Educated at Eton and Harvard, the young king set out as an enlightened reformer, taking steps to curb the bureaucracy and cronyism that had flourished under his father. Reacting to Mahendra's laissez-faire policies on tourism – which had become Nepal's major industry – he cracked down on the growing hippie population by tightening visa restrictions. In 1975, in what was to be the shrewdest and most popular move of his career, the new king proposed designating Nepal a **Zone of Peace**, a Swiss-style neutrality pledge that would at first glance appear to be completely unassailable. India, however, has consistently opposed the measure as a violation of the 1950 "peace and friendship" treaty, which provides for mutual defence, while cynics like to point out the irony of Nepal – home of the Gurkhas, the world's most formidable mercenary soldiers – declaring itself a peace zone.

Birendra's domestic reforms soon ran out of steam, and discontent grew over corruption and the slow pace of development. Widespread uprisings broke out in 1979, forcing the king to promise a national **referendum** in which voters could choose between the *panchaayat* system and multiparty democracy. Democracy lost by a margin of 55 to 45 – many say the vote was rigged – and the *panchaayat* system was retained.

During the 1980s Birendra proved himself to be an earnest but weak leader, easily manipulated by advisers and the queen – forever chaperoned by minders with walkie-talkies, he simply fell out of touch with the people. Despite token tinkerings with the system, the gravy train got more crowded throughout the decade, and insiders, sensing that the regime's days were numbered, tried to grab everything they could in the time remaining. In 1988 the king's brother, Dhirendra, was forced to relinquish his title as prince to avoid wide-ranging corruption charges. The king himself was rumoured to have Swiss bank accounts and an island in the Maldives (or Greece). Political opponents were imprisoned, while freedom of speech and the press was nonexistent. Diplomats insist Birendra was uninvolved with any shady dealings, but he would have had to be incredibly naive not to have known what was going on in his name.

DEMOCRACY RESTORED

The chickens started coming home to roost in March 1989, when India, outraged by (among other things) Nepal's purchase of anti-aircraft guns from China, retaliated with a crippling **trade embargo**. Indian Prime Minister Rajiv Gandhi – who had long professed a deep distaste for Birendra's antiquated monarchy – apparently believed shortages of fuel and medicines would touch off a popular uprising and topple the regime in a matter of weeks. Only his timing was off. The government rode out the immediate crisis by closing the universities, rationing fuel and whipping up traditional anti-Indian sentiment, until the Indian elections in December, when Gandhi's more conciliatory successor, V. P. Singh, eased the embargo.

But after eight months of hardship, inflation and police action, Nepalis were fed up, and India could no longer be cast as the villain. The previous year had witnessed China's failed pro-democracy movement at Tiananmen Square and the spectacularly successful revolutions in Eastern Europe: Nepalis were enormously stirred by these examples. Seeing their chance, the banned opposition parties united in the so-called **Movement to Restore Democracy**, demanding an end to the *panchaayat* system and the creation of a constitutional monarchy. They called for a national day of protest on February 18, 1990 – a date already designated by the government, with unintended irony, as Democracy Day. Hundreds of opposition members were duly placed under house arrest, and the planned revolt got off to a shaky start. Yet Faagun 7 (the Nepali date of Democracy Day) marked the true launch of the **Jana Andolan** ("People's Movement"), which in subsequent weeks gathered strength, resulting in violent clashes and deaths in Bhaktapur, Narayanghat and Hetauda. Even while under detention, opposition leaders were able to call strikes and blackouts at will. The king, counselled by hardliners, kept silence.

On April 3, protesters overran Patan, and three days later an estimated 200,000 people marched up Kathmandu's Durbar Marg towards the Royal Palace. The army fired into the crowd, **killing** at least 45 people, and an ominous shoot-on-sight curfew was imposed. Finally moved to action by the massacre, the king dissolved his cabinet, legalized political parties and invited the opposition to form an interim government with Bhattarai as prime minister. The *panchaayat* system was dead.

After a few hiccups, the changeover to democracy proceeded in an orderly, if leisurely, fashion. By November 1990 the interim government had ratified a **new constitution** guaranteeing free speech, human rights and a constitutional monarchy. Under its provisions, the king "reigns but does not rule": he remains the commander-in-chief of the armed forces, but cannot make any executive decisions without consulting the prime minister and cabinet. The old Rastriya Panchaayat was replaced by a Parliament consisting of a directly elected House of Representatives and a smaller National Assembly.

After a suitable interval to allow the news of democracy to percolate into the remoter regions, Nepal's first free **elections** in more than thirty years were held in May 1991. The Nepal Congress Party, which had paid its dues in exile for three decades and could claim much of the credit for bringing down the *panchaayat* system, won a majority – but not by much. While the rest of the world was backpedalling from communism as fast as it could, Nepal's several Communist parties put in a strong showing, maintaining their traditional strongholds in the east and, incredibly, sweeping the comfortable Kathmandu Valley. The National Democratic Party, largely packed with former *panchaayat*-wallahs, went down in a ball of flames. It was a clear referendum against the old guard, but a less than enthusiastic vote of confidence for the Congress Party.

CONGRESS, COMMUNISM AND BREAKDOWN

Any government inheriting such immense challenges with so slender a mandate was probably doomed to disappoint, and the first **Nepali Congress** government's honeymoon was short-lived. Prime Minister Girija Prasad Koirala, brother of the late B. P. Koirala, Nepal's first democratically elected prime minister, lost little time not only in attracting the enmity of the

NEPAL'S MAOIST INSURGENCY

Despite outward appearances, Nepal is not at peace. Since 1996, an underground **Maoist** movement has been waging a campaign of violent opposition against the government. As of this writing, the so-called **People's War** had claimed more than 600 lives; no incidents had involved foreigners, as the fighting has largely been confined to remote rural areas where tourists don't go. However, the insurgency has the potential to escalate into a full-scale civil war.

Before turning to guerrilla warfare, the **Nepal Communist Party (Maoist)** was one of several bona fide factions that participated in the 1990 democracy movement. Dissatisfied with the deals struck by the major parties after the restoration of democracy, extremists in the group went underground; the failure of the 1994–95 Communist government apparently confirmed their belief that change wasn't possible by working within the system. In 1996 they launched the People's War with sporadic attacks on police stations in the mid-western hills, and subsequently expanded the conflict to encompass more than half the districts of Nepal. Intimidation and disruption – kidnapping and assassinating government officials, bombing telecommunications facilities and other infrastructure – have been their main tactics in an effort to undermine support for the status quo, while at the same time playing for the public's sympathies through populist stunts such as raiding banks and destroying loan papers. They're able to call general strikes (*bandh*) at will, although it's debatable whether their success at this indicates true support or merely shopkeepers' and bus owners' fear of getting their windows smashed.

True to their name, Nepal's Maoists hope to bring about an agrarian, **peasant-based revolution** modelled after the one led by Mao Zedong;

like China in the 1940s, Nepal is overwhelmingly rural, with relatively few of the urban proletarians glorified in the Marxist-Leninist strain of communism. The insurgents have therefore sought first to consolidate their power in the countryside, recruiting cadres from among the disaffected youth and driving out the forces of the establishment. The plan is eventually to encircle the cities with "liberated" villages and finally to overpower the urban areas.

Successive governments have considered the Maoists terrorists and responded with force. This approach has made dialogue impossible, and has left the underlying cause of the uprising – lack of development in rural areas – unaddressed. And while to its credit the government has so far refrained from calling out the army, it has used the **police** force to conduct purges that, according to Amnesty International, have included widespread arbitrary arrests, disappearances and extrajudicial killings. It's notable that 500 of the 600 people who have died in the People's War have been Maoists. All of this has helped force the rebels into a position where they feel they have no alternative but to fight, and nothing to lose.

The People's War is essentially a symptom of poverty, unemployment and bad governance – it's a desperate struggle by desperate people. Nepalis are amazingly tolerant of oppression, so by the time they get fed up enough to take up arms the situation is probably very bad, and may be irreconcilable. That's not to say the Maoists have the support of enough of the populace to overthrow the government; what popularity they enjoy seems to be mainly an expression of frustration with the mainstream parties. But the government would do well to heed that message, rather than shooting the messenger.

opposition Communists but also alienating many in his own party.

Antagonism between the Indian-sponsored Congress Party and the Communists, who looked to China as their only remaining ideological mentor, produced strong political polarities on almost every issue. For example, Congress supported the cause of Tibetan refugees in a way that the *panchaayat* regime never did, which the Communists viewed as provocative to China. Yet the Communists certainly spoke for many Nepalis when they accused Congress leaders of selling out Nepal's interests to India. This frustration coalesced into a long squabble over the **Tanakpur project** – a $65 million

hydroelectric diversion built by India on the Mahakali River, which forms the western border between the two countries – in which the government was accused of signing away most of Nepal's rights to the water and power generated from the river.

Unemployment, unrest, Indianization and political infighting produced widespread disillusion, forcing Koirala to step down in 1994. The ensuing election produced a hung parliament, with the **Communist Party of Nepal–United Marxist-Leninist (CPN-UML)**, the largest of several communist parties, stepping forward to form a minority government. Among supporters, Asia's first democratically elected Communist government kindled much idealism, but lacking a parliamentary majority, CPN-UML leader Manmohan Adhikari could only pursue a modest programme of reform.

The Communists' leadership came to an abrupt end after only nine months, when in 1995 the **Supreme Court** nullified the earlier election results and reinstated the previous parliament. This controversial decision, in which the Court interpreted the Constitution as barring the prime minister from calling midterm polls, was to have a crippling effect on the functioning of the Nepalese state: in effect, it saddled the country with a hung parliament and prevented the voters from doing anything about it until the next scheduled election. This set in train five years of political chaos, with no fewer than six governments attempting to cobble together coalitions in every combination: left, centre-right, left-right and centre-left.

A Nepali Congress-led government, headed by Sher Bahadur Deuba, lasted eighteen months with a slim majority before falling in early 1997. The **Rastriya Prajanatantra Party (RPP)**, a rightist group comprised mainly of Panchaayat-era veterans, presided over the two short-lived governments that followed. However, the RPP proceeded to self-destruct in early 1998, provoking a constitutional crisis and causing power to return to the Nepali Congress Party under G. P. Koirala. As if things weren't unstable enough, the CPN-UML then split in two, adding further fragmentation and acrimony. That opened the door for the Nepali Congress to take on the breakaway **CPN-ML** as its minority partner, but the bitter rivalry between the CPN-ML and the UML opposition created paralysis. By the end of 1998, the ML had pulled out of the coalition, and the Nepali Congress, seeing the writing on the wall, formed a caretaker government with essentially no role but to conduct fresh elections the following May.

These **political upheavals** took a toll on Nepal and its already lagging development. Preoccupied by short-term concerns and petty crises, successive governments were in no position to take decisive action or follow through on earlier plans. Nepalis looked on helplessly as their unaccountable leaders engaged in unseemly squabbles, forged Machiavellian alliances and lined their pockets at the public's expense. **Corruption** and cronyism became institutionalized as political parties relied on kickbacks to support themselves and created elaborate systems of patronage, and as constant political infighting meant that any accusation of wrongdoing could be dismissed as party-political. Frequent changes of government gave politicians a further incentive to grab it while they could. All this caused Nepalis to lose faith in their new democracy. Many concluded that it had merely transferred power from one set of elites to another, and some sought to overthrow the system through armed rebellion (see box on p.441). Even the normally apolitical donor community began sending a clear message that foreign aid to Nepal was in jeopardy if the government didn't clean up its act.

This book went to press before the results of the 1999 election were known. Whatever the outcome, Nepal's next government will have a tough job defusing long-simmering political tensions and reclaiming the people's trust.

RELIGION: HINDUISM, BUDDHISM, SHAMANISM

To say that religion is an important part of Nepali life is a considerable understatement: it *is* life. In the Nepali world view, just about every act has spiritual implications; the gods are assumed to have a hand in every success or misfortune and must be appeased continuously. Belief and ritual form the basis of the whole social order, governing the way husbands relate to wives, parents to children and even the king to his subjects.

Three religious strands intertwine in Nepal: Hinduism, Buddhism and shamanism. In theory, these faiths are philosophically incompatible, but Nepalis, being an exceptionally tolerant lot, tend to overlook the differences. As practised by the masses, each employs superstition and rites of passage to get followers through the present life, and codes of behaviour to prepare them for the next; Hindu priests, Buddhist lamas and tribal shamans play similar roles in their respective communities. Indeed, it's really only outside observers who bother to distinguish between the religions and dwell on their outward differences – most Nepalis find such distinctions needlessly academic.

Hinduism is the state religion of Nepal, and the government claims that 90 percent of the population is Hindu. However, there are social advantages to professing Hinduism in Nepal, and official statistics don't reflect the extent to which many Nepalis blithely combine Hinduism with Buddhist or shamanist beliefs. In general, Hinduism prevails at the lower elevations and Buddhism in the Himalaya, while shamanism is strongest among the ethnic minorities of the hills.

HINDUISM

Hinduism doesn't conform to Western notions of what a religion should be, and indeed the word "religion" is totally inadequate to describe it. Hindus call it *dharma*, a much more sweeping term that conveys faith, duty, a way of life and the entire social order. Having no common church or institution, its many sects and cults preach different dogmas and emphasize different scriptures. On social matters, Hinduism can be tragically rigid – witness the caste system – and when it comes to rituals, rather petty. Yet it's a highly individualistic system, offering worshippers an almost limitless choice of deities and admitting many paths to enlightenment. By absorbing and neutralizing opposing doctrines, rather than condemning them as heresies, it has flourished longer than any other major religion.

Hinduism has been evolving since approximately 1600 BC, when **Aryan** invaders swept down from central Asia and subjugated the native Dravidian peoples of the Indus and Ganges plains. They brought with them a pantheon of nature gods and goddesses, some of whom are still in circulation: Indra (sky and rain) is popular in Kathmandu, while Surya (sun), Agni (fire), Vayu (wind) and Yama (death) retain bit parts in contemporary mythology. These so-called Vedic gods were first immortalized in the **Vedas** ("Books of Wisdom"), which were probably written between the twelfth and eighth centuries BC, and it was during this period that most of the principles now identified with Hinduism were thrashed out.

To make sure they stayed on top of the conquered Dravidians, the Aryans banned intermarriage and codified the apartheid-like **caste system**; *varna*, the Sanskrit word for caste, means "colour", and to this day members of the higher castes generally have lighter skin. Initially, four castes were established: Brahmans (priests), Kshatriyas (warriors and rulers), Vaisyas (traders and farmers) and Sudras (artisans and menials); over time, the lower two divisions spawned innumerable occupational subcastes. The Rig Veda, Hinduism's oldest text, put a divine seal of approval on the arrangements by proclaiming that Brahmans had issued from the mouth of the supreme creator, Kshatriyas from his arms, Vaishyas from his thighs and Sudras from his feet.

Brahmans (called Baahuns in Nepal), entrusted with the brain work, proceeded to exploit their position by inventing preposterously complex rituals and sacrifices, and making themselves the indispensable guardians of these mysteries (cow-worship probably dates from this period). Despite this stagnation, the philosophical foundations of Hinduism were laid during the late Vedic period and recorded in a series of discourses known as the **Upanishads**. Ever since, Hinduism has run along two radically different tracks: the Brahmans' hocus-pocus popular religion, with its comic-book deities and bloody sacrifices, and the profound, intuitive insights of gurus and *rishi* (teachers).

The essence of Hinduism, unchanged since the Upanishads were written, is that the soul (*atman*) of each living thing is like a lost fragment of the universal soul – **brahman**, the ultimate reality – while everything in the physical universe is mere illusion (*maya*). To reunite with *brahman*, the individual soul must go through a **cycle of rebirths** (*samsara*), ideally moving up the scale with each reincarnation. Determining the soul's progress is its **karma** – its accumulated "just deserts" – which is reckoned by the degree to which the soul conformed to **dharma**, or correct Hindu behaviour, in its previous lives. Thus a low-caste Hindu must accept his or her lot to atone for past sins, and follow *dharma* in the hopes of achieving a higher rebirth. The theoretical goal of every Hindu is to cast off all illusion, achieve release (*moksha*) from the cycle of rebirths, and dissolve into *brahman*.

Hinduism has assembled a vast and rich body of mythology over the past three millennia, largely in an effort to personalize *brahman* for the masses. Early on, a few of the Vedic gods were renamed, relieved of their old nature associations and given personalities to illustrate divine attributes. The concept of the **Hindu "trinity"** – Brahma the creator, Vishnu the preserver and Shiva the destroyer – was developed, and the process of god-creation was speeded by the invention of numerous **avatar**, or manifestations of gods. Hinduism's best-loved epics, the *Mahabharata* (pronounced *Mahabharat* in Nepal) and the *Ramayana* (*Ramayan*), portray two of Vishnu's *avatar*, Krishna and Ram, as models of human conduct (although as often as not Hindu gods, like their Greek counterparts, are made out to be vain and foolish).

The explosion of deities has given rise to a succession of **devotional cults** over the centuries, the most important of which nowadays are Vaishnava (followers of Vishnu), Shaiva (Shiva) and Mahadevi (the mother goddess); the last often goes by the name Shakti, a tantric term explained below. Brahma is rarely icono-

AUM

"AUM" is a word that represents to our ears that sound of the energy of the universe of which all things are manifestations. You start in the back of the mouth, "ahh," then "oo," you fill the mouth, and "mm" closes the mouth. When you pronounce this properly, all vowel sounds are included in the pronunciation. AUM. Consonants are here regarded simply as interruptions of the essential vowel sound.

All words are thus fragments of AUM, just as all images are fragments of the Form of forms. AUM is a symbolic sound that puts you in touch with that resounding being that is the universe. If you heard some of the recordings of Tibetan monks chanting AUM, you would know what the word means, all right. That's the AUM of being in the world. To be in touch with that and to get the sense of that is the peak experience of all.

A-U-M. The birth, the coming into being, and the dissolution that cycles back. AUM is called the "four-element syllable." A-U-M – and what is the fourth element? The silence out of which AUM arises, and back into which it goes, and

which underlies it. My life is the A-U-M, but there is a silence underlying it, too. That is what we would call the immortal. This is the mortal and that's the immortal, and there wouldn't be the mortal if there weren't the immortal. One must discriminate between the mortal aspect and the immortal aspect of one's own existence . . . that's why it is a peak experience to break past all that, every now and then, and to realize, "Oh . . . ah . . ."

From "The Power of Myth",
by Joseph Campbell, reproduced by
permission of Bantam Doubleday Dell.

graphically depicted and consequently not widely worshipped.

THE HINDU PANTHEON

If you're daunted by Hinduism's technicolour array of gods and goddesses, don't worry: your average Hindu would be hard-pressed to name most of them. While Hinduism is said to boast of 33 million deities, they can all be thought of as representations of the one supreme god – a paradox which isn't hard to deal with if you've been trained that everything is illusion anyway. The most important gods, described below, can easily be identified by certain trademark implements, postures and "vehicles" (animal carriers). As for gods' multiple arms and heads, these aren't meant to be taken literally: they symbolize the deity's "universal" (omnipotent) form, while severed heads and trampled corpses signify ignorance and evil.

VISHNU

Vishnu (often known as Narayan in Nepal) is the face of dignity and equanimity, typically shown standing erect holding a wheel (*chakra*), mace (*gada*), lotus (*padma*) and conch (*sankha*) in his four hands, or, as at Budhanilkantha, reclining on a serpent's coil. A statue of **Garuda** (**Garud** in Nepal), Vishnu's bird-man vehicle, is always close by. Vishnu is also sometimes depicted in one or more of his ten incarnations (*das avatar*), which follow an evolutionary progression from fish, turtle and boar to man-lion, dwarf, axe-wielding Brahman and the legendary heroes **Ram** and **Krishna**.

Ram is associated with **Hanuman**, his loyal monkey-king ally in the *Ramayan*, while Krishna is most commonly seen on calendars as a chubby blue baby, flute-player or charioteer. Interestingly, Vishnu's ninth *avatar* is the Buddha – this was a sixth-century attempt by Vaishnavas to bring Buddhists into their fold – and the tenth is Kalki, a messiah figure invented in the twelfth century when Hindus were being persecuted at the hands of Muslim invaders.

Vishnu's consort is **Lakshmi**, the goddess of wealth, to whom lamps are lit during the festival of Tihaar. Like Vishnu, she assumed mortal form in two great Hindu myths, playing opposite Ram as the chaste princess Sita, and opposite Krishna as the passionate Radha.

SHIVA

Shiva's incarnations are countless, ranging from the hideous Bhairab, who alone is said to take 64 different forms, to the benign Pashupati ("Lord of the Animals") and Nataraj ("King of the Dance"). To many devotees he is simply Mahadev: Great God. The earliest and still the most widespread icon of Shiva is the **linga**, a phallic stone fertility symbol* commonly housed in a boxy stone *shivalaya* ("Shiva home"). Shiva temples can be identified by the presence of a *trisul* (trident) and the bull **Nandi**, Shiva's mount, who is himself something of a fertility symbol.

Many sadhus worship Shiva the *yogin* (one who practises yoga), the Hindu ascetic supreme, who is often depicted sitting in meditative repose on a Himalayan mountaintop, perhaps holding a chilam of *ganja*. Pashupatinath is the national shrine to Shiva as **Pashupati**, and is patronized by Pashupata, Kaplika and other Shaiva sects, who take it to be Shiva's winter home. Another popular image of Shiva is as the loving husband with his consort, Parvati: the two can be seen leaning from an upper window of a temple in Kathmandu's Durbar Square. Nearby stand two famous statues of **Bhairab**, the tantric (see below) interpretation of Shiva in his role as destroyer: according to Hindu philosophy, everything – not only evil – must be destroyed in its turn to make way for new things.

MAHADEVI

The mother goddess is similarly worshipped in many forms, both peaceful and wrathful, and many of these are reckoned to be the consorts of corresponding Shiva forms. As **Kali** ("Black") she is the female counterpart of Bhairab, wearing a necklace of skulls and sticking out her tongue with bloodthirsty intent; as **Durga** she is the demon-slayer honoured in the great Dasain festival. In Nepal she is widely worshipped as **Bhagwati**, the embodiment of female creative

---

*The phallic aspect of the *linga* is perhaps overplayed by non-Hindus. Gandhi wrote: "It has remained for our Western visitors to acquaint us with the obscenity of many practices which we have hitherto innocently indulged in. It was in a missionary book that I first learned that the Shiva *linga* had any obscene significance at all." Then again, Gandhi denied most things to do with sex.

power. In all these forms, the mother goddess is appeased by sacrifices of uncastrated male animals. On a more peaceful level, she is also Parvati ("Hill", daughter of Himalaya), Gauri ("Golden") or just **Mahadevi** ("Great Goddess").

GANESH AND OTHERS

Several legends tell how **Ganesh**, Shiva and Parvati's son, came to have an elephant's head: one states that Shiva accidentally chopped the boy's head off, and owing to an obscure restriction on the god's restorative powers, was forced to replace it with that of the first creature he saw. The god of wisdom and remover of obstacles, Ganesh must be worshipped first to ensure offerings to other gods will be effective, which is why a Ganesh shrine or stone will invariably be found near other temples. Underscoring Hinduism's great sense of the mystical absurd, Ganesh's vehicle is a rat.

Of the other Hindu deities, only **Annapurna**, the goddess of grain and abundance (her name means "Full of Grain"), and **Saraswati**, the goddess of learning and culture, receive much attention in Nepal. Saraswati is normally depicted holding a *vina*, a musical instrument something like a sitar.

BUDDHISM

The Buddha was born Siddhartha Gautama in what is now Nepal (see p.320) in the fifth or sixth century BC, and his teachings were in many ways a protest against the ritualism to which popular Hinduism had by then been reduced. The Buddha rejected the Hindu caste system and the belief in a creator God, while adapting its doctrines of reincarnation and *karma*, along with many yogic practices; the result was a non-theistic, pragmatic philosophy that placed a greater emphasis on the active pursuit of enlightenment.

Whereas the Hindu ideal is to reunite with the Creator, the Buddhist goal is **nirvana**, a state of being where wisdom and compassion have completely uprooted the "three poisons" of greed, hatred and delusion. The essence of the Buddha's teaching is encapsulated in the **four noble truths**: existence is suffering; suffering is caused by desire; the taming of desire ends suffering; and desire can be tamed by following the **eightfold path**, a set of deceptively

simple guidelines for achieving *dharma*. He called the whole prescription the **Middle Way** because it avoided the extremes of sensual indulgence and asceticism, both of which were popularly believed to lead to enlightenment if pursued with sufficient vigour (and the Buddha had tried them both pretty vigorously before rejecting them).

As it developed, Buddhism became for many followers a full-time monastic pursuit. But for most lay people, the lonely quest for enlightenment was too hard-core and impersonal; to restore emotional elements that had been lost in the monastic movement, Buddhism evolved a populist strand known as **Mahayana** ("Great Vehicle"). Reintroducing elements of worship and prayer, Mahayana Buddhism developed its own pantheon of *bodhisattva* – enlightened intermediaries, something akin to Catholic saints, who have forgone *nirvana* until all humanity has been saved. Many of these were a repackaging of older Hindu deities, who were now given new names and roles as protectors of the *dharma*.

Followers of the original teachings called their school **Theravada** ("Way of the Elders"), but to Mahayana Buddhists it came to be known, somewhat disparagingly, as **Hinayana** ("Lesser Vehicle"). This tradition remains active in Sri Lanka and much of southeast Asia. It was the Mahayana doctrine that came to Nepal, around the fifth century, and also spread to China, Korea and Japan, adapting differently to each. Buddhism in India was dealt a death blow in the seventh century by Muslim invasions, which destroyed the great monastic universities and the thousands of monks who lived in them; what was left of Buddhism was effectively absorbed into the ocean of Hinduism.

TANTRA AND VAJRAYANA

Even as Hinduism was on the wane in India, a new religious movement was developing in Bengal and Bihar that would give a radically new bent to both Buddhism and Hinduism. **Tantra** erupted like the punk rock of religion, proclaiming that *everything* in life can be used to reach enlightenment: the five things normally shunned in orthodox Hinduism and Buddhism as poisons – meat, fish, parched grains, alcohol and sex – are embraced wholeheartedly on the tantric path. Sex, in particular, is regarded as the central metaphor for spiritual enlightenment, and it is this inversion of the sacred and profane that has given *tantra* its somewhat risqué reputation. *Tantra* abounds in esoteric imagery, *mantra* (verbal formulas) and *mandala* (diagrams used to aid meditation), which together make up a sort of mystic code intended only for initiates.

According to **Hindu tantra**, the female principle (**shakti**) possesses the creative energy which is capable of activating the male force. The gods are powerless until joined with their female counterparts – in tantric art, Bhairab is often shown locked in a fierce sexual embrace – and in many of her guises the mother goddess has become Shakti, one half of a tantric union of sexual opposites. The human psyche, too, is held to consist of male and female forces that must be harnessed: followers of Hindu *tantra* are trained to visualize the body's female energy rising like a snake from the level of the sexual organs, ascending the seven psychic centres (*chakra*) of the spinal column to reach the male principle at the top of the head, resulting in realization.

Buddhist tantra, known as **Vajrayana** ("Thunderbolt Way"), reverses the symbolism of these two forces and makes the male principle of "skill in means" or compassion the active force, and the female principle of "wisdom" passive. In tantric rituals, these forces are symbolized by the the hand-held "lightning-bolt sceptre" (*vajra; dorje* in Tibetan), which represents the male principle, and the bell (*ghanti*), representing the female. Expanding on Mahayana's all-male pantheon, Vajrayana introduces female counterparts to the main Buddha figures and some of the *bodhisattva*, and sometimes depicts them in sexual positions.

LAMAISM (TIBETAN BUDDHISM)

Vajrayana Buddhism found its greatest expression in Tibet, which it reached (by way of Nepal) in the eighth century. At the time, Tibet was under the sway of a native shamanic religion (see below) known as **Bön**: Vajrayana eventually overcame Bön*, but only by taking on board

---

* Unrepentant Bön priests were banished to the Himalayan periphery, and even today vestiges of the Bön tradition may be encountered while trekking in Nepal: for example, a follower of Bön will circle a religious monument anticlockwise, the opposite direction to a Buddhist.

---

many of its symbols and rituals, thus creating the spectacularly distinct branch of Buddhism that outsiders call **Lamaism**.

Lamaism turned Bön's demons into fierce guardian deities (*dharmapala*) – these can usually be seen flanking monastery (*gompa*) entrances – and incorporated elements of Bön magic into its meditational practices. Since blood sacrifices were out of the question, they were adapted into "vegetarian" offerings in the form of conical dough cakes called *torma*. The *Bardo Thödol* ("Tibetan Book of the Dead") is basically a shamanic guide to the after-death experience that probably owes much to Bön.

While its underlying principles aren't much different from that of Mahayana Buddhism, Lamaism has a tendency to express them in incredibly esoteric symbolism. The **Wheel of Life**, often depicted in *thangka* and frescoes at monastery entrances, is an intricate exposition of the different levels of rebirth and the limitations of the unenlightened state. The **stupa** (*chorten* in Tibetan), an ancient abstract representation of the Buddha, is developed into a complex statement of Buddhist cosmology, and Buddhahood is refracted into five aspects, symbolized by the five transcendent or *dhyani* (meditating) Buddhas, which can be seen in niches surrounding the Swayambhu stupa. **Prayer wheels**, usually bearing the *mantra, Om mani padme hum* ("Hail to the jewel in the lotus"), are Tibetan innovations that aid meditative concentration, and **prayer flags** bear *mantra* and wishes for compassion which are meant to be picked up and spread by the wind.

By far the most important feature of Tibetan Buddhism are its **bodhisattva**, which are often mistaken for deities. Held to be emanations of the *dhyani* Buddhas, they are used in meditation and rituals to help develop the qualities they symbolize, and also serve as objects of devotion. The most popular figures are **Avalokiteshwara** (**Chenrezig** in Tibetan), a white male figure with four arms (or, sometimes, a thousand), who represents compassion; **Tara**, a white or green female figure, also representing compassion; and **Manjushri**, an orange-yellow male youth gracefully holding a sword above his head, who represents wisdom. Though these figures are peaceful and benign, there are also wrathful ones with bulging eyes, often wearing human skins and drinking blood, who symbolize the energy and potency of the enlightened state and the sublimation of our crudest energies.

From the beginning, Tibetan Buddhism placed great emphasis on close contact with a **lama**, or spiritual guide, who can steer the student through the complex meditations and rituals. Teachings were passed on orally from lama to disciple, so the divergence of various sects over the centuries has had more to do with different lineages than with major doctrinal differences. The leader of each sect, and indeed of each monastery, is venerated as the reincarnation (*tulku*) of his or her predecessor, and is expected to carry on the same spiritual tradition. Of the **four main sects**, the oldest is the Nyingma-pa ("Red Hats"), founded in the eighth century by Guru Padma Sambhava, who, if all the stories told about him were true, meditated in every cave in Nepal. The Sakya-pa broke away in the eleventh century, tracing their line from the second-century Indian philosopher Nagarjuna. The Kagyu-pa order emerged in the

eleventh and twelfth centuries, inspired by the Tibetan mystic Marpa and his enlightened disciple Milarepa, who also meditated his way around Nepal. The Gelug-pa ("Yellow Hats") sect, led by the Dalai Lama, is the only one that takes a significantly different theological line; born out of a fifteenth-century reform movement to purge Lamaism of its questionable religious practices, it places greater emphasis on study and intellectual debate.

THE NEWAR SYNTHESIS

Ask a Newar whether he's Hindu or Buddhist, the saying goes, and he'll answer "yes": after fifteen centuries of continuous exposure to both faiths, the Newars of the Kathmandu Valley have concocted a unique **synthesis** of the two. To religious scholars, the Newar religion is as exciting as a biologist's missing link, for some believe that it provides a picture of the way Mahayana and Vajrayana Buddhism functioned historically in India.

A VISIT TO THE ASTROLOGER

His name is Joshi – in Newar society, all members of the astrologer subcaste are called Joshi – and to get to his office I have to duck through a low doorway off a courtyard in the old part of Patan and feel my way up two flights of wooden steps in the dark, climbing towards a glimmer of light and the sounds of low murmuring. At the landing I take off my shoes and enter the sanctum. Joshi-ji doesn't even look up. He's sitting cross-legged on the floor behind a low desk, glasses perched on the end of his nose, scowling over a sheaf of papers and, except for his Nepali-style clothes, looking exactly the way I'd always pictured Professor Godbole in *A Passage to India*. Shelves of books and scrolls are heaped behind him, and over in one corner a small shrine is illuminated by a low-watt bulb and a smouldering stick of incense. An older couple is seated in front of Joshi-ji's desk, nervously asking a question of the great man; he pushes his glasses up on his forehead, scribbles something, then pulls himself up to answer in melodic, nasal tones. I settle down on the floor next to two other waiting couples and together we keep a respectful silence.

To Newars, the **astrologer** is a counsellor, confessor, general practitioner and guide through the maze of life. With the priest and the doctor, he acts as mediator between the self and the universe (which are one); and since astrology is but one branch of Hindu knowledge, his prognostica-

tions on important occasions are considered as important as a priest's blessings, and he is often called upon to provide a second opinion on a doctor's diagnosis. He knows most of his clients from birth. For new parents, the astrologer will prepare complex planetary charts based on the baby's precise time and place of **birth**, together with a lengthy interpretation detailing personality traits, health hazards, vocational aptitude, characteristics of the ideal marriage partner, and a general assessment of the newborn's prospects. When a **marriage** is contemplated, he will study the horoscopes of the prospective couple to make sure the match is suitable, and if so, he'll perform further calculations to determine the most auspicious wedding date. During an **illness**, he may prescribe a protective amulet, gemstone or herbal remedy corresponding to the planets influencing the patient. He may also be consulted on the advisability of a business decision or a major purchase.

While Western astrology is well suited to an independent, egocentric culture, **Hindu astrology** is much more at ease with the insignificance of the individual in the midst of the vast cosmos. And unlike the Western system, which is regarded more as a tool for personal fulfilment, the Hindu tradition emphasizes external events and how – and when – to deal with them. The **horoscope** represents a snapshot of the subject's *karma*: at

Until only the past two centuries, the Newars held fast to the original monastic form of tantric Buddhism – as the *bahal* of Kathmandu and Patan still bear witness – while their rulers pursued the Hindu tantric path. However, the Kathmandu Valley has become progressively "Hinduized" since the unification of Nepal in the eighteenth century: the monasteries have largely disappeared, their monks have married, and the title of **Vajracharya** (Buddhist priest) has become a hereditary caste like that of the Baahun (Brahman) priests. Today, Newar Buddhists are perhaps the only Buddhist culture that no longer maintains active communities of monks or nuns. Although the acceptance of caste and the decline of monasticism have shifted the balance in favour of Hinduism, at the popular level the synthesis remains as well bonded as ever.

When Newars refer to themselves as **Buddha margi** (Buddhist) or **Shiva margi** (Hindu), they often do so only to indicate that they employ a Vajracharya or Baahun priest; even this doesn't always hold true, though, as many *jyapu* (farmers) call themselves "Hindu" and attend Hindu festivals, yet still use Vajracharyas. In any case, Newar rituals vary little from Hindu to Buddhist.

Puja (an act of worship) is performed to gain the favour of deities for material requests as often as for "spiritual" reasons. It is a profound and very personal ritual. An integral part of all Newar rituals is the "*puja* of five offerings", consisting of flowers (usually marigolds), incense, light (in the form of butter lamps), *sindur* (coloured powder) and various kinds of purified food (usually rice, dairy products, sometimes sweets). Before **darshan** (audience with a deity), the devotee or the priest uses consecrated water to wash him or herself and to bathe the deity. After the deity has symbolically accepted and eaten some food, the remainder is taken back by the devotee as **prasad** (consecrated food). This, along with a **tika** made with

---

the precise moment of reincarnation, the planets display the tally, and although it's misleading to speak in terms of planetary "influences", the *karma* that they reveal strongly implies the future course of one's life. The astrologer's role, then, is to suggest the best way to play the hand one was dealt.

The Hindu method of generating horoscopes follows the same essential principles as in the Western tradition, although technical differences between the two will produce somewhat different results. Hindu astrology recognizes the same twelve **signs of the zodiac**, albeit under different (Sanskrit) names, and assigns many of the same attributes to the planets and houses. The basic **birth chart** indicates the **sun sign** (the sign corresponding to the sun's position at the time of birth), the ascendant or **"rising" sign** (the sign rising above the eastern horizon at the time of birth) and the positions of the moon and the five planets known to the ancients, plus a couple of other non-Western points of reference. The positions of all of these are also noted in relation to the twelve **houses**, each of which governs key aspects of the subject's life (health, relationships and so on). The chief technical difference between Western and Hindu horoscopy is in how they line up the signs of the zodiac with respect to the earth. Western astrologers use the **tropical zodiac**, in which Aries is always assumed to start on the spring equinox (March 21, give or take a day), even though a wobble in

the earth's axis causes the actual constellations to drift out of sync by about 30° (one sign) every 2000 years or so – that's why it's now Pisces that the sun enters on March 21, and pretty soon, New Agers say, we'll be into the age of Aquarius. Hindu astrologers, on the other hand, go by the **sidereal zodiac**, which takes all its measurements from the *actual* positions of the constellations. (Technically speaking, this is a pretty profound difference, but since the Western and Hindu methods of interpretation are different, it all comes out in the wash.) If you have a horoscope done in Nepal, you'll probably be presented with a beautifully calligraphed scroll detailing all these measurements in chart and tabular form, using both tropical and sidereal measurements.

If charting a horoscope is largely a matter of mathematical donkey work, **interpretation** is an intuitive art requiring great eloquence and finesse. The astrologer can draw on numerous texts describing every conceivable conjunction of planets, and the positive and negative effects of every planet on every house; but at the end of the day, the usefulness of the reading must come down to the astrologer's own skill and experience. As I found on my visit to Joshi-ji, the specifics aren't everything. The astrologer isn't peddling facts; he's offering insight, hope, reassurance, and a dash of theatre.

David Reed

the coloured powder, confers the deity's blessing and protection.

Priests are ordinarily engaged for the more important **life-cycle rites** (birth, marriage, death) or for larger seasonal festivals; wealthier Newars may also seek private consultations at times of illness or important decisions. Baahun priests don't perform animal **sacrifices**, but they do preside over the rituals that precede them. This brings up one of the rare differences between Hindu and Buddhist Newars: while Hindu Newars are enthusiastic sacrificers – they call the bloody ninth day of the Dasain festival *Syako Tyako* (roughly, "the more you kill, the more you gain") – Buddhists seldom participate. During Dasain, Tibetan monasteries in Nepal hold special services to pray for good rebirths of the sacrificed animals.

THE NEWAR PANTHEON

All the Hindu and Buddhist deities already discussed are fair game for Newars, along with a few additional characters of local invention. Some deities specialize in curing diseases, others bring good harvests – as far as Newars are concerned, it doesn't matter whether they're Hindu or Buddhist so long as they do the job. The following are some of the figures uniquely adapted by the Newars.

Machhendranath, honoured as a rainmaker par excellence, typifies the layering of religious motifs that so frequently takes place among the Newars. To be accurate, only Hindus call the god Machhendranath; Buddhist Newars know him as **Karunamaya** or by any of a number of local names. He is commonly associated with Avalokiteshwara, the *bodhisattva* of compassion, who is invoked by the mantra *Om mani padme hum*. Depending on his incarnation (he is said to have 108), he may be depicted as having anything up to a thousand arms and eleven heads. While it's unclear how Avalokiteshwara came to be associated with the historical figures of Machhendranath and Gorakhnath – who are considered saints by Hindus – it was certainly in part the result of a conscious attempt by Hindu rulers to establish religious and social bonds by grafting two Hindu saints on to a local Buddhist cult.

Kumari, the "Living Goddess", is another often-cited example of Newar syncretism (religious fusing): although acknowledged to be an incarnation of the Hindu goddess Durga, she is picked from a Buddhist-caste family. **Bhimsen**, a mortal hero in the Hindu *Mahabharat*, who is rarely worshipped in India, has somehow been elevated to be the patron deity of Newar shopkeepers, both Hindu and Buddhist.

Manjushri, the *bodhisattva* of wisdom, has been pinched from the Buddhist pantheon to play the lead part in the Kathmandu Valley's creation myth (although he is often confused with Saraswati, the Hindu goddess of knowledge). He is always depicted with a sword, with which he cuts away ignorance and attachment, and sometimes also with a book, bow, bell and *vajra*. Likewise **Tara**, the embodiment of the female principle in Vajrayana Buddhism, assumes special meaning for Newars, who consider her the deification of an eighth-century Nepali princess.

Quintessentially tantric, the **Bajra Joginis** (or Vajra Yoginis) command their own cult centred at four temples around the Kathmandu Valley. They are regarded as the female aspect of the Buddha and are the subjects of esoteric cults and closely guarded secrets. Harati, the Buddhist protector of children, is zealously worshipped by Newars under the name **Ajima**, the grandmother goddess.

Throughout Nepal, stones and trees marked with *sindur* may be seen: vestiges of older animist practices, these may mark the place where a nature or mother goddess (generically known as **Mai**), local spirit or serpent (**nag**) is supposed to live. There are many types of these lesser spirit beings who require offerings to safeguard passage through their respective domains.

SHAMANISM

More ancient than Hinduism or Buddhism, **shamanism** is followed in diverse ways throughout the world by peoples fortunate enough to have been overlooked by the institutional religions. Variously described as medicine men, witch doctors or oracles, shamans perform mystical rituals to mediate between the physical and spiritual realms on behalf of their flock. (Western society has its "shamans", too – faith healers and mediums, for example.)

Shamanism is the traditional religion of most of Nepal's native ethnic groups, and while many have adopted at least outward forms of Hinduism or Buddhism (depending on their location), it is still widely practised in the eastern and western hills. In Nepali, the generic words for shaman are **jhankri** and **dhami**, although each ethnic group has its own term as well. Forms and practices vary from one tribe to another, but a *jhankri* – usually carrying a double-sided drum and often wearing a headdress of peacock feathers – is always unmistakable.

The *jhankri*'s main job is to maintain spiritual and physical balance, and to restore it when it has been upset. As a healer, he may examine the entrails of animals for signs, gather medicinal plants from the forest, perform sacrifices, exorcize demons, chant magical incantations to invoke helper deities, or conduct any number of other rituals. As an oracle, he may fall into a trance and act as a mouthpiece of the gods, advising, admonishing and consoling listeners. As the spiritual sentry of his community, he must ward off ghosts, evil spirits and angry ancestors – sometimes by superior strength, often by trickery. All this, plus his duties as funeral director, dispenser of amulets, teller of myths and consecrator of holy ground and so on, put the *jhankri* at the very heart of religious and social life in the hills. Little wonder that Hinduism and Buddhism have been so shaped in Nepal by these shamanistic traditions, producing a unique melting pot of religions.

Charles Leech and David Reed

MUSIC AND DANCE

There are as many different styles of Nepali music and dance as there are ethnic groups. These traditional arts are rarely performed outside Nepal, which means that you'll be in a position to appreciate some wonderfully rare sounds and sights as you travel around the country. Meanwhile, a new wave of non-traditional Nepali music is beginning to break into the world-music charts, and as a traveller in Nepal you'll be able to sample the full range and pick up the latest releases.

CLASSICAL AND RELIGIOUS

Little attempt has been made to chart the history of Nepali music. However, one of the earliest influences surely must have been **Indian classical music**, which goes back to a time when there was no distinction between India and Nepal, and to a region that extended well beyond the present borders of India. Classical music of the north Indian style flourished at the courts of the Malla kings and reached its zenith in Nepal under the Rana prime ministers, who patronized Indian musicians in their court to the exclusion of Nepali folk performers. Though it was always primarily an aristocratic genre, there is still a lively classical music network in Kathmandu, with tourist culture shows supplementing public performances and private recitals (for example, bimonthly at the royal palace).

Newar Buddhist priests still sing esoteric **tantric hymns** which, when accompanied by **mystical dances** and hand postures, have immense occult power. The secrets of these are closely guarded by initiated priests, but a rare public performance is held on Buddha Jayanti, when five *vajracharya* costumed as the Pancha Buddha dance at Swayambhu.

The contemporary layman's form of sacred music is **bhajan** – devotional hymn-singing, usually performed in front of temples and in rest houses. *Bhajan* groups gather on auspicious evenings to chant praises to Ram, Krishna or other Hindu deities; during festivals they may carry on through the night, and round-the-clock vigils are sometimes sponsored by wealthy patrons. Like a musical *puja*, the haunting verses are repeated over and over to the mesmeric beat of the tabla and the drone of the harmonium.

Sherpas and other Bhotiyas have their own ritualistic music rooted in **Tibetan Buddhist** traditions. Rhythm is more important than melody in this crashing, banging music, which is the exclusive preserve of monks. There's a hierarchy of instruments in the lamaist orchestra, from the *ghanti* (bell), *sankha* (conch shell) and *jhyaamta* (small cymbals), through the *bugcham* (large cymbals), *kangling* (small trumpet, made from a human thigh bone) and *dhyangro* (bass drum), to the *gyaling* (jewel-encrusted shawm, or oboe) and *radung* (a ten-foot-long telescopic trumpet, which looks like a Swiss alpenhorn and produces a sound like a subsonic fart). The human voice forms a separate instrument in the mix, as monks recite prayers in deep, dirge-like, "self-harmonizing" chanting – a unique practice lately introduced to the West by touring Tibetan ensembles.

FOLK

For Nepalis where electricity and videos haven't yet reached, **folk music** and dancing is still just about the only form of entertainment available. On holidays and festival days, the men of a village or neighbourhood will typically gather in a circle for an evening session of singing and socializing; as a rule only the men perform on these occasions, while the women look on.

The musical backing always consists of a **maadal** (horizontally held two-sided drum), and often also includes other drums, harmonium and *murali* (bamboo flute). After some preliminary tapping on the *maadal*, a member of the group will strike up a familiar verse, and all join in on the chorus; the first singer runs through as many verses as he can remember, at which point someone else takes over, often making up comical verses to suit the occasion. Members of the group dance to the music one at a time, each entertaining onlookers with his interpretation of the song in swirling body movements, facial expressions and hand gestures.

Young men and women sing and dance together (though again, not at the same time) at **rodi ghar**, the Nepali equivalent of a sock hop. Originally a Gurung institution, *rodi* has been embraced by many other hill groups as an informal, musical means of courtship. Young men and women of the hill tribes also sing improvised, flirtatious duets; the woman may even take the lead in these, forcing the man to come up with rejoinders to her jesting verses. In addition, women also sing in the fields to ease the burden of manual work – especially during *ropai* (rice transplanting), which has its own traditional songs.

Folk musical traditions vary among Nepal's many ethnic groups, but the true sound of Nepal may be said to be the soft and melodic music of the hills. Of several hill styles, **jhyaure**, the *maadal*-based music of the western hills, has emerged as the most popular. **Selo**, the musical style of the Tamangs that's performed to the accompaniment of the *damphu* (a one-sided, flat, round drum), has also been adopted by other ethnic communities. The music of the **Jyapu** farming caste has a lively rhythm, provided by the *dhime* (big two-sided drum) and a host of other drums, percussion instruments and woodwinds, though the singing has an extremely nasal quality that's hard for outsiders to appreciate.

Although folk music is, by definition, a pursuit of amateurs, two traditional castes of professional musicians exist in Nepal. **Gaaine** – wandering minstrels – have always served as an important unifying force in the hills, relaying not only news but also songs and musical styles from village to village. Accompanying themselves on *sarangi* (four-stringed fiddles), *gaaine* once thrived under patronage from local chieftains, whose deeds were the main topics of their songs. They're on the decline nowadays, but a few still ply their trade in the villages north of Pokhara, in the far west, and in Kirtipur in the Kathmandu Valley (needless to say, the

so-called *gaaine* in Thamel and Lakeside aren't worthy of the title). Their repertoire includes sacred songs in praise of Hindu deities, bittersweet ballads of toil and triumph, great moments in Nepali history and political commentary and even government propaganda.

Much more numerous are the **damai**, members of the tailor caste, who for generations have served as the exclusive guardians of the *paanchai baajaa* (see below), and may also be employed at shrines to play during daily offerings and blood sacrifices. The tailor-musician combination isn't as strange as it might sound: Nepalis traditionally used to have just one set of clothes made each year, for the autumn Dasain festival, so tailors needed an occupation to tide them over during the winter and spring. Handily, that's the wedding season, when musicians are much in demand.

WEDDINGS AND FESTIVALS

No wedding would be complete without the **paanchai baajaa** (five instruments), a traditional Nepali ensemble of *sahanai* (shawm), *damaha* (large kettledrum), *narsinga* (C-shaped horn), *jhyaali* (cymbals) and *dholaki* (two-sided drum). ("They got married without *paanchai baajaa*" is a euphemism for living together.) Despite the name, bands ideally number nine members – eleven is the legal maximum, set to keep wedding costs down. In the Kathmandu Valley, *paanchai baajaa* musicians have largely traded in their traditional instruments for Western brass horns and clarinets, and their ceremonial dress for fanciful, military-style uniforms, but the music remains distinctly Nepali.

Raucous and jubilant, *paanchai baajaa* music is considered an auspicious accompaniment to processions, Hindu rituals and life-cycle rites. During a **wedding**, the band accompanies the groom to the home of the bride, plays during the wedding ceremony, and again during the return procession. Apart from playing popular folk songs and film favourites, the musicians have a traditional repertoire of numbers for specific occasions – for example, the "bride-requesting tune", in which the shawm player mimics the bride's wailing as she departs from her family home, and the music of the rice-transplanting season, which imitates the body rhythm of the workers.

Festivals bring their own interwoven forms of music and dance, especially in the

Kathmandu Valley. The Newars of the valley are renowned for their spectacular **masked dances**, in which the dancers enter a trance-like state to become the embodiments of the gods they portray, gesturing and gyrating behind elaborately painted papier-mâché masks. Best known of these are Bhaktapur's Nawa Durga dancers and their supporting musicians: their vigorous dance-drama, held on the tenth day of Dasain, recounts the victory of the goddess Durga over a buffalo demon. In Kathmandu, several different troupes take the stage during Indra Jaatra, performing the famous dance of the demon Lakhe, the sword-spinning Sawo Bhaku dance, and tableaux of the Das Avatar (ten incarnations) of Vishnu. The dancing is in a more humorous vein during Gaai Jaatra, when boys and young men play female roles in drag, since women aren't normally supposed to dance in public.

Virtuoso **drummers**, the Jyapus (Newar farmers) of the valley provide the rolling beat for processions on festival days: generally they beat enormous cylindrical drums (*dhime baajaa*) in groups with two sizes of cymbal. At some shrines, in addition to a singing group, there is a complement of nine drums (*nawa daaphaa*), which are played in sequence during festivals with various accompanying instruments. Another type of popular processional band, *bansuri baajaa*, combines flutes and barrel drums.

Tibetans and Bhotiyas have their own form of dance-drama, **cham**. Tengboche hosts the most famous of such performances, Mani Rimdu, on the day after the full moon of October–November (another performance is held at Thami in May), when monks wearing masks and costumes represent various good and bad guys in the story of Buddhism's victory over the ancient Bön religion in Tibet. Monasteries at Boudha and Swayambhu also present *cham* dances around Losar (Tibetan New Year).

MODERN MUSIC

Pre-1951, Nepal had no radio and no recording industry, and those few artists who travelled to Calcutta to record their songs on 78rpm were known only to a handful of aristocrats with record-players. The dawn of modern Nepali music came in 1952, the year after the fall of the Ranas, when **Radio Nepal** was established; only a year later, Dharma Raj Thapa made recording history, selling 3000 copies of a novelty song about the conquest of Everest by Hillary and Tenzing Norgay.

A homegrown **recording industry** took root under King Mahendra (1955–72), himself something of a patron of the arts, and with it came Nepal's first wave of **recording stars**. Still the best loved of these, though he died in 1991, is Narayan Gopal, whose songs are praised for their poignant *sukha-dukha* (happiness-sadness); the late Aruna Lama is also remembered for her renditions of sad and sentimental songs. Kumar Basnet remains popular for his folk songs, while Meera Rana is still in her prime, belting out classical, folk and even pop tunes. Several of Nepal's foremost composers also came out of this era, including Amber Gurung, Nati Kazi and the late Gopal Yonjan.

More recently, the growth of the Nepali **film industry** has opened up new horizons for composers and singers; television, introduced in the mid-1980s, has provided a further boost. These have in turn contributed to the establishment of new recording studios and cassette-reproduction concerns. That said, cinema and TV have also done their share of harm. By copying third-rate Indian productions, Nepali films have mainly enlarged the market for lowest-common-denominator music, turning audiences and musicians away from traditional styles and opening the floodgates to slick Indian-produced *masaala* ("spicy": a little of this . . . a little of that).

Other recent developments have cut both ways, too. Tourist culture shows have inevitably led to the commercialization of Nepali culture and music, yet they've also helped preserve folk arts by providing a source of income for musicians and dancers. **Ghazal**, another Indian import (see p.132), has done nothing for Nepali music, but it too pays the rent for Nepali musicians. Even Radio Nepal gives with one hand and takes away with the other, by providing an important outlet for musicians but at the same time blurring regional differences.

A few Nepali groups have recently achieved crossover success with East-meets-West **fusion music**, employing traditional instruments in non-traditional arrangements and recording to high production standards. The flute-sitar-tabla trio Sur Sudha has defined this sound: members Prem Rana (flute), Bijaya Vaidya (sitar) and Surendra Shrestha (tabla) are the closest thing Nepal has to international stars, and have done much to advance Nepali music by establishing a musical institute and producing albums by other artists.

Pop music is of course a growing proposition with young urban Nepalis. Locally produced material is pretty unlistenable, but with Indian music videos now available in Nepal via satel-

lite, we can expect quantity, if not quality, to increase.

**Gopal Yonjan, Carol Tingey
and David Reed**

Gopal Yonjan, the main author of this essay, was one of Nepal's most beloved musicians. Like Narayan Gopal, with whom he is often compared, Yonjan wrote and performed songs that touched Nepalis deeply, though they were unknown to non-Nepali-speakers. He was also a source of great pride and inspiration for members of his Tamang ethnic group, who suffer considerable racial discrimination in Nepal. He died in 1997.

DISCOGRAPHY

FOLK/CLASSICAL

Prem Avatari *Flute Recital.* Classical ragas (musical movements).

Kumar Basnet *The Best of Kumar Basnet.* A collection of old and new tunes from the reigning king of Nepali folk.

Vijaya Kumar Sunam *Traditional Folk Tunes of Nepal.* Instrumental renditions of Nepali standards, often with unconventional instruments.

Tarabir Tuladher *Sitar Recital.* Classical ragas.

Various artists (Stefano Castelli, ed) *Folk Songs of Nepal. Jhyaure,* Tamang and shaman songs; sleeve notes in Italian.

Various artists (produced by Sur Sudha) *The Himalayan Lores.* An excellent compilation of classic recordings of favourite Nepali folk songs by the original artists.

Various artists (John Melville Bishop, ed) *Music of a Sherpa Village.* Introduction to folk music from Helambu.

Various artists (Laurent Aubert & M Lobsiger-Dellenbach, eds) *Musique de Fête chez les Newars.* Archival collection of 1950s and contemporary recordings.

Various artists (produced by Sur Sudha) *Nepal My Nepal.* Instrumental renditions of folk standards featuring solo *saranghi.*

Various artists (Caspar Cronk, ed) *Songs and Dances of Nepal.* A varied collection of short samples of Bhotiya, Thakali, Newar and Sherpa songs; excellent sleeve notes.

MODERN/POPULAR

Ranjit Gazmer *Chino* and *Lahuray.* Nepali film music.

Narayan Gopal *Blue Notes: Modern Songs by Narayan Gopal.* A recent compilation of folk and *ghazal* hits by the late number-one vocalist.

Amber Gurung *Kahiry Lahar Kahiry Tarang.* Good lyrics and music, although Gurung is a better composer than singer.

Prakash Gurung *Jhooma.* Nepali film music.

Prem Raj Mahat & Rekha Shaha *Simsimi Panima.* Nepali pop rooted in the folk tradition, by a male–female duo.

Gopal Yonjan *Kanchi* and *Sindoor.* Nepali film music.

FUSION

Moment *Music for Relaxation.* The addition of violin to the standard tabla and flute ensemble lends accessibility to this fusion music based on classical ragas. (Tarang and Inside Nepal – groups that feature most of the same musicians – make very similar music.)

Shristi *Made in Thamel.* Tabla/guitar space jams; the title track is an overt homage to flower power.

Sur Sudha *Festivals of Nepal, Images of Nepal, Melodies of Nepal* and others. Nepal's musical ambassadors adapt traditional tunes to create a distinctive instrumental sound featuring airy, birdlike flute backed by sitar and tabla.

Homnath Upadhya *Prastar Improvisation III: Towards the Peace.* East–West fusion music on traditional Nepali and Indian instruments.

Vajra *Relaxation Music of Nepal.* More Sur Sudha-inspired music, featuring flute and water bowls.

TIBETAN EXILES IN NEPAL

On October 7, 1950, the People's Republic of China, which had concluded its own communist revolution only a year earlier, invaded – or, as Beijing still insists, "liberated" – Tibet. The Tibetan Army was easily overpowered, and by May 1951 Tibet was forced to sign a treaty accepting Chinese rule, on the understanding that China would not interfere with Tibetan government or culture.

During the following eight years, however, Chinese troops gathered in increasing numbers in Lhasa, the Tibetan capital; Tibetan monks were tortured, women raped and children taken from their homes for "re-education" in China. The Chinese imposed disastrous new agricultural methods on Tibetans, causing widespread famine. Tension mounted, fighting flared up in the east, and in March 1959 a full-scale **uprising** erupted in Lhasa. It was brutally crushed by the Chinese and thousands of Tibetans were executed or imprisoned, while Tibet was formally annexed to China. The **Dalai Lama**, Tibet's spiritual and political leader, fled to India; he still resides in Dharmsala, where the Tibetan government-in-exile is based. Tens of thousands of Tibetans followed, making their way into Nepal and India by various routes through the Himalaya.

For three decades, Tibet has endured outright **genocide** at the hands of the Chinese: the Dalai Lama's Bureau of Information calculates that 1.2 million Tibetans have been executed, tortured, killed in battle, or have starved or died in Chinese labour camps; during the 1966–76 Cultural Revolution, virtually every monastery was deliberately destroyed. An organized **guerrilla movement**, supported by the CIA, fought the Chinese along the Nepalese border until the early 1970s, when the US–China thaw led to its dissolution. Until a few years ago, Tibet's plight was largely ignored by the major powers, but China's Tiananmen Square massacre and the Dalai Lama's receipt of the 1989 Nobel Peace Prize put discussion of Tibetan independence back on the agenda.

Today, 15,000 out of a total of 110,000 **Tibetan exiles** live in Nepal, predominantly in the Kathmandu and Pokhara valleys. A large number of these industrious immigrants have by now achieved success in the carpet and handicrafts businesses, to the point where they can no longer be regarded as an underprivileged group. Many are playing an active role in establishing Boudha as a centre of Buddhist study, thus sustaining Tibetan religion and culture until the Chinese occupation of Tibet is ended.

Given Nepal's reliance on Chinese aid, the Tibetans are a source of discomfort for the government. China regards the exile communities as potential counter-revolutionary hotbeds, and exerts pressure on Nepal to supress any political activities there. While the "Free Tibet" movement is much bigger in India, where the Dalai Lama and the Tibetan government-in-exile are based, a **Tibetan underground** does exist in Nepal, chiefly among the disaffected youth of the former refugee camps. Don't expect anyone to discuss it openly, however, since Tibetan leaders have been warned that any "political" remarks could be grounds for prompt eviction. Recent political changes don't appear to have benefited the Tibetans, either. Nepal's powerful Communist Party has links with Beijing and is therefore keen to help keep Tibetan nationalism in check.

The following profiles contrast the experiences of two Tibetans now living in Nepal.

CHOKYI NYIMA RINPOCHE: A LAMA

Chokyi Nyima Rinpoche ("Sun Lotus of the Precious One") was born in Runying, a village about 150 miles north of Lhasa, in the year of the Iron-Hare, 1951, the son of a recognized *tulku* (reincarnate lama) and an aristocratic mother. At the age of one and a half, after successfully completing numerous tests prescribed by Tibetan Buddhist tradition, he was identified as the seventh incarnation of Gar Druchen, a spiritual emanation of Nagarjuna, the second-century Indian Buddhist philosopher. Soon after, the young *rinpoche* ("precious one", a title given to revered Tibetan Buddhist teachers) was enthroned at his predecessor's monastery, Drong Gon Thubten Dargyeling, in central Tibet.

Chokyi Nyima recalls how 35 of the monastery's 500 monks were involved in lifelong retreats, as opposed to the more common three- to nine-year retreats, living in caves with "no door, only a window to pass food through, and they would never come out for the rest of their life" – a testament to the extreme faith with which some 200,000 monks and nuns devoted their lives in over 6000 monasteries and nunneries prior to China's occupation of Tibet.

Following the failed Tibetan uprising and subsequent upheavals of 1959, Chokyi Nyima and his family were whisked into exile in Gangtok, Sikkim, where, along with 53 other young *rinpoche*, he studied briefly in an English boarding school. He soon resumed his traditional monastic education, however, and for the next fifteen years studied under a series of famous Buddhist teachers.

Chokyi Nyima relates how one day, when he was nineteen or twenty, he and another young *tulku* approached their tutor, Gyalwa Karmapa, head of the Kagyu-pa sect of Tibetan Buddhism, with the intention of entering a three-year retreat. "He scolded us, saying, 'You are foolish, you just want to go in a cave to sleep. You are *tulku*, you need to save and help the sentient beings . . . why do you think you are being educated like this? Even though I am very happy that you have a willingness to go on a retreat at such a young age – on the one hand it is a good quality, but on the other hand it is not good *enough!*'" Finally sealing Chokyi Nyima's future, Gyalwa Karmapa said, "I think it is your *karma* to teach, especially to foreigners. You will go to Nepal and help your father (Urgyen Rinpoche) build a monastery." Chokyi Nyima still fondly recalls the wisdom of his teacher: "His mind was like the ocean, whereas our minds were but a drop in that ocean."

In 1974, Chokyi Nyima came to Boudha to help his father build the Ka Nying Shedrupling Monastery, and soon after, on the instructions of Gyalwa Karmapa, was made its abbot. Ka Nying Shedrupling today houses some 120 monks and lay people, who are dedicated to preserving and spreading Tibetan Buddhism through traditional wood-block printing of *pechha* (Tibetan liturgical texts), translating and publishing Buddhist books in English, and maintaining a large library of books on Buddhist topics.

Following the wish of his tutor, Chokyi Nyima began teaching not only the local community but also a growing number of foreigners. "I like to find out what kind of people they are, why they came here and what they are searching for," he says. In fact, one of his first Western

dharma students is now undertaking a three-year retreat at a Buddhist centre in Scotland. Tibetan Buddhists aren't surprised by the spread of Buddhism in the West, for they regard it as the fulfilment of an eighth-century prophecy attributed to Guru Padma Sambhava, the legendary founder of Buddhism in Tibet: "When the iron bird flies and horses run on wheels, the Tibetan people will be scattered across the face of the earth, and the *dharma* will come to the land of the red men."

One morning, during one of his daily public audiences, where there are invariably two or three Westerners, Chokyi Nyima explains his thoughts on the increasing number of Westerners interested in Tibetan Buddhism. Thoughout the informal talk he is occasionally interrupted by pilgrims and the faithful coming to receive his blessings and exchange *kata*, the white scarves Tibetans give as an offering of good luck. "I've found that the teachings are touching more and more people from different countries, because they ring true," he says. "Many Westerners, especially the younger generation, are putting more faith in Western science only to discover that there are still many unexplained things. But because they have grown up with the idea of always searching for new answers to old phenomena, they usually have a very open mind. This is very much like what the Buddha said: 'Don't take my word for it, but find out the truth for yourself.'"

To this end, one of the aims of Ka Nying Shedrupling, as well as of many other monasteries, is to make Mahayana Buddhism readily available in the West. In Chokyi Nyima's words, "If peace comes to every individual, then there will be no conflicts, no problems, because nowadays too many people think often only of themselves. That's why we train more monks to be sent all over the world to help others to share their knowledge of the peace and caring message of the Buddha."

The often serious tone that Chokyi Nyima uses to make a point never overshadows his humble and good-natured personality. As we leave the morning teaching, he gives us a mischievous look and says, "You must meditate! Don't be lazy and forget what I've said," throwing three oranges at us from a pile given as offerings.

Andy Balestracci

GEN TASHI: A KHAMPA

A boyishly trim man with a chiselled jaw is making the last stitches on a brown *chuba* (Tibetan wrap-around dress). "There! In time for Losar (Tibetan New Year)," he says to a Manang woman, who is wearing several raw-looking chunks of turquoise and coral strung around her neck.

"Please, won't you –"

"No, I said *no*. Your aunt will just have to wear something else. It's two days to Losar, and you want me to stitch another *chuba*? It's Losar, woman; we Tibetans drop all work. You go home and get the altars prepared, and leave me to my preparations."

Gen Tashi takes off his thick glasses, revealing curiously brown-bluish eyes. He bought the round-cut glasses in Lhasa on his way back from his hometown a few years ago; folding them, he puts them away with great care.

In the same room sits a younger man, Karma, shaking out black snuff onto his thumb from an aspirin bottle. He inhales with gusto, then digs out a square piece of woollen cloth from under the rug on his bed to blow his nose. "Drop everything, do your *puja*, and enjoy yourself at Losar – it's only once a year," he tells the woman.

"All right, all right. Losar is Losar I know," she says, laughing. "I won't bother you anymore. *Tashi delek* (Good day) to you – but please, after Losar . . ." And with her new *chuba* wrapped in newspaper under her arm, she leaves Gen's workroom.

For a man of 70, Gen Tashi cuts a trim figure. He sits cross-legged, ramrod straight. When people comment about his lithe figure, he says he is light because of his daily *kora* (circumambulations) around the Swayambhu hill. "The *kora* make you feel you can walk on and on," he says.

Considering his present occupation and boyish good nature, it's hard to believe that Gen spent more than a decade as a guerrilla fighter just south of the Tibetan border. He was born to a peasant family in the valley of Gyelthang, at the southeastern edge of the Tibetan plateau (the district is today part of the so-called Tibetan Autonomous Prefecture of Dechen). At the age of 14 he became a monk at Gyelthang's Sumtseling Monastery, which at the time supported 2000 monks, and for the next 18 years spent at least part of each year at the monastery observing special prayers and liturgies. For the rest of the year, when he was old enough, Gen went on family trading trips east to Dali and Lijiang in Yunnan (China), and west to Lhasa and southwest Kalimpong in Sikkim, where Chinese tea and Indian cotton and manufactured goods were traded. The trade helped finance Gen's monastic exams and initiations.

Chinese troops marched into Gen's district in 1954 and began imposing exorbitant taxes on traders, though they held back from enforcing immediate political changes. At the time of the 1959 uprising, Gen – who had just turned 36, an age considered inauspicious by Tibetans – and his family were on a butter-buying trip near Lhasa, attempting to raise money for their lama's examinations. Joining other Khampas (people of Kham, a province in eastern Tibet) caught away from home by the uprising, Gen rushed to help guard the Norbu Lingka, the Dalai Lama's summer palace in Lhasa, until the Dalai Lama could escape. Anticipating reprisals from the Chinese after the uprising, Gen fled south to Gangtok, Sikkim, where he and many compatriots found work building mountain roads.

Later the same year, the news of a re-formed guerrilla movement known as the "Four Rivers and Six Ranges" reached Sikkim. Gen and a dozen fellow Gyelthangbas quickly joined up and were deployed to Mustang, the arid, rugged area north of Pokhara, where he participated in a variety of sabotage activities against the Chinese garrisoned across the border in Tibet. "I became good at hiding arms and ammunition underground," he says, not with bravado but with a sigh at being engaged in martial activities anathema to his vows as a Buddhist monk. (Several years have passed since he relinquished his vows.)

But lacking in international support, the guerrilla operations in Nepal gradually petered out, and the military camps became semi-permanent settlements. Gen dropped out of the movement and took up tailoring, earning a living by sewing *chuba* for the camp. Finally, after twelve years in Mustang, he and Karma, a fellow Khampa, together with Karma's wife, decided to move down to Kathmandu: their lives and the struggle didn't seem to be leading anywhere.

What had it all been for? "Well, we carried the hope that we could return to our fatherland," says Gen, for the first time showing emotion.

For their new lives in the capital, they found themselves hopelessly handicapped. By then, the efforts of other Tibetans to turn the folk art of carpet-weaving into a commercially viable venture was paying off; most of them were no longer refugees. In contrast, Gen, Karma and his wife had to adjust to a new environment, learn a new language and start from scratch. The only livelihood they could turn to was stitching *chuba*.

For years they were barely able to make ends meet, but recently Karma has started earning large commissions selling antique carpets. Now only Gen needs to stitch *chuba*, while Karma's wife manages the household. She and Karma have a twelve-year-old son, Dhendup, who attends a Tibetan school in the valley. Unlike Gen and his parents, Dhendup can write and speak in English, Tibetan and Nepali. He calls Gen grandfather.

Among the shrinking number of first-generation Tibetan exiles in Nepal, especially those of Kham, Gen's story is a common one. Many spent a large part of their adult lives fighting for their country. Now, with just as much hope, though perhaps with less urgency, they still look to the day when they can return to their homeland. Until then, they continue to circumambulate and pray and work for their younger ones.

Kesang Tseten

To get involved in the Tibetan cause, contact:

Australia *Tibet Australia Council*, 16-22 Wentworth Ave, Surry Hills, Sydney (☎02/9283 3466).

Ireland *Tibet Support Group Ireland*, 120 Upper Glenageary Rd, Glenageary, Dublin (☎01/285 3443).

New Zealand *Friends of Tibet New Zealand*, PO Box 5991, Auckland (☎09/436 066).

UK *Tibet Support Group UK*, 9 Islington Green, London N1 2XH (☎0171/359 7573); Office of Tibet, 1 Culworth St, London NW8 7AF (☎0171/722 5378).

USA *International Campaign For Tibet*, 1825 K St NW, Suite 520, Washington DC 20006 (☎202/785-1515); Office of Tibet, 241 E 32nd St, New York, NY 10016 (☎212/213-5010).

DEVELOPMENT DILEMMAS

With a per-capita income of just $220, Nepal is one of the world's poorest nations. Its population of 22 million is rising at such a rate that it will double by 2030. With agriculture unable to keep pace with demand, Nepal's "food deficit" is widening yearly. Incidence of disease is shockingly high, life expectancy is dismally low, the economy is stagnating, and the country's leaders are all but stealing food out of the people's mouths.

Nepali schoolchildren are frequently asked to write essays on "What I Would Do if I Were King". There are, of course, no right answers. Nepal is sloshing with foreign experts, all clamouring to offer their suggestions – and money – yet despite the efforts of the past five decades the country remains economically poor. Some say Nepal's underlying problems, and the inefficacy of foreign aid, will keep it forever backward. Others point to tangible improvements that have been made, such as improvements in child mortality and literacy. Still others claim that Nepal's problems have been vastly overstated by the government (to ensure continued aid) and development agencies (to justify their payrolls).

"Development" is a word like "progress": it means different things to different people, and all too often is assumed uncritically to be a desirable end in itself. Throughout the world – not only in Nepal – no one has yet worked out whether development is in fact a Good Thing, and if so what form it should take. But after spending time in the field, many aid workers conclude that Nepalis – who lead rich and elegantly simple lives, nearly self-sufficient and unencumbered by many modern problems – have more to teach the "developed" (some would say *over*developed) world than it has to teach them.

Pragmatists usually argue that development is going to come anyway, and communities should at least be given a fair choice as to what kind of development they want, rather than being forced to choose between development and non-development. But while no one advocates withholding aid or denying Nepalis' aspirations to certain material improvements, many in the development world reckon that Nepali schoolchildren are probably better able to solve their own problems than foreign experts, and that Nepalis ought to be the ones who decide what is appropriate development for Nepal.

Most people agree that Nepal's overarching problem ("challenge", in development parlance) is **poverty**, which can be traced to a number of factors: steep terrain, which makes farming inefficient and communications difficult; landlocked borders; few natural resources; a rigid social structure that entrenches the rich against the poor; ineffective national government; and a

THIS IS HOW A NATION PRETENDS TO SURVIVE

This is Machhapuchhre, Your Excellency!
And that's Annapurna.
And, beyond that are
The ranges of Dhaulagiri.
You can see them with your naked eyes.
I don't think you'll need any binocular, sir.
We want to open a three-star hotel, Your Excellency!
Will you give us some loan?

Your Excellency!
This is Koshi, that's Gandaki
And, that one, yes, that blue one, is Karnali.
You might have read in some newspapers
That rivers in Nepal are on sale.
But that's not true, sir.
In fact, we have named our zones

In the name of these rivers.
It's our plan to generate electricity from them.
Will you give us some loan?

This is Kathmandu Valley, Your Excellency!
I mean country's capital,
Which contains three cities –
Kathmandu, Lalitpur and Bhaktapur.
Please mind the smell!
You may use your handkerchief, if you like.
It's true we have not been able to build
Either the sewer or public lavatories.
But in the next five-year plan
We are definitely going to introduce
"Keep the City Clean" programme.
Will you give us some loan, Your Excellency!

Min Bahadur Bista

comparatively late start (the Nepalese government did essentially nothing for its people before 1951). Unable to do anything about these causes, most development organizations have devoted themselves to alleviating symptoms.

All too often, foreigners (and, it has to be said, some Nepalis) have tended to view Nepal's situation as a set of problems that could be identified, measured and solved in isolation. Trouble is, life isn't like that: tackling one problem often only succeeds in shifting it to another area. For example, better health and sanitation are obvious requirements, but providing them increases the rate of population growth, at least in the short term. Curbing population is no simple task, for it is rooted in poverty and the low status of women. In the meantime, agriculture has to be improved to feed the growing population, deforestation reversed to stop the fuelwood crisis, and industry developed to provide jobs. Irrigation projects, roads, hydroelectric diversions are needed . . . you get the idea. Even if you resolve that development should be left to Nepalis, education, or at least "awareness-raising" programmes, will be required to get the ball rolling, and that means not so much building schools as addressing the poverty that keeps children from attending classes.

Nepal, being a proverbial Third World "basket case", has afforded aid organizations and donor nations an opportunity to test a long list of development theories. One that seemed very promising in the 1980s and 1990s was the **integrated rural development project (IRDP)**, a more holistic approach in which various subprojects are coordinated to complement each other. The Swiss IRDP at Jiri and the British one in Dhankuta, now both handed over to Nepali management, are prominent examples. Unfortunately, such projects run counter to the "small is beautiful" maxim: they're terribly expensive (and therefore unsustainable without foreign aid), prone to corruption and, in the end, limited to tiny geographic areas. Again, there are no easy, pat answers – only dilemmas.

The following sections only scratch the surface of complex issues. Many simplifications have been made. Some dilemmas are unique to Nepal, but many – if not most – are common to the entire "developing" world. The vast majority of people in the "developed" world are dangerously ignorant of the terrible pressures building in the poorer nations; travelling in Nepal offers a chance to witness the inequities firsthand and grapple with some of the dilemmas, which cannot help but make you re-examine your own lifestyle.

HEALTH

People rarely starve to death – usually **malnutrition** weakens their systems to a point where simple infections prove fatal. It may seem hard to believe, but more than 50 percent of Nepal's cute little children are undernourished, and up to 15 percent are clinically malnourished. As a result, **child mortality** is estimated at 118 per 1000. That means that, on average, one out of every nine Nepali children will die before he or she reaches the age of five; the chances of survival are better in places like Kathmandu, but conversely, they're even worse in remote areas. Still, this is an improvement over 1960, when the figure was 300 per 1000 – almost one in three. The introduction of cheap oral rehydration packets, together with simple immunization programmes, are largely responsible for saving these lives.

Nepal is one of the few countries in the world where men live longer than women: **life expectancy** is 55 for males, 54 for females. Females are the last in the family to eat (one study found that Nepali girls under the age of five suffer 50 percent higher malnutrution than boys) and are expected to work harder (another study estimated women do 57 percent of all farm work in Nepal). And childbirth is still a very real hazard for Nepali women: due to poor prenatal care and unsterile conditions during delivery, the odds of a given pregnancy or birth resulting in the death of the mother are 1 in 20 – which is especially scary when you consider that the average Nepali woman has 4.6 children.

Poor sanitation, unsafe water and crowded, smoky conditions contribute to Nepal's high incidence of disease. Up to 80 percent of the population are reckoned to be suffering from **parasitic infections** at any one time, and 8 percent have **tuberculosis**. TB kills 16,000 Nepalis annually, making it the number-one cause of death among adults age 16–49; 50,000 new cases are reported each year, a quarter of them of the "muliple-drug resistant" strain, which is virtually untreatable. Nepal's per-capita **leprosy** rate is among the highest in the world – higher, even, than India's – with an esti-

THE DEVELOPMENT INDUSTRY

Everyone loves to give aid to Nepal. Although tourism is officially listed as the country's top source of foreign exchange, the development industry is even bigger. Aid to Nepal brings in $300–500 million annually in direct grants and concessional loans, not counting the value of technical assistance.

Foreign development projects in Nepal fall roughly into three categories. **Bilateral** (and multilateral) aid – that is, money given or lent by foreign governments directly to Nepal – has financed most of the infrastructure (roads, dams, airports), as well as the biggest IRDPs. Many smaller projects are carried out by hundreds of international **non-governmental organizations (NGOs)**; some of these are well known, such as Oxfam, CARE and Save the Children, while others are just one person doing fieldwork and raising sponsorship money in his or her home country. Voluntary NGOs, such as Britain's Voluntary Service Overseas (VSO) and the US Peace Corps, generally don't run their own projects, but instead slot volunteers into existing HMG programmes. Finally, **international lending bodies** like the World Bank and Asian Development Bank act as brokers to arrange loans for big projects with commercial potential – usually irrigation and hydroelectric schemes.

Many of these organizations do excellent work; almost all are motivated by the best possible intentions. However, money cannot automatically solve Nepal's problems, as some of the biggest projects have learned to their cost. By paying their imported experts ten or twenty times more than Nepalis to do the same job, the big bilateral missions can cause resentment or, worse, encourage Nepalis to gather round the aid trough instead of doing useful work. And to the extent that they import experts and materials, they undermine Nepalis' ability to do things for themselves, fostering a crippling **aid dependency** that now permeates almost every level of society. In 1983, foreign handouts made up 40 percent of Nepal's development budget; by 1998 it was up to 70 percent, and accounted for a full 10 percent of GNP. Some wags joke that the country can't *afford* to develop, lest it jeopardize development funding.

So why is everybody clamouring to give aid to Nepal? For bilateral donors, foreign aid is a handy way of buying **political influence**. China and India are forever one-upping each other with offers to Nepal, which they regard as a crucial buffer state; and while Nepal is of less strategic interest to the main Western powers, they're happy to throw some small change Nepal's way just to ensure a compliant regime.

Aid is also a means of stimulating the donor country's own domestic economy: for example, more than half of British aid to Nepal (which amounts to £12 million annually) is paid directly to British **contractors**. Thus the emphasis of aid is usually on Western-style techno-fixes and economic growth, rather than appropriate technology and self-sufficiency. Encouraging farmers to, say, irrigate and buy fertilizers to grow cash crops may raise their income, but not necessarily their quality of life. It will, however, give Western banks a capital project to finance, Western contractors an irrigation system to build, Western chemical companies a new market for fertilizers, and Western consumer-goods companies new consumers. Meanwhile, Nepalese cash crops will be exported out of the area, even as Nepalis suffer malnutrition.

For their part, institutions like the World Bank and its sister organization, the International Monetary Fund, have reputations for pushing expensive **megaprojects** that often prove inappropriate for their impoverished recipients, and for imposing harsh "structural adjustment" programmes when debtor nations can't repay their loans. Fortunately, these institutions finally seem to be moving with the times. In 1995 the new head of the World Bank scrapped plans for a mega-hydroelectric project in eastern Nepal (see p.468), in what seems to be an effort to steer the Bank towards smaller, more environmentally sensitive projects.

But even when foreign governments and agencies try to step back and do the right thing, their charity may still have a corrupting influence. The latest fashionable philosophy is that the best way to get things done is to finance **local NGOs**, which, it's assumed, have a better handle on local problems and solutions than foreign experts. Sounds great in theory, but what's the result? An explosion in local NGOs for every conceivable cause, all sounding just as right-on as could be: "small-scale" this, "women's development" that, "environmental" whatever. (There are now so many local NGOs in Nepal that at least one exists simply to coordinate them all.) Unfortunately, some of these organizations aren't doing much besides writing grant proposals, and the only development they're assisting is their director's bank balance.

mated 24,500 cases. And while Nepal avoided the **AIDS** epidemic for many years, it now appears on the verge of a major outbreak that will strain its meagre medical resources: an estimated 50,000 to 100,000 Nepalis are now infected with HIV, the virus that causes AIDS. Women employed in the sex industry (see below) and men performing seasonal work away from home have been the main agents in transmitting the disease from India, while poor blood screening, medical re-use of needles and ignorance of the proper use of condoms all threaten to aid its spread. On the bright side, mosquito spraying in the Tarai has reduced **malaria** cases to about 25,000 annually (compared with two million a year during the 1950s), although even this is on the way back up.

Improved public **sanitation** is gradually being introduced, and is seen as the surest way to combat a number of debilitating diseases. However, in the booming Tarai cities, covered sewers are barely keeping pace with growth, while village latrines are still rarely found off the popular trekking routes. Communal taps and wells have been built in many villages to provide **drinking water**, yet only about 40 percent of Nepalis have access to safe water (see below).

Alcohol and **tobacco consumption** are also significant public-health problems in Nepal, though as yet they've hardly appeared on the political radar. In a poor country with low life expectancy, saving babies is arguably more urgent than fighting cancer and alcoholism in people who haven't got that many years left to live anyway. However, it's worth noting that the Nepalese government has a vested interest in ignoring these problems: it owns the country's biggest tobacco company, and (like all governments) it obtains substantial tax revenue from the sale of tobacco and alcohol.

Although the government, aided by United Mission to Nepal and others, has constructed more than 110 hospitals to date, Western-style facilities are neither affordable nor appropriate for most villages. Many of these parochial hospitals lack even a single resident doctor, since the vast majority of qualified physicians prefer to practise in the Kathmandu Valley, where they can make much more money in private practice. A better measure of progress on this front has been the creation of some 800 primary **health-care posts**, where health assistants (often

local people) are trained in traditional ayurvedic practices.

POPULATION

Slowing **population growth** isn't just a matter of passing out condoms. In Nepal, as in other countries, children are relied on to do many time-consuming chores – fetching water, gathering fuel, tending animals – and are also considered an investment for old age, since there's only a token state pension to draw on. Moreover, Nepalis tend to have large families because they can't be sure all their children will survive. Hindus, especially, keep trying until they've produced at least one son, who alone can perform the prescribed rites (*shradha*) for his parents after they've died.

While it's not the place of aid workers to contradict Hindu beliefs, population-control efforts can have little impact unless the **status of women** (see p.468) is raised, which to a great extent is a matter of providing them with paid employment opportunities. Earning income doesn't merely empower women; it makes it more expensive for them to have children, since to do so means stopping work. Education can also play an important part in bringing down birth rates – but the education must be targeted not so much at women, who already know they're repressed, but at men, who do the repressing. Many "women's programmes" have failed because they've assumed that women only need to be provided with the awareness and skills to improve their situation; in fact they can do little if their husbands still hold the power.

The other reasons for **high fertility** could be removed by reducing the current high levels of poverty and child mortality, and by providing ready sources of fuel and water to reduce the usefulness of extra hands. It's often said that "development is the best contraceptive", and indeed, there is a close correlation between rising standards of living and declining birth rates. Unfortunately, in most countries this so-called **demographic transition** involves a period of rapid population growth until the birth rate settles down to match the lower death rate. Some East Asian countries have seen their birth rates fall more or less simultaneously with their economies' rise, but Nepal is not, alas, in the same economic league.

At the moment, Nepal's population is still very much in growth mode. Currently doubling every 30 years, the population has a biological momentum that is unlikely to be checked in the present generation, simply because of the number of girls already approaching child-bearing age. Meanwhile, the government's **family planning** efforts are still woefully inadequate: only 15 percent of Nepalis practise any form of contraception at all. The remoteness of villages makes it all the more difficult to get the message out.

If Nepal's population doubles or triples, where will all the extra people live? As it happens, this is not a brand-new situation, for some parts of the middle hills have probably been overpopulated for a century or more. **Emigration** – to the Tarai, India and, more recently, to Kathmandu and overseas – has always regulated the people pressure. Significantly, the latest estimates show a notable decline in the annual rate of population growth – to 2.37 percent, down from 2.6 percent a decade earlier – most of which is probably due to emigration. Even so, it's estimated that the country's urban population will double in the next decade, and most of this increase will be taken up by the Kathmandu Valley and a half-dozen Tarai cities.

AGRICULTURE

If Nepal's population doubles, **food production** must theoretically double, too – a seemingly unattainable goal, given that in the past decade the country has gone from being a net exporter of food to a net importer.

Nepal's farmland is already among the most intensely cultivated in the world. A mere 20 percent of the country's land area is arable; clearing new land for cultivation only adds to deforestation, so it's preferable to find ways of increasing the productivity per hectare. Yields are currently very low even by regional standards – for example, rice and wheat yields are less than half that of those in China – but of course that means there's plenty of room for improvement. Various methods have been tried in Nepal, as in other countries. Agriculture experiment stations have achieved some success in showcasing **high-yielding seeds** and animal breeds. **Pesticides** and chemical **fertilizers** are now widely used in the Kathmandu Valley and Tarai, though nationwide the use of these inputs is still relatively low (one-fifteenth that of China's). Moreover, they're often misused, due to poorly thought-out subsidy

programmes and a lack of information: for example, many farmers apply urea (nitrogen), which is heavily subsidized, but not phosphorous and potash, which aren't, with the result that yields actually decrease. And in the Kathmandu Valley, where produce used to be organic by default, it is now often laced with unhealthy levels of agricultural chemicals.

Since Nepal experiences huge seasonal fluctuations in rainfall, **irrigation** – which allows monsoon rain to be stored and then used later in the dry season – is another high priority for improving productivity. Small-scale community projects are being built with generally good results, but the big canal systems built by the government and foreign donors are often inefficient and poorly maintained, and tend to benefit only the most well-off farmers. It's been estimated that a big government-built system costs at least eight times more per hectare than a community-built one. Shallow tubewells are another economical way to exploit groundwater in the Tarai, where the water table is high.

Tractors and other **mechanized equipment** don't do much for the yield per hectare, but they do improve the yield per *farmer*. Aided by agricultural loans, an increasing number of Tarai farmers are investing in machinery; in most parts of the hills, smaller landholdings and stair-stepped terraces make mechanized farming impractical. While this makes hill farms uncompetitive in the regional market for staple grains, landowners with access to roads are compensating by turning to vegetables and other cash crops. This shift makes a virtue out of Nepal's widening food deficit, since cash crops earn foreign exchange with which to buy staples; for this reason, the government has identified **road extension** as another agricultural priority.

Stark inequities prevail in Nepal's agriculturally based economy. Controlled by vested interests, the government has done a poor job of enforcing **land reform**, with the result that 63 percent of cultivable land is still owned by 16 percent of the population. Despite a 1964 law prohibiting landlords from charging tenant farmers annual rents of more than 15 percent of their crop, many farmers are locked in a hopeless cycle of debt and victimized by unscrupulous lenders. **Credit** is therefore a pressing need. Various government programmes extend credit to poor farmers to tide them over lean months, with variable success, but the official

THE END OF THE ROAD

Gazing down from the hill, over terraces of paddy fields, we could see the first truck making its hesitant journey up the spiralling new dust road. Local people ran down the main street of the bazaar to meet the first iron monster to complete the ascent.

For them it was the excitement of seeing a machine that moved along the ground. For me it was the feeling that here, at last, was a link with the outside world. There was the weekly plane to Kathmandu, of course. But with only eighteen seats – and $30 a seat at that – it was hardly significant to most people.

Excitement about the road lasted quite a while. Then people became less frightened and awe-struck, and the verges were no longer dotted with rapt, admiring observers. Those who could afford the fare became seasoned travellers and were no longer to be seen vomiting out of the windows as the truck lurched along. In fact it became an accepted part of daily life – rather like the plane, it came and went, affecting few people.

GOODIES

But down by the airstrip, a shantytown of temporary shacks sprang up overnight with the coming of the road. Here was where all the goodies that came by truck from India were to be found: plastic snakes that wriggled, gilt hair-slides, iron buckets, saucepans and – best of all – fresh fruit and vegetables.

For us foreigners, and the paid office workers, accustomed to going for weeks with nothing but potatoes and rice in the shops, it seemed like paradise. Every day more and more apples, oranges, onions, cabbages and tomatoes would make their way up the hill. There was even a rumour that ten bottles of Coca-Cola had been sighted in the bazaar.

One morning, as I was eyeing a big plastic bucket full of huge Indian tomatoes in a local shop, a woman pulled my arm. "Don't you want to buy mine?" she asked. And there, in her *doko*, were a few handfuls of the small green local tomatoes.

Just a fortnight earlier I would have followed her eagerly, begging to be allowed to buy some. Now the shopkeeper laughed at her: who would want to buy little sour green tomatoes when there were big sweet red ones to be had?

For women like her, trudging in for miles from one of the surrounding villages to sell her few vegetables, there was no longer a market. The influential bazaar shopkeepers negotiated deals with the Indian traders with their truckloads of vegetables. The new road meant new money for the shopkeepers – but less for the poor, whose livelihood was undermined and who had no way of buying the wonderful new merchandise.

CASUALTIES

There were other casualties, too. Gaggles of poor women, who had made a living out of carrying people's baggage from the airstrip to the bazaar, were once a common sight, haggling in angry, spirited voices over the price of their services. But with the coming of the new road, people simply boarded one of the trucks – baggage and all. Ragged and downtrodden at the best of times, these women were reduced to silently and gratefully accepting any rate people were prepared to pay for their help.

I began to wonder about the road. But I needn't have worried. Soon the monsoon rains arrived and the swelling river took charge of things. Within days the bridge was completely washed away, leaving several trucks stranded on the wrong side of the river, never to return to India.

AFTER THE MONSOON

The original truck continued to creak up and down the winding road between the airstrip and the bazaar, its fuel being hoisted across the river by rope-pulley, but became so overcrowded that one day it broke down halfway up the hill. As the road had been almost completely washed away by the rain, it was simply left there in the middle of the road.

When the monsoon ended, the truck was overgrown with creepers and made a very pleasant home for a local family.

By then the grand new road was little more than a memory. The women porters went back to climbing regularly up and down the hill; the shantytown vanished as quickly as it had appeared; and everyone went back to eating rice and potatoes as before.

Last I heard, a foreign-aid agency had decided to rebuild the road, with a proper bridge this time: in the interests of development.

Anna Robinson

Anna Robinson worked for three years as a VSO volunteer in Doti District, in the far western hills, and is now field officer for VSO Nepal.
Reproduced by permission of New Internationalist Publications.

Agriculture Development Bank, which was created to make loans for simple improvements, has unfortunately grown so bureaucratic that only wealthier farmers can avail themselves of it.

Most people agree that agriculture must receive the main thrust of development efforts in Nepal. With about 80 percent of Nepalis still making their living from the land, it's unrealistic to look for miracles elsewhere.

DEFORESTATION AND EROSION

In the Nepal hills, population, agriculture and environmental damage combine in a worrying vicious cycle: the need for more food leads to more intensive use of the land, which degrades the environment and lowers productivity, which further increases pressure on the land. An expanding population needs not only more **firewood**, but also more **fodder** for animals, which provide manure to maintain soil fertility. Overuse of firewood and fodder results in **deforestation**, as does any expansion of farmland, and as a result Nepal's forest area is shrinking by as much as 1 percent per year. Trees help anchor the fragile Himalayan topsoil – removing them causes **erosion** and landslides, which not only reduce the productivity of the land but also send silt down to the Bay of Bengal, contributing to disastrous **floods** in Bangladesh.

Or so goes the theory. In practice, emigration seems to stabilize the cycle, and studies give wildly differing estimates for the rate of deforestation. The most that can be said is that the situation is definitely bad in some areas, but not so bad in others. Experts still don't know to what extent deforestation contributes to erosion, but most agree that the prime cause is simply the natural sloughing and shifting of very young mountains.

Even the government now admits it got it wrong in the 1950s when it **nationalized the forests** to protect them. Before that, the forests had been competently managed by local communities; but when the trees were taken away from them, locals felt they had no stake in their preservation, and because government enforcement was weak they easily plundered them. HMG's current policy of **community forestry** gives local forests back to the people, recognizing that villagers are in fact very ecologically minded and will manage their forests responsi-

bly and sustainably so long as they don't fear re-nationalization. The latest evidence suggests that this policy has helped to check deforestation in many areas, and in some cases has even reversed it.

Deforestation is a separate issue **in the Tarai**, where the trees have been felled as a matter of policy, to make way for settlers and to earn money for the government through state-sanctioned timber sales. Although the vast majority of the Tarai's magnificent native forest has gone in the past four decades, the rate of logging has almost come to a standstill in recent years – ironically, because of the collapse of the government-owned timber corporation. Meanwhile, Nepal has won praise abroad for setting aside large chunks of what remains as **national parks** and wildlife reserves. However, the government can expect mounting resistance from its own people, who question why such valuable land should be set aside for tourists and crop-destroying animals (see p.304).

In recent years numerous other environmental problems have arisen in Nepal, most seriously in the Kathmandu Valley – see below.

ELECTRICITY, ROADS AND OTHER TECHNOLOGY

Many see **electricity** – specifically hydroelectricity – as Nepal's greatest natural resource and a vital engine for development. The country's steep, mountain-fed rivers are estimated to have hydroelectric potential to the tune of 83 million megawatts – enough to power the British Isles. Unfortunately, due to the cost of getting materials and technical experts into Nepal's rugged backcountry, this potential is rather expensive to harness. Ironically for a country so richly endowed, only 15 percent of Nepalis have access to electricity, and the supply falls so short of demand that the national electricity authority must resort to frequent load-shedding (scheduled power cuts) during the dry season.

Yet Nepal's electricity use is soaring at an annual clip of 15 percent, fuelled mainly by **rural electrification** and urbanites' growing use of electrical appliances. Most economic planners see this as a healthy trend, and regard a growing supply of electricity as essential for stimulating domestic industry and creating employment. It can also encourage local economic development, reduce fuel wood use, and benefit women and children by freeing up time otherwise spent gathering wood. However, electricity is of no use to people who can't afford it, and it can only play a limited role in offsetting deforestation: as far as most rural Nepalis are concerned, wood is free, whereas electricity costs rupees – and electric appliances cost dollars.

At the national level, however, the increasing reliance on electricity locks Nepal into an expensive quest for power. Fortunately, the country has always been able to rely on foreign donors to finance the showcase **large-scale hydroelectric** projects which provide most of its electricity. Diversions have been built on the Kulekhani (south of Kathmandu) and the Marsyangdi (along the Prithvi Highway), and others are under construction on the Kali Gandaki (southwest of Pokhara) and Bhote Koshi (along the road to the Tibet border). Such major projects have serious drawbacks – they're environmentally disruptive, require vast inputs of foreign aid (and often give-away-the-store economic concessions), are magnets for corruption, and put Nepal at the mercy of foreign experts to operate and maintain them – but if Nepal is to keep up with its demand for electricity they are probably a necessary evil.

Some economic planners are enamoured with the idea of building even bigger hydro diversions, not to satisfy domestic energy demand but to **export electricity** to neighbouring countries for foreign exchange. Several are in the planning stages, awaiting a willing funding partner. One, the so-called Karnali–Chisapani Project, would be one of the world's biggest: a high dam on the Karnali River in far-western Nepal, it would have a capacity of 10,800 megawatts (about 20 times Nepal's entire installed capacity), cost $4–8 billion to build, and displace 60,000 people upstream; the American energy giant Enron is seriously interested. Another megaproject, Arun III (see box on p.468), was spiked in 1995 but could conceivably be resurrected – HMG is still trolling for other funders.

Microhydro projects can't deliver the kind of power industry needs, but they are appropriate technology for mountain villages too remote to be economically connected to the grid. Scores of these have been installed (both with foreign and private Nepalese funding) to supply electricity for a few hundred households each.

Nepal is also a good candidate for **solar power**. The introduction of locally manufactured solar water heaters is helping to take some of the pressure off the electric grid and the forests. Though photovoltaics are relatively expensive for so poor a country, so too is the cost of extending the grid ($60,000 per kilometre), which means that in remote areas without hydroelectric potential it can actually work out cheaper to install solar cells. **Biogas** – gaseous fuel produced by the fermentation of organic material such as manure and agricultural waste – is also proving to be cost-effective; the Dutch government has subsidized the establishment of local small-scale plants throughout Nepal.

But at the household level, appropriate technology has to be something the average Nepali peasant can afford, which isn't much. Several groups have worked hard to introduce "**smokeless" chulo** (stoves), which burn wood more efficiently and reduce unhealthy kitchen smoke. Yet even this simple innovation illustrates the dilemmas of tampering with traditional ways: Nepalis complain that the new stoves aren't as easy to regulate and don't emit enough light, while the lack of smoke allows insects to infest their thatched roofs. That's one reason why many Nepali households are converting from thatch to corrugated metal.

Roads, like big hydroelectric and irrigation projects, don't come out well in cost-benefit analyses in Nepal, though planners insist that they're necessary for development. They cost far more than Nepal could ever afford without aid, and are almost as expensive to maintain; many are hastily built, only to wash away with the next monsoon (see box on p.465). The wealthy – bus owners, truckers, merchants, building contractors – benefit from road-building, while porters and shopkeepers along the former walking route lose out. Nevertheless, roads form an important part of Nepal's development strategy because it's virtually impossible to deliver services, administer projects, maintain order or even collect taxes in areas not served by roads. By contrast, **footbridges** put villages within easier reach of jobs and health facilities, and enable villagers to get their produce to market more efficiently, making them perhaps the most useful and popular type of public-works project.

DEATH OF A MEGAPROJECT

In 1987, the World Bank selected the upper reaches of the Arun River in eastern Nepal to be the site of a world-class hydroelectric diversion projected to cost $770 million. The so-called **Arun III** project was conceived as a strategic effort for Nepal not only to meet its growing demand for electricity but also to earn significant revenue by exporting surplus power.

Early concerns about the environmental consequences of building an access road to the site were silenced by the establishment of the huge Makalu–Barun National Park and Conservation Area, to the west of the Arun. Some observers questioned the wisdom of a poor country like Nepal putting all its eggs into such a costly basket, but no organized opposition surfaced until 1993, when the small **Alliance for Energy** charged that HMG had failed to properly investigate more appropriate alternatives to Arun III. The following year another ad-hoc organization, **Arun Concerned Group** lodged a formal appeal with the World Bank's newly formed Inspection Panel. It was a David-versus-Goliath proposition if ever there was one: Arun III was precisely the sort of Third World megaproject the World Bank had been sponsoring for decades despite objections from the world's biggest environmental groups.

But change was afoot within the lending giant, and Arun III was to become one of the first indicators of it. Reassessing every aspect of the project, the Inspection Panel concluded that it was **too big** an undertaking for Nepal, allowing too little margin for error and claiming too great a share of the country's slender development budget. The panel also found that Arun III would probably drive up Nepal's electricity tariffs – already the highest in South Asia – by 50 percent, calling into question the economic justification for building it. In 1995, incoming World Bank president James Wolfensohn **cancelled** Arun III, pledging to redirect the Bank's share of the funding towards eighteen small- and medium-scale hydro projects and a package of development assistance to the Arun region.

The decision rocked Nepal's political establishment and, for many, underscored the humiliating extent to which outside interests control Nepal's development agenda. Some warned that the loss of Arun III would mean even more serious power shortages and economic stagnation in the coming decade. Others expressed relief that Nepal would now be free to pursue smaller, less sophisticated projects that it could build, operate and maintain with less foreign involvement.

WOMEN

Outside the relative sophistication of Kathmandu, Hindu **women** are a long, long way from liberation. In remote rural areas, they're considered their husband's or father's chattel, given or taken in marriage for the price of, say, a buffalo – a status reinforced by law. Orthodox Baahuns, while in the minority, reveal the extent of female subjugation. They believe a woman is ritually unclean during menstruation and for ten days after giving birth, and that she must remain apart during that period and drink cow's urine to cleanse herself. One study found that 73 percent of Nepali women suffer from **domestic violence**. **Polygamy**, though officially outlawed, is widely practised in the hills, and if a woman doesn't produce a son she's liable to be replaced. **Abortion** is illegal in nearly all circumstances – even in cases of rape or incest – and is only allowed when the mother's life is in danger. The maximum sentence for abortion is three years, and women whose babies are stillborn risk being charged with infanticide, which carries a sentence of 20 years. Predictably, this results in unsafe backstreet abortions, which are believed to be the cause of up to half of all maternal mortality in Nepal.

Sherpanis and other Buddhist women are treated much more equally, and high-caste Hindu women may easily flout conventions, but even these women don't enjoy true power-sharing. (Indeed, when it comes to gender roles, wealthy urbanites can be as traditional as any villager: the popularity of fetal ultrasound testing services in Kathmandu and the Tarai suggests that some couples are seeking to eliminate unwanted females.)

Several development problems already touched on – inequities between the sexes in health care and education, and the failure of population-control efforts – arise directly from the low status of women in Nepal. Another tragic consequence is the **trafficking** of Nepali girls for Indian brothels. It's estimated that between 150,000 and 225,000 Nepali girls and women – 20 percent of them under the age of 16 – have been sold into sexual slavery in India, where patrons prize them for their beauty and supposed lack of inhibitions. To poor Hindu families in Nepal, daughters are often regarded as burdens, costing money to be married off and then becoming another family's asset; when a broker comes offering, say, Rs15,000 for a pubescent daughter, many readily agree. This horrific trade is most pronounced in the central hills, where it has historical roots, since Tamang girls were for generations forced to serve as concubines in the courts of the Kathmandu rulers. A prostitute may eventually buy her freedom, but ordinarily she won't be released until she's been "damaged" – which these days means she has AIDS (see above). Prostitution is also on the rise in Kathmandu and other Nepali cities.

So far, the government has shown little inclination to confront this national disgrace. Concerned NGOs have been left to set up homes for former prostitutes, who would otherwise be shunned by family and friends if they returned to their villages. Others are working to address the underlying causes of the problem – not only poverty in general, but specifically women's low education and earning power. If women are educated and enabled to earn money, they won't be seen as a drag on family finances and are less likely to be sold off.

The **women's movement** is embryonic in Nepal. Women weren't granted the vote until 1948, and though the All Nepal Women's Organization was formed in 1951, women working for social change were forced to operate underground until the 1990 restoration of democracy. Aid projects and agencies have been chiefly concerned with setting up cottage-industry employment for women, so they can earn spare cash as a first step to some sort of self-determination. Two very successful efforts, the Bangladesh-based Grameen Bank and the Nepalese government's Production Credit for Rural Women programme, have targeted women's development by making "**microenterprise loans**" to small, self-organizing groups of women and supporting the borrowers with literacy, family-planning and other training.

CHILDREN AND THE ELDERLY

Children, like women, are often victims of poverty in Nepal. As already mentioned, however much their parents love them, in poor families they are counted as an economic resource from an early age. **Child labour** has always been essential in agriculture, and in the past it was common for children to work as unpaid servants for village landowners simply so there would be one less mouth to feed. In the growing cash economy, children are increasingly being relied on to earn wages as porters, *kanchha* ("boys"), and labourers in the carpet, brick and construction industries. According to one study, 2.6 million Nepali children – 60 percent of the population between 6 and 14 – are engaged in labour. Another survey suggests that two-thirds of the carpet industry's workforce is made up of children under the age of 16, a fact that has led to a boycott of Nepalese-produced carpets in some European countries.

Not only are these youngsters often forced to work long hours in unhealthy conditions, and are frequently abused, they are deprived of their childhood – the right to play, be loved and be educated. The government has passed laws against child labour, but this is yet another problem that can only be effectively addressed by attacking its root cause: poverty. (See p.108 for information on Kathmandu's street children.)

The **elderly** in Nepal are traditionally looked after by their sons, but economic development – which brings increased mobility and beguiling new possibilities – is breaking down such traditions. Moreover, Nepal's demographic transition will require an adjustment, as it has in other countries, as there are fewer young people to support more old people. All of this means there will be a need for more elder care facilities and a meaningful national pension (currently a meagre Rs100 per month is doled out to widows over 60 and men over 75).

EDUCATION

Nepal's education system has come a long way in a short time. There were few state **schools** before 1951, and they were open only to the children of elites – now there are primary schools within walking distance of most villages, and legions of private schools in the Kathmandu Valley. However, primary-school enrolment is probably well below the official figure of 68 percent, and actual attendance may be less than 25 percent. Only 13 percent of boys – and just 3 percent of girls – finish secondary school. The trouble is that "free" public education is actually quite expensive for families who depend on their children for labour, and so in a poor country like Nepal, government-subsidized schools don't always help the most needy children. The country has made great strides in increasing **literacy**, though the gulf between adult males (55 percent) and females (25 percent) is telling.

Nepal's proportion of qualified **teachers** is very low (only 39 percent are trained), so most aid programmes have focused on teacher training. Low pay is another problem, sapping teachers' motivation and contributing to an estimated 50-percent *teacher* absentee rate. Western workers believe education could be a powerful catalyst for change in Nepal, but many complain that the current curriculum is geared for churning out bureaucrats and should be made more vocational and relevant to a peasant population. Others worry that the sponsorship of education programmes by foreign agencies leads to a lack of accountability and a sense that the curriculum is externally designed.

Those who do finish high school and go on to one of Nepal's many **colleges** or **universities** often find that there's no work for them when they graduate – a common problem in most countries, but all the more acute in Nepal, whose non-agricultural sectors are particularly poorly developed. A further cultural complication is the prevalent attitude towards education in Nepal: equated with high status, it is all too often pursued merely to avoid physical labour, which carries low status. This, ironically, has the effect of removing many of Nepal's most highly trained people from the productive workforce. Frustrated by a lack of opportunities or just plain bored, the educated youth of the Kathmandu Valley make up a growing class of angry young men given to revolutionary talk and *goonda* antics.

INDUSTRY AND TRADE

Nepal needs to create jobs – agriculture simply cannot absorb all of the country's growing workforce. Unemployment stands at around 14 percent, while some 40 percent of Nepalis are considered underemployed. Moreover, a developing nation like Nepal has to produce things, not only for domestic consumption but also for export, so that it can earn foreign exchange to pay for the imported technology and materials it needs for development. That means boosting **industry**,

which in Nepal's case accounts for a relatively low 16 percent of gross domestic product.

Tourism is Nepal's top foreign-exchange earner, and many see it as the country's most promising economic engine. But while the industry creates tens of thousands of much-needed jobs, plus indirect employment in related industries, this work tends to be menial and seasonal. Moreover, the economic benefits of tourism are highly localized, and an estimated 60 percent of the foreign exchange earned from tourism goes right back out of the country to pay for imported materials. True, tourism can claim some credit for shaping HMG's mostly progressive environmental record – but it's an open question whether the revenue earned really offsets the ecological and cultural costs. The fruits of tourism, so arbitrarily awarded, have turned legions of Nepalis into panhandlers, in much the same way that aid has done to politicians and institutions.

There are various strategies for exploiting tourism as a development tool. The one employed by nearby Bhutan is to admit only a small number of very high-paying tourists, thus maximizing revenue while minimizing impacts. Another approach, exemplified by independent trekking, is to encourage tourists to disperse and spend as much of their money as possible at the local level. Unfortunately, Nepal has so far failed to pursue any clear strategy. It has tended to go for quantity rather than quality, and to allow visitors to cram themselves into a few overused areas, which only degrades the tourist experience and undermines the industry's long-term viability; this commodity approach to tourism seems particularly short-sighted in Nepal's case, given its unique assets (after all, there is only one Mount Everest). The government's big tourism push, **Visit Nepal Year '98**, was a fiasco, as it was hardly publicized outside of the country, and was accompanied by no improvements to tourist infrastructure. The resulting bad publicity has actually produced a decline in visitors.

Until the mid-1990s, **carpet manufacture** was Nepal's fastest-growing industrial sector, and looked poised to overtake tourism in annual revenue. Highly labour-intensive, the industry still generates plenty of employment and adds lots of value to relatively cheap materials, and it has also helped to diversify the economy away from an overreliance on tourism. However, quality-control problems and bad PR over child labour have turned the boom into something of a bust, while the industry's economic benefits are now seen to be largely offset by the hidden costs of exploitation, social disruption and pollution. (See p.187 for more on this.) Nepal's **garment industry** has seen a similar rise and fall in exports, though on a smaller scale.

In many other industries, Nepal finds itself in a classic Third World bind. It can't profitably produce things like vehicles and computers because its domestic market is so small (and poor), and importing even modest amounts of these items quickly runs up a nasty **trade deficit**. The government has therefore put much of its energy into stimulating the production of run-of-the-mill goods for domestic consumption, achieving dubious successes in some sectors. Beer production, to take one example, has increased 400 percent in the past decade. In development economics, this is known as **import substitution**: for a country short on foreign exchange, a penny saved is a penny earned. Washing powder, paper, cement and shoes have seen similarly dramatic increases in output.

Many of these factories have been set up as licensed **monopolies**, which give the government more control over the pace of development, but tend to concentrate wealth in the hands of a few Kathmandu fat cats. (In most sectors the law requires that all businesses have a majority Nepali ownership, which makes for some very well-off silent partners.) A few dozen industries are still run as state-owned enterprises, most of which are slated for eventual **privatization**. However, this is a highly politicized process, and ripe for corruption, since those in charge of a sale can deliberately undervalue the enterprise and award the sale to whoever gives the juiciest kickback.

The presence of **India** as Nepal's neighbour to the south inevitably complicates matters. Nepal's main trading partner, India has traditionally levied high import duties to protect its own industries, thus benefiting Nepali border traders (who can sell imported goods for less than their Indian competitors), but crippling Nepali exporters (whose goods become uncompetitive with duty added on). Nepal's closer ties with India's leadership since the restoration of democracy have resulted in more favourable **terms of trade**, and the decision of both countries to make their currencies fully convertible has begun to make their goods more competitive in the world market. However, critics charge that the Congress Party, when it has been in power, has tended to turn a blind eye while Indian entrepreneurs bought up Nepal's choicest businesses.

ECONOMIC STRATEGY

Development workers advocate all sorts of wonderful-sounding ways to bring Nepal out of poverty. Economists ask: how do we pay for it? Hard work and good ideas will amount to nothing unless they're accompanied by a sound **economic strategy**.

Alas, Nepal's leaders have paid little attention to economics since the restoration of democracy. Their tendency to accept whatever foreign aid is offered, without analyzing how or whether it fits into the country's long-term plans, has produced crippling economic distortions and wasted much time in the race to achieve real development. Constant political upheavals have played havoc with planning, and have made virtually all decisions subservient to short-term political calculations. These factors, along with the high costs and risks of doing business in Nepal (corruption, inflation, exchange-rate fluctuations), have in turn frightened off foreign investment.

Economists estimate that if Nepal is to make significant progress in alleviating poverty, it will have to achieve long-term **economic growth** of at least 6 percent annually. The country achieved that target for a few years in the early 1990s, but since then the annual growth rate has averaged about 3 percent – only just keeping ahead of population growth. Furthermore, most of the growth has been confined to a few urban areas, and with inflation eroding people's purchasing power, the average Nepali has experienced a steadily declining standard of living.

One policy pursued fairly consistently by recent governments is **economic liberalization**, which has meant selling off loss-making state enterprises, reducing restrictions and tariffs on imports, making the currency fully convertible, and allowing for easier licensing of banks and other businesses. These actions have helped open the door to a flood of foreign goods and capital, resulting in a dramatic increase in wealth and economic activity in the Kathmandu Valley and to a lesser extent in the urban centres of the Tarai. However, it should be noted that such policies are designed by and for those who already have the capital, and they offer little benefit to Nepal's subsistence farmers and labourers. Wealth is slow to trickle down in a country like Nepal.

Lazily addicted to foreign aid, the government for many years made almost no effort to support itself through **taxation**, leading to potentially serious fiscal imbalances in the 1990s. Under pressure from international donors and lending institutions, the government has finally begun to increase its collection of income tax (though this still contributes only 10 percent of the national budget) and has instituted a 10-percent value-added tax (VAT) on the sale of most goods and services. The latter has attracted predictable opposition from the business community, and may indeed prove to be an unworkable funding mechanism due to its high susceptibility to graft. Chronically short of funds, the government is unable to operate its infrastructure efficiently, makes short-sighted decisions, and has little left over to invest in improvements; indeed, the government's fiscal inefficiency is such that it can't even utilize much of the foreign aid being offered to it.

KATHMANDU VALLEY PROBLEMS

Solutions often create their own problems. For five decades, people have been trying to get Nepal to develop – now that it has, in the **Kathmandu Valley**, many are nervously fumbling for the "off" switch.

Kathmandu appears to be following in the footsteps of other Asian capitals like Delhi and Bangkok, albeit on a smaller scale. Overpopulation is driving a growing **rural exodus**; new roads and bus services are carrying the landless poor away from their villages, while jobs in the tourism and carpet industries attract them to the Kathmandu Valley. Many immigrants land jobs and begin the difficult process of finding a place for themselves in the **big city**, and a few even find their fortune there. But there's no safety net for those who don't. They may end up squatting in the most primitive conditions imaginable – in unhealthy shacks by the river, in empty buildings, in the streets – and scrounging a living from the rubbish heaps or prostitution.

While poverty is a perennial problem in the valley, it's prosperity that's creating the brand-

new headaches, starting with **traffic** and **pollution**. Industrial workers get to their factories by tempo or bus. The more affluent drive their own motorbikes or cars. Goods must be moved by truck. Tourists take taxis. The result is ever-growing gridlock and an increasing smog problem from a fleet of vehicles that is doubling every six to eight years. Those who can afford to are moving out to the suburbs, and their commuting only worsens the problem. Vehicle emissions are blamed for an alarming increase in respiratory problems, which occur at twelve times the national average in Kathmandu. Health experts warn that children are particularly vulnerable to asthma, allergies and lead-related developmental problems caused by the appalling air quality. As discussed in the box on p.88, the causes of this environmental catastrophe are largely political, and require political will to solve. In the meantime, the introduction of electric-powered Safaa ("clean") tempos, made possible by a Danish government grant, is providing a highly visible reminder that there are cleaner alternatives.

Meanwhile, sheer numbers of people are taxing the valley's other infrastructure. In Kathmandu, demand for **drinking water** exceeds the supply by 50 to 100 percent (depending on season), with the result that residents in many neighbourhoods have pressure only on alternate mornings or evenings – most pump what water they can get up to rooftop storage tanks, and supplement it with deliveries by tanker. Leaks in underground pipes account for most of the shortfall, but of the water that is delivered, much of it is monopolized by wasteful tourist hotels and restaurants. Nobody seems to be talking about fixing the leaks or improving efficiency of the water supply; instead, most believe the solution lies in a big $250 million diversion project from the Malemchi Khola, northeast of the valley, but as of this writing the World Bank was threatening to withhold its share of the funding due to government mismanagement.

Not only is water scarce in the valley, it's also highly contaminated. A 1998 study deemed 50 percent of the capital's tap water to be "unsatisfactory" – and that was based on samples taken in the dry season, when the water is cleanest. Most of the contamination comes from **sewage** permeating the soil and infiltrating into old, leaky pipes. Only 30 percent of the valley's sewage is properly treated before being discharged: municipal treatment plants are old and don't operate properly, and in many areas raw waste is allowed to drain directly into rivers. (A new regional sewage-treatment facility is supposed to come on line in 2000, which might help.) Meanwhile, many industries – notably carpet-washing factories – discharge **toxic effluents** into the rivers. Such dumping is illegal, but the Ministry of Population and the Environment doesn't have a single inspector to enforce the law. **Garbage** is another problem, not only because the valley's growing population is generating more of it, but also because its municipalities still haven't agreed on a permanent dumping site; and in the meantime, much of it is simply burnt, adding to air pollution.

The damage that has been done to the valley's **culture** in the name of progress is less easy to quantify, but is arguably more profound. Traditional architecture is no longer valued. Members of the younger generation are drifting away from the religion of their parents. *Guthi* (charitable organizations) are in decline and have been forced to leave the upkeep of many temples to foreign preservationists. Tourism has robbed crafts of their proper use, and many performance arts of their meaning. Work outside the home has disrupted family life, and the influx of strangers has introduced social tensions and crime.

To some extent, valley residents are prepared to accept these problems as the price of progress: a little pollution or crime may seem a fair trade for improvements that keep children from dying and give people greater control over their lives. But increasingly, Kathmanduites are worrying that they might have a "Silent Spring" in the making. What will be the effects on their children of growing up breathing air, drinking water and eating food that is not only contaminated with germs but also laced with chemicals and heavy metals? In another generation, when Nepalis are presumably more prosperous and living longer and expecting more out of life, will they be haunted by elevated levels of cancer, birth defects and allergies? And will the nation be able to afford the cost of treating all the victims of these anthropogenic diseases?

BUREAUCRACY, CORRUPTION AND FATALISM

Many aid workers identify the root cause of Nepal's slow development as "institutional problems", a euphemism that covers a multitude of sins. They speak of management bottlenecks, where **bureaucrats** hoard power to such an extent that project managers have to spend most of their time in Kathmandu queueing for signatures instead of getting things done in the field. They complain that Nepali managers are overly fond of desk jobs in the capital, regarding remote hill postings as punishment and making no secret of their disdain for the local people they're supposed to be helping. (The most coveted position in Nepal is a job that involves no work and produces a regular pay cheque.) Managers frequently leave the important work to untrained underlings, preferring instead to pass their time in seminars and "talk programmes". Slogans and planning targets are more in evidence than action, while planners tend to favour rigid, top-down approaches without consulting experts in the field. These traits aren't unique to Nepal, of course, and indeed many aid organizations are themselves centralized and top-down-oriented.

But unquestionably, Nepal's gravest institutional problem is **corruption**, which seems to plumb new depths with each short-lived government. There is little tradition of public service at the national level in Nepal, and a government job with decision-making authority has long been regarded as a licence to collect kickbacks ("commissions") from those who desire a favourable decision. The graft is perpetuated by artificially low salaries and, no doubt, by the sight of apparently limitless piles of development loot. Government procedures have even been devised to streamline the process – most bilateral aid, for instance, is required to be disbursed by HMG "line agencies", each with its own hierarchy of bureaucrats who expect a piece of the action.

Under the old *panchaayat* system, corruption was endemic but discreet; since the restoration of democracy, it has become part of the modus operandi of all parties, and extends to the very highest levels. The intense competition for power has **politicized**, and corrupted, every branch of the bureaucracy: jobs are awarded on the basis of party loyalty, not merit; the appointees are essentially ordered to skim off as much as they can for the party (plus a bit for themselves), and are given political cover to do so. With each new government comes a wave of new appointees, producing administrative upheavals. Some observers have equated such systematic corruption with genocide, because the damage it's doing to Nepal's economy, and the money it's diverting from needed projects, is responsible for countless needless deaths. Over the years, foreign donors have abetted the corruption by looking the other way, not wanting to jeopardize their projects, but the situation has now become so bad, with so little aid money actually reaching its target, that some of the big donor nations have started threatening to cut off the funds.

These institutional problems are themselves only projections of Nepal's culture, elements of which seem almost designed to thwart Western-style development. One of Nepal's foremost anthropologists, Dor Bahadur Bista, argues compellingly that Nepal's greatest handicap is the **fatalism** peddled by its Baahun (Brahman) elite. According to Bista, along with Nepalis' admirable *ke garne* ("what to do?") attitude comes an exasperating apathy, and an obstructive suspicion that development efforts are merely futile attempts to resist fate. Responsibility for actions and decisions is often passed on to higher-ups (whether a boss, an astrologer or a deity), and the relationship between present work and future goals (at least in this life) is glossed over, resulting in haphazard planning and follow-through. Moreover, Nepali society places a great emphasis on **connections** and old-boy networks (called *aafno maanche* in Nepali: "one's own people"), which make it hard for members of ethnic minorities to advance, and on patronage, in which dependents are rewarded for loyalty rather than skill or innovation. Invaluable as these traits may be in a traditional village society, in a modern nation they tend to produce inept government, and foster a grovelling dependency on foreign patrons.

PROSPECTS

The foregoing isn't intended to make it sound as if Nepal's situation is hopeless, nor that there is no way for outsiders to help. Newcomers to the field tend to be the gloomiest ones, while people with a longer perspective are able to cite many major improvements. The political situation does indeed look very bad, but as of this writing, on the eve of the first general elections in five years, Nepalis were finally in a position to vote out the dead wood and bring in more accountable leaders. One is tempted to say that things can only get better. But regardless of who occupies power, Nepal will continue on its fitful development journey.

As a traveller, you too are playing a part in Nepal's development. With the right mixture of know-how and humility, you can be an agent of social change just by being yourself. Spent wisely, your money can bring tangible improvements to villages and families. In addition, there are plenty of good causes you may feel inclined to donate money to when you get home: with a little effort you should be able to see a few in action during your travels, and judge them by their fruits.

NATURAL HISTORY

The Himalaya are not only the world's tallest mountains, they're also the youngest – and still growing. Because of them, most of Tibet and parts of northern Nepal are high-altitude deserts, hidden in the Himalayan rain shadow, while many southern slopes, which bear the full brunt of the monsoon, are rainforest: nowhere in the world is there a transition of flora and fauna so abrupt as the one between the Tarai and the Himalayan crest, a distance of as little as 60km. As a result, Nepal can boast an astounding diversity of life, from rhinos to snow leopards.

GEOLOGY

The Himalaya provide graphic evidence for the **plate tectonics** (formerly known as continental drift) theory of mountain-building. According to this theory, the earth's crust is divided into a dozen or so massive plates which collide, separate and grind against each other with unimaginable force. The Himalaya are the result of the Indian subcontinental plate ramming northwards with particular force into the Asian plate – something like a car smashing into the side of a truck. It has been estimated that a 2000-kilometre cross-section of land along the collision zone has been compressed into 1000km, doubling the thickness of the crust and producing not only the Himalaya but also the vast Tibetan Plateau.

The shallow **Tethys Sea**, which once covered the entire region, was the main casualty in the process; its sedimentary deposits, now contorted and metamorphosed, can be seen at all elevations of the Himalaya. The first phase of mountain-building began around 45 million years ago, as the edge of the Asian plate, buckling under pressure from the advancing Indian plate, rose out of the sea to a height of about 2000m. Although it has since been lifted much higher, this **Tibetan Marginal Range**, which parallels the main Himalayan chain to the north, still stands as the divide between the Ganges and Tsangpo/Brahmaputra rivers. Unique among the world's major mountain ranges, the Himalaya don't form a watershed: rivers like the Kali Gandaki, Bhote Koshi (there are several by that name) and Arun cut right through the Himalaya because their courses were established by this earlier Tibetan Marginal Range.

The next major uplift occurred between 10 and 25 million years ago, when great chunks of the Asian plate were thrust southwards on top of the Indian plate, creating a low-altitude forerunner of the Himalayan range. Things appear to have remained more or less unchanged until just 600,000 years ago – practically yesterday, in geological time – when what is now the **Tibetan Plateau** was suddenly jacked up to an average elevation of 5000m, and the Tibetan Marginal Range to about 7000m. From this point on, monsoonal rains became an important erosive force on the south (Nepalese) side of the mountains, while the north, left in the rain shadow, turned into a high desert. Southward-flowing rivers, fuelled by phenomenal gradients of up to 6000m in 100km, further eroded the landscape.

Most of Nepal's present features were created at the geological last minute. Beginning around 500,000 years ago, the Tibetan rim lunged forward along numerous separate fronts to form the modern **Himalaya**. Averaging 8000m, Nepal's *himal* (massifs) show a freeze-frame of the current state of play.

But mountain-building produces downs as well as ups: around 200,000 years ago, a broad belt of foothills subsided, creating Nepal's **midland valleys**, while the southern edge of this zone curled up to form the **Mahabharat Lek** and, still further south, the **Chure Hills** (called the Siwaliks in India). These ridges rose so rapidly that they forced many southbound rivers to make lengthy east–west detours and permitted only three principal outlets to the Tarai; the Bagmati and Seti rivers were initially dammed up by the Mahabharat Lek, flooding the Kathmandu and Pokhara valleys respectively.

The Himalaya are rising still, albeit at a slower rate than previously. Periodic and severe **earthquakes** (see p.26) demonstrate that the earth continues to rearrange itself – one in eastern Nepal in 1988 killed 700 people – while **hot springs**, sometimes found near streams along trekking trails, are indicators of tectonic faultlines. **Erosion** is a particular problem in the Himalaya, where the mountains are continually sloughing off their skins, and landslides occur regularly during the monsoon. While **glaciers** play a part in shaping the terrain above about 5000m, the Himalaya aren't highly glaciated due to their sheer slopes (which can't support glacier-breeding snowfields) and relatively low precipitation at high elevations. On the whole, Himalayan glaciers are in a retreating phase, as they are in most parts of the world, and old moraines (piles of rubble left behind by melting glaciers) are commonly seen above 4000m.

Nepal's valleys are like vast cutaway diagrams of geological history, and trekking or rafting in them you'll be able to imagine the forces that have shaped the Himalaya. Igneous intrusions (usually granite) are common, but most outcrops consist of metamorphic rocks (schist, gneiss, limestone and dolomite), deposited as underwater sediments and later mashed and contorted under tremendous pressure; the wavy light and dark bands of the Lhotse-Nuptse Wall, in the Everest region, illustrate this. **Fossils** found in many of these layers have helped geologists date the phases of Himalayan mountain-building. The famous *shaligram* stones of Muktinath in the Annapurna region contain fossilized ammonites (spiral-shaped molluscs) dating from 150–200 million years ago. Of a much more recent origin, the bones of Peking Man and primitive stone tools have been found in the Chure Hills – proving that the Himalaya are so young that early humans were present during their creation.

FLORA

Nepal's **vegetation** is largely determined by altitude and can be conveniently grouped into three main divisions. The lowlands include the Tarai, Chure Hills and valleys up to about 1000m; the midlands extend roughly from 1000m to 3000m; and the Himalaya from 3000m to the upper limit of vegetation (typically about 5000m). Conditions vary tremendously within these zones, however: south-facing slopes usually receive more moisture, but also more sun in their lower reaches, while certain areas that are less protected from the summer monsoon – notably around Pokhara – are especially wet. In general, rainfall is higher in the east, and a greater diversity of plants can be found there.

THE LOWLANDS

Most of the Tarai's remaining forest consists of **sal**, a tall, straight tree much valued for its wood – a factor which is hastening its steady removal. *Sal* prefers well-drained soils and is most often found in pure stands along the Bhabar, the sloping alluvial plain at the base of the foothills; in the lower foothills, stunted specimens are frequently lopped for fodder. In spring, its cream-coloured flowers give off a heady jasmine scent. Other species sometimes associated with *sal* include *saj*, a large tree with crocodile-skin bark; *haldu*, a tree used for making dugout canoes; and *bauhinia*, a strangling vine that corkscrews around its victims.

The wetter **riverine forest** supports a larger number of species, but life here is more precarious, as rivers regularly flood and change course during the monsoon. *Sisu*, related to rosewood, and *khair*, an acacia, are the first trees to colonize newly formed sandbanks. *Simal*, towering on mangrove-like buttresses, follows close behind; also known as the silk-cotton tree, it produces bulbous red flowers in February, and in May its seed pods explode with a cottony material that is used for stuffing mattresses. *Palash* – the "flame of the forest tree" – puts on an even more brilliant show of red flowers in February. All of these trees are deciduous, shedding their leaves during the dry spring. Many other species are evergreen, including *bilar*, *jamun* and *curry*, an understorey tree with thin, pointed leaves that smell just like their name.

Grasses dominate less stable wetlands. Of the more than fifty species native to the Tarai, several routinely grow to a height of 8m. Even experts tend to pass off any tall, dense stand as "elephant grass", because the only way to get through it is on an elephant; the most common genera are *Phragmites*, *Saccharum*, *Arundo* and

Themeda. Most grasses reach their greatest height just after the monsoon and flower during the dry autumn months. Locals cut *khar*, a medium-sized variety, for thatch in winter and early spring; the official thatch-gathering season in the Tarai parks (two weeks in January) is a colourful occasion, although the activity tends to drive wildlife into hiding. Fires are set in March and April to burn off the old growth and encourage tender new shoots, which provide food for game as well as livestock.

THE MIDLANDS

The decline in precipitation from east to west is more marked at the middle elevations – so much so that the dry west shares few species in common with the moist eastern hills. Central Nepal is an overlap zone where western species tend to be found on south-facing slopes and eastern ones on the cooler northern aspects.

A common tree in dry western and central areas is **chir pine** (needles in bunches of three), which typically grows in park-like stands up to about 2000m. Various **oak** species often take over above 1500m, especially on dry ridges, and here you'll also find *ainsilo*, a cousin of the raspberry, which produces a sweet, if rather dry, golden fruit in May.

Although much of the wet midland forest has been lost to cultivation, you can see fine remnants of it above Godavari in the Kathmandu Valley and around the lakes in the Pokhara Valley. Lower elevations are dominated by a zone of **chestnut** and **chilaune**, the latter being a member of the tea family with oblong concave leaves and, in May, small white flowers. In eastern parts, several species of **laurel** form a third major component to this forest, while alder, cardamom and tree ferns grow in shady gullies.

The magical, mossy oak-rhododendron forest is still mostly intact above about 2000m, thanks to the prevalent fog that makes farming unviable at this level. **Khasru**, the predominant oak found here, has prickly leaves and is often laden with lichen, **orchids** and other epiphytes, which grow on other plants and get their moisture directly from the air. It's estimated that more than 300 orchid varieties grow in Nepal, and although not all are showy or scented, the odds are you'll be able to find one flowering at almost any time of year. **Tree rhododendron**

(*lali guraas*), Nepal's national flower, grows over 20m high and blooms with gorgeous red or pink flowers in March–April. Nearly thirty other species occur in Nepal, mainly in the east – the Milke Danda, a long ridge east of the Arun River, is the best place to view rhododendron, although impressive stands can also be seen between Ghodapani and Ghandrung in the Annapurna region. Most of Nepal's 300 species of **fern** are found in this forest type, as are many medicinal plants whose curative properties are known to ayurvedic practitioners but have yet to be studied in the West. Also occurring here are **lokta**, a small bush with fragrant white flowers in spring, whose bark is pulped to make paper, and **nettles**, whose stems are used by eastern hill-dwellers to make a hard-wearing fabric.

Holly, magnolia and maple may replace oak and rhododendron in some sites. **Dwarf bamboo**, the red panda's favourite food, grows in particularly damp places, such as northern Helambu and along the trail to the Annapurna Sanctuary. Cannabis thrives in disturbed sites throughout the midlands.

THE HIMALAYA

Conifers form the dominant tree cover in the Himalaya. Particularly striking are the forests around Rara Lake in western Nepal, where **Himalayan spruce** and **blue pine** (needles grouped in fives) are interspersed with meadows. Elsewhere in the dry west you'll find magnificent **Himalayan cedar** (*deodar*) trees, which are protected by villagers, and a species of cypress. Two types of **juniper** are present in Nepal: the more common tree-sized variety grows south of the main Himalayan crest (notably around Tengboche in the Everest region), while a dwarf scrub juniper is confined to northern rain-shadow areas. Both provide incense for Buddhist rites. In wetter areas, hemlock, fir (distinguished from spruce by its upward-pointing cones) and even the deciduous larch may be encountered.

One of the most common (and graceful) broadleafed species is **white birch**, usually found in thickets near the tree line, especially on shaded slopes where the snow lies late. **Poplars** stick close to watercourses high up into the inner valleys – Muktinath is full of them – while **berberis**, a shrub whose leaves turn scarlet in autumn, grows widely on exposed sites. Trekking up the Langtang or Marsyangdi valleys you pass through many of these forest types in rapid succession, but the most dramatic transition of all is found in the valley of the Thak Khola (upper Kali Gandaki): the monsoon jungle below Ghasa gives way to blue pine, hemlock, rhododendron and horse chestnut; then to birch, fir and cypress around Tukche; then the apricot orchards of Marpha; and finally the blasted steppes of Jomosom.

Alpine vegetation predominates on the forest floor and in moist meadows above the treeline, and – apart from the **dwarf rhododendron** (some species of which give off a strong cinnamon scent and are locally used as incense) – many **flowers** found here will be familiar to European and North American walkers. There are too many to do justice to them here, but primula, buttercup, poppy, iris, larkspur, gentian, edelweiss, buddleia, columbine and sage are all common. Most bloom during the monsoon, but rhododendrons and primulas can be seen flowering in the spring and gentians and larkspurs in the autumn.

MAMMALS

Most of Nepal's rich **animal life** inhabits the Tarai and, despite dense vegetation, is most easily observed there. In the hill regions, wildlife is much harder to spot due to population pressure – along trekking trails, at least – while very few mammals live above tree line. The following overview progresses generally from Tarai to Himalayan species.

The **Asian one-horned rhino** (*gaida*) is one of five species found in Asia and Africa, all endangered. In Nepal, about 500 rhinos – a quarter of the species total – live in Chitwan, and about 40 have been introduced to Bardia; they graze singly or in small groups in the marshy elephant grass, where they can remain surprisingly well hidden.

Although trained **elephants** (*hatti*) are a lingering part of Nepali culture (see "Chitwan National Park"), their wild relatives are seen only rarely in Nepal. Since they require vast territory for their seasonal migrations, the settling of the Tarai is putting them in increasing conflict with man, and the few that survive tend to spend much of their time in India.

Koshi Tappu is the only remaining habitat in Nepal for another species better known as a domestic breed, **wild buffalo** (*arnaa*), which graze the wet grasslands in small herds. Majestic and powerful, the **gaur** (*gauri gaai*), or Indian bison, spends most of its time in the dry lower foothills, but descends to the Tarai in spring for water.

Perhaps the Tarai's most unlikely mammals, **gangetic dolphins** – one of four freshwater species in the world – are present in small numbers in the Karnali and Sapt Koshi rivers. Curious and gregarious, dolphins tend to congregate in deep channels where they feed on fish and crustaceans; they may betray their presence with a puffing sound which they make through their blow-holes when surfacing. They're considered sacrosanct by Nepali Tharus, but are cruelly hunted in India.

The most abundant mammals of the Tarai, *chital*, or **spotted deer**, are often seen in herds around the boundary between riverine forest and grassland. Hog deer – so called because of their porky little bodies and head-down trot – take shelter in wet grassland, while the aptly named barking deer, measuring less than two feet high at the shoulder, are found throughout lowland and midland forests. Swamp deer gather in vast herds in Sukla Phanta, and males of the species carry impressive sets of antlers (their Nepali name, *barasingha*, means "twelve points"). *Sambar*, heavy-set animals standing five feet at the shoulder, are more widely distributed, but elusive. Two species of antelope, the graceful, corkscrew-horned **blackbuck** and the ungainly **nilgai** (blue bull), may be seen at Bardia and Koshi Tappu respectively; the latter was once assumed to be a form of cattle, and thus spared by Hindu hunters, but no longer.

Areas of greatest deer and antelope concentrations are usually prime territory for **tiger** (*bagh*), their main predator. However, your chances of spotting one of Nepal's endangered Bengal tigers are slim: they're mainly nocturnal, never very numerous, and incredibly stealthy. In the deep shade and mottled sunlight of dense riverine forest, a tiger's orange- and black-striped coat provides almost total camouflage. A male may weigh 250kg and measure 3m from nose to tail. Tigers are solitary hunters; some have been known to consume up to 20 percent of their body weight after a kill, but they may go several days between feeds. Males and females maintain separate but overlapping territories, regularly patrolling them, marking the boundaries with scent and driving off interlopers. Some Nepalis believe tigers to be the unquiet souls of the deceased.

Leopards are equally elusive, but much more widely distributed: they may be found in any deep forest from the Tarai to the timber line. As a consequence, leopards account for many more maulings than tigers in Nepal, and are more feared. A smaller animal (males weigh about 45kg), they prey on monkeys, dogs and livestock. **Other cats** – such as the fishing cat, leopard cat and the splendid clouded leopard – are known to exist in the more remote lowlands and midlands, but are very rarely sighted. Hyenas and wild dogs are scavengers of the Tarai, and **jackals**, though seldom seen (they're nocturnal), produce an eerie howling that is one of the most common night sounds in the Tarai and hills.

While it isn't carnivorous, the dangerously unpredictable **sloth bear**, a Tarai species, is liable to turn on you and should be approached with extreme caution. Its powerful front claws are designed for unearthing termite nests, and its long snout for extracting the insects. The **Himalayan black bear** roams midland forests up to tree line and is, if anything, more dangerous. **Wild boars** can be seen rooting and scurrying through forest anywhere in Nepal.

Monkeys, a common sight in the Tarai and hills, come in two varieties in Nepal. Comical **langurs** have silver fur, black faces and long, ropelike tails; you'll sometimes see them sitting on stumps like Rodin's *Thinker*. Brown **rhesus macaques** are more shy in the wild, but around temples are tame to the point of being nuisances. Many other small mammals may be spotted in the hills, among them porcupines, flying squirrels, foxes, civets, otters, mongooses and martens. The **red panda**, with its rust coat and bushy, ringed tail, almost resembles a tree-dwelling fox; like its Chinese relative, it's partial to bamboo, and is very occasionally glimpsed in the cloud forest of northern Helambu.

Elusive animals of the rhododendron and birch forests, **musk deer** are readily identified by their tusk-like canine teeth; males are hunted for their musk pod, which can fetch $200 an ounce on the international market. Though by no means common, **Himalayan tahr** is the most frequently observed large mammal of the high country; a goat-like animal with long, wiry fur and short horns, it browses along steep cliffs below the tree line. **Serow**, another goat rela-tive, inhabits remote canyons and forested areas, while **goral**, sometimes likened to chamois, occurs from middle elevations up to the tree line.

The Himalaya's highest residents are **blue sheep**, who graze the barren grasslands above the tree line year-round. Normally tan, males go a slaty colour in winter, accounting for their name. Herds have been sighted around the Thorung La in the Annapurna region, but they occur in greater numbers north of Dhorpatan and in She-Phoksundo National Park. Their chief predator is the **snow leopard**, a secretive cat whose habits are still little understood.

AMPHIBIANS AND REPTILES

Native to the Tarai's wetlands, crocodiles are most easily seen in winter, when they sun themselves on muddy banks to warm up their cold-blooded bodies. The endangered **mugger crocodile** favours marshes and oxbow lakes, where it may lie motionless for hours on end until its prey comes within snapping distance. Muggers mainly pursue fish, but will eat just about anything they can get their jaws around – including human corpses thrown into the river by relatives unable to afford wood for a cremation. The even more endangered **gharial crocodile** lives exclusively in rivers and feeds on fish; for more on its precarious state, see p.310.

Nepal has many kinds of **snakes**, but they are rarely encountered: most hibernate in winter, even in the Tarai, and shy away from humans at other times of year. Common cobras – snake charmers' favourites – inhabit low elevations near villages; they aren't found in the Kathmandu Valley, despite their abundance in religious imagery there. Kraits and pit vipers, both highly poisonous, have been reported, as have pythons up to twenty feet long. However, the commonest species aren't poisonous and are typically less than two feet long.

Chances are you'll run into a **gecko** or two, probably clinging to a guest-house wall. Helpful insect-eaters, these lizard-like creatures are able to climb almost any surface with the aid of amazing suction pads on their feet. About fifty species of **fish** have been recorded in Nepal, but only *mahseer*, a sporty relative of carp that attains its greatest size in the lower Karnali River, is of much interest; most ponds are stocked with carp and catfish.

BIRDS

Over 800 **bird species** – one tenth of the earth's total – have been sighted in Nepal. The country receives a high number of birds migrating between India and central Asia in spring and autumn and, because it spans so many ecosystems, provides habitats for a wide range of year-round residents. The greatest diversity of species is found in the Tarai wildlife parks, but even the Kathmandu Valley is remarkably rich in birdlife. The following is only a listing of the major categories – for the complete picture, get hold of *Birds of Nepal* (see "Books").

In the **Tarai** and lower hills, raptors (birds of prey) such as ospreys, cormorants, darters, gulls and kingfishers patrol streams and rivers for food; herons and storks can also be seen fishing, while cranes, ducks and moorhens wade in or float on the water. Many of these migratory species are particularly well represented at Koshi Tappu, which is located along the important Arun Valley corridor to Tibet. Peafowl make their meowing mating call – and peacocks occasionally deign to unfurl their plumage – while many species of woodpeckers can be heard, if not seen, high up in the *sal* canopy. Cuckoos and "brain fever" birds repeat their idiotic two- or four-note songs in an almost demented fashion. Parakeets swoop in formation; bee-eaters, swifts, drongos, swallows and rollers flit and dive for insects, while jungle fowl look like chickens as Monet might have painted them. Other oddities of the Tarai include the paradise flycatcher, with its lavish white tail-feathers and dragonfly-like flight; the lanky great adjutant stork, resembling a prehistoric reptile in flight; and the giant hornbill, whose beak supports an appendage that looks like an upturned welder's mask.

Many of the above birds are found in **the midlands** as well as the Tarai – as are mynas, egrets, crows and magpies, which tend to scavenge near areas of human habitation. Birds of prey – falcons, kestrels, harriers, eagles, kites, hawks and vultures – may also be seen at almost any elevation. Owls are common, but not much liked by Nepalis. Babblers and laughing thrushes populate the oak-rhododendron forest and are as noisy as their names suggest. Over twenty species of flycatchers are present in the Kathmandu Valley alone.

Nepal's national bird, the iridescent, multi-coloured *danphe* (impeyan pheasant), can often be spotted scuttling through the undergrowth in the Everest region; a range of house paints has been named after it. *Kalij* and *monal*, two other native pheasants, also inhabit the higher hills and lower **Himalaya**. Migrating waterfowl often stop over at high-altitude lakes –ruddy shelducks are a trekking-season attraction at Gokyo – and snow pigeons, grebes, finches and choughs may all be seen at or above the tree line. Mountaineers have reported seeing choughs at up to 8200m on Everest.

INVERTEBRATES AND INSECTS

Perhaps no other creature in Nepal arouses such squeamishness as the **leech** (*jukha*). Fortunately, these segmented, caterpillar-sized annelids remain dormant underground during the trekking seasons; during the monsoon, however, they come out in force everywhere in the Tarai and hills, making any hike a bloody business. Leeches are attracted to body heat, and will inch up legs or drop from branches to reach their victims. The bite is completely painless – the bloodsucker injects a local anesthetic and anticoagulant – and often goes unnoticed until the leech drops off of its own accord. To dislodge one, apply salt or burn it with a cigarette; don't pull it off or the wound could get infected.

Over 600 species of **butterflies** have been recorded in Nepal, with more being discovered all the time. Although the monsoon is the best time to view butterflies, many varieties can be seen before and especially just after the rains – look beside moist, sandy banks or atop ridges; Phulchoki is an excellent place to start in the Kathmandu Valley. Notable hill varieties include the intriguing orange oakleaf, whose markings enable it to vanish into forest litter, and the golden birdwing, a large, angular species with a loping wingbeat. **Moths** are even more numerous – around 5000 species are believed to exist in Nepal, including the world's largest, the giant atlas, which has a wingspan of almost a foot.

Termites are Nepal's most conspicuous social insects, constructing towering, fluted mounds up to eight feet tall in the western Tarai. Organized in colonies much the same as ants and bees, legions of termite workers and "reproductives" serve a single king and queen. The mounds function as cooling towers for the busy nest below; monuments to insect industry, they're made from tailings excavated from the colony's galleries and bonded with saliva for a wood-hard finish. **Honey bees** create huge, drooping nests in the Tarai and especially in the lush cliff country north of Pokhara. **Spiders** aren't very numerous in Nepal, although one notable species grows to be six inches across and nets birds (it's not poisonous to humans).

Fireflies, with orange and black bodies, give off a greenish glow at dusk in the Tarai. For many travellers, however, the extent of their involvement with the insect kingdom will be in swatting **mosquitoes**: two genera are prevalent in the lowlands, one of them *Anopheles*, the infamous vector of malaria.

BOOKS

Most of these books are a lot easier to come by in Kathmandu, and some will be available only in Nepal. Where the UK and US publishers are different, the UK publisher is given first – books published in other countries are indicated accordingly. Out of print (o/p) books may still be found in Nepal, or in your library.

GENERAL

Lynn Andrews *Windhorse Woman* (Warner, US). One woman's spiritual quest in Nepal; very New Age.

Barbara Crossette *So Close to Heaven* (Knopf, US). A survey of the "vanishing Buddhist kingdoms of the Himalayas", including a chapter focusing on Nepal's Tibetans, Bhotiyas and Newars.

Jeff Greenwald *Mister Raja's Neighborhood: Letters from Nepal* (John Daniel, US). The author went to Kathmandu to write the Great Asian Novel and ended up writing a series of letters – though perhaps contemplating his navel a bit too much in the process. *Shopping for Buddhas* (Harper & Row, US) is something of a sequel.

Harka Gurung *Vignettes of Nepal* (Sajha Prakashan, Nepal). Probably the best book written by a Nepali in English about his country, a vivid travelogue illuminated by a native's insights.

Pico Iyer *Video Night in Kathmandu* (Black Swan/Random House). A collection of essays on popular traveller hang-outs in Asia that are stronger on style than substance.

Peter Matthiessen *The Snow Leopard* (Collins Harvill/Viking Penguin). Matthiessen joins biologist George Schaller in a pilgrimage to Dolpo to track one of the world's most elusive cats, and comes up with characteristically Zen insights. A magnificent piece of writing, filled with beautiful descriptions of the landscape – and ever-perceptive observations of how Matthiessen's quest for the snow leopard became one of self-discovery.

Dervla Murphy *The Waiting Land* (John Murray/Overlook Press). A personal account of working with Pokhara's Tibetan refugees in 1965, written in the author's usual entertaining and politically on-the-ball style.

COFFEE-TABLE BOOKS

Kevin Bubriski *Portrait of Nepal* (Chronicle Books, US). An extraordinary collection of large-format portraits that does for Nepal's indigenous peoples what E. S. Curtis's photography did for Native Americans. With great subtlety and dignity, Bubriski has documented cultures and lifestyles that are passing within our generation. A truly important book.

Kevin Bubriski and Keith Dowman *Power Places of the Kathmandu Valley* (Inner Traditions International, US). A collaboration by two eminently qualified authorities: rich colour photographs accompanied by well-researched text.

John Everingham and Galen Rowell *Pokhara: In the Shadow of the Annapurnas* (Book Faith India). Nice photos and informative text about Pokhara, its valley and the Annapurna region.

Jim Goodman and Thomas Kelly *Kathmandu Valley* (Book Faith India). A collection of sumptuous photos and accompanying cultural essays.

Toni Hagen and Deepak Thapa *Nepal: The Kingdom of the Himalaya* (Himal Books, Nepal). No person alive has seen as much of Nepal as Hagen, who literally surveyed the entire country in the 1950s. His ground-breaking book, first published in 1961, has now been impressively updated.

Thomas Kelly and Patricia Roberts *Kathmandu: City at the Edge of the World* (Weidenfeld & Nicolson/Abbeville Press). Stunning photography and extensive essays on culture and religion.

Eric Valli and Diane Summers *Caravans of the Himalaya* (Thames & Hudson). Travelogue of a journey along the Nepal–Tibet trade route, packaged for maximum armchair impact. Valli and Summers have collaborated on several other books of the same lavish ilk, notably *Hunting for Honey: Adventures with the Rajis of Nepal* (Thames & Hudson), which features amazing photos of men clinging to branches while raiding beehives.

HISTORY

Byron Farwell *The Gurkhas* (Penguin). One of many books lionizing Nepal's famous Gurkha soldiers.

Percival Landon *Nepal* (Ratna Pustak Bhandar, Nepal). In two volumes, this was the most comprehensive study of the country at the time (1928) and is regarded as a classic – but having been commissioned by the Maharaja, it has a distinct political bias.

Michel Peissel *Tiger for Breakfast* (Time Books International, India). This biography of Boris Lissanevitch, the Russian emigré who ran Kathmandu's first tourist hotel, opens a fascinating window on 1950s Nepal.

Ludwig Stiller *The Rise of the House of Gorkha* (Ratna Pustak Bhandar, Nepal). An academic but readable account of Nepal's unification and war with Britain, written by a Jesuit priest turned Nepalese citizen.

David Tomory *A Season in Heaven: True Tales from the Road to Kathmandu* (HarperCollins, India). Disjointed but engrossing oral histories of the hippie trail to Kathmandu in the 1960s and '70s.

CULTURE AND ANTHROPOLOGY

Association of Nepalis in the Americas *The Nepal Cookbook* (Motilal Benarsidass, India). Easy-to-follow recipes of most standard Nepali dishes.

Mary M. Anderson *The Festivals of Nepal* (Rupa, Nepal). Despite the title, this only covers the Kathmandu Valley's festivals, but it's quite readable.

Dor Bahadur Bista *Peoples of Nepal* (Ratna Pustak Bhandar, Nepal). The standard overview of Nepal's ethnic groups, though much of the information is now superseded by more recent work.

Jim Goodman *Guide to Enjoying Nepalese Festivals* (Pilgrims Book House, Nepal). All the arcane whys and wherefores of the Kathmandu Valley's festivals: authoritative, though not very user-friendly.

Eva Kipp *Bending Bamboo, Changing Winds: Nepali Women Tell Their Life Stories* (Faith Book India). Powerful oral histories and photographs of women from all over Nepal, revealing not only the country's amazing cultural diversity but also the universal trials of being a Nepali woman.

Barbara J. Scot *The Violet Shyness of Their Eyes: Notes from Nepal* (Calyx Books, US). A woman's perspective on life in the Nepali hills, striking a nice balance between observation and introspection.

Irene Taylor *Buddhas in Disguise: Deaf People of Nepal* (Dawn Sign Press, US). A photojournal of the author's experiences among "those whose ears do not hear", examining the socio-religious perceptions of deaf people in a mostly non-literate society.

BHOTIYAS

Christoph von Fürer-Haimendorf *Himalayan Traders* (John Murray, US). An anthropological study of the impact of China's occupation of Tibet on Bhotiya and Sherpa traders.

David L. Snellgrove *Himalayan Pilgrimage* (Shambhala, US). An insightful travelogue/anthropological account of a trip through north-western Nepal in the 1950s.

CHHETRIS

Monica Connell *Against a Peacock Sky* (Penguin/Viking Penguin). Beautiful, impressionistic rendering of life among the *matawaali* (alcohol-drinking) Chhetris of Jumla District, capturing the subtleties of village life in Nepal.

GURUNGS

Broughton Coburn *Nepali Aama: Portrait of a Nepalese Hill Woman* (Moon Publications, US). Delightful study of a Gurung woman in a village south of Pokhara, in her own words, with photos.

Stan Royal Mumford *Himalayan Dialogue: Tibetan Lamas and Gurung Shamans in Nepal*

(University of Wisconsin Press). An account of myths and rituals practised in a village along the Annapurna Circuit – fascinating, once you get past the anthropological jargon.

MAGARS

Gary Shepherd *Life Among the Magars* (Sahayogi, Nepal). A personal account, with plenty of pertinent insights.

MAITHILIS

Ram Dayal Rakesh *Folk Festivals of Mithila* (Book Faith India). A delightful account of this Tarai region's festivals, along with related folk tales and traditional song lyrics.

SHERPAS

Hugh R. Downs *Rhythms of a Himalayan Village* (Harper & Row, US). An extraordinarily sensitive synthesis of black-and-white photos, text and quotes, describing rituals and religion in a Solu village.

James F. Fisher *Sherpas: Reflections on Change in Himalayan Nepal* (University of California Press, US). A before-and-after account, written by a member of Edmund Hillary's 1964 school-building team, who concludes that Sherpas are more resilient than we give them credit for.

RELIGION

HINDUISM

P. Lal (trans) *The Ramayana of Valmiki* (Tarang, Nepal). A condensed version of the classic epic.

K. M. Sen *Hinduism* (Penguin/Viking Penguin). An accessible survey, explanatory without being too obscure.

Shri Purohit Swami (trans) *The Geeta* (Faber & Faber, UK). A portable, robust translation of the Bhagavad Gita.

TIBETAN BUDDHISM

Tenzin Gyatso (the Dalai Lama) *The Way to Freedom: Core Teachings of Tibetan Buddhism* (HarperCollins, US). Good primer, though perhaps a bit evangelical.

Christmas Humphries *Buddhism: An Introduction and Guide* (Penguin). First published in 1951, this classic but demanding overview puts all the major sects into perspective.

Vicki Mackenzie *Reincarnation: The Boy Lama* (Bloomsbury, UK). An intriguing book, recounting the lives of Lama Yeshe, the abbot of Kopan Monastery, who died in 1984, and Osel Hita Torres, who was born in 1985 and enthroned as Yeshe's reincarnation at the age of two.

Robert A F Thurman *Essential Tibetan Buddhism* (HarperCollins, US). A survey of basic teachings, weaving together classic texts with modern commentary. Not for beginners.

Chögyam Trungpa *The Myth of Freedom* (Shambhala, Nepal). A useful primer on the metaphysics of Buddhist meditation, one of a welter of books by a master who was instrumental in packaging Buddhism for the West.

ART AND ARCHITECTURE

Lydia Aran *The Art of Nepal* (Sahayogi, Nepal). Surprisingly good overview of Nepalese religion as well as stone, metal and wood sculpture and *thangka* paintings.

Claire Burkert *Janakpur Art: A Living Tradition* (Janakpur Women's Development Center, Nepal). As simple and understated as its subject, this slim booklet highlights the dignity of the women who create Maithili art.

Susi Dunsmore *Nepalese Textiles* (British Museum Press, UK). A labour of love, this handsome, full-colour book details the patterns and techniques of all of Nepal's major ethnic groups.

Handicraft Association of Nepal *A Short Description of Gods, Goddesses and Ritual Objects of Buddhism and Hinduism in Nepal* (Handicraft Association of Nepal). An inexpensive booklet that may help in sorting out iconography.

Michael Hutt *Nepal: A Guide to the Art and Architecture of the Kathmandu Valley* (Kinscadale, UK). An in-depth discussion of iconography, design and construction, in hard cover.

Eva Rudy Jansen *The Book of Buddhas: Ritual Symbolism Used in Buddhist Statuary and Ritual Objects* and *The Book of Hindu Imagery: The Gods and Their Symbols* (Binkey Kok Publications, Holland). Good introductory guides to the iconography of religious statuary found in Nepal.

Philip Rowson *The Art of Tantra* (Thames & Hudson/Norton). A survey of tantric iconography and the theology behind it.

FICTION AND POETRY

NEPALI AUTHORS

Laxmi Prasad Devkota *Muna Madan* (Nirala, India). The most famous work by Nepal's best-loved poet recounts the tragic, almost Shakespearean tale of a young Newar trader who leaves his young wife to travel to Lhasa.

Kesar Lall and Tej R. Kansakar (trans) *Forbidden Fruit and Other Stories* (Ratna Pustak Bhandar, Nepal). Some of these stories, translated from the Newari, are better than others, but all shed light on Nepali culture, dealing with themes of family duty, class relationships, fate and the ever-present spectre of *dukha* (sadness).

B. P. Koirala *Faulty Glasses* (Book Faith India). Short stories that capture everyday life and concerns in 1940s Nepal. Koirala was Nepal's first elected prime minister.

Shankar Koirala *Khairini Ghat* (Pilgrims Book House, Nepal). A haunting, elliptical novella depicting the ignorance and cruelty of life in a Nepali village in the 1950s.

Tara Nath Sharma *Blackout* (Nirala, Nepal). A dark novel of life in the Nepal hills, by an author who has served time in jail for his views.

FOREIGN AUTHORS

W. E. Bowman *The Ascent of Rum Doodle* (Pimlico, UK). Reprint of the classic 1956 parody of the mountaineering-account genre.

Philip Kerr *Esau* (Chatto & Windus, UK). An appallingly bad thriller set in Nepal with an absolutely cartoonish plot that includes a rogue CIA agent, a *sadhu* with magic powers and a yeti.

Frederick Lenz *Surfing the Himalayas* and *Snowboarding to Nirvana* (St Martin's). Dreadful, unaccountably popular books set in a fantasy Nepal that propound a New-Agey, don't-worry-be-happy form of Buddhism.

Kim Stanley Robinson *Escape From Kathmandu* (Unwin/Tor). Pure potboiler, but it might be fun for the real-life *mise en scène* (action starts at the Hotel Star in Thamel).

CHILDREN'S BOOKS

Kanak Mani Dixit *Adventures of a Nepali Frog* and *The Leech and I* (Rato Bangala Kitab, Nepal). Fun, fanciful romps through Nepal with animal protagonists.

Joy Stephens *Where's the Hasiya, Sanu Maya?* (Rhim-Jim Kitaab, Nepal). A bilingual story of village life in Nepal.

Joanne Stephenson *Two Rams* (Book Faith India). A Nepali boy meets his first Westerners.

Agatha Pakhrin Thapa *The Adventures of the Mice* (Rhim-Jim Kitaab, Nepal). A cute story in bilingual verse.

NATURAL HISTORY

Robert Fleming, Jr *The General Ecology, Flora and Fauna of Midland Nepal* (Tribhuwan University, Nepal). A simple ecology text drawing on examples mainly from around the Kathmandu Valley.

Robert Fleming Sr, Robert Fleming Jr and Lain Singh Bangdel *Birds of Nepal* (Nature Himalayas, Nepal). The authoritative field guide.

K. K. Gurung *Heart of the Jungle* (André Deutsch, US). The essential guide to Chitwan's flora and fauna, written by the former manager of *Tiger Tops Jungle Lodge*.

Carol Inskipp *A Popular Guide to the Birds and Mammals of the Annapurna Conservation Area* (ACAP, Nepal). A slim volume with some colour plates.

Dorothy Mierow and Tirtha Shrestha *Himalayan Flowers and Trees* (Sahayogi, Nepal). A pocket-sized guide with colour plates and some useful information at the back.

George Schaller *Stones of Silence: Journeys in the Himalaya* (University of Chicago Press, US). Written by the wildlife biologist who accompanied Peter Matthiessen on his quest for the snow leopard, this book provides a detailed view of ecosystems of the high Himalaya.

Colin Smith *Illustrated Checklist of Nepal's Butterflies* (Rohit Kumar, Nepal). Beautiful colour plates showing nearly 600 species, by the curator of the Annapurna Regional Museum.

Martin Woodcock *Birds of India* (HarperCollins, US). A stand-in for Fleming (see above) if the latter is unavailable.

DEVELOPMENT AND POLITICS

When you're in Nepal, look out for *Himal*, a bimonthly magazine devoted to development and environmental issues. It's published in Kathmandu and is available in many bookshops there.

Lynn Bennett *Dangerous Wives and Sacred Sisters* (Columbia University Press, US). Good insight into the life and position of Hindu women in Nepal.

Dor Bahadur Bista *Fatalism and Development* (Orient Longman, India). An insightful analysis of the cultural factors that stand in the way of Nepal's development, by the country's best-known anthropologist.

Indra Majpuria *Nepalese Women* (M Devi, Nepal). Though it wanders quite a bit, this forcibly gets across the hardships and problems facing women in Nepal.

Charlie Pye-Smith *Travels in Nepal* (Penguin/Viking Penguin). A cross between a travelogue and a progress report on aid projects, this succeeds in giving plenty of facts and analysis without getting bogged down in institutional waffle.

David Seddon *Nepal: A State of Poverty* (Vikas, Nepal). A hard look at the issues by one of the longest-serving foreign critics of Nepal's development efforts.

Ludmilla Tüting and Kunda Dixit *Bikas-Binas, Development-Destruction* (Ratna Pustak Bhandar, Nepal). Excellent collection of articles which covers the whole gamut of dilemmas arising out of development, environmental degradation and tourism. It's supposed to speak for the entire Himalayan region, but it really focuses on Nepal.

HEALTH

Jim Duff and Peter Gormly *The Himalayan First Aid Manual* (World Expeditions, Nepal). Handy pocket-sized booklet, sold by the Kathmandu Environmental Education Project.

Andrew J. Pollard and David R. Murdoch *The High Altitude Medicine Handbook* (Book Faith India). Everything you need to know for a trek; the "micro" edition contains the same text in a much more portable form.

Dr Ravi P. Thapaliya *Your Health in Nepal* (Musk, Nepal). A thorough manual on health and safety for travelling, trekking, rafting and visiting the Tarai wildlife parks.

MOUNTAINS AND MOUNTAINEERING

Chris Bonington *Everest South West Face* (Hodder & Stoughton, UK, o/p). An exhaustive tome covering every aspect of a major Himalayan assault – in this case, an unsuccessful one. Also look out for Bonington's *The Everest Years* (Hodder, UK) and his retrospective, *Mountaineer* (The Mountaineers, US).

Anatoli Boukreev and G. Weston deWalt *The Climb* (St Martin's). Boukreev was one of the central actors in the 1996 Everest drama, and this book provides a *Rashomon*-like alternative version of the events described in Jon Krakauer's *Into Thin Air* (see below).

Maurice Herzog *Annapurna* (Paladin, US). One of the greatest true adventure stories ever written, describing the first successful ascent of an 8000-metre peak. Herzog's dreamlike description of his altitude- and hypothermia-induced stupor on the summit, the desperate descent, and the state of his mind as he contemplated death are riveting.

Jon Krakauer *Into Thin Air* (Random House, US). The best-selling first-person account of the disastrous events on Everest in 1996. It's an efficient and balanced telling of a story that has all the elements of (excuse the pun) high tragedy: hubris, heroism, angry mountain gods, rivalry, vanity, triumph, agony. Ironically, perhaps tragically, this book will probably do as much as anything ever written about Everest to make more foolish people want to climb it.

Reinhold Messner *The Crystal Horizon* (Crowood Press/The Mountaineers). Not very well written (or maybe it's the translation), but a nonetheless compelling account of Messner's 1980 solo ascent of Everest. Messner's *All 14 Eight-Thousanders* (Crowood Press, UK) has awesome photos and an interesting appendix of Himalayan mountaineering statistics.

Andrew Stevenson *Annapurna Circuit: A Himalayan Journey* (Constable, UK). One trekker's diary: standard experiences and a few insights.

H. W. Tilman *Nepal Himalaya* (Cambridge University Press, UK, o/p). A chatty account of the first mountaineering reconnaissance of Nepal in 1949–51, reprinted as part of *The*

Seven Mountain-Travel Books (Diadem/The Mountaineers). Though crusty, and at times racist, Tilman was one of the century's great adventurers, and his writing remains fresh and witty.

Walt Unsworth *Everest* (Grafton/Cloudcap). Exhaustive history of mountaineering on the world's highest peak.

TREKKING GUIDES

Stan Armington *Trekking in the Nepal Himalaya* (Lonely Planet). A less perceptive, but more portable, alternative to Bezruchka (below). Some people prefer its "Day 1–Day 2" route descriptions.

Stephen Bezruchka *Trekking in Nepal: A Traveler's Guide* (Cordee/The Mountaineers). The most thorough, even-handed and sensitive book on trekking, containing background pieces on Nepali culture and natural history.

Alton C. Byers III *Treks on the Kathmandu Valley Rim* (Sahayogi, Nepal). Mainly day hikes and overnights.

Amy R. Kaplan and Michael Keller *Nepal: An Essential Handbook for Trekkers* (Mandala, Nepal). A primer on trek preparations and cultural and environmental sensitivity. Includes tips on health, porters and trekking with kids.

Wendy Brewer Lama *Trekking Gently in the Himalaya* (Sagarmatha Pollution Control Project, Nepal). An excellent, concise pamphlet on trekkers' environmental and cultural responsibilities.

Jamie McGuinness *Trekking in the Everest Region* and *Trekking in Langtang, Helambu and Gosainkund* (Trailblazer, UK). Exhaustive and perceptive guides to all the routes in these regions.

Bill O'Connor *The Trekking Peaks of Nepal* (Crowood Press, UK). Describes climbing routes and trek approaches for eighteen trekking peaks.

Kev Reynolds *Dolpo* and *Manaslu: A Trekker's Guide* (Book Faith India). Slim but welcome guidebooks to these areas.

Hugh Swift *Trekking in Nepal, West Tibet and Bhutan* (Hodder/Sierra Club). Gives vivid area accounts instead of hour-by-hour route descriptions; getting a little dated now.

Bryn Thomas *Trekking in the Annapurna Region* (Trailblazer, UK). The best guide to this popular region, though not as comprehensive as the other Trailblazer titles.

OTHER GUIDES

Dubby Bhagat *Peak Hour: A Handbook of the Everest Flight* (Rupa, India). Chatty, first-person travelogue of the sights seen from the standard "mountain flight".

John Burbank *Culture Shock! Nepal* (Graphic Arts Center, US). Sensitivity training for tourists, with valuable insights into social mores, religion, caste and cross-cultural relations.

James Giambrone *Kathmandu Valley Bikes & Hikes* (APA). Two dozen itineraries, accompanied by an excellent fold-out route map.

Peter Knowles and Dave Allardice *White Water Nepal* (Rivers Publishing, UK). An indispensable companion for all rafters and kayakers, written with great wit and no nonsense; useful maps, stream profiles and hydrographs. *Rafting Nepal: A Consumer's Guide* is a cheaper, locally printed version for the casual rafter.

Rajendra Khadka (ed) *Travelers' Tales Nepal* (O'Reilly and Associates, US). Interesting anecdotes and musings by expats, climbers and ordinary travellers, including excerpts by Rheinhold Messner and Peter Matthiessen and the most disgusting leech story ever committed to paper.

John Sanday *Odyssey Guide to the Kathmandu Valley* (Collins, UK). The author is the leading authority on restoration of the valley's monuments.

LANGUAGE

Basic Nepali is surprisingly easy to learn, and local people are always thrilled when travellers make the effort to pick up a few phrases. Knowing a little bit of the language certainly comes in handy, too, since while nearly all Nepalis who deal with tourists speak English, few people do off the beaten track.

Nepali (sometimes called Gurkhali) is closely related to Hindi and other Sanskrit-based languages, so Nepali-speakers and Indians can usually catch the gist of what each other is saying. However, nearly half of all Nepalis speak Tibetan, Sherpa or one of several dozen other Tibeto-Burman dialects, which are completely unrelated to Nepali – almost all speak Nepali as a second language, but sometimes with difficult to understand regional accents.

Nepali is written in a script known as **Devanaagari**: there's fortunately no need for travellers to learn it since signs, bus destinations and so on are usually written in Roman script. This transliteration, though, often leads to problems of inconsistency – see the note in "Information and maps" in Basics for more on this. For a **glossary of food terms**, see "Eating and drinking" in Basics.

The most useful **phrasebooks** on the market are Lonely Planet's *Nepal Phrasebook* and Shyam P Wagley's *Nepali Phrasebook* (Ratna Pustak Bhandar, Nepal). *A Simple Nepali for Trekkers* (Rupa, Nepal), available only in Nepal, goes a little deeper into grammar, but isn't as good for quick reference. For a full-blown **teach-yourself book**, try *A Basic Course in Spoken Nepali*, by Tika Karki and Chij Shrestha (self-published) or David Matthews' *A Course in Nepali* (School of Oriental and African Studies, UK), both widely available in Nepal.

PRONUNCIATION

Even when Nepali is transliterated from the Devanaagari script into the Roman alphabet using phonetic spellings, there are a number of peculiarities in pronunciation:

A as in *a*lone

AA as in f*a*ther

B sounds like a cross between "b" and "v"

E as in caf*é*

I as in pol*i*ce

J as in *j*ust

O as in n*o*te

R sounds like a cross between "r" and "d"

S sounds almost like "sh"

U as in b*oo*t

W sounds like a cross between "w" and "v"

Z sounds like "dj" or "dz"

The "a" and "aa" distinction is crucial. *Maa* (in) is pronounced as it looks, with the vowel stretched out, but *ma* (I) sounds like "muh" and *mandir* (temple) like "mundeer". The accent almost always goes on the syllable with "aa" in it, or if there's no "aa", on the first syllable.

Some Nepali vowels are nasalized – to get the right effect, you have to block off your nasal passage, producing a slightly honking sound like a French "n". Nasalized vowels aren't indicated in this book, but they're something to be aware of. To hear how they should sound, listen to a Nepali say *tapaai* (you) or *yahaa* (here).

ASPIRATED CONSONANTS

The combinations "ch" and "sh" are pronounced as in English, but in all other cases where an "h" follows a consonant the sound is meant to be aspirated – in other words, give it an extra puff of air. Thus *bholi* (tomorrow) sounds like b'*h*oli and Thamel sounds like T'*h*amel. Note these combinations:

CHH sounds like a very breathy "ch", as in "pi*tch h*ere"

PH sometimes sounds like an "f" (as in *ph*one) but may also be pronounced like a breathy "p" (as in hap*h*azard)

TH is pronounced as in "pu*t here*" (not as in *th*ink)

RETROFLEX CONSONANTS

Finally, the sounds "d", "r" and "t" also occur in retroflex forms – ie they're pronounced by rolling the tip of the tongue back towards the roof of the mouth. Again, it's not worth going into too much detail about this here, but it's a safe bet that whenever these letters are followed by an "h" they'll be retroflex – an obvious example is Kathmandu, which sounds a little like "Kardmandu". Sometimes retroflexion results in a difference in meaning: *saathi* means friend, but with a retroflex "th" it means sixty.

A BRIEF GUIDE TO SPEAKING NEPALI

GREETINGS AND BASIC PHRASES

For advice on the nuances of some of these basic phrases, see "Cultural Hints" in Basics.

Hello, Goodbye	*Namaste* (said with palms together as if praying)	I didn't understand that	*Maile tyo bujina*
		Please speak more slowly	*Bistaarai bolnus*
Hello (very formal)	*Namaskar*	I only speak a little Nepali	*Ma ali ali Nepali bolchhu*
Yes/No (It is/isn't)	*Ho/Hoina*		
Yes/No (There is/isn't)	*Chha/Chhaina*	Pardon?	*Hajur?*
Thank you (formal)	*Dhanyabaad*	Please	*Kripaya*
How are things? (informal);	*Kasto chha?*	No thanks	*Nai; Pardaina (I don't want it)*
(polite)	*Sanchai chha?*	I'm sorry, excuse me	*Maph garnus*
Okay, fine (informal);	*Thik chha*	Let's go	*Jaun*
(polite)	*Sanchai chha*	It was an honour to meet you	*Hajur lai bhetera dherai kushi laagyo*
What's your name? (to an adult);	*Tapaaiko naam ke ho?*	Thank you (very much) for everything	*Sapai kurako laagi (dherai) dhanyabaad*
(to a child);	*Timro naam ke ho?*	See you again	*Pheri betaunla*
My name is . . .	*Mero naam . . . ho*		
My country is . . .	*Mero desh . . . ho*		
I don't know	*Malaai thaahaa chhaina*		

FORMS OF ADDRESS

Excuse me . . .	*0 . . .*	Younger brother (men or boys younger than you)	*Bhaai*
(more polite)	*Hajur . . .*		
Elder brother (said to men your age or older)	*Daai; Daaju* (more respectful)	Father (a man old enough to be your father)	*Bua*
		Mother (women old enough to be your mother)	*Aama*
Elder sister (women your age or older)	*Didi*	Grandfather (old men)	*Baje*
		Grandmother (old women)	*Bajei*
Younger sister (women or girls younger than you)	*Bahini*	Shopkeeper, Innkeeper (male)	*Saahuji*
		Shopkeeper, Innkeeper (female)	*Saahuni*

BASIC QUESTIONS AND REQUESTS

Whether you're making a statement or asking a question, the word order is the same in Nepali – to indicate that you're asking, not telling, make sure you raise your voice at the end.

Do you speak English?	*Tapaai Angreji bolnuhunchha?*	Is/Isn't there a . . .?	*. . . chha/chhaina?*
		Is . . . available?	*. . . painchha?*
Is there someone who speaks English?	*Angreji bolne kohi chha?*	Is . . . okay?	*. . . hunchha?*
		Please help me	*Kripaya malaai madhat garnus*
I don't speak Nepali	*Ma Nepali boldina*		

Continues over

BASIC QUESTIONS AND REQUESTS (continued)

Please give me . . .	*Kripaya . . . dinus*	What does . . mean?	*. . . ko mane ke ho?*
I'm (hungry)	*Malaai (bhok) laagyo*	Really?	*Saachinai? or Hora?*
I'm not (hungry)	*Malaai (bhok) laageko chhaina*	How	*Kasari*
		What	*Ke*
I like . . . (very much)	*Malaai . . . (dherai) manparchha*	When	*Kahile*
I want/don't want	*Ma . . . chaahanchhu/ chaahunna*	Where	*Kahaa*
		Who	*Ko*
What's (this) for?	*(Yo) ke ko laagi?*	Why	*Kina*
What's the matter?	*Ke bhayo?*	Which	*Kun*
What's (this) called in Nepali?	*Nepali maa (yo) ke bhanchha?*		

NEGOTIATIONS

How much does this cost?	*Esko kati parchha?*	I don't have any change	*Masanga khudra chhaina*
How much for a (room)?	*(Rum) ko kati parchha?*	Please use the meter	*Malaai meter-maa laijaanus*
How many people?	*Kati jana?*	Just a moment	*Ek chin* (literally, "One blink")
For (two) people	*(Dui) jana ko laagi*		
Only one person	*Ek jana maatrai*	I'll come back	*Ma pharkanechhu*
Can I see it?	*Herna sakchhu?*	Good job, Well done	*Kyaraamro*
It's very/too expensive	*Dherai mahango bhayo*	Don't worry	*Chinta nagarnus*
Is there a cheaper one?	*Kunai sasto chha?*	The bill, please	*Bil dinus*
I don't need it	*Malaai chahindaina*		

DIRECTIONS

Where is the . . . ?	*. . . kahaa chha?*	Where are you coming from?	*Tapaai kahaabaata aaunu bhayeko?*
Where is this (bus) going?	*Yo (bas) kahaa jaanchha?*	Here	*Yahaa*
Which is the way/trail/ road to . . . ?	*. . . -jaane baatokun ho?*	There/Yonder	*Tyahaa/Utyahaa*
		(To the) right	*Daayaa (tira)*
Which is the best way?	*Kun baato sabhanda raamro chha?*	(To the) left	*Baayaa (tira)*
		Straight	*Sidhaa*
How far is it?	*Kati taadhaa chha?*	North	*Uttaar*
Where are you going?	*Tapaai kahaa jaadai hununchha?*	South	*Dakshin*
		East	*Purba*
I'm going to . . .	*Ma . . . jaadai chhu*	West	*Pashchim*
		Near/Far	*Najik/Taadhaa*

TIME

What time is it?	*Kati bajyo?*	(Five) past (six)	*(Chha) bajer (paanch) minet gayo*
What time does the bus leave?	*Yo bas kati baaje jaanchha?*	(Ten) to (eight)	*(Aath) bajana (das) minet bakichha*
When does it arrive?	*Kati baaj pugchha?*		
How many hours does it take?	*Kati ghanta laagchha?*	Minute	*Minet*
		Hour	*Ghanta*
(Two) o'clock	*(Dui) bajyo*	Day	*Din*
(Nine)-thirty	*Saadhe (nau) bajyo*	Day (of week)	*Bar*

Week	Haptaa	Ago, Before	Pahile
Month	Maina	Next week	Aarko haptaa
Year	Barsa	Last month	Gayeko maina
Today	Aaja	(Two) years ago	(Dui) barsa agi
Tomorrow	Bholi	Morning	Bihaana
Yesterday	Hijo	Afternoon	Diuso
Now	Ahile	Evening	Belukaa
Later	Pachhi	Night	Raati

DEALING WITH KIDS

There's no foolproof way to silence pesky kids, but the following phrases might help you parry the taunts. (For more on the problem of begging among Nepali children, see p.108.)

Begging is bad	Maagnu raamro hoina	Rude boy/person	Naraamro keta maanchhe
Don't beg	Namaago		
I don't give to beggars	Maagnelai dinna	Don't you have any manners?	Bhudi chhaina?
So loud!	Kasto karaieko!		
Am I deaf?	Ma bahiro chhura?	Don't you have anything better to do?	Aru kaam chhaina?
Be quiet	Chup laaga		
Go back/Go away	Pharka/Jaaun	Don't do that	Teso nagara
		Don't touch that	Tyo nachalau

NOUNS

Bag, baggage	Jholaa	Mistake	Galti
Bed	Bistaara	Money	Paisa
Blanket, quilt	Sirak	Mother	Aama
Boy	Keta	Mouth	Mukh
Bus	Bas	Nose	Naak
Candle	Mainbatti	Pain	Dukhyo
Child, children	Ketaketi	Paper	Kaagat
Clothes	Luga	Person	Maanchhe
Daughter	Choraa	Place	Thau
Ear	Kan	Problem	Samasya
Eye	Ankha	Restaurant	Resturent, bhojanalaya
Family	Pariwaar	Road	Baato, rod
Father	Buwa	Room	Rum, kothaa
Fever	Joro	School	Skul
Foot	Khutta	Seat	Sit
Friend	Saathi	Shoe	Jutta
Food	Khaanaa	Shop	Pasal
Girl	Keti	Son	Chori
Hand	Haat	Stomach	Pet
Head	Taauko	Success	Safal
Hotel/Lodge	Hotel/Laj	Teahouse	Chiya pasal, chiya dokan
House	Ghar	Ticket	Tiket
Husband	Srimaan	Toilet	Chaarpi, toilet
Job, work	Kaam	Town, village	Gaaun
Lamp	Batti	Trail/main trail	Baato/mul baato
Mattress	Danlap	Water	Paani
Medicine	Ausadhi	Wife	Srimati

Continues over

ADJECTIVES AND ADVERBS

One tricky thing about Nepali adjectives: the ones that describe feelings behave like nouns. Thus to express the notion "I'm thirsty", you have to say *Malaai thirkaa laagyo* ("To me thirst has struck").

A little	Alikati	Early	Chaadai	Only	Maatrai
Already	Pahilei	Easy	Sajilo	Open	Khulaa
After	Pachhi	Empty	Khali	Often	Kahilekahi
Again	Pheri	Enough	Prasasta	Quickly	Chitto
All	Sabai	Expensive	Mahango	Right (correct)	Thik
Alone	Eklai	Far	Taadhaa	Rude	Naraamro, phohori
A lot	Dherai	Full (thing)	Bhari		
Always	Sadai	Full (person)	Agaayo	Sad	Dukhi
Another	Aarko	Fun	Majaa	Same	Eutai
Bad	Kharaab, naraamro	Good	Raamro	Similar	Ustai
		Happy	Kushi	Slowly	Bistaarai
Beautiful	Raamro	Heavy	Garungo	Small	Saano
Best	Sabhanda raamro	Hot (person or weather)	Garam	Soon	Chaadai, chittai
Better	Ajai raamro	Hot (liquid)	Taato	Stolen	Choreko
Big	Thulo	Hungry	Bhokayeko	Strong	Baliyo
Cheap	Sasto	Interesting	Majaa	Stupid	Murkha
Clean	Safaa	Late	Dhilo	Tall	Aglo
Clever	Chalakh	Less	Thorai	Tasty	Mitho
Closed	Bhanda	Lost	Haraayeko	Terrible	Jhur
Cold (person or weather)	Jaado	Loud	Charko	Thirsty	Tirkha
		More (quantity)	Aru	Tired	Thakai
Cold (liquid)	Chiso	More (degree)	Ekdum, ajai	Too much	Asadei
Crazy	Paagal	Near(er)	Najik(ai)	Uphill	Ukaalo
Dark	Adhyero	Never	Kahilei	Very	Dherai
Different	Pharak	New	Naya	Wet	Bhijyo
Difficult	Gaaro	Noisy	Halla	Worse	Khattam
Dirty	Phohor	Old (thing)	Purano	Worst	Sabhanda naraamro
Dishonest	Bemaani	Old (person)	Budho (male), Budhi (female)		
Downhill	Oraallo			Wrong	Galti
Dry	Sukeko				

VERBS

The following verbs are in the infinitive form. To turn a verb into a polite command (eg, "Please sit"), just add -*s* (*Basnus*); for an informal command, replace the -*nu* with -*un* (*Basun*). For an all-purpose tense, drop the -*u* ending and replace it with -*e* (eg *Jaane* can mean go, going or will go, depending on the context). The easiest way to negate any verb is to put *na*- in front of it (*Nabasnus, Ma najaane*).

Arrive	Aaipugnu	Forget	Birsanu	Make	Banaunu
Ask	Sodhnu	Get	Paunu, linu	Need	Chaahinu
Believe	Biswas garnu	Give	Dinu	Open	Kholnu
Break	Bhaanchnu	Go	Jaanu	Put	Raakhnu
Buy	Kinnu	Hear, listen	Sunnu	Receive	Paunu
Carry	Boknu	Help	Madhat garnu	Remember	Samjhinu
Close	Banda garnu	Hurry	Hatar garnu	Rent	Bhadama linu
Come	Aunu	Learn	Siknu	Rest	Aaram garnu
Cook	Pakaaunu	Leave	Chodnu	Return	Pharkanu
Do	Garnu	Lie (speak untruthfully)	Jhutho bolnu	Run	Dagurnu
Eat	Khaanu			Say, tell	Bhannu
Feel	Mahasus garnu	Look, see	Hernu	Sit	Basnu
Fix	Thoknu	Lose	Haraunu	Sell	Bechnu

Sleep	Sutnu			Want	Chahanu
Speak	Bolnu	Try	sochnu	Wash	Dhunu (face,
Steal	Chornu	Understand	Kosis garnu		clothes),
Stop	Roknu	Use	Bujnu		nuhaaunu
Take	Linu	Wait	Prayog garnu		(body)
Think	Bichaar garnu,	Walk	Parkhinu	Work	Kaam garnu
			Hidnu		

OTHER HANDY WORDS

Most of the following words are what we would call prepositions.
However, those marked with an asterisk (*) are actually postpositions in Nepali,
meaning they come *after* the thing they're describing (eg, "with me" comes out *masanga*).

Above, over, up	Maathi*	If	Yedi
And	Ra	Near	Nira*
Below, under, down	Talla*	Or	Ki
Because	Kinabhane	Out, Outside	Bahira*
Behind	Pachhadi*	That	Tyo
But	Tara	This	Yo
Each	Pratyek	To, Towards	Tira*
From	Baata*	With	Sanga*
In, Inside	Bhitra*	Without	Chhaina*
In front of	Agaadi*		

NUMBERS

Unlike the English counting system, which starts using compound numbers above 20 (twenty-one, twenty-two, etc), Nepali numbers are irregular all the way up to 100 –the following are the ones you're most likely to use. A slight further complication is the use of "counters" when quantifying nouns. In English, we sometimes use counters – for example, two pieces of paper, five plates of rice – but in Nepali the use is more systematic. Fortunately, you can get by with just two counters: *wotaa* for things, *jana* for people. Thus "five books" is *paanch wotaa kitaab*, "twelve girls" is *baarha jana keti*. But note these irregular counters: *ek wotaa = euta; dui wotaa = duita; tin wotaa = tintaa*.

half	aada	12	baara	50	pachaas
1	ek	13	tera	60	saathi
2	dui	14	chaudha	70	sattari
3	tin	15	pandra	80	asi
4	chaar	16	sora	90	nabbe
5	paanch	17	satra	100	ek sae
6	chha	18	athaara	1000	ek hajaa
7	saat	19	unnais	first (time)	pahilo (palta)
8	aath	20	bis	second	dosro
9	nau	25	pachhis	third	tesro
10	das	30	tis	fourth	chautho
11	eghaara	40	chaalis	fifth	paachau

DAYS AND MONTHS

It's unlikely you'll ever have to use these.
Nepali months start around the middle of our months, and vary from 27 to 32 days.

Sunday	Aitabar	Jan–Feb	Magh	July–August	Saaun
Monday	Sombar	Feb–March	Faagun		(or Shrawan)
Tuesday	Mangalbar	March–April	Chaitra	Aug–Sept	Bhadau (or Bhadra)
Wednesday	Budhabar	April–May	Baisaakh	Sept–Oct	Ashoj (or Ashwin)
Thursday	Bihibar	May–June	Jeth (or Jestha)	Oct–Nov	Khattik
Friday	Sukrabar	June–July	Asaar (or	Nov–Dec	Mangsir
Saturday	Sanibar		Ashadh)	Dec–Jan	Puus

SOME NEWARI PHRASES

Newari is still the first language for many in Kathmandu Valley. It's a difficult language to learn, with many local dialects, and knowing it is no more necessary than, say, knowing Welsh in Wales, yet trying out even the tiniest smidgen of it will astound and delight your innkeeper. The following phrases will get you going.

Hello	*Namaste*	this cost?	
Yes/No	*Ji/Maji*	No thanks	*Mha*
Thank you	*Dhanyabaad*	Please give me that	*Wo chhaka biya*
How are things?	*Chhitang gaya chong?*		*deshang*
Fine	*Bala*	Begging is bad	*Phonegu jya baamalaa*
What's your name?	*Chigu naang chhu?*	A little	*Bhachaa*
My name is . . .	*Jigu naang . . . kha*	Bad	*Mabaalaa*
My country is . . .	*Jigu chhey . . . kha*	Cheap	*Dang*
I don't understand	*Jing mathu*	Good	*Baalaa*
Can you repeat?	*Chhaka dhaya dis-*	Hungry	*Naiya pityaa*
hang?		Thirst	*Pyaas*
Do you speak English?	*Chhi Englis*	Tired	*Thakejula*
	khalhayadhiya?	1	*Chharkaa*
I don't speak Newari	*Jing Newa kha*	2	*Nirkaa*
	lhayemasa	3	*Sorhkaa*
Please help me	*Jitang gwali yana*	4	*Perkaa*
	dishang	5	*Nyarkaa*
Excuse me	*Maph biya*	6	*Khurkaa*
Can I go in?	*Ji wone jilaa?*	7	*Nerkaa*
What's this called in	*Thuyatang chhu*	8	*Chyarkaa*
Newari?	*dhaigu?*	9	*Gurkaa*
How far is it?	*Guli taappaa?*	10	*Jhirkaa*
How much does	*Thukiya guli?*		

NEPALI NUMBERS

१	२	३	४	५	६	७	८	९	१०
1	**2**	**3**	**4**	**5**	**6**	**7**	**8**	**9**	**10**

A GLOSSARY OF NEPALI, NEWARI AND TIBETAN TERMS

ANNAPURNA goddess of grain and abundance (literally, "Full of Grain"); form of Lakshmi.

ASHTA MANGALA the eight auspicious symbols of Buddhism.

AVALOKITESHWARA the *bodhisattva* of compassion (also known as Chenrezig).

AVATAR bodily incarnation of a deity.

BAAHUN Brahman, Hindu priest.

BABA holy man.

BAGH tiger.

BAHAL (or **BAHA**) buildings and quadrangle of a former Buddhist Newar monastery (a few are still active).

BAHIL (or **BAHI**) Newari term for Buddhist monastery.

BAJRA see "Vajra".

BAJRA JOGINI (or **VAJRA YOGINI**) female tantric counterpart to Bhairab.

BAKSHISH not a bribe, but a tip in advance.

BAN forest.

BARAHI (or **VARAHI**) Vishnu incarnated as a boar.

BAZAAR commercial area of a town – not necessarily a covered market.

BENI confluence of rivers.

BETAL symbol of death, often represented by a pair of skeletons flanking a temple entrance.

BETEL see "*paan*".

BHAAT cooked rice; food.

BHAIRAB terrifying tantric form of Shiva.

BHAJAN hymn, hymn-singing.

BHANJYANG a pass (Nepali).

BHARAT India.

BHATTI simple tavern, usually selling food as well as alcohol.

BHIMSEN patron god of Newar merchants.

BHOJANALAYA Nepali restaurant.

BHOT Tibet.

BHOTIYA highland peoples of Tibetan ancestry (the term is often considered pejorative).

BIDESHI foreigner (but many Nepalis call all foreigners *Aamerikan* – even Japanese).

BIDI cheap rolled-leaf cigarette.

BODHISATTVA in Mahayana Buddhism, one who forgoes *nirvana* until all other beings have attained enlightenment.

BRAHMA the Hindu creator god, one of the Hindu "trinity".

BRAHMAN member of the Hindu priestly caste (*baahun* in Nepali); metaphysical term meaning the universal soul.

CHAARPI latrine.

CHAITYA small Buddhist monument.

CHARES hashish.

CHAUTAARA resting platform beside a trail with trees for shade.

CHHETRI member of the ruling or warrior caste.

CHHANG (or **CHHYANG**) homemade beer brewed from rice or other grains.

CHILAM vertical clay pipe for smoking tobacco or *ganja*.

CHOLO traditional half-length woman's blouse.

CHORTEN another name for a *chaitya* in high mountain areas.

CHOWK intersection, square or courtyard (pronounced "choke").

CHUBA Tibetan sheepskin coat; Tibetan dress.

CHULO clay stove.

DAADA (or **DANDA**) a ridge.

DAMARU two-sided drum.

DANPHE Nepal's national bird, a pheasant with brilliant plumage.

DAPHNE shrub used in paper-making.

DAS AVATAR the ten incarnations of Vishnu.

DAURA SURUWAL traditional dress of hill men: wrap-around shirt and jodhpur-like trousers.

DEWAL stepped temple platform; temple with prominent steps.

DEVI see "*Mahadevi*".

DHAARA communal water tap or tank.

DHABA Indian-style fast-food restaurant.

DHAKA colourful hand-loomed material made in the Nepalese hills.

DHAMI shaman, similar to *jhankri*.

DHARMA religion; correct behaviour (applies to both Hinduism and Buddhism).

DHARMSALA rest house for pilgrims.

DHOKA gate.

DHOTI Indian-style loincloth.

DHYANI BUDDHAS meditating figures representing the five aspects of Buddha nature.

DOKO conical cane basket carried by means of a headstrap.

DORJE Tibetan word for *vajra*.

DUN low-lying valleys just north of the Tarai (sometimes called inner Tarai, or *bhitri madesh* – "inner plains").

DURBAR palace; royal court.

DURGA demon-slaying goddess.

DYOCHHEN tantric temple or meeting hall.

DZOPKIO sturdy yak-cattle crossbreed; the female is called a *dzum*.

GAIDA (or **GAINDA**) rhinoceros.

GAAINE wandering minstrel of the hills.

GAJUR brass or gold finial at the peak of a temple.

GANESH elephant-headed god of wisdom and remover of obstacles.

GANJA cannabis, marijuana.

GARUD Vishnu's man-bird carrier.

GAUN village, town.

GELUG-PA one of four main Lamaist sects.

GHAMA central wooden beam of a festival chariot.

GHANTA a bell, usually rung at temples as a sort of "amen".

GHAT riverside platform for worship and cremations; any waterside locality.

GHAZAL Indian form of popular music.

GIDDA vulture; Nepali slang for Israeli.

GOMPA Buddhist monastery (Tibetan).

GOONDA hooligan, thug.

GUPHA cave.

GURKHAS Nepali soldiers who serve in special regiments in the British and Indian armies.

GUTHI Newar benevolent association that handles upkeep of temples, organizes festivals, etc.

HANUMAN valiant monkey king in the *Ramayan*.

HATTI elephant.

HIMAL massif or mountain range with permanent snow.

HITI Newari word for *dhaara*.

HMG His Majesty's Government.

JAAND unstrained *chhang*.

JAATRA festival.

JAL holy water.

JANAI sacred thread worn over left shoulder by high-caste Hindu men.

JHANKRI shaman, or medicine man, of the hills.

JYAPU member of the Newar peasant farming caste.

KAGYU-PA one of four main Lamaist sects.

KALI the mother goddess in her most terrifying form.

KARMA the soul's accumulated merit, determining its next rebirth.

KAROD 10 million (*crore* in India).

KATA white scarf given to lamas by visitors.

KHAT a litter or platform on which a deity is carried during a festival.

KHOLA stream or river.

KHUKURI curved knife carried by most Nepali hill men.

KIRTIMUKHA common temple motif, a gargoyle-like face grappling with a snake.

KORA circumambulation or pilgrimage around a Buddhist monument.

KOT fort (pronounced "coat").

KRISHNA one of Vishnu's *avatar*, hero of the *Mahabharat*.

KUMARI a girl worshipped by Nepalis as the living incarnation of Durga.

KUNDA pond, water tank.

KWERI Nepali slang for foreigner.

LA pass (Tibetan).

LALI GURAAS tree rhododendron.

LAKH 100,000.

LAKSHMI consort of Vishnu, goddess of wealth.

LAMA Tibetan Buddhist priest: hence Lamaism.

LEK mountain range without permanent snow.

LHAKANG interior of a *gompa*.

LINGA (or **LINGAM**) the phallic symbol of Shiva, commonly the centrepiece of temples and sometimes occurring in groups in the open.

LOKESHWAR see "*Avalokiteshwara*".

MACHAAN watchtower used by Tarai farmers to ward off wild animals.

MACHHENDRANATH rain-bringing deity of the Kathmandu Valley; also known as Karunamaya or Bungadeo.

MAHABHARAT (or **MAHABHARATA**) Hindu epic of the battle between two families, featuring Krishna and containing the Bhagavad Gita.

MAHABHARAT LEK highest range of the Himalayan foothills.

MAHADEV "Great God", an epithet for Shiva.

MAHADEVI mother goddess.

MAHAYANA non-monastic form of Buddhism followed in Nepal, Tibet and east Asia.

MAHOUT elephant handler.

MANDALA mystical diagram, meditation tool.

MANDAP pavilion.

MANDIR temple.

MANI STONE slate inscribed with the mantra *Om mani padme hum*.

MANTRA religious incantation.

MASAALA spice; any mixture (thus *masaala* films, with their mixture of drama, singing, comedy, etc).

MASAN riverside cremation platform.

MATH Hindu priest's home.

MELA religious fair or gathering.

NAAMLO tumpline, headstrap for carrying a *doko*.

NADI river.

NAG snake or snake spirit, believed to have rain-bringing powers.

NAGAR city.

NAK female yak.

NAMASTE traditional Nepali greeting.

NANGLO cane tray, used for winnowing.

NANDI Shiva's mount, a bull.

NARAYAN common name for Vishnu.

NATH "Lord".

NIRVANA in Buddhism, enlightenment and release from the cycle of rebirth.

NYINGMA-PA one of four main Lamaist sects.

OM MANI PADME HUM the mantra of Avalokiteshvara, roughly translating as "Hail to the jewel in the lotus".

PAAN mildly addictive mixture of areca nut and lime paste, wrapped in a leaf and chewed, producing blood-red spit.

PADMA SAMBHAVA alias Guru Rinpoche, the eighth-century saint who brought Buddhism to Tibet.

PAHAAD hill.

PANCHAAYAT council or assembly, the basis for Nepal's pre-democratic government.

PANDIT Hindu priest.

PARBAT mountain.

PARBATI (or **PARVATI**) Shiva's consort.

PASHMINA Nepali equivalent of cashmere.

PATAASI traditional black and red-trimmed sari worn by women around Bhaktapur.

PATAKA (or **DHWAJA**) necktie-shaped brass ornament hanging from a temple, to be used by the deity when descending to earth.

PATI open shelter erected as a public resting place.

PAUBHA Newar scroll painting.

PHANIT elephant driver.

PHANTA grassland surrounded by jungle.

PHEDI foot (of a hill, pass, etc).

PIPAL common shade tree of the fig genus; also known as *bodhi*, the tree under which Buddha attained enlightenment.

POKHARI pond, usually man-made.

PRAJNA wisdom (Sanskrit).

PRASAD food consecrated after being offered to a deity – a sort of spiritual souvenir.

PUJA an act of worship.

PUJARI Hindu priest or caretaker of a particular temple.

PUL bridge.

PURETH Hindu priest who makes house calls.

RAJPATH, RAJMARGA "King's Way", "King's Road".

RAKSI distilled spirit.

RAM mortal *avatar* of Vishnu, hero of the *Ramayan*.

RAMAYAN (or **RAMAYANA**) popular Hindu epic in which Sita, princess of Janakpur, is abducted and eventually rescued by Ram and Hanuman.

RATH chariot used in religious processions.

RINPOCHE "precious jewel": title given to revered lamas.

RUDRAKSHA furrowed brown seeds, prized by *Shaivas*; it's said that the wearer of a *rudraksha* necklace must always tell the truth.

SADHU Hindu ascetic.

SAHIB honorific term given to male foreigners, pronouced "sahb"; women are called *mem-sahib*.

SAJHA cooperative; the name of a quasi-governmental bus company.

SAKYA-PA one of four main Lamaist sects.

SAL tall tree of the Tarai and lower hills, valued for its timber.

SARANGI Nepali four-stringed violin.

SARASWATI Hindu goddess of learning and the arts.

SATI (or **SUTTEE**) practice of Hindu widows throwing themselves on their husbands' funeral pyres.

SATTAL public rest house.

SHAIVA member of the cult of Shiva (pronounced "Shaib").

SHAKTI in Hindu *tantra*, the female principle that empowers the male; the mother goddess in this capacity.

SHALIGRAM fossil-bearing stones found near Muktinath, revered by *Vaishnavas*.

SHIKRA Indian-style temple, shaped like a square bullet.

SHIVA "the destroyer", one of the Hindu "trinity" – a god of many guises.

SHIVALAYA one-storey Shiva shrine containing a *linga*.

SHIVA MARGI a Hindu Newar.

SHRADHA Hindu death rites performed for a parent.

SHRI an honorific prefix.

SINDUR red paste used in making *tika* and decorating idols.

SIRDAR Nepali trek leader.

SITA Ram's wife, princess of Janakpur, heroine of the *Ramayan*.

STOL "short takeoff and landing" (read "hair-raising") landing strip.

STUPA large dome-shaped Buddhist monument, usually said to contain holy relics.

SUDRA member of the lowest, menial caste of Hinduism.

SUNYASAN Hindu who has renounced the world, usually in old age.

TAAL lake.

TANTRA esoteric psycho-sexual path to enlightenment, a major influence on Nepali Hinduism and Buddhism.

TARA Buddhist goddess; female aspect of Buddha nature.

TASHI DELEK Tibetan for welcome, *namaste*.

TEMPO three-wheeled scooter, autoriksha.

THAKURI very orthodox Chhetri subcaste.

THANGKA Buddhist scroll painting.

TIKA auspicious mark placed on the forehead during *puja* or festivals or before making a journey.

TOL neighbourhood.

TOLA traditional unit of weight (11.5g); precious metals are sold by the *tola*, as is hashish.

TOPI traditional Nepalese cap.

TORANA elaborate wooden carving, or metal shield, above a temple door.

TORMA dough offerings made by Buddhist monks.

TRISUL the trident, a symbol of Shiva.

TSAMPA toasted barley flour, a staple food of Tibetans and Bhotiyas.

TUDIKHEL parade ground.

TULKU reincarnation of a late great teacher in the Tibetan Buddhist tradition.

UPAYA compassion (Sanskrit).

VAISHNAVA follower of the cult of Vishnu (pronounced "Baishnab").

VAISYA (or **BAISYA**) Hindu caste of traders and farmers.

VAJRA sceptre-like symbol of tantric power (pronounced "bajra").

VAJRACHARYA Buddhist Newar priest.

VAJRAYANA "Thunderbolt Way": tantric Buddhism.

VEDAS the oldest Hindu scriptures; hence Vedic gods, extolled in the *Vedas*.

VIHARA (or **MAHAVIHARA**) Buddhist monastery (Sanskrit).

VIPASSANA ancient and austere Buddhist meditation practice.

VISHNU "the preserver", member of the Hindu "trinity", worshipped in ten main incarnations (pronounced "Bishnu").

YANGSI reincarnated successor of a Tibetan lama.

YONI symbol of the female genitalia, usually carved into the base of a *linga* as a reservoir for offerings.

INDEX

Introducing Tekware.

(What to wear when your biggest fashion concern is hypothermia.)

Lynn Hill climbing Three Sisters,
Photo: Clint Clemens

Made from advanced synthetic fabrics, **TEKWARE®** is clothing that dries faster, lasts longer and maintains overall comfort better than cotton. Its design combines the experience of world-class outdoor athletes and the expertise of our research and development teams. The result is a line of technologically superior outdoor equipment that makes cotton obsolete. For the dealer nearest you or to receive a free catalogue call: First Ascent, Units 2-5, Limetree Business Park, Matlock, Derbyshire, England DE4 3EJ, Freephone: 0800 146034.

THE NORTH FACE

NEVER STOP EXPLORING